Lecture Notes in Artificial Intellig

Edited by J. G. Carbonell and J. Siekmann

Subseries of Lecture Notes in Computer Science

Francesca Toni   Paolo Torroni (Eds.)

Computational Logic in Multi-Agent Systems

6th International Workshop, CLIMA VI
London, UK, June 27-29, 2005
Revised Selected and Invited Papers

 Springer

Series Editors

Jaime G. Carbonell, Carnegie Mellon University, Pittsburgh, PA, USA
Jörg Siekmann, University of Saarland, Saarbrücken, Germany

Volume Editors

Francesca Toni
Imperial College London
Department of Computing
180 Queen's Gate, SW7 2BZ London, UK
E-mail: ft@doc.ic.ac.uk

Paolo Torroni
Università di Bologna
Dipartimento di Elettronica, Informatica e Sistemistica
Viale Risorgimento 2, 40136 Bologna, Italy
E-mail: paolo.torroni@unibo.it

Library of Congress Control Number: Applied for

CR Subject Classification (1998): I.2.11, I.2, C.2.4, F.4

LNCS Sublibrary: SL 7 – Artificial Intelligence

ISSN   0302-9743
ISBN-10   3-540-33996-5 Springer Berlin Heidelberg New York
ISBN-13   978-3-540-33996-0 Springer Berlin Heidelberg New York

Springer is a part of Springer Science+Business Media

springer.com

© Springer-Verlag Berlin Heidelberg 2006
Printed in Germany

Typesetting: Camera-ready by author, data conversion by Scientific Publishing Services, Chennai, India
Printed on acid-free paper   SPIN: 11750734   06/3142   5 4 3 2 1 0

Preface

Computational Logic in Multi-Agent Systems (CLIMA) is a series of workshops aimed at promoting activity and exchange in the intersection of two vivid research areas. Since 2000, CLIMA has provided an opportunity to researchers to present their work on the application of general and declarative theories grounded on computational logic to multi-agent systems specification, semantics and procedures, and to confront ideas such as autonomy, deliberation, knowledge, commitment, openness, and trust with the computational logic paradigms. This research has encouraged the use of formal approaches to multi-agent systems research, and it has dealt with disparate issues such as implementations, environments, tools, and verification of computational systems.

The sixth edition of CLIMA was held at City University London, UK, on June 27–29, 2005. The workshop lasted three days and included an invited lecture by Robert A. Kowalski (Imperial College London) based on his last book. Sixty delegates from 15 countries (UK, Italy, France, Japan, Norway, The Netherlands, Cyprus, Germany, Canada, Ireland, Lithuania, Poland, Spain, Sweden, and Switzerland) attended the three-day event. Many of them were students.

CLIMA VI was innovative in many respects: beside the regular paper sessions, where the speakers presented papers selected from around 30 submissions, and the invited lecture, it hosted:

– a small tutorial program, with six lectures on cutting-edge CL-based agent technology,
– the first edition of the CLIMA contest, organized by Jürgen Dix and Mehdi Dastani, and
– the SOCS dissemination event reporting important results of an EU-funded project at the intersection of MAS and Logic Programming.

As we felt that we had enough material in our hands, motivated by the success of CLIMA VI we decided to propose a special edition to Springer. This volume features an invited article by Robert Kowalski, five tutorial papers presenting a view on the state of the art in CL-based MAS programming, four papers describing the implemented systems that participated in the contest, introduced by an invited paper by Jürgen Dix, Mehdi Dastani, and Peter Novak, a selection of technical papers, and an article about SOCS. All in all, this book is a state-of-the-art survey, authored by 56 researchers worldwide. A Program Committee of 26 top-level researchers and 40 additional reviewers contributed with their hard work and very fruitful comments and suggestions to the technical quality of this book: each of the 14 technical papers, 4 contest papers, and 7 invited papers enjoyed 3 to 5 reviews, in a 2-round process in which authors could reply to the reviewers' comments and argue in favor of their claims.

This volume opens with an invited article by Kowalski, presenting abductive logic programming (ALP) and its application in intelligent agents research. In

The Logical Way to Be Artificially Intelligent, Kowalski shows that ALP can be used to model reactive, proactive and preactive thinking, which can be performed by an agent as needed, or in advance, transforming high-level goals and beliefs into lower-level condition-action rule form. Kowalski also shows how ALP, proposed as a framework for constructing artificial agents, can also be used as a cognitive model of human agents.

The book continues with three sets of papers, covering *foundational aspects of agency, agent programming*, and *agent interaction and normative systems*. The articles of these sections are partly extended versions of papers presented at CLIMA VI, are partly novel, invited contributions that present, in a didactic style, advanced topics in CL-based MAS research.

Foundational Aspects of Agency

Setting the foundations of a theory of agency involves reasoning about notions such as agent knowledge, trust, beliefs, competence, abilities, and their relation with the environment, e.g., through actions or access to information. To this end, several formalisms have been used, adapted and refined, such as epistemic and doxastic logics and the situation calculus. This part of the book presents a selection of papers presented at CLIMA VI dealing with such foundational aspects of agency.

In *Ability in a Multi-Agent Context: a Model in the Situation Calculus*, Cholvy et al. provide a model of the notion of ability and its relation with the notion of action in a multi-agent context in the situation calculus. The authors provide a formal definition of the notion of ability of an agent to perform an action as the combination of its competences and some favorable conditions that allow it to perform that action, through the intermediary notion of "theoretical ability." The article is also concerned with the notion of ability of a group of agents. It deals with the dynamic notion of "occasional ability" (depending on the state of the world in which it is evaluated) and with the nontrivial problem of inferring the ability of the group from the abilities of the individuals of the group.

Nguyen advocates the use of modal logic programming to deal with reasoning about epistemic states of agents. In *Reasoning about Epistemic States of Agents by Modal Logic Programming*, he starts from the consideration that an agent should have knowledge about other agents in the system, and when such knowledge is only partial, it should nevertheless be able to reason about their epistemic states, possibly by simulating them, using some assumptions. To this end, Nguyen proposes an SLD-resolution calculus for modal logic programs in the multi-modal logic $KD4I_g5_a$. Such logic is intended for reasoning about belief and common belief of agents. The author provides soundness and completeness results and a formalization of McCarty's wise men puzzle using $KD4I_g5_a$ to demonstrate his ideas.

Epistemic logic frameworks for agents is also dealt within the paper *Strongly Complete Axiomatizations of "Knowing At Most" in Syntactic Structures*. The authors extend the logic language of syntactic structures based on syntactic assignments to model knowledge, with a new operator used to represent the position that an agent "knows at most" a given finite set of formulae. The syntactic approach is presented as a complementary approach to the modal approach, which can be used to model certain types of agents and certain types of situations that are difficult if not impossible to model with the modal approach, e.g., non-ideal – rather than ideal – agents, and situations where one is interested in explicit – rather than implicit – knowledge. In this paper, Ågotnes and Walicki present a strongly complete infinitary system and a strongly complete finitary system for a slightly weaker variant of the language.

Logical Spaces in Multi-Agent Only Knowing Systems presents a weak multi-agent system of "only knowing" and an analysis of the logical spaces that can be defined in it. Logical spaces can be used to express one agent's apprehension of the relations between concepts as understood by another agent, or, as the authors demonstrate, to define a situation in which an agent cannot conceive of a situation in which another agent has certain assumptions. Solhaug and Waaler's logic complements the approach to generalizing Levesque's "All I Know" system made by Halpern and Lakemeyer. The logic is defined entirely at the object level, with no reference to meta-concepts in the definition of the axiom system.

Trustworthiness by Default opens with an epigraph taken from Moses' address to the Israelites, which the authors use to introduce a framework for reasoning about relative trustworthiness. The framework considers sets of information sources as the basic trusted units, and is applied to conflict resolution and belief formation at various degrees of reliability. Klüwer and Waaler show how to construct a lattice of degrees of trustworthiness based on an assignment of relative trustworthiness to information source sets, to derive a priority structure, and apply it to the problem of forming the right opinion. Consolidated with an unquestioned knowledge base, this provides an unambiguous account of what an agent should believe, conditionally on which information sources are trusted.

Decision Procedure for a Fragment of Mutual Belief Logic with Quantified Agent Variables presents a deduction-based decision procedure for a fragment of mutual belief logic with quantified agent variables, $MBQL$. The language of $MBQL$ contains belief, everybody believes and mutual belief modalities, variables and constants for agents. The language of $MBQL$ is especially convenient to describe the properties of rational agents when the number of agents is not known in advance, and helps simplifying expressions when the exact number of agents is known instead. In this article, Pliuškevičius and Pliuškevičienė also propose a sequent calculus with invertible rules MBQ^* for the language of $MBQL$, and a loop-check-free sequent calculus for a fragment of $MBQL$.

Agent Programming

While modal logics have proven very useful to model and reason about agent mental states and their relations, the use of temporal logics and declarative programming is favored by many researchers when it comes to constructing operational agent systems and to implementing MAS based on their logical specifications. This volume includes four papers about state-of-the-art (multi-)agent frameworks based on extensions of logic programming, and one presenting tools for execution and proof based on temporal logic. This part contains four of them, followed by two CLIMA papers about agent programming.

In *Implementing Temporal Logics: Tools for Execution and Proof*, Fisher presents an overview of a selection of tools for execution and proof based on temporal logic, and outlines both the general techniques used and problems encountered in implementing them. The tools considered are mainly theorem-provers and (logic-based) agent programming languages, including clausal temporal resolution and executable temporal logics, and several of their implementations. This tutorial paper concentrates on general principles, with the aim of giving the reader an overview of the ways temporal logics are handled and used as the basis for both programming and verification.

Jason is a multi-agent systems development platform based on an interpreter for an extended version of AgentSpeak: an elegant, logic-based programming language based on the best known and most studied architecture for cognitive agents (the BDI architecture). In the tutorial paper *BDI Agent Programming in AgentSpeak Using **Jason***, Bordini and Hübner give an overview of the various features available in ***Jason***. The paper is intended for a general audience although some parts might be clearer for readers familiar with agent-oriented programming. The authors focus on the main features of ***Jason***, so that readers can assess whether ***Jason*** might be of interest, and give plenty of references to other papers and documentation where more detail and examples can be found.

The $\mathcal{KGP}$ model of agency, defined within the SOCS project, gives concrete guidelines for the formal specification of the knowledge of agents based on LP via a modular knowledge base and of the behavior of computees via a cycle theory providing flexible, declarative control of operation. In the tutorial paper *Using the $\mathcal{KGP}$ Model of Agency to Design Applications*, Sadri describes the main features of the $\mathcal{KGP}$ and gives user guidance on how the model can be used to develop applications. The paper concentrates on the abstract component of the $\mathcal{KGP}$, which consists of formal specifications of a number of different modules, including the knowledge bases, capabilities, transitions and control. For each of these, Sadri summarizes what is provided by the model, and through the platform implementing the model, and what is left to the users to specify according to the application requirements.

In *Multi-threaded Communicating Agents in Qu-Prolog*, Clark et al. summarize the key features of the multi-threaded Qu-Prolog language for implementing communicating agent applications. Internal threads of an agent communicate using the shared dynamic database used as a generalization of Linda tuple store. Threads in different agents communicate using either a thread-to-thread store and forward communication system or by a publish and subscribe mechanism in which messages are routed to their destinations based on content test subscriptions. The authors illustrate the features using an auction house application, which makes essential use of the three forms of inter-thread communication of Qu-Prolog. The agent bidding behavior is specified graphically as a finite state automaton and its implementation is essentially the execution of its state transition function.

Is an agent that focuses on one goal at a time better than an agent that frequently re-examines his commitments to ensure that he honors only those that are feasible? Or, how can such behaviors be compared with each other? The cycle theories of $\mathcal{KGP}$ agents define declaratively the possible alternative behaviors of agents, depending on their internal state and their perception of the external environment in which they are situated. In *Variety of Behaviors Through Profiles in Logic-based Agents*, Sadri and Toni show how by using this form of control specification one can specify different profiles of agents. In the paper, three different profiles are introduced, called "careful," "focussed," and "full planner" profile. The authors demonstrate how agent profiles would vary agent behaviors and what advantages they have with respect to factors in the application and in the environment, such as time-criticality.

This part is concluded by Knottenbelt and Clark's proposal: a simple event calculus representation of contracts and a reactive BDI agent architecture can be used to enable the monitoring and execution of contract terms and conditions. In *Contract-Related Agents*, the authors use the event calculus to deduce current and past obligations, obligation fulfilment and violation. By associating meta-information with the contracts, the agent is able to select which of its contracts with other agents are relevant to solving its goals by outsourcing. The agent is able to handle an extendable set of contract types such as standing contracts, purchase contracts and service contracts, without the need for a first-principles planner.

Agent Interaction and Normative Systems

A great deal of MAS research is devoted to studying specification and verification of interaction protocols, design of normative systems, representation of contexts, modelling other agents' mental states during interaction, and operational procedures for distributed intelligent reasoning, such as composition of information sources and reasoning using default beliefs about the possible outcomes of agent interaction. A tutorial and six technical papers compose this part, whose focus is not on individual agents but on social agents, their interaction and the norms that govern their systems.

Specification and Verification of Agent Interaction Using Abductive Reasoning, based on Chesani and Gavanelli's tutorial, provides an overview of the theory and tools produced within SOCS to design, define and test agent interaction protocols. The SOCS language for protocol specification is grounded on ALP. Its main element are social integrity constraints, used to specify relationships among happened events (e.g., messages or timeouts), expectations about future events, and predicates defined in the social knowledge base. This language aims to define open, extensible and not over-constrained protocols, following a social approach to agent interaction. A software tool called SOCS-SI allows one to verify *at execution time* if the agents conform to the defined protocols.

A complementary approach to verification of agents' conformance to protocols consists of inspecting the programs that encode their communicative behavior ("policies"), and verifying *a priori*, rather than at execution time, that they will actually produce interactions conforming to the public protocols. In this case, an issue is whether the test preserves the agents' capability of interacting, besides certifying the legality of their possible conversations. In the paper *Verification of Protocol Conformance and Agent Interoperability*, Baldoni and colleagues propose an approach based on the theory of formal languages. The conformance test is based on the acceptance of both the policy and the protocol by a special finite state automaton and it guarantees the interoperability of agents that are individually proven conformant.

How to connect norms specified by means of abstract terms ("persons driving vehicles may not access public parks") to norms specified via more concrete ones ("persons wheeling bicycles are allowed to access public parks")? An answer to this question is found in Grossi and coworkers' contextual taxonomies ("A counts as B in context C") for representing categorizing features of normative systems. *Contextual Terminologies* builds on work done on contextual taxonomies so as to add the possibility to deal with attributes or roles, i.e., binary relations besides concepts. This shift from simple taxonomies to rich description logic terminologies allows one to model more complex scenarios. The formalization is obtained by means of a formal semantics framework to reason within contexts and about contexts and their interplay.

Boella and van der Torre consider the design of normative multi-agent systems composed of both constitutive and regulative norms in their paper *Constitutive Norms in the Design of Normative Multiagent Systems*. They analyze the properties of constitutive norms, in particular their lack of reflexivity, and the trade-off between constitutive and regulative norms in the design of normative systems. As a methodology they use the metaphor of describing social entities as agents and of attributing mental attitudes to them. In this agent metaphor, regulative norms expressing obligations and permissions are modelled as goals of social entities, and constitutive norms expressing "counts as" relations are their beliefs.

Sakama and Inoue address the issue of combining knowledge of different information sources. Suppose a multi-agent system in which each agent has a knowledge base written in a common logic programming language. When two programs do not contradict each other, they may be combined into one by taking the union of programs. In non-monotonic logic programs, however, simple merging does not always reflect the meaning of individual programs. In *Combining Answer Sets of Nonmonotonic Logic Programs*, the authors study the compositional semantics of non-monotonic logic programs, supposing the answer set semantics of extended disjunctive programs. They provide methods for computing program composition and discuss their properties.

Speculative computation was first defined to cope with the incompleteness generated by communication failure or response delays. The idea is to allow the asking agent, while waiting for the slave agents to reply, to reason using default beliefs until replies are sent. *Speculative Constraint Processing with Iterative Revision for Disjunctive Answers* extends the framework proposed by Satoh and Yamamoto for speculative computation and iterative answer revision for yes/no questions. In this paper, Ceberio et al. present an extension of the framework for more general types of questions using constraint logic programming. They equip the framework with a sound operational model, which provably gives a correct answer with respect to the most recent replies.

When two agents have to interact it is important for each agent to know the other agent's intentions because this knowledge allows one to anticipate his future behavior. A method for this is presented in Demolombe and Otermin Fernandez's *Intention Recognition in the Situation Calculus and Probability Theory Frameworks*, and instantiated in the particular context of a pilot that interacts with an aircraft. The method is restricted to contexts where the agent only performs procedures in a given library of procedures, and where the system that intends to recognize the agent's intentions has a complete knowledge of the actions performed by the agent. An original aspect is that the procedures are defined for human agents and not for artificial agents, which makes the problem more complex than the standard one of plan recognition.

The First CLIMA Contest

The first CLIMA contest represented an important step towards collecting important benchmarks, identifying advantages/shortcomings, and advertising the use of CL to the broader MAS audience, and fostering integration of CL into existing agent-oriented software engineering frameworks. Dastani et al. open this section with the article *The First Contest on Multi-Agent Systems Based on Computational Logic*. In this paper, the authors describe the contest scenario and the winning criteria, and compare the performance of the competitors in the difficult task of determining the winning system. The other four short articles contain the description of the competing systems.

Coffey and Gaertner used ant-style pheromone trails as the basis for a pseudorandom walk procedure. Their agents, implemented in the concurrent LP language Qu-Prolog described in this book by Clark et al., explore the world uniformly based on information disseminated globally via a publish/subscribe mechanism. Interesting features of this approach, presented in *Implementing Pheromone-Based, Negotiating Forager Agents*, are the distribution of roles (collector/explorer) and the ability of agents to negotiate so as to increase the performance of collection/delivery task allocation. All in Prolog! (or almost all).

Cares et al. took the challenge from an agent-oriented software engineering perspective. The paper *Extending Tropos for a Prolog Implementation: a Case Study Using the Food-Collecting Agent Problem* uses the contest scenario as a case study to illustrate a method of obtaining a Prolog MAS implementation starting from a Tropos design. This solution includes autonomous behavior, beliefs, multiple role playing, communication and cooperation, and it ranked first in the contest together with the one implemented by Coffey and Gaertner.

In *Reactive Food Gathering*, Logie et al. describe a simple system, implemented as a collection of purely reactive agents, with no internal representation of their environment, which dynamically switch between a number of behaviors depending on interaction with their environment. The agents co-operate indirectly via environmental markers, generating an emerging global behavior that solves the problem.

This part closes with *Strategies for Multi-Agent Coordination in a Grid World Using Petri Nets*, by Nunes Gonçalves and Bittencourt. A distinguishing feature of the authors' solution is the focus on coordination. Their agents implement a strategy to select the most capable agent in the environment so as to execute tasks that they cannot execute themselves. The specification of the multi-agent system is made using Petri Nets.

Project Report

The SOCS dissemination event, affiliated to CLIMA VI, presented several key aspects of the EU-funded European project SOCS (SOcieties of ComputeeS), one of the main sponsors of CLIMA VI. Computees are agents in computational logic. From January 2001 to June 2005, in a joint research effort involving six European academic institutions, SOCS pushed the state of the art in LP and in MAS research, producing as its main results the KGP model of agency and the SOCS social model based on social integrity constraints. During this event, the speakers Toni, Kakas, Bracciali, and Alberti presented the declarative and operational models for agents and multi-agent systems and the formal properties of agents and agent systems developed within SOCS. Torroni discussed possible guidelines for evaluating intelligent systems of reasoning agents, building on the SOCS experience. In the last paper of this volume, Toni presents the challenges and outcomes of SOCS.

Further information about CLIMA VI is available from the website `http://clima.deis.unibo.it/`. General information about the workshop series, with links to past and future events, can be found on the CLIMA workshop series home page, `http://centria.di.fct.unl.pt/~clima/`. The next CLIMA edition is organized by Katsumi Inoue, Ken Satoh and Francesca Toni. It will take place in Hakodate, Japan, on May 8-9, 2006, in conjunction with AAMAS and it will host the second CLIMA contest.

While wishing you a good read, we thank the local organizer, the contest organizers, the website administrators, the Program Committee members, the additional reviewers, the authors and the delegates, who contributed to a very interesting and inspiring event, and the sponsors: the Association for Logic Programming, AgentLink III, and the Fifth Framework EU Programme through the SOCS Project.

March 2006   Francesca Toni
                                                                  Paolo Torroni

Organization

Workshop Chairs

Francesca Toni, Imperial College London, UK
Paolo Torroni, University of Bologna, Italy

Program Committee

José Alferes, New University of Lisbon, Portugal
Rafael Bordini, University of Durham, UK
Gerd Brewka, University of Leipzig, Germany
Jürgen Dix , Technical University of Clausthal, Germany
Thomas Eiter, Vienna University of Technology, Austria
Klaus Fischer, DFKI, Germany
Michael Fisher, The University of Liverpool, UK
James Harland, Royal Melbourne Institute of Technology, Australia
Katsumi Inoue, National Institute of Informatics, Japan
Antonis Kakas, University of Cyprus, Cyprus
Evelina Lamma, University of Ferrara, Italy
João Leite, New University of Lisbon, Portugal
Paolo Mancarella, University of Pisa, Italy
Paola Mello, University of Bologna, Italy
John-Jules Ch. Meyer, Utrecht University, The Netherlands
Leora Morgenstern, IBM, USA
Wojciech Penczek, Polish Academy of Sciences, Poland
Jeremy Pitt, Imperial College, London, UK
Enrico Pontelli, New Mexico State University, USA
Fariba Sadri, Imperial College London, UK
Ken Satoh, National Institute of Informatics, Japan
Renate Schmidt, The University of Manchester, UK
Tran Cao Son, New Mexico State University, USA
Kostas Stathis, City University London, UK
Wiebe van der Hoek, The University of Liverpool, UK
Cees Witteveen, Delft University of Technology, The Netherlands

CLIMA Steering Committee

Jürgen Dix, Technical University of Clausthal, Germany
Michael Fisher, The University of Liverpool, UK
João Leite, New University of Lisbon, Portugal
Fariba Sadri, Imperial College London, UK
Ken Satoh, National Institute of Informatics, Japan

Francesca Toni, University of Pisa, Italy
Paolo Torroni, University of Bologna, Italy

Contest Organizers

Mehdi Dastani, Utrecht University, The Netherlands
Jürgen Dix, Technical University of Clausthal, Germany

Additional CLIMA Reviewers

Marco Alberti	Jomi Hubner	Rossella Rubino
Federico Banti	Ullrich Hustadt	Claudio Schifanella
Jamal Bentahar	Magdalena Kacprzak	Kostas Stathis
Andrea Bracciali	Peep Küngas	Andrzej Szałas
Andreas Brüning	Sławomir Lasota	Giacomo Terreni
Lisette van der Burgh	Ambra Molesini	Arianna Tocchio
Marco Cadoli	Àlvaro Moreira	Satoshi Tojo
Carlos Cares	Adriaan ter Mors	Krzysztof Trojanowski
Federico Chesani	Yasuo Nagai	Francesco Viganò
Pierangelo Dell'Acqua	Brendan Neville	Gregory Weeler
Agostino Dovier	Peter Novak	Mathijs de Weerdt
Nivea Ferreira	Regimantas Pliuškevičius	Pınar Yolum
Marco Gavanelli	Ian Pratt-Hartmann	
Davide Grossi	Daniel Ramirez-Cano	

Web Support

Fabio Bucciarelli   Federico Chesani

Local Organisation

Kostas Stathis

Sponsoring Institutions

Table of Contents

Agent Interaction and Normative Systems

The First CLIMA Contest

Project Report

The Logical Way to Be Artificially Intelligent

Robert Kowalski

Imperial College London
rak@doc.ic.ac.uk
http://www.doc.ic.ac.uk/~rak/

Abstract. Abductive logic programming (ALP) can be used to model reactive, proactive and pre-active thinking in intelligent agents. Reactive thinking assimilates observations of changes in the environment, whereas proactive thinking reduces goals to sub-goals and ultimately to candidate actions. Pre-active thinking generates logical consequences of candidate actions, to help in deciding between the alternatives. These different ways of thinking are compatible with any way of deciding between alternatives, including the use of both decision theory and heuristics.

The different forms of thinking can be performed as they are needed, or they can be performed in advance, transforming high-level goals and beliefs into lower-level condition-action rule form, which can be implemented in neural networks. Moreover, the higher-level and lower-level representations can operate in tandem, as they do in dual-process models of thinking. In dual process models, intuitive processes form judgements rapidly, sub-consciously and in parallel, while deliberative processes form and monitor judgements slowly, consciously and serially.

ALP used in this way can not only provide a framework for constructing artificial agents, but can also be used as a cognitive model of human agents. As a cognitive model, it combines both a descriptive model of how humans actually think with a normative model of humans can think more effectively.

1 Introduction

Symbolic logic is one of the main techniques used in Artificial Intelligence, to develop computer programs that display human intelligence. However, attempts to use symbolic logic for this purpose have identified a number of shortcomings of traditional logic and have necessitated the development of various improvements and extensions. This paper - and the draft book [6] on which it is based - aims to show that many of these developments can also be used for the original purpose of logic – to improve the quality of human thinking.

I have written the book informally, both to reach a wider audience and to demonstrate that the enhanced logic is in fact relevant and congenial for human thinking. However, in this paper, I will draw attention to some of the more technical issues, for the consideration of a more academic audience.

The logic used in the book is based on an extension of abductive logic programming (ALP) to logic-based agents [7]. In ALP agents, *beliefs* are represented by logic programs and *goals* are represented by integrity constraints. The agent's

F. Toni and P. Torroni (Eds.): CLIMA VI, LNAI 3900, pp. 1 – 22, 2006.

observations and *actions* are represented by abducible predicates. Beliefs and goals have both a declarative interpretation in logical terms, as well as a procedural interpretation in computational terms.

ALP agents are both *reactive* to changes they observe in the environment and *proactive* in planning ahead and reducing goals to sub-goals. In this paper I show that ALP agents can also be *pre-active* in thinking about the possible consequences of actions before deciding what to do.

In conventional ALP, the logical consequences of abductive hypotheses are checked to determine whether they violate any integrity constraints. However, in ALP agents, where abductive hypotheses include alternative, candidate actions, the pre-actively generated consequences of candidate actions are used to decide between the alternatives. This decision can be made in different ways. One way is to use conventional Decision Theory, judging the utilities and probabilities of the consequences of the alternative candidates and choosing an action that maximizes expected utility. However, other ways of deciding between actions are also compatible with ALP, including ways that compile decision making into heuristics.

The combination of reactive, proactive and pre-active thinking is obtained in ALP agents by combining forward and backward reasoning. This reasoning can be performed whenever the need arises, or it can be performed once and for all by reasoning in advance. Reasoning in advance transforms and compiles higher-level goals and beliefs into lower-level goals, which are similar to condition-action rules, which implement stimulus-response associations compiled into neural networks.

In modern computing, it is common to develop programs in a high-level representation and then to transform or compile them into a lower-level representation for the sake of efficiency. If it later becomes necessary to correct or enhance the resulting lower-level program, this is generally done by first modifying the higher-level representation and then recompiling it into a new lower-level form.

However, many existing computer systems are legacy systems developed before the existence of higher-level programming languages. It is often possible to decompile these lower-level programs into higher-level form, although, because of the undisciplined nature of lower-level languages, sometimes the relationship is only approximate.

The relationship between higher-level and lower-level computer programs is analogous to the relationship between higher-level and lower-level representations in ALP agents. It is also similar to the relationship between deliberative and intuitive thinking in the *dual process model* of human thinking [10]. In the dual process model, one system, which is older in evolutionary terms, is responsible for *intuitive thinking*. It is associative, automatic, unconscious, parallel, and fast. The other system, which is distinctively human, is responsible for *deliberative thinking*. It is rule-based, controlled, conscious, serial, and slow.

In computing, high-level and low level representations normally operate separately, but can be compiled or decompiled from one into the other. In the dual process model, however, intuitive and deliberative thinking can operate in tandem, as when the intuitive, subconscious level "quickly proposes intuitive answers to judgement problems as they arise", while the deliberative, conscious level "monitors the quality of these proposals, which it may endorse, correct, or override" [3]. This interaction between intuitive and deliberative thinking can be mimicked in part by the use of pre-active thinking in ALP agents, to monitor and evaluate candidate actions generated by reactive thinking. In ALP agents both the deliberative level and the intuitive level are represented in logical form.

These topics are expanded upon in the remainder of the paper. Section 2 outlines the basic features of the ALP agent model, including reactive, proactive, and pre-active thinking. Section 3 investigates the relationship between thinking and deciding. Section 4 discusses the transformation of high-level representations into lower-level, more efficient form, and the way in which high-level and lower-level representations interact. Section 5 shows how low-level feed-forward neural networks can be represented in logical form and can be simulated by forward reasoning. Section 6 discusses some of the implications of this for the notion that logic can serve as a wide-spectrum language of thought. Section 7 addresses some of the arguments against logic as a model of human thinking, and section 8 is the conclusion.

2   The Basic ALP Agent Model

2.1   Putting Logic in its Place in the Agent Cycle

The logic used in the book is based on an extension of abductive logic programming (ALP) to logic-based agents [7]. The most important feature of the extension is that it embodies logic in the thinking component of an agent's observe-think-decide-act cycle:

> To cycle,
> observe the world,
> *think*,
> decide what actions to perform,
> act,
> cycle again.

The agent cycle can be viewed as a generalisation of production systems, in which thinking is performed by using condition-action rules of the form:

> If conditions then candidate actions.

Condition-action rules look a lot like logical implications, but they do not have the declarative semantics of implications. Nonetheless, as we will later see, in ALP agents, condition-action rules are represented by goals expressed in logical form.

This view of logic in the mind of an agent embodied in the world is pictured in figure 1. In this picture, the agent uses logic to represent its goals and beliefs, and to help control its interactions with the world. It transforms its experience into observations in logical form and uses its goals and beliefs to generate candidate actions, to satisfy its goals and to maintain itself in a satisfactory relationship with the changing world.

The agent's body, in addition to being a part of the world, transforms both raw experience into observations and the will to act into physical changes in the world. This is analogous to the way in which hardware and software are related in a computer. The hardware transforms stimuli from the environment into inputs and transforms outputs into physical changes in the environment. The internal processing of inputs into outputs is performed by the hardware, but is controlled conceptually by software. In this analogy, the brain and body of an agent are to the mind as hardware is to software.

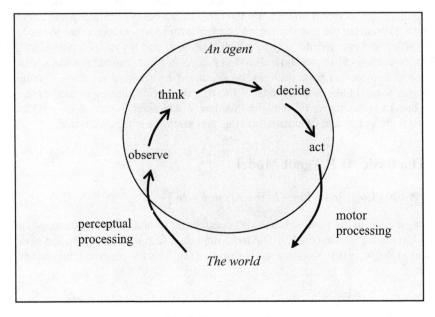

Fig. 1. The agent cycle

In general, the result of thinking is a set of candidate actions, which are the input to the decision-making component of the agent cycle. In the same way that Logic is only one way of thinking, there are many ways of deciding what to do. Decision theory, which combines judgements about the utility of the outcomes of actions with judgements about their probability, is one such way of deciding. As we will see in an example later, it is also possible to compile decision-making directly into lower-level goals and beliefs. In production systems, decision making is called "conflict resolution".

An agent's ultimate goal is to maintain itself in a satisfactory relationship with the surrounding world, and thinking and deciding are only one way of achieving that goal. An agent can also act to satisfy its goals instinctively, by means of *stimulus-response associations*, in a way that might be characterised as acting without thinking. Instinctive behaviour can be hardwired into an agent's body, without entering into its mind. Or it might be learned as the result of repeated performance and feedback. Instinctive behaviour is a near relation of intuitive thinking in the dual process model.

The agent cycle, as described above, concerns the real time behaviour of an agent, and does not address the processes involved in learning new behaviours and updating old ones. Suffice it to say that learning, belief revision and goal revision are essential activities for a real agent interacting with the real world. Because of the logical nature of ALP agents, such techniques as inductive logic programming are especially suitable to model such activities. They are, however, beyond the scope of this paper.

2.2 ALP Combines Forward and Backward Reasoning

Abductive logic programming [4] comes in many forms and variations, both in terms of its semantics and in terms of its proof procedures. However, in all of these forms, abductive logic programs have two components: ordinary logic programs and integrity constraints. They also have two, corresponding kinds of predicates – *ordinary predicates* that are defined by logic programs and *abducible predicates* that are, directly or indirectly, constrained by integrity constraints.

In ALP agents, logic programs are used to represent an agent's *beliefs*, and integrity constraints to represent its *goals*. The abducible predicates are used to represent the agent's *observations* and *actions*. The integrity constraints are *active*, in the sense that they can generate representations of actions that the agent can perform, in order to maintain integrity.

Consider, for example, the goal of getting help in an emergency on the London underground.

Goal   If there is an emergency then I get help.

Beliefs   There is an emergency if there is a fire.
           There is an emergency if one person attacks another.
           There is an emergency if someone becomes seriously ill.
           There is an emergency if there is an accident.

           There is a fire if there are flames.[1]
           There is a fire if there is smoke.

           A person gets help
           if the person alerts the driver.

           A person alerts the driver
           if the person presses the alarm signal button.

Here, for simplicity, the abducible predicates associated with observations are the predicates "there are flames", "there is smoke", "one person attacks another", "someone becomes seriously ill", and "there is an accident". The only abducible predicate associated with candidate actions is "the person presses the alarm signal button". All of these abducible predicates are indirectly constrained by the goal of getting help whenever there is an emergency. All the other predicates, including the higher-level actions of getting help and alerting the driver are ordinary predicates, defined by the agent's beliefs.

---

[1] These two rules, relating fire, flames and smoke are the converse of the causal rules, which state that if there is a fire then there are flames and smoke. The causal rules are a higher-level representation, whereas the rules used here are a lower-level, more efficient representation. The higher-level, causal representation would need abduction to explain that an observation of smoke or flames can be caused by fire. In fact, the term "abduction" normally refers to such generation of hypotheses to explain observations. The lower-level representation used here replaces abduction by deduction.

The goal itself is a *maintenance goal*, which an agent can use to derive actions to maintain itself in a desired relationship with the changes that it observes in its environment. Maintenance goals can be viewed as a generalization of condition-action rules.

Maintenance goals are triggered as a consequence of observations, similarly to the way in which integrity constraints in a database are triggered as the result of updates. An agent reasons forwards from its beliefs, to derive consequences of its observations. Suppose, for example, that I am travelling as a passenger on the underground and that my body experiences a combination of sensations that my mind interprets as an observation of smoke. The observation triggers my beliefs, which I use to reason forward in two steps, to recognize that there is an emergency.

The conclusion that there is an emergency triggers the maintenance goal, which I then use to reason forward one more step, to derive the achievement goal of getting help. The achievement goal triggers other beliefs, which I use to reason backwards in two steps, to reduce the achievement goal to the action sub-goal of pressing the alarm signal button. Since there are no other candidate actions in this simple example, I decide to press the alarm signal button, which my body then transforms into a combination of motor activities that is intended to accomplish the desired action.

The fact that pure logic programs are declarative means that they can be used to reason in many different ways. In the procedural interpretation, they are used only to reason backwards, as procedures that reduce goals to sub-goals. However, in ALP they are used to reason both backwards and forwards.

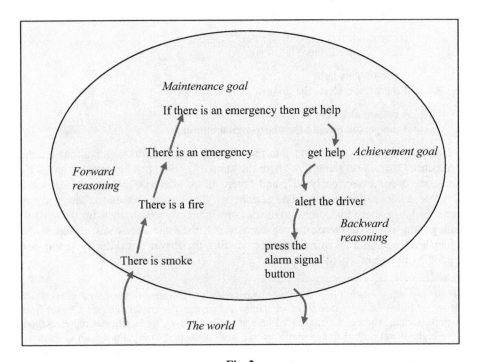

Fig. 2

This combination of forward and backward reasoning, together with the interface between the agent's mind and the world, is pictured in figure 2. Arguably, this treatment of maintenance goals as integrity constraints generalizes condition-action rules in production systems. Condition-action rules are the special case where no forward reasoning is needed to trigger the maintenance goal and no backward reasoning is needed to reduce the achievement goal to actions. Thus maintenance goals include condition-action rules as a special case, but in general are much higher-level.

Vickers [12], in particular, championed the idea that human activity and organizations should be viewed as maintaining relationships with the changing environment. He characterized Simon's view of management and problem solving as the narrower view of only solving achievement goals. Vickers view-point has been taken up by in recent years by the soft systems school of management [2].

2.3 ALP Combines Reactive and Proactive Thinking

The combination of forward and backward reasoning enables ALP agents to be both reactive and proactive. They are reactive when they use forward reasoning to respond to changes in the environment, and they are proactive when they use backward reasoning to achieve goals by reducing them to sub-goals. In everyday life, human agents are both reactive and proactive to varying degrees.

Consider, as another example, a simplified ALP version of Aesop's fable of the fox and the crow. Suppose the fox has the following achievement goal and beliefs:

Goal   I have the cheese.

Beliefs   The crow has the cheese.

An animal has an object
if the animal is near the object
and the animal picks up the object.

I am near the cheese
if the crow has the cheese
and the crow sings.

The crow sings if I praise the crow.

The fox can use its beliefs as a logic program, to reason backwards, to reduce its goal to the actions of praising the crow and picking up the cheese.[2] The fox's reduction of its goal to sub-goals is pictured in figure 3.

In keeping with the view that the primary goals of an agent are all maintenance goals, the fox's achievement goal almost certainly derives from a maintenance goal, such as this:

If I become hungry, then I have food and I eat it.

---

[2] The story is simplified partly because the element of time has been ignored. Obviously, the fox needs to praise the crow before picking up the cheese.

Here the condition of being hungry is triggered by an observation of being hungry, which the fox receives from its body. Notice that the achievement goal of having the food is only half of the story. To satisfy the maintenance goal, the fox also needs to eat the food.

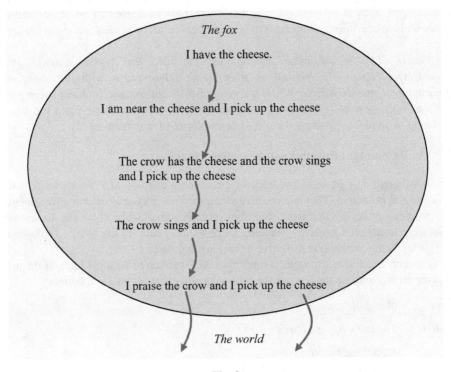

Fig. 3

In Aesop's fable, the fox's belief about the behaviour of the crow is true. The crow is a purely reactive agent, which responds to praise as the fox believes. The reactivity of the crow can be viewed as reasoning forwards in one step from an observation to derive an achievement goal, which is an action, from a maintenance goal. This is pictured in figure 4.

This view of the crow's behaviour is a logical abstraction of behaviour that might be hardwired into the crow as a system of lower-level stimulus-response associations. The relationship between such a logical abstraction and the stimulus-response associations is, arguably, like the relationship between software and hardware.

Notice the difference between the sentence

If the fox praises me, then I sing.

which is a goal for the crow, and the sentence

The crow sings if I praise the crow.

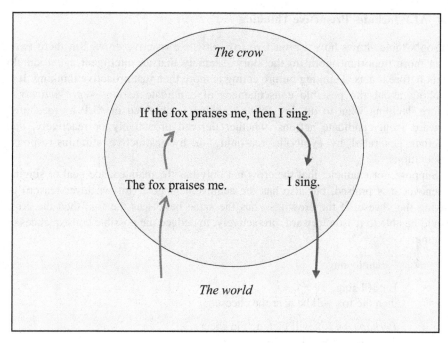

Fig. 4

which is a belief for the fox. Both sentences are implications. However, for the crow, the implication is used as a goal, to generate its behaviour. But for the fox, the implication is used as a belief, to describe the crow's behaviour and to reduce goals to sub-goals.

The difference between the two sentences has nothing to do with the order in which the conclusion and condition of the implication is written, because there is no semantic difference between writing an implication forwards in the form

If conditions then conclusion.

and writing it backwards in the form

Conclusion if conditions.

Semantically both implications have the same declarative meaning. (In the same way that both inequalities $1 < 2$ and $2 > 1$ have the same meaning.)

However, no matter how implications are written, there is an important distinction between them depending upon whether they are used as goals or as beliefs. When they are used as beliefs, they represent the world as it actually is. When they are used as goals, they represent the world as the agent would like it to be. When a goal is an implication, the agent performs actions to make the implication true. It only needs to perform these actions to make the conclusion of the implication true when the world makes the conditions of the implication true. It need not worry about performing actions when the world makes the conditions of the implication false. The analogous distinction in deductive databases between implications used as integrity constraints and implications used as rules was first investigated by Nicolas and Gallaire [17].

2.4 ALP Includes Pre-active Thinking

Aesop's fable shows how a proactive fox outwits a reactive crow. But there is an even more important moral to the story - namely that an intelligent agent should think before it acts. Thinking before acting is more than just proactive thinking. It is thinking about the possible consequences of candidate actions - *pre-actively* – before deciding what to do. Pre-active thinking is obtained in ALP by reasoning forward from candidate actions, whether derived proactively or reactively, and whether generated by symbolic reasoning or by instinctive stimulus-response associations.

Suppose, for example, that the crow not only has the maintenance goal of singing whenever it is praised, but also has the achievement goal (for whatever reason) of having the cheese. If the crow also has the same beliefs as the fox, then the crow would be able to reason forward, pre-actively, to deduce the possible consequences of singing:

> I want to sing.
>
> But if I sing,
> then the fox will be near the cheese.
>
> *Perhaps* the fox will pick up the cheese.
> Then the fox will have the cheese,
> and I will not have the cheese.
>
> Since I want to have the cheese,
> I will not sing.

Notice that the crow can not consistently achieve the goal of having the cheese and also maintain the goal of singing whenever it is praised. In real life, an agent needs to weigh its goals, trading one goal off against another.[3]

Notice too that the outcome of an agent's actions typically depends also on external events, over which the agent may have little or no control. In the story of the fox and crow, the outcome of the crow's singing depends on whether or not the fox decides to pick up the cheese.

3 Thinking Needs to be Combined with Deciding What to Do

In ALP, pre-active thinking simply checks whether candidate actions satisfy the integrity constraints. However, in real life, we also have to choose between actions, taking into consideration the relative utilities and probabilities of their possible consequences. In Decision Theory, the agent uses these considerations to choose an action that has maximum expected utility.

---

[3] Alternatively, if the crow wants to have the cheese in order to eat it, then the crow could satisfy both goals by first eating the cheese and then singing.

3.1 Combining ALP with Decision Theory

Suppose, for example, that I have the following beliefs:

> I get wet if it rains and I do not carry an umbrella.
> I stay dry if I carry an umbrella.
> I stay dry if it doesn't rain.

Assume also that I am about to leave home, and that as a sub-goal of leaving home I have to decide what to take with me, and in particular whether or not to take an umbrella. I can control whether to take an umbrella, but I can not control whether it will rain. At best I can only judge the probability of rain.

Reasoning forward from the assumption that I take an umbrella and then have to carry it, I can derive the certain outcome that I will stay dry. However, reasoning forward from the assumption that I do not carry an umbrella, I derive the uncertain outcome that I will get wet or I will stay dry, depending on whether or not it will rain.

In classical logic, that would be the end of the story. But, in Decision Theory, I can judge the likelihood that it is going to rain, judge the positive utility of staying dry compared with the negative utility of having to carry the umbrella, weigh the utilities by their associated probabilities, and then choose an action that has the maximum expected utility.

For the record, here is a simple, example calculation:

$$
\begin{aligned}
\text{Utility of getting wet} &= -8. \\
\text{Utility of staying dry} &= 2. \\
\text{Utility of carrying an umbrella} &= -3 \\
\text{Utility of not carrying an umbrella} &= 0 \\
\text{Probability of raining} &= .1 \\
\text{Probability of not raining} &= .9
\end{aligned}
$$

Assume   I take an umbrella.
Then   Probability of staying dry = 1
           Expected utility = 2 – 3 = - 1

Assume   I do not take an umbrella .
Then   Probability of staying dry = .9
           Probability of getting wet =.1
           Expected utility = .9 ·2 - .1 ·8 = 1.8 - .8 = 1

Decide   I do not take an umbrella!

Given the same utilities, the probability of rain would have to be greater than .3 before I would decide to take an umbrella.

Because thinking and deciding are separate components of the agent cycle, any way of thinking is compatible with any way of deciding. Thus the use of ALP for thinking can be combined with Decision Theory or any other way of deciding what to do. This combination of thinking and deciding in ALP agents is pictured in figure 5.

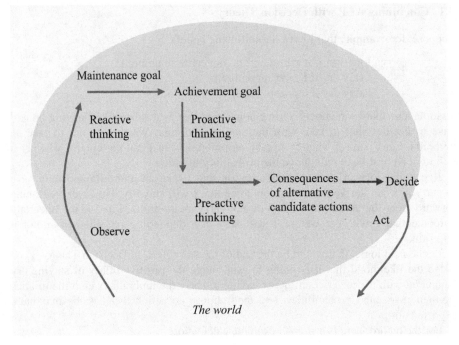

Fig. 5

A combination of abductive logic programming and Decision Theory has been developed by David Poole in his Independent Choice Logic [8]. He shows how the logic can be used to represent Bayesian networks, influence diagrams, Markov decision processes and the strategic and extensive form of games.

Poole focuses on the semantics of ICL, whereas I focus on the logical and computational procedures an individual agent might use in practice. One consequence of this difference is that he views condition-action rules as *policies*, and represents them by ordinary logic programs, whereas I view them as goals, and represent them as integrity constraints.

3.2 Decision Making Can Often Be Compiled into the Thinking Component of the Agent Cycle

The problem with Decision Theory is that it requires an unrealistic amount of information about utilities and probabilities and too much computation. Nonetheless, Decision Theory represents a normative ideal against which other, more practical decision-making methods can be evaluated.

In the case of taking or not taking an umbrella, a more practical alternative might be to use maintenance goals or condition-action rules instead[4]:

---

[4] In this representation the decision not to take an umbrella is implicit. It holds if the decision to take an umbrella does not hold.

> If I leave home and it is raining then I take an umbrella.
> If I leave home and there are dark clouds in the sky then I take an umbrella.
> If I leave home and the weather forecast predicts rain then I take an umbrella.

The maintenance goals in this example compile decision-making into the thinking component of the agent cycle. In some cases, the compilation might be an exact implementation of the Decision Theoretic specification. In other cases, it might only be an approximation.

Other alternatives to Decision Theory include the use of priorities between different actions, goals or condition-action rules, and the use of default reasoning.

4 Combining Higher-Level and Lower-Level Thinking

4.1 Higher Levels of Thinking Can Be Compiled into Lower Levels

Abductive logic programs have a computational, as well as a logical, interpretation. Goals and beliefs expressed in logical form can be viewed as programs written in a high-level programming language. Programs written at this high, logical level are executed by backward and forward reasoning.

For the sake of efficiency, high-level programs are often compiled into lower-level programs and are executed using corresponding lower-level computational mechanisms. Usually the higher and lower-level programs are written in distinct programming languages. However, they can also be written in the same language.

Compiling a high level program into a more efficient, lower level program written in the same language is called *program transformation*. Program transformation typically gains efficiency by performing at compile time, once and for all, execution steps that would otherwise have to be performed repeatedly, at run time. In the case of abductive logic programs, higher-level programs can be transformed into lower-level, more efficient programs, by performing reasoning steps in advance, before they are needed.

This is easy to see in the London underground example. The original high-level ALP representation can be compiled/transformed into the equivalent, more efficient condition-action rule representation:

> If there are flames then I press the alarm signal button.
> If there is smoke then I press the alarm signal button.
> If one person attacks another then I press the alarm signal button.
> If someone becomes seriously ill then I press the alarm signal button.
> If there is an accident then I press the alarm signal button.

This lower-level program is written in the same higher-level ALP language as the original representation, but it now consists of five maintenance goals, rather than one maintenance goal and eight beliefs. It is obtained by reasoning in advance, replacing the concept of "emergency" by all of the alternative types of emergency, replacing the concept of "fire" by the two different ways of recognizing a fire, and reducing "getting help" to the action of pressing the alarm signal button.

The two representations are computationally equivalent, in the sense that they give rise to the same externally observable behaviour. However, the lower-level program is more efficient. Not only does it require fewer steps to execute at run time, but it uses simpler reasoning techniques, consisting of forward reasoning alone, instead of the combination of forward and backward reasoning needed by the higher-level program.

The two representations are not logically equivalent. The high-level representation logically implies the lower-level representation, but not vice versa. In particular, the higher-level representation has an explicit representation of the concepts of there being an emergency and of getting help, which are only implicit in the lower-level representation. Moreover, the higher-level representation also has an explicit representation of the purpose of the agent's behaviour, namely to get help whenever there is an emergency, which is only implicit as an *emergent goal* in the lower-level representation.

In computing, higher-level representations (including program specifications) are generally developed, before they are compiled/transformed into lower-level representations for the sake of efficiency. However, if anything then goes wrong with the lower-level representation, it is generally easier to debug and correct the higher-level representation and to recompile it into the lower-level form, than it is to change the lower-level representation itself.

For example, if something goes wrong with the condition-action rule formulation of the London underground rules - if the button doesn't work, or if the driver doesn't get help - then the rules will fail, but the passenger might not even recognise there is a problem. Or, if the environment changes – if new kinds of emergencies arise or if better ways of getting help are developed – then it is easier to extend the higher-level representation than it is to modify the lower-level rules.

In computing, it is common to iterate the compilation of programs into a number of increasingly lower-levels, and ultimately into hardware. Historically, however, lower-level languages were used before higher-level, more human-oriented languages were developed. Because legacy systems originally developed and implemented in such lower-level languages are difficult to maintain, it is common to re-implement them in modern higher-level languages. This can sometimes be done by an inverse process of *decompiling* lower-level programs into higher-level programs. However, because of the undisciplined nature of low-level programming languages, the attempt to decompile such programs may only be partially successful. In many cases it may only be possible to approximate the lower-level programs by higher-level ones, sometimes only guessing at their original purpose.

4.2 Combining Deliberative and Intuitive Thinking

The relationship between deliberative and intuitive thinking is analogous to the relationship between higher-level and lower-level program execution.

The simplest relationship is when, as the result of frequent repetition, deliberative thinking migrates to the intuitive level – when, for example, a person learns to use a keyboard, play a musical instrument, or drive a car. This is like compiling or transforming a high-level program into a lower-level program. After a particular combination of high-level, general-purpose procedures has been used many times over, the combination is compressed into a computationally equivalent, lower-level shortcut. The shortcut is a special-purpose procedure, which achieves the same result as the combination of more general procedures, but it does so more efficiently and with less awareness of its purpose.

Conversely, intuitive thinking and tacit knowledge can sometimes be made explicit – for example, when a linguist constructs a formal grammar for a natural language, a coach explains how to swing a golf club, or a knowledge engineer develops an expert system. This is like decompiling a low-level representation into a higher-level representation. In many cases it can be hard to distinguish whether the low-level representation is implemented in hardware or in software, and the resulting higher-level representation may only be approximate.

In computing, higher-level and lower-level programs can operate in tandem, as when the lower-level program is used on a routine basis, but the higher-level program is used to modify and recompile the lower-level program when it goes wrong or needs to be updated. In human thinking, however, intuitive and deliberative thinking are often coupled together more closely. Intuitive thinking generates candidate judgments and actions rapidly and unconsciously, while deliberative thinking consciously monitors the results. This close coupling of deliberative and intuitive thinking is like the use of pre-active thinking in ALP agents to monitor candidate actions generated reactively by condition-action rules.

These relationships between different levels of thinking are pictured, somewhat imperfectly, in figure 6.

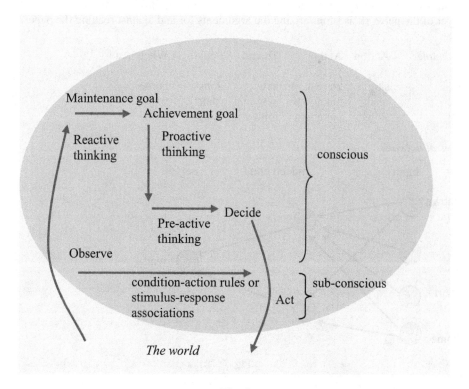

Fig. 6

5 Neural Networks

It is a common view in Cognitive Science that intuitive thinking is best modelled by sub-symbolic neural networks [13], which employ distributed representations with hidden nodes that do not have a symbolic interpretation. However, in their text book, *Computational Intelligence: A Logical Approach*, Poole *et al* [9] show how to represent any feed-forward neural network as a logic program. Forward reasoning with the logic program simulates forward execution of the neural network.

Poole *et al* illustrate their representation with the example (figure 7) of a person's decision whether to read an article. The decision is based upon such factors as whether the author is known or unknown, the article starts a new thread or is a follow-up article, the article is short or long, and the person is at home or at work.

The weights on the arcs are obtained by training an initial version of the network with a training set of examples. In the logic program, "f" is a sigmoid function that coerces the real numbers into the range [0,1]. Similarly, the "strengths" of the inputs lie in the range [0,1], where 0 is associated with the Boolean value *false* and 1 with *true*.

It is generally held that neural networks are unlike logic, in that they can have hidden units that can not be interpreted as concepts or propositions. Indeed, Poole *et al* characterize their example as illustrating just that point. However, in my formulation of the logic program, to make it more readable, I have given the predicate symbols "meaningful" predicate names, interpreting the hidden units in the middle layer of the network as summarizing the arguments for and against reading the paper.

Example	Action	Author	Thread	Length	Where read
E1	skip	known	new	long	home
E2	reads	unknown	new	short	work
E3	skips	unknown	follow-up	long	work

Neural network

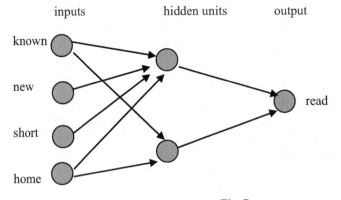

Fig. 7

Logic program

I read with strength S_3
if   there is an argument for reading with strength S_1
and   there is an argument against reading with strength S_2
and $S_3 = f(-2.98 + 6.88 S_1 - 2.1 S_2)$

There is an argument for reading with strength S_1
if   known with strength S_4
and   new with strength S_5
and   short with strength S_6
and   home with strength S_7
and $S_1 = f(-5.25 + 1.98 S_4 + 1.86 S_5 + 4.71 S_6 - .389 S_7)$

There is an argument against reading with strength S_2
if   known with strength S_4
and   new with strength S_5
and   short with strength S_6
and   home with strength S_7
and $S_2 = f(.493 - 1.03 S_4 - 1.06 S_5 - .749 S_6 + .126 S_7)$

The logic program is an exact, logical representation of the neural network. However, it employs numerical values and functions, which can only be approximated by a natural language representation, such as this:

I read an article
if the argument for reading the article is strong
and the argument against reading the article is weak.

There is an argument for reading an article
if the article is short.

There is an argument against reading an article
if the thread is a follow-up and the author is unknown.

The terms "strong" and "weak" are explicitly vague, whereas the notions of "an article being short", "a thread being new" and "an author being known" are implicitly vague. Taking this into account, the representation can be transformed into a simpler form, where all vagueness is implicit and where the arguments for and against reading an article are also implicit:

I read an article
if the article is short and the thread is new.

I read an article
if the article is short and the thread is a follow-up and the author is known.

Expressed in this way and treating the sentences as goals rather than as beliefs, the problem of deciding whether to read an article is similar to the problem of deciding whether to take an umbrella when leaving home. In both cases, the decision depends upon the interpretation of implicitly vague concepts, such as an article being short or there being dark clouds in the sky.

In both cases, moreover, the decision can also be made at a higher-level, by analysing the goals and other outcomes that the decision might be expected to achieve. In the case of reading an article, is the higher-level goal to gain information? Or is it simply to be entertained? If it is to gain information, how likely is it that the article will contain the information I am looking for? Is it worth the effort involved? Or would it be better to consult an expert instead?

In the case of taking an umbrella when I leave home, is the higher-level goal to keep my hair and clothing neat and tidy? Or is it to avoid catching a chill and coming down with a cold? In the first case, maybe it should just wear a hat and some suitable outdoor clothing. In the second case, if I am so fragile, then maybe I should stay home or travel by taxi.

6 Logic as Wide-Spectrum Language of Thought

The neural network example suggests that logic can represent a wide spectrum of levels of thought, ranging from subconscious thought at the neural network level to conscious thought in natural language. At the neural network level, logic programs can represent connections among vague concepts that hold with varying degrees of strength. Although these degrees might have precise values at the neurological level, they are not accessible to higher-levels of consciousness and can only be approximated in natural language.

A number of authors have investigated the relationship between neural networks and logic programs. One of the earliest of these investigations, by Holldobler and Kalinke [15], studied the problem of translating normal logic programs into neural networks. More recently, Stenning and van Lambalgen [16] have argued that the implementation of logic programs by neural networks shows that logic can model intuitive thinking in the dual process model. D'Avila Garcez, Broda and Gabbay [14], on the other hand, studied the problem of extracting higher-level, "meaningful" logic programs from neural networks. Taken together with the direct translation of neural networks into correspondingly low-level logic programs of Poole et al [9], these studies suggest that logic can model different levels of thought, from neural networks to natural language.

The relationship between logic and natural language is normally viewed from the linguistic perspective, by studying the problem of extracting logical meaning from natural language. But it can also be viewed from the knowledge representation perspective, by comparing the logical form of an agent's thoughts with the communication of those thoughts to another agent in natural language.

Although logical representations are normally presented in symbolic, mathematical form, they can also be expressed in a stylized form of natural language, as in this paper. Both of these forms are unambiguous and context-independent. Thus, to the extent that some form of logic is adequate for knowledge representation, this provides evidence that human agents might think in a mental language that is a logical form of natural language.

In contrast with the thoughts we have in our mind, our natural language communication of those thoughts is generally more ambiguous and context-sensitive than we intend. This suggests that our thoughts may be more logical than their natural language expression might suggest. Even natural language communications that seem to be in explicit logical form can be more ambiguous than they seem on the surface.

As Stenning and van Lambalgen [16] argue, natural language communications need to be interpreted to determine their intended logical form, even when those communications are already expressed in logical form. They argue that the gap between the surface logical structure of sentences and the deeper logical structure of their intended meanings helps to explain and refute certain psychological experiments that suggest that people are not logical. They show, moreover, that human performance in these experiments is compatible with the thesis that people apply logical reasoning to the intended meanings of sentences rather than to their surface form. In fact, in their main example, they show, not only that the intended meanings of sentences can be expressed in logical form, but that they have logic programming form, and that the minimal model semantics of logic programs gives a better analysis of human performance in these experiments than the classical semantics of traditional logic.

This difference between the surface structure of natural language and its underlying logical form is illustrated also by the second sentence of the London underground Emergency Notice:

> If there is an emergency then you press the alarm signal button.
> The driver will stop if any part of the train is in a station.

The second sentence has an explicitly logical form, due to its use of the logical connective "if" and the quantifier "any". However, taken literally, the sentence doesn't express what its authors probably had in mind:

> The driver will stop *the train* if *someone presses the alarm signal button*
> and any part of the train is in a station.

It is likely that most people interpret the second sentence of the Notice as it is intended, rather than as it is expressed. This suggests that people are more logical than many psychologists are inclined to believe.

7   Thinking = Logic + Control

The view that logic can serve as a wide-spectrum language of thought is in marked contrast with conventional views of logic in cognitive science. Paul Thagard [11], for example, in his introductory textbook, "Mind: Introduction to Cognitive Science" (page 45) writes:

> "In logic-based systems the fundamental operation of thinking is *logical deduction*, but from the perspective of rule-based systems the fundamental operation of thinking is *search*."

Here he uses the term "rule-based system" to refer to condition-action rule production systems. He then goes on to say that among the various models of thinking investigated in cognitive science, rule-based systems have "the most psychological applications" (page 51).

Jonathan Baron [1] in his textbook, "Thinking and Deciding" writes, page 4:

> "Thinking about actions, beliefs and personal goals can all be described in terms of a common framework, which asserts that thinking consists of *search* and *inference*. We *search* for certain objects and then *make inferences* from and about the objects we have found."

Baron associates logic with making inferences, but not with performing search. He also distinguishes thinking from deciding, but restricts the application of logic to the pre-active, inference-making component of thinking.

Both Thagard and Baron fail to recognize that, to be used in practice, logic needs to be controlled. This could be put in the form of a pseudo-equation[5]:

$$Thinking = Logic + Control.$$

Here the term "Logic" refers to goals and beliefs expressed in logical form and "Control" refers to the manner in which the inference rules of logic are applied. Control includes the use of forward and backward reasoning. In the case of backwards reasoning, it includes strategies for selecting sub-goals, as well as strategies for searching for alternative ways of solving goals and sub-goals. It also includes the application of inference rules in sequence or in parallel.

Frawley [13] argues that the analysis of algorithms into logic plus control also applies to mental algorithms and helps to explain different kinds of language disorders. He argues that Specific Language Impairment, for example, can be understood as a defect of the logic component of mental algorithms for natural language, whereas Williams syndrome and Turner syndrome can be understood as defects of the control component.

In fairness to Thagard and Baron, it has to be acknowledged that they are simply reporting generally held views of logic, which do not take into account some of the more recent developments of logic in Artificial Intelligence. Moreover, both, in their different ways, draw attention to characteristics of thinking that are missing both from traditional logic and from the simple pro-active model of thinking associated with logic programming. Thagard draws attention to the importance of reactive thinking with condition-action rules, and Baron to the importance of pre-active thinking by inference after search.

8   Conclusions

There isn't space in this paper to discuss all of the arguments that have been made against logic. Instead, I have considered only some of the most important alternatives that have been advocated – production systems, decision theory, and neural networks, in particular.

In the case of production systems, I have argued that condition-action rules are subsumed by maintenance goals in logical form. They are the special case of

---

[5] In the same sense that *Algorithm = Logic + Control* [5].

maintenance goals in which no forward reasoning is necessary to process observations, and no backward reasoning is necessary to reduce goals to sub-goals.

In the case of decision theory, I have argued that forward reasoning can be used pre-actively to derive possible consequences of candidate actions, and can be combined with any way of deciding between the alternatives. One such possibility is to use decision theory directly to choose a candidate action having maximum expected utility. Another is to compile such decisions into heuristic maintenance goals that approximate the decision-theoretic normative ideal.

In the case of neural networks, I have considered how the low-level logic-programming representation of feed-forward networks, given by *Poole et al*, might be approximated by higher-level logical representations. I have also suggested that such lower-level and higher-level logical representations might interact in a manner similar to the way in which intuitive and deliberative thinking interact in the dual process model. The lower-level representation proposes intuitive answers to problems as they arise, and the higher-level representation monitors and modifies the proposals as time allows.

I have restricted my attention in this paper to the way in which logic can be used to help control the routine, real-time behaviour of an intelligent agent. Except for program transformation, in which a higher-level representation is compiled into a more efficient, lower-level form, I have not considered the wider issues of learning and of revising goals and beliefs. Fortunately, there has been much work in this area, including the work on inductive logic programming, which is relevant to this issue.

Again for lack of space, I have not been able to discuss a number of extensions of logic that have been developed in Artificial Intelligence and that are important for human thinking. Among the most important of these is the treatment of default reasoning and its interpretation in terms of argumentation. Also, I do not want to give the impression that all of the problems have been solved. In particular, the treatment of vague concepts and their approximations is an important issue that needs further attention.

Despite the limitations of this paper, I hope that it will suggest, not only that logic deserves greater attention in Cognitive Science, but that it can be applied more effectively by ordinary people in everyday life.

Acknowledgements

Many thanks to the anonymous reviewers and to Ken Satoh for their helpful comments on an earlier draft of this paper.

References

1. Baron, J.: Thinking and Deciding (second edition). Cambridge University Press(1994)
2. Checkland, P.: Soft Systems Methodology: a thirty year retrospective. John Wiley Chichester (1999)
3. Kahneman, D., Shane F.: Representativeness revisited: Attributive substitution in intuitive judgement. In: Heuristics of Intuitive Judgement: Extensions and Applications, Cambridge University Press (2002)

4. Kakas, T., Kowalski, R., Toni, F.: The Role of Logic Programming in Abduction. In: Gabbay, D., Hogger, C.J., Robinson, J.A. (eds.): Handbook of Logic in Artificial Intelligence and Programming 5. Oxford University Press (1998) 235-324

5. Kowalski, R.: Logic for Problem Solving. North Holland Elsevier (1979)

6. Kowalski, R.: How to be artificially intelligent. http://www.doc.ic.ac.uk/~rak/ (2002-2006)

7. Kowalski, R., Sadri, F.: From Logic Programming towards Multi-agent Systems. Annals of Mathematics and Artificial Intelligence. Vol. 25 (1999) 391-419

8. Poole, D.L.: The independent choice logic for modeling multiple agents under uncertainty. Artificial Intelligence. Vol. 94 (1997) 7-56

9. Poole, D.L., Mackworth, A.K., Goebel, R.: Computational intelligence: a logical approach. Oxford University Press (1998)

10. Smith, E.R., DeCoster, J.: Dual-Process Models in Social and Cognitive Psychology: Conceptual Integration and Links to Underlying Memory Systems. Personality and Social Psychology Review. Vol. 4 (2000) 108-131

11. Thagard, P.: Mind: Introduction to Cognitive Science. MIT Press (1996)

12. Vickers, G.: The Art of Judgement. Chapman and Hall, London (1965)

13. Frawley, W.: Control and Cross-Domain Mental Computation: Evidence from Language Breakdown. *Computational Intelligence,* 18(1), (2002) 1-28

14. d'Avila Garcez, A.S., Broda, K., Gabbay, D.M.: Symbolic knowledge extraction from trained neural networks: A sound approach. Artificial Intelligence 125 (2001) 155–207

15. Holldobler, S. Kalinke, Y. : Toward a new massively parallel computational model for logic programming. In *Proceedings of the Workshop on Combining Symbolic and Connectionist Processing, ECAI 94,* (1994) 68-77

16. Stenning, K., van Lambalgen, M.: Semantic interpretation as computation in non-monotonic logic. Cognitive Science (2006)

17. Nicolas, J.M., Gallaire, H.: Database: Theory vs. interpretation. In Gallaire, H.,Minker, J. (eds.): Logic and Databases. Plenum, New York (1978)

Ability in a Multi-agent Context: A Model in the Situation Calculus

Laurence Cholvy[1], Christophe Garion[2], and Claire Saurel[1]

[1] ONERA Centre de Toulouse,
2 Avenue Édouard Belin,
31055 Toulouse, France
{cholvy, saurel}@cert.fr
[2] SUPAERO,
10 Avenue Édouard Belin,
31055 Toulouse, France
garion@supaero.fr

Abstract. This paper studies the notion of ability and its relation with the notion of action in a multi-agent context. It introduces the distinction between two notions respectively called "theoretical ability" and "ability". The main contribution of this paper is a model of these notions in the Situation Calculus.

1 Introduction

Allocating tasks or planning in a multi-agent context [8, 3], requires taking into account what the agents are able to do, *i.e.* the agents abilities, in order to assign tasks to agents who are able to perform them. The notion of ability must then be modelled and this implies to explicit the parameters which define this notion.

Obviously, the agent itself, or the group of agents, is one of these parameters. But what is the nature of what the ability applies on? For instance, when we say that *John is able to paint the door*, do we mean that John is able to perform a particular action which consists in applying paint with a specific brush on the door? Or do we mean that John is able to see to it that the door is painted, by the means he wants, for instance by delegating this task to someone else? Modelling ability thus implies modelling actions.

In the literature, there are two main approaches to action theory. The first one consists in giving in the language means to explicitly represent actions. This is the case of dynamic logic for instance [9], which offers modal operators to speak about the execution of an action, and also the execution of an action by an agent. This is also the case of situation calculus [14, 16], which allows one to represent actions, their preconditions and their effects, but also situations considered as results of the successive application of actions in an initial situation. On the contrary, actions are not explicitly represented in the second approach. The operators defined there only allow to express the fact that the agent sees about some property to be true (cf. the *stit* operator [11] and the notion of *agency* in [7]).

F. Toni and P. Torroni (Eds.): CLIMA VI, LNAI 3900, pp. 23–36, 2006.

As the notion of ability is strongly linked to the notion of action, it has been studied according to these two approaches. For instance, the multi modal dynamic logic KARO [18] aims at defining agent's ability to perform an action according to the first approach. Primitive concepts are the agent's knowledge, its capacity to perform an action, the effects of an action and the opportunity associated with an action. Ability and opportunity are two intertwined notions, we will come back on it later.

Concerning the second approach, the notion of ability does not bear on actions, but on the fact that a property is true [10, 7]. These two formalisms are based on propositional modal logics. In [7], Elgesem defines ability and action as primitive notions. He considers a function f which determines for a given world w and a goal φ the worlds in which the agent has realized its ability to see to it that φ is true from w. Thus, an agent is able to see to it that φ is true if and only if the set of worlds $f(w, \varphi)$ is not empty. With this definition, ability and action, which is also defined by f, are two binded notions. For instance, if an agent sees to it that φ is true, then this agent is able to see to it that φ. In [10], Horty uses temporal models to represent actions: an agent sees to it that φ is true at a moment m if it restricts the "histories" which m belongs to in order that φ is true. The ability for an agent to see to it that φ is true is defined as the possibility (in the classical sense, see [2]) for the agent to see to it that φ is true. Let us notice that with this formalism, Horty avoids several paradoxes. In particular, it cannot be deduced that if φ is true, then the agent has the ability to see to it that φ.

We must also mention [12], in which the authors use the situation calculus to model the notion of "ability to reach a goal", *i.e.* "ability to make a proposition true". Two definitions are given in a mono-agent context. According to the one the authors find the simplest to use, the agent has the ability in a situation s to make φ true (*i.e.* the agent is able to reach the goal φ) if there exists a sequence of actions such that the agent knows in s that executing these actions will make φ true. In other terms, the agent has the ability to make φ true if he knows a plan to achieve φ.

This brief state of the art shows that there is no consensus on what the ability applies on. However, we find in the literature several points of agreement relatively to the notion of ability.

First, the notion of ability must not be confused with the notion of possibility nor with the notion of permission [17]. These possible confusions are due to ambiguities of the natural language. For instance, the sentence "I can open the door" is sometimes used to say "I am able to open the door" according to the notion of ability we study here. But this sentence is also sometimes used to say "I have now the possibility to open the door" (because, for instance, the door is now unlocked), but this does not mean that I am able to do so. Here, it refers to a notion of possibility. Finally, this sentence is sometimes used to mean "I have the permission to open the door", which still does not imply that I am able to do so and which refers here to a deontic notion.

Secondly, several people agree on the fact that two kinds of ability must be distinguished [17, 18, 5, 1].

One can first distinguish what is called "generic ability" by some people (or "ability" by others) and which refers to the agent's competences to perform an action in normal conditions. "I can open the door" means here that I know what to do to open the door, independently of my current intellectual or physical state and of the current state of the world. Thus, with this point of view, I can say "I am able to open the door" even if my arms are broken or the door is locked.

One can also distinguish what is called "occasional ability" by some people (or "pragmatic possibility", or "opportunity to exercise an ability" by others) and which refers to the current situation. Here, "I can open the door" means that I have the generic ability to open the door *and* the current situation is such that conditions are favourable for me to use this generic ability (for instance, my arms are not broken and the door is unlocked).

Finally, in a multi-agent context, one of the main problems is to define the notion of ability relatively to a group of agents, and in particular to infer the ability of the group from the abilities of the individuals of the group. For instance, what are the conditions for saying that a group of people is able to paint the door? Or a group of people is able to first sand the door, then to paint it? The problem is not trivial since the notion of ability previously called "occasional" is a dynamic notion which depends on the state of the world in which it is evaluated. But in a multi-agent context, the dynamic of the world is hard to foresee because several agents may change the world.

This paper presents a preliminary study of the notion of ability in a multi-agent context. As far as we know, no previous work has already attacked the same question in a multi-agent context. In particular, it must be noticed that the notion we are trying to model here is different from the one Pauly has studied [15]. Indeed, in his work "an agent (or a group of agents) can bring about a proposition" means that this agent (or group of agents) has a (collective) efficient strategy which makes this proposition true, whatever the other people do. In particular, the logic defined by Pauly does not apply when a first agent can bring about a proposition and another one can bring about its contrary.

This paper is organized as follows. In section 2, we informally discuss some requirements about the notion of ability. In section 3 we propose a formal model, in the Situation Calculus, of concepts related to ability and we justify the use of such formalism. Some properties of this model are given in 4, and an example is detailed in 5. Section 6 presents an implementation of our modelling and section 7 is devoted to a discussion and presents some perspectives.

2   Informal Requirements About Ability

Our modelling lies on the following choices:

- The ability we focus on bears on actions. We aim at characterizing the meaning of being able to perform actions, *i.e.* to perform a procedure [6].

- We aim at explicitly representing actions, their preconditions and their effects. We consider the general case when some primitive actions may require several agents to be performed (for instance, lifting an heavy door requires two agents).
- We aim at defining the ability of an agent to perform an action as the combination of its competences and some favourable conditions that allow it to perform that action. But we also aim at making a difference between the conditions which are related to the agent only from those which are not. For doing so, we introduce an intermediary notion called "theoretical ability".

2.1 Model of Action

In our model of action, any primitive action is specified by its preconditions which are the conditions under which it can be performed, independently of any agent. When these conditions are true, we say that *the action is possible* [16].

Example 1. For instance, "painting" is only possible if there is some paint and a brush.

2.2 Model of Ability

In our model, the primitive notion is the notion of competence described as follows:

Competence. Competence represents the knowing-how of the agent (or agents) relatively to an action. This knowledge may be inborn or may result from a learning phase. In our model, this information is considered as *primitive*.

For instance, we will have initial data like: "John is competent to paint a door" or "John and Peter are competent together to lift the door". The first sentence means that John knows the successive gestures he has to make so that the door is painted. The second sentence means that they both know how to coordinate their gestures in order to lift the door.

In this work, we will assume that the competences of the agents can not be deleted: once an agent is competent to perform an action, he will always be. This assumption seems to be justified in many applications with rather short temporal horizon where it can be assumed that the agents do not loose their competences. As we will see, this assumption can be easily removed.

It must be noticed that this notion of competence is different from the one Cohen and Levesque consider in [4], where, if an agent competent for a proposition p believes p, then p is true.

Theoretical Ability. From the notion of competence, we first define the notion of theoretical ability as follows:

Definition 1. *Let A be a non empty group of agents (possibly a singleton) and α be a primitive action. A is theoretically able to perform α if:*

1. *A is competent to perform α*
2. *some conditions, related to the agents of A, are true.*

Remember that competence is considered to be a primitive notion. The conditions expressed in point 2 concern the agent (its physical state for instance), but not all the environment.

Example 2. For instance, an agent is theoretically able to paint a door if it is competent for paint a door and if it is not tired.

Notice that this notion is close to the notion of *ability* of [18].

Ability. The notion of ability is finally defined from the notion of theoretical ability by taking into account the conditions which define the possibility to perform the action.

Definition 2. *Let A be a non empty group of agents (possibly a singleton) and α be a primitive action. A is able to perform α if:*

1. *A is theoretically able to perform α*
2. *α is possible.*

Notice that the notion of possibility in this definition is the one defined by Reiter in [16]. The possibility here is a set of conditions concerning the state of the world excepting the agent.

Example 3. For instance, an agent is able to paint a door if it is theoretically able to paint the door (i.e, competent for painting the door, not tired) and if there is some paint and a brush.

This notion of ability is a kind of occasional ability in the sense of section 1.

It can also be noticed that the previous condition "α is possible" is very close to the notion of "opportunity to exercise an ability" mentioned in [5], as well as the one mentioned in [18]. It means that, in our approach, an agent is able to perform an action if it has the opportunity to exercise the theoretical ability to perform this action.

2.3   Extensions to More Complex Actions

Considering only primitive actions is not enough and we must also consider more complex actions obtained by composition of primitive ones. In this preliminary work, we focus on sequences (like for instance: "lift the door, then paint it".)

We would like to validate the following assertion (cf. [18]): agent a is able to perform the sequence α then β if a is able to perform α and, once a has performed α, a is able to perform β.

Example 4. For instance, assume that sanding a door is tiring. Then, we would like to deduce that John is not able to sand then to paint the door (i.e, not able to perform the action "sand then paint"). Indeed, even if John is able to sand the door, once he will have sanded it, he will be tired. Thus, he will not be able to paint the door.

2.4   Deriving Ability of a Group from Abilities of Individuals

In a multi-agent context, it is necessary to extend these previous notions for a group of agents. We will say that a group of agents is able to perform a primitive action if one of its sub-group (possibly a singleton) is able to perform it. Notice that in some cases, only a subgroup may be competent to do some action: an agent does not have the competence to carry a piano, but a group of three agents may have it.

As for the sequences, we would like to validate the fact that a group is able to perform the action "α then β" if one of its sub-group is able to perform α and, once this sub-group has performed α, the group is able to perform β.

Example 5. Consider now that Peter is also competent to paint the door and is not tired. Then the group {John, Peter} is able to sand the door then to paint it. Indeed, John is able to sand it (see previously) and, once John has sanded the door, the group is still able to paint the door (because Peter has remained not tired).

3   Model of Ability in the Situation Calculus

3.1   The Situation Calculus

We suggest to use the Situation Calculus to model these notions for two reasons:

- firstly, this formalism is a good candidate for modelling actions since it offers means to explicitly express preconditions and effects of actions;
- secondly, an important problem underlying this present work, the frame problem (i.e, how to express what are the changings induced by the performance of an action by an agent and how to express what remains unchanged), has been provided a solution in the Situation Calculus by Reiter.

3.2   The Language

We consider a first order language $\mathcal{L}_{CS}$ which will allow us to model and reason about actions and ability. In this language, the changes of the world are resulting from action performances. It is defined as follows:

- a set of constants to represent agents A.
- a set of functions and constants used to represent primitive actions, with parameters or without.
  For instance the term "*paint(x)*" will represent the action "to paint the object x".
- A unary predicate *primitive(.)* used to list the primitive actions.
  Thus, *primitive(paint(x))* means that *paint(x)* is a primitive action.
- a binary function ; used to represent the sequence of actions.
  sand(x); paint(x) will represent the action which consists in sanding the object x then painting it.

- a constant S_0 used to represent the initial situation.
- a ternary function do.

  $do(\mathcal{A}, paint(x), s)$ represents the situation which follows from the situation s, when the group of agents $\mathcal{A}$ has painted the object x.

  Notice that here, unlike the "classical" Situation Calculus, the agent is not a parameter of the function which represents the action, but is a parameter of the function do which represents the performance of the action.
- a set of predicates called relational *fluents* which represent properties which may be changed by the performance of an action. The last argument of a fluent is a situation.

  For instance, $painted(door, S_0)$ expresses that the door is painted in the initial situation S_0.
- a particular binary fluent *Poss* used to express that an action is possible in a situation.
- a particular binary fluent *competent* used to represent the fact that an agent (or a group) is competent for performing a primitive action.

  For instance, $competent(\{a\}, paint(door), s)$ expresses that agent a is competent to paint the door in situation s.
- a particular ternary fluent *able_t* used to represent the fact that an agent (or a group) is theoretically able to perform an action.

  $able\_t(\{a\}, paint(door), S_0)$ expresses that agent a is, in situation S_0, theoretically able to paint the door.
- a particular ternary fluent *able* used to represent the fact that an agent (or a group) is able to perform an action.

  $able(\{a\}, paint(door), S_0)$ expresses that agent a is, in situation S_0, able to paint the door.

3.3   The Axioms

Description of the Initial Situation. First, the initial state of the world must be represented. For doing so, for any fluent f and for any tuples $t_1, \ldots, t_n$ of ground terms such that $f(t_1, \ldots, t_n)$ is true in the initial situation, we consider the following axiom:

$$f(t_1, \ldots, t_n, S_0) \tag{1}$$

In particular, since *competent* is a fluent, for any group G competent for performing the primitive action α in the initial situation S_0, we consider the following axiom:

$$competent(G, \alpha, S_0) \tag{2}$$

Primitive Actions. For any primitive action α, we consider an axiom of the following form:

$$primitive(\alpha) \tag{3}$$

Precondition Axioms for Primitive Actions. We represent the preconditions of the primitive actions (*i.e.* the conditions that make the performance of the action possible) by an axiom of the following type:

$$\forall \alpha \forall S \; Poss(\alpha, S) \leftrightarrow pre(\alpha, S) \tag{4}$$

Precondition Axioms for Sequence. We then extend this kind of axioms for a sequence $\alpha; \beta$ where α is a primitive action and β is a complex action as follows:

$$\forall S \forall G \forall \alpha \forall \beta \quad Poss(\alpha, S) \wedge Poss(\beta, do(G, \alpha, S)) \leftrightarrow Poss(\alpha; \beta, S) \qquad (5)$$

Axiom (5) expresses that $\alpha; \beta$ is possible in S iff α is possible in S and β is possible after the performance of α in S.

Successor State Axioms. Following Reiter [16], for any fluent $f(t_1, \ldots, t_n)$, we consider a successor state axiom which specifies all the ways the value of the fluent may change.

$$\forall S \forall G \forall \alpha \quad Poss(\alpha, S) \rightarrow f(t_1, \ldots, t_n, do(G, \alpha, S)) \leftrightarrow \qquad (6)$$

$$\gamma_f^+(t_1, \ldots, t_n, \alpha, S) \vee (f(t_1, \ldots, t_n, S) \wedge \neg \gamma_f^-(t_1, \ldots, t_n, \alpha, S))$$

$\gamma_f^+(t_1, \ldots, t_n, \alpha, S)$ represents the conditions which make f true after α has been performed in S. $\gamma_f^-(t_1, \ldots, t_n, \alpha, S)$ represents the conditions which make f false after α has been performed in S.

Since *competent* is a *fluent*, we have to express a successor state axiom for it. In this paper, we assume that the competence is not deleted, *i.e.* once an agent is competent to perform an action. This is expressed by:

$$\forall \alpha \forall \beta \forall G \forall S \quad Poss(\beta, S) \rightarrow (competent(G, \alpha, do(G, \beta, S)) \leftrightarrow competent(G, \alpha, S)) \qquad (7)$$

One can wonder why we have chosen to use a fluent to represent competence if we assume that competence does not change during execution of action. Let us claim that our modelling allows to relax this assumption easily by modifying axiom (7).

Theoretical Ability Axioms. For any primitive action α, we consider an axiom of the following form:

$$\forall G \forall S \quad competent(G, \alpha, S) \wedge conditions\_t(G, \alpha, S) \rightarrow able\_t(G, \alpha, S) \qquad (8)$$

It expresses that a group G is theoretically able to perform α in situation S if G is competent for α in S and if some conditions related to G and α are satisfied.

Finally, in order to derive the theoretical ability for a group of agents, we consider:

$$\forall G \forall G' \forall \alpha \forall S \quad primitive(\alpha) \wedge (G' \subseteq G) \wedge able\_t(G', \alpha, S) \rightarrow able\_t(G, \alpha, S) \qquad (9)$$

$$\forall G \forall G' \forall \alpha \forall \beta \forall S \quad (G' \subseteq G) \wedge able\_t(G', \alpha, S) \wedge able\_t(G, \beta, do(G', \alpha, S)) \rightarrow able\_t(G, \alpha; \beta, S) \qquad (10)$$

Axiom (9) expresses the fact that if a sub group G' of G is theoretically able to perform a primitive action α, then the group G is also theoretically able to perform α. Axiom (10) expresses that if a sub-group G' of G is theoretically able to perform α and if G is theoretically able to perform β once G' has performed α, then G is theoretically able to perform $\alpha; \beta$ (*i.e.* to perform α then β).

Ability Axioms. Finally, the following axiom allows to derive the ability of a group:

$$\forall G \forall \alpha \forall S \; able\_t(G, \alpha, S) \wedge Poss(\alpha, S) \rightarrow able(G, \alpha, S) \tag{11}$$

4   Some Properties of This Model

Proposition 1. *Let* $\Sigma = \{(1), \ldots, (11)\}$ *be the set of axioms presented previously. Then :*

$$\Sigma \vdash \forall \alpha \forall \beta \forall G \forall G' \forall S \; able(G, \alpha, S) \wedge able(G', \beta, do(G, \alpha, S)) \rightarrow able(G \cup G', \alpha; \beta, S)$$

Proof. This proposition is proved by an inductive proof on the length of the sequence $\alpha; \beta$.

This proposition means that if the group G is able to perform α in the situation s and if the group G' is able to perform β after G has performed α in S, then the group $G \cup G'$ is able to perform $\alpha; \beta$ in S.

A corollary is the following:

Proposition 2. *Let* $\Sigma = \{(1), \ldots, (11)\}$ *be the set of axioms presented previously. Then :*

$$\Sigma \vdash \forall \alpha \forall \beta \forall G \forall S \; able(G, \alpha, S) \wedge able(G, \beta, do(G, \alpha, S)) \rightarrow able(G, \alpha; \beta, S)$$

Proposition 3. *Let* $\Sigma = \{(1), \ldots, (11)\}$ *be the set of axioms presented previously, f be a fluent and α a primitive action.* $\Sigma \vdash \forall G \forall S \quad Poss(\alpha, S) \rightarrow f(\ldots, do(G, \alpha, S)) \not\Longrightarrow \Sigma \vdash \forall S \forall G' \; f(\ldots, S) \rightarrow able(G', \alpha, S).$

Proof. This proposition is proved by finding a counter example. Let us consider an action α such that a postcondition of α is that f is true (i.e, after any performance of α by a group of agents G, f is true). Let us suppose that f is true in a situation S, then if we consider a group of agents G' such that each agent in G' is not competent for doing α (for instance), then G' is not able to perform α according to axiom (8)[1].

This result guaranties that we do not validate the paradox mentioned in introduction: "if φ is true, then the agent has the ability to see to it that φ".

5   Example

5.1   Description of the Example

Let a, b and c be three agents.

- Primitive actions we consider are: to lift the door (*lift*), to sand the door (*sand*), to paint the door (*paint*).

---

[1] Notice that this is true because *able_t* cannot be deduced in our model without using *competent*.

- Competence of agents are: a is competent for sanding the door and for painting it. b is only competent for painting the door. a and b together are competent for lifting the door. c is not competent for any action.
- The initial situation is such that there is a sander ($sander(S_0)$) and it works, there is some paint and the agents are not tired (for each agent a, $ok(a, S_0)$ holds).
- Sanding is possible if the sander works.
- Painting is possible if there is some paint ($paint_r$).
- An agent is theoretically able to sand the door if it is competent for doing so and if it is not tired ; an agent is theoretically able to paint the door is it is competent for doing so and if it is not tired ; two agents are together theoretically able to lift the door is they are together competent for doing so and if they are not tired.
- Successive state axioms are defined as follows:
  An agent is tired iff it has sanded the door, or it has participated in lifting the door.
  There is paint left after the execution of an action, except if it is a painting action.
  No action makes the sander out.

5.2   Formulas in the Situation Calculus

Description of the Initial Situation (Axioms (1) and (2))

$$ok(a, S_0)$$
$$ok(b, S_0)$$
$$ok(c, S_0)$$
$$paint\_r(S_0)$$
$$sander(S_0)$$
$$competent(\{a, b\}, lift, S_0)$$
$$competent(\{b, a\}, lift, S_0)$$
$$competent(a, sand, S_0)$$
$$competent(a, paint, S_0)$$
$$competent(b, paint, S_0)$$

Primitive Actions (Axioms (3))

$$primitive(lift)$$
$$primitive(sand)$$
$$primitive(paint)$$

Preconditions Axioms for Primitive Actions (Axioms (4))

$$\forall S \quad Poss(lift, S)$$

$$\forall S \quad sander(S) \leftrightarrow Poss(sand, S)$$

$$\forall S \quad paint\_r(S) \leftrightarrow Poss(paint, S)$$

Successive State Axioms (Axioms (6))

$$\forall B \forall Y \forall S \ \ Poss(Y, S) \rightarrow (sander(do(B, Y, S)) \leftrightarrow sander(S))$$

$$\forall A \forall X \forall S \ \ Poss(X, S) \rightarrow (paint\_r(do(A, X, S)) \leftrightarrow paint\_r(S) \wedge \neg(X = paint))$$

$$\forall A \forall B \forall X \forall S \ \ poss(X, S) \rightarrow (ok(A, do(B, X, S)) \leftrightarrow$$
$$((ok(A, S) \wedge (B = A) \wedge \neg(X = sand)) \vee$$
$$(ok(A, S) \wedge (A \in B) \wedge \neg(X = lift)) \vee$$
$$(ok(A, S) \wedge \neg(A \in B))))$$

Theoretical Ability Axioms (Axioms (8))

$$\forall A \forall B \forall S \ \ competent(A, B, lift, S) \wedge ok(A, S) \wedge ok(B, S) \rightarrow able\_t(\{A, B\}, lift, S)$$

$$\forall A \forall S \ \ competent(A, sand, S) \wedge ok(A, S) \rightarrow able\_t(A, sand, S)$$

$$\forall A \forall S \ \ competent(A, paint, S) \wedge ok(A, S) \rightarrow able\_t(A, paint, S)$$

5.3   Some Conclusions

Let us denote Σ the set of axioms (1),..., (11). Then,

- $\vdash \Sigma \rightarrow able\_t(a, paint, S_0)$
  In the initial situation, a is theoretically able to paint the door because it is competent for doing it and it is not tired.
- $\vdash \Sigma \rightarrow able\_t(a, paint, do(a, paint, S_0))$
  Since painting does not make the agent tired, a is still theoretically able to paint after he has painted.
- $\nvdash \Sigma \rightarrow able(a, paint, do(a, paint, S_0))$
  But, after a has painted the door, there is no more paint, so it cannot be proved that a is able to paint the door again (even if it is theoretically able as it is shown previously)
- $\nvdash \Sigma \rightarrow able\_t(a, sand; paint, S_0)$
  Indeed, after having sanded the door, a will be tired, so he will not be theoretically able to paint the door.
- $\nvdash \Sigma \rightarrow able\_t(a, paint, do(\{a, b\}, lift, S_0))$
  After the group a, b has lifted the door, a and b are tired. Thus, a is not theoretically able to paint the door.
- $\vdash \Sigma \rightarrow able(\{a, b\}, paint; lift, S_0)$
  The group a, b is able to paint then lift the door. Indeed once a or b will have painted the door, a and b will not be tired. So they will be able to lift the door.
- $\nvdash \Sigma \rightarrow able(\{a, b\}, lift; paint, S_0)$
  The group a, b is not able to lift then to paint the door. Indeed once a and b will have lifted the door, a and b will both be tired. So none of them will be able to paint the door.

– Let us add now that agent c is competent for painting the door:
Let Σ' the set obtained by adding the formula $competent(c, paint, S_0)$ to Σ.
Thus $\vdash \Sigma' \rightarrow able(\{a, b, c\}, lift; paint, S_0)$
The group a, b, c is now able to lift then to paint the door. Indeed, if agents a and b lift the door, then this does not make c tired. So c is able to paint the door after a and b have lifted the door.

6 Implementation

This model has been implemented in Prolog. As in [13], we use a binary predicate holds in order to represent fluents. For instance, $ok(a, S_0)$ is represented by holds(ok([a]), S0). The successor state axiom for fluent ok is expressed by the following clause:

```
holds(ok(A), do(B,X,S))  :- B=A, \+ (X=sand), holds(ok(A),S), Poss(X,S).
holds(ok(A), do(B,X,S))  :- member(A,B), \+ (X=lift), holds(ok(A),S),
                                                          Poss(X,S).
holds(ok(A), do(B,X,S))  :- \+ member(A,B), holds(ok(A),S), Poss(X,S).
```

We can show that, given a group of agents G and an action α primitive or not, we have $\Sigma \vdash able\_t(G, \alpha, S_0)$ (resp. $\Sigma \vdash able(G, \alpha, S_0)$) if and only if Prolog with negation as failure proves holds(able_t(G,alpha),S0) (resp. holds(able(G,alpha),S0)). For instance, resuming the example presented in section 5.3 using negation as failure, we can now show that the answer to the question holds(able([a,b], [paint,lift], S0)) is yes and the answer to holds(able([a,b], [lift,paint], S0) is no[2].

7 Discussion

In this paper, we have presented an attempt to model in the Situation Calculus the notions of theoretical ability and ability of an agent towards an action in a multi-agent context. Definitions of these two notions to groups of agents has also been given.

In this model, agents' theoretical ability depends on their competence and on some conditions depending on the agents. Agents' ability is then defined from theoretical ability and from some conditions which do not depend on the agents.

Introducing the notion of theoretical ability is of course interesting from a modelling point of view since it makes a distinction between conditions which are related to the agents who perform the actions and conditions which are not. But it may also be interesting in the preliminary phase of planning when choosing the agents who will be in charge of the task to be performed. Indeed, proving that the chosen agents are not even theoretically able to perform the global task is enough to prove that the task will never be performed by these agents and that changing agents is required.

---

[2] Notice that we implement sequence of actions as lists in Prolog.

However, if one is only interested in proving that a group of agents is able to perform an action, the intermediary notion of theoretical ability is not useful and definitions have to be compacted as follows:

$$\forall G \forall S \quad competent(G, \alpha, S) \wedge conditions\_t(G, \alpha, S) \wedge Poss(\alpha, S) \rightarrow able(G, \alpha, S)$$

This preliminary work has many perspectives.

First, some more formal properties on this model must be proved. In particular, formal relations with existing works mentioned in the introduction have to be established.

Secondly, another assumption could be made when inferring the ability of a group from the abilities of its agents. Indeed, the model presented here assumes that a group of agents is able to perform an action if one of its member is able to do so. But this assumes that the conditions for an agent to be theoretically able to perform an action do not depend on the fact that this agent belongs or not to a group. But it could happen that a single agent is theoretically able to perform an action but when it belongs to a group, it is no longer able (not because the others agents prevent him to do so but because belonging to a group changes the conditions sufficient for him to be theoretically able to perform the action).

Thirdly, we have to extend this work by considering more types of complex actions like concurrence, iteration or conditionals. We must also take into account time and action durations. For doing so, the solution provided in [6] can be adopted.

Finally, the model presented here does not take external actions into account. In particular, fluents are changed only by actions performed by the agents we consider. But in many applications, the world may change because some other agents we don't know change it. An immediate solution we could study, consists in introducing an "external agent" who could be used to model the evolution of the world which are independent from the other agents.

Acknowledgements

This work has been funded by DGA (Délégation Générale de l'Armement) under contract: SPOTI/0373088.

References

1. B. Chaib-Draa and R. Demolombe. L'interaction comme champ de recherche. *Information - Interaction - Intelligence, numéro spécial Modèles Formels de l'Interaction*, pages 5–24, 2001.
2. B.F. Chellas. *Modal logic. An introduction*. Cambridge University Press, 1980.
3. L. Cholvy and C. Garion. Distribution of goals addressed to a group of agents. In J. S. Rosenschein, T. Sandholm, M. Wooldridge, and M. Yokoo, editors, *Proceedings of the Second International Joint Conference on Autonomous Agents and Multiagent Systems*, pages 765–772. ACM Press, July 2003.
4. P.R. Cohen and H.J. Levesque. Intention is choice with commitment. *Artificial Intelligence*, 42:213–261, 1990.

5. R. Demolombe. Formalisation en logique des interactions entre agents : quels concepts formaliser ? Technical report, ONERA/DTIM, 2000. In French.

6. R. Demolombe and E. Hamon. What does it mean that an agent is performing a typical procedure: a formal definition in the Situation Calculus. In *Proceedings of the First International Joint Conference an Autonomous Agents and Multiagent Systems (AAMAS'02)*, pages 905–911, Bologna, Italy, 2002.

7. D. Elgesem. The modal logic of agency. *Nordic Journal of Philosophical Logic*, 2(2):1–46, 1997.

8. B.J. Grosz, L. Hunsberger, and S. Kraus. Planning and acting together. *AI Magazine*, 20(4):23–34, 1999.

9. D. Harel. Dynamic logic. In D. Gabbay and F. Guenthner, editors, *Handbook of Philosophical Logic*, volume 2, pages 497–604. D. Reidel Publishing Company, 1984.

10. J.F. Horty. Agency and obligation. *Synthese*, 108:269–307, 1996.

11. J.F. Horty and N. Belnap. The deliberative stit : a study of action, omission, ability and obligation. *Journal of Philosophical Logic*, 24:583–644, 1995. Reprinted in *The Philosopher's Annual, Volume 18-1995*, Ridgeview Publishing Company, 1997.

12. Y. Lespérance, H.J. Levesque, F. Lin, and R.B. Scherl. Ability and knowing how in the situation calculus. *Studia Logica*, 66(1):165–186, oct 2000.

13. H.J. Levesque, R. Reiter, Y. Lespérance, F. Lin, and R. Scherl. GOLOG: A logic programming language for dynamic domains. *Journal of Logic Programming*, 31:59–84, 1997.

14. J. MacCarthy and P. Hayes. Some philosophical problems from the standpoint of artificial intelligence. In D. Michie and B. Melzer, editors, *Machine Intelligence 4*, pages 463–502. Edinburgh University Press, 1969.

15. M. Pauly. A modal logic for conditional power in games. *Journal of Logic and Computation*, 12(1):149–166, 2000.

16. R. Reiter. The frame problem in the situation calculus: a simple solution (sometimes) and a completeness result for goal regression. In *Artificial Intelligence and Mathematical Theory of Computation: Papers in Honor of John McCarthy*, pages 359–380. Academic Press, New York, 1991.

17. R. Thomason. Ability, action and context. Presentation at the Temporality and Discourse Context: Dynamic and Modal Approaches Workshop, 2001.

18. B. van Linder, W. van der Hoek, and J.-J. Ch. Meyer. Formalizing abilities and opportunities of agents. *Fundamenta Informaticae*, 34(1-2):53–101, 1998.

Reasoning About Epistemic States of Agents by Modal Logic Programming

Linh Anh Nguyen

Institute of Informatics, University of Warsaw,
ul. Banacha 2, 02-097 Warsaw, Poland
`nguyen@mimuw.edu.pl`

Abstract. Modal logic programming is one of appropriate approaches to deal with reasoning about epistemic states of agents. We specify here the least model semantics, the fixpoint semantics, and an SLD-resolution calculus for modal logic programs in the multimodal logic $KD4I_g5_a$, which is intended for reasoning about belief and common belief of agents. We prove that the presented SLD-resolution calculus is sound and complete. We also present a formalization of the wise men puzzle using a modal logic program in $KD4I_g5_a$. This shows that it is worth to study modal logic programming for multi-agent systems.

1 Introduction

Reasoning is an important aspect of agents. In order to be able to make right actions, an agent should have general knowledge of the field it works on, information about the environment, and abilities to interact with the environment, to make inferences, and to revise its knowledge base. In multi-agent systems, agents should be able to communicate, collaborate, and sometimes compete with each other. For this aim, an agent should have knowledge about other agents in the system and be able to reason about their epistemic states. It is not that an agent can have all information it wants or can reason exactly as the others, but at least it can simulate epistemic states of the other agents, using some assumptions. The wise men puzzle introduced by McCarthy [20] is an example of reasoning about epistemic states of agents. We will study it in Section 3.

Modal logics and logic programming are useful instruments for multi-agent systems. Using modal logics is a natural way to represent and reason about knowledge and belief of agents (see, e.g., [11, 33, 32, 17, 8, 1]). Logic programming is also useful because logical implication is probably the inference form humans use most and want to adopt for multi-agent systems. Thus, one can think about modal logic programming as an approach to deal with reasoning about epistemic states of agents.

Modal logic programming has been studied in a number of works (see the earlier surveys [29, 13] and the later works [28, 5, 22, 26]). There are two approaches: the direct approach [12, 3, 5, 22, 26] and the translation approach [9, 28]. The first approach directly uses modalities, while the second one translates modal logic

F. Toni and P. Torroni (Eds.): CLIMA VI, LNAI 3900, pp. 37–56, 2006.

programs to classical logic programs. In this paper we will use the direct approach. This approach is justifiable, as the direct approach deals with modalities more closely, and modalities allow us to separate object-level and epistemic-level notions nicely.

In [22], we developed a fixpoint semantics, the least model semantics, and an SLD-resolution calculus in a direct way for modal logic programs in all of the basic serial monomodal logics. In that work we do not assume any special restriction on occurrences of $\square$ and $\diamond$ in programs and goals. In [26], we generalized the methods of [22] and gave a general framework for developing fixpoint semantics, the least model semantics, and SLD-resolution calculi for logic programs in normal multimodal logics whose frame restrictions consist of the conditions of seriality and some classical first-order Horn formulas.

In this work, we instantiate the above mentioned framework for the multimodal logic $KD4I_g5_a$, which was introduced in [23] for reasoning about belief and common belief. We prove that the obtained SLD-resolution calculus is sound and complete. We also give a purely logical formalization of the wise men puzzle using a modal logic program in $KD4I_g5_a$.

The rest of this paper is structured as follows. In Section 2, we give definitions for multimodal logics, define the multimodal logic $KD4I_g5_a$ and the modal logic programming language MProlog. In Section 3, we recall the wise men puzzle and formalize it by an MProlog program in $KD4I_g5_a$. In Section 4, we instantiate the framework given in [26] for $KD4I_g5_a$ in order to specify the least model semantics, the fixpoint semantics, and an SLD-resolution calculus for MProlog programs in $KD4I_g5_a$. Soundness and completeness of the obtained SLD-resolution calculus is proved in Section 5. In Section 6, we give two more examples illustrating the usefulness of modal logic programming for multi-agent systems. In Section 7, we briefly mention related works and discuss how to extend our system to deal with actions and time. Finally, Section 8 contains some concluding remarks.

2   Preliminaries

2.1   Syntax and Semantics of Quantified Multimodal Logics

A language for quantified multimodal logics is an extension of the language of classical predicate logic with modal operators $\square_i$ and $\diamond_i$, for $1 \le i \le m$ (where m is fixed). The modal operators $\square_i$ and $\diamond_i$ can take various meanings. For example, $\square_i$ can stand for "the agent i believes" and $\diamond_i$ for "it is considered possible by agent i". The operators $\square_i$ are called universal modal operators, while $\diamond_i$ are called existential modal operators. Terms and formulas are defined in the usual way, with an emphasis that if φ is a formula then $\square_i\varphi$ and $\diamond_i\varphi$ are also formulas.

A *Kripke frame* is a tuple $\langle W, \tau, R_1, \ldots, R_m \rangle$, where W is a nonempty set of possible worlds, $\tau \in W$ is the *actual world*, and R_i is a binary relation on W, called the *accessibility relation* for the modal operators $\square_i$, $\diamond_i$. If $R_i(w, u)$ holds then we say that the world u is accessible from the world w via R_i.

A *fixed-domain Kripke model with rigid terms*, hereafter simply called a (Kripke) model, is a tuple $M = \langle D, W, \tau, R_1, \ldots, R_m, \pi \rangle$, where D is a set called the *domain*, $\langle W, \tau, R_1, \ldots, R_m \rangle$ is a Kripke frame, and π is an interpretation of symbols. For a constant symbol a, $\pi(a)$ is an element of D, denoted by a^M. For an n-ary function symbol f, $\pi(f)$ is a function from D^n to D, denoted by f^M. For an n-ary predicate symbol p and a world $w \in W$, $\pi(w)(p)$ is an n-ary relation on D, denoted by $p^{M,w}$. (We adopt here the version with fixed-domain and rigid terms, as it is most popular. This work can be extended for other versions of Kripke semantics, e.g. with varying domain and flexible terms; see a discussion in [26].)

A *model graph* is a tuple $\langle W, \tau, R_1, \ldots, R_m, H \rangle$, where $\langle W, \tau, R_1, \ldots, R_m \rangle$ is a Kripke frame and H is a function that maps each world of W to a set of formulas.

Every model graph $\langle W, \tau, R_1, \ldots, R_m, H \rangle$ corresponds to a Herbrand model $M = \langle \mathcal{U}, W, \tau, R_1, \ldots, R_m, \pi \rangle$ specified by: $\mathcal{U}$ is the Herbrand universe (i.e. the set of all ground terms), $c^M = c$, $f^M(t_1, \ldots, t_n) = f(t_1, \ldots, t_n)$, and $((t_1, \ldots, t_n) \in p^{M,w}) \equiv (p(t_1, \ldots, t_n) \in H(w))$, where $t_1, \ldots, t_n$ are ground terms. We will sometimes treat a model graph as its corresponding model.

A *variable assignment* V w.r.t. a Kripke model M is a function that maps each variable to an element of the domain of M. The value of $t^M[V]$ for a term t is defined as usual.

Given some Kripke model $M = \langle D, W, \tau, R_1, \ldots, R_m, \pi \rangle$, some variable assignment V, and some world $w \in W$, the *satisfaction relation* $M, V, w \models \psi$ for a formula ψ is defined as follows:

$$M, V, w \models p(t_1, \ldots, t_n) \text{ iff } (t_1^M[V], \ldots, t_n^M[V]) \in p^{M,w};$$
$$M, V, w \models \Box_i \varphi \quad \text{iff for all } v \in W \text{ such that } R_i(w, v), \, M, V, v \models \varphi;$$
$$M, V, w \models \forall x. \varphi \quad \text{iff for all } a \in D, \, (M, V', w \models \varphi),$$
$$\text{where } V'(x) = a \text{ and } V'(y) = V(y) \text{ for } y \neq x;$$

and as usual for other cases (treating $\Diamond_i \varphi$ as $\neg \Box_i \neg \varphi$, and $\exists x. \varphi$ as $\neg \forall x. \neg \varphi$). We say that M satisfies φ, or φ is true in M, and write $M \models \varphi$, if $M, V, \tau \models \varphi$ for every V. For a set Γ of formulas, we call M a model of Γ and write $M \models \Gamma$ if $M \models \varphi$ for every $\varphi \in \Gamma$.

If as the class of admissible interpretations we take the class of all Kripke models (with no restrictions on the accessibility relations) then we obtain a quantified multimodal logic which has a standard Hilbert-style axiomatization denoted by K_m. Other *normal (multi)modal logics* are obtained by adding certain axioms to K_m. Mostly used axioms are ones that correspond to a certain restriction on the Kripke frame defined by a classical first-order formula using the accessibility relations. For example, the axiom $(D) : \Box_i \varphi \rightarrow \Diamond_i \varphi$ corresponds to the frame restriction $\forall x \exists y \, R_i(x, y)$.

For a normal modal logic L whose class of admissible interpretations can be characterized by classical first-order formulas of the accessibility relations, we call such formulas *L-frame restrictions*, and call frames with such properties *L-frames*. We call a model M with an L-frame an *L-model*. We say that φ is *L-satisfiable* if there exists an L-model of φ, i.e. an L-model satisfying φ. A formula

φ is said to be *L-valid* and called an *L-tautology* if φ is true in every *L*-model. For a set Γ of formulas, we write $\Gamma \models_L \varphi$ and call φ a *logical consequence* of Γ in *L* if φ is true in every *L*-model of Γ.

2.2   The Multimodal Logic $KD4I_g5_a$

Suppose that there are n agents and $m = 2^n - 1$. Let g be an one-to-one function that maps every natural number less than or equal to m to a non-empty subset of $\{1, \ldots, n\}$. Suppose that an index $1 \leq i \leq m$ stands for the group of agents whose indices form the set $g(i)$. To capture belief and common belief of agents, we can extend K_m with the following axioms

- $(D) : \Box_i\varphi \rightarrow \neg\Box_i\neg\varphi$ (belief is consistent),
- $(4) : \Box_i\varphi \rightarrow \Box_i\Box_i\varphi$ (belief satisfies positive introspection),
- $(I_g) : \Box_i\varphi \rightarrow \Box_j\varphi$ if $g(i) \supset g(j)$ (if i indicates a supergroup of a group j then every common belief of i is also a common belief of j).
- $(5_a) : \neg\Box_i\varphi \rightarrow \Box_i\neg\Box_i\varphi$ if $g(i)$ is a singleton (belief of a single agent satisfies negative introspection).

Thus, for reasoning about belief and common belief, we can use:

$$KD4I_g5_a = K_m + (D) + (4) + (I_g) + (5_a)$$

Here we want to catch the most important properties of belief and common belief, and the aim is not to give an exact formulation of belief or common belief. The logic $KD4I_g5_a$ was introduced in [23]. It is different in the nature from the well-known multimodal logic of common knowledge. It also differs from the modal logic with mutual belief [1].

In [15] (an extension of [14]), Goré and Nguyen show that the satisfiability problem in the propositional version of $KD4I_g5_a$ is in EXPTIME. Clearly, the problem is PSPACE-hard (as $KD4I_g5_a$ contains KD4). We guess that the problem is EXPTIME-hard when $n \geq 3$ (i.e. $m \geq 7$). It is an open problem.

The given axioms correspond to the following frame restrictions:

Axiom	Corresponding Condition
(D)	$\forall u \, \exists v \, R_i(u, v)$
(4)	$\forall u, v, w \, (R_i(u, v) \wedge R_i(v, w) \rightarrow R_i(u, w))$
(I_g)	$R_j \subseteq R_i$ if $g(i) \supset g(j)$
(5_a)	$\forall u, v, w \, (R_i(u, v) \wedge R_i(u, w) \rightarrow R_i(w, v))$ if $g(i)$ is a singleton

For further reading on epistemic logics, see, e.g., [11, 33, 8, 1].

2.3   Modal Logic Programs

A *modality* is a (possibly empty) sequence of modal operators. A *universal modality* is a modality which contains only universal modal operators. We use $\triangle$ to denote a modality and $\boxdot$ to denote a universal modality. Similarly as in classical logic programming, we use a clausal form $\boxdot(\varphi \leftarrow \psi_1, \ldots, \psi_n)$ to denote the formula $\forall(\boxdot(\varphi \vee \neg\psi_1 \ldots \vee \neg\psi_n))$. We use E to denote a classical atom and A, $B_1, \ldots, B_n$ to denote formulas of the form E, $\Box_i E$, or $\Diamond_i E$.

A *program clause* is a formula of the form $\boxdot(A \leftarrow B_1, \ldots, B_n)$, where $n \geq 0$. $\boxdot$ is called the *modal context*, A the *head*, and $B_1, \ldots, B_n$ the *body* of the program clause. An *MProlog program* is a finite set of program clauses.

An *MProlog goal atom* is a formula of the form $\boxdot E$ or $\boxdot \Diamond_i E$. An *MProlog goal* is a formula written in the clausal form $\leftarrow \alpha_1, \ldots, \alpha_k$, where each α_i is an MProlog goal atom. The *empty goal* (i.e. the *empty clause*) is denoted by $\Diamond$.

In $KD4I_g5_a$, if $g(i)$ is a singleton then we have the equivalence $\nabla_i \nabla'_i \varphi \equiv \nabla'_i \varphi$ for any modal operators ∇_i and ∇'_i with the same modal index i. For this reason, we adopt some restrictions to simplify the form of MProlog programs and goals in $KD4I_g5_a$. An MProlog program is called a $KD4I_g5_a$-*MProlog program* if the modal contexts of its program clauses do not contain subsequences of the form $\Box_i \Box_i$ if $g(i)$ is a singleton. An MProlog goal is called a $KD4I_g5_a$-*MProlog goal* if each of its goal atoms $\triangle E$ satisfies the condition that $\triangle$ does not contain subsequences of the form $\Box_i \Box_i$ or $\Box_i \Diamond_i$ if $g(i)$ is a singleton.

Let P be an $KD4I_g5_a$-MProlog program and $G = \leftarrow \alpha_1, \ldots, \alpha_k$ be an $KD4I_g5_a$-MProlog goal. An *answer* θ for $P \cup \{G\}$ is a substitution whose domain is the set of all variables of G. We say that θ is a *correct answer* in $KD4I_g5_a$ for $P \cup \{G\}$ if θ is an answer for $P \cup \{G\}$ and $P \models_{KD4I_g5_a} \forall((\alpha_1 \wedge \ldots \wedge \alpha_k)\theta)$.

It is shown in [23] that MProlog has the same expressiveness power as the general Horn fragment in normal modal logics. Moreover, the restrictions adopted for $KD4I_g5_a$-MProlog do not reduce expressiveness of the language (see [23]).

3   The Wise Men Puzzle

Before considering technical details of semantics of $KD4I_g5_a$-MProlog, we give a formalization of the three wise men puzzle in MProlog. The puzzle is a famous benchmark introduced by McCarthy [20] for AI. It can be stated as follows (cf. [18]). A king wishes to know whether his three advisors (A, B, C) are as wise as they claim to be. Three chairs are lined up, all facing the same direction, with one behind the other. The wise men are instructed to sit down in the order A, B, C. Each of the men can see the backs of the men sitting before them (e.g. C can see A and B). The king informs the wise men that he has three cards, all of which are either black or white, at least one of which is white. He places one card, face up, behind each of the three wise men, explaining that each wise man must determine the color of his own card. Each wise man must announce the color of his own card as soon as he knows what it is. All know that this will happen. The room is silent; then, after a while, wise man A says "My card is white!".

The wise men puzzle has been previously studied in a number of works (e.g., [20, 18, 10, 7, 2, 28, 4]). McCarthy [20] directly used possible worlds to formalize the puzzle. Konolige [18], Nonnengart [28], and Baldoni [4] also used modal logics for the puzzle. Konolige [18] focused on limited reasoning, Nonnengart [28] used semi-functional translation for modal logic programming, and Baldoni [4] used a prefixed tableau system. Both McCarthy [20] and Nonnengart [28] used some feature of mutual belief, but they did not define it purely. Baldoni [4] adopted too strong versions of axioms 4 and 5, which are rather not suitable for the puzzle. As other approaches for the wise men puzzle, Elgot-Drapkin [10] used step-logics, while Cimatti and Serafini [7], Attardi and Simi [2] studied reasoning in belief-contexts. Our formalization of the wise men puzzle given below uses $KD4I_g5_a$-MProlog. It is more elegant than the above-mentioned formalizations, as it uses a modal logic with a clear semantics of common belief in a direct way.

As reported in [24], we have designed and implemented a modal logic programming system, also called MProlog. In that system, SLD-resolution calculi for MProlog can be specified according to the theoretical framework given in [26]. An instantiation of that framework for $KD4I_g5_a$ is presented in the next section. Its implementation (of SLD-resolution) is denoted by ccKD4Ig5a. In that implementation, *bel* denotes belief and *pos* denotes possibility, and modalities are represented by lists, e.g. $\Box_i \langle X \rangle_j \Diamond_k q(a)$ is represented by $[bel(I), pos(J, X), pos(K)] : q(a)$. The implemented calculus requires definitions of predicates $singleton\_group/1$, $subgroup/2$, and $union\_group/3$. Denote the wise men by a, b, c, and the possible groups by gAB, gAC, gBC, $gABC$, where, e.g., $gABC = \{a, b, c\}$. Thus, $[bel(gABC)] : \varphi$ means that φ is a common belief of the group $\{a, b, c\}$. Define the mentioned required predicates in the usual way. The three wise men problem can be formalized by the following program:

```
:- calculus ccKD4Ig5a.
```

% If Y sits behinds X then X's card is white if Y considers this as possible.
```
[bel(gABC)]: (white(X) :-
     member(X, [a,b,c]), member(Y, [a,b,c]), X @< Y, [pos(Y)]:white(X)).
```

% The following formula is "dual" to the above formula.
```
[bel(gABC)]: ([bel(Y)]:black(X) :-
     member(X, [a,b,c]), member(Y, [a,b,c]), X @< Y, black(X)).
```

% At least one of the wise men has a white card.
```
[bel(gABC)]: (white(a) :- black(b), black(c)).
[bel(gABC)]: (white(b) :- black(c), black(a)).
[bel(gABC)]: (white(c) :- black(a), black(b)).
```

/* Each of B and C does not know the color of his own card. In particular, each of the men considers that it is possible that his own card is black. */
```
[bel(gABC),pos(b)]:black(b).
[bel(gABC),pos(c)]:black(c).
```

The question is whether A believes that his card is white. It is passed to the interpreter as $mcall([bel(a)] : white(a))$ and solved in less than 1 second[1] using certain option settings.

The above program uses the syntax of the implemented system. We give below a version using the purely logical formalism of MProlog. For clarity, instead of numeric indices we use a, b, c, ab, ac, bc, abc with the meaning that

---

[1] On TravelMate 230X, 1.7GHz-M.

$g(a) = \{a\}$, $g(b) = \{b\}$, $g(c) = \{c\}$, ..., and $g(abc) = \{a, b, c\}$. Let P_{wise_men} be the following program:

$$
\begin{aligned}
\varphi_1 &= \Box_{abc}\,(white(a) \leftarrow \Diamond_b\,white(a)) \\
\varphi_2 &= \Box_{abc}\,(white(a) \leftarrow \Diamond_c\,white(a)) \\
\varphi_3 &= \Box_{abc}\,(white(b) \leftarrow \Diamond_c\,white(b)) \\
\varphi_4 &= \Box_{abc}\,(\Box_b\,black(a) \leftarrow black(a)) \\
\varphi_5 &= \Box_{abc}\,(\Box_c\,black(a) \leftarrow black(a)) \\
\varphi_6 &= \Box_{abc}\,(\Box_c\,black(b) \leftarrow black(b)) \\
\varphi_7 &= \Box_{abc}\,(white(a) \leftarrow black(b), black(c)) \\
\varphi_8 &= \Box_{abc}\,(white(b) \leftarrow black(c), black(a)) \\
\varphi_9 &= \Box_{abc}\,(white(c) \leftarrow black(a), black(b)) \\
\varphi_{10} &= \Box_{abc}\Diamond_b\,black(b) \\
\varphi_{11} &= \Box_{abc}\Diamond_c\,black(c)
\end{aligned}
$$

The goal is $\leftarrow \Box_a white(a)$. We will continue this example in Section 4.5. For a formalization of the puzzle with n wise men, see [26].

4 Semantics of $KD4I_g5_a$-MProlog Programs

In this section, we present the least model semantics, the fixpoint semantics and an SLD-resolution calculus for $KD4I_g5_a$-MProlog programs. For abbreviation, *from now on we use L to denote $KD4I_g5_a$.*

4.1 Labeled Modal Operators

When applying the direct consequence operator $T_{L,P}$ for an MProlog program P in L, if we obtain an "atom" of the form $\triangle\Diamond_i E$, then to simplify the task we label the modal operator $\Diamond_i$. Labeling allows us to address the chosen world(s) in which this particular E must hold. A natural way is to label $\Diamond_i$ by E to obtain $\langle E \rangle_i$. On the other hand, when dealing with SLD-derivation, we cannot change a goal $\leftarrow \Diamond_i(A \wedge B)$ to $\leftarrow \Diamond_i A, \Diamond_i B$. But if we label the operator $\Diamond_i$, let's say by X, then we can safely change $\leftarrow \langle X \rangle_i(A \wedge B)$ to $\leftarrow \langle X \rangle_i A, \langle X \rangle_i B$.

We will use the following notations:

- $\top$: the *truth* symbol, with the usual semantics[2];
- E, F : classical atoms (which may contain variables) or $\top$;
- X, Y, Z : variables for classical atoms or $\top$, called *atom variables*;
- $\langle E \rangle_i$, $\langle X \rangle_i$: $\Diamond_i$ labeled by E or X;
- ∇ : $\Box_i$, $\Diamond_i$, $\langle E \rangle_i$, or $\langle X \rangle_i$, called a *modal operator*;
- $\triangle$: a (possibly empty) sequence of modal operators, called a *modality*;
- $\boxdot$: a *universal modality*;
- A, B : formulas of the form E or ∇E, called *simple atoms*;
- α, β : formulas of the form $\triangle E$, called *atoms*;
- φ, ψ : *(labeled) formulas* (i.e. formulas that may contain $\langle E \rangle_i$ and $\langle X \rangle_i$).

---

[2] i.e. it is always true that $M, V, w \models \top$.

We use subscripts beside ∇ to indicate modal indexes in the same way as for $\square$ and $\diamond$. To distinguish a number of modal operators we use superscripts of the form (i), e.g. $\square^{(1)}$, $\square^{(2)}$, $\nabla^{(i)}$, $\nabla^{(i')}$.

A *ground formula* is a formula with no variables and no atom variables. A modal operator is said to be *ground* if it is $\square_i$, $\diamond_i$, or $\langle E \rangle_i$ with E being $\top$ or a ground classical atom. A *ground modality* is a modality that contains only ground modal operators. A *labeled modal operator* is a modal operator of the form $\langle E \rangle_i$ or $\langle X \rangle_i$.

Denote $EdgeLabels = \{\langle E \rangle_i \mid E \in \mathcal{B} \cup \{\top\}$ and $1 \leq i \leq m\}$, where $\mathcal{B}$ is the Herbrand base (i.e. the set of all ground classical atoms). The semantics of $\langle E \rangle_i \in EdgeLabels$ is specified as follows. Let $M = \langle D, W, \tau, R_1, \ldots, R_m, \pi \rangle$ be a Kripke model. A $\diamond$-*realization function on* M is a partial function $\sigma :$ $W \times EdgeLabels \to W$ such that if $\sigma(w, \langle E \rangle_i) = u$, then $R_i(w, u)$ holds and $M, u \models E$. Given a $\diamond$-realization function σ, a world $w \in W$, and a ground formula φ, the satisfaction relation $M, \sigma, w \models \varphi$ is defined in the usual way, except that $M, \sigma, w \models \langle E \rangle_i \psi$ iff $\sigma(w, \langle E \rangle_i)$ is defined and $M, \sigma, \sigma(w, \langle E \rangle_i) \models \psi$. We write $M, \sigma \models \varphi$ to denote that $M, \sigma, \tau \models \varphi$. For a set I of ground atoms, we write $M, \sigma \models I$ to denote that $M, \sigma \models \alpha$ for all $\alpha \in I$; we write $M \models I$ and call M a model of I if $M, \sigma \models I$ for *some* σ.

4.2   Model Generators

We define that a modality $\nabla_{i_1}^{(1)} \ldots \nabla_{i_k}^{(k)}$ is in the *L-normal form* if for all $1 \leq j < k$ if $g(i_j)$ is a singleton then $i_j \neq i_{j+1}$. (Note that if $g(i)$ is a singleton then $\nabla_i \nabla'_i \varphi \equiv \nabla'_i \varphi$ is $KD4I_g5_a$-valid.) A modality is in *L-normal labeled form* if it is in L-normal form and does not contain modal operators of the form $\diamond_i$ or $\langle \top \rangle_i$. An atom is in *L-normal (labeled) form* if it is of the form $\triangle E$ with $\triangle$ in L-normal (labeled) form. An atom is in *almost L-normal labeled form* if it is of the form $\triangle A$ with $\triangle$ in L-normal labeled form.

A *model generator* is a set of ground atoms not containing $\diamond_i$, $\langle \top \rangle_i$, $\top$. An *L-normal model generator* is a model generator consisting of atoms in L-normal labeled form.

We will define the *standard L-model* of an L-normal model generator I so that it is a *least L-model* of I (where a model M is *less than or equal to* a model M' if for every positive ground formula φ without labeled operators, if $M \models \varphi$ then $M' \models \varphi$). In the construction we will use the operator Ext_L defined below.

A *forward rule* is a schema of the form $\alpha \to \beta$, while a *backward rule* is a schema of the form $\alpha \leftarrow \beta$. A rule can be accompanied with some conditions specifying when the rule can be applied.

The *operator Ext_L* is specified by the corresponding forward rules given in Table 1. Given an L-normal model generator I, $Ext_L(I)$ is the least extension of I that contains all ground atoms in L-normal labeled form that are derivable from some atom of I using the rules specifying Ext_L. Note that $Ext_L(I)$ is an L-normal model generator if so is I.

Denote $Serial_L = \{\boxdot \langle \top \rangle_i \top \mid 1 \leq i \leq m$ and $\boxdot \langle \top \rangle_i$ is in L-normal form$\}$.

Table 1. A schema for semantics of $KD4I_g5_a$-MProlog

$L = KD4I_g5_a$,   L-MProlog

$\preceq_L$ is defined in page 46.
The L-normal form of modalities is defined in page 44.

Rules specifying operators Ext_L, Sat_L, NF_L, rNF_L, $rSat_L$:
(*Both sides of each rule are in almost L-normal labeled form.*)

Ext_L $\triangle\square_i\alpha \rightarrow \triangle\square_j\alpha$ if $g(i) \supset g(j)$ $\hspace{2cm}$ (1)

$\hspace{1.2cm}$ $\triangle\square_i\alpha \rightarrow \triangle\square_i\square_i\alpha$ $\hspace{4cm}$ (2)

Sat_L the rules specifying Ext_L plus

$\hspace{1.2cm}$ $\triangle\langle F\rangle_i E \rightarrow \triangle\square_i\Diamond_i E$ if $g(i)$ is a singleton $\hspace{1.5cm}$ (3)

$\hspace{1.2cm}$ $\triangle\nabla\nabla' E \rightarrow \triangle\Diamond_i E$ if $\Diamond_i \preceq_L \nabla$ and $\Diamond_i \preceq_L \nabla'$ $\hspace{1cm}$ (4)

NF_L $\triangle\nabla_i\nabla'_i E \rightarrow \triangle\nabla'_i E$ if $g(i)$ is a singleton and

$\hspace{1.8cm}$ ∇'_i is of the form $\square_i$ or $\langle E\rangle_i$ $\hspace{3.5cm}$ (5)

rNF_L $\triangle\nabla_i E \leftarrow \triangle\langle X\rangle_i\nabla_i E$ if $g(i)$ is a singleton,

$\hspace{1.8cm}$ ∇_i is of the form $\square_i$ or $\langle E\rangle_i$, and X is a fresh atom variable $\hspace{0.3cm}$ (6)

$rSat_L$ $\triangle\Diamond_i E \leftarrow \triangle\langle X\rangle_i E$ for X being a fresh atom variable $\hspace{0.6cm}$ (7)

$\hspace{1.3cm}$ $\triangle\nabla_i\alpha \leftarrow \triangle\square_j\alpha$ if $g(i) \subseteq g(j)$ $\hspace{3.2cm}$ (8)

$\hspace{1.3cm}$ $\triangle\Diamond_i E \leftarrow \triangle\Diamond_j E$ if $g(i) \supset g(j)$ $\hspace{3.3cm}$ (9)

$\hspace{1.3cm}$ $\triangle\square_i\square_i\alpha \leftarrow \triangle\square_i\alpha$ $\hspace{5.3cm}$ (10)

$\hspace{1.3cm}$ $\triangle\nabla_i\Diamond_i E \leftarrow \triangle\Diamond_i E$ if $g(i)$ is a singleton $\hspace{2.2cm}$ (11)

$\hspace{1.3cm}$ $\triangle\Diamond_i E \leftarrow \triangle\langle X\rangle_j\Diamond_i E$ if $g(i) \supseteq g(j)$ and

$\hspace{1.8cm}$ X is a fresh atom variable $\hspace{5cm}$ (12)

Let I be an L-normal model generator. The *standard L-model* of I is constructed by building an L-model for $Ext_L(I) \cup Serial_L$ according to the semantics of ground labeled modal operators, and formally is defined as follows. Let $W' = EdgeLabels^*$ (i.e. the set of finite sequences of elements of $\{\langle E\rangle_i \mid E \in \mathcal{B} \cup \{\top\}$ and $1 \leq i \leq m\}$), $\tau = \epsilon$, $H(\tau) = Ext_L(I) \cup Serial_L$. Let $R'_i \subseteq W' \times W'$ and $H(u)$, for $u \in W'$, $u \neq \tau$, be the least sets such that:

- if $\langle E\rangle_i\alpha \in H(w)$, then $R'_i(w, w\langle E\rangle_i)$ holds and $\{E, \alpha\} \subseteq H(w\langle E\rangle_i)$;
- if $\square_i\alpha \in H(w)$ and $R'_i(w, w\langle E\rangle_i)$ holds, then $\alpha \in H(w\langle E\rangle_i)$.

Let R_i, for $1 \leq i \leq m$, be the least[3] extension of R'_i such that $\{R_i \mid 1 \leq i \leq m\}$ satisfies all the L-frame restrictions except seriality (which is cared by $Serial_L$). Let W be W' without worlds not accessible directly nor indirectly from τ via the accessibility relations R_i. We call the model graph $\langle W, \tau, R_1, \ldots, R_m, H\rangle$

---

[3] The least extension exists due to the assumption that all L-frame restrictions not concerning seriality are classical first-order Horn formulas.

the *standard L-model graph* of I, and its corresponding model M the *standard L-model* of I. $\{R_i' \mid 1 \le i \le m\}$ is called the *skeleton* of M. By the *standard $\diamond$-realization function on M* we call the $\diamond$-realization function σ defined as follows: if $R_i'(w, w\langle E \rangle_i)$ holds then $\sigma(w, \langle E \rangle_i) = w\langle E \rangle_i$, else $\sigma(w, \langle E \rangle_i)$ is undefined.

It can be shown that *the standard L-model of an L-normal model generator I is a least L-model of I.*

4.3 Fixpoint Semantics

We now consider the direct consequence operator $T_{L,P}$. Given an L-normal model generator I, how can $T_{L,P}(I)$ be defined? Based on the axioms of L, I is first extended to the *L-saturation* of I, denoted by $Sat_L(I)$, which is a set of atoms. Next, *L-instances of program clauses* of P are *applied* to the atoms of $Sat_L(I)$. This is done by the operator $T_{oL,P}$. The set $T_{oL,P}(Sat_L(I))$ is a model generator but not necessary in L-normal form. Finally, the *normalization operator NF_L* converts $T_{oL,P}(Sat_L(I))$ to an L-normal model generator. $T_{L,P}(I)$ is defined as $NF_L(T_{oL,P}(Sat_L(I)))$.

To compare modal operators we define $\preceq_L$ to be the least reflexive and transitive relation between modal operators such that $\diamond_i \preceq_L \langle E \rangle_i \preceq_L \square_i$, $\diamond_i \preceq_L \langle X \rangle_i \preceq_L \square_i$, and if $g(i) \subseteq g(j)$ then $\square_i \preceq_L \square_j$ and $\diamond_j \preceq_L \diamond_i$.

An atom $\nabla^{(1)} \dots \nabla^{(n)} \alpha$ is called an *L-instance* of an atom $\nabla^{(1')} \dots \nabla^{(n')} \alpha'$ if there exists a substitution θ such that $\alpha = \alpha'\theta$ and $\nabla^{(i)} \preceq_L \nabla^{(i')}\theta$ for all $1 \le i \le n$ (treating $\nabla^{(i')}$ as an expression). For example, if $g(1) \subseteq g(2)$ then $\square_1 \diamond_2 E$ is an L-instance of $\square_2 \langle F \rangle_1 E$.

A modality $\triangle$ is called an *L-instance* of $\triangle'$, and we also say that $\triangle'$ is *equal to or more general in L than* $\triangle$ (hereby we define a *pre-order between modalities*), if $\triangle E$ is an L-instance of $\triangle' E$ for some ground classical atom E.

Let $\square$ and $\square'$ be universal modalities in L-normal form. We say that $\square$ is an *L-context instance* of $\square'$ if $\square'\varphi \to \square\varphi$ is L-valid (for every φ). (It can be shown that the propositional version of the logic L is decidable. So, the problem of checking whether a given universal modality is an L-context instance of another one is also decidable.)

Let $\square$ and $\square'$ be universal modalities in L-normal form, φ and φ' be program clauses with empty modal context. We say that $\square\varphi$ is an *L-instance* of (a program clause) $\square'\varphi'$ if $\square$ is an L-context instance of $\square'$ and there exists a substitution θ such that $\varphi = \varphi'\theta$.

For example, if $g(1) \subseteq g(2)$ then $\square_2\square_1$ is an L-context instance of $\square_2$ and $\square_2\square_1(p(a) \leftarrow q(a))$ is an L-instance of $\square_2(p(x) \leftarrow q(x))$.

We now give definitions concerning Sat_L, $T_{oL,P}$, and NF_L.

The *saturation operator Sat_L* is specified by the corresponding forward rules given in Table 1. Given an L-normal model generator I, $Sat_L(I)$ is the least extension of I that contains all ground atoms in almost L-normal labeled form that are derivable from some atom in I using the rules specifying Sat_L. For example, if $g(1)$ is a singleton and $g(2)$ is not, then $\square_2\square_2\square_1\diamond_1 p(a) \in Sat_L(\{\square_2\langle q(b)\rangle_1 p(a)\})$.

When computing the least fixpoint of a modal logic program, whenever an atom of the form $\triangle \diamond_i E$ is introduced, we "fix" the $\diamond$ by replacing the atom by $\triangle \langle E \rangle_i E$. This leads to the following definition. The *forward labeled form* of an atom α is the atom α' such that if α is of the form $\triangle \diamond_i E$ then $\alpha' = \triangle \langle E \rangle_i E$, else $\alpha' = \alpha$. For example, the forward labeled form of $\diamond_1 s(a)$ is $\langle s(a) \rangle_1 s(a)$.

Let P be an L-MProlog program. The *operator* $T_{oL,P}$ is defined as follows: for a set I of ground atoms in almost L-normal labeled form, $T_{oL,P}(I)$ is the least (w.r.t. $\subseteq$) model generator such that if $\boxdot(A \leftarrow B_1, \ldots, B_n)$ is a ground L-instance of some program clause of P and $\triangle$ is a maximally general[4] ground modality in L-normal labeled form such that $\triangle$ is an L-instance of $\boxdot$ and $\triangle B_i$ is an L-instance of some atom of I (for every $1 \le i \le n$), then the forward labeled form of $\triangle A$ belongs to $T_{oL,P}(I)$.

For example, if $g(1) \subseteq g(2)$ and P contains the clause $\Box_2(\diamond_1 p(x) \leftarrow q(x), r(x), \Box_1 s(x), \diamond_2 t(x))$ and $I = \{\langle q(a) \rangle_1 q(a), \langle q(a) \rangle_1 r(a), \Box_2 \Box_2 s(a), \Box_2 \langle t(a) \rangle_1 t(a)\}$, then $\langle q(a) \rangle_1 \langle p(a) \rangle_1 p(a) \in T_{oL,P}(I)$.

The *normalization operator* NF_L is specified by the corresponding forward rules given in Table 1. Given a model generator I, $NF_L(I)$ is the set of all ground atoms in L-normal labeled form that are derivable from some atom of I using the rules specifying NF_L. For example, if $g(1)$ is a singleton then $NF_L(\{\langle q(a) \rangle_1 \langle p(a) \rangle_1 p(a)\}) = \{\langle p(a) \rangle_1 p(a)\}$.

Define $T_{L,P}(I) = NF_L(T_{oL,P}(Sat_L(I)))$. By definition, the operators Sat_L, $T_{oL,P}$, and NF_L are all increasingly monotonic and compact. Hence the operator $T_{L,P}$ is monotonic and continuous. By the Kleene theorem, it follows that $T_{L,P}$ has the least fixpoint $T_{L,P} \uparrow \omega = \bigcup_{n=0}^{\omega} T_{L,P} \uparrow n$, where $T_{L,P} \uparrow 0 = \emptyset$ and $T_{L,P} \uparrow n = T_{L,P}(T_{L,P} \uparrow (n-1))$ for $n > 0$. Denote the least fixpoint $T_{L,P} \uparrow \omega$ by $I_{L,P}$ and the standard L-model of $I_{L,P}$ by $M_{L,P}$.

It can be shown that for an L-MProlog program P, $M_{L,P}$ *is a least L-model of P.* See also Lemma 1 given in Section 5.

4.4   SLD-Resolution

The main work in developing an SLD-resolution calculus for L-MProlog is to specify a reverse analogue of the operator $T_{L,P}$. The operator $T_{L,P}$ is a composition of Sat_L, $T_{oL,P}$, and NF_L. So, we have to investigate reversion of these operators.

A *goal* is a clause of the form $\leftarrow \alpha_1, \ldots, \alpha_k$, where each α_i is an atom.

The following definition concerns reversion of the operator $T_{oL,P}$.

Let $G = \leftarrow \alpha_1, \ldots, \alpha_i, \ldots, \alpha_k$ be a goal and $\varphi = \boxdot(A \leftarrow B_1, \ldots, B_n)$ a program clause. Then G' is *derived* from G and φ in L using mgu θ, and called an *L-resolvent* of G and φ, if the following conditions hold:

- $\alpha_i = \triangle' A'$, with $\triangle'$ in L-normal labeled form, is called the *selected atom*, and A' is called the *selected head atom*;

---

[4] W.r.t. the pre-order between modalities described earlier for L.

- $\triangle'$ is an L-instance of a universal modality $\boxdot'$ and $\boxdot'(A \leftarrow B_1, \ldots, B_n)$ is an L-instance of the program clause φ;
- θ is an mgu of A' and the forward labeled form of A;
- G' is the goal $\leftarrow (\alpha_1, \ldots, \alpha_{i-1}, \triangle'B_1, \ldots, \triangle'B_n, \alpha_{i+1}, \ldots, \alpha_k)\theta$.

For example, if $g(1) \subseteq g(2)$ then $\leftarrow \Box_1 \Diamond_2 q(x), \Box_1 r(x)$ is an L-resolvent of $\leftarrow \Box_1 p(x)$ and $\Box_2(p(x) \leftarrow \Diamond_2 q(x), r(x))$ (here, $\boxdot = \Box_2$ and $\triangle' = \boxdot' = \Box_1$).

As a reverse analogue of the operator Sat_L, we provide the operator $rSat_L$, which is specified by the corresponding backward rules given in Table 1. We say that $\beta = rSat_L(\alpha)$ *using an $rSat_L$ rule* $\alpha' \leftarrow \beta'$ if $\alpha \leftarrow \beta$ is of the form $\alpha' \leftarrow \beta'$. We write $\beta = rSat_L(\alpha)$ to denote that "$\beta = rSat_L(\alpha)$ using some $rSat_L$ rule".

As a reverse analogue of the operator NF_L, we provide the operator rNF_L, which is specified by the corresponding backward rules given in Table 1. We say that $\beta =_\theta rNF_L(\alpha)$ *using an rNF_L rule* $\alpha' \leftarrow \beta'$ if θ is an mgu such that $\alpha\theta \leftarrow \beta$ is of the form $\alpha' \leftarrow \beta'$. We write $\beta =_\theta rNF_L(\alpha)$ to denote that "$\beta =_\theta rNF_L(\alpha)$ using some rNF_L rule". For example, if $g(1)$ is a singleton then we have $\langle Y \rangle_1 \langle E \rangle_1 E =_\theta rNF_L(\langle X \rangle_1 E)$ with $\theta = \{X/E\}$ and Y being a fresh atom variable.

Let $G = \leftarrow \alpha_1, \ldots, \alpha_i, \ldots, \alpha_k$ be a goal. If $\alpha_i' = rSat_L(\alpha_i)$ using an $rSat_L$ rule φ, then $G' = \leftarrow \alpha_1, \ldots, \alpha_{i-1}, \alpha_i', \alpha_{i+1}, \ldots, \alpha_k$ is *derived* from G and φ, and we call G' an *(L-)resolvent* of G and φ, and α_i the *selected atom* of G.

Similarly, G' is *derived* from G and an rNF_L rule φ using an mgu θ, and called an *(L-)resolvent* of G and φ, if α_i is called the *selected atom*, $\alpha_i' =_\theta rNF_L(\alpha_i)$ using φ, and $G' = \leftarrow \alpha_1\theta, \ldots, \alpha_{i-1}\theta, \alpha_i', \alpha_{i+1}\theta, \ldots, \alpha_k\theta$.

For example, resolving $\leftarrow \Box_1\Box_1 p(x)$ with the rule $\triangle\Box_i\Box_i\alpha \leftarrow \triangle\Box_i\alpha$ results in $\leftarrow \Box_1 p(x)$, since $\triangle$ is instantiated to the empty modality, i is instantiated to 1, and α is instantiated to $p(x)$.

Observe that $rSat_L$ rules and rNF_L rules are similar to program clauses and the way of applying them is similar to the way of applying classical program clauses, except that we do not need mgu's for $rSat_L$ rules.

We now define SLD-derivation and SLD-refutation.

Let P be an L-MProlog program and G a goal. An *SLD-derivation* from $P \cup \{G\}$ in L consists of a (finite or infinite) sequence $G_0 = G, G_1, \ldots$ of goals, a sequence $\varphi_1, \varphi_2, \ldots$ of variants of program clauses of P, $rSat_L$ rules, or rNF_L rules, and a sequence $\theta_1, \theta_2, \ldots$ of mgu's such that if φ_i is a variant of a program clause or an rNF_L rule then G_i is derived from G_{i-1} and φ_i in L using θ_i, else $\theta_i = \varepsilon$ (the empty substitution) and G_i is derived from G_{i-1} and (the $rSat_L$ rule variant) φ_i. Each φ_i is called an *input clause/rule* of the derivation.

We assume *standardizing variables apart* as usual (see [19]).

An *SLD-refutation* of $P \cup \{G\}$ in L is a finite SLD-derivation from $P \cup \{G\}$ in L with the empty clause as the last goal in the derivation.

Let P be an L-MProlog program and G a goal. A *computed answer* θ in L of $P \cup \{G\}$ is the substitution obtained by restricting the composition $\theta_1 \ldots \theta_n$ to the variables of G, where $\theta_1, \ldots, \theta_n$ is the sequence of mgu's used in an SLD-refutation of $P \cup \{G\}$ in L.

4.5   Example

We give here an SLD-refutation of $P_{wise\_men} \cup \{\leftarrow \Box_a white(a)\}$ in $KD4I_g5_a$, where P_{wise_men} is the $KD4I_g5_a$-MProlog program given in Section 3.

Goals	Input clauses/rules	MGUs
$\leftarrow \Box_a white(a)$		
$\leftarrow \Box_a \Diamond_b white(a)$	φ_1	
$\leftarrow \Box_a \langle X_2 \rangle_b white(a)$	(7)	
$\leftarrow \Box_a \langle X_2 \rangle_b \Diamond_c white(a)$	φ_2	
$\leftarrow \Box_a \langle X_2 \rangle_b \langle X_4 \rangle_c white(a)$	(7)	
$\leftarrow \Box_a \langle X_2 \rangle_b \langle X_4 \rangle_c black(b), \Box_a \langle X_2 \rangle_b \langle X_4 \rangle_c black(c)$	φ_7	
$\leftarrow \Box_a \langle X_2 \rangle_b black(b), \Box_a \langle X_2 \rangle_b \langle X_4 \rangle_c black(c)$	φ_6	
$\leftarrow \Box_a \langle black(b) \rangle_b \langle X_4 \rangle_c black(c)$	φ_{10}	$\{X_2/black(b)\}$
$\Diamond$	φ_{11}	$\{X_4/black(c)\}$

5   Soundness and Completeness

In this section, we prove soundness and completeness of the SLD-resolution calculus given for $KD4I_g5_a$-MProlog, which is stated as follows.

Theorem 1. *Let P be an $KD4I_g5_a$-MProlog program and G an $KD4I_g5_a$-MProlog goal. Then every computed answer in $KD4I_g5_a$ of $P \cup \{G\}$ is a correct answer in $KD4I_g5_a$ of $P \cup \{G\}$. Conversely, for every correct answer θ in $KD4I_g5_a$ of $P \cup \{G\}$, there exists a computed answer γ in $KD4I_g5_a$ of $P \cup \{G\}$ such that $G\theta = G\gamma\delta$ for some substitution δ.*

In [26], we presented a general framework for developing fixpoint semantics, the least model semantics, and SLD-resolution calculi for logic programs in multi-modal logics, and proved that under certain expected properties of a concrete instantiation of the framework for a specific multimodal logic, the SLD-resolution calculus is sound and complete. The semantics of $KD4I_g5_a$-MProlog presented in the previous section and summarized in Table 1 is based on and compatible with the framework given in [26].

By the results of [26], to prove soundness and completeness of SLD-resolution of $KD4I_g5_a$-MProlog, we can prove Expected Lemmas 4 – 10 of [26] (w.r.t. the schema given in Table 1). The Expected Lemma 6 is trivial, and the Expected Lemmas 7 – 10, which concern properties of the operators Sat_L, NF_L, $rSat_L$, and rNF_L, can be verified in a straightforward way. The remaining Expected Lemmas 4 and 5 are renumbered respectively as Lemmas 1 and 2 given below.

A model generator I is called an *L-model generator of P* if $T_{L,P}(I) \subseteq I$.

Lemma 1. *Let P be an L-MProlog program and I an L-model generator of P. Then the standard L-model of I is an L-model of P.*

Lemma 2. *Let I be an L-normal model generator, M the standard L-model of I, and α a ground L-MProlog goal atom. Suppose that $M \models \alpha$. Then α is an L-instance of some atom of $Sat_L(I)$.*

To prove these lemmas we need Lemmas 3 and 4 given below.

If a modality $\triangle$ is obtainable from $\triangle'$ by replacing some (possibly zero) ∇_i by $\square_i$ then we call $\triangle$ a $\square$-*lifting form* of $\triangle'$. If $\triangle$ is a $\square$-lifting form of $\triangle'$ then we call an atom $\triangle\alpha$ a $\square$-*lifting form* of $\triangle'\alpha$. For example, $\square_1\langle p(a)\rangle_1\square_2 q(b)$ is a $\square$-lifting form of $\langle X\rangle_1\langle p(a)\rangle_1\Diamond_2 q(b)$.

Lemma 3. *Let I be an L-normal model generator and $M = \langle W, \tau, R_1, \ldots, R_m, H\rangle$ the standard L-model graph of I. Let $w = \langle E_1\rangle_{i_1} \ldots \langle E_k\rangle_{i_k}$ be a world of M and $\triangle = w$ be a modality. Then for α not containing $\top$, $\alpha \in H(w)$ iff there exists a $\square$-lifting form $\triangle'$ of $\triangle$ such that $\triangle'\alpha \in Ext_L(I)$.*

This lemma can be easily proved by induction on the length of $\triangle$.

The following lemma is labeled Expected Lemma 2 in [26]. It states that the standard L-model of I is really an L-model of I.

Lemma 4. *Let I be an L-normal model generator, M the standard L-model of I, and σ the standard $\Diamond$-realization function on M. Then M is an L-model and $M, \sigma \models I$.*

Proof. By the definition, M is an L-model. Let $\{R'_i \mid 1 \le i \le m\}$ be the skeleton of M. We prove by induction on the length of α that for any $w \in W$, if $\alpha \in H(w)$ then $M, \sigma, w \models \alpha$. The cases when α is a classical atom or $\alpha = \langle E\rangle_i\beta$ are trivial. Consider the remaining case when $\alpha = \square_i\beta$. Let u be a world such that $R_i(w, u)$ holds. Because $Ext_L(I)$ contains only atoms in L-normal form and $\square_i\beta \in H(w)$, there does not exist v such that $R'_i(v, w)$ holds. Consequently, since $R_i(w, u)$ holds, there exist worlds $w_0 = w$, w_1, $\ldots$, w_{h-1}, $w_h = u$ and indices $j_1, \ldots, j_h$ with $h \ge 1$ such that $R'_{j_1}(w_0, w_1)$, $\ldots$, $R'_{j_h}(w_{h-1}, w_h)$, and $g(k) \subseteq g(i)$ for all $k \in \{j_1, \ldots, j_h\}$. Since $\square_i\beta \in H(w)$, by Lemma 3, there exists a $\square$-lifting form $\triangle'$ of $\triangle = w$ such that $\triangle'\square_i\beta \in Ext_L(I)$. By the rules specifying Ext_L, it follows that $\triangle'\square_{j_1} \ldots \square_{j_h}\beta \in Ext_L(I)$. Hence, by Lemma 3, $\beta \in H(u)$. By the inductive assumption, $M, \sigma, u \models \beta$. Hence $M, \sigma, w \models \square_i\beta$.

Proof of Lemma 1. Let M be the standard L-model of I and σ the standard $\Diamond$-realization function on M. By the definition of L-instances of program clauses and the construction of M, it is sufficient to prove that for any ground L-instance $\boxdot(A \leftarrow B_1, \ldots, B_n)$ of some program clause of P, for any $w \in W$ being an L-instance of $\boxdot$, $M, w \models (A \leftarrow B_1, \ldots, B_n)$. Suppose that $M, w \models B_i$ for all $1 \le i \le n$. We show that $M, w \models A$.

Let $\triangle = w = \langle E_1\rangle_{i_1} \ldots \langle E_k\rangle_{i_k}$. We first show that for any ground simple atom B of the form E, $\square_i E$, or $\Diamond_i E$, if $M, w \models B$ then $\triangle B$ is an L-instance of some atom from $Sat_L(I)$. Suppose that $M, w \models B$. If $k \ge 1$ and $i = i_k$ and $g(i)$ is a singleton, then let $v = \langle E_1\rangle_{i_1} \ldots \langle E_{k-1}\rangle_{i_{k-1}}$, else let $v = w$.

If $B = E$, then by Lemma 3, some $\square$-lifting form of $\triangle B$ belongs to $Ext_L(I)$, and hence $\triangle B$ is an L-instance of some atom from $Sat_L(I)$.

Now suppose that $B = \square_i E$. Let $u = v\langle \top\rangle_i$ and $\triangle' = v\square_i$. We have $R_i(w, u)$, and hence $M, u \models E$. By Lemma 3, it follows that some $\square$-lifting form of $\triangle'E$ belongs to $Ext_L(I)$. Hence, $\triangle B$ is an L-instance of some atom from $Sat_L(I)$.

Next, suppose that $B = \Diamond_i E$. Consider the case $w \neq v$ (i.e. $i = i_k$ and $g(i)$ is a singleton). Since $M, w \models B$, there exists F such that $v\langle F \rangle_i$ is a world of M and $M, v\langle F \rangle_i \models E$. Let $\triangle' = v\langle F \rangle_i$. By Lemma 3, some $\square$-lifting form of $\triangle' E$ belongs to $Ext_L(I)$. Hence, by the rules (2) and (3) of Sat_L, $\triangle B$ is an L-instance of some atom from $Sat_L(I)$. Now consider the case $w = v$ (i.e. $k = 0$ or $i \neq i_k$ or $g(i)$ is not a singleton). Since $M, w \models \Diamond_i E$, there exists $u = w\langle F_1 \rangle_{j_1} \ldots \langle F_h \rangle_{j_h}$ such that $M, u \models E$, $h \geq 1$, and $g(l) \subseteq g(i)$ for all $l \in \{j_1, \ldots, j_h\}$. By Lemma 3, some $\square$-lifting form of $w\langle F_1 \rangle_{j_1} \ldots \langle F_h \rangle_{j_h} E$ belongs to $Ext_L(I)$. It follows that some $\square$-lifting form of $\triangle\langle F_1 \rangle_{j_1} \ldots \langle F_h \rangle_{j_h} E$ belongs to $Sat_L(I)$. By the rules of Sat_L, some $\square$-lifting form of $\triangle\Diamond_i E$ belongs to $Sat_L(I)$. Hence $\triangle B$ is an L-instance of some atom from $Sat_L(I)$.

Since $M, w \models B_i$ for $1 \leq i \leq n$, it follows that $\triangle B_i$ is an L-instance of some atom from $Sat_L(I)$. Consequently, $\triangle A$ is an L-instance of some atom α from $T_{oL,P}(Sat_L(I))$. Let α' be the L-normal form of α, i.e. $NF_L(\{\alpha\}) = \{\alpha'\}$. We have $\alpha' \in T_{L,P}(I) \subseteq I$. By Lemma 4, $M, \sigma \models \alpha'$. If $\alpha' = \alpha$ then we can derive from $M, \sigma \models \alpha'$ that $M, w \models A$. Suppose that $\alpha' \neq \alpha$. Thus, α is of the form $\triangle'' \nabla_i \nabla_i' E$, where $\triangle'' \nabla_i = \triangle$, $g(i)$ is a singleton, and ∇_i' is $\square_i$ or $\langle E \rangle_i$. If $\nabla_i' = \langle E \rangle_i$ then $A = \Diamond_i E$. We have that $\alpha' = \triangle'' \nabla_i' E$. Since $M, \sigma \models \alpha'$ and $g(i)$ is a singleton, it follows that $M, \sigma \models \triangle'' \square_i A$. Hence $M, w \models A$. This completes the proof.

Proof of Lemma 2. Let $\langle W, \tau, R_1, \ldots, R_m, H \rangle$ be the standard L-model graph of I, $\boxed{\cdot} = \square_{i_1} \ldots \square_{i_k}$ be a modality, and $w = \langle \top \rangle_{i_1} \ldots \langle \top \rangle_{i_k}$. Suppose that α is of the form $\boxed{\cdot} E$. Since $M \models \alpha$, we have $M, w \models E$. Hence, by Lemma 3, $\boxed{\cdot} E \in Ext_L(I)$, and we also have $\boxed{\cdot} E \in Sat_L(I)$. Now suppose that α is of the form $\boxed{\cdot}\Diamond_i E$ with the property that if $g(i)$ is a singleton then $i \neq i_k$. Since $M \models \alpha$, we have $M, w \models \Diamond_i E$. Hence there exists $u = w\langle F_1 \rangle_{j_1} \ldots \langle F_h \rangle_{j_h}$ such that $E \in H(u)$, $h \geq 1$, and $g(l) \subseteq g(i)$ for all $l \in \{j_1, \ldots, j_h\}$. By Lemma 3, some $\square$-lifting form of $w\langle F_1 \rangle_{j_1} \ldots \langle F_h \rangle_{j_h} E$ belongs to $Ext_L(I)$. It follows that some $\square$-lifting form of $\boxed{\cdot}\langle F_1 \rangle_{j_1} \ldots \langle F_h \rangle_{j_h} E$ belongs to $Ext_L(I)$ and $Sat_L(I)$. Hence $\boxed{\cdot}\Diamond_i E$ is an L-instance of some atom from $Sat_L(I)$.

We have proved Lemmas 1 and 2, which completes the proof of Theorem 1.

6   More Examples

In this section, we give two more examples illustrating the usefulness of modal logic programming for multi-agent systems.

6.1   Inheritance in a Hierarchy of Classes

In [5], Baldoni et al. formalizes an example taken from [6] of inheritance in a hierarchy of classes by a modal logic program. We adopt here their example with a small modification. Let us consider four classes: *animal, horse, bird,* and *tweety.* Since what is true for animals is also true for birds and horses, the *bird* and *horse* classes inherit from the *animal* class. Moreover, the class *tweety* inherits from *bird* and thus from *animal.*

Animals are not agents in the normal sense, but there is a similarity between the mentioned hierarchy of classes with a multi-agent system. We can treat the class *animal* as a group of agents, the class *bird* as its subgroup of agents, and so on. Program clauses with modal context *animal* can be applied for *horse*, *bird*, and *tweety*. Apparently, this feature is useful for defining epistemic states of groups of agents.

In the following, we use the mentioned classes as modal indices and write, e.g., $[animal]$ and $\langle animal \rangle$ respectively for $\Box_{animal}$ and $\Diamond_{animal}$ (and $\langle X \rangle_{animal}$ can be denoted by $\langle animal, X \rangle$). We use $KD4I_g5_a$, and for the hierarchy, we adopt the conditions that $g(animal) \supset g(horse)$, $g(animal) \supset g(bird)$, and $g(bird) \supset g(tweety)$. Furthermore, treating *tweety* as an object, we assume that $g(tweety)$ is a singleton.

As an example, we have the following clauses:

$$[animal]mode(walk).$$
$$[animal](mode(run) \leftarrow no\_of\_legs(X), X \geq 2).$$
$$[animal](mode(gallop) \leftarrow no\_of\_legs(X), X = 4).$$
$$[horse]no\_of\_legs(4).$$
$$[horse]covering(hair).$$
$$[bird]no\_of\_legs(2).$$
$$[bird]covering(feather).$$
$$[tweety]owner(fred).$$

The atom $[tweety]mode(run)$ can be derived from the above program in $KD4I_g5_a$. If the program contains also $[bird](mode(fly) \leftarrow light)$ or $[bird](mode(fly) \leftarrow \langle bird \rangle light)$, and $\langle tweety \rangle light$, then we can derive $\langle tweety \rangle mode(fly)$ (i.e. have a refutation for the goal $\leftarrow \langle tweety \rangle mode(fly)$). This and the example about the wise men puzzle demonstrate that using $KD4I_g5_a$-MProlog we can reason about possibility. This feature was not incorporated in the work [5] by Baldoni *et al.* (as they studied only modal logic programs without existential modal operators).

6.2   An Example for Modal Deductive Databases

For distributed systems of belief we can use the logic system

$$KD4_s5_s = K_m + (D) + (4_s) + (5_s)$$

where axioms (4_s): $\Box_i \varphi \rightarrow \Box_j \Box_i \varphi$ and (5_s): $\neg \Box_i \varphi \rightarrow \Box_j \neg \Box_i \varphi$ say that agents have full access to belief bases of each other. They are members of a united system and viewed as "friends". An SLD-resolution for MProlog in $KD4_s5_s$ is given in [23]. The following example is taken from our paper [27].

Let us consider the situation when a company has some branches and a central database. Each of the branches can access and update the database, and suppose that the company wants to distinguish data and knowledge coming from different branches. Also assume that data coming from branches can contain noises and statements expressed by a branch may not be highly recognized by other branches. This means that data and statements expressed by branches are treated as "belief" rather than "knowledge". In this case, we can use the multimodal logic $KD4_s5_s$, where each modal index represent a branch of the company, also called an *agent*. Recall that in this logic each agent has a full access to the belief bases of the other agents. Data put by agent i are of the form $\Box_i E$ (agent i believes in E) or $\Diamond_i E$ (agent i considers that E is possible). A statement expressed by agent i is a clause of the form $\Box_i(A \leftarrow B_1, \ldots, B_n)$, where A is an atom of the form E, $\Box_i E$, or $\Diamond_i E$, and $B_1, \ldots, B_n$ are simple modal atoms that may contain modal operators of the other agents. For communicating with normal users, the central database may contain rules with the empty modal context, i.e. in the form $E \leftarrow B_1, \ldots, B_n$, which hide sources of information. As a concrete example, consider the following program/database in $KD4_s5_s$:

agent 1:

$$\Box_1(\Diamond_1 likes(x, Coca) \leftarrow likes(x, Pepsi)) \tag{1}$$
$$\Box_1(\Diamond_1 likes(x, Pepsi) \leftarrow likes(x, Coca)) \tag{2}$$
$$\Box_1 likes(Tom, Coca) \leftarrow \tag{3}$$
$$\Box_1 likes(Peter, Pepsi) \leftarrow \tag{4}$$

agent 2:

$$\Box_2(likes(x, Coca) \leftarrow likes(x, Pepsi)) \tag{5}$$
$$\Box_2(likes(x, Pepsi) \leftarrow likes(x, Coca)) \tag{6}$$
$$\Box_2 likes(Tom, Pepsi) \leftarrow \tag{7}$$
$$\Box_2 likes(Peter, Coca) \leftarrow \tag{8}$$
$$\Box_2 likes(Peter, beer) \leftarrow \tag{9}$$

agent 3:

$$\Box_3(very\_much\_likes(x, y) \leftarrow likes(x, y), \Box_1 likes(x, y), \Box_2 likes(x, y)) \tag{10}$$
$$\Box_3 likes(Tom, Coca) \leftarrow \tag{11}$$
$$\Diamond_3 likes(Peter, Pepsi) \leftarrow \tag{12}$$
$$\Diamond_3 likes(Peter, beer) \leftarrow \tag{13}$$

for communicating with users:

$$very\_much\_likes(x, y) \leftarrow \Box_3 very\_much\_likes(x, y) \tag{14}$$
$$likes(x, y) \leftarrow \Diamond_3 very\_much\_likes(x, y) \tag{15}$$
$$possibly\_likes(x, y) \leftarrow \Diamond_i likes(x, y) \ (\text{for } i \in \{1, 2, 3\}) \tag{16}$$

In the above example, we assume that data and rules are stored in a central database. They can be stored also in a distributed database, where each agent (i.e. branch) has its own database. Such a distributed database can be treated as a multi-agent system.

7   Related Works and Possible Extensions

This paper considers only one of different aspects of multi-agent systems. In particular, we did not consider temporal dimension, actions, and events. Thus the current version of MProlog is not yet an agent programming language like AgentSpeak(L) [30], 3APL [16], and KARO [21]. In this work, we concentrated on reasoning about common/mutual belief, which was also considered in the paper [21] on KARO, but neglected in [31, 30, 16].

To deal with actions and time, possible solutions are to adopt CTL like the BDI-architecture [31], (concurrent) dynamic logic like the KARO system [21], or discrete linear temporal logic. Extending MProlog with dynamic logic or discrete linear temporal logic is possible, because such logics can be treated as modal logics. In our opinion, extending MProlog with concurrent dynamic logic is an interesting problem. Some temporal operators can be defined by modal operators of actions. Interaction between time and belief/knowledge is also a problem to be considered. For simplicity, one can study the case when temporal operators are outside the scope of belief/knowledge.

However, this is still not sufficient for practical multi-agent systems. There remain a lot of problems to be solved. In our opinion, multi-agent planning deserves for more attention. Also, perhaps we should use rewards and penalties for cooperative and competitive[5] multi-agent systems to deal with negotiation and cooperation. But in that case, it seems not easy to adopt logics for specification and verification of multi-agent systems.

Our related works are listed in the next section. Works involving with the wise men puzzle have been discussed in Section 3.

8 Conclusions

Our contributions in this paper are: the schema for semantics of $KD4I_g5_a$-MProlog given in Table 1, proofs of the soundness and completeness of SLD-resolution for $KD4I_g5_a$-MProlog, and a formalization of the wise men puzzle in the purely logical formalism of $KD4I_g5_a$-MProlog together with its SLD-refutation.

In this text, we recalled a large number of definitions and constructions from [26] (which in turn is an extension of [22]) in order to make the paper self-contained and understandable. Thus, the method used in this work for specifying and proving correctness of semantics of $KD4I_g5_a$-MProlog is not new. It originates or relates to our other works [22, 23, 24, 25, 26]. However, this does not reduce the originality of the above-mentioned contributions. They are first published in this paper.

The SLD-refutation given in Section 4.5 for the wise men puzzle does not uses rules or properties involving with axiom (5_a). Consequently, the puzzle can be solved in the logic $KD4I_g = K_m + (D) + (4) + (I_g)$. The choice of $KD4I_g5_a$ is justified as one of possible multimodal logics of belief and common/mutual belief that can be used to formalize the wise men puzzle. Our framework for modal logic programming [26] is applicable for a wide class of multimodal logics (see [23, 25]) and it can be extended for other versions of Kripke semantics, e.g. with varying domain or flexible terms (see a discussion in [26]).

In summary, this paper is on reasoning about common/mutual belief. It shows that the wise men puzzle can be nicely formalized in a multimodal logic of belief

---

[5] Environment can be treated as a competitive agent.

using modal logic programming. Our system is goal-driven and we focused on theoretical aspects like soundness and completeness. We did not incorporate actions and temporal dimension into our system, and this remains as an interesting problem.

Acknowledgements

I would like to thank the reviewers for helpful comments and suggestions.

References

1. H. Aldewereld, W. van der Hoek, and J.-J.Ch. Meyer. Rational teams: Logical aspects of multi-agent systems. *Fundamenta Informaticae*, 63(2–3):159–183, 2004.
2. G. Attardi and M. Simi. Proofs in context. In J. Doyle, E. Sandewall, and P. Torasso, editors, *KR'94: Principles of Knowledge Representation and Reasoning*, pages 16–26, San Francisco, 1994. Morgan Kaufmann.
3. Ph. Balbiani, L. Fariñas del Cerro, and A. Herzig. Declarative semantics for modal logic programs. In *Proceedings of the 1988 International Conference on Fifth Generation Computer Systems*, pages 507–514. ICOT, 1988.
4. M. Baldoni. Normal multimodal logics with interaction axioms. In D. Basin, M. D'Agostino, D.M. Gabbay, and L. Viganò, editors, *Labelled Deduction*, pages 33–57. Kluwer Academic Publishers, 2000.
5. M. Baldoni, L. Giordano, and A. Martelli. A framework for a modal logic programming. In *Joint International Conference and Symposium on Logic Programming*, pages 52–66. MIT Press, 1996.
6. A. Brogi, E. Lamma, and P. Mello. Inheritance and hypothetical reasoning in logic programming. In *Proceedings of ECAI'90*, pages 105–110, Stockholm, 1990.
7. A. Cimatti and L. Serafini. Multi-agent reasoning with belief contexts: The approach and a case study. In M. Wooldridge and N.R. Jennings, editors, *Proceedings of ECAI-94, LNCS 890*, pages 71–85. Springer, 1995.
8. N. de Carvalho Ferreira, M. Fisher, and W. van der Hoek. Practical reasoning for uncertain agents. In J.J. Alferes and J.A. Leite, editors, *Proceedings of JELIA'2004*, volume 3229 of *LNCS*, pages 82–94. Springer-Verlag, 2004.
9. F. Debart, P. Enjalbert, and M. Lescot. Multimodal logic programming using equational and order-sorted logic. *Theoretical Comp. Science*, 105:141–166, 1992.
10. J.J. Elgot-Drapkin. Step-logic and the three-wise-men problem. In *AAAI*, pages 412–417, 1991.
11. R. Fagin, J.Y. Halpern, Y. Moses, and M.Y. Vardi. *Reasoning About Knowledge*. MIT Press, 1995.
12. L. Fariñas del Cerro. Molog: A system that extends Prolog with modal logic. *New Generation Computing*, 4:35–50, 1986.
13. M. Fisher and R. Owens. An introduction to executable modal and temporal logics. In M. Fisher and R. Owens, editors, *Executable Modal and Temporal Logics, IJCAI'93 workshop*, pages 1–20. Springer, 1995.
14. R. Goré and L.A. Nguyen. A tableau system with automaton-labelled formulae for regular grammar logics. In B. Beckert, editor, *Proceedings of TABLEAUX 2005, LNAI 3702*, pages 138–152. Springer-Verlag, 2005.

15. R. Goré and L.A. Nguyen. Tableaux for regular grammar logics of agents using automaton-modal formulae. To be submitted to JAR, 2006.

16. K.V. Hindriks, F.S. de Boer, W. van der Hoek, and J.-J.Ch. Meyer. Agent programming in 3APL. *Autonomous Agents and Multi-Agent Systems*, 2(4):357–401, 1999.

17. M. Kacprzak, A. Lomuscio, and W. Penczek. Bounded versus unbounded model checking for interpreted systems (invited talk at FAAMAS'03). In B. Dunin-Keplicz and R. Verbrugge, editors, *Proceedings of FAAMAS'03*, pages 5–20, 2003.

18. K. Konolige. Belief and incompleteness. Technical Report 319, SRI Inter., 1984.

19. J.W. Lloyd. *Foundations of Logic Programming, 2nd Ed.* Springer-Verlag, 1987.

20. J. McCarthy. First order theories of individual concepts and propositions. *Machine Intelligence*, 9:120–147, 1979.

21. J.-J.Ch. Meyer, F.S. de Boer, R.M. van Eijk, K.V. Hindriks, and W. van der Hoek. On programming KARO agents. *Logic Journal of the IGPL*, 9(2), 2001.

22. L.A. Nguyen. A fixpoint semantics and an SLD-resolution calculus for modal logic programs. *Fundamenta Informaticae*, 55(1):63–100, 2003.

23. L.A. Nguyen. Multimodal logic programming and its applications to modal deductive databases. Manuscript (served as a technical report), available on Internet at http://www.mimuw.edu.pl/~nguyen/papers.html, 2003.

24. L.A. Nguyen. The modal logic programming system MProlog. In J.J. Alferes and J.A. Leite, editors, *Proceedings of JELIA 2004, LNCS 3229*, pages 266–278. Springer, 2004.

25. L.A. Nguyen. An SLD-resolution calculus for basic serial multimodal logics. In D.V. Hung and M. Wirsing, editors, *Proceedings of ICTAC 2005, LNCS 3722*, pages 151–165. Springer, 2005.

26. L.A. Nguyen. The modal logic programming system MProlog: Theory, design, and implementation. Manuscript, available at http://www.mimuw.edu.pl/~nguyen/mprolog, 2005.

27. L.A. Nguyen. On modal deductive databases. In J. Eder, H.-M. Haav, A. Kalja, and J. Penjam, editors, *Proceedings of ADBIS 2005, LNCS 3631*, pages 43–57. Springer, 2005.

28. A. Nonnengart. How to use modalities and sorts in Prolog. In C. MacNish, D. Pearce, and L.M. Pereira, editors, *Proceedings of JELIA'94, LNCS 838*, pages 365–378. Springer, 1994.

29. M.A. Orgun and W. Ma. An overview of temporal and modal logic programming. In D.M. Gabbay and H.J. Ohlbach, editors, *Proc. First Int. Conf. on Temporal Logic - LNAI 827*, pages 445–479. Springer-Verlag, 1994.

30. A.S. Rao. AgentSpeak(L): BDI agents speak out in a logical computable language. In *Proceedings of the 7th European Workshop MAAMAW*, volume 1038 of *LNCS*, pages 42–55. Springer, 1996.

31. A.S. Rao and M.P. Georgeff. Modeling rational agents within a BDI-architecture. In *KR*, pages 473–484, 1991.

32. R.A. Schmidt and D. Tishkovsky. Multi-agent logic of dynamic belief and knowledge. In S. Flesca, S. Greco, N. Leone, and G. Ianni, editors, *Proceedings of JELIA'2002*, volume 2424 of *LNAI*, pages 38–49. Springer, 2002.

33. W. van der Hoek and J.-J. Meyer. Modalities for reasoning about knowledge and uncertainties. In P. Doherty, editor, *Partiality, Modality, and Nonmonotonicity*. CSLI Publications, 1996.

Strongly Complete Axiomatizations of "Knowing at Most" in Syntactic Structures

Thomas Ågotnes and Michal Walicki

Department of Informatics, University of Bergen,
PB. 7800, N-5020 Bergen, Norway
{agotnes, walicki}@ii.uib.no

Abstract. Syntactic structures based on standard syntactic assignments model knowledge directly rather than as truth in all possible worlds as in modal epistemic logic, by assigning arbitrary truth values to atomic epistemic formulae. This approach to epistemic logic is very general and is used in several logical frameworks modeling multi-agent systems, but has no interesting logical properties — partly because the standard logical language is too weak to express properties of such structures. In this paper we extend the logical language with a new operator used to represent the proposition that an agent "knows at most" a given finite set of formulae and study the problem of strongly complete axiomatization of syntactic structures in this language. Since the logic is not semantically compact, a strongly complete *finitary* axiomatization is impossible. Instead we present, first, a strongly complete *infinitary* system, and, second, a strongly complete finitary system for a slightly weaker variant of the language.

1 Introduction

Epistemic logic [1, 2] describe the knowledge of one or several agents. The by far most popular approach to epistemic logic has been to interpret knowledge as truth in all worlds considered possible. To this end, the formalisms of modal logic (see, e.g., [3]) are used: the logical language includes formulae of the form $K_i\phi$, and the semantics is defined by Kripke structures describing the possible worlds. While the modal approach to epistemic logic has been highly successful in many applications, in some contexts it is less applicable. An example of the latter is when we need to model the explicit knowledge an agent has computed, e.g., stored in his knowledge base, at a specific point in time. In modal epistemic logic, an agent necessarily knows all the logical consequences of his knowledge – *the logical omniscience problem* [4]. Furthermore, an agent cannot know a *contradiction* without knowing *everything*. Modal epistemic logic fails as a logic of the explicitly computed knowledge of real agents, because it assumes a very particular and extremely powerful mechanism for reasoning. In reality, different agents have different reasoning mechanisms (e.g. non-monotonic or resource-bounded) and representations of knowledge (e.g. as propositions or as syntactic formulae).

F. Toni and P. Torroni (Eds.): CLIMA VI, LNAI 3900, pp. 57–76, 2006.

In this paper we study a radically different approach to epistemic logic – the *syntactic approach*. In the syntactic approach, a formula $K_i\phi$ can be assigned a truth value independently of the truth value assigned to any other formula of the form $K_i\psi$. Thus the syntactic approach allows, e.g., an agent's knowledge to not be closed under logical consequence or other conditions, and to contain contradictions. Several logical frameworks modeling agents in general [5, 6, 7, 1, 8, 9, 10] and multi-agent systems in particular [11, 12, 13, 14, 15] are based on the syntactic approach. Of particular recent interest has been the body of work on *the Logic of General Awareness* [16, 17, 18, 11, 19, 20, 21], which combine an awareness operator with syntactic semantics with a traditional epistemic operator with possible worlds semantics.

We use the formalisation of the syntactic approach by [1], called *syntactic structures*, and present several new results about the axiomatisation of certain properties of such structures. A syntactic structure is an isolated abstraction of syntactic knowledge, but the results we obtain are also relevant for logics with, e.g., a combination of syntactic and semantic operators.

Knowledge can also be modeled directly by a semantic, rather than a syntactic, approach, by using, e.g., *Montague-Scott* structures [22, 23, 24]). Syntactic structures are generalizations of both Kripke structures and Montague-Scott structures. The literature contains numerous proposed solutions to the logical omniscience problem, see, e.g., [25, 26, 1] for reviews. Wansing [27] shows that many of these approaches can be modeled using Rantala models [28, 29], and that Rantala models can be seen as the most general models of knowledge. It is easy to see that syntactic structures are as general as Rantala models; any Rantala model can be simulated by a syntactic structure. However, syntactic structures are so general that they have no interesting logical properties that can be expressed in the traditional language of epistemic logic – indeed, they are completely axiomatized by propositional logic.

In this paper, in order to be able to express interesting properties of syntactic structures, we extend the logical language with an epistemic operator $\triangledown_i$ for each agent. $\triangledown_i X$, where X is a finite set of formulae, expresses the fact that agent i knows *at most* X. The main problem we consider is the construction of a strongly complete axiomatization of syntactic structures in this language. A consequence of the addition of the new operator is that semantic compactness is lost, and thus that a strongly complete finitary axiomatization is impossible. Instead we, first, present a strongly complete *infinitary* system, and, second, a strongly complete finitary system for syntactic structures for a slightly weaker variant of the epistemic operators.

Our motivation for pursuing the syntactic approach is not that we view it as an *alternative* to the modal approach for all purposes. Rather, we view it as a *complementary approach*, which can be more suitable than the modal approach in some circumstances. A disadvantage of the syntactic approach is that it does not explain knowledge in terms of more fundamental concepts such as possible worlds. But on the other hand, in some cases knowledge of formulae *is* the fundamental concept, for example when an agent stores its knowledge as syntactic strings in a database. Advantages of the syntactic approach include the fact that it can be used to model certain types of agents and certain types of situations which are difficult if not impossible to model with the modal approach; e.g., non-ideal – rather than ideal – agents, and situations where we are interested in explicit – rather than implicit – knowledge. As a concrete example, consider the explicitly computed knowledge of a (non-ideal) agent at a point in time at which it has computed $p \rightarrow q$ and p but not (yet) q. The formulae $K(p \rightarrow q)$, Kp and $\neg Kq$ can never be true at the same time in modal epistemic logic, but they can in the syntactic approach.

Rather than dictating the properties of knowledge, the syntactic approach is a general framework in which different properties can be explored. In this paper we are interested in logical systems describing syntactic knowledge which are strongly complete. If these systems are extended with a set of axioms, the resulting systems are automatically strongly complete with respect to the models of the axioms. For example, if we want to include the assumption that an agent cannot know both a formula and its negation at the same time, we can add the axiom schema $K_i\alpha \rightarrow \neg K_i\neg\alpha$ to one of the systems we discuss, and the resulting system will again be strongly complete with respect to syntactic structures with the mentioned property.

In Section 2 syntactic structures based on standard syntactic assignments and their use in epistemic logic are introduced, before the "at most" operator ∇_i and its interpretation in syntactic structures are presented in Section 3. The completeness results are presented in Section 4, and we discuss some related work and conclude in Sections 5 and 6. We presently define some logical concepts and terminology used in the remainder.

1.1 Logic

By "a logic" we henceforth mean a language of formulae together with a class of semantic structures and a satisfiability relation $\models$. The semantic structures considered in this paper each have a set of *states*, and satisfiability relations relate a formula to a pair consisting of a structure M and a state s of M. A formula ϕ is *satisfiable* if there is a model M with a state s such that $(M, s) \models \phi$. A formula ϕ is a (local) *logical consequence* of a theory (set of formulae) Γ, $\Gamma \models \phi$, iff $(M, s) \models \psi$ for all $\psi \in \Gamma$ implies that $(M, s) \models \phi$. The usual terminology and notation for Hilbert-style proof systems are used: $\Gamma \vdash_S \phi$ means that formula ϕ is derivable from theory Γ in system S, and when Δ is a set of formulae, $\Gamma \vdash_S \Delta$ means that $\Gamma \vdash_S \delta$ for each $\delta \in \Delta$. We use the following definition of maximality: a theory in a language L is maximal if it contains either ϕ or $\neg\phi$ for each $\phi \in L$. A logical system is *weakly complete*, or just *complete*, if $\models \phi$ (i.e. $\emptyset \models \phi$, ϕ is *valid*) implies $\vdash_S \phi$ (i.e. $\emptyset \vdash_S \phi$) for all formulae ϕ, and *strongly complete* if $\Gamma \models \phi$ implies $\Gamma \vdash_S \phi$ for all formulae ϕ and theories Γ. If a logic has a (strongly) complete logical system, we say that the logic *is* (strongly) complete. A logic is semantically *compact* if for every theory Γ, if every finite subset of Γ is satisfiable then Γ is satisfiable. It is easy to see that under the definitions used above:

Fact 1. A weakly complete logic has a sound and strongly complete finitary axiomatization iff it is compact.

2   The Epistemic Logic of Syntactic Structures

Syntactic structures are defined, and used to interpret the standard epistemic language, as follows. Given a number of agents n we write Σ for the set $\{1, \ldots, n\}$. The standard epistemic language:

Definition 2 ($\mathcal{L}$). Given a set of primitive propositions Θ and a number of agents n, $\mathcal{L}(\Theta, n)$ (or just $\mathcal{L}$) is the least set such that:

- $\Theta \subseteq \mathcal{L}$
- If $\phi, \psi \in \mathcal{L}$ then $\neg\phi, (\phi \wedge \psi) \in \mathcal{L}$
- If $\phi \in \mathcal{L}$ and $i \in \Sigma$ then $K_i\phi \in \mathcal{L}$ □

The set of *epistemic atoms* is $\mathcal{L}^{At} = \{K_i\phi : \phi \in \mathcal{L}, i \in \Sigma\}$. An epistemic formula is a propositional combination of epistemic atoms. A syntactic structure [1] assigns a truth value to the primitive propositions and epistemic atoms.

Definition 3 (Syntactic Structure). A *syntactic structure* is a tuple

$$(S, \sigma)$$

where S is a set of states and

$$\sigma(s) : \Theta \cup \mathcal{L}^{At} \to \{\mathbf{true}, \mathbf{false}\}$$

for each $s \in S$. The function σ is called a *standard syntactic assignment*.   □

Satisfaction of an $\mathcal{L}$ formula ϕ by a state s of a syntactic structure M, written $(M, s) \models \phi$, is defined as follows:

$$
\begin{aligned}
(M, s) &\models p & &\Leftrightarrow & \sigma(s)(p) &= \mathbf{true} \\
(M, s) &\models \neg\phi & &\Leftrightarrow & (M, s) &\not\models \phi \\
(M, s) &\models (\phi \wedge \psi) & &\Leftrightarrow & (M, s) &\models \phi \text{ and } (M, s) \models \psi \\
(M, s) &\models K_i\phi & &\Leftrightarrow & \sigma(s)(K_i\phi) &= \mathbf{true}
\end{aligned}
$$

We note that although [1] define syntactic structures in a possible worlds framework, the question of satisfaction of ϕ in a state s does not depend on any other state $(((S, \sigma), s) \models \phi \Leftrightarrow ((\{s\}, \sigma), s) \models \phi)$. We nevertheless keep the possible worlds framework in this paper, while pointing out that it does not play any significant role, for easier comparison with the standard formalisation. A consequence of this independence of states is the following: if a system is strongly complete with respect to all syntactic structures, then the system extended with a set of axioms Γ is strongly complete with respect to the models of Γ. For example, a strongly complete system extended with the axiom schema $K_i\alpha \to \neg K_i\neg\alpha$

will be strongly complete with respect to syntactic structures never assigning **true** to both α and $\neg\alpha$ for any formula α in any state.

Syntactic structures are very general descriptions of knowledge – in fact so general that no epistemic properties of the class of all syntactic structures can be described by the standard epistemic language:

Theorem 4. Propositional logic, with substitution instances for the language $\mathcal{L}$, is sound and complete with respect to syntactic structures.   □

In the next section we increase the expressiveness of the epistemic language.

3   Knowing at Most

The formula $K_i\phi$ denotes that fact that i knows *at least* ϕ – he knows ϕ but he may know more. We can generalize this to finite sets $X \subseteq \mathcal{L}$ of formulae:

$$\triangle_i X \equiv \bigwedge \{K_i\phi : \phi \in X\}$$

representing the fact that i knows at least X. The new operator we introduce here[1] is a dual to $\triangle_i$, denoting the fact that i knows *at most* X:

$$\triangledown_i X$$

denotes the fact that every formula an agent knows is included in X, but he may not know all the formulae in X. If $\mathcal{L}$ was finite, the operator $\triangledown_i$ could (like $\triangle_i$) be defined in terms of K_i:

$$\triangledown_i X = \bigwedge \{\neg K_i\phi : \phi \in \mathcal{L} \setminus X\}$$

But since $\mathcal{L}$ is not finite (regardless of whether or not Θ is finite), $\triangledown_i$ is not definable by K_i. We also use a third, derived, epistemic operator: $\diamondsuit_i X \equiv \triangle_i X \wedge \triangledown_i X$ meaning that the agent knows exactly X. The extended language is called $\mathcal{L}_\triangledown$.

Definition 5 ($\mathcal{L}_\triangledown$). Given a set of primitive propositions Θ, and a number of agents n, $\mathcal{L}_\triangledown(\Theta, n)$ (or just $\mathcal{L}_\triangledown$) is the least set such that:

- $\Theta \subseteq \mathcal{L}_\triangledown$
- If $\phi, \psi \in \mathcal{L}_\triangledown$ then $\neg\phi, (\phi \wedge \psi) \in \mathcal{L}_\triangledown$
- If $\phi \in \mathcal{L}$ and $i \in \Sigma$ then $K_i\phi \in \mathcal{L}_\triangledown$
- If $X \in \wp^{fin}(\mathcal{L})$ and $i \in \Sigma$ then $\triangledown_i X \in \mathcal{L}_\triangledown$ □

The language $\mathcal{L}_\triangledown(\Theta, n)$ is defined to express properties of syntactic structures over the language $\mathcal{L}(\Theta, n)$ (introduced in Section 2), and thus the epistemic

---

[1] The $\triangledown_i X$ operator was also used in a similar logic for the special case of agents who can know only *finitely* many formulae at one time in [30]. The results in the current paper has been used to further investigate the case with the finiteness assumption [31].

operators K_i and ∇_i operate on formulae from $\mathcal{L}(\Theta, n)$. We assume that Θ is countable, and will make use of the fact that it follows that $\mathcal{L}_\nabla(\Theta, n)$ is (infinitely) countable.

If X is a finite set of $\mathcal{L}_\nabla$ formulae, we write $\triangle_i X$ as discussed above (i.e., as a shorthand for $\bigwedge_{\phi \in X} K_i \phi$). In addition, we use $\Diamond_i X$ for $\triangle_i X \wedge \nabla_i X$, and the usual derived propositional connectives.

The interpretation of $\mathcal{L}_\nabla$ in a state s of a syntactic structure M is defined in the same way as the interpretation of $\mathcal{L}$, with the following clause for the new epistemic operator:

$$(M, s) \models \nabla_i X \qquad \Leftrightarrow \qquad \{\phi \in \mathcal{L} : \sigma(s)(K_i \phi) = \textbf{true}\} \subseteq X$$

It is easy to see that

$$(M, s) \models \triangle_i X \qquad \Leftrightarrow \qquad \{\phi \in \mathcal{L} : \sigma(s)(K_i \phi) = \textbf{true}\} \supseteq X$$
$$(M, s) \models \Diamond_i X \qquad \Leftrightarrow \qquad \{\phi \in \mathcal{L} : \sigma(s)(K_i \phi) = \textbf{true}\} = X$$

3.1   Properties

The following schemata, where X, Y, Z range over finite sets of formulae and ϕ over single formulae, show some properties of syntactic structures, in the language $\mathcal{L}_\nabla$.

$\triangle_i \emptyset$		E1
$(\triangle_i X \wedge \triangle_i Y) \rightarrow \triangle_i (X \cup Y)$		E2
$(\nabla_i X \wedge \nabla_i Y) \rightarrow \nabla_i (X \cap Y)$		E3
$\neg(\triangle_i X \wedge \nabla_i Y)$	when $X \not\subseteq Y$	E4
$(\nabla_i(Y \cup \{\phi\}) \wedge \neg K_i \phi) \rightarrow \nabla_i Y$		E5
$\triangle_i X \rightarrow \triangle_i Y$	when $Y \subseteq X$	**KS**
$\nabla_i X \rightarrow \nabla_i Y$	when $X \subseteq Y$	**KG**

The properties are self-explanatory. **KS** and **KG** stands for knowledge *specialisation* and *generalisation*, respectively.

It is straightforward to prove the following.

Lemma 6. E1–E5, **KG**, **KS** are valid.   □

4   Axiomatizations of Syntactic Structures

In this section we discuss axiomatizations of syntactic structures in the language $\mathcal{L}_\nabla$. The following lemma shows that the logic is not compact, and thus it does not have a strongly complete finitary axiomatization (Fact 1).

Lemma 7. The logic of syntactic structures in the language $\mathcal{L}_\triangledown$ is not compact.□

PROOF. Let $p \in \Theta$ and let Γ_1 be the following $\mathcal{L}_\triangledown$ theory:

$$\Gamma_1 = \{K_i p, \neg \triangledown_i \{p\}\} \cup \{\neg K_i \phi : \phi \neq p\}$$

Let Γ' be a finite subset of Γ_1. Clearly, there exists a ϕ' such that $\neg K_i \phi' \notin \Gamma'$. Let $M = (\{s\}, \sigma)$ be such that $\sigma(s)(K_i \phi) = \textbf{true}$ iff $\phi = p$ or $\phi = \phi'$. It is easy to see that $(M, s) \models \Gamma'$. If there was some (M', s') such that $(M', s') \models \Gamma_1$, then $(M', s') \models \neg \triangledown_i \{p\}$ i.e. there must exist a $\phi \neq p$ such that $\sigma(s)(K_i \phi) = \textbf{true}$ – which contradicts the fact that $(M', s') \models \neg K_i \phi$ for all $\phi \neq p$. Thus, every finite subset of Γ_1 is satisfiable, but Γ_1 is not. ∎

We present a strongly complete *infinitary* axiomatization in Section 4.1. Then, in Section 4.2, a finitary axiomatization for a slightly weaker language than $\mathcal{L}_\triangledown$ is proven strongly complete for syntactic structures.

4.1   An Infinitary System

We define a proof system EC^ω for the language $\mathcal{L}_\triangledown$ by using properties presented in Section 3 as axioms, in addition to propositional logic. In addition, EC^ω contains an infinitary derivation clause **R***. After presenting EC^ω, the rest of the section is concerned with proving its strong completeness with respect to the class of all syntactic structures. This is done by the commonly used strategy of proving satisfiability of maximal consistent theories. Thus we need an infinitary variant of the Lindenbaum lemma. However, the usual proof of the Lindenbaum lemma for finitary systems is not necessarily applicable to infinitary systems. In order to prove the Lindenbaum lemma for EC^ω, we use the same strategy as [32] who prove strong completeness of an infinitary axiomatization of PDL (there with canonical models). In particular, we use the same way of defining the derivability relation by using a weakening rule **W**, and we prove the deduction theorem in the same way by including a cut rule **Cut**.

Definition 8 (EC^ω). EC^ω is a logical system for the language $\mathcal{L}_\triangledown$ having the following axiom schemata

All substitution instances of tautologies of propositional calculus		**Prop**
$\neg(\triangle_i X \wedge \triangledown_i Y)$	when $X \not\subseteq Y$	E4
$(\triangledown_i(Y \cup \{\gamma\}) \wedge \neg K_i \gamma) \rightarrow \triangledown_i Y$		E5
$\triangledown_i X \rightarrow \triangledown_i Y$	when $X \subseteq Y$	**KG**

The derivation relation $\vdash_{EC^\omega}$ – written $\vdash_\omega$ for simplicity – between sets of $\mathcal{L}_\triangledown$ formulae and single $\mathcal{L}_\triangledown$ formulae is the smallest relation closed under the following conditions:

$$\vdash_\omega \phi \qquad\qquad\qquad \text{when } \phi \text{ is an axiom} \quad \textbf{Ax}$$

$$\{\phi, \phi \to \psi\} \vdash_\omega \psi \qquad\qquad\qquad\qquad\qquad \textbf{MP}$$

$$\bigcup_{j\in J}\{\alpha_j \to \neg K_i\gamma : \gamma \notin X_j\} \vdash_\omega \bigwedge_{j\in J}\alpha_j \to \triangledown_i X \qquad \textbf{R*}$$

$$\text{when } X = \bigcap_{j\in J} X_j \text{ and } X \text{ and } J \text{ are finite}$$

$$\frac{\Gamma \vdash_\omega \phi}{\Gamma \cup \Delta \vdash_\omega \phi} \qquad\qquad\qquad\qquad\qquad \textbf{W}$$

$$\frac{\Gamma \vdash_\omega \Delta, \Gamma \cup \Delta \vdash_\omega \phi}{\Gamma \vdash_\omega \phi} \qquad\qquad\qquad\qquad \textbf{Cut}$$

In the above schemata, X, Y, Z, X_j range over sets of $\mathcal{L}$ formulae, γ over $\mathcal{L}$ formulae, Γ, Δ over sets of $\mathcal{L}_\triangledown$ formulae, ϕ, ψ, α_j over $\mathcal{L}_\triangledown$ formulae, i over agents, and J over sets of indices. $\qquad\qquad\qquad\qquad\qquad\qquad\qquad\qquad$ □

It is easy to see that E1, E2, E3 and **KS** are derivable in EC^ω.

In order to understand the meaning of the **R*** rule, first consider the following instance, obtained by taking $J = \{1, \ldots, k\}$ and α_j to be a tautology for every $j \in J$, where $X_1, \ldots, X_k$ are arbitrary sets of $\mathcal{L}$ formulae and i an agent:

$$\{\neg K_i\gamma : \gamma \notin X_1\} \cup \cdots \cup \{\neg K_i\gamma : \gamma \notin X_k\} \vdash_\omega \triangledown_i \bigcap_{1\le j\le k} X_j$$

This expression says that if it is the case that, for each X_j, the agent (i) does not know anything which is not in X_j, then the agent knows *at most* the intersection of $X_1, \ldots, X_k$. The general case when α_j is not necessarily an tautology is easily understood in light of this special case: if, for each X_j, α_j implies that i does not know any formula outside X_j, then the conjunction of $\alpha_1, \ldots, \alpha_k$ implies that i knows *at most* the intersection of $X_1, \ldots, X_k$.

The use of the weakening rule instead of more general schemata makes inductive proofs easier, but particular derivations can sometimes be more cumbersome. For example:

Lemma 9.

$$\Gamma \cup \{\phi\} \vdash_\omega \phi \qquad\qquad\qquad\qquad\qquad \textbf{R1}$$

$$\frac{\vdash_\omega \psi \to \phi}{\Gamma \cup \{\psi\} \vdash_\omega \phi} \qquad\qquad\qquad\qquad\qquad \textbf{R2}$$

$$\qquad\qquad\qquad\qquad\qquad\qquad\qquad\qquad\qquad\qquad □$$

PROOF.

R1: $\{\phi, \phi \to \phi\} \vdash_\omega \phi$ by **MP**; $\vdash_\omega \phi \to \phi$ by **Ax**; $\{\phi\} \vdash_\omega \phi \to \phi$ by **W**; $\{\phi\} \vdash_\omega \phi$ by **Cut** and $\Gamma \cup \{\phi\} \vdash_\omega \phi$ by **W**.

R2: Let $\vdash_\omega \psi \to \phi$. By **W**, $\{\psi\} \vdash_\omega \psi \to \phi$; by **MP** $\{\psi, \psi \to \phi\} \vdash_\omega \phi$ and thus $\{\psi\} \vdash_\omega \phi$ by **Cut**. By **W**, $\Gamma \cup \{\psi\} \vdash_\omega \phi$. ■

In order to prove the Lindenbaum lemma, we need the deduction theorem. The latter is shown by first proving the following rule.

Lemma 10. The following rule of *conditionalization* is admissible in EC^ω.

$$\frac{\Gamma \cup \Delta \vdash_\omega \phi}{\Gamma \cup \{\psi \to \delta : \delta \in \Delta\} \vdash_\omega \psi \to \phi} \qquad \textbf{Cond}$$

$\square$

PROOF. The proof is by infinitary induction over the derivation $\Gamma \cup \Delta \vdash_\omega \phi$ (derivations are well-founded). The base cases are **Ax**, **MP** and **R***, and the inductive steps are **W** and **Cut**.

Ax: $\Gamma = \Delta = \emptyset$. We must show that $\vdash_\omega \psi \to \phi$ when $\vdash_\omega \phi$. By **W** we get $\phi \to (\psi \to \phi) \vdash_\omega \phi$, then $\phi, \phi \to (\psi \to \phi) \vdash_\omega \psi \to \phi$ is an instance of **MP**, and by **Cut** we get $\phi \to (\psi \to \phi) \vdash_\omega \psi \to \phi$. By **Prop**, $\vdash_\omega \phi \to (\psi \to \phi)$, so by **Cut** once more we get $\vdash_\omega \psi \to \phi$.

MP: $\Gamma \cup \Delta = \{\phi', \phi' \to \phi\} \vdash_\omega \phi$. That $\Gamma \cup \{\psi \to \delta : \delta \in \Delta\} \vdash_\omega \psi \to \phi$ can be shown for each of the four possible combinations of Γ and Δ in a similar way to the **Ax** case.

R*: $\phi = \bigwedge_{j \in J} \alpha_j \to \bigtriangledown_i X$ and $\Gamma \cup \Delta = \bigcup_{j \in J}\{\alpha_j \to \neg K_i \phi' : \phi' \in \mathcal{L} \setminus X_j\}$ where J is finite and $X = \bigcap_{j \in J} X_j$ is finite, i.e. there exist for each $j \in J$ sets Y_j and Z_j such that $\mathcal{L} \setminus X_j = Y_j \uplus Z_j$ and

$$\Gamma = \bigcup_{j \in J}\{\alpha_j \to \neg K_i \phi' : \phi' \in Y_j\}$$

$$\Delta = \bigcup_{j \in J}\{\alpha_j \to \neg K_i \phi' : \phi' \in Z_j\}$$

Let

$$\Gamma' = \bigcup_{j \in J}\{(\psi \wedge \alpha_j) \to \neg K_i \phi' : \phi' \in Y_j\}$$

$$\Delta' = \bigcup_{j \in J}\{(\psi \wedge \alpha_j) \to \neg K_i \phi' : \phi' \in Z_j\}$$

$\Gamma' \cup \Delta' = \bigcup_{j \in J}\{(\psi \wedge \alpha_j) \to \neg K_i \phi' : \phi' \in \mathcal{L} \setminus X_j\}$, and thus $\Gamma' \cup \Delta' \vdash_\omega \gamma'$, where $\gamma' = \bigwedge_{j \in J}(\psi \wedge \alpha_j) \to \bigtriangledown_i X$, by **R***. By **W**, $\Gamma' \cup \Delta' \cup \Gamma \vdash_\omega \gamma'$. By **Prop**, $\vdash_\omega (\alpha_j \to \neg K_i \phi') \to ((\psi \wedge \alpha_j) \to \neg K_i \phi')$ for each $\alpha_j \to \neg K_i \phi' \in \Gamma$, and by R2 (once for each formula in Γ) $\Delta' \cup \Gamma \vdash_\omega \Gamma'$. By **Cut**, $\Delta' \cup \Gamma \vdash_\omega \gamma'$, and it only remains to convert the conjunctions in Δ' and γ' to implications: $\Delta' \cup \Gamma \cup \{\gamma'\} \vdash_\omega \psi \to \phi$ by **Prop** and R2, and by **Cut** and **W** it follows that $\Delta' \cup \Gamma \cup \{\psi \to \delta : \delta \in \Delta\} \vdash_\omega \psi \to \phi$. By **Prop** and R2 (once of each formula in Δ), $\Gamma \cup \{\psi \to \delta : \delta \in \Delta\} \vdash_\omega \Delta'$, and by **Cut** $\Gamma \cup \{\psi \to \delta : \delta \in \Delta\} \vdash_\omega \psi \to \phi$, which is the desired conclusion.

W: $\Gamma' \cup \Delta' \vdash_\omega \phi$ for some $\Gamma' \subseteq \Gamma$ and $\Delta' \subseteq \Delta$. By the induction hypothesis we can use **Cond** to obtain $\Gamma' \cup \{\psi \to \delta : \delta \in \Delta'\} \vdash_\omega \psi \to \phi$, and thus $\Gamma \cup \{\psi \to \delta : \delta \in \Delta\} \vdash_\omega \psi \to \phi$ by **W**.

Cut: $\Gamma \cup \Delta \vdash_\omega \Delta'$ and $\Gamma \cup \Delta \cup \Delta' \vdash_\omega \phi$, for some Δ'. By the induction hypothesis on the first derivation (once for each $\delta' \in \Delta'$), $\Gamma \cup \{\psi \to \delta : \delta \in \Delta\} \vdash_\omega \phi \to \delta'$ for each $\delta' \in \Delta'$. By the induction hypothesis on the second derivation, $\Gamma \cup \{\psi \to \delta : \delta \in \Delta \cup \Delta'\} \vdash_\omega \psi \to \phi$. By **Cut**, $\Gamma \cup \{\psi \to \delta : \delta \in \Delta\} \vdash_\omega \psi \to \phi$.   ∎

Theorem 11 (Deduction Theorem). The rule

$$\frac{\Gamma \cup \{\phi\} \vdash_\omega \psi}{\Gamma \vdash_\omega \phi \to \psi} \qquad \textbf{DT}$$

is admissible in EC^ω.   □

PROOF. If $\Gamma \cup \{\phi\} \vdash_\omega \psi$, then $\Gamma \cup \{\phi \to \phi\} \vdash_\omega \phi \to \psi$ by **Cond**. $\Gamma \vdash_\omega \phi \to \phi$ by **Ax** and **W**, and thus $\Gamma \vdash_\omega \phi \to \psi$ by **Cut**.   ∎

Now we are ready to show that consistent theories can be extended to maximal consistent theories. The proof relies on **DT**.

Lemma 12 (Lindenbaum lemma for EC^ω). If Γ is EC^ω-consistent, then there exists an $\mathcal{L}_\nabla$-maximal and EC^ω-consistent Γ' such that $\Gamma \subseteq \Gamma'$.   □

PROOF. Recall **R***:

$$\bigcup_{j \in J} \{\alpha_j \to \neg K_k \psi : \psi \notin X_j\} \vdash_\omega \bigwedge_{j \in J} \alpha_j \to \nabla_k X.$$

Formulae which can appear on the right of $\vdash_\omega$ in its instances will be said to have **R***-form. A special case of this schema is when $\bigwedge_j \alpha_j$ is a tautology (i.e., each α_j is), from which

$$\bigcup_{j \in J} \{\neg K_k \phi : \psi \notin X_j\} \vdash_\omega \nabla_k X.$$

can be obtained. Now, $\Gamma' \supset \Gamma$ is constructed as follows. $\mathcal{L}_\nabla$ is countable, so let $\phi_1, \phi_2, \ldots$ be an enumeration of $\mathcal{L}_\nabla$ respecting the subformula relation (i.e., when ϕ_i is a subformula of ϕ_j then $i < j$).

$\Gamma_0 = \Gamma$

$$\Gamma_{i+1} = \begin{cases} \Gamma_i \cup \{\phi_{i+1}\} & \text{if } \Gamma_i \vdash_\omega \phi_{i+1} \\ \Gamma_i \cup \{\neg\phi_{i+1}\} & \text{if } \Gamma_i \not\vdash_\omega \phi_{i+1} \text{ and } \phi_{i+1} \text{ does not have the } \textbf{R*}\text{-form} \\ \Gamma_i \cup \{\neg\phi_{i+1}, K_k\psi\} & \text{if } \Gamma_i \not\vdash_\omega \phi_{i+1} \text{ and } \phi_{i+1} \text{ has the } \textbf{R*}\text{-form, where } \psi \\ & \text{is arbitrary such that } \psi \notin X \text{ and } \Gamma_i \not\vdash_\omega \neg K_k\psi \end{cases}$$

$$\Gamma' = \bigcup_{i=0}^{\omega} \Gamma_i$$

The existence of ψ in the last clause in the definition of Γ_{i+1} is verified as follows: since $\Gamma_i \not\vdash_\omega \phi_{i+1}$, there must be, to prevent an application of **R***, at least one

α_j and $\psi \notin X$ such that $\Gamma_i \nvdash_\omega \alpha_j \to \neg K_k \psi$. By construction (and the ordering of formulae), each α_j or its negation is included in Γ_i. If $\Gamma_i \vdash_\omega \neg \alpha_j$ then also $\Gamma_i \vdash_\omega \alpha_j \to \neg K_k \psi$, and this would be the case also if $\Gamma_i \vdash_\omega \neg K_k \psi$. So $\Gamma_i \vdash_\omega \alpha_j$ and $\Gamma_i \nvdash_\omega \neg K_k \psi$.

It is easy to see that Γ' is maximal.

We show that each Γ_i is consistent, by induction over i. For the base case, Γ_0 is consistent by assumption. For the inductive case, assume that Γ_i is consistent. Γ_{i+1} is constructed by one of the three cases in the definition:

1. Γ_{i+1} is obviously consistent.
2. If $\Gamma_{i+1} = \Gamma_i \cup \{\neg \phi_{i+1}\} \vdash_\omega \bot$, then $\Gamma_i \vdash_\omega \phi_{i+1}$ by **DT** and **Prop**, contradicting the assumption in this case.
3. Consider first the special case (when all α_j are tautologies). Assume that $\Gamma_{i+1} = \Gamma_i \cup \{\neg \triangledown_k X, K_k \psi\} \vdash_\omega \bot$. Then $\Gamma_i \vdash_\omega K_k \psi \to \triangledown_k X$ by **DT** and **Prop** and by E4, since $\psi \notin X$, $\Gamma_i \vdash_\omega K_k \psi \to \neg \triangledown_k X$, and thus $\Gamma_i \vdash_\omega \neg K_k \psi$ contradicting the assumption in this case.

   In the general case, assume that $\Gamma_{i+1} = \Gamma_i \cup \{\neg(\bigwedge_j \alpha_j \to \triangledown_k X), K_k \psi\} \vdash_\omega \bot$:

   i Then $\Gamma_i \vdash_\omega K_k \psi \to (\neg(\bigwedge_j \alpha_j \to \triangledown_k X) \to \bot)$, i.e., $\Gamma_i \vdash_\omega K_k \psi \to (\bigwedge_j \alpha_j \to \triangledown_k X)$, i.e., $\Gamma_i \vdash_\omega \bigwedge_j \alpha_j \to (K_k \psi \to \triangledown_k X)$.

   ii By assumption in the construction, $\Gamma_i \nvdash_\omega \neg(\bigwedge_j \alpha_j)$ (for otherwise it would prove $\bigwedge_j \alpha_j \to \triangledown_k X$), but since $\bigwedge_j \alpha_j$ (as well as each α_j) is a subformula of ϕ_{i+1}, it or its negation is already included in Γ_i. But this means that $\Gamma_i \vdash_\omega \bigwedge_j \alpha_j$. Combined with (i), this gives $\Gamma_i \vdash_\omega K_k \psi \to \triangledown_k X$, i.e., $\Gamma_i \vdash_\omega \neg K_k \psi \vee \triangledown_k X$.

   iii On the other hand, by E4, since $\psi \notin X$: $\Gamma_i \vdash_\omega \neg(K_k \psi \wedge \triangledown_k X)$, i.e., $\Gamma_i \vdash_\omega \neg K_k \psi \vee \neg \triangledown_k X$. Combined with (ii) this means that $\Gamma_i \vdash_\omega \neg K_k \psi$, but this contradicts the assumption in the construction of Γ_{i+1}.

Thus each Γ_i is consistent.

To show that Γ' is consistent, we first show that

$$\Gamma'' \vdash_\omega \phi \Rightarrow (\Gamma'' \subseteq \Gamma' \Rightarrow \phi \in \Gamma') \tag{1}$$

holds for all derivations $\Gamma'' \vdash_\omega \phi$, by induction over the derivation. The base cases are **Ax**, **MP** and **R***, and the inductive steps are **W** and **Cut**. Let i be the index of the formula ϕ, i.e. $\phi = \phi_i$.

Ax: If $\vdash_\omega \phi$, then $\phi \in \Gamma_i$ by the first case in the definition of Γ_i.

MP: $\Gamma'' = \{\phi', \phi' \to \phi\}$. If $\Gamma'' \subseteq \Gamma'$, there exists k, l such that $\phi' \in \Gamma_k$ and $\phi' \to \phi \in \Gamma_l$. If $\phi \notin \Gamma'$, $\neg \phi \in \Gamma'$ by maximality, i.e. there exists a m such that $\neg \phi \in \Gamma_m$. But then $\neg \phi, \phi', \phi' \to \phi \in \Gamma_{\max(k,l,m)}$, contradicting consistency of $\Gamma_{\max(k,l,m)}$.

R*: $\Gamma'' = \bigcup_{j \in J} \{\alpha_j \to \neg K_k \psi : \psi \notin X_j\}$ and $\phi = \bigwedge_j \alpha_j \to \triangledown_k X$, where $X = \bigcap_j X_j$, and $\Gamma'' \subseteq \Gamma'$. If $\phi \notin \Gamma'$ then, by maximality, $\neg \phi \in \Gamma'$, and thus $\neg \phi \in \Gamma_i$. Then, by construction of Γ_i, $\Gamma_{i-1} \nvdash_\omega \phi$ (otherwise $\phi \in \Gamma'$) and $K_k \psi \in \Gamma_i$ for some $\psi \notin X$. By the same argument as in point 3.(ii) above, $\Gamma_i \vdash_\omega \bigwedge_j \alpha_j$, and hence also $\Gamma' \vdash_\omega \bigwedge_j \alpha_j$. But then, for an appropriate m

(namely, for which $\phi_m = \alpha_j \to \neg K_k\psi$): $\Gamma_{m-1} \vdash_\omega \alpha_j$ and $\Gamma_{m-1} \vdash_\omega K_k\psi$, i.e., $\neg(\alpha_j \to \neg K_k\psi) \in \Gamma_m$, and so $\alpha_j \to \neg K_k\psi \notin \Gamma'$, which contradicts the assumption that $\Gamma'' \subseteq \Gamma'$.

W: $\Gamma'' = \Gamma''' \cup \Delta$, and $\Gamma''' \vdash_\omega \phi$. If $\Gamma'' \subseteq \Gamma'$, $\Gamma''' \subseteq \Gamma$ and by the induction hypothesis $\phi \in \Gamma'$.

Cut: $\Gamma'' \vdash_\omega \Delta$ and $\Gamma'' \cup \Delta \vdash_\omega \phi$. Let $\Gamma'' \subseteq \Gamma'$. By the induction hypothesis on the first derivation (once for each of the formulae in Δ), $\Delta \subseteq \Gamma'$. Then $\Gamma'' \cup \Delta \subseteq \Gamma'$, and by the induction hypothesis on the second derivation $\phi \in \Gamma'$.

Thus (1) holds for all $\Gamma'' \vdash_\omega \phi$; particularly for $\Gamma' \vdash_\omega \phi$. Consistency of Γ' follows: if $\Gamma' \vdash_\omega \perp$, then $\perp \in \Gamma'$, i.e. $\perp \in \Gamma_l$ for some l, contradicting the fact that each Γ_l is consistent. ∎

The following Lemma is needed in the proof of the thereafter following Lemma stating satisfiability of maximal consistent theories.

Lemma 13. Let $\Gamma' \subseteq \mathcal{L}_\nabla$ be an $\mathcal{L}_\nabla$-maximal and EC^ω-consistent theory. If there exists an X' such that $\Gamma' \vdash_\omega \nabla_i X'$, then there exists an X such that $\Gamma' \vdash_\omega \Diamond_i X$. □

PROOF. Let Γ' be maximal consistent, and let $\Gamma' \vdash_\omega \nabla_i X'$. Let

$$X = \bigcap_{Y \subseteq X' \text{ and } \Gamma' \vdash_\omega \nabla_i Y} Y$$

Since every Y is included in the finite set X', X is finite, and $\Gamma' \vdash_\omega \nabla_i X$ can be obtained by a finite number of applications of E3. Let

$$Z = \bigcup_{\Gamma' \vdash_\omega \Delta_i Y} Y$$

If $\Gamma' \vdash_\omega \Delta_i Y$, then $Y \subseteq X$, since otherwise Γ' would be inconsistent by E4. Thus Z is finite. By a finite number of applications of E2, $\Gamma' \vdash_\omega \Delta_i Z$. If $Z \not\subseteq X$, then Γ' would be inconsistent by E4, so $Z \subseteq X$. We now show that $X \subseteq Z$. Assume the opposite: $\phi \in X$ but $\phi \notin Z$ for some ϕ. Let $X^- = X \setminus \{\phi\}$. $\Gamma' \nvdash_\omega K_i\phi$, since otherwise $\phi \in Z$ by definition of Z. By maximality, $\Gamma' \vdash_\omega \neg K_i\phi$. By E5, $\Gamma' \vdash_\omega \nabla_i X^-$ – but by construction of X it follows that $X \subseteq X^-$ which is a contradiction. Thus, $X = Z$, and $\Gamma' \vdash_\omega \Diamond_i X$. ∎

Lemma 14. Every maximal EC^ω-consistent $\mathcal{L}_\nabla$ theory is satisfiable. □

PROOF. Let Γ be maximal and consistent. We construct the following syntactic structure, which is intended to satisfy Γ:

$$M^\Gamma = (\{s\}, \sigma^\Gamma)$$
$$\sigma^\Gamma(s)(p) = \mathbf{true} \Leftrightarrow \Gamma \vdash_\omega p \text{ when } p \in \Theta$$
$$\sigma^\Gamma(s)(K_i\phi) = \mathbf{true} \Leftrightarrow \phi \in X_i^\Gamma$$

where:

$$X_i^\Gamma = \begin{cases} Z \text{ where } \Gamma \vdash_\omega \Diamond_i Z \text{ if there is an } X' \text{ such that } \Gamma \vdash_\omega \nabla_i X' \\ \{\gamma : \Gamma \vdash_\omega K_i \gamma\} \qquad \text{otherwise} \end{cases}$$

In the definition of X_i^Γ, the existence of a Z such that that $\Gamma \vdash_\omega \Diamond_i Z$ in the case that there exists an X' such that $\Gamma \vdash_\omega \nabla_i X'$ is guaranteed by Lemma 13. We show, by structural induction over ϕ, that

$$(M^\Gamma, s) \models \phi \Longleftrightarrow \Gamma \vdash_\omega \phi \tag{2}$$

This is a stronger statement than the lemma; the lemma is given by the direction to the left. We use three base cases: when ϕ is in Θ, $\phi = K_i \psi$ and $\phi = \nabla_i X$. The first base case and the two inductive steps negation and conjunction are trivial, so we show only the two interesting base cases. For each base case we consider the situations when X_i^Γ is given by a) the first and b) the second case in its definition.

- $\phi = K_i \psi$: $(M^\Gamma, s) \models K_i \psi$ iff $\psi \in X_i^\Gamma$.
  $\Rightarrow$) Let $\psi \in X_i^\Gamma$. In case a), $X_i^\Gamma = Z$ where $\Gamma \vdash_\omega \Diamond_i Z$ and by **KS**, $\Gamma \vdash_\omega K_i \psi$. In case b), $\Gamma \vdash_\omega K_i \psi$ by construction of X_i^Γ.
  $\Leftarrow$) Let $\Gamma \vdash_\omega K_i \psi$. In case a), $\Gamma \vdash_\omega \nabla_i Z$ and thus $\psi \in Z = X_i^\Gamma$ by E4 and consistency of Γ. In case b), $\psi \in X_i^\Gamma$ by construction.
- $\phi = \nabla_i X$: $(M^\Gamma, s) \models \nabla_i X$ iff $X_i^\Gamma \subseteq X$.
  $\Rightarrow$) Let $X_i^\Gamma \subseteq X$. In case a), $\Gamma \vdash_\omega \Diamond_i Z$ where $Z = X_i^\Gamma \subseteq X$, so $\Gamma \vdash_\omega \nabla_i X$ by **KG**. In case b), X_i^Γ must be finite, since X is finite. For any $\psi \notin X_i^\Gamma$, $\Gamma \nvdash_\omega K_i \psi$ by construction of X_i^Γ, and $\Gamma \vdash_\omega \neg K_i \psi$ by maximality. Thus, by **R*** (with $J = \{1\}$, $\alpha_1 = \top$ and $X_1 = X_i^\Gamma$), $\Gamma \vdash_\omega \nabla_i X_i^\Gamma$, contradicting the assumption in case b). Thus, case b) is impossible.
  $\Leftarrow$) Let $\Gamma \vdash_\omega \nabla_i X$. In case a), $\Gamma \vdash_\omega \triangle_i Z$ and by E4 and consistency of Γ $X_i^\Gamma = Z \subseteq X$. Case b) is impossible by definition. ∎

Theorem 15. EC^ω is a sound and strongly complete axiomatization of syntactic structures, in the language $\mathcal{L}_\nabla$. ☐

PROOF. Soundness follows from Lemma 6, and the easily seen facts that $\Gamma \models \phi$ for every instance $\Gamma \vdash_\omega \phi$ of both **MP** and of **R***, and that **W** and **Cut** preserve logical consequence, by induction over the definition of the derivation relation. Strong completeness follows from Lemmas 12 and 14.

4.2 A System for a Weaker Language

In the previous section we proved strong completeness of EC^ω by using **R***. It turns out that strong completeness can be proved without **R***, if we restrict the logical language slightly. The restriction is that for some arbitrary primitive proposition $\hat{p} \in \Theta$, $K_i \hat{p}$ and $\nabla_i X$ are not well-formed formulae for any i and any X with $\hat{p} \in X$. The semantics is not changed; we are still interpreting the language in syntactic structures over $\mathcal{L}(\Theta, n)$ as described in Sections 2 and 3. Thus, in the restricted logic agents can know something which is not expressible in the logical language.

$\mathcal{L}_{\bigtriangledown}^{\hat{p}} \subset \mathcal{L}_{\bigtriangledown}$ is the restricted language for a given primitive proposition $\hat{p}$.

Definition 16 ($\mathcal{L}_{\bigtriangledown}^{\hat{p}}$). Given a set of primitive propositions Θ, a proposition $\hat{p} \in \Theta$ and a number of agents n, $\mathcal{L}_{\bigtriangledown}^{\hat{p}}(\Theta, n)$ (or just $\mathcal{L}_{\bigtriangledown}^{\hat{p}}$) is the least set such that:

- $\Theta \subseteq \mathcal{L}_{\bigtriangledown}^{\hat{p}}$
- If $\phi, \psi \in \mathcal{L}_{\bigtriangledown}^{\hat{p}}$ then $\neg\phi, (\phi \wedge \psi) \in \mathcal{L}_{\bigtriangledown}^{\hat{p}}$
- If $\phi \in (\mathcal{L} \setminus \{\hat{p}\})$ and $i \in \Sigma$ then $K_i\phi \in \mathcal{L}_{\bigtriangledown}^{\hat{p}}$
- If $X \in \wp^{fin}(\mathcal{L} \setminus \hat{p})$ and $i \in \Sigma$ then $\bigtriangledown_i X \in \mathcal{L}_{\bigtriangledown}^{\hat{p}}$ □

The finitary logical system $EC^{\hat{p}}$ is defined by the same axiom schemata as EC^ω. The two systems do not, however, have the same axioms since they are defined for different languages – the extensions of the schemata are different. The derivation relation for $EC^{\hat{p}}$ is defined by the axioms and the derivation rule modus ponens. Particularly, the infinitary derivation clause **R*** from EC^ω is not included.

Definition 17 ($EC^{\hat{p}}$). $EC^{\hat{p}}$ is the logical system for the language $\mathcal{L}_{\bigtriangledown}^{\hat{p}}$ consisting of the following axiom schemata:

All substitution instances of tautologies of propositional calculus		**Prop**
$\neg(\triangle_i X \wedge \bigtriangledown_i Y)$	when $X \not\subseteq Y$	**E4**
$(\bigtriangledown_i(Y \cup \{\gamma\}) \wedge \neg K_i\gamma) \to \bigtriangledown_i Y$		**E5**
$\bigtriangledown_i X \to \bigtriangledown_i Y$	when $X \subseteq Y$	**KG**

The derivation relation $\vdash_{EC^{\hat{p}}}$ – written $\vdash_{\hat{p}}$ for simplicity – between sets of $\mathcal{L}_{\bigtriangledown}^{\hat{p}}$ formulae and single $\mathcal{L}_{\bigtriangledown}^{\hat{p}}$ formulae is the smallest relation closed under the following conditions:

$\Gamma \vdash_{\hat{p}} \phi$	when $\phi \in \Gamma$	**Prem**
$\Gamma \vdash_{\hat{p}} \phi$	when ϕ is an axiom	**Ax**
$\dfrac{\Gamma \vdash_{\hat{p}} \phi, \Gamma \vdash_{\hat{p}} \phi \to \psi}{\Gamma \vdash_{\hat{p}} \psi}$		**MP**

□

It is easy to see that E1, E2, E3, **KS** and **DT** are derivable in EC^ω.

The restriction $\mathcal{L}_{\bigtriangledown}^{\hat{p}} \subset \mathcal{L}_{\bigtriangledown}$ is sufficient to prove strong completeness without **R*** in a manner very similar to the proof in Section 4.1. The first step, existence of maximal consistent extensions, can now be proved by the standard proof since the system is finitary.

Lemma 18 (Lindenbaum lemma for $EC^{\hat{p}}$). If Γ is $EC^{\hat{p}}$-consistent, then there exists an $\mathcal{L}_{\bigtriangledown}^{\hat{p}}$-maximal and $EC^{\hat{p}}$-consistent Γ' such that $\Gamma \subseteq \Gamma'$.   □

Second, we establish the result corresponding to Lemma 13 for $\mathcal{L}_{\bigtriangledown}^{\hat{p}}$ and $EC^{\hat{p}}$.

Lemma 19. Let $\Gamma' \subseteq \mathcal{L}_{\bigtriangledown}^{\hat{p}}$ be a $\mathcal{L}_{\bigtriangledown}^{\hat{p}}$-maximal and $EC^{\hat{p}}$-consistent theory. If there exists a X' such that $\Gamma' \vdash_{\hat{p}} \bigtriangledown_i X'$, then there exists a X such that $\Gamma' \vdash_{\hat{p}} \Diamond_i X$. $\square$

PROOF. The proof is essentially the same as for Lemma 13, for the language $\mathcal{L}_{\bigtriangledown}^{\hat{p}}$ instead of $\mathcal{L}_{\bigtriangledown}$ (note that in that proof we did not rely on **R***, and that $\hat{p} \notin X$ since $X \subseteq X'$). ∎

Third, we show satisfiability.

Lemma 20. Every maximal $EC^{\hat{p}}$-consistent $\mathcal{L}_{\bigtriangledown}^{\hat{p}}$ theory is satisfiable. $\square$

PROOF. Let Γ be maximal and consistent. The proof is very similar to that of the corresponding result for EC^{ω} (Lemma 14). We construct the following syntactic structure, which is intended to satisfy Γ:

$$M^{\Gamma} = (\{s\}, \sigma^{\Gamma})$$
$$\sigma^{\Gamma}(s)(p) = \textbf{true} \Leftrightarrow \Gamma \vdash_{\hat{p}} p \text{ when } p \in \Theta$$
$$\sigma^{\Gamma}(s)(K_i\phi) = \textbf{true} \Leftrightarrow \phi \in X_i^{\Gamma}$$

where:

$$X_i^{\Gamma} = \begin{cases} Z \text{ where } \Gamma \vdash_{\hat{p}} \Diamond_i Z & \text{if there is an } X' \text{ such that } \Gamma \vdash_{\hat{p}} \bigtriangledown_i X' \\ \{\gamma : \Gamma \vdash_{\hat{p}} K_i\gamma\} \cup \{\hat{p}\} & \text{if } \forall_{X'} \Gamma \nvdash_{\hat{p}} \bigtriangledown_i X' \text{ and } \bigcup_{\Gamma \vdash_{\hat{p}} \triangle_i Y} Y \text{ is finite} \\ \{\gamma : \Gamma \vdash_{\hat{p}} K_i\gamma\} & \text{if } \forall_{X'} \Gamma \nvdash_{\hat{p}} \bigtriangledown_i X' \text{ and } \bigcup_{\Gamma \vdash_{\hat{p}} \triangle_i Y} Y \text{ is infinite} \end{cases}$$

The existence of Z is guaranteed by Lemma 19, and, again, we show, by structural induction over ϕ, that

$$(M^{\Gamma}, s) \models \phi \Longleftrightarrow \Gamma \vdash_{\hat{p}} \phi \tag{3}$$

for all $\phi \in \mathcal{L}_{\bigtriangledown}^{\hat{p}}$. As in the proof of Lemma 14 we only show the epistemic base cases. For each base case we consider the situations when

a) there is an X' such that $\Gamma \vdash_{\hat{p}} \bigtriangledown_i X'$ or
b) $\Gamma \nvdash_{\hat{p}} \bigtriangledown_i X'$ for every X'

corresponding to the first and to the second and third cases in the definition of X_i^{Γ}, respectively.

- $\phi = K_i\psi$: $(M^{\Gamma}, s) \models K_i\psi$ iff $\psi \in X_i^{\Gamma}$.
  $\Rightarrow$) Let $\psi \in X_i^{\Gamma}$. In case a), $X_i^{\Gamma} = Z$ where $\Gamma \vdash_{\hat{p}} \Diamond_i Z$ and by **KS**, $\Gamma \vdash_{\hat{p}} K_i\psi$. In case b), $\psi \neq \hat{p}$ (since $K_i\psi \in \mathcal{L}_{\bigtriangledown}^{\hat{p}}$) and thus $\Gamma \vdash_{\hat{p}} K_i\psi$ by construction of X_i^{Γ}.
  $\Leftarrow$) Let $\Gamma \vdash_{\hat{p}} K_i\psi$. In case a), $\Gamma \vdash_{\hat{p}} \bigtriangledown_i Z$ and thus $\psi \in Z = X_i^{\Gamma}$ by E4 and consistency of Γ. In case b), $\psi \in X_i^{\Gamma}$ by construction.
- $\phi = \bigtriangledown_i X$: $(M^{\Gamma}, s) \models \bigtriangledown_i X$ iff $X_i^{\Gamma} \subseteq X$.

$\Rightarrow$) Let $X_i^\Gamma \subseteq X$. In case a), $\Gamma \vdash_{\hat{p}} \Diamond_i Z$ where $Z = X_i^\Gamma \subseteq X$, so $\Gamma \vdash_{\hat{p}} \bigtriangledown_i X$ by **KG**. In case b), if $\hat{p} \in X_i^\Gamma$ then $\hat{p} \in X$ which is impossible since $\bigtriangledown_i X$ is a formula. But if $\hat{p} \notin X_i^\Gamma$ then X_i^Γ is infinite (by construction) which is also impossible since X is finite – thus case b) is impossible.

$\Leftarrow$) Let $\Gamma \vdash_{\hat{p}} \bigtriangledown_i X$. In case a), $\Gamma \vdash_{\hat{p}} \triangle_i Z$ and by **E4** and consistency of Γ $X_i^\Gamma = Z \subseteq X$. Case b) is impossible by definition. ∎

Theorem 21. $EC^{\hat{p}}$ is a sound and strongly complete axiomatization of syntactic structures, in the language $\mathcal{L}_{\bigtriangledown}^{\hat{p}}$. □

PROOF. Soundness follows from the soundness of EC^ω and the fact that $\Gamma \vdash_{\hat{p}} \phi$ implies $\Gamma \vdash_\omega \phi$, the latter which can be seen by induction on the length of a proof in $EC^{\hat{p}}$ (every $\mathcal{L}_{\bigtriangledown}^{\hat{p}}$ formula is also a $\mathcal{L}_{\bigtriangledown}$ formula): the base case **Prem** follows by R1 (Lemma 9), the base case **Ax** follows by **Ax** and **W**, and the inductive case **MP** follows by **MP**, **W** and **Cut**. Strong completeness follows from Lemmas 20 and 18. ∎

5   Only Knowing

Apart from the syntactic approaches mentioned in the introduction, the work maybe most closely related to the ideas discussed in this paper is the body of work on *only knowing* [33] which try to model concepts similar to our "knowing at most" and "knowing exactly". Here, we compare these ideas.

Several authors have analyzed the knowledge state of an agent who knows a (set of) formula(e) [34, 35, 36, 37]. Levesque [33] introduced a logic in which *only knowing* can be expressed in the logical language. Briefly speaking, Levesque's language is of first order[2] and has two unary epistemic connectives **B** and **O**.[3] Semantically, a *world* is a truth assignment to the primitive sentences, and satisfaction of a formula is defined relative to a pair W, w where W is the set of worlds the agent considers possible and w is the "real" world[4] (the world corresponding to the correct state of affairs). A sentence $\mathbf{B}\alpha$ is true in W, w iff α is true in W, w' for every $w' \in W$; **B** is the traditional belief/knowledge operator in modal epistemic logic. A sentence $\mathbf{O}\alpha$ is true in W, w iff $\mathbf{B}\alpha$ is true in W, w and $w' \in W$ for every w' such that α is true in W, w'. $\mathbf{O}\alpha$ expresses that the agent only knows α; the set of possible worlds is as large as possible consistent with believing α. The **O** operator can be modeled by a "natural dual" to the **B** operator — an operator **N**. The intended meaning of $\mathbf{N}\alpha$ is that α at most is believed to be false, and $\mathbf{N}\alpha$ is true in W, w iff α is true in W, w' for every $w' \notin W$. Then, $\mathbf{O}\alpha$ is true iff $\mathbf{B}\alpha$ and $\mathbf{N}\neg\alpha$ is true; **B** specifies a lower bound and **N** specifies an upper bound on what is believed.

---

[2] The logic was only shown to be complete for the unquantified version of the language, the full version was later shown to be incomplete [38].

[3] Levesque only considers a single agent, but his approach has later been extended to the multi-agent case [39].

[4] Note that this corresponds to the semantical assumptions of the modal logic $S5$ for one agent.

Levesque's logic of only knowing and the extended syntactic epistemic logic we have discussed in this paper set out to model similar concepts, i.e. *all an agent knows* — expressed as $\mathbf{O}\alpha$ by Levesque and $\Diamond X$ by us (for simplicity, we here assume the single-agent case and write the epistemic operators without subscript). In order to compare these two notions, we take a closer look at a possible correspondence between the operators $\mathbf{N}$ and $\triangledown$.

The first question is whether given a formula α there is an X such that $\triangledown X$ corresponds to $\mathbf{N}\alpha$. The intended interpretation of $\mathbf{N}\alpha$ is that the agent "knows at most $\neg\alpha$", so "corresponds" should at least require that $\neg\alpha \in X$. However, the following is a sound inference rule in Levesque's logic:

$$\frac{\alpha \to \beta}{\mathbf{N}\alpha \to \mathbf{N}\beta}$$

and it should thus be the case that $\neg\beta \in X$ too. That does not follow automatically in our logic, and we cannot define X to include all such $\neg\beta$s since there are infinitely many and X must be finite. Thus, we cannot express $\mathbf{N}\alpha$ directly by $\triangledown_i X$.

The second question is the other direction: given a set X, is there an α such that $\mathbf{N}\alpha$ corresponds to $\triangledown X$? Again, we should at least require $\mathbf{N}\neg \bigwedge X$ to hold, since otherwise the agent might know something which is not specified by X. It follows that, to get the proper semantics for negation, we should require that $\neg\mathbf{N}\neg \bigwedge X$ holds whenever $\neg \triangledown X$ holds. But take X such that the conjunction is an inconsistency: $\bigwedge X = \bot$. Now $\mathbf{N}\neg\bot$ does hold — but it holds trivially: it is in fact valid in Levesque's logic. So if $\neg \triangledown X$, for the given X, it can never be the case that $\neg\mathbf{N}\neg \bigwedge X$ holds. Thus, for inconsistent X, these two formulae $\triangledown X$ and $\mathbf{N}\alpha$ do not have corresponding semantics since the latter can never be false while the former can. In other words, we cannot express $\triangledown X$ directly by $\mathbf{N}\alpha$, either.

As an illustration of a situation where our $\Diamond$ operator might express an agent's knowledge more realistically than the $\mathbf{O}$ operator is when we want to model an agent's explicit knowledge at a point in time when it has computed *only* the formulae $p \to q$ and p (and not yet q). From $\mathbf{O}((p \to q) \land p)$ it follows that $\mathbf{B}q$ – which is not true – but from $\Diamond\{p \to q, p\}$ it does not follow that Kq.

Although these observations are not a full formal analysis of the respective expressive power of the two logics, they seem to confirm the idea that the syntactic and semantic approaches are fundamentally different.

6 Conclusions

In this paper we investigated syntactic operators, similar to those used in several logical models of multi-agent systems such as the logic of general awareness [11].

We introduced a "knows at most" operator in order to increase the expressiveness of the epistemic language with respect to syntactic structures, and investigated strong axiomatization of the resulting logic. The new operator destroyed semantic compactness and thus the possibility of a strongly complete finitary axiomatization, but we presented a strongly complete infinitary axiomatization. An interesting result is that we have a strongly complete finitary axiomatization if we make the assumption that the agents can know something which is not expressible in the logical language. The results are a contribution to the logical foundation of multi-agent systems.

Related work include the classical syntactic treatment of knowledge mentioned in the introduction and modeled in a possible worlds framework by [1] as described in Section 2. The $\bigtriangledown_i$ operator is new in the context of syntactic models. It is however, as we discussed in Section 5, similar to Levesque's **N** operator [33]. Although a full formal comparison between the relative expressive power of these two logics are outside the scope of this paper, and is left as an opportunity for future work, the discussion in Section 5 indicates that despite apparent similarities the syntactic and the semantic approaches are fundamentally different — also when it comes to "only knowing". We saw that a correspondence between the operators was obstructed by that fact that the syntactic logic has no closure condition (in the first "question" in Section 5) and the fact that it has no consistency condition (in the second "question" in Section 5). The syntactic "at most" operator is an alternative to the "only knowing" operator when these two conditions cannot be assumed.

In [31] we investigate the $\triangle_i$ and $\bigtriangledown_i$ operators in the special case of agents who can know only *finitely* many syntactic formulae at the same time. Completeness results for such finitely restricted agents build upon the results presented in this paper. Another possibility for future work is to study other special classes of syntactic structures.

In this paper we have only studied the *static* aspect of syntactic knowledge. In [14], we discuss how syntactic knowledge can evolve as a result of reasoning and communication, i.e. a *dynamic* aspect of knowledge.

Acknowledgements. The work in this paper has been partly supported by grants 166525/V30 and 146967/431 (MoSIS) from the Norwegian Research Council.

References

1. Fagin, R., Halpern, J.Y., Moses, Y., Vardi, M.Y.: Reasoning About Knowledge. The MIT Press, Cambridge, Massachusetts (1995)
2. Meyer, J.J.C., van der Hoek, W.: Epistemic Logic for AI and Computer Science. Cambridge University Press, Cambridge, England (1995)
3. Blackburn, P., de Rijke, M., Venema, Y.: Modal Logic. Cambridge University Press, Cambridge University Press (2001)
4. Hintikka, J.: Impossible possible worlds vindicated. Journal of Philosophical Logic **4** (1975) 475–484
5. Eberle, R.A.: A logic of believing, knowing and inferring. Synthese **26** (1974) 356–382
6. Moore, R.C., Hendrix, G.: Computational models of beliefs and the semantics of belief sentences. Technical Note 187, SRI International, Menlo Park, CA (1979)

7. Halpern, J.Y., Moses, Y.: Knowledge and common knowledge in a distributed environment. Journal of the ACM **37** (1990) 549–587
8. Konolige, K.: A Deduction Model of Belief and its Logics. PhD thesis, Stanford University (1984)
9. Konolige, K.: Belief and incompleteness. In Hobbs, J.R., Moore, R.C., eds.: Formal Theories of the Commonsense World. Ablex Publishing Corporation, New Jersey (1985) 359 – 403
10. Konolige, K.: A Deduction Model of Belief. Morgan Kaufmann Publishers, Los Altos, California (1986)
11. Fagin, R., Halpern, J.Y.: Belief, awareness and limited reasoning. Artificial Intelligence **34** (1988) 39–76 A preliminary version appeared in [16].
12. Drapkin, J., Perlis, D.: Step-logics: An alternative approach to limited reasoning. In: Proceedings of the European Conference on Artificial Intelligence, Brighton, England (1986) 160–163
13. Elgot-Drapkin, J., Kraus, S., Miller, M., Nirkhe, M., Perlis, D.: Active logics: A unified formal approach to episodic reasoning. Techn. Rep. CS-TR-4072 (1999)
14. Ågotnes, T., Walicki, M.: Syntactic knowledge: A logic of reasoning, communication and cooperation. In Ghidini, C., Giorgini, P., van der Hoek, W., eds.: Proceedings of the Second European Workshop on Multi-Agent Systems (EUMAS), Barcelona, Spain (2004)
15. Alechina, N., Logan, B., Whitsey, M.: A complete and decidable logic for resource-bounded agents. In: Proc. of the Third Intern. Joint Conf. on Autonomous Agents and Multi-Agent Syst. (AAMAS 2004), ACM Press (2004) 606–613
16. Fagin, R., Halpern, J.Y.: Belief, awareness and limited reasoning. In: Proceedings of the Ninth International Joint Conference on Artificial Intelligence, Los Angeles, CA (1985) 491–501
17. Hadley, R.F.: Fagin and halpern on logical omniscience: A critique with an alternative. In: Proc. Sixth Canadian Conference on Artificial Intelligence, Montreal, University of Quebec Press (1986) 49 – 56
18. Konolige, K.: What awareness isn't: A sentential view of implicit and explicit belief. In Halpern, J.Y., ed.: Theoretical Aspects of Reasoning About Knowledge: Proceedings of the First Conference, Los Altos, California, Morgan Kaufmann Publishers, Inc. (1986) 241–250
19. Huang, Z., Kwast, K.: Awareness, negation and logical omniscience. In van Eijk, J., ed.: Logics in AI, Proceedings JELIA'90. Volume 478 of Lecture Notes in Computer Science. Springer-Verlag, Berlin (1991) 282–300
20. Thijsse, E.: On total awareness logics. In de Rijke, M., ed.: Diamonds and Defaults. Kluwer Academic Publishers, Dordrecht (1993) 309–347
21. Halpern, J.: Alternative semantics for unawareness. Games and Economic Behaviour **37** (2001) 321–339
22. Montague, R.: Pragmatics. In Klibansky, R., ed.: Contemporary Philosophy: A Survey. I. La Nuova Italia Editrice, Florence (1968) 102–122 Reprinted in [40, pp. 95 – 118].
23. Montague, R.: Universal grammar. Theoria **36** (1970) 373–398 Reprinted in [40, pp. 222 – 246].
24. Scott, D.S.: Advice on modal logic. In Lambert, K., ed.: Philosophical Problems in Logic. D. Reidel Publishing Co., Dordrecht (1970) 143–173
25. Moreno, A.: Avoiding logical omniscience and perfect reasoning: a survey. AI Communications **11** (1998) 101–122
26. Sim, K.M.: Epistemic logic and logical omniscience: A survey. International Journal of Intelligent Systems **12** (1997) 57–81

27. Wansing, H.: A general possible worlds framework for reasoning about knowledge and belief. Studia Logica **49** (1990) 523–539
28. Rantala, V.: Impossible worlds semantics and logical omniscience. Acta Philosophica Fennica **35** (1982) 106–115
29. Rantala, V.: Quantified modal logic: non-normal worlds and propositional attitudes. Studia Logica **41** (1982) 41–65
30. Ågotnes, T., Walicki, M.: A logic for reasoning about agents with finite explicit knowledge. In Tessem, B., Ala-Siuru, P., Doherty, P., Mayoh, B., eds.: Proc. of the 8th Scandinavian Conference on Artificial Intelligence. Frontiers in Artificial Intelligence and Applications, IOS Press (2003) 163–174
31. Ågotnes, T., Walicki, M.: Complete axiomatizations of finite syntactic epistemic states. In Baldoni, M., Endriss, U., Omicini, A., Torroni, P., eds.: The Third International Workshop on Declarative Agent Languages and Technologies (DALT 2005), Workshop Notes, Utrecht, the Netherlands (2005) To appear in Lecture Notes in Artificial Intelligence (LNAI), Springer-Verlag, 2006.
32. de Lavalette, G.R., Kooi, B., Verbrugge, R.: Strong completeness for propositional dynamic logic. In Balbiani, P., Suzuki, N.Y., Wolter, F., eds.: Preliminary Proceedings of AiML2002, Institut de Recherche en Informatique de Toulouse IRIT (2002) 377–393
33. Levesque, H.J.: All I know: a study in autoepistemic logic. Artificial Intelligence **42** (1990) 263–309
34. Konolige, K.: Circumscriptive ignorance. In Waltz, D., ed.: Proceedings of the National Conference on Artificial Intelligence, Pittsburgh, PA, AAAI Press (1982) 202–204
35. Moore, R.C.: Semantical considerations on nonmonotonic logic. In Bundy, A., ed.: Proceedings of the 8th International Joint Conference on Artificial Intelligence, Karlsruhe, FRG, William Kaufmann (1983) 272–279
36. Halpern, J.Y., Moses, Y.: Towards a theory of knowledge and ignorance. In Apt, K.R., ed.: Logics and Models of Concurrent Systems. Springer-Verlag, Berlin (1985) 459–476
37. Halpern, J.Y.: A theory of knowledge and ignorance for many agents. Journal of Logic and Computation **7** (1997) 79–108
38. Halpern, J.Y., Lakemeyer, G.: Levesque's axiomatization of only knowing is incomplete. Artificial Intelligence **74** (1995) 381–387
39. Halpern, J.Y., Lakemeyer, G.: Multi-agent only knowing. In Shoham, Y., ed.: Theoretical Aspects of Rationality and Knowledge: Proceedings of the Sixth Conference (TARK 1996). Morgan Kaufmann, San Francisco (1996) 251–265
40. Montague, R.: Formal Philosophy. Yale University Press, New Haven, CT (1974)

Logical Spaces in Multi-agent Only Knowing Systems

Bjørnar Solhaug[1,2] and Arild Waaler[3,4]

[1] SINTEF ICT, Norway
[2] Dep. of Information Science and Media Studies, University of Bergen, Norway
[3] Finnmark College, Norway
[4] Dep. of Informatics, University of Oslo, Norway

Abstract. We present a weak multi-agent system of Only knowing and an analysis of the logical spaces that can be defined in it. The logic complements the approach to generalizing Levesque's All I Know system made by Halpern and Lakemeyer. A novel feature of our approach is that the logic is defined entirely at the object level with no reference to meta-concepts in the definition of the axiom system. We show that the logic of Halpern and Lakemeyer can be encoded in our system in the form of a particular logical space.

1 Introduction

Designing systems capable of representing defeasible patterns of reasoning within a multi-agent context is a non-trivial exercise, especially since most non-monotonic systems are not equipped with modalities and hence do not generalize smoothly to multi-agent situations. Exceptions to this are systems in the autoepistemic family, for which multi-modal generalizations exist. Both Halpern and Lakemeyer [2, 3, 4, 6] and Waaler [12] have proposed such generalizations of Levesque's system of only knowing [7], and we have recently introduced a formal Kripke-semantics [13] for these systems. A variety of multi-modal only knowing languages have been analyzed semantically in [5].

A basic idea underlying all the above cited systems is to generalize a notion of consistency. Halpern and Lakemeyer [4] achieves this by formalizing a semantic notion of satisfiability, while Waaler [12] takes the syntactical definition of consistency as his point of departure and builds this into the definition of his multi-agent system L_I. In both cases this gives a compact formalization which in many cases is an advantage. However, from a conceptual point of view the systems hide a number of details, a fact which makes them hard to penetrate. The precise effect of the circular "consistency" axioms is particularly difficult to grasp, even though the formal semantics come to aid.

Building so closely on a notion of logical consistency, the above mentioned systems sacrifice the ability to naturally distinguish propositions that an agent believes because they cannot possibly be conceived false, from propositions that the agent believes only by virtue of explicit evidence. This distinction can be

F. Toni and P. Torroni (Eds.): CLIMA VI, LNAI 3900, pp. 77–95, 2006.
© Springer-Verlag Berlin Heidelberg 2006

expressed in the single agent system Æ [11], a system relative to Levesque's only knowing system in which the "consistency axiom" is replaced by an explicit axiomatization of what the authors call a *logical space*. A logical possibility of the form $\Diamond\varphi$, φ purely Boolean, is in the system of Levesque deduced from the consistency of φ. A logical space in Æ is a formula λ such that for each purely Boolean φ, either $\lambda \vdash \Diamond\varphi$ or $\lambda \vdash \neg\Diamond\varphi$. We may then e.g. define a logical space λ such that $\lambda \vdash \Box(\mathsf{penguin}(\mathsf{Tweety}) \supset \mathsf{bird}(\mathsf{Tweety}))$, expressing that the agent cannot conceive of a penguin not being a bird.

Compared to the only knowing system of Levesque, the system Æ has an increased expressive power due to the possibility of varying the logical space. In particular, the "consistency axiom" of Levesque corresponds to one of many possibilities. In Levesque's system [7], as in the generalizations found in [4] and [13], the necessity operator only captures the *logical relation* between concepts.

The aim of this paper is to present a multi-agent only knowing system along the lines of Æ. A feature of this is, first, that we can express multi-agent generalizations of logical spaces. We can use a well-known example of Frege to illustrate a situation in which this expressiveness can be needed. Suppose that an agent has reason to believe that another agent is unaware of the identity of "The morning star" and "The evening star". Since the reference in this case is a matter of definition, it is natural for him to think that the other agent is simply unaware of the definition and hence that the other agent finds it inconceivable that the two names denote one and the same object. The system proposed in this paper can naturally express that an agent a has a model of another agent's logical space, and that this space differs from the space of agent a.

The previous example illustrates the use of logical spaces to express one agent's apprehension of the relations between concepts as understood by another agent. The situation is slightly more complex in situations involving three agents. Assume for instance a scenario in which there are two agents a and b that are studying together, both holding the degree of bachelor. Being familiar with the educational system, agent a cannot conceive of a master not being a bachelor. This may be captured by a logical space λ_a such that $\lambda_a \vdash \Box_a(\mathsf{master}(\mathsf{Fred}) \supset \mathsf{bachelor}(\mathsf{Fred}))$ for any given agent Fred. The common background of a and b may furthermore be encoded into the logical space of agent a such that $\lambda_a \vdash \Box_a\Box_b(\mathsf{master}(\mathsf{Fred}) \supset \mathsf{bachelor}(\mathsf{Fred}))$. This expresses that agent a cannot conceive of a situation in which agent b assumes that a master is not a bachelor. Assume, now, a third agent, let us say a's younger brother c, that does not share this background. In fact he is almost totally unfamiliar with the educational system. Agent a, knowing his brother well, may then have a logical space λ_a such that $\lambda_a \vdash \Diamond_a\Diamond_c(\mathsf{bachelor}(\mathsf{Fred}) \wedge \neg\mathsf{master}(\mathsf{Fred}))$.

The logical space is hence of conceptual importance by introducing more flexibility and expressiveness to the representations of epistemic states. The notion of necessity embedded in the logical space also has implications for the formalization of defeasible reasoning as we shall see in Sect. 4.

A second feature of the logic that we propose here is that it is closed under uniform substitution. The reason for this is that it employs no meta-concepts in the definition of its rules. Third, it can naturally accommodate all the systems cited in this introduction by virtue of being more general than them. Fourth, it explicates what the complex, circular "consistency axioms" hide, a point which makes it interesting as a foundational study.

In order to bring the task of defining a multi-agent logical space to a manageable level, we will address the problem inductively at different levels of complexity, each level corresponding to a sub-language within which the set of possibilities is outlined. The base case is equivalent to the single-agent case: Let $\mathcal{L}_0$ denote the language of propositional logic. The set of possibilities is derived by closing a subset of $\mathcal{L}_0$, each element of which describes a possibility, under the $\Diamond_a$-operator for each agent a. The resulting set of formulae is then a subset of the language of the next level, denoted $\mathcal{L}_1$. Inductively, the set of possibilities for agent a at level $k+1$ is derived from a subset of *the a-objective formulae of* $\mathcal{L}_k$ ("objective" because it does not contain any modal operators).

The main task of this paper is to construct the sets of formulae that, for each agent and each language level, express each and every logical possibility. In Sect. 4, we will show how the logic of $\mathcal{Æ}_I$ applies to examples from the paper of Halpern and Lakemeyer [4] as well as some new examples. In Sect. 6, we relate $\mathcal{Æ}_I$ to the systems of Halpern and Lakemeyer [4] and Waaler [12]. Specifically we show the equivalence of the three systems when a particular logical space is added to the axioms of $\mathcal{Æ}_I$.

In [13] a modal reduction property for L_I is established, which states that any "only knowing" expression is provably equivalent to a disjunction of "only knowing" expressions of a particular simple form. Each of these latter expressions provides us with an explicit syntactical representation of a particular model of the original formula. The latter expressions explicitly characterize the possible cognitive states of the agent, given the initial "only knowing" expression. In Sect. 5 we shall see that the same property holds also in $\mathcal{Æ}_I$.

2   The Logic $\mathcal{Æ}_I$

2.1   Syntax

The object language $\mathcal{L}$ contains a countable set of propositional letters $\mathcal{P}$, the propositional constant $\bot$, the Boolean connectives $\neg$ and $\wedge$ and the modal operators $\mathbf{B}_a$ and $\mathbf{C}_a$ for each a in a countable non-empty set of indices I. The index set I represents the set of agents, $\mathbf{B}_a$ is a belief operator, and $\mathbf{C}_a$ is a complementary *co-belief* operator for agent $a \in I$. The propositional constant $\top$ is defined as $\neg\bot$, while the Boolean connectives $\vee$, $\supset$ and $\equiv$ are the usual abbreviations. Other modal operators defined as abbreviations are the following: $\mathbf{b}_a\varphi$ (φ is compatible with belief) is $\neg\mathbf{B}_a\neg\varphi$, $\mathbf{c}_a\varphi$ (φ is compatible with co-belief) is $\neg\mathbf{C}_a\neg\varphi$, $\Box_a\varphi$ (φ is necessary) is $\mathbf{B}_a\varphi \wedge \mathbf{C}_a\varphi$ and $\Diamond_a\varphi$ (φ is possible) is $\mathbf{b}_a\varphi \vee \mathbf{c}_a\varphi$. Observe that necessity and possibility are relative to the extension of a given agent's belief and co-belief; the notion of necessity hence captures *personal* necessity.

The more accurate interpretation of the $\mathbf{B}_a$-operator is that a formula $\mathbf{B}_a\varphi$ states that agent a believes at least φ to be true, but perhaps more. The $\mathbf{B}_a$-operator thus puts a *lower* bound on the extension of belief. The complementary operator $\mathbf{C}_a$ puts an *upper* bound on the belief in the sense that a formula $\mathbf{C}_a\varphi$ states that agent a believes at most φ to be false, but perhaps less. The formula $\mathbf{B}_a\varphi \wedge \mathbf{C}_a\neg\varphi$ states that φ is *exactly* what is believed. The introduction of the $\mathbf{C}_a$-operator thus allows an "All a knows"-proposition $\mathbf{O}_a\varphi$ to be defined as $\mathbf{B}_a\varphi \wedge \mathbf{C}_a\neg\varphi$.

A formula not mentioning any modal operator is called *purely Boolean*. φ is an *a-modal atom* if it is of the form $\mathbf{B}_a\psi$ or $\mathbf{C}_a\psi$, $a \in I$. An *a*-modal *literal* is an *a*-modal atom or the negation of an *a*-modal atom. φ is a *completely a-modalized formula* if it is a Boolean combination of *a*-modal atoms. φ is *free of modality a* if it is a Boolean combination of propositional letters and modal atoms not of modality a. Notice, however, that a formula free of modality a may have occurrences of *a*-modal operators within the scope of a *b*-modal operator, $a \neq b$. φ is a *first-order formula* if, for each $a \in I$ and each subformula $\mathbf{B}_a\psi$ and $\mathbf{C}_a\psi$ in φ, ψ is free of modality a. If Γ is a set of formulae, $\Gamma^{\backslash a} = \{\varphi \in \Gamma \mid \varphi$ free of modality $a\}$ and $\Gamma^a = \{\varphi \in \Gamma \mid \varphi$ completely *a*-modalized$\}$. If Γ is a set of formulae, $\mathsf{Sf}(\Gamma)$ denotes the set of subformulae of the formulae in Γ. When Γ is a singleton set containing φ, $\mathsf{Sf}(\varphi)$ denotes $\mathsf{Sf}(\{\varphi\})$.

The *modal depth* $\mathsf{d}(\varphi)$ of a formula φ expresses the nesting of alternating modalities in φ. Formally, the modal depth of a purely Boolean φ is 0. Otherwise, if φ is $\mathbf{B}_a\psi$ or $\mathbf{C}_a\psi$, let Ψ be the set of modal atoms which occur as subformulae in ψ. Then $\mathsf{d}(\varphi)$ is the maximal number in $\{\mathsf{d}(\chi)+1 \mid \chi \in \Psi$ and χ is not *a*-modalized$\}$ $\cup \{\mathsf{d}(\chi) \mid \chi \in \Psi$ and χ is *a*-modalized$\}$. Otherwise, the modal depth of φ is the maximal $\mathsf{d}(\psi)$ for a subformula ψ of φ. The modal depth of an *a*-modal formula φ is hence increased by prefixing φ with any other modal operator than an *a*-modal operator.

Example 1. Let φ and ψ be purely Boolean. Then $\mathsf{d}(\varphi) = 0$, $\mathsf{d}(\mathbf{B}_a\varphi) = 1$, $\mathsf{d}(\mathbf{B}_a\varphi \wedge \mathbf{B}_b\psi) = 1$, $\mathsf{d}(\mathbf{B}_a\mathbf{C}_a\varphi) = 1$ and $\mathsf{d}(\mathbf{B}_a\mathbf{B}_b\varphi) = 2$.

If Γ is a set of formulae, $\Gamma_k = \{\varphi \in \Gamma \mid \mathsf{d}(\varphi) \leq k\}$. We will in this paper be interested in sub-languages relative to a given modal depth and a given agent. Since $\mathcal{L}$ denotes the language of $\mathcal{E}_I$ (which is just a set of formulae) these sub-languages are denoted $\mathcal{L}_k$, $\mathcal{L}_k^{\backslash a}$ and $\mathcal{L}_k^a$ following the set indexing notation introduced above.

A *tautology* is a substitution instance of a formula valid in propositional logic, e.g. $\Box_a\varphi \supset \Box_a\varphi$. The deducibility relation '$\vdash$' of the logic $\mathcal{E}_I$ is defined as the least relation that contains all tautologies, is closed under all instances of the rules

$$\frac{\vdash \varphi}{\vdash \Box_a\varphi} \ (\mathrm{RN}) \qquad \frac{\vdash \varphi \quad \vdash \varphi \supset \psi}{\vdash \psi} \ (\mathrm{MP})$$

and contains all instances of the following schemata for each $a \in I$:

$$K_{\mathbf{B}}: \quad \mathbf{B}_a(\varphi \supset \psi) \supset (\mathbf{B}_a\varphi \supset \mathbf{B}_a\psi) \qquad \overline{B}_\Box: \quad \neg\mathbf{B}_a\varphi \supset \Box_a\neg\mathbf{B}_a\varphi$$
$$K_{\mathbf{C}}: \quad \mathbf{C}_a(\varphi \supset \psi) \supset (\mathbf{C}_a\varphi \supset \mathbf{C}_a\psi) \qquad \overline{C}_\Box: \quad \neg\mathbf{C}_a\varphi \supset \Box_a\neg\mathbf{C}_a\varphi$$
$$B_\Box: \quad \mathbf{B}_a\varphi \supset \Box_a\mathbf{B}_a\varphi \qquad\qquad\qquad T: \quad \Box_a\varphi \supset \varphi$$
$$C_\Box: \quad \mathbf{C}_a\varphi \supset \Box_a\mathbf{C}_a\varphi$$

We write $\vdash \varphi$ if φ is theorem of $\cancel{E}_I$, and $\varphi_1, \ldots, \varphi_n \vdash \psi$ for $\vdash (\varphi_1 \wedge \cdots \wedge \varphi_n) \supset \psi$. $\Gamma \vdash \varphi$ means that there is a finite number of formulae $\gamma_1, \ldots, \gamma_n$ in Γ such that $\gamma_1, \ldots, \gamma_n \vdash \varphi$. If $\Gamma \vdash \bot$, Γ is *inconsistent* otherwise Γ is consistent. We will without reference use the well-known principles of modal logic, especially substitution of provable equivalents, the derived rule

$$\frac{\varphi_1, \ldots, \varphi_n \vdash \psi}{\mathbf{B}_a\varphi_1, \ldots, \mathbf{B}_a\varphi_n \vdash \mathbf{B}_a\psi}$$

and the corresponding rule for $\mathbf{C}_a$.

Lemma 1. $\Box_a$ *is an S5 modality.*

Lemma 2. *Any formula is provably equivalent to a first-order formula with the same modal depth.*

The former of these two results is Lemma 1 of [13]; the latter is Lemma 2 of [12]. For proofs and further details about the results in the rest of this section, the reader may consult [13].

2.2 Semantics

A *frame* is a structure $(W, \{R_a, S_a \mid a \in I\})$, where W is a non-empty set of points and R_a and S_a are binary relations satisfying the following two conditions:

$(f1)$ Let X be either R_a or S_a and Y be either R_a or S_a or their complements $\overline{R_a}$ or $\overline{S_a}$. Then the composition $X \circ Y \subseteq Y$.
$(f2)$ $E_a = R_a \cup S_a$ is reflexive.

Note that in standard terminology two of the eight sub-conditions of $(f1)$ state that R_a and S_a are transitive, e.g. $R_a \circ R_a \subseteq R_a$, while two of them state that they are Euclidean, e.g. $R_a \circ \overline{R_a} \subseteq \overline{R_a}$.

Lemma 3. E_a *is an equivalence relation.*

An *a-cluster* is an equivalence class of W modulo E_a. Let C be an a-cluster. We define the *belief part* C^+ and the *co-belief part* C^- of C by: $C^+ = \{x \in C \mid xR_ax\}$ and $C^- = \{x \in C \mid xS_ax\}$. C is *bisected* if $C^+ \cap C^- = \emptyset$.

Lemma 4. $C = C^+ \cup C^-$.

A *model* $\mathcal{M} = (W, \{R_a, S_a \mid a \in I\}, V)$ is a frame with a valuation function V, which maps each propositional letter onto a subset of W. The satisfiability relation $\vDash_x$, $x \in W$, is defined by

$$\mathcal{M} \vDash_x p \quad \leftrightarrow x \in V(p),\ p \text{ a propositional letter,}$$
$$\mathcal{M} \vDash_x \neg\varphi \leftrightarrow \mathcal{M} \nvDash_x \varphi,$$
$$\mathcal{M} \vDash_x \mathbf{B}_a\varphi \leftrightarrow \forall y\,(xR_ay \rightarrow \mathcal{M} \vDash_y \varphi),$$
$$\mathcal{M} \vDash_x \mathbf{C}_a\varphi \leftrightarrow \forall y\,(xS_ay \rightarrow \mathcal{M} \vDash_y \varphi),$$

and in the usual way for the other Boolean connectives. We write $\mathcal{M} \models_X \varphi$ iff $(\forall x \in X)(\mathcal{M} \models_x \varphi)$. A formula is valid in a frame if it is true at all points in all models on the frame. If φ is valid in all frames, we write $\models \varphi$, and say that φ is *valid*. $\Gamma \models \varphi$ means that for all models, φ is true at all points which satisfy all formulae in Γ. Note that if C is an a-cluster, all points in C agree on every completely a-modalized formula in every model on the frame.

Theorem 1. *Æ$_I$ is sound, complete and decidable.*

Proof. This can be proved by the use of standard techniques from modal logic, see [13].   □

3 Finitely Bounded Sub-languages

The analysis of a belief representation designed for the formalization of defeasible reasoning depends on the set of formulae that is considered possible by the agent in question. A particular logical possibility is represented by a formula of the form $\Diamond_a \varphi$. What we aim to do is to encode the logical possibilities into a logical space λ_a such that for all formulae φ from a particular set of formulae free of modality a, either $\lambda_a \vdash \Diamond_a \varphi$ or $\lambda_a \vdash \neg \Diamond_a \varphi$. The way to do this is to generalize the single-agent notion of an *atom* to the multi-agent case.

In the single-agent system Æ, assuming a finite set of propositional letters in the language, say $p_1, \ldots, p_m$, an *atom* is defined as a conjunction $\pm p_1 \wedge \cdots \wedge \pm p_m$, where $\pm p$ means either p or $\neg p$. The notion of an atom is a twin to the notion of a *complete theory*: Given any language $\mathcal{L}^*$, a formula $\varphi \in \mathcal{L}^*$ is a complete theory for $\mathcal{L}^*$ iff for all formulae $\psi \in \mathcal{L}^*$, either $\varphi \vdash \psi$ or $\varphi \vdash \neg \psi$. As an atom can be interpreted as a propositional valuation, it is easy to see that each atom is a complete theory for the language of propositional logic.

There are 2^m non-equivalent atoms given the set $\{p_1, \ldots, p_m\}$ of propositional letters. Each atom represents a complete characterization of a state of affairs, and where $\alpha_1, \ldots, \alpha_n$ characterize the states of affairs conceivable to a given agent, the logical space is defined as the formula

$$\Diamond \alpha_1 \wedge \cdots \wedge \Diamond \alpha_n \wedge \Box(\alpha_1 \vee \cdots \vee \alpha_n).$$

In the *maximal* logical space, all atoms are possible, i.e. $n = 2^m$.

In order to generalize the notion of an atom, and hence the notion of a logical space, to the multi-agent case we must be precise about the properties that must be satisfied by the atoms. To begin with, the set of atoms is defined over an *objective language*, i.e. a language free of modalities. In the multi-agent case, we need for each agent a to operate with a language that is a-*objective*, i.e. free of modality a.

An agent's epistemic state is in the single-agent case furthermore represented in the language $\mathcal{L}_1$ whereas the atoms are defined over $\mathcal{L}_0$, i.e. the language of propositional logic. In the multi-agent case we hence want for each agent a to represent the generalized atoms over a language $\mathcal{L}_k^{\backslash a}$ while the logical space is given in the language $\mathcal{L}_{k+1}^a$, which is the former language closed under the a-modal operators.

The explication of the set of propositional atoms requires the assumption of a propositional language defined over a finite set of propositional letters. For the set of generalized atoms to be finite, they must be defined over a *finite multi-modal language*. For such a language to be finite, the set of propositional letters and the set of different modalities, i.e. the index set I, obviously need to be finite. As we may construct new formulae by prefixing a formula free of modality a with any a-modal operator, the finite language must moreover be bounded by an upper modal depth. Under the assumption that the set of propositional letters and the set of agents are finite, we will for each modal depth k operate with the finitely bounded sub-language $\mathcal{L}_k$.

The crucial property of an atom in the single agent case is that it is a complete theory for the language of propositional logic. This property will serve as a test for for deciding whether a suggested multi-modal logical space is a correct generalization of the single-agent logical space. In other words, if

$$\Diamond_a \varphi_1 \wedge \cdots \wedge \Diamond_a \varphi_n \wedge \Box_a(\varphi_1 \vee \cdots \vee \varphi_n)$$

is a multi-modal logical space for a given agent a, where $\{\varphi_1, \ldots, \varphi_n\} \subseteq \mathcal{L}_k^{\backslash a}$ for a given integer k, then each $\varphi \in \{\varphi_1, \ldots, \varphi_n\}$ should be a complete theory for $\mathcal{L}_k^{\backslash a}$. The formula φ is then a complete characterization of the material content of a state of affairs as well as a complete characterization of the epistemic state of every agent $b \in I \backslash \{a\}$.

Observe finally that the set of propositional atoms completely characterizes the language of propositional logic in the sense that for all PL formulae ψ, there exists a set of atoms the disjunction of which is equivalent to ψ. The set of generalized atoms from a sub-language $\mathcal{L}_k^{\backslash a}$ over which the logical space of agent a is defined must hence satisfy this property with respect to the formulae of $\mathcal{L}_k^{\backslash a}$.

Convention. We will use the following notation for the distribution of a modality over a set of formulae: $\mathbf{B}_a \Gamma = \{\mathbf{B}_a \gamma \mid \gamma \in \Gamma\}$, and the same for any other modality.

Definition 1. *Let $\Phi \subseteq \mathcal{L}^{\backslash a}$. The functions Bel_a, Cobel_a and Lspace_a, all of them from a set of formulae free of modality a to a completely a-modalized formula, are defined as follows:*

$$\mathsf{Bel}_a(\Phi) = \bigwedge b_a \Phi \wedge \mathbf{B}_a(\bigvee \Phi),$$

$$\mathsf{Cobel}_a(\Phi) = \bigwedge c_a \Phi \wedge C_a(\bigvee \Phi),$$

$$\mathsf{Lspace}_a(\Phi) = \bigwedge \Diamond_a \Phi \wedge \Box_a(\bigvee \Phi).$$

$\mathsf{Lspace}_a(\Phi)$ *is the logical space for agent a spanned by Φ. If $\Phi^+ \cup \Phi^- = \Phi$, then $\mathsf{Bel}_a(\Phi^+) \wedge \mathsf{Cobel}_a(\Phi^-)$ is a doxastic a-alternative spanned by Φ. Notice that a doxastic a-alternative spanned by Φ entails $\mathsf{Lspace}_a(\Phi)$. The set of all doxastic a-alternatives spanned by every nonempty subset of Φ is denoted $\mathsf{Dox}_a(\Phi)$.*

Two properties will play a central role in our analysis. A set of formulae Φ satisfies the property of *mutual inconsistency* if every two elements of Φ are consistent iff they are equivalent. Φ is *representationally complete for* $\mathcal{L}^*$ if $\Phi \subseteq \mathcal{L}^*$ and every formula $\varphi \in \mathcal{L}^*$ is equivalent to a disjunction of formulae in Φ ($\mathcal{L}^*$ any language addressed in this paper).

Lemma 5. *If* $\Phi \subseteq \mathcal{L}^{\backslash a}$ *satisfies mutual inconsistency, then so does* $\mathsf{Dox}_a(\Phi)$.

Proof. Let δ_1 and δ_2 be two distinct elements of $\mathsf{Dox}_a(\Phi)$. Then δ_1 and δ_2 must disagree on the belief set or the co-belief set. We treat the former. Let $\delta_1 \vdash \mathsf{Bel}_a(\Gamma_1)$ and $\delta_2 \vdash \mathsf{Bel}_a(\Gamma_2)$. There is then a formula φ such that either $\varphi \in \Gamma_1$ and $\varphi \notin \Gamma_2$ or vice verca. In the first case, $\varphi \wedge \gamma \vdash \bot$ for each $\gamma \in \Gamma_2$ by mutual inconsistency. Hence $\varphi \wedge \bigvee \Gamma_2 \vdash \bot$. By modal logic, $\mathbf{B}_a(\bigvee \Gamma_2) \vdash \mathbf{B}_a \neg \varphi$. Since $\delta_2 \vdash \mathbf{B}_a(\bigvee \Gamma_2)$ and $\delta_1 \vdash \mathbf{b}_a \varphi$, we get $\delta_1 \wedge \delta_2 \vdash \bot$. The latter case is symmetrical. $\square$

Lemma 6. *Let* $\mathcal{L}^*$ *be any Boolean closed set of formulae and* Φ *be representationally complete for* $\mathcal{L}^*$. *Then* $\vdash \bigvee \Phi$.

Proof. Assume that $\neg \bigvee \Phi$ is consistent. Since Φ is representationally complete for $\mathcal{L}^*$ and $\mathcal{L}^*$ is Boolean closed, there must then be a non-empty set $\Gamma \subseteq \Phi$ such that $\vdash \bigvee \Gamma \equiv \neg \bigvee \Phi$. But this is clearly impossible. $\square$

Lemma 7. *Let* Φ *be representationally complete for* $\mathcal{L}_k^{\backslash a}$. *Then* $\mathsf{Dox}_a(\Phi)$ *is representationally complete for* $\mathcal{L}_{k+1}^a$.

Proof. Let $\varphi \in \mathcal{L}_{k+1}^a$. We may without loss of generality assume that φ is first-order. Since Φ is representationally complete for $\mathcal{L}_k^{\backslash a}$, the formulae inside the scope of the a-modalities are equivalent to disjunctions of formulae from Φ. By standard propositional reasoning and normal modal logic and, φ is equivalent to a formula on DNF, where each disjunct is of the form $\psi = \bigwedge \mathbf{b}_a \Gamma_1 \wedge \mathbf{B}_a(\bigvee \Gamma_2) \wedge \bigwedge \mathbf{c}_a \Gamma_3 \wedge \mathbf{C}_a(\bigvee \Gamma_4)$, $\Gamma_1, \dots, \Gamma_4$ subsets of Φ. Let

$$\Delta = \{\delta \in \mathsf{Dox}_a(\Phi) \mid \delta = \mathsf{Bel}_a(\Phi^+) \wedge \mathsf{Cobel}_a(\Phi^-), \Gamma_1 \subseteq \Phi^+ \subseteq \Gamma_2, \Gamma_3 \subseteq \Phi^- \subseteq \Gamma_4\}.$$

Then $\vdash \psi \equiv \bigvee \Delta$. To see that $\bigvee \Delta \vdash \psi$, observe that if $\Gamma_1 \subseteq \Phi^+$, then $\mathsf{Bel}_a(\Phi^+) \vdash \mathbf{b}_a \gamma$ for each $\gamma \in \Gamma_1$, and if $\Phi^+ \subseteq \Gamma_2$, then $\mathbf{B}_a(\bigvee \Phi^+) \vdash \mathbf{B}_a(\bigvee \Gamma_2)$. Conversely, assume that $\psi \nvdash \bigvee \Delta$, i.e. that ψ is consistent with $\neg \bigvee \Delta$. This entails that ψ is consistent with a formula θ constructed as a conjunction out of the negation of one conjunct from each δ in Δ. But by construction of ψ there is no such θ which is consistent with ψ. $\square$

Lemma 8. *Let* Φ *be representationally complete for* $\mathcal{L}_k^{\backslash a}$ *and satisfy mutual inconsistency, and let* δ *be a doxastic* a-*alternative spanned by* $\Gamma \subseteq \Phi$. *Then* δ *is a complete theory over* $\mathcal{L}_{k+1}^a$.

Proof. We need to prove that either $\delta \vdash \psi$ or $\delta \vdash \neg \psi$ for every $\psi \in \mathcal{L}_{k+1}^a$. By Lemma 2, we may without loss of generality assume that ψ is first-order. The result for Boolean combinations of formulae follows easily once the result is established for modal atoms. It suffices to deal with the case where ψ is of the form $\mathbf{B}_a\varphi$, as the other cases are symmetrical.

Let $\delta \vdash \mathsf{Bel}_a(\varGamma_1)$ and $\vdash \varphi \equiv \bigvee \varGamma_2$, $\varGamma_1$ and $\varGamma_2$ subsets of $\varPhi$. There are two cases. Either $\varGamma_1 \subseteq \varGamma_2$, or there is a formula γ such that $\gamma \in \varGamma_1$ and $\gamma \notin \varGamma_2$. In the first case, $\bigvee \varGamma_1 \vdash \bigvee \varGamma_2$. By modal logic, $\mathbf{B}_a(\bigvee \varGamma_1) \vdash \mathbf{B}_a(\bigvee \varGamma_2)$, and so $\delta \vdash \mathbf{B}_a\varphi$. In the second case, $\gamma \wedge \bigvee \varGamma_2 \vdash \bot$ by mutual inconsistency. By modal logic, $\mathbf{b}_a\gamma \vdash \mathbf{b}_a\neg(\bigvee \varGamma_2)$. Since $\delta \vdash \mathbf{b}_a\gamma$, we get that $\delta \vdash \mathbf{b}_a\neg(\bigvee \varGamma_2)$, i.e. $\delta \vdash \neg\mathbf{B}_a\varphi$. $\square$

We are now ready to generalize the single-agent notion of an atom to the multi-agent case. In the single-agent case, an atom α can be interpreted as a complete characterization of the material content of a state of affairs. In the multi-agent case, we want for each agent $a_i \in I$, $I = \{a_1, \ldots, a_m\}$, and each modal depth k to define a doxastic alternative δ_i, such that δ_i completely characterizes the cognitive state of agent a_i. A conjunction $\alpha \wedge \delta_1 \wedge \cdots \wedge \delta_m$ is then a complete characterization of the material content of a state of affairs, as well as a complete characterization of the cognitive state of every agent. As we shall see, the conjunction $\alpha \wedge \delta_1 \wedge \cdots \wedge \delta_m$ is a complete theory for $\mathcal{L}_k$. This conjunction will be referred to as *an I-atom with depth k*.

Given a set of I-atoms with depth k, the doxastic alternatives for agent a with depth $k + 1$ will be defined over this set. Intuitively, where $\varPhi$ is the set of I-atoms with depth k, the set of formulae $\mathsf{Dox}_a(\varPhi)$ is the set of doxastic a-alternatives with depth $k + 1$. This is, however, not the correct generalization of the single-agent case, since in the single-agent case, a doxastic alternative is defined over a set of *purely Boolean formulae*. Generalizing this is to define a doxastic alternative for agent a_i over a set of formulae *free of modality a*. To this end, we will define a set of formulae from $\mathcal{L}_k^{\backslash a}$ each formula of which forms a complete theory for $\mathcal{L}_k^{\backslash a}$.

Convention. Let $\varphi = \alpha \wedge \delta_1 \wedge \cdots \wedge \delta_m$ be a formula such that $\alpha \in \mathcal{L}_0$ and δ_i is a doxastic a-alternative. Then $\varphi[a_i/\top] = \alpha \wedge \delta_1 \wedge \cdots \wedge \delta_{i-1} \wedge \top \wedge \delta_{i+1} \wedge \cdots \wedge \delta_m$. If $\varPhi$ is a set of I-atoms, $\varPhi[a_i/\top] = \{\varphi[a_i/\top] \mid \varphi \in \varPhi\}$.

Definition 2 (I-atoms). *The set of I-atoms $\varPhi_k$ with depth k is defined as follows: $\varPhi_0$ is the set of atoms, while $\varPhi_{k+1}$ is all formulae $\alpha \wedge \delta_1 \wedge \cdots \wedge \delta_m$ such that*

- α *is an atom,*
- δ_i *is a doxastic a_i-alternative spanned by the set $\varGamma_i \subseteq \varPhi_k[a_i/\top]$,*
- $\exists \varphi \in \varPhi_k$ *such that $\varphi \vdash \alpha$ and for each a_i, $\varphi[a_i/\top] \in \varGamma_i$.*

From now on $\varPhi_k$ refers to the set of I-atoms with depth k. The third condition in the definition above is a consistency condition as witnessed by the following result.

Lemma 9. *Assume that each $\varPhi_k$ satisfies mutual inconsistency and that $\varPhi_k[a/\top]$ is representationally complete for $\mathcal{L}_k^{\backslash a}$ for each agent a. Let α be an atom and δ_i be a doxastic a_i-alternative spanned by $\varGamma_i \subseteq \varPhi_k[a_i/\top]$. Then $\alpha \wedge \delta_1 \wedge \cdots \wedge \delta_m$ is consistent if and only if $\exists \varphi \in \varPhi$ such that $\varphi \vdash \alpha$ and for each a_i, $\varphi[a_i/\top] \in \varGamma_i$.*

Proof. Note that if δ_i is spanned by the set $\Gamma_i \subseteq \Phi_k[a_i/\top]$, then $\delta_i \vdash \Box_{a_i}(\bigvee \Gamma_i)$. By axiom T, $\delta_i \vdash \bigvee \Gamma_i$. Since the conjuncts of ψ are of different modalities (the atom purely Boolean, however), inconsistency of ψ can stem from axiom T only. Hence, it suffices to prove that the consistency condition ensures consistency of $\psi = \alpha \wedge \bigvee \Gamma_1 \wedge \cdots \wedge \bigvee \Gamma_m$.

Also note that Φ_0 is the set of atoms (which trivially is representationally complete for $\mathcal{L}_0$) and that the condition for $k = 1$ then simply states that there is an atom α such that $\alpha \in \Gamma_i$ for each Γ_i. If there is a Γ_i such that $\alpha \notin \Gamma_i$, Lemma 6 gives that $\bigvee \Gamma_i \vdash \neg\alpha$. Hence ψ is inconsistent. Conversely, if ψ is inconsistent, there must be a Γ_i such that $\alpha \notin \Gamma_i$, and hence the condition is not satisfied.

If $k > 1$, suppose that the condition is not satisfied. Then, for each $\varphi \in \Phi_k$ which entails α there is a Γ_i such that $\varphi[a_i/\top] \notin \Gamma_i$. It follows from this that given any two distinct sets Γ_i and Γ_j, each two elements $\varphi_1[a_i/\top] \in \Gamma_i$ and $\varphi_2[a_j/\top] \in \Gamma_j$ must disagree on a doxastic a_l-alternative, $a_i \neq a_j \neq a_l$. In other words, there are two distinct doxastic a_l-alternatives δ_1 and δ_2 such that $\varphi_1[a_i/\top] \vdash \delta_1$ and $\varphi_2[a_j/\top] \vdash \delta_2$. By the mutual inconsistency assumption, $\delta_1 \wedge \delta_2 \vdash \bot$, and so $\varphi_1[a_i/\top] \wedge \varphi_2[a_j/\top] \vdash \bot$. Since this holds for any two distinct sets Γ_i and Γ_j, ψ must be inconsistent.

Suppose conversely that ψ is inconsistent. There are two cases. In the first case, there is a set Γ_i such that $\bigvee \Gamma_i \vdash \neg\alpha$, i.e. for each $\varphi \in \Phi_k$ such that $\varphi \vdash \alpha$, there is a set Γ_i such that $\varphi[a_i/\top] \notin \Gamma_i$. Then the condition is not satisfied. In the second case, there are two distinct sets Γ_i and Γ_j such that $\bigvee \Gamma_i \wedge \bigvee \Gamma_j \vdash \bot$. Then, for each two elements $\varphi_1[a_i/\top] \in \Gamma_i$ and $\varphi_2[a_j/\top] \in \Gamma_j$, $\varphi_1[a_i/\top] \wedge \varphi_2[a_j/\top] \vdash \bot$. We may assume that α is entailed by both φ_1 and φ_2 since this was treated in the first case. Since $\varphi_1[a_i/\top] \wedge \varphi_2[a_j/\top] \vdash \bot$, the two formulae must disagree on a doxastic a_l-alternative, and hence φ_1 and φ_2 are two distinct elements of Φ_k. The condition is then not satisfied. □

Lemma 10. *The set $\Phi_k[a/\top]$ satisfies mutual inconsistency.*

Proof. The base case is when $k = 0$. $\Phi_0[a/\top]$ is the set of atoms, and it is immediate that the set of atoms satisfies mutual inconsistency. Suppose inductively that φ and ψ are two distinct elements of $\Phi_{k+1}[a/\top]$. Then φ and ψ either disagree on an atom or on a doxastic b-alternative, $b \neq a$. In the first case, it is immediate that $\varphi \wedge \psi \vdash \bot$. In the second case, let $\varphi \vdash \delta_b^1$ and $\psi \vdash \delta_b^2$, where δ_b^1 and δ_b^2 are doxastic b-alternatives spanned by Γ_1 and Γ_2, respectively, Γ_1 and Γ_2 subsets of $\Phi_k[b/\top]$. By the induction hypothesis, $\Phi_k[b/\top]$ satisfies mutual inconsistency. By Lemma 5, $\delta_b^1 \wedge \delta_b^2 \vdash \bot$. Hence $\varphi \wedge \psi \vdash \bot$. □

Corollary 1. *The set of doxastic a-alternatives spanned by subsets of $\Phi_k[a/\top]$ satisfies mutual inconsistency.*

Proof. Immediate from Lemma 10 and Lemma 5. □

Lemma 11. *$\Phi_k[a/\top]$ is representationally complete for $\mathcal{L}_k^{\backslash a}$ and $\mathsf{Dox}_a(\Phi_k[a/\top])$ is representationally complete for $\mathcal{L}_{k+1}^a$.*

Proof. Both properties are proved by simultaneous induction on k. In the base case $\Phi_0 = \Phi_0^{\backslash a}$. It is easy to see that the first condition holds. Since Φ_0 is representationally complete for $\mathcal{L}_0$, the second holds by Lemma 7.

$\Phi_{k+1}[a/\top]$ is representationally complete for $\mathcal{L}_{k+1}^{\backslash a}$ (induction step). We have to prove that for each $\varphi \in \mathcal{L}_{k+1}^{\backslash a}$ there is a subset of $\Phi_{k+1}[a/\top]$ the disjunction of which is equivalent to φ. It is easy to see (using the DNF equivalent of each formula) that it is sufficient to prove this for φ of the form $\varphi^{\mathcal{P}} \wedge \varphi^{a_1} \wedge \cdots \wedge \varphi^{a_m}$ where $\varphi^{\mathcal{P}}$ is purely Boolean, φ^a is $\top$ and every other φ^{a_i} is in $\mathcal{L}_{k+1}^{a_i}$. Let the atom set $\widehat{\varphi}^{\mathcal{P}}$ be the set of atoms which imply $\varphi^{\mathcal{P}}$, $\widehat{\varphi}^a$ be $\{\top\}$ and $\widehat{\varphi}^{a_i}$ be the set of all $\delta \in \mathsf{Dox}_{a_i}(\Phi_k[a_i/\top])$ such that $\delta \vdash \varphi$. Let $\widehat{\varphi}$ be the set of every formula $\alpha \wedge \delta_1 \wedge \cdots \wedge \delta_m$ in $\Phi_{k+1}[a/\top]$ such that $\alpha \in \widehat{\varphi}^{\mathcal{P}}$ and $\delta_i \in \widehat{\varphi}^{a_i}$.

It follows by construction that $\bigvee \widehat{\varphi} \vdash \varphi$. Conversely, assume that φ is consistent with $\neg \bigvee \widehat{\varphi}$. By induction hypothesis and Lemma 6, $\vdash \mathsf{Dox}_{a_i}(\Phi_k[a_i/\top])$. This entails that there must be a consistent ψ of the form $\alpha \wedge \delta_1 \wedge \cdots \wedge \delta_m$ which implies φ and which is not in $\Phi_{k+1}[a/\top]$. But this is only possible if δ violates the third subcondition in the definition of Φ_{k+1} (Definition 2). By Lemma 9, ψ is inconsistent. Contradiction. Hence $\vdash \varphi \equiv \bigvee \widehat{\varphi}$.

$\mathsf{Dox}_a(\Phi_k[a/\top])$ is representationally complete for $\mathcal{L}_{k+1}^a$ (induction step). By the induction hypothesis, $\Phi_k[a/\top]$ is representationally complete for $\mathcal{L}_k^{\backslash a}$. Then, by Lemma 7, $\mathsf{Dox}_a(\Phi_k[a/\top])$ is representationally complete for $\mathcal{L}_{k+1}^a$. □

Theorem 2. *Each formula $\varphi \in \Phi_k^{\backslash a}$ is a complete theory over $\mathcal{L}_k^{\backslash a}$. Each doxastic alternative $\delta \in \mathsf{Dox}_a(\Phi_k[a/\top])$ is a complete theory over $\mathcal{L}_{k+1}^a$.*

Proof. By Lemma 10, $\Phi_k[a/\top]$ satisfies mutual inconsistency and by Lemma 11 $\Phi_k[a/\top]$ is representationally complete for $\mathcal{L}_k^{\backslash a}$. By Lemma 8, each $\delta \in \mathsf{Dox}_a(\Phi_k[a/\top])$ is a complete theory over $\mathcal{L}_{k+1}^a$. Since each $\delta \in \mathsf{Dox}_a(\Phi_{k-1}[a/\top])$ is a complete theory over $\mathcal{L}_k$, it follows that each $\varphi \in \Phi_k[a/\top]$ is a complete theory over $\mathcal{L}_k^{\backslash a}$. □

Having defined the set of I-atoms, we may now define the logical space for the multi-agent case. A *logical space of agent a up to depth k* is defined over a subset Γ of $\Phi_k[a/\top]$ by the formula $\mathsf{Lspace}_a(\Gamma)$. Observe that for $k = 0$, the logical space is defined by the formula $\mathsf{Lspace}_a(\Delta)$, $\Delta \subseteq \Phi_0$, which is a logical space as defined for the single-agent system Æ.

Corollary 2. *Let λ_a be a logical space for agent a up to k and $\varphi \in \mathcal{L}_k^{\backslash a}$. Then either $\lambda_a \vdash \Diamond_a \varphi$ or $\lambda_a \vdash \neg \Diamond_a \varphi$.*

4   Examples: Belief Representations with Defaults

Generally we represent the beliefs of an agent a by formulae of the form $\lambda_a \wedge \mathbf{O}_a \varphi$ where φ is the conjunction of a knowledge base κ and a number of *default conditionals* $\mathbf{b}_a \psi \supset \psi$, κ and ψ free of modality a. We may read the default conditionals as "agent a believes ψ provided that ψ is compatible with the rest of the beliefs". κ captures the rest of the beliefs whereas the logical space determines whether or not ψ is compatible with κ.

A crucial point illustrated in this section is that the logical space serves as a possibility operator and as such determines whether or not two formulae are compatible; the logical space hence also determines whether or not a default conditional is triggered.

This is in contrast to both the approach formalized in the system L_I [13] and the approach by Halpern and Lakemeyer [4]. In these approaches the set of possibilities is fixed and determined by the axiomatic system: The axiom system L_I refers to consistency within the system while the system of Halpern and Lakemeyer has a number of axioms and rules for reasoning about satisfiability. Formulae that as such are consistent or satisfiable within the system then constitute the set of logical possibilities.

The difference between $Æ_I$ and these approaches is shown in the formal analyses of belief representations by the fact that the logical possibilities are *explicitly given* in $Æ_I$, while the other approaches need additional formal reasoning for determining these possibilities.

In Section 6.1 of [4], Halpern and Lakemeyer give examples of how their logic can be used to represent default reasoning in a multi-agent situation. We will show how the inferences are carried out in the logic $Æ_I$. (Notice that in these examples the knowledge base is empty, i.e. $\kappa = \top$.)

Example 2. The first example of Halpern and Lakemeyer is this. Let p be agent a's secret and suppose he makes the assumption that unless he believes that b knows his secret, he assumes that she does not know it. We will now prove that if this is all he believes and if it is conceivable that b does not know his secret, then he believes that she does not know his secret. Formally, we show

$$\lambda_a \wedge \mathbf{O}_a(\neg \mathbf{B}_a \mathbf{B}_b p \supset \neg \mathbf{B}_b p) \vdash \mathbf{B}_a \neg \mathbf{B}_b p,$$

where λ_a is the logical space of agent a. Let φ denote $\neg \mathbf{B}_a \mathbf{B}_b p \supset \neg \mathbf{B}_b p$. Note that the assumption that it is conceivable to a that b does not know his secret implies that $\lambda_a \vdash \Diamond_a \neg \mathbf{B}_b p$. Let us turn to the formal derivation.

1. $\lambda_a \wedge \mathbf{O}_a \varphi \vdash \mathbf{B}_a \varphi$ PL
2. $\lambda_a \wedge \mathbf{O}_a \varphi \vdash \mathbf{C}_a \neg \varphi$ PL
3. $\vdash (\mathbf{B}_a \varphi \wedge \neg \mathbf{B}_a \mathbf{B}_b p) \supset \mathbf{B}_a \neg \mathbf{B}_b p$ normal logic, $Æ_I$
4. $\vdash \mathbf{C}_a \neg \varphi \supset (\mathbf{C}_a \neg \mathbf{B}_a \mathbf{B}_b p \wedge \mathbf{C}_a \mathbf{B}_b p)$ normal logic
5. $\lambda_a \wedge \mathbf{O}_a \varphi \vdash \Diamond_a \neg \mathbf{B}_b p$ assumption
6. $\lambda_a \wedge \mathbf{O}_a \varphi \vdash \mathbf{C}_a \mathbf{B}_b p \supset \neg \mathbf{B}_a \mathbf{B}_b p$ 5, PL
7. $\lambda_a \wedge \mathbf{O}_a \varphi \vdash \neg \mathbf{B}_a \mathbf{B}_b p$ 2, 4, 6, PL
8. $\lambda_a \wedge \mathbf{O}_a \varphi \vdash \mathbf{B}_a \neg \mathbf{B}_b p$ 1, 3, 7, PL

In the third line, we made use of the modal reductive strength of the logic. The critical point in the derivation is of course the fifth line. This theorem rests on the assumption that $\neg \mathbf{B}_b p$ is conceivable to agent a. The derivation in the system of Halpern and Lakemeyer is somewhat longer, since they need to apply some extra machinery to reason about validity and satisfiability.

The non-monotonicity becomes apparent when we add $\mathbf{B}_b p$ to the belief set of agent a, or we define the logical space such that $\lambda_a \vdash \neg\Diamond_a\neg\mathbf{B}_b p$. Then $\mathbf{B}_a\mathbf{B}_b p$ is deducible.

Example 3. In their next example, Halpern and Lakemeyer show how one agent reasons about another agent's ability to reason non-monotonically. The letter p stands for "Tweety flies". It is then shown that if a believes that all b believes is that by default Tweety flies, then a believes that b believes that Tweety flies.

Again, it is the logical space that makes the deduction go through in our system. But here, since a is reasoning about b's ability to reason non-monotonically, if a is to derive the conclusion that b believes p, a must believe that p is conceivable to b, i.e that the logical space λ_b of b implies $\Diamond_b p$. Note that since the non-monotonicity in this example is about b, we need not consult the logical space of a.

What we want to prove is thus that $\mathbf{B}_a(\lambda_b \wedge \mathbf{O}_b(\mathbf{b}_b p \supset p)) \vdash \mathbf{B}_a\mathbf{B}_b p$. The formal derivation is as follows:

1. $\lambda_b \wedge \mathbf{O}_b(\mathbf{b}_b p \supset p) \vdash \mathbf{B}_b(\mathbf{b}_b \supset p)$ PL
2. $\lambda_b \wedge \mathbf{O}_b(\mathbf{b}_b p \supset p) \vdash \mathbf{C}_b\neg(\mathbf{b}_b \supset p)$ PL
3. $\vdash (\mathbf{B}_b(\mathbf{b}_b p \supset p) \wedge \neg\mathbf{B}_b\neg p) \supset \mathbf{B}_b p$ normal logic, $\mathcal{E}_I$
4. $\vdash \mathbf{C}_b\neg(\mathbf{b}_b \supset p) \supset (\mathbf{C}_b\mathbf{b}_b p \wedge \mathbf{C}_b\neg p)$ normal logic
5. $\lambda_b \wedge \mathbf{O}_b(\mathbf{b}_b p \supset p) \vdash \Diamond_b p$ assumption
6. $\lambda_b \wedge \mathbf{O}_b(\mathbf{b}_b p \supset p) \vdash \mathbf{C}_b\neg p \supset \neg\mathbf{B}_b\neg p$ 5, PL
7. $\lambda_b \wedge \mathbf{O}_b(\mathbf{b}_b p \supset p) \vdash \neg\mathbf{B}_b\neg p$ 2, 4, 6, PL
8. $\lambda_b \wedge \mathbf{O}_b(\mathbf{b}_b p \supset p) \vdash \mathbf{B}_b p$ 1, 3, 7, PL
9. $\mathbf{B}_a(\lambda_b \wedge \mathbf{O}_b(\mathbf{b}_b p \supset p)) \vdash \mathbf{B}_a\mathbf{B}_b p$ 8, normal logic

The assumption to the effect that a believes λ_b is stronger than what we actually need. The assumption we need is that every logical space of agent b compatible with a's beliefs implies $\Diamond_b p$.

In these examples the logical space is essential by serving as a possibility operator. The logical space may also be decisive in the interpretation of belief representations with defaults. In Section 1 we addressed a scenario in which one agent b, being familiar with the educational system, had a logical space λ_b such that $\lambda_b \vdash \Box_b(\mathsf{master}(\mathsf{Fred}) \supset \mathsf{bachelor}(\mathsf{Fred}))$ where Fred is any given agent. Assume now that agent c, which is quite ignorant about educational matters, has confused the two concepts and that his logical space λ_c is such that $\lambda_c \vdash \Box_c(\mathsf{bachelor}(\mathsf{Fred}) \supset \mathsf{master}(\mathsf{Fred}))$. Should they both learn that, with very few exceptions, a person holding the degree of master may apply for the admission to candidature for the PhD, they will add this to their belief set as a default. They both know that agent a is a bachelor. Agent b furthermore knows that $\neg\mathsf{master}(a)$, and so the default is not relevant for his beliefs about a. Agent c on the other hand deduces that a indeed is a master since $\Box_c(\mathsf{bachelor}(a) \supset \mathsf{master}(a)) \vdash \mathbf{B}_c(\mathsf{bachelor}(a) \supset \mathsf{master}(a))$. If c does not already believe otherwise, he will by default deduce that a may apply for the admission to the PhD candidature. Two agents that believe the same set of default conditionals may hence interpret them differently because of the different ways in which they relate concepts as represented by their respective logical spaces.

We will in the rest of the section list a number of illuminating theorems of $Æ_I$ that show the relation between the logical space one the one hand and a belief representation with defaults on the other hand.

Assume first a belief representation $\lambda_a \wedge \mathbf{O}_a\varphi_1$ where $\varphi_1 = \kappa \wedge (\mathbf{b}_a\psi \supset \psi)$. The formula $\mathbf{O}_a\varphi_1$ should be related to the following theorems of $Æ_I$:

1. $\neg\Diamond_a(\kappa \wedge \psi) \vdash \mathbf{O}_a\varphi_1 \equiv \mathbf{O}_a\kappa$
2. $\Diamond_a(\kappa \wedge \psi) \vdash \mathbf{O}_a\varphi_1 \equiv \mathbf{O}_a(\kappa \wedge \psi)$

It is now easy to see that an analysis of the belief representation $\lambda_a \wedge \mathbf{O}_a\varphi_1$ is determined by the logical space λ_a. If $\lambda_a \vdash \neg\Diamond_a(\kappa \wedge \psi)$, then $\lambda_a \vdash \mathbf{O}_a\varphi_1 \equiv \mathbf{O}_a\kappa$, and if $\lambda_a \vdash \Diamond_a(\kappa \wedge \psi)$, then $\lambda_a \vdash \mathbf{O}_a\varphi_1 \equiv \mathbf{O}_a(\kappa \wedge \psi)$.

Observe that the case in which $\lambda_a \vdash \Diamond_a(\kappa \wedge \psi)$ generalizes Example 2 above and that the theorem $\lambda_a \vdash \mathbf{O}_a\varphi_1 \equiv \mathbf{O}_a(\kappa \wedge \psi)$ is a stronger result than what was proven in the example: It immediately follows here that $\lambda_a \wedge \mathbf{O}_a\varphi_1 \vdash \mathbf{B}_a(\kappa \wedge \psi)$ which corresponds to the result in Example 2 when $\kappa = \top$, i.e. when the knowledge base is empty.

Let us now turn to the more interesting case in which there are two default conditionals. Assume the belief representation $\lambda_a \wedge \mathbf{O}_a\varphi_2$ where $\varphi_2 = \kappa \wedge (\mathbf{b}_a\psi \supset \psi) \wedge (\mathbf{b}_a\gamma \supset \gamma)$. The logical space λ_a is again the key in the analysis of this representation as illustrated as follows.

1. If $\lambda_a \vdash \neg\Diamond_a(\kappa \wedge \psi) \wedge \neg\Diamond_a(\kappa \wedge \gamma)$, then $\lambda_a \vdash \mathbf{O}_a\varphi_2 \equiv \mathbf{O}_a\kappa$.
2. If $\lambda_a \vdash \neg\Diamond_a(\kappa \wedge \psi) \wedge \Diamond_a(\kappa \wedge \gamma)$, then $\lambda_a \vdash \mathbf{O}_a\varphi_2 \equiv \mathbf{O}_a(\kappa \wedge \gamma)$
3. If $\lambda_a \vdash \Diamond_a(\kappa \wedge \psi) \wedge \neg\Diamond_a(\kappa \wedge \gamma)$, then $\lambda_a \vdash \mathbf{O}_a\varphi_2 \equiv \mathbf{O}_a(\kappa \wedge \psi)$
4. If $\lambda_a \vdash \Diamond_a(\kappa \wedge \psi) \wedge \Diamond_a(\kappa \wedge \gamma) \wedge \neg\Diamond_a(\kappa \wedge \psi \wedge \gamma)$,
   then $\lambda_a \vdash \mathbf{O}_a\varphi_2 \equiv \mathbf{O}_a(\kappa \wedge \psi) \vee \mathbf{O}_a(\kappa \wedge \gamma)$
5. If $\lambda_a \vdash \Diamond_a(\kappa \wedge \psi \wedge \gamma)$, then $\lambda_a \vdash \mathbf{O}_a\varphi_2 \equiv \mathbf{O}_a(\kappa \wedge \psi \wedge \gamma)$

The first theorem corresponds to the situation in which none of the defaults apply, whereas the second and third theorem correspond to the situation in which one of the defaults apply but not the other. In the fourth case both defaults apply in isolation, but are mutually exclusive. The belief representation is hence ambiguous in the sense that there are more than one interpretations. In the fifth case both defaults apply.

Formal proofs of the above theorems are not easily obtained syntactically. Given the semantics of $Æ_I$ together with the soundness and completeness theorems, the proofs are however quite straightforward. This illustrates an important technical advantage over the system by Halpern and Lakemeyer [4].

We will not provide the semantic proofs here as they are very similar to the proofs of the examples in Section 4 of [13]. We will, however, in the following point out the aspects in which the analysis here differs from the reasoning in [13].

A given logical space λ_a is by construction consistent and hence, by completeness, satisfiable. By soundness $\lambda_a \vdash \neg\Diamond_a\psi$ implies $\lambda_a \vDash_C \neg\Diamond_a\psi$ for every

a-cluster C in all models $\mathcal{M}$. By definition of the satisfiability relation $\mathcal{M} \models_x \neg\psi$ for all points $x \in C$. By similar reasoning, if $\lambda_a \vdash \Diamond_a\psi$, there exists a point $x \in C$ such that $\mathcal{M} \models_x \psi$ for all a-clusters C in all models $\mathcal{M}$ satisfying λ_a.

Given these observations about models satisfying a specific logical space, we semantically prove theorems of the form $\lambda_a \vdash \mathbf{O}_a\varphi \equiv \mathbf{O}_a\varphi'$ by showing that $\lambda_a \models \mathbf{O}_a\varphi \equiv \mathbf{O}_a\varphi'$ and then argue by completeness. The way of reasoning is to prove that for any a-cluster C in any model $\mathcal{M}$ such that $\mathcal{M} \models_C \lambda_a \wedge \mathbf{O}_a\varphi$, then $\mathcal{M} \models_x \varphi \equiv \varphi'$ for all points $x \in C$. The desired result then follows.

The contrast to the system L_I in the semantic argument lies in the role of the logical space. The semantics of L_I is identical to the semantics of $\mathcal{E}_I$ except that the models in L_I additionally satisfy three specific properties. These properties are used in an essential way in the semantic analysis of the belief representations with defaults. In the system $\mathcal{E}_I$ the essence lies in the properties of the a-clusters satisfying a logical space λ_a.

Observe finally that a reduction property of the system is used in the analysis of belief representations with defaults: We start with a formula $\mathbf{O}_a\varphi$ where φ is a conjunction of formulae some of which are not free of modality a and deduce a disjunction of formulae $\mathbf{O}_a\varphi'$ in which φ' is free of modality a. This is a special case of the modal reduction theorem that is addressed in the following section.

5 The Modal Reduction Theorem

We will in this section assume a sub-language $\mathcal{L}_k$ bounded by a finite set of propositional letters $\mathcal{P}$, a finite set of indices I and a given modal depth k. Let the logical space λ of agent a be given, and let β be any formula. The modal reduction theorem states that there are formulae $\beta_1, \ldots, \beta_n$ free of modality a, such that

$$\lambda \vdash \mathbf{O}_a\beta \equiv \mathbf{O}_a\beta_1 \vee \cdots \vee \mathbf{O}_a\beta_n.$$

Moreover, each formula $\mathbf{O}_a\beta_i$, $i \leq n$, is defined directly from one of the a-clusters satisfying $\lambda \wedge \mathbf{O}_a\beta$, and each such a-cluster is represented by a formula $\mathbf{O}_a\beta_i$.

Let $\lambda \wedge \mathbf{O}_a\varphi$ have depth k. We will say that $\lambda \wedge \mathbf{O}_a\varphi$ is an *explicit belief representation* if for any formula $\psi \in \mathcal{L}_k^a$, either $\lambda \wedge \mathbf{O}_a\varphi \vdash \psi$ or $\lambda \wedge \mathbf{O}_a\varphi \vdash \neg\psi$. In other words, an explicit belief representation is a formula that determines the agent's attitude towards any formula in the language.

Theorem 3. *Let φ be any formula free of modality a. Then $\lambda \wedge \mathbf{O}_a\varphi$ is an explicit belief representation.*

Related to the notion of an explicit belief representation is the notion of an *implicit* belief representation, i.e. formulae of the form $\lambda \wedge \mathbf{O}_a\varphi$ that allow ambiguity with respect to a-modalized formulae. An implicit belief representation is a formula $\lambda \wedge \mathbf{O}_a\varphi$ where φ is not free of modality a. By applying the modal reduction theorem, such formulae are reduced to disjunctions of formulae, each of them an explicit belief representation.

6   Related Work

We will in this section prove the equivalence of the system $Æ_I$ with two earlier attempts of generalizing the system of Levesque [7]. The first of these other systems is the system HL of Halpern and Lakemeyer [4], where a generalization of Levesque's system is provided by coding the satisfiability relation into the system. Notice that the language of HL is an extension of $\mathcal{L}$. We will prove the equivalence with $Æ_I$ with respect to the common part of the languages. The second system is the system L_I of Waaler [12], where the $\Diamond$-axiom of Levesque's system is generalized to the statement that $\Diamond_a\varphi$ is a theorem provided that φ is a consistent formula free of modality a.

The deducibility relations of HL and L_I are denoted $\vdash_{HL}$ and $\vdash_{L_I}$, respectively. In [12], the equivalence of L_I and HL was established. We will in this section prove the equivalence of the system $Æ_I$ and the system L_I. The equivalences of the three systems then follow as a corollary.

6.1   The System L_I

Let $\vdash'$ be the deducibility relation given by removing the axiom schema T from the system $Æ_I$. The deducibility relation $\vdash_{L_I}$ of the system L_I is defined as the least relation extending $\vdash'$ containing every instance of the following schema for each agent $a \in I$:

$$\Diamond_a : \Diamond_a\varphi \text{ provided } \varphi \nvdash_{L_I} \bot, \quad \varphi \text{ free of modality } a.$$

There is a circular pattern to the $\Diamond_a$-axiom, but in [12], it is shown that the circularity is not vicious. This result is captured by Lemma 12 below.

As in $Æ_I$ any formula is provably equivalent to a first-order formula in L_I. Moreover, T is a theorem of L_I. Hence, L_I is an extension of $Æ_I$. For proof of these claims consult [13].

6.2   Equivalence of $Æ_I$ and L_I

L_I is a proper extension of $Æ_I$. However, equivalence between the systems can be established for sub-languages up to a given depth by strengthening $Æ_I$ with a particular set of formulae. In the single-agent case, when the maximal logical space is added to the axioms of $Æ$, the system $Æ$ is equivalent to the propositional fragment of Levesque's system. What we need to do in the multi-agent case is to identify a set of formulae that, when added to the axioms of $Æ_I$, yields equivalence of $Æ_I$ and L_I.

Definition 3 (Maximal I-atoms). *The set of maximal I-atoms with depth k is defined as follows: Φ_0 is the set of atoms, while Φ_{k+1} is all formulae $\alpha \wedge \delta_1 \wedge \cdots \wedge \delta_m$ such that*

- *α is an atom,*
- *δ_i is a doxastic a_i-alternative spanned by $\Phi_k[a_i/\top]$,*

The critical difference between the definition of a maximal I-atom and the definition of an I-atom as defined in Definition 2 is that δ_i in the inductive step of the definition of a maximal I-atom is spanned by $\Phi_k[a_i/\top]$, and *not subsets* of $\Phi_k[a_i/\top]$. The consistency condition is furthermore omitted. This is because formulae $\alpha \wedge \delta_1 \wedge \cdots \wedge \delta_m$ trivially satisfy the consistency condition in the definition of the maximal I-atoms. (We omit the easy proof of this claim.)

The maximal logical space of agent a_i with depth k is now defined as $\lambda_i = \mathsf{Lspace}_a(\Phi_{k-1}[a_i/\top])$. We will prove that the set of formulae $\Lambda = \{\lambda_i \mid a_i \in I\}$ added to the axioms of $\mathcal{E}_I$ yields equivalence with L_I up to depth k.

Before we proceed, we need an important result from [12]. This result states that L_I-consistency of a formula φ free of modality a is established without reference to the theorem $\Diamond_a \varphi$.

Lemma 12. *Let φ be L_I-provable. Then there is an L_I-proof π of φ such that $\mathsf{d}(\psi) < \mathsf{d}(\varphi)$ for every instance of an axiom $\Diamond_a \psi$ which is used in π.*

Theorem 4. *Let Λ be the set of maximal logical spaces with depth k for each agent $a_i \in I$ and $\mathsf{d}(\varphi) \leq k$. Then $\Lambda \vdash \varphi$ iff $\vdash_{L_I} \varphi$.*

Proof. The proof is by induction on the depth of the logical spaces, and both directions are proved simultaneously. As $\vdash \subseteq \vdash_{L_I}$, we need for the 'only if' direction to prove that $\vdash_{L_I} \bigwedge \Lambda$. For the 'if' direction, we need to prove that L_I is a strengthening of $\mathcal{E}_I$ by $\bigwedge \Lambda$ only. That is, we need to prove that $\Diamond_{a_i} \varphi$ is deducible in $\mathcal{E}_I$ from Λ, where $\Diamond_{a_i} \varphi$ is derivable in L_I by an application of $\Diamond_{a_i}$ to a formula φ, where $\mathsf{d}(\varphi) < \mathsf{d}(\lambda_i)$.

The base case is when each λ_i is spanned by the set of atoms Φ_0. 'Only if': As every atom α is L_I-consistent, $\vdash_{L_I} \Diamond_{a_i} \alpha$ by the $\Diamond_{a_i}$-axiom, and since $\bigvee \Phi_0$ is a PL-tautology, we get $\vdash_{L_I} \Box_{a_i}(\bigvee \Phi_0)$ by RN. So $\vdash_{L_I} \lambda_i$ for every $\lambda_i \in \Lambda$. 'If': Suppose $\vdash_{L_I} \Diamond_{a_i} \varphi$ is deduced in L_I by an application of $\Diamond_{a_i}$. It must then be the case that φ is a purely Boolean formula such that $\varphi \nvdash_{L_I} \bot$. Since L_I extends $\mathcal{E}_I$, $\varphi \nvdash \bot$. There is then an atom α such that $\alpha \vdash \varphi$. By modal logic, $\Diamond_{a_i} \alpha \vdash \Diamond_{a_i} \varphi$, and so $\lambda_i \vdash \Diamond_{a_i} \varphi$.

In the inductive step, let $\mathsf{d}(\lambda_i) = k+1$, λ_i spanned by $\Phi_k[a_i/\top]$. 'Only if': We need to establish that $\psi \nvdash_{L_I} \bot$ for every $\psi \in \Phi_k[a_i/\top]$ and that $\vdash_{L_I} \bigvee \Phi_k[a_i/\top]$. Once these two properties are established, we may apply $\Diamond_{a_i}$ to the first and RN to the latter to get the desired result.

Note that ψ is a conjunction of an atom and a doxastic a_j-alternative δ_j for each $a_j \neq a_i$. Each δ_j entails the maximal logical space λ_j', $\mathsf{d}(\delta_j) = k$. Let Λ' be the set of maximal logical spaces with depth k for each $a_j \neq a_i$. By construction of the logical space, we have $\psi \wedge \Lambda' \nvdash \bot$. By the induction hypothesis, $\psi \nvdash_{L_I} \bot$. By axiom $\Diamond_{a_i}$, we get $\vdash_{L_I} \Diamond_{a_i} \psi$.

Let Δ_j be the doxastic a_j-alternatives spanned by $\Phi_{k-1}[a_j/\top]$. Observe that for each $\delta_j \in \Delta_j$, $\mathsf{d}(\delta_j) = k$ and $\delta_j \vdash \lambda_j'$, where λ_j' is the maximal logical space with depth k for agent a_j. Notice that the set of conjunctions of an atom and a formula $\delta_j \in \Delta_j$ for each $a_j \neq a_i$ is exactly the set of formulae $\Phi_k[a_j/\top]$. In order to prove $\vdash_{L_I} \bigvee \Phi_k[a_i/\top]$, we will prove that $\vdash_{L_I} \bigvee \Delta_j$ for each $a_j \neq a_i$.

The result then follows by standard propositional reasoning and the fact that $\vdash_{L_I} \bigvee \Phi_0$.

We will first prove that $\lambda'_j \vdash \bigvee \Delta_j$. Suppose that $\lambda'_j \nvdash \bigvee \Delta_j$, i.e. $\lambda'_j \wedge \neg (\bigvee \Delta_j) \nvdash \perp$. By Lemma 11, there is a doxastic a_j-alternative δ'_j with depth k such that $\delta'_j \vdash \lambda'_j \wedge \neg (\bigvee \Delta_j)$. But then $\delta'_j \vdash \lambda'_j$, and so $\delta_j \in \Delta_j$. Contradiction. Since $\lambda'_j \vdash \bigvee \Delta_j$, we get $\vdash_{L_I} \bigvee \Delta_j$ by the induction hypothesis. $\vdash_{L_I} \bigvee \Phi_k[a_i/\top]$ follows by standard propositional reasoning, and $\vdash_{L_I} \Box_{a_i}(\bigvee \Phi_k[a_i/\top])$ by RN.

'If': Suppose $\vdash_{L_I} \Diamond_{a_i}\varphi$, $\mathsf{d}(\varphi) < \mathsf{d}(\lambda_i)$, $\lambda_i \in \Lambda$, is deduced in L_I by an application of $\Diamond_{a_i}$. It must then be the case that φ is a formula free of modality a_i such that $\varphi \nvdash_{L_I} \perp$. By Lemma 12, any application of the $\Diamond_{a_i}$-axiom to establish the consistency of φ is to formulae with depth $< \mathsf{d}(\varphi)$. By the induction hypothesis, $\Lambda' \wedge \varphi \nvdash \perp$, where Λ' is the set of maximal logical spaces with depth k for each $a_j \neq a_i$.

We may without loss of generality assume that φ is first-order and on DNF. Since $\Lambda' \wedge \varphi \nvdash \perp$, there is a disjunct ψ of ϕ such that $\Lambda' \wedge \psi \nvdash \perp$. ψ is a conjunction of a purely Boolean formula $\psi^{\mathcal{P}}$ and a completely a_j-modalized formula ψ^{a_j} for each $a_j \neq a_i$. Since $\lambda'_j \wedge \psi^{a_j} \nvdash \perp$, $\lambda'_j \in \Lambda'$, there is by Lemma 11 a doxastic a_j-alternative δ_j with depth k such that $\delta_j \vdash \lambda'_j \wedge \psi^{a_j}$. Let Δ be the set of these formulae δ_j for each $a_j \neq a_i$. As to $\psi^{\mathcal{P}}$, there is an atom α such that $\alpha \vdash \psi^{\mathcal{P}}$. Since each δ_j entails the maximal logical space, the consistency condition is trivially satisfied, and so $\alpha \wedge \Delta \nvdash \perp$. Since each element of $\{\alpha\} \cup \Delta$ entails a respective conjunct of ψ, we have $\alpha \wedge \Delta \vdash \psi$, and so $\alpha \wedge \Delta \vdash \varphi$. Observe that the conjunction $\alpha \wedge \bigwedge \Delta$ is an element of $\Phi_k[a_j/\top]$ and that $\Diamond_{a_i}(\alpha \wedge \bigwedge \Delta)$ is a conjunct of the maximal logical space λ_i with depth k. Since $\alpha \wedge \Delta \vdash \varphi$, we have $\Diamond_{a_i}(\alpha \wedge \bigwedge \Delta) \vdash \Diamond_{a_i}\varphi$ by modal logic, and so $\lambda_i \vdash \Diamond_{a_i}\varphi$ as desired.   □

Corollary 3. $\Lambda \vdash \varphi$ iff $\vdash_{L_I} \varphi$ iff $\vdash_{HL} \varphi$, $\varphi \in \mathcal{L}$, provided $\mathsf{d}(\varphi) \leq \mathsf{d}(\lambda_i)$ for each $\lambda_i \in \Lambda$.

Proof. Follows immediately from Theorem 15 of [12] and Theorem 4.   □

7   Conclusion and Future Work

The focus of this paper is on the logical foundation of multi-agent systems. We have successfully developed a notion of logical space for agents in a multi-modal only knowing language. Clearly, a practical application will require a more economical way of representing and reasoning within logical spaces, typically achieved by means of highly restricted languages. However, to implement constraints like this, one needs to know what "all the options" are. This paper presents an answer to this fundamental and conceptually important question.

A number of interesting questions can be raised on the basis of this logical clarification. First, we have not presented any complexity analysis. The size of a logical space grows quickly beyond any tractable level. However, in a particular situation one will not need to span the entire space syntactically, exactly like one in Æ can provide an implicit definition of a logical space by means of a characteristic formula [8, 11]. We plan to address this question in a subsequent paper. We also plan to extend the reduction method used to give a constructive proof of the Modal Reduction Theorem in Æ to Æ$_I$ and to extend the language with language constructs to express different degrees of confidence for each agent (like in Æ). The latter task is in itself straightforward; however, a non-trivial use of this would be to develop a theory of multi-agent default reasoning within this language which generalizes the encoding of default logic in Æ [1].

References

1. Engan, I., Lian, E. H., Langholm, T. and Waaler, A.: Default Reasoning with Preference within Only Knowing Logic. The 8th International Conference on Logic Programming and Nonmonotonic Reasoning (LPNMR'05), Lecture Notes in Computer Science **3662** (2005) 304–316

2. Halpern, J. Y.: Reasoning about Only Knowing with Many Agents. Proceedings of the 11th National Conference on Artificial Intelligence (AAAI-93) (1993) 655–661

3. Halpern, J. Y.: A Theory of Knowledge and Ignorance for many agents. Journal of Logic and Computation **7:1** (1997) 79–108

4. Halpern, J. Y. and Lakemeyer, G.: Multi-Agent Only Knowing. Journal of Logic and Computation **11:1** (2001) 40–70

5. Hoek, W. and Thijsse, E.: A General Approach to Multi-Agent Minimal Knowledge: With Tools and Samples. Studia Logica **72:1** (2002) 61–84

6. Lakemeyer, G.: All They Know: A Study in Multi-Agent Autoepistemic Reasoning. Proc. of the 13th International Joint Conference on Artificial Intelligence (IJCAI-93) (1993) 376–381

7. Levesque, H. J.: All I know: A study in autoepistemic logic. Artificial Intelligence **42** (1990) 263–309

8. Lian, E. H., Langholm, T. and Waaler, A.: Only Knowing with Confidence Levels: Reductions and Complexity. In J. J. Alferes and J. Leite, editors, Proceedings of JELIA'04, Lecture Notes in Artificial Intelligence **3229** (2004) 500–512

9. Solhaug, B.: Logical Spaces in Multi-Modal Only Knowing Logics. Master's Thesis, University of Oslo (2004)

10. Waaler, A.: Logical Studies in Complementary Weak S5. Doctoral thesis, University of Oslo (1994)

11. Waaler, A., Klüwer, J.W., Langholm, T. and Lian, E.: Only Knowing with Degrees of Confidence. *Journal of Applied Logic*, 2006. To appear. A preprint is available at http://folk.uio.no/johanw/ok-doc.pdf.

12. Waaler, A.: Consistency proofs for systems of multi-agent only knowing. *Advances in Modal Logic*, **5** (2005) 347–366

13. Waaler, A. and Solhaug, B.: Semantics for Multi-Agent Only Knowing (extended abstract). In R. van der Meyden, editor, Proceedings of the 10th Conference on Theoretical Aspects of Rationality and Knowledge (TARK X), ACM Digital Library (2005) 109–125

Trustworthiness by Default

Johan W. Klüwer[1] and Arild Waaler[2]

[1] Dep. of Philosophy, University of Oslo
johanw@filosofi.uio.no
[2] Finnmark College and Dep. of Informatics, University of Oslo
arild@ifi.uio.no

But never put a person to death on the testimony of only one witness. There must always be at least two or three witnesses.
Deuteronomy 17:6 (New Living Translation)

Abstract. We present a framework for reasoning about information sources, with application to conflict resolution and belief formation at various degrees of reliability. On the basis of an assignment of relative trustworthiness to sets of information sources, a lattice of degrees of trustworthiness is constructed; from this, a priority structure is derived and applied to the problem of forming the right opinion. Consolidated with an unquestioned knowledge base, this provides an unambiguous account of what an agent should believe, conditionally on which information sources are trusted. Applications in multi-agent doxastic logic are sketched.

1 Introduction

To trust an information source, in the simplest, unconditional form, is to believe every piece of information that the source provides. While providing a paradigm, this notion of trust has limited application to realistic scenarios. In general, the trust we have in our information sources, which may vary in kind from teachers to newspapers to legal witnesses, is not unconditional: we believe what we are told by a trusted source only as long as we don't possess knowledge to the contrary. This simple observation motivates the approach to trust that we will be discussing in this paper. Conditional trust in an information source is a *default* attitude: To believe what you are told, unless you know better.

When looking for information, we often need to consider several sources. Sources may vary widely with regard to their reliability, and a cautious default approach then informs us to let the more trustworthy ones take priority over those that are less trustworthy. Furthermore, we often need to consider more than one source at a time. Notions of agreement or corroboration, as well as the consolidation of information drawn from different sources, are essential.

What we present here is a framework for reasoning about relative trustworthiness, with sets of information sources as the basic trusted units. The main part of the paper is structured as follows. Section 2 addresses properties of the trustworthiness relation itself, making only informal reference to notions of information. Building on a simple relation between sets of sources (2.1), rational

F. Toni and P. Torroni (Eds.): CLIMA VI, LNAI 3900, pp. 96–111, 2006.

trust attitudes are identified and ordered according to strength (2.2, 2.3), and ordered in a tree structure of "fallbacks" (2.4). Section 3 employs this structure to provide an account of trust in terms of default conditionals. Notions of information, as provided by individual sources as well as collections of sources, are defined in 3.1. The prioritized default logic $Æ_T$ is briefly presented in section 3.2. The defaults approach is then made explicit in section 3.3, which presents a method for expressing trust attitudes as formulae of $Æ_T$.

The expression of trusting attitudes in terms of prioritized defaults provides an answer to the following non-trivial question: Given that we possess a body of antecedent knowledge, and are provided with information from a set of variously trusted sources, what is it reasonable to believe?

For the presentation of the core theory, we assume that the information provided by sources is expressed in propositional logic, but the approach to relative trustworthiness is equally applicable if one wants to use a more, or less, complex language. Looking forward, section 3.4 outlines how the analysis can be applied to multi-agent doxastic logic, to enable the representation of doxastic agents with varying degrees of trust that the beliefs of other agents are true.

This work builds on two main sources. For the theory of trustworthiness, the most important is the work of John Cantwell [1, 2], in which the basic relation of trustworthiness is defined in a way that is close to the one given here. For the aspects that relate to default inference and belief, the prioritized belief logic $Æ$ [9, 10, 12], which is closely related to that of [7], has been the primary source of reference.

We consider the following to be guiding principles for what follows.

Given a collection of sources, what all sources agree on is at least as trustworthy as what only some agree on. $\qquad$ (1)

If some unit x is trusted, and y is at least as trustworthy as x, then rationality demands that y should be trusted too. $\qquad$ (2)

Accept information from a trusted unit as true, unless it is inconsistent with what you have already accepted. $\qquad$ (3)

2   A Trustworthiness Relation

2.1   The Basic Pre-order on Information Sources

Let $\mathfrak{S}$ be a (possibly empty) finite set of *sources*. The *trustworthiness relation* $\trianglelefteq$ is a relation between subsets of $\mathfrak{S}$; we will often refer to these as *source units*. A source unit is an entity that is capable of providing information, as follows: A singleton unit $\{a\}$ provides exactly what the single source a does. A non-singleton unit provides only what follows from the contribution of every member. Informally, think of a non-singleton source unit as making a "common statement", i.e., the strongest that its members all agree on.

Notation: Small Latin letters a, b, c denote sources, small variable letters x, y, z range over source units, capital Latin letters A, B, C denote particular sets of source units, and capital variable letters X, Y, Z range over arbitrary sets of source units. We will sometimes have to collect sets of source units, for which we shall use capital Greek letters Γ, Δ.

We assume that the trustworthiness relation is reflexive and transitive (a *preorder*). Two source units x and y may be *trustworthiness-equivalent*, written $x \sim y$.

$$x \sim y \quad =_{\text{def}} \quad x \trianglelefteq y \text{ and } y \trianglelefteq x \tag{4}$$

We write $x \lhd y$ to express that y is strictly more trustworthy than x.

$$x \lhd y \quad =_{\text{def}} \quad x \trianglelefteq y \text{ and not } x \sim y \tag{5}$$

Source units that are unrelated by $\trianglelefteq$ will be called *independent*, denoted $x \wr y$. Intuitively, we interpret independence as a consequence of lack of evidence; neither of $x \rhd y$, $x \lhd y$, and $x \sim y$ is believed to obtain. If no two source units are independent, we say $\trianglelefteq$ is *connected*.

We assume that every source, however it is combined with other sources, makes a non-negative contribution of information. Together with (1), this implies that enlargement of a source unit with new members may never yield a unit that provides a stronger set of information. Hence, a source unit will be at least as trustworthy as every unit that it contains as a subset. This motivates taking the following principle, which we will refer to as *monotonicity*, to be valid.

$$x \trianglelefteq x \cup y . \tag{6}$$

It follows that for each source unit x, the following hold.

$$x \trianglelefteq \mathfrak{S} , \tag{7}$$

$$\emptyset \trianglelefteq x . \tag{8}$$

To see why (7) is valid, note that $\mathfrak{S}$ only provides information which is agreed upon by all the sources. At the other extreme, we stipulate that the empty set is a limit case that always provides inconsistent information, motivating (8).

In referring to particular source units in examples we will consistently simplify notation by omitting brackets: $a \lhd bc$ is, e.g., shorthand for $\{a\} \lhd \{b, c\}$. Likewise, the set $\{\{a\}, \{a, b\}\}$ will be denoted a, ab. Observe that the symbol a should, depending on the context, either be taken as a reference to the source a or to the singleton source set $\{a\}$ or to the singleton source set collection $\{\{a\}\}$.

2.2 The Poset of Trust-Equivalent Source Units

We will use the term *trust attitude*, given a set of sources $\mathfrak{S}$, to mean the belief that a set of source units can be trusted. (Note that this employs the non-relative sense of trust in an entity, as opposed to the relative notion of trusting one entity more than another.) Our aim in this and the following section is to identify the *permissible* trust attitudes.

We start by noting that the empty set represents the attitude of placing trust in none of the sources. This maximally sceptical attitude is obviously permissible, and it amounts to regarding even information that all the sources support as unreliable. Given a trust relation $\lhd$, we can distinguish those further trust attitudes that respect the relation, according to principle (2), that x may only be trusted if every $y \unrhd x$ is trusted as well. In the following, we allow ourselves to talk about attitudes as being the sets of source units themselves, and to say that a source unit is "included" in an attitude of trust, meaning that that source unit is among those trusted.

We use the following standard terminology. In a *poset* $(S, \leq)$ the $\leq$-relation is reflexive, transitive and anti-symmetric. The poset has a unique cover relation $\prec$, defined as $x \prec y$ iff $x < y$ and $x \leq z < y$ implies $z = x$. $C \subseteq S$ is an *antichain* if every two distinct elements in C are incomparable by $\leq$. Note in particular that $\emptyset$ is an antichain. Every subset of S has $\leq$-minimal elements, and the set of these elements is an antichain. $\uparrow C$ denotes an *up-set*, defined as $\{x \mid (\exists y \in C)(y \leq x)\}$. The set of antichains in a poset is isomorphic to the set of up-sets under set inclusion.

If an attitude of trust includes a source unit x, but not an equivalently trustworthy source unit y, then the attitude is not permissible. This motivates a focus on the equivalence classes of $\mathfrak{S}$ modulo $\sim$. Where $x \subseteq \mathfrak{S}$,

$$[x] \quad =_{\text{def}} \quad \{y : x \sim y\} \tag{9}$$

Let $\dot{\mathfrak{S}}$ be the set of all equivalence classes of $\mathfrak{S}$ modulo $\sim$. We will say a source unit x is *vacuous* with regard to trustworthiness if $x \in [\emptyset]$. In the extreme case that every source unit is a member of $[\emptyset]$, the trustworthiness relation itself is said to be vacuous.

Where X and Y are in $\dot{\mathfrak{S}}$, define a relation $\dot{\lhd}$ of relative strength between them as follows.

$$X \dot{\lhd} Y \quad =_{\text{def}} \quad (\exists x \in X)(\exists y \in Y)(x \lhd y) \tag{10}$$

Let $X \dot{\trianglelefteq} Y$ designate $X \dot{\lhd} Y$ or $X = Y$ and let $X \dot{\wr} Y$ designate independence.

Lemma 1. $(\dot{\mathfrak{S}}, \dot{\trianglelefteq})$ *is a poset in which* $[\emptyset]$ *is the unique minimum and* $[\mathfrak{S}]$ *the unique maximum.* $(\dot{\mathfrak{S}}, \dot{\trianglelefteq})$ *is a linear order iff* $(\wp \mathfrak{S}, \trianglelefteq)$ *is connected.*

Proof. Monotonicity entails the unique minimum and maximum. The other properties follow easily from the construction of $(\dot{\mathfrak{S}}, \dot{\trianglelefteq})$.

Example 1. Assume that the set of sources $\mathfrak{S}$ contains just a and b, and that $a \lhd ab$, $b \lhd ab$, $\emptyset \lhd a$, and $\emptyset \lhd b$ (i.e., the source units a, b, and ab are non-vacuous, and ab is more trustworthy than both a and b). The following figure shows Hasse diagrams of the poset $(\dot{\mathfrak{S}}, \dot{\trianglelefteq})$, given 1. $a \lhd b$, 2. $a \sim b$, and 3. $a \wr b$.

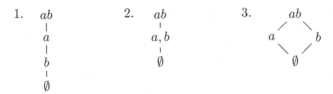

1. ab
    |
    a
    |
    b
    |
    $\emptyset$

2. ab
    |
    a, b
    |
    $\emptyset$

3. ab
    a b
    $\emptyset$

Relation 1 requires information provided by a to take precedence over information provided by b. Relation 2 emerges from taking a to be precisely as reliable as b. This implies it is only rational to accept a's contribution given that b's is accepted as well, and in the event that a and b contradict each other, it is ruled out that either can be trusted separately. Relation 3 reflects a situation in which less is known about the relative trustworthiness of a and b than in 1 and 2: neither is known to be better than or equivalent to the other. With this relation, trusting b but not a is not irrational, so the range of admissible attitudes is wider. In particular, if the information a provides is incompatible with what b provides, the relation does not rule out making a *choice* of trusting just one of the two.[1] Compared to 1 and 2, this relation offers more freedom, but less guidance.

The following example, which is developed further in later sections, describes a reasonably realistic scenario in which assessment of the relative trustworthiness of source units is called for.

Example 2 (Traffic accident). A traffic accident has occurred. We have been assigned the task of finding witnesses, assessing their relative trustworthiness, gathering their statements on what came to pass, weighing the evidence according to trustworthiness and finally presenting an account of the accident that meets a reasonable standard (threshold) of reliability.

At the outset, we know that there are three witnesses, a, b, and c, but nothing about their respective trustworthiness. We are however provided with a drawing, illustrating the accident ⊛ and the positions of the witnesses.

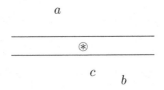

Assume that the criterion according to which sources are deemed trustworthy or not is their viewpoint relative to the incident, and nothing else. Making no prior assumptions, we start out with the weakest possible trust relation (relation 0 below). By applying information provided by the drawing, we are able to considerably strengthen the trust relation. We will consider a sequence of three steps.

---

[1] When the case arises that a and b contradict each other, a choice will implicitly favour a revision of the trust relation to be like 1 or 2. If the subject opts to trust a over b, 1 is favored; if neither, this favors 2.

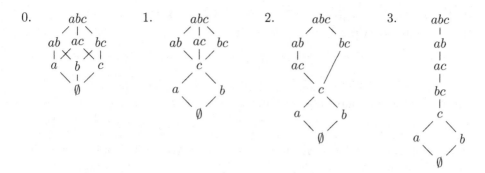

1. Seeing that c was closer to where the accident took place than the others, we take c to be more trustworthy than both: $a \lhd c$ and $b \lhd c$.

2. Because a and b are farther apart than a and c, their viewpoints are likely to be more divergent. Whatever can be observed from widely different perspectives is likely to hold true. Therefore, we will assume $ac \lhd ab$.

3. Because b and c are close together, we add $bc \lhd ac$ as well.

We choose to make no further additions to the relation. In particular, we refrain from making a judgment whether a is more trustworthy than b, or vice versa, or just as trustworthy as b: we consider a and b to be independent. This means it will be consistent with the trust relation to make a choice between which of a and b to trust. If they should happen to contradict each other, our lack of commitment as to which is more trustworthy then presents us with the option to trust just one of the two.

In steps 2 and 3, the unit c is more trustworthy than the unit b, but this relationship is reversed when the units are enlarged with source a, as $ac \lhd ab$ holds. Indeed, the following substitution principles are not valid; given $z[y/x] = (z \setminus x) \cup y$,

$$\text{If } x \lhd y \text{ and } x \subset z, \text{ then } z \lhd z[y/x],$$
$$\text{If } x \sim y \text{ and } x \subset z, \text{ then } z \sim z[y/x].$$

2.3   A Lattice of Trust Levels

We know from Lemma 1 that $(\dot{\mathfrak{S}}, \mathrel{\dot{\trianglelefteq}})$ is a poset. Given the poset it is straightforward to identify the permissible trust attitudes: a trust attitude is permissible if it is an up-set in $(\dot{\mathfrak{S}}, \mathrel{\dot{\trianglelefteq}})$. Technically, we will represent an attitude by its set of minima, or equivalently, by an antichain in the partial order $(\dot{\mathfrak{S}}, \mathrel{\dot{\trianglelefteq}})$. We define the set $\mathfrak{T}$ of permissible trust attitudes as follows,

$$\mathfrak{T} = \{ \cup \Gamma \mid \Gamma \text{ is an antichain in } (\dot{\mathfrak{S}}, \mathrel{\dot{\trianglelefteq}}) \}.$$

Let the symbol λ denote the attitude that no source unit is trusted, $\cup \emptyset$.

Having a weak trust attitude means trusting only what many sources agree on, or perhaps none; a strong attitude means trusting many sources, or perhaps all. Let Γ and Δ be antichains in $(\acute{\mathfrak{S}}, \trianglelefteq)$. Then we define the natural relation of strength between permissible trust attitudes $\leq$,

$$\sqcup\Gamma \leq \sqcup\Delta \text{ iff } \uparrow\!\Delta \subseteq \uparrow\!\Gamma.$$

By definition, λ is $\leq$-maximal in $\mathfrak{T}$. This is natural, as the corresponding attitude of trusting no source unit will always have a maximal degree of reliability. Ordered by $\leq$, the members of $\mathfrak{T}$ form a lattice in which lesser nodes represent stronger trust attitudes. It is natural to talk about the permissible trust attitudes as corresponding to a hierarchy of degrees of trust. We shall hence occasionally refer to $\mathfrak{T}$ as the set of *trust levels*. The following figure displays the lattices of trust levels corresponding to the posets of example 2.

Example 3 (Lattices for example 2).

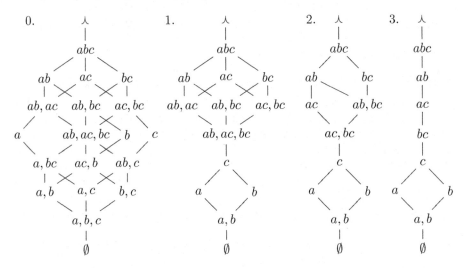

In the lattice $(\mathfrak{T}, \leq)$ $A < B$ intuitively means that B is a level of trustworthiness that is genuinely greater than A. The lattice of trust levels makes *explicit* what the permissible trust attitudes are and how they are related with regard to strength. This can form the basis for choosing, in a given scenario, a *threshold* of trust: a level that is deemed sufficiently trustworthy.

Let $\sqcap$ denote meet and $\sqcup$ denote join. Then $A \sqcup B$ is the weakest trust level that is at least as strong as both A and B; if A and B are not comparable by $\leq$, then it is stronger. $A \sqcap B$ is the strongest trust level that is at least as weak as both A and B. A threshold of trust can be conveniently specified by reference to the source units trusted. Observe that each member of $\acute{\mathfrak{S}}$ is a member of $\mathfrak{T}$. Therefore, any expression using members of $\acute{\mathfrak{S}}$ (i.e., equivalence classes of source units), $\sqcap$ and $\sqcup$ denotes a unique level of trust.

The function of a threshold may also be described in terms of *risk*. If $A < B$, then to choose A as the threshold of trust is to take a greater risk with regard to trusting sources than if B is chosen. Fixing a threshold of trustworthiness amounts to fixing a "limit" of risk, to draw a line between what is trusted, and not trusted, in the non-relative sense of the word. For example, with a threshold at $A \sqcup B$, if A and B are comparable, risk is limited to what follows from commitment to the more reliable of the two; if incomparable, then to the greatest degree of risk that represents comparably less risk than both A and B. To say that $A \sqcap B$ lies above the risk limit means that A and B are both considered reliable (i.e., that all source units in both A and B provide only true information).

Example 4 (Threshold for example 3). Say that we adopt the attitude to "trust all that ab and ac deliver, as long as it is confirmed by bc" as a threshold. This attitude is expressible as $([ab] \sqcap [ac]) \sqcup [bc]$. Given relations 0, 1, and 2, the attitude amounts to trusting only what a, b, and c agree on, because $(ab \sqcap ac) \sqcup bc = (ab, ac) \sqcup bc = abc$. With the stronger relation 3, it denotes the level ab.

2.4   A Tree of *Fallbacks* for Broken Trust

The core of a default conception of trust in information sources is the default rule (3) to accept what you are told, as long as it does not contradict what you have already accepted. We presently interpret this rule with respect to relative trustworthiness. Let us consider a trusting subject that has only permissible trust attitudes. In the non-relative sense of trust, $\curlywedge$ is always trusted, and a level X is trusted, on condition that every $Y \geq X$ is also trusted, by default.

Now, if trusting the source units at level X is incompatible with trusting the units at a superior level Y, trust at X is blocked; X is not trustable. This will obtain whenever information provided by the source units at X is inconsistent either with antecedent knowledge, or with information accepted at a superior level. The significance of of trusting at X should in such a case be identified with trusting some superior, trustable level; call this the *fallback* of X. The fallback, as the value of a blocked default, is the key notion that allows us to view relative trust as a default attitude.

Let X be an element of $\mathfrak{T}$ different from $\curlywedge$, and let Γ be the $\leq$-cover of X. Given that Γ is singleton, we straightforwardly identify $\bigcup \Gamma$ as the appropriate fallback of X. Where not, note that by construction of the lattice, X is a level composed of a set of simpler levels, the members of Γ. That trust is broken at X means at least one of these levels is not trustable. In this case, the fallback of X should be identified as a level with greater trustworthiness than every Y immediately superior to X. Let the fallback $\mathfrak{f}(X)$ of X be defined as

$$\mathfrak{f}(X) = \mathrm{lub}(\Gamma) \text{ in } (\mathfrak{T}, \leq).$$

The fallback function is undefined for $\curlywedge$; otherwise every node has a unique fallback. $\curlywedge$, representing the trust level of antecedent knowledge, is always the fallback of $[\mathfrak{S}]$. Note that every path from the lattice maximum $\curlywedge$ to a trust level X must go through $\mathfrak{f}(X)$, and that $\mathfrak{f}(X)$ is the $\leq$-minimal node with this property.

The *fallback tree* $(\mathfrak{T}, \prec)$ is defined as the weakest relation such that for all $X \in \mathfrak{T}$, $\mathfrak{f}(X) \prec X$. It is easy to show that the fallback tree is indeed a tree with root $\curlywedge$. The following figure illustrates fallback trees to match the lattices of example 3.

Example 5 (Fallback trees for example 3).

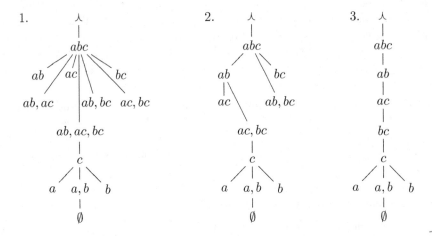

3   Trust in Terms of Defaults

The aim of this section is to implement the default approach to the information trust model based on a function i which assigns propositional content to each source in $\mathfrak{S}$. The basic assignment of information to sources is a mapping from members of $\mathfrak{S}$ to expressions in a formal language. In section 3.1 we use the simple language of propositional logic to this end. Besides the basic assignment we must also specify information processing operations corresponding to the constructions of source units and trust attitudes.

The default interpretation of fallback trees is then encoded into the logic $Æ_T$. Encoding fallback trees in $Æ_T$ will allow us to give precise answers to questions such as, "which trustworthiness levels support a belief in a proposition ϕ?", and "is ϕ entailed by the beliefs of a given degree of trustworthiness?". $Æ_T$ is a natural choice as representation language for default inferences; in particular it allows a simple representation of ordered supernormal defaults theories. There is a natural encoding of prescriptively ordered default logic into $Æ_T$ [3], and the encoding of supernormal defaults exploits this encoding. Contrary to the language of Reiter-style default logic $Æ_T$ has a natural extension to multi-agent languages

However, there is no intrinsic reason for restricting the co-domain of the assignment function to a language of propositional logic; one can easily conceive of using more complex languages for this purpose. Section 3.4 explores possibilities for using multi-agent languages. The encoding of the fallback tree is in this case a straightforward application of the technique to multi-modal $Æ_T$.

3.1   Agreement and Consolidation

Basically the information interpretation of the trust model assigns formal expressions to each source in $\mathfrak{S}$. The assignment function i must be extended to source units (sets of sources) and trust attitudes (sets of source units). To implement this we identify the corresponding operations of *agreement* and *consolidation* of information content. Identifying these operations is one of the key factors in the default interpretation of the trust theory.

In propositional logic these operations will be implemented simply by means of disjunctions and conjunctions. Let us denote the informational content of a source a in $\mathfrak{S}$ by i_a, which is a formula of propositional logic. Intuitively, the information i_x provided by a source unit is defined to be the strongest proposition that every member of the unit supports – the strongest that the members all agree on. If $x = \{a_1, \ldots, a_n\}$, $a_i \in \mathfrak{S}$, then $i_x = i_{a_1} \vee \cdots \vee i_{a_n}$. The value of $i_{\emptyset}$, on the common understanding of 0-ary disjunctions, will be assumed to be the propositional falsity constant $\perp$. The empty set hence gives a contribution which is always unacceptable.

We define the *consolidated* informational contribution of $x_1, \ldots, x_n \subseteq \mathfrak{S}$ as $i_X = i_{x_1} \wedge \cdots \wedge i_{x_n}$, where $X = \{x_1, \ldots, x_n\}$. That is, we define the informational contribution of a set of source units as the strongest consequence that would follow from taking each unit as a source of evidence. Observe in particular that $i_{\{\emptyset\}}$ will always be $\perp$ since $\perp$ is always one of its conjuncts. By convention i_λ is $\top$.

3.2   Intermezzo: The Logic $\mathcal{Æ}_\top$

$\mathcal{Æ}_\top$ is an "Only knowing" logic, generalizing the pioneering system of Levesque [7] with language constructs for the representation of various degrees of confidence for a doxastic subject.

The object language of $\mathcal{Æ}_\top$ extends the language of propositional logic by the addition of modal operators: $\square$ (necessity) and modalities B_k (belief) and C_k (co-belief) for each k in a finite index set I. The index set represents the distinct degrees of confidence and comes along with a partial order which gives the indices relative strength. $b_k\varphi$ is defined as $\neg B_k \neg \varphi$ and denotes that φ is compatible with belief at degree of confidence k.

A formula φ is *completely modalized* if every occurrence of a propositional letter occurs within the scope of a modal operator and *purely Boolean* if it contains no occurrences of modal operators. The "all I know at k" expression $O_k\varphi$ abbreviates $B_k\varphi \wedge C_k\neg\varphi$, meaning that *precisely* φ is believed with degree of confidence k. A formula of the form $\bigwedge_{k \in I} O_k\varphi_k$ is called an O_I-*block*. If each φ_k is purely Boolean, the O_I-block is said to be *prime*.

$\mathcal{Æ}_\top$ is a special instance of the system $\mathcal{Æ}_\rho$ introduced in [8] and further analyzed and motivated in [12]; the references contain in particular an axiomatization, a formal semantics and proofs of soundness, completeness and the finite model property. A particularly strong property of $\mathcal{Æ}_\top$ is the Modal Reduction Theorem: for each O_I-block φ^I and for some $m \geq 0$, there are prime O_I-blocks $\psi_1^I, \ldots, \psi_m^I$ such that $\vdash \varphi^I \equiv (\psi_1^I \vee \cdots \vee \psi_m^I)$.[2]

---

[2] In the sequel $\vdash$ denotes the provability relation of $\mathcal{Æ}_\top$ (which extends the provability relation of classical logic).

A prime O_I-block determines the belief state of the agent in a unique and transparent way; if such a formula is satisfiable, it has essentially only one model. A non-prime O_I-block only implicitly defines the belief state and has in general a number of different models. The Modal Reduction Theorem relates an implicit belief representation to an explicit representation by a provable equivalence. It is is Σ_2^p-hard to determine whether $m > 0$ in the statement of the theorem.

If there is only one degree of confidence, $Æ_T$ is equivalent to Levesque's system of only knowing, for which there is a direct correspondence between a stable expansion in autoepistemic logic and a prime formula $O\varphi$. A prime O_I-block is a natural generalization of the notion of stable expansion to a hierarchical collection of expansions.

3.3   Encoding the Fallback Tree as Defaults in $Æ_T$

We now describe how to use a fallback tree to extract information, both between contributions of the sources, which may be more or less mutually compatible, and between these contributions and a set of antecedently given information.

To facilitate the discussion let us say that a fallback tree is *information labelled* if each node X in the tree is labelled with i_X. The labels express the information contribution attached to the trust level X.

We will assume that a *knowledge base*, denoted κ, is given with unconditional trustworthiness. Informally, say that (precisely) κ, a formula of propositional logic, is believed with full conviction. The notion of trustworthiness is directly relevant to the notions of confidence and belief, as is clear by the simple observation that information stemming from highly trustworthy sets of sources will be considered reliable with a greater degree of confidence than that which is provided by less trustworthy sources. Following the default interpretation formulated in principle (3), we can define a simple procedure which reveals what information may reliably be said to be supported at each level of trustworthiness. Define the following formula by induction over the fallback tree.

$$\beta_\lambda = \kappa$$

$$\beta_X = \begin{cases} \beta_{f(X)} \wedge i_X & \text{if } \beta_{f(X)} \wedge i_X \text{ is PL-consistent,} \\ \beta_{f(X)} & \text{otherwise.} \end{cases}$$

Then β_X denotes what a rational agent should believe at a degree of confidence corresponding to the trust attitude X.

The modal logic $Æ_T$ is suitable for the representation of fallback trees and the associated default principle. In the encoding we use the set of trust levels $\mathfrak{T}$ as the index set which individuates modalities in the language of $Æ_T$. Let $(\mathfrak{T}, \prec)$ be the fallback tree and $\prec^*$ be the reflexive, transitive closure of $\prec$. For $X \in \mathfrak{T}$ we define

$$\delta_X = b_X i_X \supset i_X.$$

Note that δ_X is equivalent to $\neg i_X \supset B_X \neg i_X$, i.e., should φ be false, the subject will believe that it is. We will refer formulae of this form as *default conditionals* when they occur within a modal O-context, since the conditional then has the force of formalizing the property corresponding to the statement "the proposition i_X holds by default".

The default interpretation of the default structure is formalized by the following encoding:

$$[\![\mathfrak{T}, \prec, \kappa]\!]_{\curlywedge} = O_{\curlywedge}\kappa$$

$$[\![\mathfrak{T}, \prec, \kappa]\!]_X = O_X(\kappa \wedge \bigwedge_{Y \prec^* X} \delta_Y)$$

$$[\![\mathfrak{T}, \prec, \kappa]\!] = \bigwedge_{X \in \mathfrak{T}}[\![\mathfrak{T}, \prec, \kappa]\!]_X$$

The encoding is structurally similar to the encoding of ordered default theories into Æ_T in [3].

Theorem 1. $\vdash [\![\mathfrak{T}, \prec, \kappa]\!] \equiv \bigwedge_{X \in \mathfrak{T}} O_X \beta_X$.

Proof. The proof uses simple properties from the model theory of Æ_T, cf. [12]. In an Æ_T model M all points agree on the truth value of every completely modalized formula. We will hence use the notation $M \models \varphi$ whenever a completely modalized φ is satisfied at some point in M. We use the following two facts in the proof. Let M satisfy $O_X \varphi$ for an index X.

1. If M satisfies $O_X \psi$, then $\varphi \equiv \psi$ is true at every point in M.
2. If φ and ψ are purely Boolean, M satisfies $b_X \psi$ iff $\varphi \not\vdash \neg\psi$.

We show, by induction on X, the more general result that for any $Z \in \mathfrak{T}$

$$\vdash \bigwedge_{X \prec^* Z}[\![\mathfrak{T}, \prec, \kappa]\!]_X \equiv \bigwedge_{X \prec^* Z} O_X \beta_X \ .$$

Note that the base case is trivial since X in this case is $\curlywedge$. For the induction step, it is sufficient to show that $M \models [\![\mathfrak{T}, \prec, \kappa]\!]_X \equiv O_X \beta_X$ for any Æ_T-model satisfying both $[\![\mathfrak{T}, \prec, \kappa]\!]_{f(X)}$ and $O_{f(X)}\beta_{f(X)}$. By fact 1, every such model M satisfies

$$M \models (\kappa \wedge \bigwedge_{Y \prec^* f(X)} \delta_Y) \equiv \beta_{f(X)}$$

and hence trivially

$$M \models (\kappa \wedge \bigwedge_{Y \prec^* X} \delta_Y) \equiv (\beta_{f(X)} \wedge \delta_X) \ .$$

Thus $M \models [\![\mathfrak{T}, \prec, \kappa]\!]_X \equiv O_X(\beta_{f(X)} \wedge \delta_X)$. It only remains to show

$$M \models O_X(\beta_{f(X)} \wedge (b_X i_X \supset i_X)) \equiv O_X \beta_X \ .$$

But since $M \models O_{f(X)}\beta_{f(X)}$, it follows directly from the definition of β_X and fact 2 that $M \models b_X i_X$ iff $\beta_{f(X)} \not\vdash \neg i_X$, and we are done. ☐

The theorem shows that the encoding of a node X and its information content can be reduced to the $O_{\mathfrak{T}}$-block $\bigwedge_{X \in \mathfrak{T}} O_X \beta_X$ within the logic itself, where at each node X in the tree the formula β_X is the proposition that the rational agent will entertain at this level of trust.

Example 6 (Example 5, with information). The witnesses a, b, and c are interviewed for their accounts of the accident scenario. We assign content to propositional variables as follows: p = The green car was veering; q = There was a cat in the road; r = The red car was veering; s = The red car was speeding. The following figure records the witnesses' statements (left), and the resulting post-evaluation propositions at each trust level decorate the fallback tree (3.).[3]

$a \; : \; q \wedge (r \vee s)$

$b \; : \; p \wedge \neg q$

$c \; : \; p \wedge r$

3. $\curlywedge \; : p \vee r$
    $|$
$abc \; : (p \vee r) \wedge (q \wedge (r \vee s) \vee p \wedge (\neg q \vee r))$
    $|$
$ab \; : (p \vee r) \wedge (q \wedge (r \vee s) \vee p \wedge \neg q)$
    $|$
$ac \; : (p \vee r) \wedge (q \wedge s \vee (q \vee p) \wedge r)$
    $|$
$bc \; : p \wedge r$
    $|$
$c \; : p \wedge r$

$p \wedge r \wedge q : a \quad\quad\quad b \; : p \wedge r \wedge \neg q$

$a, b \; : p \wedge r \, [\perp]$
    $|$
$\emptyset \; : p \wedge r \, [\perp]$

For nodes a, b and $\emptyset$, the value $\perp$ is displayed in brackets to emphasize that the information contribution of these nodes is inconsistent with information provided at more trustworthy levels. These nodes will then take values from the consistent fallback node c, i.e., $p \wedge r$. Note that even though a and b may not both be fully trusted, choosing either of them is consistent. Also note that the proposition s, which figures as a disjunct in a's account, is eliminated from the node bc onwards.

3.4   From Information Sources to Doxastic Agents

There is no intrinsic reason to use the language of propositional logic to represent the information delivered by sources. This section addresses the use of multi-modal languages for this purpose. The expressive power of such languages is needed in cases where the sources deliver information about agents; typically, about what the agents believe. To generalize the approach of section 3.3 we need to extend the language of $Æ_T$ such that it extends the information representation language.

The logic $Æ_T$ has been extended to a multi-modal language. An interesting proof-theoretical property of this extension of $Æ_T$ is that it has a sequent calculus formulation which admits constructive cut-elimination and hence cut-free proofs; this is proved in [11] for a multi-agent language in which the beliefs of

---

[3] Formulae computed using *The Logics Workbench*, http://www.lwb.unibe.ch/.

each subject are represented relative to different degrees of confidence. A Kripke semantics for the logic has been presented in [13].[4]

Let us assume that the modalities in the multi-agent language is defined by a collection $I_0, \ldots, I_m$ of index sets, one for each agent. The indices in each index set are partially ordered, while two indices in different index sets are unrelated.

The notion of an O_I-block transfers to the multi-modal language: An O_{I_j}-block is a formula $\bigwedge_{k \in I_j} O_k \varphi_k$. If each formula φ_k is I_j-objective, i.e. all occurrences of a I_j-modality occurs within the scope of a modality which belongs to another agent, the O_{I_j}-block is prime. An O_I-block can now be defined as a conjunction of O_{I_j}-blocks, one for each agent. Given these concepts the Modal Reduction Theorem transfers to the multi-modal logic.

Let us first assume that the sources deliver information about the beliefs of agents $\alpha_1, \ldots, \alpha_m$ without being agents themselves, i.e. they do not deliver information about other sources, or about themselves, or about the observer who collects the information. Assume also that the beliefs of these agents are represented in the multi-modal system $K45_m$, i.e., a sub-language of multi-modal $\text{Æ}_\top$, so that the i function now delivers $K45_m$ formulae.

The index sets for the multi-modal $\text{Æ}_\top$-representation are $\mathfrak{T}, \{\alpha_1\}, \ldots, \{\alpha_m\}$. We will use the same simple functions for agreement and consolidation as introduced for propositional logic in section 3.1, and since the two facts of $\text{Æ}_\top$-models which we use in the proof of Theorem 1 can be lifted to models of multi-modal $\text{Æ}_\top$, the multi-modal generalization of Theorem 1 is straightforward. The two following examples illustrate some simple properties that we can express within this framework.

Example 7 (Modal information). A simple case in which sources provide formulae in a modal language. Let the trustworthiness relation be given as in example 1, relation 3. Let the knowledge base be empty, and assign information to sources as below (left). The fallback tree shows the outcome of evaluation (right). Here, trusting what a and b agree on (source unit ab) implies accepting that agent 1 has a full belief regarding p. Trusting both sources (node a, b) implies accepting that 1 is inconsistent.

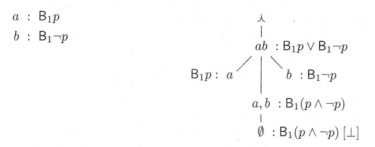

---

[4] The semantics has been given for a multi-agent language without confidence levels. An extension to the language addressed in this section is straightforward.

Example 8 (Modal information II). Trusting both a and b implies accepting that agent 2 is ignorant about the truth value of p if agent 1 believes p.

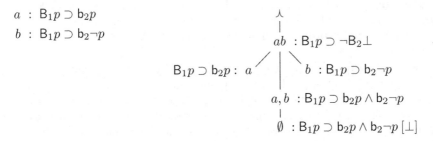

a : $\mathsf{B}_1 p \supset \mathsf{b}_2 p$

b : $\mathsf{B}_1 p \supset \mathsf{b}_2 \neg p$

λ

ab : $\mathsf{B}_1 p \supset \neg \mathsf{B}_2 \bot$

$\mathsf{B}_1 p \supset \mathsf{b}_2 p$: a b : $\mathsf{B}_1 p \supset \mathsf{b}_2 \neg p$

a, b : $\mathsf{B}_1 p \supset \mathsf{b}_2 p \wedge \mathsf{b}_2 \neg p$

$\emptyset$: $\mathsf{B}_1 p \supset \mathsf{b}_2 p \wedge \mathsf{b}_2 \neg p \, [\bot]$

If the information sources are themselves agents, the same representation scheme can clearly be used as long as we do not take the information supplied by an agent as an expression of what that agent believes.

It is, however, in many cases natural to take an a report of agent a that φ precisely as evidence for $\mathsf{B}_a \varphi$, in which case we have to modify the structure of the representation. Basically, we now want to include the formula $\mathsf{B}_a \varphi$ in the representation (one solution is to add this to the knowledge base κ), and still infer a belief that φ by default at the trust level at hand (as we do in the two examples above). However, the situation is now more subtle since forms of Moore's paradox (i.e., "φ, but I do not believe it!") can arise while the fallback tree is processed. It is not clear what the appropriate analyses of these situations amount to. Interestingly, the agreement function will in these cases give rise to a kind of group belief, while consolidation gives rise to a kind of distributed belief (see e.g. [4]).

We plan to address this subtle and interesting application domain in a follow-up paper, along with an analyses of how one can make use of the full expressive power of multi-modal Æ_T to specify very complex formulae delivered by each agent.

4 Related Work

The present account of trustworthiness generalizes and clarifies the approach introduced by John Cantwell [1, 2]. Our approach improves on Cantwell's by making a clear separation between the notion of trustworthiness on the one hand, and information and belief on the other, which allows for the notion of trustworthiness level to be separated from a given model. Furthermore, the present theory gives informative results for various weak kinds of trustworthiness relations that yield vacuous output on Cantwell's approach. (Cantwell incorporates his theory of trustworthiness into a theory of *belief revision*. This is an application that we have not gone into.)

In this paper, no attempt has been made to give an account of the basic, non-relative notion of trust; for this, we refer to Jones [5]. We have however shown that a generalization of the present theory is possible, in [6], where the relative trustworthiness structures are reinterpreted to fit Jones' general analysis of trust. This complements the present paper by demonstrating that the relational framework is applicable to any type of trust, within the scope of Jones' theory.

We believe there are several areas in which the theory we have presented can be applied as a framework for trust in information sources. Consider two examples: A security protocol may employ the concept of trust levels, to assess input from multiple sources in authentication procedures, as well as for managing trust thresholds in response to threats. A query tool for the Semantic Web could use the method of fallbacks to consolidate information from a variety of complementary databases, and to track relative reliability of query results. Each such application of a relative-trust perspective will have different requirements with regard to representation languages. It is also likely that domain-specific, efficient algorithms for evaluating outcomes at trust levels can be found. One major issue we have not discussed is the proper construction of a trust relation; however, it is clear that the relevant parameters will vary widely with the application at hand. (A minimal account of relation revision is given in [6].) We hope this theory provides a suitable starting point for domain-specific investigations of relative trustworthiness.

Bibliography

[1] John Cantwell. Resolving conflicting information. *Journal of Logic, Language, and Information*, 7:191–220, 1998.

[2] John Cantwell. *Non-Linear Belief Revision*. Doctoral dissertation, Uppsala University, Uppsala, 2000.

[3] Iselin Engan, Tore Langholm, Espen H. Lian, and Arild Waaler. Default reasoning with preference within only knowing logic. In *Proceedings of LPNMR'05*, volume 3662 of *Lecture Notes in Artificial Intelligence*, 2005.

[4] Ronald Fagin, Joseph Y. Halpern, Yoram Moses, and Moshe Y. Vardi. *Reasoning about Knowledge*. MIT Press, Cambridge, Mass., 1995.

[5] Andrew J. I. Jones. On the concept of trust. *Decision Support Systems*, 33:225–232, 2002.

[6] Johan W. Klüwer and Arild Waaler. Relative trustworthiness. In *Proceedings of FAST 2005*, volume 3866 of *Lecture Notes in Computer Science*, pages 158–170, 2006.

[7] Hector J. Levesque. All I know: A study in autoepistemic logic. *Artificial Intelligence*, 42:263–309, 1990.

[8] E. H. Lian, T. Langholm, and A Waaler. Only knowing with confidence levels: Reductions and complexity. In J. J. Alferes and J. Leite, editors, *Proceedings of JELIA'04*, volume 3225 of *Lecture Notes in Artificial Intelligence*, pages 500–512, 2004.

[9] K. Segerberg. *Some modal reduction theorems in autoepistemic logic*. Uppsala Prints and Preprints in Philosophy. Uppsala University, 1995.

[10] Arild Waaler. *Logical Studies in Complementary Weak S5*. Doctoral thesis, University of Oslo, 1994.

[11] Arild Waaler. Consistency proofs for systems of multi-agent only knowing. *Advances in Modal Logic*, 5:347–366, 2005.

[12] Arild Waaler, Johan W. Klüwer, Tore Langholm, and Espen H. Lian. Only knowing with degrees of confidence. *Journal of Applied Logic*, 2006. To appear.

[13] Arild Waaler and Bjørnar Solhaug. Semantics for multi-agent only knowing (extended abstract). In R. van der Meyden, editor, *Proceedings of TARK X*, ACM Digital Library, pages 109–125, 2005.

Decision Procedure for a Fragment of Mutual Belief Logic with Quantified Agent Variables

Regimantas Pliuškevičius and Aida Pliuškevičienė

Institute of Mathematics and Informatics,
Akademijos 4, Vilnius 08663, Lithuania
{regis, aida}@ktl.mii.lt

Abstract. A deduction-based decision procedure is presented for a fragment of mutual belief logic with quantified agent variables ($MBQL$). The language of $MBQL$ contains belief, everybody believes and mutual belief modalities, variables and constants for agents. The language of $MBQL$ is convenient to describe the properties of rational agents when the number of agents is not known in advance. On the other hand, even if the exact number of agents is known, a language with quantified agent variables allows us to use more compact expressions. For the $MBQL$ a sequent calculus MBQ^* with invertible (in some sense) rules is proposed. The presented decision procedure is realized by means of the calculus MBQ^* that allows us to simplify a procedure of loop-check sharply. For a fragment of $MBQL$ (without positive occurrences of mutual belief modality), the loop-check-free sequent calculus is proposed. To this end, special rules for belief and everybody believes modalities (introducing marked modalities and indices) and special sequents serving as a termination criterion for non-derivability are introduced. For sequents containing positive occurrences of mutual belief modality sequents of special shape are used to specialize a loop-check and to find non-logical (loop-type) axioms.

1 Introduction

Mutual belief (common knowledge) logics are multi-modal logics extended with mutual belief (common knowledge) and everybody believes (everybody knows) modalities. Sequent-like calculi (with an analytic cut rule instead of loop-type axioms) and Hilbert-style calculi for propositional common knowledge logics (based on a finite set of agents) are constructed in several works (see, e.g., [1], [4], [14]). In [7], the Hilbert-style calculus for the common knowledge logic with an infinite set of agents is presented. This calculus involves some restrictions on cardinality of the set of agents and contains rather a complex axiom for an everybody knows operator. A propositional Hilbert-type calculus for the mutual belief logic (based on a finite set of agents) is constructed in several works (see, e.g., [2]).

Propositional agent-based logics are often insufficient for more complex real world situations. First-order extensions of these logics are necessary whenever the cardinality of an application domain and/or the number of agents are not known in advance. On the other hand, even if the exact number of agents is known, we get more compact expressions using quantified agent variables. In [19], it is described a rich logic

F. Toni and P. Torroni (Eds.): CLIMA VI, LNAI 3900, pp. 112–128, 2006.

$LORA$ (Logic of Rational Agents), based on a three-sorted first-order logic (containing variables for agents, actions, and other individuals), a multi-agent BDI logic, and a dynamic logic. In [13], a logic QLB (quantified logic for belief) with the Barcan axiom containing variables for agents and other individuals is presented. The same idea as in [13] and [19], namely, *use of term as an agent*, is utilized in term-modal logics [5]. The variables for agents are used to define the notions of alternating belief and mutual belief [20]. In [16], a decision procedure for a fragment of temporal logic of belief and actions with restricted occurrences of quantified agent and action variables is presented.

In this paper, a fragment of mutual belief logic with quantified agent variables ($MBQL$) is considered. Unlike [5], [13], and [19], the language of $MBQL$ does not contain function symbols. The aim of this paper is to present a deduction-based decision procedure for $MBQL$. For the $MBQL$ a sequent calculus MBQ with invertible (in some sense) rules is proposed. The invertibility property is very significant because it allows us to preserve a derivability backward applying the rules. The calculus MBQ^* contains so called separation and splitting rules. The separation rules incorporate "bad" quantifier rules for agent variables, the rules for everybody believes modality, as well as rules for belief modalities. Some deduction tools similar to the separation rules are used informally in [15] for the propositional (single agent) BDI logic. The splitting rule is used to separate belief, everybody believes, and mutual belief modalities in a succedent of a special shape sequent. The splitting rule and some of separation rules are not invertible in the usual sense but they are existentially invertible. In contrast to the usual deterministic invertibility, the existential invertibility is non-deterministic. Despite this non-determinism, we get a possibility to preserve derivability when constructing derivations. The decision procedure for a subset of $MBQL$ (without positive occurrences of mutual belief modality) is an important point of the decision procedure presented. For this fragment of $MBQL$, a loop-check-free sequent calculus is proposed. This calculus corresponds to the contraction-free sequent calculus. However, the loop-check-free type sequent calculus *differs* from a contraction-free sequent calculus. In the contraction-free sequent calculus (see [3], [9]) the duplication of the main formula in the premise of any rule is *eliminated at all*. In the loop-check-free sequent calculus there are rules with the duplication of the main formula in the premise of a rule, but backward applications of the rules that can induce loops are *restricted*. It allows us to eliminate loop-check and does not require to translate sequents to a certain normal form as in [9]. Special rules for belief and everybody believes modalities and special sequents serving as a termination criterion for non-derivability are introduced. These special rules introduce marked modalities and indices allowing us to terminate backward applications of these rules. These tools enable us to use sequents *without histories* employed in several works (e.g., [8]). Constructing derivations of the sequents containing positive occurrences of mutual belief modality, sequents of special shape are used to specialize a loop-check and to find non-logical (loop-type) axioms. Special weakening rules are backward applied *implicitly* (together with other rules). Backward application of special weakening rules works as special contraction rules. These rules play the essential role in terminating the procedure proposed.

A procedural approach of decidable logical calculi is used here and we assume that the notions of a decidable calculus and a deduction-based decision procedure are identical.

The paper is organized as follows. In Section 2, the language and semantics of the $MBQL$ are presented. In Section 3, auxiliary tools for the presented decision procedure are described. In Section 4, a decision algorithm based on the sequent calculus MBQ^* is presented, and examples demonstrating the algorithm presented are given. In Section 5, a foundation of the decision algorithm is presented.

2   Language and Semantics of $MBQL$

The $MBQL$ consists of the multi-modal logic $KD45_n$ (doxastic logic or weak-$S5_n$), extended with restricted occurrences of quantifiers for agent variables, and a logic containing mutual belief and everybody believes modalities [2].

The *language* of $MBQL$ contains: (1) a set of propositional symbols $P, P_1, \ldots, Q,$ $Q_1, \ldots$; (2) a set of agent constants $i, i_1, \ldots, a_1, \ldots, b_1, \ldots$ $(i, i_j, a_k, b_l \in \{1, 2, \ldots\})$; (3) a set of agent variables $x, x_1, \ldots, y, y_1, \ldots$; (4) a set of belief modality of the shape $\mathbf{B}(t)$, where t is an agent term, i.e., an agent constant or an agent variable; everybody believes modality $\mathbf{EB}$; mutual belief modality $\mathbf{MB}$; (5) logical operators: $\supset, \wedge, \vee, \neg,$ $\forall, \exists$.

The *formula* of $MBQL$ is defined inductively as follows: every propositional symbol is a formula; if A, B are formulas, then $A \supset B, A \wedge B, A \vee B, \neg A$ are formulas; if i is an agent constant, A is a formula, then $\mathbf{B}(i)A$ is a formula; if x is an agent variable, A is a formula, $Q \in \{\forall, \exists\}$, then $Qx\,\mathbf{B}(x)A$ is a formula; if A is a formula, then $\mathbf{EB}A$ and $\mathbf{MB}A$ are formulas. The formula A is a *logical* one if A contains only logical operators and propositional symbols.

As it follows from the definition of a formula, we do not consider, for example, expressions of the shape $\forall x \exists y\,\mathbf{B}(x)\,\mathbf{B}(y)A$, while the expressions of the shape $\forall x\,\mathbf{B}(x)\exists$ $y\,\mathbf{B}(y)A$ are considered.

When the formula under consideration contains occurrences of operators $\mathbf{EB}$ and/or $\mathbf{MB}$, it is assumed that the number of agents is *finite*. In this case, the formula $\forall x\,\mathbf{B}(x)A$ means informally the same as the formula $\bigwedge_{i=1}^{n}\mathbf{B}(i)A$, and the formula $\exists x\,\mathbf{B}(x)A$ – as the formula $\bigvee_{i=1}^{n}\mathbf{B}(i)A$, where n is the number of agents. Since, in general, the exact number of agents is not known *in advance*, it is convenient to use formulas with quantified agent variables. On the other hand, even if the exact number of agents is known, a language with quantified agent variables allows us to use more compact expressions. Such expressions are used in [13], [19], [20].

The formula $\mathbf{B}(i)A$ means "agent i believes A". Formal semantics of the formula $\mathbf{B}(i)A$ satisfies the semantics of the logic $KD45_n$ (see, e.g., [14]). The formula $\mathbf{EB}A$ means "every agent believes A", i.e., $\mathbf{EB}A \equiv \bigwedge_{i=1}^{n}\mathbf{B}(i)A$, where n is the number of agents. The formula $\mathbf{MB}A$ means "A is mutual belief of all agents". Therefore we use only the so-called *public* mutual belief modality and assume that there is *perfect communication* between agents. For simplicity we consider only one group of agents. The formula $\mathbf{MB}A$ has the same meaning as the infinite formula $\bigwedge_{k\geq 1}\mathbf{EB}^k A$, where $\mathbf{EB}^1 A = \mathbf{EB}A$, and $\mathbf{EB}^k A = \mathbf{EB}^{k-1}\mathbf{EB}A$, if $k > 1$. Infinitary nature of the modality **MB** is explained in [19]. The modality **MB** behaves as that of logic $KD4$. In addition, this modality along with the modality **EB** satisfies the following powerful properties:

  EB$A \wedge$ **MB**$(A \supset$ **EB**$A) \supset$ **MB**A (induction);
  MB$A \equiv$ **EB**$A \wedge$ **EB** **MB**A (fixed point).

All belief modalities can be nested. For example, the formula $\mathbf{B}(i_1)\,\mathbf{B}(i_2)P$, where P is a proposition "John is a good programmer", means "agent i_1 believes that agent i_2 believes that John is a good programmer". The formula $\exists x\,\mathbf{B}(x)\forall y\,\mathbf{B}(y)P$, where P means the same as above, means "some agent believes that each agent believes that John is a good programmer".

To define the formal semantics of the formula $Qx\,\mathbf{B}(x)A$ ($Q \in \{\forall, \exists\}$) we must present an interpretation of agent variables. This interpretation is obtained by means of an assignment: $V \to D$ (agent assignment), where V is a set of agent variables, D is a domain of agent constants. The model M is a pair $< \mathcal{I}, \mathbf{a} >$, where $\mathbf{a}$ is an agent assignment, $\mathcal{I}$ is a tuple $< D, St, \pi, \mathbf{R} >$, where D is a domain of agent constants; St is a set of states; π is an interpretation function of the propositional variables; $\mathbf{R}$ are the accessibility relations. All these relations satisfy transitive, serial, and Euclidean properties (e.g., [14]).

The concept "formula A is valid in $M = < \mathcal{I}, \mathbf{a} >$ at the state $s \in St$" (in symbols $M, s \models A$) is defined by induction on the structure of the formula of $MBQL$. Let us define only the cases where A is $Qx\,\mathbf{B}(x)N$ ($Q \in \{\forall, \exists\}$). Other cases are defined in the usual way (see, e.g., [2], [4], [14], [19]).

$M, s \models \forall x\,\mathbf{B}(x)N$ if and only if for every agent assignment $\mathbf{a}'$ which differs from $\mathbf{a}$ at most with respect to the agent constant i, $< \mathcal{I}, \mathbf{a}' > \models \mathbf{B}(i)N$;

$M, s \models \exists x\,\mathbf{B}(x)N$ if and only if for some agent assignment $\mathbf{a}'$ which differs from $\mathbf{a}$ at most with respect to the agent constant i, $< \mathcal{I}, \mathbf{a}' > \models \mathbf{B}(i)N$.

Along with formulas we consider *sequents*, i.e., formal expressions $A_1, \ldots, A_k \to B_1, \ldots, B_m$, where $A_1, \ldots, A_k$ ($B_1, \ldots, B_m$) is a multiset of formulas. A sequent is interpreted as the formula $\bigwedge_{i=1}^{k} A_i \supset \bigvee_{j=1}^{m} B_j$. The sequent S is a *logical* one if S contains only logical formulas.

Recall the notions of positive and negative occurrences.

A formula (or some symbol) occurs *positively* in some formula B if it appears within the scope of no negation sign or in the scope of an even number of the negation sign, once all the occurrences of $A \supset C$ have been replaced by $\neg A \vee C$; in the opposite case, the formula (symbol) occurs *negatively* in B. For a sequent $A_1, \ldots, A_k \to B_1, \ldots, B_m$ positive and negative occurrences are determined just like for the formula $\bigwedge_{i=1}^{k} A_i \supset \bigvee_{j=1}^{m} B_j$.

3   Some Auxiliary Tools of the Decision Algorithm

The decision procedure presented here is based on the sequent calculus with invertible (in some sense, see Section 5) rules. All derivations are constructed as backward derivations. In this section, we present the main auxiliary tools of the decision algorithm: logical calculus, reduction, separation and splitting rules, and special weakening rules.

Let (j) be any rule of a sequent calculus. The rule (j) is applied to get the conclusion of (j) from the premises of (j). If the rule (j) is backward applied, i.e., to get
premises of (j) from the conclusion of (j) we have a "bottom-up application of (j)"
instead of "application of (j)". The rule (j) is called *invertible* in the sequent calculus I, if the derivability in I of the conclusion of (j) implies the derivability in I of
each premise of (j). If all rules of the calculus I are invertible, then, constructing the
backward derivation of a derivable sequent, in each step bottom-up applying the rule
we get premises which are derivable, i.e., bottom-up application of any invertible rule
preserves a derivability (see, e.g., [10]).

The decidable *calculus Log* is defined by the axiom: $\Gamma, A \rightarrow \Delta, A$ (where A is
the main formula of the axiom) and traditional invertible rules for logical operators
$\supset, \vee, \wedge, \neg$ (see, e.g., [10]).

A derivation in the calculus *Log* is constructed as a tree using bottom-up applications of the rules. The derivation V is *successful*, if each leaf of V is an axiom, and
unsuccessful, if there exists a leaf which is not an axiom.

Let us define reduction rules by means of which a sequent is reduced to a set of
sequents in some canonical forms (see below).

Reduction rules consist of the following rules:

– Logical rules: all the rules of the calculus *Log* and the following rules:

$$\frac{\Gamma \rightarrow \Delta, \mathbf{B}(c)A}{\Gamma \rightarrow \Delta, \forall x\, \mathbf{B}(x)A} \ (\rightarrow \forall) \qquad \frac{\mathbf{B}(c)A, \Gamma \rightarrow \Delta}{\exists x\, \mathbf{B}(x)A, \Gamma \rightarrow \Delta} \ (\exists \rightarrow),$$

where the variable x is an agent variable and the agent constant c (called an eigen-
constant) does not enter the conclusion of the rules.

– Modal rules:

$$\frac{\Gamma \overset{c}{\rightarrow} \Delta, \mathbf{EB}A; \ \Gamma \rightarrow \Delta, \mathbf{EB\,MB}A}{\Gamma \rightarrow \Delta, \mathbf{MB}A} \ (\rightarrow \mathbf{MB}),$$

where the letter c over $\rightarrow$ in a sequent means that a sequent is a *critical* one and
it will be used to define non-logical axioms (see next section). If the conclusion of
an application of the rule (i), where $(i) \neq (\rightarrow \mathbf{MB})$, is a critical sequent, then the
premises of this application are also critical ones, i.e., they are of the shape $\Gamma \overset{c}{\rightarrow} \Delta$.
In the rule $(\rightarrow \mathbf{MB})$, the left premise is a critical sequent, while the right premise
is not a critical sequent.

$$\frac{\mathbf{EB}A, \mathbf{EB\,MB}A, \Gamma \rightarrow \Delta}{\mathbf{MB}A, \Gamma \rightarrow \Delta} \ (\mathbf{MB} \rightarrow).$$

$$\frac{\Gamma \rightarrow \Delta, \bigwedge_{i=1}^{n} \mathbf{B}(i)A}{\Gamma \rightarrow \Delta, \mathbf{EB}A} \ (\rightarrow \mathbf{EB}) \qquad \frac{\bigwedge_{i=1}^{n} \mathbf{B}(i)A, \Gamma \rightarrow \Delta}{\mathbf{EB}A, \Gamma \rightarrow \Delta} \ (\mathbf{EB} \rightarrow),$$

where n is the number of agents.

To define separation rules and the splitting rule, some canonical forms of sequents
are introduced.

The sequent S is *a primary* sequent, if S is of the following shape:
$$\Sigma_1, \forall \mathcal{B}\Gamma, \mathbf{EB}\Pi_1, \mathbf{MB}\Theta_1 \rightarrow \Sigma_2, \exists \mathcal{B}\Delta, \mathbf{EB}\Pi_2, \mathbf{MB}\Theta_2, \text{ where}$$

- for every i ($i \in \{1, 2\}$) Σ_i is empty or consists of logical formulas;
- $\forall \mathcal{B}\Gamma$ denotes a list $\forall x\, \mathbf{B}(x)\Gamma_0$, $\mathcal{B}\tilde{\Gamma}$, where $\forall x\, \mathbf{B}(x)\Gamma_0$ is empty or consists of formulas of the shape $\forall x_j\, \mathbf{B}(x_j)M_j$, $j \in \{1, 2, \ldots\}$; $\mathcal{B}\tilde{\Gamma}$ denotes a list $\mathbf{B}(1)\Gamma_1, \ldots,$ $\mathbf{B}(n)\Gamma_n$, where n is the number of agents and $\mathbf{B}(l)\Gamma_l$ ($1 \leq l \leq n$) is *empty* or consists of formulas of the shape $\mathbf{B}(l)C$;
- $\exists \mathcal{B}\Delta$ denotes a list $\exists x\, \mathbf{B}(x)\Delta_0$, $\mathcal{B}\tilde{\Delta}$, where $\exists x\, \mathbf{B}(x)\Delta_0$ is empty or consists of formulas of the shape $\exists x_j\, \mathbf{B}(x_j)N_j$, $j \in \{1, 2, \ldots\}$; $\mathcal{B}\tilde{\Delta}$ denotes a list $\mathbf{B}(1)\Delta_1, \ldots,$ $\mathbf{B}(n)\Delta_n$, where n is the number of agents and $\mathbf{B}(r)\Delta_r$ ($1 \leq r \leq n$) is *empty* or consists of formulas of the shape $\mathbf{B}(r)D$;
- for every i ($i \in \{1, 2\}$) $\mathbf{EB}\Pi_i$ ($\mathbf{MB}\Theta_i$) is empty or consists of formulas of the shape $\mathbf{EB}A$ ($\mathbf{MB}A$, correspondingly).

A primary sequent S is a $\mathbf{B}$-*reduced primary* one, if S is of the following shape $\Sigma_1, \forall \mathcal{B}\Gamma \rightarrow \Sigma_2, \exists \mathcal{B}\Delta$, where Γ, Δ may contain modalities $\mathbf{MB}$, $\mathbf{EB}$.

By definition of a primary sequent, it follows that each member M of the primary sequent S is either a logical formula, or has the shape γA, where $\gamma \in \{Qx\, \mathbf{B}(x^\circ),\ \mathbf{MB},\ \mathbf{EB}\}$, $Qx \in \{\varnothing, \forall x, \exists x\}$, $x^\circ = i$ (i is an agent constant), if $Qx = \varnothing$, and $x^\circ = x$, if $Qx \neq \varnothing$ (in this case, $Q = \forall$, if M is in antecedent of S and $Q = \exists$, if M is in succedent of S). By definition of the $\mathbf{B}$-reduced primary sequent, it follows that the $\mathbf{B}$-reduced primary sequent S contains the same members as the primary sequent except for members of the shape γA, where $\gamma \in \{\mathbf{MB},\ \mathbf{EB}\}$.

For example, let S' be a sequent $P, \forall x\, \mathbf{B}(x)A,\ \mathbf{B}(2)P,\ \mathbf{B}(5)Q \rightarrow \mathbf{MB}Q, \exists x\, \mathbf{B}(x)$ $\mathbf{MB}Q,\ \mathbf{B}(1)P$ and S^* be a sequent $P, \forall x\, \mathbf{B}(x)A \wedge \mathbf{B}(2)P,\ \mathbf{B}(5)Q \rightarrow \mathbf{MB}Q \vee \exists x\, \mathbf{B}(x)\,\mathbf{MB}Q \vee \mathbf{B}(1)P$, where $A = \mathbf{EB}P \supset \mathbf{MB}Q$. Then S' is a primary sequent but S^* is not a primary one. However, bottom-up applying logical rules ($\wedge \rightarrow$) and ($\rightarrow \vee$), we get S' from S^*.

In general, it is easy to see that, bottom-up applying logical rules, *each sequent* can be reduced to a *set of primary sequents*. In turn, a *primary sequent* can be reduced to a *set of* $\mathbf{B}$-*reduced primary sequents*.

For example, in order to reduce the primary sequent S', considered just now, to a set of $\mathbf{B}$-reduced primary sequents, let us bottom-up apply the reduction rule ($\rightarrow \mathbf{MB}$) to S'. Then we get two primary sequents: $S_1 = P, \forall x\, \mathbf{B}(x)A,\ \mathbf{B}(2)P,\ \mathbf{B}(5)Q \xrightarrow{c} \mathbf{EB}Q, \exists x\, \mathbf{B}(x)\,\mathbf{MB}Q,\ \mathbf{B}(1)P$ and $S_2 = P, \forall x\, \mathbf{B}(x)A,\ \mathbf{B}(2)P,\ \mathbf{B}(5)Q \rightarrow \mathbf{EB}\,\mathbf{MB}Q,$ $\exists x\, \mathbf{B}(x)\,\mathbf{MB}Q,\ \mathbf{B}(1)P$. Let a set $\{1, 2, 3, 4, 5\}$ be a set of agent constants, then bottom-up applying the reduction rules ($\rightarrow \mathbf{EB}$), ($\rightarrow \wedge$) from S_1 we get five $\mathbf{B}$-reduced primary sequents of the shape: $S_{1i} = P, \forall x\, \mathbf{B}(x)A,\ \mathbf{B}(2)P,\ \mathbf{B}(5)Q \xrightarrow{c} \mathbf{B}(i)Q, \exists x\, \mathbf{B}(x)\,\mathbf{MB}Q,\ \mathbf{B}(1)P$, where $i \in \{1, 2, 3, 4, 5\}$. Analogously, from S_2 we get five $\mathbf{B}$-reduced primary sequents of the shape: $S_{2i} = P, \forall x\, \mathbf{B}(x)A,\ \mathbf{B}(2)P,\ \mathbf{B}(5)Q \rightarrow \mathbf{B}(i)\,\mathbf{MB}Q, \exists x\, \mathbf{B}(x)\,\mathbf{MB}Q,\ \mathbf{B}(1)P$. In general, bottom-up applying modal reduction rules and logical reduction rules ($\rightarrow \wedge$) and ($\wedge \rightarrow$), *each primary sequent* can be reduced to a *set of* $\mathbf{B}$-*reduced primary sequents*. Therefore a $\mathbf{B}$-reduced primary sequent is a general canonical form of an arbitrary sequent of $MBQL$.

Using the notation from the definition of a primary sequent, let us introduce the following specific canonical forms. These forms are helpful because they allow us to decrease the space of derivation and to find non-logical axioms (see next section).

The primary sequent S is a **B**-*primary* one, if S is of the following shape:

$$\Sigma_1, \forall \mathcal{B}\Gamma, \text{EB}\Pi_1, \text{MB}\Theta_1 \rightarrow \Sigma_2, \exists \mathcal{B}\Delta.$$

From the shape of the **B**-primary sequent it is easy to see that, bottom-up applying non-branching reduction rules (**MB** $\rightarrow$), (**EB** $\rightarrow$), *each* **B**-*primary sequent* can be reduced to a **B**-reduced primary sequent.

The primary sequent S is an **EB**-*primary* one, if S is of the following shape:

$$\Sigma_1, \forall \mathcal{B}\Gamma, \text{EB}\Pi_1, \text{MB}\Theta_1 \rightarrow \Sigma_2, \text{EB}A.$$

The primary sequent S is an **MB**-*primary* one, if S is of the following shape:

$$\Sigma_1, \forall \mathcal{B}\Gamma, \text{EB}\Pi_1, \text{MB}\Theta_1 \rightarrow \Sigma_2, \text{MB}A.$$

The primary sequent S is a *non-splittable primary* one, if S is either a **B**-primary or an **EB**-primary or an **MB**-primary sequent. Otherwise, the primary sequent S is a *splittable primary* one.

The primary sequent S is an **EB**-*reduced primary* one, if S is of the following shape $\Sigma_1, \forall x\, \mathbf{B}(x)\Gamma_0, \text{EB}\Pi_1, \text{MB}\Theta_1 \rightarrow \Sigma_2, \text{EB}A$. Otherwise, the sequent S is not an **EB**-reduced primary one. The **EB**-reduced primary sequent is a special case of the **EB**-primary sequent which allows us to bottom-up apply the separation rule (SR_1) (see below).

To specify loop-check in $MBQL$ let us introduce indices and marked modalities. The marked modalities are used in the separation rules for modalities $\mathbf{B}(t)$ and **EB**. The *marked modalities* have the shape Υ^* ($\Upsilon^* \in \{ \mathbf{B}^*(t), \text{EB}^*, \text{MB}^* \}$). The marked modalities are defined as follows: $A^* = A$, where A is a logical formula; $(A \odot B)^* = A^* \odot B^*$, where $\odot \in \{\wedge, \vee, \supset\}$; $(\neg A)^* = \neg A^*$; $(\Upsilon A)^* = \Upsilon^* A^*$ and $\Upsilon^{**} = \Upsilon^*$, where $\Upsilon \in \{ \mathbf{B}(t), \text{EB}, \text{MB} \}$. The notation $\Upsilon^* \Pi$ means $(\Upsilon A_1)^*, \ldots, (\Upsilon A_n)^*$, where $n \geq 1$ and $\Upsilon \Pi$ is a sequence of formulas $\Upsilon A_1, \ldots, \Upsilon A_n$.

Along with the marked modalities, we use *indexed formulas*. These formulas are of the following shape $\exists x^\circ \, \mathbf{B}^k(x^\circ)A$, where $k \in \{0, \ldots, m\}$, $\exists x^\circ \in \{\varnothing, \exists x\}$ and $x^\circ = i$ if $\exists x^\circ = \varnothing$. At the very beginning, a formula has no index and the index k is treated as zero. Only *positive occurrences* of formulas of the shape $\exists x^\circ \, \mathbf{B}(x^\circ)A$ in the succedent of a sequent may contain indices. The index k denotes the number of bottom-up applications of the separation rule (SR_2) to belief modality with the same main formula. The marked modalities and indices allow us to use sequents *without histories* employed in several works (e.g., [8]).

The primary sequent S is a **B**-*saturated* one, if $S = \Sigma_1, \forall \mathcal{B}^*\Gamma, \text{EB}^*\Pi_1, \text{MB}^*\Theta_1 \rightarrow \Sigma_2, \exists \mathcal{B}^l\Delta$, where $\exists \mathcal{B}^l\Delta$ denotes a list $\exists x\, \mathbf{B}(x)\Delta_0, \mathcal{B}\tilde{\Delta}$ (see definition of a primary sequent) and $Log \nvdash \Sigma_1 \rightarrow \Sigma_2$. Otherwise, S is not a **B**-saturated sequent. **B**-saturated sequents will be used as a *termination criterion for non-derivability*.

The primary sequent S is an **EB**-*saturated* one, if $S = \Sigma_1, \forall \mathcal{B}^*\Gamma, \text{EB}^*\Pi_1, \text{MB}^*\Theta_1 \rightarrow \Sigma_2, \text{EB}^*A$, where $Log \nvdash \Sigma_1 \rightarrow \Sigma_2$. Otherwise, S is not an **EB**-saturated sequent. **EB**-saturated sequents will be used as a *stopping device* for bottom-up *application of the separation rule* (SR_1) (see below).

Let us introduce a separation rule for the everybody believes modality **EB**. *The conclusion* of this separation rule is an **EB**-*reduced primary sequent* S such that $Log \nvdash \Sigma_1 \rightarrow \Sigma_2$ and S is not an **EB**-saturated sequent.

Separation rule (SR_1) for everybody believes modality EB:

$$\frac{\forall x\, \mathbf{B}^*(x)\Gamma_0, \Gamma_0, \Pi_1^*, \Theta_1, \mathbf{MB}^*\Theta_1 \to A^\circ}{\Sigma_1, \forall x\, \mathbf{B}(x)\Gamma_0, \mathbf{EB}\Pi_1, \mathbf{MB}\Theta_1 \to \Sigma_2, \mathbf{EB}A^\circ} (SR_1),$$

where $\mathbf{EB}A^\circ$ is either empty or a formula $\mathbf{EB}A$; if $\mathbf{EB}A^\circ$ is empty, then A° is empty, otherwise $A^\circ = A$.

Remark 1. *(a) Let S be an* **EB**-*primary sequent* $\mathbf{B}(1)P \to \mathbf{EB}P$. *This sequent is not an* **EB**-*reduced primary one. Therefore we cannot apply the rule (SR_1) to S. A modified rule (SR_1), when $\forall x\, \mathbf{B}(x)\Gamma_0$ is replaced by $\forall \mathcal{B}\Gamma$, can be applied to S. It is obvious that S is invalid. Bottom-up applying the modified rule (SR_1) to S, we get a valid sequent $\mathbf{B}^*(1)P, P \to P$. Thus, the restriction that the separation rule (SR_1) can be applied only to an* **EB**-*reduced primary sequent but not to any* **EB**-*primary sequent, is essential.*

(b) Bottom-up applications of (SR_1) to an **EB**-*saturated primary sequent can induce loops. Therefore if an* **EB**-*saturated sequent S is obtained, then S is reduced to a set of* **B**-*reduced primary sequents and the rules (SR_2) and (SR_3) (see below) are bottom-up applied to these sequents.*

Let us introduce two separation rules for the belief modality $\mathbf{B}(t)$ denoted as (SR_2) and (SR_3). *The conclusion* of these separation rules is a **B**-*reduced primary sequent S* such that $Log \nvdash \Sigma_1 \to \Sigma_2$ and S is not a **B**-saturated sequent.

Separation rule (SR_2) for belief modality $\mathbf{B}(t)$:

$$\frac{\Theta_1^*, \Gamma_0, \mathbf{B}^*(l)\Gamma_l, \Gamma_l \to \Theta_2, \mathbf{B}(r)\Delta_r, \exists x^\circ\, \mathbf{B}^{k+1}(x^\circ)M, M}{\Sigma_1, \forall \mathcal{B}\Gamma \to \Sigma_2, \exists \mathcal{B}\Delta, \exists x^\circ\, \mathbf{B}^k(x^\circ)M} (SR_2),$$

where $\forall \mathcal{B}\Gamma, \exists \mathcal{B}\Delta$ are determined in the definition of a primary sequent; Θ_1 means $\forall x\, \mathbf{B}(x)\Gamma_0$ and Θ_2 means $\exists x\, \mathbf{B}(x)\Delta_0$; $\exists x^\circ \in \{\varnothing, \exists x\}$ and it is assumed that $\exists x^\circ\, \mathbf{B}^{*k}(x^\circ)M = \exists x^\circ\, \mathbf{B}^k(x^\circ)M$. The formula $\exists x^\circ\, \mathbf{B}^k(x^\circ)M$ is the *main formula* of (SR_2).

To define the values of the agent constants l and r let us consider two cases.

(1) $\exists x^\circ = \varnothing$, then $x^\circ = i$ and $\exists x^\circ\, \mathbf{B}^k(x^\circ)M$ is of the shape $\mathbf{B}^k(i)M$. In this case, $l = r = i$, i.e., $\mathbf{B}(l)\Gamma_l$, and $\mathbf{B}(r)\Delta_r$ consist of formulas of the shape $\mathbf{B}(i)D$.

(2) $\exists x^\circ = \exists x$. In this case, the pairs consisting of $\mathbf{B}^*(l)\Gamma_l$ $(1 \leq l \leq n)$ and $\mathbf{B}(r)\Delta_r$ $(1 \leq r \leq n)$, where $l = r$, must be reset, i.e., all possible values of agent constants must be tested.

The separation rule (SR_2) corresponds to transitivity and Euclidean properties of belief modality.

Separation rule (SR_3) for belief modality $\mathbf{B}(t)$:

$$\frac{\Theta_1^*, \Gamma_0, \mathbf{B}^*(l)\Gamma_l, \Gamma_l \to}{\Sigma_1, \forall \mathcal{B}\Gamma \to \Sigma_2, \exists \mathcal{B}\Delta} (SR_3),$$

where $\forall \mathcal{B}\Gamma, \exists \mathcal{B}\Delta$, and Θ_1 are the same as in the rule (SR_2). Applying the rule (SR_3) all the possible values of the agent constant l must be tested.

The rule (SR_3) corresponds to the serial property of belief modality.

It should be noted that the rule (SR_3) is a special case of the rule (SR_2) where $\exists \mathcal{B}\Delta$ is empty, or all the formulas from $\exists \mathcal{B}\Delta$ are not essential.

Splitting rule:

$$\frac{S_1 \quad \text{or} \quad S_2 \quad \text{or} \quad S_3}{\Sigma_1, \forall \mathcal{B}\Gamma, \mathbf{EB}\Pi_1, \mathbf{MB}\Theta_1 \ \rightarrow \ \Sigma_2, \exists \mathcal{B}\Delta, \mathbf{EB}\Pi_2, \mathbf{MB}\Theta_2} \ (Sp),$$

where the conclusion of the rule is a splittable primary sequent S such that the logical part $\Sigma_1 \rightarrow \Sigma_2$ of S is not derivable in the calculus Log; S_1 is a **B**-primary sequent of the shape $\Sigma_1, \forall \mathcal{B}\Gamma, \mathbf{EB}\Pi_1, \mathbf{MB}\Theta_1 \rightarrow \Sigma_2, \exists \mathcal{B}\Delta$; S_2 is an **EB**-primary sequent of the shape $\Sigma_1, \forall \mathcal{B}\Gamma, \mathbf{EB}\Pi_1, \mathbf{MB}\Theta_1 \rightarrow \Sigma_2, \mathbf{EB}A$, where $\mathbf{EB}A$ is a formula from $\mathbf{EB}\Pi_2$; S_3 is an **MB**-primary sequent of the shape $\Sigma_1, \forall \mathcal{B}\Gamma, \mathbf{EB}\Pi_1, \mathbf{MB}\Theta_1 \rightarrow \Sigma_2, \mathbf{MB}A$, where $\mathbf{MB}A$ is a formula from $\mathbf{MB}\Theta_2$.

Remark 2. *In the succedent of the premises S_2 and S_3 of the splitting rule (Sp) we choose only one modalized formula (however we must test all possible modalized formulas). Whereas in the succedent of the premise S_1 all formulas from $\exists \mathcal{B}\Delta$ must be left. Indeed, it is easy to see, for example, that a **B**-primary sequent $\mathbf{B}(1)(\mathbf{B}(1)P_1 \vee \mathbf{B}(1)P_2) \rightarrow \mathbf{B}(1)P_1, \mathbf{B}(1)P_2$ is valid, but the sequent $S_j = \mathbf{B}(1)(\mathbf{B}(1)P_1 \vee \mathbf{B}(1)P_2) \rightarrow \mathbf{B}(1)P_j$ $(j \in \{1,2\})$ is invalid.*

Special weakening rules:

$$\frac{\Gamma \rightarrow \Delta, A}{\Gamma \rightarrow \Delta, A, A_1} \ (\rightarrow W) \qquad \frac{A, \Gamma \rightarrow \Delta}{A, A_1, \Gamma \rightarrow \Delta} \ (W \rightarrow),$$

$$\frac{\Gamma \rightarrow \Delta, \mathbf{\Upsilon}_1^* A}{\Gamma \rightarrow \Delta, \mathbf{\Upsilon}_1^* A, \mathbf{\Upsilon}_1 A_1} \ (\rightarrow W^*) \qquad \frac{\forall x^\circ \mathbf{\Upsilon}^* A, \Gamma \rightarrow \Delta}{\forall x^\circ \mathbf{\Upsilon}^* A, \forall x^\circ \mathbf{\Upsilon} A_1, \Gamma \rightarrow \Delta} \ (W^* \rightarrow),$$

$$\frac{\Gamma \rightarrow \Delta, \exists x^\circ \mathbf{B}^k(x^\circ)A}{\Gamma \rightarrow \Delta, \exists x^\circ \mathbf{B}^k(x^\circ)A, \exists x^\circ \mathbf{B}^+(x^\circ)A_1} \ (\rightarrow W^k) \quad (+ \in \{\varnothing, *\}),$$

where A and A_1 are coincidental or congruent [12], $\mathbf{\Upsilon}_1 \in \{\mathbf{EB}, \mathbf{MB}\}$, $\mathbf{\Upsilon} \in \{\mathbf{B}(t), \mathbf{EB}, \mathbf{MB}\}$, $\forall x^\circ \in \{\varnothing, \forall x\}$, $\exists x^\circ \in \{\varnothing, \exists x\}$.

Remark 3. *(a) The separation rules (SR_i) $(i \in \{2,3\})$ incorporate the quantifier rules for agent variables, the traditional structural rules of weakening, and the rule of Shwarts for a single belief modality [17] (see also [15]).*

(b) A bottom-up application of the separation rule (SR_1) can be replaced by bottom-up applications of the reduction rules $(\rightarrow \mathbf{EB})$, $(\mathbf{EB} \rightarrow)$, separation rules (SR_2), (SR_3), and traditional weakening rules. However, the rule (SR_1) is convenient because it allows us to shorten derivations.

4   Description of the Decision Algorithm

The decision algorithm for an arbitrary sequent is realized by means of a calculus MBQ for a considered fragment of the mutual belief logic. The *calculus MBQ* is obtained from the calculus Log adding the separation rules (SR_l) $(1 \leq l \leq 3)$, reduction rules, special weakening rules, the splitting rule (Sp), and non-logical axioms (defined below). When constructing derivations in the calculus MBQ, *termination criteria* are used for *derivability* and *non-derivability*. Along with non-derivability of logical sequents in Log, **B**-saturated sequents (defined in the previous section) serve as special sequents determining the *termination criterion for non-derivability*.

Let us describe the *termination criterion for derivability*. As indicated in Section 2, the modality **MB** satisfies the induction axiom, i.e., a deductive principle involving the periodicity property. This fact necessitates a departure from ordinary Gentzen-like calculi. The logical axiom $\Gamma, A \rightarrow \Delta, A$ of the calculus Log (described in the previous section) is a traditional *termination criterion for derivability*. But it is not sufficient for an arbitrary sequent containing positive occurrences of the modality **MB**. For such sequents, non-logical axioms are introduced as another *termination criterion for derivability* of sequents. To this end, inspection of sequents other than a logical axiom in a leaf of derivation is required. This inspection always terminates because nothing essentially new can be generated in constructing derivations (it will be shown later and is demonstrated in Example 3). Such a situation is a common phenomenon for other temporal and agent-like logics with induction-type axioms. For the first time this idea was realized in [6], [18] for a propositional linear temporal logic.

Let us introduce some notions to define non-logical axioms.

First we define parametrically identical formulas and sequents. Namely, formulas A and A' are *parametrically identical* ones (in symbols $A \approx A'$) if either $A = A'$, or A and A' are congruent (see, e.g., [12]), or differ only by respective occurrences of eigen-constants of the rules $(\rightarrow \forall)$, $(\exists \rightarrow)$; moreover, the occurrences of modality Υ and marked modality Υ^* ($\Upsilon \in \{ \mathbf{B}(t), \mathbf{EB}, \mathbf{MB} \}$), as well as $\mathbf{B}^j(t)$ and $\mathbf{B}^k(t)$, are treated as coincidental.

Sequents $S = A_1, \ldots, A_k \rightarrow A_{k+1}, \ldots, A_{k+m}$ and $S' = A'_1, \ldots, A'_k \rightarrow A'_{k+1}, \ldots,$ A'_{k+m} are *parametrically identical* (in symbols $S \approx S'$), if for all j $(1 \leq j \leq k + m)$ formulas A_j and A'_j are parametrically identical ones.

A sequent $S = \Gamma \rightarrow \Delta$ *subsumes* a sequent $S' = \Pi, \Gamma' \rightarrow \Delta', \Theta$ (in symbols $S \succeq S'$) if $\Gamma \rightarrow \Delta \approx \Gamma' \rightarrow \Delta'$ (in a special case, $S = S'$). We always can test this relation automatically. The sequent S' is *subsumed* by S.

Let V be a derivation in the calculus MBQ and i be a branch in V. A primary sequent S' from the branch i is a *non-logical axiom* if, in the branch i below S', there exists an **MB**-primary sequent S such that $S \succeq S'$ and the sequent S' is not a critical one (a critical sequent was defined in the previous section). Therefore a non-logical axiom is a primary sequent of the shape $\Gamma \rightarrow \Delta, \mathbf{MB}A$ provided that this sequent is not a critical one.

The introduction of non-logical axioms means employment of loop-check in a specific way. From the shape of the rules of MBQ it follows that nothing new can be obtained when constructing an ordered derivation of a sequent. From this fact we get that the non-logical axioms are constructed in a *finite* way.

If there *exists* a derivation V of the sequent S such that a leaf of *each* branch i of V is an axiom (either logical or non-logical), then $MBQ \vdash S$ (termination criterion for derivability). In this case, the derivation V is *successful*.

If in *all* possible derivations V_k of the sequent S there *exists* a branch having a sequent which is either non-derivable in Log or a **B**-saturated one, then $MBQ \nvdash S$ (termination criterion for non-derivability). In this case, the derivation V is *unsuccessful*.

In the next section, it will be justified, that for any sequent the process of construction of a derivation proceeds automatically and always terminates.

To justify the termination of a derivation, it is convenient to modify the rule (SR_2) adding the following restriction: if $k > 0$ then $\exists \mathcal{B}\Delta$ is empty or consists of indexed formulas. If the succedent of the conclusion of this rule contains an indexed formula $\exists x^\circ \mathbf{B}^k(x^\circ)M$ ($k > 0$) and a non-indexed formula $\exists y^\circ \mathbf{B}(y^\circ)A$ then the main formula of this rule is the latter. As well as in the rule (SR_2), the conclusion of a modified rule must be the **B**-reduced primary sequent S such that $Log \nvdash \Sigma_1 \to \Sigma_2$ and S is not a **B**-saturated sequent. This rule, denoted as (SR_2^*), is justified in the next section. MBQ^* is a calculus obtained from the calculus MBQ replacing the rule (SR_2) by the rule (SR_2^*).

In the next section, it is shown that all the rules of the calculus MBQ^*, except for the separation rules (SR_2^*), (SR_3) and the splitting rule, are invertible. The separation rules (SR_2^*), (SR_3) and the splitting rule are *existentially invertible* (see Lemma 4). The existential invertibility of the mentioned rules means that repeating applications of these rules are necessary, in general, and a backtracking is used. The invertibility, existential invertibility and termination of backward applications of the rules of the calculus MBQ^* are crucial in the presented decision algorithm.

The decision algorithm is realized by constructing an *ordered derivation* in the calculus MBQ^*. An ordered derivation consists of several levels. Each level contains six main parts.

1. Let S be an arbitrary sequent. Then S is reduced to a set of primary sequents S_i bottom-up applying logical reduction rules. This process terminates because (a) bottom-up application of each logical reduction rule (j) eliminates the main logical symbol from the main formula of the rule and (b) the complexity of a premise of the rule (j) is less than the complexity of a conclusion of the rule (j).

2. Let the considered primary sequent S_i be such that neither the logical part of S_i is derivable in Log, nor S_i is a non-logical axiom, and S_i is a splittable sequent. Then the rule (Sp) is bottom-up applied to S_i. As a result we get a non-splittable sequent S_{iq} ($q \in \{\mathbf{B}, \mathbf{EB}, \mathbf{MB}\}$). As it follows from the shape of the rule (Sp) this process terminates.

3. Let the considered primary sequent S_i be such that either the logical part of S_i is derivable in Log, or S_i is a non-logical axiom. Then the considered branch of derivation is finished and the process of constructing the ordered derivation of the next sequent is started, i.e., a new level of construction of a derivation begins. If S_i is one of the sequents obtained during the reduction of sequent S to a set of primary sequents S_i (see points 1 and 5) and not all the sequents from this set are tested, then the next sequent is a sequent from the set of primary sequents. Otherwise, the next sequent is chosen using backtracking. The process of determination whether the sequent S_i is an axiom always terminates. In the case of the logical axiom, termination follows from the decidability of the calculus Log. In the case of the

non-logical axiom, termination follows from the fact that the relation $S_j \succeq S_i$ can always be tested automatically.

4. Let the considered primary sequent S_j be an **EB**-reduced primary sequent such that the rule (SR_1) can be applied to S_j. Then the rule (SR_1) is applied and a sequent S' is obtained. The process of constructing the ordered derivation of the obtained sequent S' is started, i.e., a new level of construction of the derivation begins.

5. Let the considered primary sequent S_j be either an **EB**-primary sequent such that the rule (SR_1) cannot be applied to S_j, or a **B**-primary sequent or an **MB**-primary one. Then S_j is reduced to a set of **B**-reduced primary sequents S_{jk} bottom-up applying modal reduction rules. Each sequent S_{jk} is such that $Log \not\vdash \Sigma_1 \to \Sigma_2$, where $\Sigma_1 \to \Sigma_2$ is the logical part of S_{jk}. The case where $Log \vdash \Sigma_1 \to \Sigma_2$ was fixed earlier and considered in point 3.

6. Let us consider the following cases:

   (a) a sequent S_{jk} from the set of **B**-reduced primary sequents is a **B**-saturated sequent. Then a sequent S_j is not derivable. If S_j is obtained as a premise of the rule (Sp), then using backtracking we must test another premise of the application of (Sp), i.e., a new level of construction of the derivation begins. If S_j is one of the sequents obtained during the reduction of sequent S to a set of primary sequents S_i (see point 1), then S is not derivable;

   (b) if the sequent S_{jk} from the set of **B**-reduced primary sequents is such that the separation rules (SR_2^*) and (SR_3) can be applied to S_{jk}, then *all possible* (using backtracking and choosing other values of agent constants and/or the main formula of the rules) bottom-up applications of the rules (SR_2^*) and (SR_3) are realized.

A *calculus* MBQ_1 is obtained from the calculus MBQ^* by removing the reduction rule $(\to \textbf{MB})$ and non-logical axioms. MBQ_1 is a loop-check-free calculus and is applied to sequents without positive occurrences of **MB**.

Let us demonstrate the performance of the described algorithm by examples. In the examples derivations are presented in a linear form. At each step of a derivation the explanation of the step is given in the brackets. For simplicity, in all the examples, presented below, it is assumed that the set $\{1, 2\}$ is a set of agent constants. First, let us construct an ordered derivation in MBQ_1 such that all the branches of the derivation end with a logical axiom.

Example 1. *Let S be an* **EB**-*primary sequent of the shape* $\mathbf{B}(1)P \to \mathbf{EB}(P \vee \neg \mathbf{B}(2)P)$. *The derivation of S is as follows.*

   (1) $\mathbf{B}(1)P \to \mathbf{EB}(P \vee \neg \mathbf{B}(2)P)$ [*considered sequent*]

   (2) $\mathbf{B}(1)P \to \mathbf{B}(1)(P \vee \neg \mathbf{B}(2)P)$ [**B**-*reduced primary sequent obtained from (1) bottom-up applying* $(\to \textbf{EB})$, $(\to \wedge)$]

   (3) $\mathbf{B}(1)P \to \mathbf{B}(2)(P \vee \neg \mathbf{B}(2)P)$ [**B**-*reduced primary sequent obtained from (1) bottom-up applying* $(\to \textbf{EB})$, $(\to \wedge)$]

   (4) $\mathbf{B}^*(1)P, P, \mathbf{B}(2)P \to \mathbf{B}^1(1)(P \vee \neg \mathbf{B}(2)P), P$ [*logical axiom obtained from (2) bottom-up applying* (SR_2^*), $(\to \vee)$, $(\to \neg)$]

   (5) $\mathbf{B}(2)P \to \mathbf{B}^1(2)(P \vee \neg \mathbf{B}(2)P), P$ [*from (3) bottom-up applying* (SR_2^*), $(\to \vee)$, $(\to \neg)$]

(6) $\mathbf{B}^*(2)P, P \to \mathbf{B}^2(2)(P \vee \neg \mathbf{B}(2)P), P$ [*logical axiom obtained from (5) bottom-up applying* (SR_2^*), $(\to \vee)$, $(\to \neg)$ *and the special weakening rule* $(W^* \to)$]

Therefore $MBQ_1 \vdash S$.

Let us demonstrate termination criterion for non-derivability in MBQ_1.

Example 2. *(a) Let S be an* **EB**-*reduced primary sequent of the shape* $\mathbf{EB}P \to$ **EB EB**P. *This sequent expresses the transitivity property for the modality* **EB**. *The derivation of S is as follows.*

(1) $\mathbf{EB}P \to \mathbf{EB}\,\mathbf{EB}P$ [*considered sequent*]

(2) $P \to \mathbf{EB}P$ [*from (1) bottom-up applying* (SR_1)]

(3) $\to P$ [*from (2) bottom-up applying* (SR_1)]

Since Log $\nvdash$ (3) we get $MBQ_1 \nvdash S$. Therefore the transitivity property fails for the modality **EB**.

(b) Let S be a **B**-*reduced primary sequent of the shape* $\to \mathbf{B}(1)A$, *where* $A = P \vee \mathbf{EB} \neg \mathbf{B}(1)P$. *The derivation of S is as follows.*

(1) $\to \mathbf{B}(1)(P \vee \mathbf{EB} \neg \mathbf{B}(1)P)$ [*considered sequent*]

(2) $\to \mathbf{B}^1(1)A, P, \mathbf{EB} \neg \mathbf{B}(1)P$ [*from (1) bottom-up applying* (SR_2^*), $(\to \vee)$; *this sequent is splittable primary sequent*]

(3) $\to \mathbf{B}^1(1)A, P$ [*from (2) bottom-up applying* (Sp) *and choosing the premise S_1; since this sequent is a* **B**-*saturated sequent we cannot bottom-up apply any rule to this sequent; thus $MBQ_1 \nvdash$ (3) and we must backtrack to sequent (2)*]

(4) $\to P, \mathbf{EB} \neg \mathbf{B}(1)P$ [*from (2) bottom-up applying (Sp) and choosing the premise S_2; this sequent is an* **EB**-*reduced primary sequent*]

(5) $\mathbf{B}(1)P \to$ [*from (4) bottom-up applying* (SR_1), $(\to \neg)$]

(6) $\mathbf{B}^*(1)P, P \to$ [*from (5) bottom-up applying* (SR_3)]

Since (6) is a **B**-*saturated sequent we cannot bottom-up apply any rule to this sequent. Therefore $MBQ_1 \nvdash S$.*

Let us construct an ordered derivation in MBQ^* containing non-logical axioms along with logical ones.

Example 3. *Let S be an* **MB**-*primary sequent of the shape* $\mathbf{MB}P \to \mathbf{MB}\,\mathbf{MB}(P \vee Q)$. *The derivation of S is as follows.*

(1) $\mathbf{MB}P \to \mathbf{MB}\,\mathbf{MB}(P \vee Q)$ [*considered sequent; since this sequent is an* **MB**-*primary one it can be used to get a non-logical axiom*]

(2) $\mathbf{EB}P, \mathbf{EB}\,\mathbf{MB}P \overset{c}{\to} \mathbf{EB}\,\mathbf{MB}(P \vee Q)$ [*from (1) bottom-up applying* $(\to \mathbf{MB})$, *and to left branch applying* $(\mathbf{MB} \to)$; *this sequent is an* **EB**-*reduced primary sequent*]

(3) $\mathbf{EB}P, \mathbf{EB}\,\mathbf{MB}P \to \mathbf{EB}\,\mathbf{MB}\,\mathbf{MB}(P \vee Q)$ [*from (1) bottom-up applying* $(\to \mathbf{MB})$, *and to right branch applying* $(\mathbf{MB} \to)$; *this sequent is an* **EB**-*reduced primary sequent*]

(4) $P, \mathbf{MB}P \overset{c}{\to} \mathbf{MB}(P \vee Q)$ [*from (2) bottom-up applying* (SR_1); *since this sequent is an* **MB**-*primary one it can be used to get a non-logical axiom*]

(5) $P, \mathbf{EB}P, \mathbf{EB}\,\mathbf{MB}P \overset{c}{\to} \mathbf{EB}(P \vee Q)$ [*from (4) bottom-up applying* $(\to \mathbf{MB})$, *and to left branch applying* $(\mathbf{MB} \to)$; *this sequent is an* **EB**-*reduced primary sequent*]

(6) $P, \mathbf{MB}^*P \overset{c}{\to} P, Q$ [*from (5) bottom-up applying* (SR_1), $(\to \vee)$; *this sequent is a logical axiom*]

$(7) P, \mathbf{EB} P, \mathbf{EB} \mathbf{MB} P \rightarrow \mathbf{EB} \mathbf{MB}(P \vee Q)$ [*from (4) bottom-up applying* ($\rightarrow$ **MB**), *and to right branch applying* (**MB** $\rightarrow$); *this sequent is an* **EB**-*reduced primary sequent*]

$(8) P, \mathbf{MB}^* P \rightarrow \mathbf{MB}(P \vee Q)$ [*from (7) bottom-up applying* (SR_1); *since this sequent is not a critical one, and in the same branch below there is an* **MB**-*primary sequent (4) such that* $(4) \succeq (8)$, *this sequent is a non-logical axiom; return to (3)*]

$(9) P, \mathbf{MB}^* P \rightarrow \mathbf{MB} \mathbf{MB}(P \vee Q)$ [*from (3) bottom-up applying* (SR_1); *since this sequent is not a critical one and in the same branch below there is an* **MB**-*primary sequent (1) such that* $(1) \succeq (9)$, *this sequent is a non-logical axiom*]

Therefore $MBQ^* \vdash S$.

(b) *Let* S_1 *be a sequent obtained from the sequent S considered in point (a) of this example replacing* $(P \vee Q)$ *by* P. *Analogously as in the previous point we can get* $MBQ^* \vdash S_1$. *Thus the modality* **MB** *(opposite to the modality* **EB**) *satisfies the transitivity property.*

5 Foundation of Presented Decision Procedure

A foundation of presented decision procedure consists of two parts: syntactical and semantical ones. The semantical part includes soundness and completeness of MBQ^*. The syntactical part includes a justification of (1) termination of the procedure, and (2) invertibility and existential invertibility of the rules of the calculus MBQ^*.

5.1 Termination of Presented Decision Procedure

First let us prove that use of the separation rule (SR_2^*) instead of the rule (SR_2) does not change the class of sequents derivable in MBQ.

Let $\Sigma_1, \forall \mathcal{B} \Gamma \rightarrow \Sigma_2, \exists \mathcal{B} \Delta, \exists x^\circ \mathbf{B}^k(x^\circ) M$, where $k > 0$, be the conclusion of bottom-up application of the rule (SR_2) and $\exists x^\circ \mathbf{B}^k(x^\circ) M$ is the main formula of this application. Let $\exists \mathcal{B} \Delta = \exists \mathcal{B} \Delta_1, \exists \mathcal{B} \Delta_2$, where $\exists x \mathcal{B} \Delta_1$ ($\exists x \mathcal{B} \Delta_2$) consists of indexed (non-indexed, correspondingly) formulas of the shape $\exists x^\circ \mathbf{B}(x^\circ) A$. Then $n = |\exists \mathcal{B} \Delta_2|$ (i.e., the number of members of $\exists \mathcal{B} \Delta_2$) is called a non-indexed degree (n-degree, in short) of the considered bottom-up application of the rule (SR_2).

Lemma 1. *If* $MBQ \vdash^V S$ *then* $MBQ^* \vdash S$.

Proof. Let in the derivation V there are l bottom-up application of the rule (SR_2). Let n_i be the n-degree of i-th application of the rule (SR_2). The proof is carried out by induction on N, where $N = max(n_1, \ldots, n_i, \ldots, n_l)$. Let $N = n_i$ and $n_i > 0$. Then let us consider an i-th bottom-up application of (SR_2). This application can be replaced by bottom-up applications of (SR_2) having n-degree less then n_i.

Let us justify the finiteness of bottom-up applications of the rules (SR_2^*) and (SR_3). Let (SR_2^D) $((SR_3^D))$ be the rule obtained from the rule (SR_2^*) $((SR_3)$, correspondingly) dropping the restriction that the conclusion of the rule is not a **B**-saturated sequent, i.e., the conclusion of the rules (SR_i^D) ($i \in \{2, 3\}$) is any reduced primary sequent logical part of which is not derivable in Log.

A bottom-up application of the rule (SR_i^D) ($i \in \{2, 3\}$) is a *degenerate* one if the conclusion of this rule is a **B**-saturated sequent. Let MBQ^D be a calculus obtained from the calculus MBQ^* replacing the rules (SR_2^*) and (SR_3) by the rules (SR_2^D) and (SR_3^D), correspondingly.

Lemma 2. *Let $MBQ^D \vdash^V S$. Then $MBQ^* \vdash^{V^*} S$, where V^* does not contain degenerate applications of the rules (SR_2^D) and (SR_3^D).*

Proof. Proof is carried out using induction on the number $n(V)$ of degenerate bottom-up applications of the rules (SR_2^D) and (SR_3^D) in the derivation V. If $n(V) = 0$ then $V = V^*$. Let $n(V) > 0$. Let us consider the lowest degenerate bottom-up application one of these rules. Let S^* (S^+) be the premise (conclusion, correspondingly) of this lowest degenerate application of (SR_i^D), $i \in \{2, 3\}$. Below this bottom-up degenerate application of the considered rule must be a non-degenerate application of the same rule. Let S^{**} be a premise of this non-degenerate bottom-up application of (SR_i^D). Using special weakening rules, and the fact that S^+ is **B**-saturated sequent we get $S^* \succeq S^{**}$. Using the admissibility of structural rule of weakening in MBQ^D we get derivation of S^{**} without the considered lowest degenerate application of the rule (SR_i^D). So by induction assumption we get derivation V^* in MBQ^*.

Now let us justify the termination criterion for non-derivability by means of **B**-saturated sequents.

Lemma 3. *Let in each possible ordered derivation V_k of a sequent S there exists a branch such that a leaf of this branch is a **B**-saturated sequent S^*. Then $MBQ^* \nvdash S$.*

Proof. Relaying on Lemmas 1, 2 it is impossible to bottom-up apply to a sequent S^* neither the rule (SR_2^*) nor the rule (SR_3). Since logical part of **B**-saturated sequent S^* is not derivable in Log we get $MBQ^* \nvdash S^*$.

From Lemmas 2, 3 it follows that the restrictions on the rules (SR_2^*) and (SR_3) are correct. Therefore the finite number of applications of the separation rules (SR_2^*) and (SR_3) in a derivation is sufficient. According to Remark 3 (b) the finiteness of bottom-up applications of the separation rule (SR_1) follows from the finiteness of bottom-up applications of (SR_2^*) and (SR_3). The finiteness of bottom-up applications of the reduction and special weakening rules as well as the splitting rule follows from the shape of these rules. From these facts termination of the presented decision procedure follows.

5.2 Soundness and Completeness of MBQ^*

To justify semantical part of the presented decision procedure and invertibility of the rules of MBQ^* let us introduce an infinite calculus MBQ_ω.

The calculus MBQ_ω is obtained from MBQ^* by dropping the non-logical axioms and replacing the reduction rule $(\rightarrow \mathbf{MB})$ by infinite reduction rule:

$$\frac{\Gamma \rightarrow \Delta, \mathbf{EB}A; \ldots; \Gamma \rightarrow \Delta, \mathbf{EB}^k A; \ldots}{\Gamma \rightarrow \Delta, \mathbf{MB}A} \ (\rightarrow \mathbf{MB}_\omega),$$

$k \in \{1, \ldots\}$; $\mathbf{EB}^1 A = \mathbf{EB}A$, $\mathbf{EB}^k A = \mathbf{EB}\,\mathbf{EB}^{k-1}A$, $k > 1$.

We can prove an invertibility of the reduction rules (including $(\rightarrow \mathbf{MB}_\omega)$), the separation rule (SR_1), and special weakening rules in calculus MBQ_ω using traditional proof-theoretical methods.

It is easy to see that the separation rules (SR_2^*), (SR_3), and the splitting rule (Sp) are not invertible in the usual sense. However, mentioned rules are *existential invertible*. Namely, using induction on the height of a derivation (see [16]) and invertibility of reduction rules we can prove the following lemma.

Lemma 4 (existential invertibility of rules (SR_2^*), (SR_3), and splitting rule).
(a) Let S be a $\mathbf{B}$-reduced primary sequent and S is not a $\mathbf{B}$-saturated. Let $MBQ_\omega \vdash S$ and $\Sigma_1 \rightarrow \Sigma_2$ be the logical part of S, such that $Log \nvdash \Sigma_1 \rightarrow \Sigma_2$. Then either
  - *there exists a formula $\exists x° \, \mathbf{B}^k(x°)M$ from $\exists \mathcal{B}\Delta$, such that $MBQ_\omega \vdash S_2$, where the sequent S_2 is a premise of the rule (SR_2^*), or*
  - *there exists $l \geq 0$ such that $MBQ_\omega \vdash S_3$, where the sequent S_3 is a premise of the rule (SR_3).*

(b) Let S be a splittable primary sequent, $MBQ_\omega \vdash S$ and $\Sigma_1 \rightarrow \Sigma_2$ is the logical part of S, such that $Log \nvdash \Sigma_1 \rightarrow \Sigma_2$. Then $MBQ_\omega \vdash S_i$, where either $i = 1$, or $i = 2$, or $i = 3$, and S_i is a premise of the splitting rule (Sp).

Using invertibility of the rules of MBQ_ω and Schütte method [11]) (other than in [11], we get more than one reduction tree used in [11]) we can prove

Theorem 1 (soundness and ω-completeness of MBQ_ω). *Let S be a sequent. Then $\forall M \models S$ if and only if $MBQ_\omega \vdash S$. The cut rule is admissible in MBQ_ω.*

From the fact that $MBQ_\omega \vdash \mathbf{MB}A \equiv \mathbf{EB}A \wedge \mathbf{EB}\,\mathbf{MB}A$ and admissibility of cut in MBQ_ω we get that the rule $(\rightarrow \mathbf{MB})$ is admissible and invertible in MBQ_ω. Thus we get the following

Lemma 5. *All reduction rules of MBQ_ω, the separation rule (SR_1), special weakening rules, and the rule $(\rightarrow \mathbf{MB})$ are invertible in MBQ_ω.*

To get an equivalence between calculi MBQ^* and MBQ_ω we introduce invariant calculus $INMBQ$. An *invariant calculus* $INMBQ$ is obtained from MBQ^* replacing the non-logical axioms by the following invariant rule:

$$\frac{\Gamma \rightarrow \Delta, I; \; I \rightarrow \mathbf{EB}(I); \; I \rightarrow \mathbf{EB}A}{\Gamma \rightarrow \Delta, \mathbf{MB}A} \; (\rightarrow \mathbf{MB}_I),$$

where an invariant formula I is constructed automatically (similarly to [16]).
Analogously as in [16] we can prove

$$MBQ^* \vdash S \text{ if and only if } INMBQ \vdash S \text{ if and only if } MBQ_\omega \vdash S \qquad (*).$$

From (*) and Lemmas 4, 5 we get that all reduction rules, the separation rule (SR_1), and special weakening rules are invertible in MBQ^*, while the separation rules (SR_2^*), (SR_3), and splitting rule are existentially invertible in MBQ^*. Therefore the non-logical axioms are constructed not only in finite way, but also in an *automatic* way.

From Theorem 1 and (*) follows that MBQ^* is *sound* and *complete*.

Using these facts, Lemmas 2, 3, we get the following

Theorem 2. *Let S be an arbitrary sequent. Then one can automatically construct a successful or an unsuccessful ordered derivation V of the sequent S in MBQ* such that V always terminates.*

References

1. Alberucci, L., The modal μ-calculus and the logic of common knowledge. *Ph.D. thesis, Institut für Informatic and angewandte mathematik, Universität Bern*, (2002).
2. Aldewereld, H., van der Hoek, W., Meyer, J.J.Ch., Rational teams: logical aspects of multi-agent systems. *Fundamenta Informaticae*, **63**(2-3), (2004), 159 – 183.
3. Dyckhoff, R., Contraction-free sequent calculi for intuitionistic logic, *Journal of Symbolic Logic*, **57**, (1992), 795–807.
4. Fagin, R., Halpern, J.Y., Moses, Y., Vardi, M.Y., *Reasoning about knowledge*, MIT Press, Cambridge, Mass. (1995).
5. Fitting M., Thalmann L., Voronkov A., Term-modal logics. *Studia Logica*, **69**(1), (2001), 133-169.
6. Gough, G.D., Decision procedures for temporal logic. *Master's thesis, Department of Computer Science, Manchester University, Oxford Rd., Manchester, M139PL, UK*, October (1984).
7. Halpern, J.Y., Shore R.A., Reasoning about common knowledge with infinitely many agents. *Information and Computation*, **191** (2004), 1–40.
8. Heuerding A., Seyfried M., Zimmermann H., Efficient loop-check for backward proof search in some non-classical propositional logics. *Lecture Notes in Computer Science*, **1071** (1996), 210–225.
9. Hudelmaier, J., A contraction-free sequent calculus for $S4$, in *Proof Theory for Modal Logic*, H. Wansing, Ed. Kluwer Academic Publishers, Dordrechts, Boston/London (1996), 3–16.
10. Kanger, S. A simplified proof method for elementary logic. *Computer Programming and Formal Systems, Studies in Logic and the Foundations of Mathematics*, North-Holland, (1963), 87-93.
11. Kawai, H., Sequential calculus for a first-order infinitary temporal logic. *Zeitchr. für Math. Logic and Grundlagen der Math.*, **33**, (1987), 423–432.
12. Kleene, S.C., *Introduction to metamathematics*, D.Van Nostrand Company, North-Holland Publishing Co., P. Noordhoff LTD (1952).
13. Lomuscio A., Colombetti M., QLB: A quantified logic for belief. *Lecture Notes in Artificial Intelligence*, **1193**, (1996), 71-85.
14. Meyer, J.J.Ch., van der Hoek, W., *Epistemic Logic for AI and Computer Science*. Cambridge University Press, Cambridge, 1995.
15. Nide, N., Takata, S., Deduction systems for BDI logics using sequent calculus. In *Proc. of AAMAS'02*, (2002), 928–935.
16. Pliuškevičius, R., Pliuškevičienė, A., Decision procedure for a fragment of temporal logic of belief and actions with quantified agent and action variables. *Annals of Mathematics, Computing & Teleinformatics*, **1**(2), (2004), 51–72.
17. Shwarts G.F., Gentzen style systems for $K45$ and $K45D$. *Lecture Notes in Computer Science*, **363**, (1989), 245–256.
18. Wolper P., The tableaux method for temporal logic: an overview. *Logique et Analyse*, **28**, (1985), 119–136.
19. Wooldridge, M., *Reasoning about Rational Agents*. The MIT Press (2000).
20. Wooldridge, M., *An introduction to multiagent systems*. John. Wiley & Sons Ltd., (2002).

Implementing Temporal Logics:
Tools for Execution and Proof

Michael Fisher

Logic and Computation Group,
Department of Computer Science,
University of Liverpool, Liverpool L69, UK
M.Fisher@csc.liv.ac.uk
http://www.csc.liv.ac.uk/~michael

1 Introduction

In this article I will present an overview of a selection of tools for execution and proof based on temporal logic, and outline both the general techniques used and problems encountered in implementing them. This selection is quite subjective, mainly concerning work that has involved researchers I have collaborated with at Liverpool (and, previously, Manchester). The tools considered will mainly be theorem-provers and (logic-based) agent programming languages. Specifically:

- clausal temporal resolution [21, 28] and several of its implementations, namely Clatter [14], TRP++ [42] and TeMP [44], together with its application to verification [35];
- executable temporal logics [24, 4] and its implementation as both METATEM [3] and Concurrent METATEM [22, 49], together with its use as a programming language for both individual agents [23, 26, 29] and multi-agent systems [33, 30, 32].

In addition, I will briefly mention work on induction-based temporal proof [5], temporal logic programming [1], and model checking [7].

Rather than providing detailed algorithms, this presentation will concentrate on general principles, outlining current problems and future possibilities. The aim here is to give the reader an overview of the ways we handle temporal logics. In particular how we use such logics as the basis for both programming and verification.

2 What Is Temporal Logic?

2.1 Some History

Temporal logic was originally developed in order to represent tense in natural language [56]. Within Computer Science, it has achieved a significant role in a number of areas, particularly the formal specification and verification of concurrent and distributed systems [55]. Much of this popularity has been achieved as a number of useful concepts, such as *safety*, *liveness* and *fairness* can be formally, and concisely, specified using temporal logics [20, 52].

F. Toni and P. Torroni (Eds.): CLIMA VI, LNAI 3900, pp. 129–142, 2006.

2.2 Some Intuition

In their simplest form, temporal logics can be seen as extensions of classical logic, incorporating additional operators relating to time. These operators are typically: '$\bigcirc$', meaning "in the next moment in time", '$\square$', meaning "at every future moment", and '$\diamondsuit$', meaning "at some future moment". These additional operators allow us to express statements such as

$$\square(send \ \Rightarrow \ \diamondsuit received)$$

to characterise the statement

> "it is always the case that if we send a message then, at some future moment it *will* be received".

The flexibility of temporal logic allows us to use formulae such as

$$\square(send \ \Rightarrow \ \bigcirc(received \vee \ send))$$

which is meant to characterise

> "it is always the case that, if we send a message then, at the next moment in time, either the message will be received or we will send it again"

and

$$\square(received \ \Rightarrow \ \neg send)$$

meaning

> "it is always the case that if a message is received it cannot be sent again".

Thus, given formulae of the above form then, if we try to send a message, i.e. '*send*', we *should* be able to show that it is *not* the case that the system continually re-sends the message (but it is never received) i.e. the statement

$$\square send \ \wedge \ \square \neg received$$

should be inconsistent.

2.3 Some Applications

The representation of dynamic activity via temporal formalisms is used in a wide variety of areas within Computer Science and Artificial Intelligence, for example Temporal Databases, Program Specification, System Verification, Agent-Based Systems, Robotics, Simulation, Planning, Knowledge Representation, and many more. While I am not able to describe all these aspects here, the interested reader should see, for example, [52, 53, 7, 62, 47]. With respect to multi-agent systems, temporal logics provide the formalism underlying basic dynamic/distributed activity, while this temporal framework is often extended to incorporate rational agent aspects such as beliefs, goals and knowledge [27].

There are many different temporal logics (see, for example [20]). The models of time which underlie these logics can be discrete, dense or interval-based, linear, branching or partial order, finite or infinite, etc. In addition, the logics can have a wide range of operators, such as those related to discrete future-time (e.g: $\bigcirc$, $\Diamond$, $\square$), interval future-time (e.g: $\mathcal{U}$, $\mathcal{W}$), past-time (e.g: $\bullet$ $\blacklozenge$, $\blacksquare$, $\mathcal{S}$, $\mathcal{Z}$), branching future-time (e.g: **A**, **E**), fixed-point generation (e.g: μ, ν) and propositional, quantified propositional or full first-order variations. Even then, such temporal logics are often combined with standard modal logics. For example, typical combinations involve TL + S5 modal logic (often representing 'Knowledge'), or TL + KD45 (Belief) + KD (Desire) + KD (Intention).

Here, I will mainly concentrate on one very popular variety, namely discrete linear temporal logic, which has an underlying model of time isomorphic to the Natural Numbers (i.e. an infinite sequence with distinguished initial point) and is also linear, with each moment in time having at most one successor. (Note that the infinite and linear constraints ensure that each moment in time has *exactly* one successor, hence the use of a single '$\bigcirc$' operator.)

3 Where's the Difficulty?

Temporal Logics tend to be complex. To give some intuition why this is the case, let us look at a few different ways of viewing (initially propositional) temporal logic.

Propositional temporal logic can be thought of as

1. *A specific decidable (PSPACE-complete) fragment of classical first-order logic.*

    For example, the semantics of (discrete, linear) propositional temporal logic can be given by translation to first-order logic as follows. Here, we interpret a temporal formula at a moment in time (indexed by i), and encode this index as an argument to the first-order formula. For simplicity, we consider just propositional symbols, such as p. Then, the question of whether the formula p is satisfied at moment i in a temporal model is translated to the question of whether $p(i)$ is satisfied in a classical first-order logic model:

    $$i \models_{TL} p \quad \rightarrow \quad \models p(i)$$
    $$i \models_{TL} \bigcirc p \quad \rightarrow \quad \models p(i+1)$$
    $$i \models_{TL} \Diamond p \quad \rightarrow \quad \models \exists j. \, (j \geq i) \wedge p(j)$$
    $$i \models_{TL} \square p \quad \rightarrow \quad \models \forall j. \, (j \geq i) \Rightarrow p(j)$$

    However, this first-order translation can be a problem as proof/execution techniques often find it hard to isolate exactly this fragment.

2. *A multi-modal logic, comprising two modalities, [1] and [∗], which interact closely.*

    The modality [1] represents a move of one step forwards, while [∗] represents all future steps.

    Thus, the induction axiom in discrete temporal logic

    $$\vdash \square(\varphi \Rightarrow \bigcirc\varphi) \ \Rightarrow \ (\varphi \Rightarrow \square\varphi)$$

    can be viewed as the *interaction* axiom between modalities

    $$\vdash [*](\varphi \Rightarrow [1]\varphi) \ \Rightarrow \ (\varphi \Rightarrow [*]\varphi)$$

    Usually, [1] is represented as '$\bigcirc$', while [∗] is represented as '$\square$'.

    However, while mechanising modal logics is relatively easy, multi-modal problems become complex when interactions occur between the modalities; in our case the interaction is of an *inductive* nature, which can be particularly complex.

3. *A characterisation of simple induction.*

 The induction axiom in discrete temporal logic

$$\vdash \Box(\varphi \Rightarrow \bigcirc\varphi) \Rightarrow (\varphi \Rightarrow \Box\varphi)$$

can alternatively be viewed as

$$[\forall i.\ \varphi(i) \Rightarrow \varphi(i+1)] \Rightarrow [\varphi(0) \Rightarrow \forall j.\ \varphi(j)]$$

Reformulated, this becomes

$$[\varphi(0) \wedge \forall i.\ \varphi(i) \Rightarrow \varphi(i+1)] \Rightarrow \forall j.\ \varphi(j)$$

which should be familiar as a version of arithmetical induction, i.e. if φ is true of 0 and if φ being true of i implies it is true of $i+1$, then we know φ is true of all Natural Numbers.

 However, this use of induction can again cause problems for first-order proof techniques.

4. *A logic over sequences, trees or partial-orders (depending on the model of time).*

 For example, a sequence-based semantics can be given for discrete linear temporal logic:

$s_i, s_{i+1}, \ldots, s_\omega \models \bigcirc p$ if, and only if, $s_{i+1}, \ldots, s_\omega \models p$

$s_i, s_{i+1}, \ldots, s_\omega \models \Diamond p$ if, and only if, there exists a $j \geq i$ such that $s_j, \ldots, s_\omega \models p$

$s_i, s_{i+1}, \ldots, s_\omega \models \Box p$ if, and only if, for all $j \geq i$ then $s_j, \ldots, s_\omega \models p$

This shows that temporal logic can be used to characterise a great variety of, potentially complex, computational structures.

5. *A syntactic characterisation of finite-state automata over infinite words (ω-automata).*

 For example
 - formulae such as $p \Rightarrow \bigcirc q$ give constraints on possible state transitions,
 - formulae such as $p \Rightarrow \Diamond r$ give constraints on accepting states within an automaton, and
 - formulae such as $p \Rightarrow \Box s$ give global constraints on states in an automaton.

 This shows some of the power of temporal logic as a variety of different ω-automata can be characterised in this way.

The decision problem for a simple propositional (discrete, linear) temporal logic is already PSPACE-complete [58]; other variants of temporal logic may be worse! When we move to *first-order* temporal logics, things begin to get unpleasant. It is easy to show that first-order temporal logic is, in general, incomplete (i.e. not recursively-enumerable [59, 2]). In fact, until recently, it has been difficult to find *any* non-trivial fragment of first-order temporal logic that has reasonable properties. A breakthrough by Hodkinson *et al.* [39] showed that *monodic* fragments of first-order temporal logic could be complete, even decidable. Monodic first-order temporal logics add quantification to temporal logic but only allow at most one free variable in any temporal subformula. Thus,

$$\forall x.\, a(x) \;\Rightarrow\; \Box b(x)$$
$$\forall x.\, a(y) \;\Rightarrow\; \Diamond c(y, y)$$
$$\forall z.\, (\exists w.\, d(w, z)) \;\Rightarrow\; \bigcirc(\forall v.\, e(z, v))$$

are all *monodic* formulae, whereas

$$\forall x.\, \forall y.\, f(x, y) \;\Rightarrow\; \bigcirc g(y, x)$$

is not. The monodic fragment of first-order temporal logic is recursively enumerable [39] and, when combined with a decidable first-order fragment, often produces a decidable first-order temporal logic [38, 10, 9, 45].

4   What Tools?

The main tools that we are interested in are used to carry out *temporal verification*, via resolution on temporal formulae, and *temporal execution*, via direct execution of temporal formulae. In our case, both of these use temporal formulae within a specific normal form, called *Separated Normal Form (SNF)* [25].

4.1   SNF

A temporal formula in Separated Normal Form (SNF) is of the form

$$\Box \bigwedge_{i=1}^{n} (P_i \Rightarrow F_i)$$

where each of the '$P_i \Rightarrow F_i$' (called *clauses* or *rules*) is one of the following

$$\textbf{start} \;\Rightarrow\; \bigvee_{k=1}^{r} l_k \qquad \text{(an initial clause)}$$

$$\bigwedge_{j=1}^{q} m_j \Rightarrow \bigcirc \bigvee_{k=1}^{r} l_k \qquad \text{(a step clause)}$$

$$\bigwedge_{j=1}^{q} m_j \Rightarrow \Diamond l \qquad \text{(a sometime clause)}$$

where each l, l_k or m_j is a literal and '**start**' is a formula that is only satisfied at the "beginning of time".

Thus, the intuition is that:

- initial clauses provide *initial* constraints;
- step clauses provide constraints on the *next* step; and
- sometime clauses provide constraints on the *future*.

We can provide simple examples showing some of the properties that might be represented directly as SNF clauses.

- Specifying initial conditions: $\textbf{start} \Rightarrow reading$
- Defining transitions between states: $(reading \wedge \neg finished) \Rightarrow \bigcirc reading$
- Introducing new eventualities (goals): $(tired \wedge reading) \Rightarrow \Diamond \neg reading$
$$reading \Rightarrow \Diamond finished$$
- Introducing permanent properties:

$$(increasing \wedge (value = 1)) \Rightarrow \bigcirc \square (value > 1)$$

which, in SNF, becomes

$$(increasing \wedge (value = 1)) \Rightarrow \bigcirc (value > 1)$$
$$(increasing \wedge (value = 1)) \Rightarrow \bigcirc r$$
$$r \Rightarrow \bigcirc (value > 1)$$
$$r \Rightarrow \bigcirc r$$

Translation from an arbitrary propositional temporal formula into SNF is an operation of polynomial complexity [25, 28].

We also need the concept of a *merged* SNF clause: any SNF clause is a merged SNF clause and, given two merged SNF clauses $A \Rightarrow \bigcirc B$ and $C \Rightarrow \bigcirc D$, we can generate a new merged SNF clause $(A \wedge C) \Rightarrow \bigcirc (B \wedge D)$.

4.2   Clausal Resolution

Given a set of clauses in SNF, we can apply resolution rules, such as

$$\text{Initial Resolution:}\quad \begin{array}{c} \textbf{start} \Rightarrow (A \vee l) \\ \textbf{start} \Rightarrow (B \vee \neg l) \\ \hline \textbf{start} \Rightarrow (A \vee B) \end{array}$$

$$\text{Step Resolution:}\quad \begin{array}{c} P \Rightarrow \bigcirc (A \vee l) \\ Q \Rightarrow \bigcirc (B \vee \neg l) \\ \hline (P \wedge Q) \Rightarrow \bigcirc (A \vee B) \end{array}$$

$$\text{Temporal Resolution (simplified)[1]:}\quad \begin{array}{c} A \Rightarrow \bigcirc \square \neg l \\ Q \Rightarrow \Diamond l \\ \hline Q \Rightarrow (\neg A) \mathcal{W} l \end{array}$$

As we will see later, it is this *temporal resolution* rule that causes much of the difficulty.

It should be noted here that the above is a basic explanation of clausal temporal resolution. A number of refinements, both in terms of what resolution rules are used, and the form of SNF, have been developed [11, 8].

There has also been considerable work on extending the clausal resolution approach to handle logics formed by combining temporal logic with one or more modal logic. In particular, resolution for a *temporal logic of knowledge* (i.e. temporal logic combined with an S5 modal logic of knowledge) have been developed [19]. More recent work in this area has concerned extending resolution to cope with more complex interactions between the knowledge and time dimensions [18, 54] and application of such logics in verification [17, 16].

---

[1] $(\neg A) \mathcal{W} l$ is satisfied either if $\neg A$ is always satisfied, or if $\neg A$ is satisfied up to a point when l is satisfied.

4.3   Executable Temporal Logics

In executing temporal logic formulae, we use the *Imperative Future* approach [4]:

- transforming the temporal specification into SNF;
- from the initial constraints, *forward chaining* through the set of temporal rules representing the agent; and
- constraining the execution by attempting to satisfy goals, such as $\Diamond g$ (i.e. g eventually becomes true).

Since some goals might not be able to be satisfied immediately, we must keep track of the outstanding goals and reconsider them later. The basic strategy used is to attempt to satisfy the oldest outstanding eventualities first and keep a record of the others, retrying them as execution proceeds.

Example. Imagine a search agent which can *search*, *speedup* and *stop*, but can also run out of resources (*empty*) and *reset*.

The agent's internal definition might be given by a temporal logic specification in SNF, for example,

$$\textbf{start} \Rightarrow \neg searching$$
$$search \Rightarrow \Diamond searching$$
$$(searching \wedge speedup) \Rightarrow \bigcirc (empty \vee reset)$$

The agent's behaviour is implemented by *forward-chaining* through these formulae.

- Thus, *searching* is false at the beginning of time.
- Whenever *search* is made true, a commitment to eventually make *searching* true is given.
- Whenever both *speedup* and *searching* are made true, then either *reset* or *empty* will be made true in the next moment in time.

This provides the basis for temporal execution, and has been extended with execution for combinations with *modal* logics, deliberation mechanisms [26], resource-bounded reasoning [29] and a concurrent operational model [22].

5   Implementations

5.1   Clausal Temporal Resolution

The essential complexity in carrying out clausal temporal resolution is implementing the temporal resolution rule itself. First, let us note that the Temporal Resolution rule outlined earlier is not in the correct form. The *exact* form of this rule is

$$\text{Temporal Resolution (full):} \quad \begin{array}{c} A_1 \Rightarrow \bigcirc B_1 \\ \ldots \Rightarrow \ldots \\ A_n \Rightarrow \bigcirc B_n \\ Q \Rightarrow \Diamond l \\ \hline Q \Rightarrow (\bigwedge_{i=1}^{n} \neg A_i) \, \mathcal{W} \, l \end{array}$$

where each $A_i \Rightarrow \bigcirc B_i$ is a merged SNF clause and each B_i satisfies $B_i \Rightarrow (\neg l \wedge \bigvee_{j=1}^{n} A_j)$.

Thus, in order to implement this rule, a *set* of step clauses satisfying certain properties must be found; such a set is called a *loop*. This process has undergone increasing refinement, as has the implementation of clausal temporal resolution provers in general:

1. The original approach proposed was to conjoin all sets of step clauses to give, so called, *merged* SNF clauses and then treat these merged clauses as edges/transitions in a graph. Finding a loop is then just a question of extracting a *strongly connected component* from the graph, which is a linear operation [60].

   The problem here is explicitly constructing the large set of merged SNF clauses.

2. Dixon [12, 13, 14] developed an improved (breadth-first) search algorithm, which formed the basis of the 'Clatter' prover. This search approach effectively aimed to generate only the merged SNF clauses that were *required* to find a loop, rather than generating all such clauses.

   The problem with the Clatter family of provers was the relatively slow link to the classical resolution system (which was used to carry out the step resolution operations).

3. Hustadt then developed TRP [46]. The idea here was to use arithmetical translations to translate as much as possible of the process to classical resolution operations and then use an efficient classical resolution system. In addition, TRP used a translation of the breadth-first loop search algorithm into a series of classical resolution problems suggested in [15]. (TRP is also able to deal with the combination of propositional temporal logic with various modal logics including KD45 and S5.) The resulting system was evaluated against other decision procedures for this form of temporal logic and was shown to be very competitive [46, 43].

   The main problems with TRP were that it was implemented in Prolog and that the data/term representation/indexing techniques could be improved.

4. A more recent variety of clausal resolution system for propositional temporal logic is TRP++, implemented by Hustadt and Konev [42]. Here, TRP is re-implemented in C++ and is refined with a number of contemporary data representation and indexing techniques.

   TRP++ currently performs very well in comparison with other provers for propositional temporal logic.

5. Finally, TeMP [44] is a clausal resolution prover specifically designed for monodic first-order temporal logic [8, 50]. This utilises the Vampire [57] system to handle much of the internal first-order proving.

Both TRP++ and TeMP are available online[2].

5.2 Executable Temporal Logics

The Imperative Future style of execution provides a relatively simple approach to executing temporal logic formulae. As described above, beginning at the initial conditions

---

[2] See http://www.csc.liv.ac.uk/~konev

we simply forward chain through the step clauses/rules generating a model, all the time constraining the execution with formulae such as '$\Diamond g$'.

The development in this area has not primarily been concerned with speed. As we will see below, the developments have essentially involved refining and extending the internal capabilities of the programs and allowing for more complex interactions between programs.

Thus, the implementations of this approach, beginning with METATEM, proceeded as follows.

1. The first approach, reported in [34], essentially used a `Prolog` meta-interpreter to implement the system. The forward chaining aspect is relatively standard, and the management of outstanding eventualities (i.e. formulae such as '$\Diamond g$') was handled with a queue structure.

   In order to maintain completeness (in the propositional case) a form of *past-time loop checking* had to be employed. This involved retaining a large proportion, and sometimes *all*, of the history of the computation and checking for loops over this as every new computation state was constructed. (Note that this loop-checking aspect is usually omitted from the later languages.)

   The main problems with this approach were the lack of features, particularly those required for programming rational agents, such as internal reasoning, deliberation and concurrency.

2. In [22], Concurrent METATEM was developed. This allowed for multiple asynchronous, communicating METATEM components and provided a clean interaction between the internal (logical) computation and the concurrent operational model.

   Concurrent METATEM was implemented in `C++` but was relatively slow and static (i.e. process scheduling was implemented directly).

3. Kellett, in [48, 49], developed more refined implementation techniques for Concurrent METATEM. Here, individual METATEM programs were compiled into (linked) pairs of I/O automata [51], one to handle the internal computation, the other to handle the interaction with the environment. Such automata can then, potentially, be cloned (for process spawning) and moved (for load balancing and mobility).

   While Concurrent METATEM provides an interesting model of simple multi-agent computation, work was still required on the internal computation mechanism for each individual agent.

4. More recently, the internal computation has been extended by providing a *belief* dimension, allowing meta-control of the deliberation[3], allowing resource-bounded reasoning and incorporating agent abilities [26, 29, 30].

   This has led to a programming language in which rational agents can be implemented, and in which complex multi-agent organisations can be developed. Recent work by Hirsch [37] has produced a `Java` implementation of both individual and group aspects, and has applied this to multi-agent and pervasive computing applications [31, 32, 36].

---

[3] Deliberation here means the process of deciding in which order to attempt outstanding eventualities at each computation step.

5.3 Other Techniques

In this section, I will briefly mention a few other systems related to temporal logic.

Induction-based Temporal Proof. As mentioned above, first-order temporal logics are complex. In particular, full first-order temporal logic is not recursively-enumerable. However, as we still wish to prove theorems within such a logic, we have been developing techniques to support this. Such a system is described in [5], where an induction-based theorem-prover is enhanced with heuristics derived from the clausal temporal resolution techniques (see above) and implemented in λClam/λProlog.

Temporal Logic Programming. Standard logic programming techniques were transferred to temporal logic in [1]. However, because of the incompleteness of first-order temporal logics, the language was severely restricted. In fact, if we think of SNF above then the fragment considered is essentially that consisting of initial and step clauses. Thus, implementation for such a language is a small extension of classical logic programming techniques and constraint logic programming techniques.

Model Checking. Undoubtedly the most popular application of temporal logic is in *model checking*. Here, a finite-state model capturing the executions of a system is checked against a temporal formula. These finite state models often capture hardware descriptions, network protocols or complex software [40, 7]. While much model-checking technology was based on automata-theoretic techniques, advances in *symbolic* [6] and *on-the-fly* [41] techniques have made model checking the success it is. Current work on abstraction techniques and Java model checking, such as [61], promise even greater advances.

6 Summary

I have overviewed a selection of tools for execution and proof within temporal logic. While this selection has been heavily biased towards those in which I have been involved, several of the techniques are at the forefront of their areas. Although these tools are generally prototypes, they are increasingly used in realistic scenarios, and more sophisticated versions appear likely to have a significant impact in both Computer Science and Artificial Intelligence.

Acknowledgments. Much of this work has been supported by funding from the UK's Engineering and Physical Sciences Research Council (EPSRC)[4], and has involved collaboration with a variety of outstanding colleagues who work (or have worked) within the Logic and Computation group at Liverpool[5]. I thank them all for their endeavours. I would also like to thank the anonymous referees of the CLIMA VI post-proceedings for their helpful comments.

---

[4] http://www.epsrc.ac.uk
[5] http://www.csc.liv.ac.uk/research/logics

References

1. M. Abadi and Z. Manna. Temporal Logic Programming. *Journal of Symbolic Computation*, 8: 277–295, 1989.
2. M. Abadi. The Power of Temporal Proofs. *Theoretical Computer Science*, 64:35–84, 1989.
3. H. Barringer, M. Fisher, D. Gabbay, G. Gough, and R. Owens. METATEM: An Introduction. *Formal Aspects of Computing*, 7(5):533–549, 1995.
4. H. Barringer, M. Fisher, D. Gabbay, R. Owens, and M. Reynolds, editors. *The Imperative Future: Principles of Executable Temporal Logics*. Research Studies Press, Chichester, United Kingdom, 1996.
5. J. Brotherston, A. Degtyarev, M. Fisher, and A. Lisitsa. Implementing Invariant Search via Temporal Resolution. In *Proceedings of LPAR-2002*, pages 86–101. Springer Verlag, 2002. Lecture Notes in Computer Science, 2514.
6. J.R. Burch, E.M. Clarke, K.L. McMillan, D.L. Dill, and L.J. Hwang. Symbolic Model Checking: 10^{20} states and beyond. In *Proceedings of the 5th Symposium on Logic in Computer Science, Philadelphia*, June 1990.
7. E.M. Clarke, O. Grumberg, and D. Peled. *Model Checking*. MIT Press, December 1999.
8. A. Degtyarev, M. Fisher, and B. Konev. Monodic Temporal Resolution. *ACM Transactions on Computational Logic* 7(1), January 2006.
9. A. Degtyarev, M. Fisher, and B. Konev. Handling equality in monodic temporal resolution. In *Proceedings of 10th International Conference on Logic for Programming, Artificial Intelligence, and Reasoning (LPAR)*, volume 2850 of *Lecture Notes in Computer Science*, pages 214–228, Almaty, Kazakhstan, 2003. Springer-Verlag.
10. A. Degtyarev, M. Fisher, and A. Lisitsa. Equality and Monodic First-Order Temporal Logic. *Studia Logica*, 72(2):147–156, November 2002.
11. A. Degtyarev, M. Fisher, and B. Konev. A simplified clausal resolution procedure for propositional linear-time temporal logic. In U. Egly and C. G. Fermüller, editors, *Automated Reasoning with Analytic Tableaux and Related Methods*, volume 2381 of *Lecture Notes in Computer Science*, pages 85–99. Springer-Verlag, July 30–August 1 2002.
12. C. Dixon. *Strategies for Temporal Resolution*. PhD thesis, Department of Computer Science, University of Manchester, Manchester M13 9PL, U.K., December 1995.
13. C. Dixon. Search Strategies for Resolution in Temporal Logics. In *Proceedings of the Thirteenth International Conference on Automated Deduction (CADE)*, volume 1104 of *Lecture Notes in Computer Science*, New Jersey, July/August 1996. Springer-Verlag.
14. C. Dixon. Temporal Resolution using a Breadth-First Search Algorithm. *Annals of Mathematics and Artificial Intelligence*, 22:87–115, 1998.
15. C. Dixon. Using Otter for Temporal Resolution. In *Advances in Temporal Logic*. Kluwer Academic Publishers, 1999.
16. C. Dixon. Using Temporal Logics of Knowledge for Specification and Verification — a Case Study. *Journal of Applied Logic*, 2005. To appear.
17. C. Dixon, M-C. Fernández Gago, M. Fisher, and W. van der Hoek. Using temporal logics of knowledge in the formal verification of security protocols. In *Proceedings of International Symposium on Temporal Representation and Reasoning (TIME)*. IEEE CS Press, 2004.
18. C. Dixon and M. Fisher. Clausal Resolution for Logics of Time and Knowledge with Synchrony and Perfect Recall. In *Proceedings of Joint International Conference on Temporal Logic and Advances in Modal Logic (AiML-ICTL)*, Leipzig, Germany, October 2000.
19. C. Dixon, M. Fisher, and M. Wooldridge. Resolution for Temporal Logics of Knowledge. *Journal of Logic and Computation*, 8(3):345–372, 1998.
20. E. A. Emerson. Temporal and Modal Logic. In J. van Leeuwen, editor, *Handbook of Theoretical Computer Science*, pages 996–1072. Elsevier, 1990.

21. M. Fisher. A Resolution Method for Temporal Logic. In *Proc. Twelfth International Joint Conference on Artificial Intelligence (IJCAI)*, Sydney, Australia, 1991. Morgan Kaufman.

22. M. Fisher. Concurrent METATEM — A Language for Modeling Reactive Systems. In *Parallel Architectures and Languages, Europe (PARLE)*, Munich, Germany, June 1993. (Published in *Lecture Notes in Computer Science*, volume 694, Springer-Verlag).

23. M. Fisher. Representing and Executing Agent-Based Systems. In M. Wooldridge and N. R. Jennings, editors, *Intelligent Agents*. Springer-Verlag, 1995.

24. M. Fisher. An Introduction to Executable Temporal Logics. *Knowledge Engineering Review*, 11(1):43–56, March 1996.

25. M. Fisher. A Normal Form for Temporal Logic and its Application in Theorem-Proving and Execution. *Journal of Logic and Computation*, 7(4):429–456, August 1997.

26. M. Fisher. Implementing BDI-like Systems by Direct Execution. In *Proceedings of International Joint Conference on Artificial Intelligence (IJCAI)*. Morgan-Kaufmann, 1997.

27. M. Fisher. Temporal Development Methods for Agent-Based Systems. *Journal of Autonomous Agents and Multi-Agent Systems*, 10(1):41–66, January 2005.

28. M. Fisher, C. Dixon, and M. Peim. Clausal Temporal Resolution. *ACM Transactions on Computational Logic*, 2(1):12–56, January 2001.

29. M. Fisher and C. Ghidini. Programming Resource-Bounded Deliberative Agents. In *Proceedings of International Joint Conference on Artificial Intelligence (IJCAI)*. Morgan Kaufmann, 1999.

30. M. Fisher and C. Ghidini. The ABC of Rational Agent Programming. In *Proc. First International Conference on Autonomous Agents and Multi-Agent Systems (AAMAS)*, pages 849–856. ACM Press, July 2002.

31. M. Fisher, C. Ghidini, and B. Hirsch. Organising Computation through Dynamic Grouping. In *Objects, Agents and Features*, volume 2975 of *Lecture Notes in Computer Science*, pages 117–136. Springer-Verlag, 2004.

32. M. Fisher, C. Ghidini, and B. Hirsch. Programming Groups of Rational Agents. In *Computational Logic in Multi-Agent Systems (CLIMA-IV)*, volume 3259 of *849–856*. Springer-Verlag, November 2004.

33. M. Fisher and T. Kakoudakis. Flexible Agent Grouping in Executable Temporal Logic. In *Proceedings of Twelfth International Symposium on Languages for Intensional Programming (ISLIP)*. World Scientific Press, 1999.

34. M. Fisher and R. Owens. From the Past to the Future: Executing Temporal Logic Programs. In *Proceedings of Logic Programming and Automated Reasoning (LPAR)*, St. Petersberg, Russia, July 1992. (Published in *Lecture Notes in Computer Science*, volume 624, Springer-Verlag).

35. M-C. Fernández Gago, U. Hustadt, C. Dixon, M. Fisher, and B. Konev. First-Order Temporal Verification in Practice. Accepted for publication in *Journal of Automated Reasoning*.

36. B. Hirsch, M. Fisher, C. Ghidini, and P. Busetta. Organising Software in Active Environments. In *Computational Logic in Multi-Agent Systems (CLIMA-V)*, volume 3487 of *Lecture Notes in Computer Science*. Springer-Verlag, 2005.

37. B. Hirsch. *Programming Rational Agents*. PhD thesis, Department of Computer Science, University of Liverpool, United Kingdom, May 2005.

38. I. Hodkinson. Monodic Packed Fragment with Equality is Decidable. *Studia Logica*, 72(2):185–197, November 2002.

39. I. Hodkinson, F. Wolter, and M. Zakharyashev. Decidable fragments of first-order temporal logics. *Annals of Pure and Applied Logic*, 2000.

40. G.J. Holzmann. *Design and Validation of Computer Protocols*. Prentice-Hall, Englewood Cliffs, New Jersey, 1991.

41. G.J. Holzmann. The model checker spin. *IEEE Trans. on Software Engineering*, 23(5):279–295, May 1997. Special issue on Formal Methods in Software Practice.

42. U. Hustadt and B. Konev. TRP++ 2.0: A temporal resolution prover. In *Proceedings of Conference on Automated Deduction (CADE-19)*, number 2741 in *Lecture Notes in Artificial Intelligence*, pages 274–278. Springer, 2003.

43. U. Hustadt and R. A. Schmidt. Scientific benchmarking with temporal logic decision procedures. In D. Fensel, F. Giunchiglia, D. McGuinness, and M.-A. Williams, editors, *Principles of Knowledge Representation and Reasoning: Proceedings of the Eighth International Conference (KR'2002)*, pages 533–544. Morgan Kaufmann, 2002.

44. U. Hustadt, B. Konev, A. Riazanov, and A. Voronkov. **TeMP**: A temporal monodic prover. In D. A. Basin and M. Rusinowitch, editors, *Proceedings of the Second International Joint Conference on Automated Reasoning (IJCAR 2004)*, volume 3097 of *Lecture Notes in Artificial Intelligence*, pages 326–330. Springer, 2004.

45. U. Hustadt, B. Konev, and R. A. Schmidt. Deciding monodic fragments by temporal resolution. In R. Nieuwenhuis, editor, *Proceedings of the 20th International Conference on Automated Deduction (CADE-20)*, volume 3632 of *Lecture Notes in Artificial Intelligence*, pages 204–218. Springer, 2005.

46. U. Hustadt and R. A. Schmidt. Formulae which highlight differences between temporal logic and dynamic logic provers. In E. Giunchiglia and F. Massacci, editors, *Issues in the Design and Experimental Evaluation of Systems for Modal and Temporal Logics*, Technical Report DII 14/01, pages 68–76. Dipartimento di Ingegneria dell'Informazione, Unversitá degli Studi di Siena, 2001.

47. M. Huth and M. Ryan. *Logic in Computer Science*. Cambridge University Press, 2000.

48. A. Kellett. *Implementation Techniques for Concurrent* METATEM. PhD thesis, Department of Computing and Mathematics, Manchester Metropolitan University, 2000.

49. A. Kellett and M. Fisher. Automata Representations for Concurrent METATEM. In *Proceedings of the Fourth International Workshop on Temporal Representation and Reasoning (TIME)*. IEEE Press, May 1997.

50. B. Konev, A. Degtyarev, C. Dixon, M. Fisher, and U. Hustadt. Mechanising first-order temporal resolution. *Information and Computation*, 199(1-2):55–86, 2005.

51. N. A. Lynch and M. R. Tuttle. An Introduction to Input/Output Automata. Technical Report MIT/LCS/TM-373, Laboratory for Computer Science, Massachusetts Institute of Technology, November 1988.

52. Z. Manna and A. Pnueli. *The Temporal Logic of Reactive and Concurrent Systems: Specification*. Springer-Verlag, New York, 1992.

53. Z. Manna and A. Pnueli. *Temporal Verification of Reactive Systems: Safety*. Springer-Verlag, New York, 1995.

54. C. Nalon, C. Dixon, and M. Fisher. Resolution for Synchrony and No Learning. In *Proceedings of Advances in Modal Logic Confernece (AiML-5)*, Manchester, UK, September 2004.

55. A. Pnueli. The Temporal Logic of Programs. In *Proceedings of the Eighteenth Symposium on the Foundations of Computer Science*, Providence, USA, November 1977.

56. A. Prior. *Past, Present and Future*. Oxford University Press, 1967.

57. A. Riazanov and A. Voronkov. Vampire 1.1 (system description). In *Proc. IJCAR 2001*, pages 376–380. Volume 2083 of *Lecture Notes in Artificial Intelligence*, Springer-Verlag, 2001.

58. A. P. Sistla and E. M. Clarke. Complexity of propositional linear temporal logics. *ACM Journal*, 32(3):733–749, July 1985.

59. A. Szalas and L. Holenderski. Incompleteness of First-Order Temporal Logic with Until. *Theoretical Computer Science*, 57:317–325, 1988.
60. R. Tarjan. Depth-First Search and Linear Graph Algorithms. *SIAM Journal on Computing*, 1:146–160, 1972.
61. W. Visser, K. Havelund, G. Brat, and S. Park. Model checking programs. In *International Conference on Automated Software Engineering (ASE)*, September 2000.
62. M. Wooldridge. *Reasoning about Rational Agents*. MIT Press, 2000.

BDI Agent Programming in AgentSpeak Using *Jason*

Rafael H. Bordini[1] and Jomi F. Hübner[2]

[1] Department of Computer Science,
University of Durham,
Durham DH1 3LE, UK
`R.Bordini@durham.ac.uk`
[2] Departamento de Sistemas e Computação,
Universidade Regional de Blumenau,
Blumenau, SC 89035-160, Brazil
`jomi@inf.furb.br`

Abstract. This paper is based on the tutorial given as part of the tutorial programme of CLIMA-VI. The tutorial aimed at giving an overview of the various features available in *Jason*, a multi-agent systems development platform that is based on an interpreter for an extended version of AgentSpeak. The BDI architecture is the best known and most studied architecture for cognitive agents, and AgentSpeak is an elegant, logic-based programming language inspired by the BDI architecture.

1 Introduction

The BDI agent architecture [27, 33, 29] has been a central theme in the multi-agent systems literature since the early 1990's. After a period of relative decline, it seems BDI agents are back in vogue, with various conference papers referring again to elements of the BDI theory. Arguably, that theory provides the grounding for some of the essential features of autonomous agents and multi-agent systems, so it will always have an important role to play in the research in this area. Besides, the software industry is beginning to use technologies that clearly derived from the academic work on BDI-based systems.

AgentSpeak is an elegant agent-oriented programming language based on logic programming, and inspired by the work on the BDI architecture [27] and BDI logics [28] as well as on practical implementations of BDI systems such as PRS [16] and dMARS [17]. However, in its original definition [26], AgentSpeak was just an abstract programming language. For these reasons, our effort in developing *Jason* was very much directed towards using AgentSpeak as the basis, but also providing various extensions that are required for the practical development of multi-agent systems.

The elegance of the AgentSpeak core of the language interpreted by *Jason* makes it an interesting tool both for teaching multi-agent systems as well as the practical development of multi-agent systems (in particular in association with existing agent-oriented software engineering methodologies for BDI-

F. Toni and P. Torroni (Eds.): CLIMA VI, LNAI 3900, pp. 143–164, 2006.
© Springer-Verlag Berlin Heidelberg 2006

like systems). **Jason** is implemented in Java and is available Open Source at `http://jason.sourceforge.net`. Some of the features available in **Jason** are:

- speech-act based inter-agent communication (and annotation of beliefs with information sources);
- annotations on plan labels, which can be used by elaborate (e.g., decision theoretic) selection functions;
- the possibility to run a multi-agent system distributed over a network (using SACI, or some other agent middleware);
- fully customisable (in Java) selection functions, trust functions, and overall agent architecture (perception, belief-revision, inter-agent communication, and acting);
- straightforward extensibility (and use of legacy code) by means of user-defined "internal actions";
- clear notion of *multi-agent environments*, which can be implemented in Java (this can be a simulation of a real environment, e.g., for testing purposes before the system is actually deployed).

This paper is based on a CLIMA-VI tutorial which aimed at giving an overview of the various features available in **Jason**. It is intended for a general audience although some parts might be clearer for readers familiar with agent-oriented programming. To keep the paper at a reasonable size, we only describe the main features of **Jason**, so that readers can assess whether **Jason** might be of interest, rather than aiming at a didactic presentation. For the interested reader, we give here plenty of references to other papers and documentation where more detail and examples can be found; a general reference giving a longer overview is [9], and see [8] for details. The paper is organised as follows. Section 2 presents the *language* interpreted by **Jason**, and its informal semantics is given in Section 3. Some other features of the language related to multi-agent communication and interaction are discussed in Section 4. We then present the main feature of the *platform* which facilitate the development of multi-agent systems in Section 5. Section 6 discusses various issues (such as formal verification) and we then make some final remarks.

2   *Jason* Extension of the AgentSpeak Language

The AgentSpeak(L) programming language was introduced in [26]. It is a natural extension of logic programming for the BDI agent architecture, and provides an elegant abstract framework for programming BDI agents. The BDI architecture is, in turn, the predominant approach to the implementation of *intelligent* or *rational* agents [33].

An AgentSpeak agent is defined by a set of *beliefs* giving the initial state of the agent's *belief base*, which is a set of ground (first-order) atomic formulæ, and a set of plans which form its *plan library*. Before explaining exactly how a plan is written, we need to introduce the notions of goals and triggering events.

AgentSpeak distinguishes two types of *goals*: achievement goals and test goals. Achievement goals are formed by an atomic formulæ prefixed with the '!' operator, while test goals are prefixed with the '?' operator. An *achievement goal* states that the agent wants to achieve a state of the world where the associated atomic formulæ is true. A *test goal* states that the agent wants to test whether the associated atomic formulæ is (or can be unified with) one of its beliefs.

An AgentSpeak agent is a reactive planning system. The events it reacts to are related either to changes in beliefs due to perception of the environment, or to changes in the agent's goals that originate from the execution of plans triggered by previous events. A *triggering event* defines which events can initiate the execution of a particular plan. Plans are written by the programmer so that they are triggered by the *addition* ('+') or *deletion* ('-') of beliefs or goals (the "mental attitudes" of AgentSpeak agents).

An AgentSpeak plan has a *head* (the expression to the left of the arrow), which is formed from a triggering event (specifying the events for which that plan is *relevant*), and a conjunction of belief literals representing a *context*. The conjunction of literals in the context must be a logical consequence of that agent's current beliefs if the plan is to be considered *applicable* at that moment in time (only applicable plans can be chosen for execution). A plan also has a *body*, which is a sequence of basic actions or (sub)goals that the agent has to achieve (or test) when the plan is triggered. Plan bodies include *basic actions* — such actions represent atomic operations the agent can perform so as to change the environment. Such actions are also written as atomic formulæ, but using a set of *action symbols* rather than predicate symbols.

Figure 1 give examples of three AgentSpeak plans, illustrating a scenario in which a robot is instructed to be especially attentive to "green patches" on rocks it observers while roving on Mars. The first plan says that whenever the rover perceives a green patch on a certain rock (a belief addition), it should try and examine that particular rock; however note that this plan can only be used (i.e., it is only applicable) in case the batteries are not too low. In order to examine the rock, it has to retrieve, from its own belief base, the coordinates it has associated with that rock (this is the test goal in the beginning of the plan's body), then achieve the goal of traversing to those coordinates and, once there, examining the rock. Recall that each of these achievement goals will trigger the execution of some other plan.

The two other plans (note the last one is only an excerpt) provide alternative courses of actions that the Mars exploration rover has to take according to what it believes about the environment when the rover has to achieve a new goal of traversing towards some given coordinates. If the rover believes that there is a safe path in that direction, then all it has to do is to take the action of moving towards those coordinates (this is a basic action via which the rover can effect changes in its environment). The alternative plan is not shown here; it should provide alternative means for the agent to reach the rock but avoiding unsafe paths.

```
+green_patch(Rock)
  : not battery_charge(low)
    <- ?location(Rock,Coordinates);
       !traverse(Coordinates);
       !examine(Rock).

+!traverse(Coords)
  : safe_path(Coords)
    <- move_towards(Coords).

+!traverse(Coords) :
  : not safe_path(Coords)
    <- ...
```

Fig. 1. Examples of AgentSpeak Plans for a Mars Rover

The main differences between the language interpreted by *Jason* and the original AgentSpeak(L) language described above are as follows. Wherever an atomic formulæ[1] was allowed in the original language, here a literal is used instead. This is either an atomic formulæ $p(t_1,\ldots,t_n)$, $n \geq 0$, or $\sim p(t_1,\ldots,t_n)$, where '$\sim$' denotes strong negation[2]. Default negation is used in the context of plans, and is denoted by 'not' preceding a literal. The context is therefore a conjunction of default literals. For more details on the concepts of strong and default negation, plenty of references can be found, e.g., in the introductory chapters of [18]. Terms now can be variables, lists (with Prolog syntax), as well as integer or floating point numbers, and strings (enclosed in double quotes as usual); further, any atomic formulæ can be treated as a term, and (bound) variables can be treated as literals (this became particularly important for introducing communication, but can be useful for various things). Infix relational operators, as in Prolog, are allowed in plan contexts.

Also, a major change is that atomic formulæ now can have "annotations". This is a list of terms enclosed in square brackets immediately following the formula. Within the belief base, annotations are used, e.g., to register the sources of information. A term source(s) is used in the annotations for that purpose; s can be an agent's name (to denote the agent that communicated that information), or two special atoms, percept and self, that are used to denote that a belief arose from perception of the environment, or from the agent explicitly adding a belief to its own belief base from the execution of a plan body, respectively. The initial beliefs that are part of the source code of an AgentSpeak agent are assumed to be internal beliefs (i.e., as if they had a [source(self)] annotation), unless the belief has any explicit annotation given by the user (this could be useful if the programmer wants the agent to have an initial belief about the environment or

---

[1] Recall that actions are special atomic formulæ with an action symbol rather than a predicate symbol. What we say next only applies to usual predicates, not actions.

[2] Note that for an agent that uses Closed-World Assumption, all the user has to do is not to use literals with strong negation anywhere in the program, nor negated percepts in the environment (see "Creating Environments" under Section 5).

as if it had been communicated by another agent). Fore more on the annotation of sources of information for beliefs, see [21].

Plans also have labels, as first proposed in [3]. However, a plan label can now be any atomic formula, including annotations, although we suggest that plan labels use annotations (if necessary) but have a predicate symbol of arity 0, as in `aLabel` or `anotherLabel[chanceSuccess(0.7), expectedPayoff(0.9)]`. Annotations in plan labels can be used for the implementation of sophisticated applicable plan (i.e., option) selection functions. Although this is not yet provided with the current distribution of *Jason*, it is straightforward for the user to define, e.g., decision-theoretic selection functions; that is, functions which use something like expected utilities annotated in the plan labels to choose among alternative plans. The customisation of selection functions is done in Java (by choosing a plan from a list received as parameter by the selection functions), and is explained in Section 5. Also, as the label is part of an instance of a plan in the set of intentions, and the annotations can be changed dynamically, this provides all the means necessary for the implementation of efficient intention selection functions, as the one proposed in [3]. However, this also is not yet available as part of *Jason*'s distribution, but can be set up by users with some customisation.

Events for handling plan failure are already available in *Jason*, although they are not formalised in the semantics yet. If an action fails or there is no applicable plan for a subgoal in the plan being executed to handle an internal event with a goal addition `+!g`, then the whole failed plan is removed from the top of the intention and an internal event for `-!g` associated with that same intention is generated. If the programmer provided a plan that has a triggering event matching `-!g` and is applicable, such plan will be pushed on top of the intention, so the programmer can specify in the body of such plan how that particular failure is to be handled. If no such plan is available, the whole intention is discarded and a warning is printed out to the console. Effectively, this provides a means for programmers to "clean up" after a failed plan and before "backtracking" (that is, to make up for actions that had already been executed but left things in an inappropriate state for next attempts to achieve the goal). For example, for an agent that persist on a goal `!g` for as long as there are applicable plans for `+!g`, it suffices to include a plan `-!g : true <- !g.` in the plan library. It is also simple to specify a plan which, under specific condition, chooses to drop the intention altogether (by means of a pre-defined internal action).

Finally, as also introduced in [3], *internal actions* can be used both in the context and body of plans. Any action symbol starting with '.', or having a '.' anywhere, denotes an internal action. These are user-defined actions which are run internally by the agent. We call them "internal" to make a clear distinction with actions that appear in the body of a plan and which denote the actions an agent can perform in order to change the shared environment (in the usual jargon of the area, by means of its "effectors"). In *Jason*, internal actions are coded in Java, or in indeed other programming languages through the use of JNI (Java Native Interface), and they can be organised in libraries of actions for specific purposes (the string to the left of '.' is the name of the library; standard internal actions have an empty library name).

There are several standard internal actions that are distributed with *Jason*, but we do not mention all them here (see [8] for a complete list). To give an example, *Jason* has an internal action that implements KQML-like inter-agent communication. The usage is: `.send(+receiver, +illocutionary_force, +prop_content)` where each parameter is as follows. The `receiver` is simply referred to using the name given to agents in the multi-agent system (see Section 5). The `illocutionary_forces` available so far are: `tell`, `untell`, `achieve`, `unachieve`, `tellHow`, `untellHow`, `askIf`, `askOne`, `askAll`, and `askHow`. The effects of receiving messages with each of these types of illocutionary acts are explained in Section 4. Finally, the message's propositional content `prop_content` is a literal.

Another important class of standard internal actions are related to querying about the agent's current desires and intentions as well as forcing itself to drop desires or intentions. The notion of desire and intention used is exactly as formalised for AgentSpeak agents in [11]. The standard AgentSpeak language has provision for beliefs to be queried (in plan contexts and by test goals) and since our earlier extensions beliefs can be added or deleted from plan bodies. However, an equally important feature, as far as the generic BDI architecture is concerned, is for an agent to be able to check current desires/intentions and drop them under certain circumstances. In *Jason*, this can be done by the use of certain special standard internal actions.

3   Informal Semantics

As we mentioned in the introduction, one of the important characteristics of *Jason* is that it implements the operational semantics of an extension of AgentSpeak. Having formal semantics also allowed us to give precise definitions for practical notions of beliefs, desires, and intentions in relation to running AgentSpeak agents, which in turn underlies the work on formal verification of AgentSpeak programs, as discussed later in this section. The formal semantics, using structural operational semantics [24] (a widely-used notation for giving semantics to programming languages) was given then improved and extended in a series of papers [20, 10, 11, 21, 31]. In particular, [31] presents a revised version of the semantics and include some of the extensions we have proposed to AgentSpeak, including rules for the interpretation of speech-act based communication. Due to space limitation, in this paper we will only provide the main intuitions behind the interpretation of AgentSpeak programs.

Besides the belief base and the plan library, the AgentSpeak interpreter also manages a set of *events* and a set of *intentions*, and its functioning requires three *selection functions*. The event selection function ($S_\mathcal{E}$) selects a single event from the set of events; another selection function ($S_\mathcal{O}$) selects an "option" (i.e., an applicable plan) from a set of applicable plans; and a third selection function ($S_\mathcal{I}$)

selects one particular intention from the set of intentions. The selection functions are supposed to be agent-specific, in the sense that they should make selections based on an agent's characteristics (though previous work on AgentSpeak did not elaborate on how designers specify such functions[3]). Therefore, we here leave the selection functions undefined, hence the choices made by them are supposed to be non-deterministic.

Intentions are particular courses of actions to which an agent has committed in order to handle certain events. Each intention is a stack of partially instantiated plans. Events, which may start off the execution of plans that have relevant triggering events, can be *external*, when originating from perception of the agent's environment (i.e., addition and deletion of beliefs based on perception are external events); or *internal*, when generated from the agent's own execution of a plan (i.e., a subgoal in a plan generates an event of type "addition of achievement goal"). In the latter case, the event is accompanied with the intention which generated it (as the plan chosen for that event will be pushed on top of that intention). External events create new intentions, representing separate focuses of attention for the agent's acting on the environment.

We next give some more details on the functioning of an AgentSpeak interpreter, which is clearly depicted in Figure 2 (reproduced from [19]). Note, however, that this is a depiction of the essential aspects of the interpreter for the original (abstract) definition of AgentSpeak; it does *not* include the extensions implemented in *Jason*. In the figure, sets (of beliefs, events, plans, and intentions) are represented as rectangles. Diamonds represent selection (of one element from a set). Circles represent some of the processing involved in the interpretation of AgentSpeak programs.

At every interpretation cycle of an agent program, the interpreter updates a list of events, which may be generated from perception of the environment, or from the execution of intentions (when subgoals are specified in the body of plans). It is assumed that beliefs are updated from perception and whenever there are changes in the agent's beliefs, this implies the insertion of an event in the set of events. This belief revision function is not part of the AgentSpeak interpreter, but rather a necessary component of the agent architecture.

After $S_{\mathcal{E}}$ has selected an event, the interpreter has to unify that event with triggering events in the heads of plans. This generates the set of all *relevant plans* for that event. By checking whether the context part of the plans in that set follows from the agent's beliefs, the set of *applicable plans* is determined — these are the plans that can actually be used at that moment for handling the chosen event. Then $S_{\mathcal{O}}$ chooses a single applicable plan from that set, which becomes the *intended means* for handling that event, and either pushes that plan on the top of an existing intention (if the event was an internal one), or

---

[3] Our extension of AgentSpeak in [3] deals precisely with the automatic generation of efficient intention selection functions. The extended language allows one to express relations between plans, as well as quantitative criteria for their execution. We then use decision-theoretic task scheduling to guide the choices made by the intention selection function.

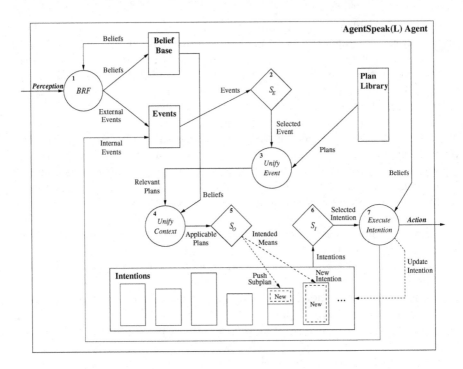

Fig. 2. An Interpretation Cycle of an AgentSpeak Program [19]

creates a new intention in the set of intentions (if the event was external, i.e., generated from perception of the environment).

All that remains to be done at this stage is to select a single intention to be executed in that cycle. The $\mathcal{S}_{\mathcal{I}}$ function selects one of the agent's intentions (i.e., one of the independent stacks of partially instantiated plans within the set of intentions). On the top of that intention there is a plan, and the formula in the beginning of its body is taken for execution. This implies that either a basic action is performed by the agent on its environment, an internal event is generated (in case the selected formula is an achievement goal), or a test goal is performed (which means that the set of beliefs has to be checked).

If the intention is to perform a basic action or a test goal, the set of intentions needs to be updated. In the case of a test goal, the belief base will be searched for a belief atom that unifies with the atomic formula in the test goal. If that search succeeds, further variable instantiation will occur in the partially instantiated plan which contained that test goal (and the test goal itself is removed from the intention from which it was taken). In the case where a basic action is selected, the necessary updating of the set of intentions is simply to remove that action from the intention (the interpreter informs to the architecture component responsible for the agent effectors what action is required). When all formulæ in the body of a plan have been removed (i.e., have been executed), the whole plan is removed from the intention, and so is the achievement goal that generated it (if that was the case). This ends a cycle of execution, and everything is repeated all over again, initially checking the state of the environment after agents have acted upon it, then generating the relevant events, and so forth.

4　Other Features of the Language

4.1　Agent Communication in *Jason*

The performatives that are currently available for agent communication in *Jason* are largely inspired by KQML. We also include some new performatives, related to plan exchange rather than communication about propositions. The available performatives are briefly described below, where s denotes the agent that sends the message, and r denotes the agent that receives the message. Note that `tell` and `untell` can be used either for an agent to pro-actively send information to another agent, or as replies to previous `ask` messages.

tell: s intends r to believe (that s believes) the sentence in the message's content to be true;

untell: s intends r not to believe (that s believes) the sentence in the message's content to be true;

achieve: s requests that r try to achieve a state of the world where the message content is true;

unachieve: s requests that r try to drop the intention of achieving a state of the world where the message content is true;

tellHow: s informs r of a plan;

untellHow: s requests that r disregard a certain plan (i.e., delete that plan from its plan library);

askIf: s wants to know if the content of the message is true for r;

askAll: s wants all of r's answers to a question;

askHow: s wants all of r's plans for a triggering event;

A mechanism for receiving and sending messages asynchronously is used. Messages are stored in a mail box and one of them is processed by the agent at the beginning of a reasoning cycle. The particular message to be handled at the beginning of the reasoning cycle is determined by a selection function, which can be customised by the programmer, as three selection functions that are originally part of the AgentSpeak interpreter.

Further, in processing messages we consider a "given" function, in the same way that the selection functions are assumed as given in an agent's specification. This function defines a set of *socially acceptable* messages. For example, the receiving agent may want to consider whether the sending agent is even allowed to communicated with it (e.g., to avoid agents being attacked by malicious communicating agents). For a message with illocutionary force `achieve`, the agent will have to check, for example, whether the sending agent has sufficient social power over itself, or whether it wishes to act altruistically towards that agent and then do whatever it is being asked.

Note that notions of trust can also be programmed into the agent by considering the annotation of the sources of information during the agent's practical reasoning. When applied to `tell` messages, the function only determines if the message is to be processed at all. When the source is "trusted" (in this limited sense used here), the information source for a belief acquired from communication is annotated with that belief in the belief base, enabling further consideration on degrees of trust during the agent's reasoning.

When the function for checking message acceptance is applied to an `achieve` message, it should be programmed to return true if, e.g., the agent has a subordination relation towards the sending agent. However this "power/subordination" relation should not be interpreted with particular social or psychological nuances: the programmer defines this function so as to account for all possible reasons for an agent to do something for another agent (from actual subordination to true altruism). Similar interpretations for the result of this function when applied to other types of messages (e.g., `askIf`) can be derived easily. For more elaborate conceptions of trust and power, see [14].

In order to endow AgentSpeak agents with the capability of processing communication messages, we annotate, for each belief, what is its source. This annotation mechanism provides a very elegant notation for making explicit the sources of an agent's belief. It has advantages in terms of expressive power and readability, besides allowing the use of such explicit information in an agent's reasoning (i.e., in selecting plans for achieving goals).

Belief sources can be annotated so as to identify which was the agent in the society that previously sent the information in a message, as well as to denote internal beliefs or percepts (i.e., in case the belief was acquired through perception of the environment). By using this information source annotation mechanism, we also clarify some practical problems in the implementation of AgentSpeak interpreters relating to internal beliefs (the ones added during the execution of a plan). In the interpreter reported in [3], we dealt with the problem by creating a separate belief base where the internal beliefs were included or removed.

Due to space restriction, we do not discuss the interpretation of received messages with each of the available illocutionary forces. This is presented both formally and informally in [31].

4.2   Cooperation in AgentSpeak

Coo-BDI (Cooperative BDI, [1]) extends traditional BDI agent-oriented programming languages in many respects: the introduction of *cooperation* among agents for the retrieval of external plans for a given triggering event; the extension of plans with *access specifiers*; the extension of *intentions* to take into account the external plan retrieval mechanism; and the modification of the interpreter to cope with all these issues.

The *cooperation strategy* of an agent *Ag* includes the set of agents with which it is expected to cooperate, the plan retrieval policy, and the plan acquisition policy. The cooperation strategy may evolve during time, allowing greater flexibility and autonomy to the agents, and is modelled by three functions:

- trusted(*Te, TrustedAgentSet*), where *Te* is a (not necessarily ground) triggering event and *TrustedAgentSet* is the set of agents that *Ag* will contact in order to obtain plans relevant for *Te*.
- retrievalPolicy(*Te,Retrieval*), where *Retrieval* may assume the values always and noLocal, meaning that relevant plans for the trigger *Te* must be retrieved from other agents in any case, or only when no local relevant plans are available, respectively.
- acquisitionPolicy(*Te,Acquisition*), where *Acquisition* may assume the values discard, add and replace meaning that, when a relevant plan for *Te* is retrieved from a trusted agent, it must be used and discarded, or added to the plan library, or used to update the plan library by replacing all the plans triggered by *Te*.

Plans. Besides the standard components which constitute BDI plans, in this extension plans also have a *source* which determines the first owner of the plan, and an *access specifier* which determines the set of agents with which the plan can be shared. The source may assume two values: self (the agent possesses the plan) and *Ag* (the agent was originally from *Ag*). The access specifier may assume three values: private (the plan cannot be shared), public (the plan can be shared with any agent) and only *(TrustedAgentSet)* (the plan can be shared only with the agents contained in *TrustedAgentSet*).

The Coo-AgentSpeak mechanism to be available in *Jason* soon will allow users to define cooperation strategies in the Coo-BDI style, and takes care of all other issues such as sending the appropriate requests for plans, suspending intentions that are waiting for plans to be retrieved from other agents, etc. The Coo-AgentSpeak mechanism is described in detail in [1].

One final characteristic of *Jason* that is relevant here is the configuration option on what to do in case there is no applicable plan for a relevant event. If an event is relevant, it means that there are plans in the agent's plan library for handling that particular event (representing that handling that event is normally a desire of that agent). If it happens that none of those plans are applicable at a certain time, this can be a problem as the agent does not know how to handle the situation at that time. Ancona and Mascardi [1] discussed how this problem is handled in various agent-oriented programming languages. In *Jason*, a configuration option is given to users, which can be set in the file where the various agents and the environment composing a multi-agent system are specified. The option allows the user to state, for events which have relevant but not applicable plans, whether the interpreter should discard that event altogether (events=discard) or insert the event back at the end of the event queue (events=requeue). Because of *Jason*'s customisation mechanisms, the only modification that were required for *Jason* to cope with Coo-AgentSpeak was a third configuration option that is available to the users — no changes to the interpreter itself was required. When Coo-AgentSpeak is to be used, the option events=retrieve must be used in the configuration file. This makes *Jason* call the user-defined selectOption function *even when no applicable plans exist for an event*. This way, part of the Coo-BDI approach can be implemented by providing a special `selectOption` function which takes care of retrieving plans externally, whenever appropriate.

5   Main Features of the *Jason* Platform

5.1   Configuring Multi-agent Systems

The configuration of a complete multi-agent system is given by a very simple text file. The EBNF grammar in Figure 3 gives the syntax that can be used in the configuration file. In this grammar, `<NUMBER>` is used for integer numbers, `<ASID>` are AgentSpeak identifiers, which must start with a lowercase letter, `<ID>` is any identifier (as usual), and `<PATH>` is as required for defining file pathnames as usual in ordinary operating systems.

The `<ID>` used after the keyword `MAS` is the name of the society. The keyword `infrastructure` is used to specify which of the two infrastructures available in *Jason*'s distribution will be used. The options currently available are either "Centralised" or "Saci"; the latter option allows agents to run on different machines over a network. It is important to note that the user's environment and customisation classes remain the same with both infrastructures.

Next an `environment` needs to be referenced. This is simply the name of Java class that was used for programming the environment. Note that an optional host name where the environment will run can be specified. This only works if the SACI option is used for the underlying system infrastructure.

The keyword `agents` is used for defining the set of agents that will take part in the multi-agent system. An agent is specified first by its symbolic name given as an AgentSpeak term (i.e., an identifier starting with a lowercase letter); this is the name that agents will use to refer to other agents in the society (e.g., for

```
mas            →  "MAS" <ID> "{"
                     [ "infrastructure" ":" <ID> ]
                     [ environment ]
                     agents
                  "}"
environment    →  "environment" ":" <ID> [ "at" <ID> ]
agents         →  "agents" ":" ( agent ";" )+
agent          →  <ASID>
                     [ filename ]
                     [ options ]
                     [ "agentArchClass" <ID> ]
                     [ "agentClass" <ID> ]
                     [ "#" <NUMBER> ]
                     [ "at" <ID> ]
filename       →  [ <PATH> ] <ID>
options        →  "[" option ( "," option )* "]"
option         →  <ID> "=" ( <ID> | <NUMBER> | <STRING> )
```

Fig. 3. EBNF of the Language for Configuring Multi-Agent Systems

inter-agent communication). Then, an optional filename can be given where the AgentSpeak source code for that agent is given; by default *Jason* assumes that the AgentSpeak source code is in file `<name>.asl`, where `<name>` is the agent's symbolic name. There is also an optional list of settings for the AgentSpeak interpreter available in *Jason* (these are explained below). An optional number of instances of agents using that same source code can be specified by a number preceded by `#`; if this is present, that specified number of "clones" will be created in the multi-agent system. In case more than one instance of that agent is requested, the actual name of the agent will be the symbolic name concatenated with an index indicating the instance number (starting from 1). As for the `environment` keyword, an agent definition may end with the name of a host where the agent(s) will run (preceded by "at"). As before, this only works if the SACI-based infrastructure was chosen.

The user can change the initial settings of the AgentSpeak interpreter available in *Jason*, or pass on settings to the agent classes by enclosing in square brackets certain configuration statements. These have the form of a keyword, followed by '=' and then the value (possibly predefined keywords) attributed to them; see [8] for further details. Finally, user-defined overall agent architecture and other user-defined functions to be used by the AgentSpeak interpreter for each particular agent can be specified with the keywords `agentArchClass` and `agentClass`.

5.2 Creating Environments

Jason agents can be situated in real or simulated environments. In the former case, the user would have to customise the "overall agent architecture", as described in the next part of this section; in the latter case, the user must provide an implementation of the simulated environment. This is done directly in a Java class that extends the *Jason* base Environment class. A general example of an environment class is shown in Figure 4.

All percepts (i.e., everything that is perceptible in the environment) should be determined using the addPercept method; the argument is a literal, so strong negation can be used in applications where there is open-world assumption. It is possible to send individualised perception; that is, in programming the environment the developer can determine what subset of the environment properties will be perceptible to individual agents. Recall that within an agent's overall architecture you can further customise what beliefs the agent will actually aquire from what it perceives. Intuitively, the environment properties available to an agent from the environment definition itself are associated to what is actually perceptible at all in the environment (for example, if something is behind my office's walls, I cannot see it). The customisation at the agent overall architecture level should be used for simulating faulty perception (i.e., even though something is perceptible for that agent in that environment, it may still not include some of those properties in its belief revision process, because it failed to perceive it). Determination of an agent's individual perception within the environment is done by using the "addPercept(`agentName`, `percept`)" method, where `agentName` is a string and `percept` is a literal.

```
public class myEnv extends Environment {

    public myEnv() {
        // environment initialisations
    }

    public String getPos(String ag) {
        // some code that returns the agent position
    }

    public boolean executeAction(String ag, Term action) {
        if (action.equals(...)) {
            // execute the action
        }
        ...
        removePercept(ag); // remove all percepts of agent ag
        addPercept(ag,Literal.parseLiteral("pos(r1," + getPos(ag) + ")"));
        addPercept(p); // add p as a percept to all agents
        return true;
    }
}
```

Fig. 4. Example of an Environment Class

Most of the code for building environments should be (referenced) in the body of the method executeAction which must be declared as described above. Whenever an agent tries to execute a basic action (those which are supposed to change the state of the environment), the name of the agent and a Term representing the chosen action are sent as parameter to this method. So the code for this method needs to check the Term (which has the form of a Prolog structure) representing the action (and any parameters) being executed, and check which is the agent attempting to execute the action, then do whatever is necessary in that particular model of an environment — normally, this means changing the percepts, i.e., what is true or false of the environment is changed according to the actions being performed. Note that the execution of an action needs to return a boolean value, stating whether the agent's attempt at performing that action on the environment was executed or not. A plan fails if any basic action attempted by the agent fails.

5.3   Customising Agents

Certain aspects of the cognitive functioning of an agent can be customised by the user overriding methods of the Agent class (see Figure 5). The three first selection functions are discussed extensively in the AgentSpeak literature (see Section 3 and Figure 2). The social acceptance function (socAcc, which is related to pragmatics, e.g., trust and power social relations) and the message selection function are discussed in [31] and Section 4. By changing the message selection function, the user can determine that the agent will give preference to messages from certain agents, or certain types of messages, when various messages have been received during one reasoning cycle. While basic actions are being executed by the environment, before the (boolean) feedback from the environment is available the intention to which that action belongs must be suspended; the last internal function allows customisation of priorities to be given when more than one intention can be resumed because feedback from the environment became available during the last reasoning cycle.

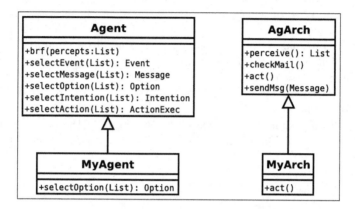

Fig. 5. Agent Customisation

Similarly, the user can customise the functions defining the overall agent architecture (see Figure 5, AgArch class). These functions handle: (i) the way the agent will perceive the environment; (ii) the way it will update its belief base given the current perception of the environment, i.e., the so called belief revision function (BRF) in the AgentSpeak literature; (iii) how the agent gets messages sent from other agents (for speech-act based inter-agent communication); and (iv) how the agent acts on the environment (for the basic actions that appear in the body of plans) — normally this is provided by the environment implementation, so this function only has to pass the action selected by the agent on to the environment, but clearly for multi-agent systems situated in a real-world environment this might be more complicated, having to interface with, e.g., available process control hardware.

For the perception function, it may be interesting to use the function defined in *Jason*'s distribution and, after it has received the current percepts, then process further the list of percepts, in order to simulate faulty perception, for example. This is on top of the environment being modelled so as to send different percepts to different agents, according to their perception abilities (so to speak) within the given multi-agent system (as with ELMS environments, see [12]).

It is important to emphasise that the belief revision function provided with *Jason* simply updates the belief base and generates the external events (i.e., additions and deletion of beliefs from the belief base) in accordance with current percepts. In particular, it does not guarantee belief consistency. As percepts are actually sent from the environment, and they should be lists of terms stating everything that is true (and explicitly false too, if closed-world assumption is dropped), it is up to the programmer of the environment to make sure that contradictions do not appear in the percepts. Also, if AgentSpeak programmers use addition of internal beliefs in the body of plans, it is their responsibility to ensure consistency. In fact, the user might be interested in modelling a "paraconsistent" agent, which can be done easily.

An important construct for allowing AgentSpeak agents to remain at the right level of abstraction is that of internal actions, which allows for straightforward extensibility and use of legacy code. As suggested in [3], internal actions that start with '.' are part of a standard library of internal actions that are distributed with **Jason**. Internal actions defined by users should be organised in specific libraries, which provides an interesting way of organising such code, which is normally useful for a range of different systems. In the AgentSpeak program, the action is accessed by the name of the library, followed by '.', followed by the name of the action. Libraries are defined as Java packages and each action in the user library should be a Java class, the name of the package and class are the names of the library and action as it will be used in the AgentSpeak programs.

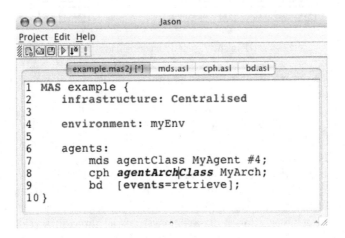

Fig. 6. *Jason* IDE

5.4   Available Tools and Documentation

Jason is distributed with an Integrated Development Environment (IDE) which provides a GUI for editing a MAS configuration file as well as AgentSpeak code for the individual agents. Figure 6 shows a screenshot of the **Jason** IDE, when the user is editing the multi-agent systems configuration file; the AgentSpeak code of each agent can also be edited (with syntax highlight) from the GUI.

Through the IDE, it is also possible to control the execution of a MAS, and to distribute agents over a network in a very simple way. There are three execution modes:

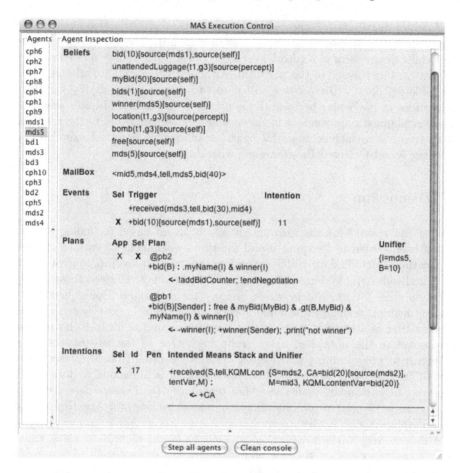

Fig. 7. *Jason*'s Mind Inspector

Asynchronous: in which all agents run asynchronously. An agent goes to its next reasoning cycle as soon as it has finished its current cycle. This is the default execution mode.

Synchronous: in which each agent performs a single reasoning cycle in every "global execution step". That is, when an agent finishes a reasoning cycle, it informs *Jason*'s execution controller, and waits for a "carry on" signal. The *Jason* controller waits until all agents have finished their current reasoning cycle and then sends the "carry on" signal to them.

Debugging: this execution mode is similar to the synchronous mode; however, the *Jason* controller also waits until the user clicks on a "Step" button in the GUI before sending the "carry on" signal to the agents.

There is another tool provided as part of the IDE which allows the user to inspect agents' internal states when the system is running in debugging mode. This is very useful for debugging MAS, as it allows "inspection of agents' minds" across a distributed system. The tool is called "mind inspector", and is shown in Figure 7.

Jason's distribution comes with documentation which is also available on-line at `http://jason.sourceforge.net/Jason.pdf`. The documentation has something of the form of a tutorial on AgentSpeak, followed by a description of the features and usage of the platform. Although it covers all of the currently available features of *Jason*, we still plan to improve substantially the documentation, in particular because the language is at times still quite academic. Another planned improvement in the available documentation, in the relatively short term, is to include material (such as slides and practical exercises) for teaching Agent-Oriented Programming with *Jason*.

6   Discussion

One of the reasons for the growing success of agent-based technology is that it has been shown to be quite useful for the development of various types of applications, including air-traffic control, autonomous spacecraft control, health care, and industrial systems control, to name just a few. Clearly, these are application areas for which *dependable systems* are in demand. Consequently, formal verification techniques tailored specifically for multi-agent systems is also an area that is attracting much research attention and is likely to have a major impact in the uptake of agent technology. One of the advantages of the approach to programming multi-agent systems resulting from the research reviewed in this paper is precisely the fact that it is amenable to formal verification. In particular, model checking techniques (and state-space reduction techniques to be used in combination with model checking) for AgentSpeak have been developed [6, 7, 5, 13].

Although very little has been considered so far in regards to using agent-oriented software engineering methodologies for the development of designs for systems to be implemented in *Jason*, existing methodologies that specifically concern BDI agents, such as Prometheus [23], should be perfectly suitable for that purpose. In that book, the authors show an example of the use of JACK (see [32]) for the implementation, but they explicitly say that any platform that provides the basic concepts of reactive planning systems (such as goals and plans) would be most useful in the sense of providing all the required constructs to support the implementation of designs developed in accordance to the Prometheus methodology. Because AgentSpeak code is considerably more readable than other languages such as JACK and Jadex (see [25]), it is arguable that *Jason* will provide at least a much more clear way of implementing such designs. However, being an industrial platform, JACK has, currently, far better supporting tools and documentation, but on the other hand, *Jason* is *open source*, whereas JACK is not.

A construct that has an important impact in maintaining the right level of abstraction in AgentSpeak code even for sophisticated systems is that of internal actions (described earlier in Section 2). Internal actions necessarily have a boolean value returned, so they are declaratively represented within a logic program in AgentSpeak — in effect, we can keep the agent program as a high-level representation of the agent's reasoning, yet allowing it to be arbitrarily sophisticated by the use of existing software implemented in Java, or indeed any programming language through the use of JNI. Thus, the way in which integration with traditional object-oriented programming and use of legacy code is accomplished in *Jason* is far more elegant than with other agent programming languages (again, such as JACK and Jadex).

As *Jason* is implemented in Java, there is no issue with portability, but very little consideration has been given so far to standards compliance and interoperability. However, components of the platform can be easily changed by the user. For example, at the moment there are two infrastructures available in *Jason*'s distribution: a centralised one (which means that the whole system runs in a single machine) and another which uses SACI for distribution. It should be reasonably simple to produce another infrastructure which uses, e.g., JADE (see [2]) for FIPA-compliant distribution and management of agents in a multi-agent system.

As yet, *Jason* has been used only for a couple of application described below, and also for simple student projects in academia. However, due to its AgentSpeak basis, it is clearly suited to a large range of applications for which it is known that BDI systems are appropriate; various applications of PRS [16] and dMARS [17] for example have appeared in the literature [34, Chapter 11].

Although we aim to use it for a wide range of applications in the future, in particular Semantic Web and Grid-based applications, one particular area of application in which we have great interest is Social Simulation [15]. In fact, *Jason* is being used as part of a large project to produce a platform tailored particularly to Social Simulation. The platform is called MAS-SOC and is described in [12]; it includes a high-level language called ELMS [22] for defining multi-agent environments. This approach was used to develop a simple social simulation on social aspects of urban growth. Another area of application that has been initially explored is the use of AgentSpeak for defining the behaviour of animated characters for computer animation (or virtual reality) [30].

7   Final Remarks

Jason is being actively improved and extended. The long term objective is to have a platform which makes available important technologies resulting from research in the area of Multi-Agent Systems, but doing this in a sensible way so as to avoid the language becoming cumbersome and, most importantly, having formal semantics for most, if not all, of the essential features available in *Jason*. There are ongoing projects to extend *Jason* with organisations, given that social structure is an essential aspect of developing complex multi-agent systems, and with ontological descriptions underlying the belief base, thus facilitating the use of *Jason* for Semantic Web and Grid-based applications. We aim to contribute, for example, to the area of e-Social Science, developing large-scale Grid-based social simulations using *Jason*.

Acknowledgments

As seen from the various references throughout this document, the research on AgentSpeak has been carried out with the help of many colleagues. We are grateful for the many contributions received over the last few years from: Davide Ancona, Marcelo G. de Azambuja, Deniel M. Basso, Ana L.C. Bazzan, Antônio Carlos da Rocha Costa, Guilherme Drehmer, Michael Fisher, Rafael de O. Jannone, Romulo Krafta, Viviana Mascardi, Victor Lesser, Rodrigo Machado, Joyce Martins, Álvaro F. Moreira, Fabio Y. Okuyama, Denise de Oliveira, Carmen Pardavila, Marios Richards, Maíra R. Rodrigues, Rosa M. Vicari, Willem Visser, Michael Wooldridge.

Rafael Bordini gratefully acknowledges the support of The Nuffield Foundation (grant number NAL/01065/G).

References

1. D. Ancona, V. Mascardi, J. F. Hübner, and R. H. Bordini. Coo-AgentSpeak: Cooperation in AgentSpeak through plan exchange. In N. R. Jennings, C. Sierra, L. Sonenberg, and M. Tambe, editors, *Proceedings of the Third International Joint Conference on Autonomous Agents and Multi-Agent Systems (AAMAS-2004), New York, NY, 19–23 July*, pages 698–705, New York, NY, 2004. ACM Press.

2. F. Bellifemine, F. Bergenti, G. Caire, and A. Poggi. JADE — a java agent development framework. In Bordini et al. [4], chapter 5, pages 125–147.

3. R. H. Bordini, A. L. C. Bazzan, R. O. Jannone, D. M. Basso, R. M. Vicari, and V. R. Lesser. AgentSpeak(XL): Efficient intention selection in BDI agents via decision-theoretic task scheduling. In C. Castelfranchi and W. L. Johnson, editors, *Proceedings of the First International Joint Conference on Autonomous Agents and Multi-Agent Systems (AAMAS-2002), 15–19 July, Bologna, Italy*, pages 1294–1302, New York, NY, 2002. ACM Press.

4. R. H. Bordini, M. Dastani, J. Dix, and A. El Fallah Seghrouchni, editors. *Multi-Agent Programming: Languages, Platforms and Applications*. Number 15 in Multi-agent Systems, Artificial Societies, and Simulated Organizations. Springer-Verlag, 2005.

5. R. H. Bordini, M. Fisher, C. Pardavila, and M. Wooldridge. Model checking AgentSpeak. In J. S. Rosenschein, T. Sandholm, M. Wooldridge, and M. Yokoo, editors, *Proceedings of the Second International Joint Conference on Autonomous Agents and Multi-Agent Systems (AAMAS-2003), Melbourne, Australia, 14–18 July*, pages 409–416, New York, NY, 2003. ACM Press.

6. R. H. Bordini, M. Fisher, W. Visser, and M. Wooldridge. Model checking rational agents. *IEEE Intelligent Systems*, 19(5):46–52, September/October 2004.

7. R. H. Bordini, M. Fisher, W. Visser, and M. Wooldridge. State-space reduction techniques in agent verification. In N. R. Jennings, C. Sierra, L. Sonenberg, and M. Tambe, editors, *Proceedings of the Third International Joint Conference on Autonomous Agents and Multi-Agent Systems (AAMAS-2004), New York, NY, 19–23 July*, pages 896–903, New York, NY, 2004. ACM Press.

8. R. H. Bordini, J. F. Hübner, et al. *Jason: A Java-based agentSpeak interpreter used with saci for multi-agent distribution over the net*, manual, version 0.6 edition, Feb 2005. http://jason.sourceforge.net/.

9. R. H. Bordini, J. F. Hübner, and R. Vieira. *Jason* and the golden fleece of agent-oriented programming. In Bordini et al. [4], chapter 1, pages 3–37.

10. R. H. Bordini and Á. F. Moreira. Proving the asymmetry thesis principles for a BDI agent-oriented programming language. In J. Dix, J. A. Leite, and K. Satoh, editors, *Proceedings of the Third International Workshop on Computational Logic in Multi-Agent Systems (CLIMA-02), 1st August, Copenhagen, Denmark, held as part of FLoC-02*, Electronic Notes in Theoretical Computer Science 70(5). Elsevier, 2002. URL: <http://www.elsevier.nl/locate/entcs/volume70.html>.

11. R. H. Bordini and Á. F. Moreira. Proving BDI properties of agent-oriented programming languages: The asymmetry thesis principles in AgentSpeak(L). *Annals of Mathematics and Artificial Intelligence*, 42(1–3):197–226, Sept. 2004. Special Issue on Computational Logic in Multi-Agent Systems.

12. R. H. Bordini, F. Y. Okuyama, D. de Oliveira, G. Drehmer, and R. C. Krafta. The MAS-SOC approach to multi-agent based simulation. In G. Lindemann, D. Moldt, and M. Paolucci, editors, *Proceedings of the First International Workshop on Regulated Agent-Based Social Systems: Theories and Applications (RASTA'02), 16 July, 2002, Bologna, Italy (held with AAMAS02) — Revised Selected and Invited Papers*, number 2934 in Lecture Notes in Artificial Intelligence, pages 70–91, Berlin, 2004. Springer-Verlag.

13. R. H. Bordini, W. Visser, M. Fisher, C. Pardavila, and M. Wooldridge. Model checking multi-agent programs with CASP. In W. A. Hunt Jr. and F. Somenzi, editors, *Proceedgins of the Fifteenth Conference on Computer-Aided Verification (CAV-2003), Boulder, CO, 8–12 July*, number 2725 in Lecture Notes in Computer Science, pages 110–113, Berlin, 2003. Springer-Verlag. Tool description.

14. C. Castelfranchi and R. Falcone. Principles of trust for MAS: Cognitive anatomy, social importance, and quantification. In Y. Demazeau, editor, *Proceedings of the Third International Conference on Multi-Agent Systems (ICMAS'98), Agents' World, 4–7 July, Paris*, pages 72–79, Washington, 1998. IEEE Computer Society Press.

15. J. Doran and N. Gilbert. Simulating societies: An introduction. In N. Gilbert and J. Doran, editors, *Simulating Society: The Computer Simulation of Social Phenomena*, chapter 1, pages 1–18. UCL Press, London, 1994.

16. M. P. Georgeff and A. L. Lansky. Reactive reasoning and planning. In *Proceedings of the Sixth National Conference on Artificial Intelligence (AAAI'87), 13–17 July, 1987, Seattle, WA*, pages 677–682, Manlo Park, CA, 1987. AAAI Press / MIT Press.

17. D. Kinny. The distributed multi-agent reasoning system architecture and language specification. Technical report, Australian Artificial Intelligence Institute, Melbourne, Australia, 1993.

18. J. A. Leite. *Evolving Knowledge Bases: Specification and Semantics*, volume 81 of *Frontiers in Artificial Intelligence and Applications, Dissertations in Artificial Intelligence*. IOS Press/Ohmsha, Amsterdam, 2003.

19. R. Machado and R. H. Bordini. Running AgentSpeak(L) agents on SIM_AGENT. In J.-J. Meyer and M. Tambe, editors, *Intelligent Agents VIII – Proceedings of the Eighth International Workshop on Agent Theories, Architectures, and Languages (ATAL-2001), August 1–3, 2001, Seattle, WA*, number 2333 in Lecture Notes in Artificial Intelligence, pages 158–174, Berlin, 2002. Springer-Verlag.

20. Á. F. Moreira and R. H. Bordini. An operational semantics for a BDI agent-oriented programming language. In J.-J. C. Meyer and M. J. Wooldridge, editors, *Proceedings of the Workshop on Logics for Agent-Based Systems (LABS-02), held in conjunction with the Eighth International Conference on Principles of Knowledge Representation and Reasoning (KR2002), April 22–25, Toulouse, France*, pages 45–59, 2002.

21. Á. F. Moreira, R. Vieira, and R. H. Bordini. Extending the operational semantics of a BDI agent-oriented programming language for introducing speech-act based communication. In J. Leite, A. Omicini, L. Sterling, and P. Torroni, editors, *Declarative Agent Languages and Technologies, Proceedings of the First International Workshop (DALT-03), held with AAMAS-03, 15 July, 2003, Melbourne, Australia (Revised Selected and Invited Papers)*, number 2990 in Lecture Notes in Artificial Intelligence, pages 135–154, Berlin, 2004. Springer-Verlag.

22. F. Y. Okuyama, R. H. Bordini, and A. C. da Rocha Costa. ELMS: an environment description language for multi-agent simulations. In D. Weyns, H. van Dyke Parunak, F. Michel, T. Holvoet, and J. Ferber, editors, *Environments for Multiagent Systems, State-of-the-art and Research Challenges. Proceedings of the First International Workshop on Environments for Multiagent Systems (E4MAS), held with AAMAS-04, 19th of July*, number 3374 in Lecture Notes in Artificial Intelligence, pages 91–108, Berlin, 2005. Springer-Verlag.

23. L. Padgham and M. Winikoff, editors. *Developing Intelligent Agent Systems: A Practical Guide*. John Wiley and Sons, 2004.

24. G. D. Plotkin. A structural approach to operational semantics. Technical report, Computer Science Department, Aarhus University, Aarhus, 1981.

25. A. Pokahr, L. Braubach, and W. Lamersdorf. Jadex: A BDI reasoning engine. In Bordini et al. [4], chapter 6, pages 149–174.

26. A. S. Rao. AgentSpeak(L): BDI agents speak out in a logical computable language. In W. Van de Velde and J. Perram, editors, *Proceedings of the Seventh Workshop on Modelling Autonomous Agents in a Multi-Agent World (MAAMAW'96), 22–25 January, Eindhoven, The Netherlands*, number 1038 in Lecture Notes in Artificial Intelligence, pages 42–55, London, 1996. Springer-Verlag.

27. A. S. Rao and M. P. Georgeff. BDI agents: From theory to practice. In V. Lesser and L. Gasser, editors, *Proceedings of the First International Conference on Multi-Agent Systems (ICMAS'95), 12–14 June, San Francisco, CA*, pages 312–319, Menlo Park, CA, 1995. AAAI Press / MIT Press.

28. A. S. Rao and M. P. Georgeff. Decision procedures for BDI logics. *Journal of Logic and Computation*, 8(3):293–343, 1998.

29. M. P. Singh, A. S. Rao, and M. P. Georgeff. Formal methods in DAI: Logic-based representation and reasoning. In G. Weiß, editor, *Multiagent Systems—A Modern Approach to Distributed Artificial Intelligence*, chapter 8, pages 331–376. MIT Press, Cambridge, MA, 1999.

30. J. A. Torres, L. P. Nedel, and R. H. Bordini. Autonomous agents with multiple foci of attention in virtual environments. In *Proceedings of 17th International Conference on Computer Animation and Social Agents (CASA 2004), Geneva, Switzerland, 7–9 July*, pages 189–196, 2004.

31. R. Vieira, A. Moreira, M. Wooldridge, and R. H. Bordini. On the formal semantics of speech-act based communication in an agent-oriented programming language. *Submitted article, to appear*, 2005.

32. M. Winikoff. JACK^{TM} intelligent agents: An industrial strength platform. In Bordini et al. [4], chapter 7, pages 175–193.

33. M. Wooldridge. *Reasoning about Rational Agents*. The MIT Press, Cambridge, MA, 2000.

34. M. Wooldridge. *An Introduction to MultiAgent Systems*. John Wiley & Sons, 2002.

Using the KGP Model of Agency to Design Applications

Fariba Sadri

Department of Computing,
Imperial College London,
180 Queen's gate, London SW7 2BZ, UK
fs@doc.ic.ac.uk

Abstract. This paper is a tutorial describing the main features of the KGP (Knowledge-Goals-Plan) model of agency and giving user guidance on how the model can be used to develop applications. The KGP model is based on computational logic. It consists of an abstract component, a computational component and an implementation. This paper concentrates on the abstract component, which consists of formal specifications of a number of different modules, including the knowledge bases, capabilities, transitions and control. For each of these we summarise what is provided by the model, and through the platform implementing the model, and what is left to the users to specify according to the requirements of the applications for which they wish to use the KGP model to design agents.

1 Introduction

1.1 The Model

The KGP (Knowledge-Goals-Plan) model of agency has been developed within the EU SOCS (Societies of Computational Entities) project in a collaborative effort involving Imperial College, City University, and the universities of Cyprus, Pisa, Bologna, and Ferrara. Information about the project can be found at http://lia.deis.unibo.it/research/socs/.

The model is general purpose and highly modular. All of its components, including its control component, are based on computational logic, and more concretely on abductive logic programming [8] and logic programming with priorities [3], both with extensions that deal with temporal constraints.

The model includes:

- an abstract model (declarative semantics): providing formal specifications, in computational logic, for all the components,
- a computational model (operational semantics): providing a computational counterpart for all the formal components of the abstract model, and
- a prototype implementation (PROSOCS) in Prolog, Java and JXTA [19].

The computational model exploits the modularity of the abstract model and has been proved correct with respect to it. It consists of:

F. Toni and P. Torroni (Eds.): CLIMA VI, LNAI 3900, pp. 165–185, 2006.

- a proof procedure, CIFF [4,5,6], that combines abduction and constraint logic programming, for the components of the model that are based on abductive logic programming, and
- a proof procedure, Gorgias [7], that combines argumentation and constraints, for the components of the model that are based on logic programming with priorities.

In this paper we concentrate on the abstract model.

The KGP model has been designed to cater for the needs of a global computing setting. To this end it provides heterogeneity, allowing agents to be designed such that they differ from each other in their knowledge and behaviour. It also incorporates features that allow agents to function in dynamic open environments, adapt to changes in the environment and interact with other agents.

The model integrates various aspects of agency, including:

- Reasoning: for example for planning and proactivity
- Reactivity: for example allowing agents to react to changes they perceive in their environment by performing actions, including sending communications to other agents
- Goal introduction: allowing agents to alter their goals according to their circumstances
- Declarative control: providing dynamic control of the operations of the agent
- (some) Belief revision: for example allowing agents to modify their beliefs in the light of their observations
- Interaction: for example allowing agents to negotiate with one another for resources.

The model and its prototype implementation have been used in applications in combinatorial auctions and negotiation for resources. The formal basis of the model facilitates formal specification and verification of properties. Such properties have been studied and are reported in [1].

A detailed description of the KGP model and its comparison with other models can be found in [9,10], a summary in [2, 11], and details of its implementation in [18]. Details of some components of the model can be found in [14] for the planning component, in [12] for the control component, and in [4, 5, 6] and [7] for the proof procedures. Extensions of the model than incorporate normative concepts can be found in [16, 17].

1.2 Examples

The following examples can help provide a quick and informal introduction to some of the main features of the KGP model.

KGP agents have individual states that are updated as they observe their environment and interact with other agents. They decide dynamically what goals to set themselves depending on their own individual preferences and what they know about their environments.

At any particular time the agent may consider a number of potential goals, for example:

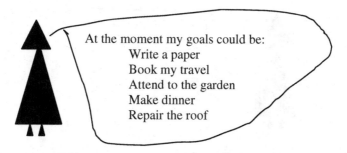

At the moment my goals could be:
    Write a paper
    Book my travel
    Attend to the garden
    Make dinner
    Repair the roof

Then depending on its knowledge of the environment, its temporal constraints (e.g. deadline for the paper) and its preferences it can decide which of the possible goals to set itself at that particular time. For example it may decide that the two goals of writing a paper and booking travel should be given highest priority.

I am going to:
    Write a paper and
    Book my travel

It may then proceed with the task of achieving its chosen goals. Concurrently with planning how to achieve its goals and executing actions, the agent observes its environment and records information and communications it receives from the environment and from other agents. For example it may observe that it is raining and that water is pouring in through the roof.

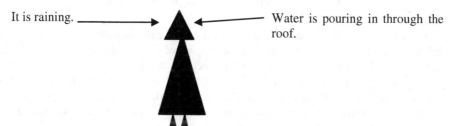

It is raining. ⟶ ⟵ Water is pouring in through the roof.

It adapts to changes that it perceives in its environment and circumstances by adjusting or changing its goals, or reacting in some other appropriate way. For example the observation that the roof is leaking may change the agent's priorities and give higher priority to the goal of repairing the roof than the other potential goals.

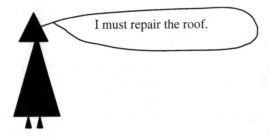

The agent plans (partially) for its goals and executes actions towards achieving them. For example (informally) the following could be a partial plan for the goal of repairing the roof.

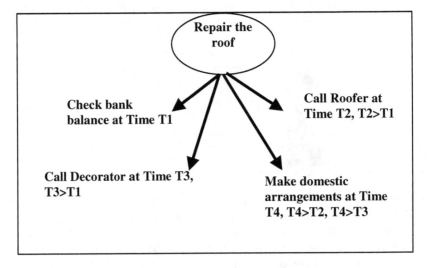

Fig. 1. A partial plan for the goal "Repair the roof"

The partial plan above consists of three actions of checking the bank balance, and calling the roofer and the decorator, and a subgoal of making domestic arrangements which has to be further planned for. All the actions and the subgoal have associated times, possibly as yet undetermined, with some constraints on them, for example that calling the roofer and the decorator should take place after checking the bank balance. Of the three actions here two are *communicative* (calling the roofer and the decorator) and one is *sensing* (checking bank balance).

KGP agents can interleave action execution with planning and observing their environment. Sometimes the result of their action execution or what they observe calls for adjustments to their plans. For example the agent with the plan above may find out that its bank balance is rather low after it executes the action of checking its bank balance. This new knowledge, in turn, can result in the agent setting itself an additional goal of finding more money, and giving this goal appropriate temporal constraints with respect to its other goals.

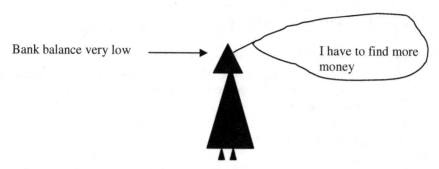

KGP agents interact with each other. Each one has its own policy on how to respond to messages it receives from others. Such interactions can be used, for example, to ask for resources:

One particularly novel feature of the model is its dynamic context-dependent control. Control is specified by cycle theories that are defined as logic programs with priorities. They allow the agent to determine at run-time what to do next and they allow us to design agents with heterogeneous behaviours.

In the remainder of this paper, we describe the abstract part of the KGP model in more detail, and explain how a designer can proceed to use the model to develop an application. For lack of space our description of the model will not give full details. More details can be found in [9]. Here we summarise the model to the extent of explaining its main features and giving guidelines to the user. Throughout this paper by "user of the model" we mean the person who uses the KGP model to design agents for an application.

2 The KGP Model in a Nutshell

In the KGP model an agent is characterised by the following components:

- An internal mental state, < KB, Goals, Plan >, consisting of a KB which is a collection of knowledge bases, and the agent's (current) goals and plan
- A set of reasoning capabilities
- A sensing capability
- A set of formal state transition rules
- A cycle theory.

The cycle theory orchestrates the application of the transitions, which, in turn, use the capabilities, which use the information in the knowledge bases in the agent's internal mental state. These knowledge bases are updated as the agent receives information from the environment and executes actions in the environment.

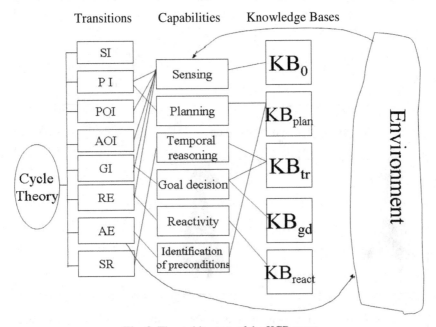

Fig. 2. The architecture of the KGP agent

Some components of the model are fixed, i.e. pre-defined and provided through the implementation platform. These are typically the domain-independent parts of the model:

- The structure of the internal mental state
- The set of capabilities and transitions
- The definition of the capabilities
- The definition of the transitions
- The syntax of the knowledge bases in KB
- Some parts of the knowledge bases

- The syntax of the rules in the cycle theories
- The definition of some of the selection operators (see Section 6) that are used in cycle theories.

Other components of the model are under the control of the application designer using the model. These should be specified by the designer to cater for the requirements and domains of his applications. These components specify domain-dependent knowledge and the specific behaviour requirements of the agent being designed. These user-specified components are:

- Some of the contents of the knowledge bases in KB:
  to cater for knowledge related to a domain or application, knowledge about the priorities of the agents being designed, and the agents' interaction policies.
- The contents of the cycle theories:
  to design the behaviour and profile of agents.
- Some of the definitions of the selection operators:
  to design heuristics affecting the agents' decision making.

Domain specific requirements and heterogeneity are provided by varying the contents of the components that are under the control of the user of the model. We now describe all the components of the model in more detail.

3   The Internal Mental State

The internal mental state of an agent is a triple $<$ KB, Goals, Plan $>$.

3.1   KB, the Agent's Knowledge Base

KB consists of several modules supporting the reasoning capabilities. These modules are:

- KB0: used to store dynamic data
- KB_{plan}: used for planning
- KB_{tr}: used for temporal reasoning
- KB_{react}: used for reactivity
- KB_{gd}: used for goal decision

Now we describe each of these in some detail.

The first (KB0) is a set of logic facts. The last (KB_{gd}) is a logic program with priorities, and the remaining three (KB_{plan}, KB_{tr}, KB_{react}) are abductive logic programs.

KB0 is a dynamic knowledge base which is *revised* as the agent observes its environment (via its sensing capability) and is *contained* within all the other knowledge bases (and is used by all capabilities).

What the model provides:

KB0 of agent a records the following types of information (for details of syntax the reader is referred to [9] or [11]):

- actions which have been executed by a, together with the time of the execution
  (executed(action, time))

- actions which have been executed by agents y other than *a*, together with the time of observation by *a* *(observed(y,action,t))*
- properties (fluent literals) observed by *a*, together with the time of observation *(observed(literal, time))*.

What the user has to provide:
The contents of KB0 are determined by the sensing capability and the Passive and Active Observation transitions (see Section 5), and, of course, by the environment of the agent. The user of the model does not need to design or provide any of the contents of KB0.

KB_{plan} is the knowledge base that is used (in conjunction with KB0) to generate plans for the agents' goals (via the Planning capability and Plan Introduction transition - see Sections 4 and 5). It is an abductive event calculus (AEC) theory. For a description of abductive logic programming see [8], for event calculus see [13], and for abductive event calculus see [14].

What the model provides:
In a nutshell $KB_{plan}= < P_{plan}, A_{plan}, I_{plan} >$. P_{plan} is a set of rules that define effects and preconditions of actions. In describing the effects of actions it defines a predicate *holds_at(Literal,Time)* in terms of *happens(Action,Time)* and *observed(Literal,Time)*.

In particular P_{plan} has two sets of rules, those that are domain-independent and those that are domain-dependent. The domain-dependent part of P_{plan} has to be specified by the user (see later). The following are some of the domain-independent rules in P_{plan}. In these and in the other rules in the remainder of this paper a comma between atoms on either side of the arrow represents the connective "and". All the variables are assumed to be universally quantified over the rule they occur in, unless stated otherwise.

```
holds_at(G,T2)←happens(A,T1),  T1 < T2,
            initiates(A,T1,G),  not clipped(T1,  G,  T2)

holds_at(G,T)←holds_initially(G),  0 < T,
            not clipped(0,G,T)

holds_at(G,T2)  ←  observed(G,T1),  T1 < T2,
            not clipped(T1,G,T2)

clipped(T1,G,T2)  ←  happens(A,T),  terminates(A,T,G),
            T1<T,  T<T2

happens(A,T)←  executed(A,T)

happens(A,T)←  assume_happens(A,T)
```

These rules express that a property G holds at a time if at an earlier time an action initiating it has been executed or assumed (via abduction), or if it held initially (at time 0), or if at an earlier time it has been observed to hold, and, in all cases, provided that G has not been clipped via a terminating action between the two times. The 3rd and 5th rules are bridge rules for connecting the AEC theory to KB0. The 6th rule allows abductions of actions in order to form a plan.

A_{plan}, the set of abducible atoms, consists of *assume_happens(Action,Time)*. A plan will contain a set of ground instances of this abducible atom providing the actions of

the plan. A brief example is given below. I_{plan}, the set of integrity constraints. Like
• P_{plan} it consists of a domain-dependent part and a domain-independent part. The latter
consists of the following integrity constraints:

```
holds_at(Literal,Time), holds_at(¬Literal,Time)→ false
assume_happens(Action,Time),precondition(Action,Time,L)
       → holds_at(L, Time)
```

The first constraint expresses that a property and its negation cannot hold at the
same time, and the second expresses that if an action is assumed to happen at a time
then at that time its precondition must hold.

What the user has to provide:
The user has to provide the domain-dependent parts of P_{plan} and I_{plan}. The domain-
dependent part of P_{plan} consists of:

- what holds initially, using the predicate *holds_initially(l)* to denote that a fluent *l*
  holds initially (at time 0), e.g. *holds_initially(at(john, home))* expresses that John is
  initially at home,
- what actions initiate and terminate what properties, using the predicates *initiates(a,
  t, l)* and *terminates(a,t,l)* to denote that action *a*, executed at time *t* initiates or
  terminates the fluent *l*, respectively, e.g. *initiates(go(X, L1,L2),T,at(X,L2))* and
  terminates(go(X, L1,L2),T,at(X,L1)) state that going from location *L1* to *L2*
  initiates being at *L2* and terminates being at *L1*, and
- the preconditions of actions, using the predicate *precondition(a,t,l)* to denote that
  fluent *l* is a precondition for executing action *a* at time *t*, e.g. *precondition(go(X,
  L1,L2),T,at(X,L1))* expresses that a precondition for going from location *L1* to *L2* is
  being at *L1*.

The domain dependent part of I_{plan} consists of any constraints that are to be
specified with respect to the particular agent or environment or application domain.
These constraints have to conform to the following syntax:

Conditions → h[t], Tc,

where Conditions is a conjunction of any of the following:

- holds_at (l,t'), where l is a fluent literal and t' is a time variable
- happens (a,t'), where a is an action operator and t' is a time variable
- assume_happens(a,t'), where a and t' are as above,
- temporal constraints,
  h[t] is any of the following:
- holds_at (l,t),
- happens (a,t),
- assume_happens(a,t),

and Tc are temporal constraints on t possibly with respect to any time variables in
Conditions.
Either of h[t] or Tc may be absent from the head. If both are absent then the head
should be *false*.

Examples of such integrity constraints are:

```
assume_happens(go(Person,L,maths_building) ,Time) →
Time>8, Time<23
```

stating that one can go to the maths building only between times 8 and 23.

```
assume_happens(work,Time), assume_happens(rest, Time) →
false
```

stating that the agent cannot work and rest at the same time. As a simple example consider the goal of John being at the maths building at time 10, i.e. holds_at (at(john,maths_building), 10). Given the domain-dependent examples above, a plan for this goal is for John to go to the maths building between the hours of 8 and 10. This plan is denoted as assume_happens(go(john, home, maths_building), T) and T>8 and T<10.

KB_{tr}: In [9] we give a formulation of KB_{tr} that is slightly different from that of KB_{plan}, but here we can assume that KB_{tr} is the same as KB_{plan}. KB_{tr}, the knowledge base for the temporal reasoning part of the model, is used to determine and predict what properties (fluents) hold at given times (via the Temporal Reasoning capability). This functionality is used, for example, when the agent wishes to determine if the preconditions of an action in its plan hold, or to check if (according to what it believes) some of its goals have been achieved.

KB_{react} is used for the reactivity part of the model (Reactivity capability and transition).

What the model provides:
KB_{react} is KB_{plan} with its I_{plan} extended to include *reactive constraints*. The syntax of the reactive constraints is as follows:

Triggers, Conditions → h[t], Tc,

where Conditions, h[t] and Tc are as in the syntax of integrity constraints in I_{plan}, described above, and Triggers is a non-empty conjunction of items of the form *observed(l,t'), observed(c,a,t'), happens(a,t'), assume_happens(a,t'), executed(a,t')*.

The intended reading of each reactive constraint is that if the constraint is "triggered" (via matches to *Triggers* found in the agent internal state) and its *Conditions* hold with respect to the internal state, then the constraint "fires", and its conclusion is added to the Goals component of the state if it contains a timed fluent, or to the Plan component if it contains a timed action operator.

What the user has to provide:
The user has to provide all the reactive constraints of KB_{react}. Reactive constraints can be used to represent a number of different things. For example they can be used to represent

- interaction policies,
- condition-action rules, and
- policies for repairing plans.

An example of a reactive constraint representing an interaction policy of agent *a* is:

```
observed(C, tell(C,a,request(R,D,T1)),T),
holds_at(have(R),T1), not holds_at(need(R),T1), T+1<T1
→assume_happens(tell(a,C,accept(request(R,D,T1))),T2),
T2>T, T2<T1
```

This says that if agent a observes that an agent C requests at time T to be given a resource R at a later time T1, and a knows that it has that resource at time T1 and does not need it then a accepts to give C the resource at time T1 and communicates this acceptance to him any time after receiving (observing) the request and before T1. The variable D is an identifier for the dialogue that includes the request and the acceptance of the request.

An example of a reactive rule representing a condition-action rule is:

```
observed(alarm-sound(Room),T), holds_at(in(Room),T)
→assume_happens(leave(Room),T1), T1<T + 2
```

This says that if an alarm sounds in the room you are in leave the room within 2 time points.

An example of a reactive rule representing a specific plan repair policy is:

```
executed(send_message(M),T), observed(network_down, T1),
T1=T+1 → assume_happens(send_message(M), T2), T2>T1+5
```

This says that if you have sent a message and then at the next time point observed that the network is down you should send the message again after waiting at least 5 time units.

Kb_{gd} contains the goal preference policies of the agent. It is used when the agent wishes to decide what goals to set itself (via the Goal Decision capability and transition).

What the model provides:
KB_{gd} has 3 main parts (it also contains KB0):

- the *lower-level part* to generate potential goals,
- the *higher-level part* to specify priorities between the other rules of the theory, effectively allowing to choose amongst the potential goals,
- the *auxiliary part* consisting of rules defining any auxiliary predicates used in the lower and higher level parts.

The syntax for the parts is fixed in the model and is based on logic programming with priorities. We describe the syntax below.

What the user has to provide:
The user has to provide the rules for the 3 parts of KB_{gd} listed above. In doing so the user will determine

- the set of all possible appropriate goals for the agent that is being designed,
- context dependency of potential goals, i.e. rules that determine under what circumstances, depending on temporal constraints, environmental factors and the agent's private knowledge, what goals should be considered, and
- the agent's preferences and priorities, i.e. under what circumstances the agent should commit to which goals.

Note that the possible appropriate goals for the agent should guide the user towards what needs to be specified in KB_{plan}, i.e. it would make sense for KB_{plan} to provide specification of actions (through the *initiates, terminates* and *precondition* predicates) that can help towards achieving some or all of these goals. In other words it would be appropriate to incorporate in the model the knowledge that can potentially be used to generate plans for the potential goals of the agent.

The lower-level part of KB_{gd} consists of rules of the form

name of the rule: G[t], Tg ← L$_1$, ..., L$_n$, Tc   (n>0 or n=0)

where

- the L_i are either time dependent conditions of the form *holds_at(l,t)*, or time dependent conditions formulated in terms of auxiliary predicates defined in the auxiliary part of KB_{gd},
- G is a goal fluent (see Section3.2 and the examples below) chosen by the user,
- Tg is a (possibly empty) set of temporal constraints,
- t is a time variable, assumed to be existentially quantified with the scope the head of the rule,
- Tc are temporal constraints on the time variables in the body of the rule.

All variables, except t, are implicitly universally quantified over the rule. Each rule in the lower-level part is given a name. Examples of lower-level rules are:

```
gd(dinner): make_dinner(T) ← holds_at(finished_work,T)

gd(repair): repair_roof(T) ← holds_at(leaky_roof,T)
```

These state that making dinner is a potential goal when work is finished and repairing the roof is a potential goal when the roof is leaking.

The higher-level part of KB_{gd} consists of rules of the form

name of the rule: h_p(rule1, rule2) ← L$_1$, ..., L$_n$, Tc   (n>0 or n=0)

where

- the L_i are Tc are as described as in the lower-level part, and
- *rule1* and *rule2* are names of other rules in KB_{gd}.

These higher-level rules represent priorities amongst rules in the lower-level part or other priority rules in the higher-level part. Each rule in the higher-level part is given a name. Examples of higher-level rules are:

```
gd_pref(X,Y):h_p(gd(X), gd(Y)) ← type(X,TX),
              type(Y,TY), more_urgent_wrt_type(TX,TY)
```

This states that the rule called gd(X) should be given higher priority than the rule called gd(Y) whenever X is a more urgent type of goal compared to Y.

The auxiliary part is simply a logic program defining any auxiliary predicates occurring in the other parts. In addition, it can contain statements of incompatibility using the predicate *incompatible(g1,g2)* denoting that two goals *g1* and *g2* are incompatible (to hold at the same time). Examples of the auxiliary part rules are:

```
type(dinner, optional)

type(repair, required)

more_urgent_wrt_type(required,optional)

incompatible(make_dinner, repair_roof)
```

These collection of example rules for the 3 parts of KB_{gd} ensure that whenever both making dinner and repairing the roof are potential goals the latter will be chosen as the one with higher priority.

3.2 Goals and Plan

What the model provides:
The representation of a goal in the state is a timed fluent   l[t], for example *has_driving_licence(john, T1)*, where T1 may be constrained in the state, for example by the temporal constraints *10<T1, T1<20*. There are two types of goals:

- Mental (under the control of the agent), e.g. *be_at_the_airport(T), T<18*
- Sensing (not under the control of the agent and observable by sensing the external environment), e.g. *request_accepted(T), raining(T)*.

When a goal l[t] in the state is selected for planning it is automatically represented as holds_at(l,t).
The representation of a Plan in the state is a set of partially ordered actions. An action is a timed operator a[t], e.g *pay_fine(john, T)*, where T may be constrained in the state, for example by the temporal constraint T1<T, T<T3. There are three types of actions:

- Physical   e.g.   *do(clear_table, T)*
- Sensing   e.g.   *sense(connection_on, T)*
- Communicative   e.g.   *tell(x, y, request(r1, d, T),T1)*

All the time variables associated with goals and actions are assumed to be existentially quantified over the whole state. Goals and actions can be viewed as organised in a tree structure, showing associations of goals/subgoals/actions for ease of revision and partial planning.
Below is an (informal) example of goals/actions tree in state of an agent called *a*.

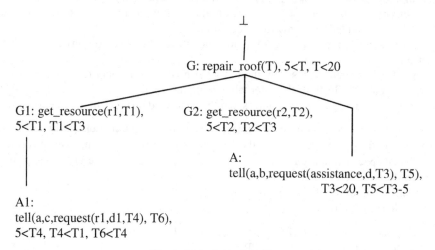

$\perp$

G: repair_roof(T), 5<T, T<20

G1: get_resource(r1,T1),   G2: get_resource(r2,T2),
5<T1, T1<T3   5<T2, T2<T3

A:
tell(a,b,request(assistance,d,T3), T5),
T3<20, T5<T3-5

A1:
tell(a,c,request(r1,d1,T4), T6),
5<T4, T4<T1, T6<T4

Fig. 3. A Goals/Actions Tree

In this tree the root is represented by the symbol $\perp$. The *top level* goal is to repair the roof at a time between times 5 and 20. A partial plan for this goal consists of the two subgoals G1 and G2 of getting two resources r1 and r2 within the specified temporal constraints, and an action A of requesting assistance from agent b. A (full) plan for goal G1 consists of action A1 of requesting the resource from agent c, with the specified temporal constraints.

What the user has to provide:
For the Goals and Plan components of the agent's internal state the user does not need to provide anything. The goals in Goals will result from the information the user provides in KB_{gd}, KB_{plan} and KB_{react}. The actions in Plan will result from the information the user provides in KB_{plan} and KB_{react}.

4 The Capabilities

As mentioned in Section 2 the model provides a sensing capability and a number of reasoning capabilities. The model provides all the necessary specifications for these. Below we summarise these capabilities.

The Sensing Capability: This allows the agent to observe the environment and to receive messages from other agents. The agent observes actions executed by other agents and fluents holding in the environment. These observations are made either passively via the Passive Observation Introduction transition (see Section 5) or actively by the agent seeking specific information, via the Active Observation Introduction transition (see Section 5). The results of the observations are recorded in KB0, as described in Section 3.

The Reasoning Capabilities: There are 5 reasoning capabilities:

1. Planning: generates partial plans for given sets of goals in the internal state of the agent
2. Temporal reasoning: makes predictions about properties holding in the environment
3. Reactivity: reacts to perceived changes in the environment by generating goals and actions to be added to the internal state of the agent
4. Identification of preconditions of actions: identifies the preconditions of given sets of actions
5. Goal decision: determines how the top level goals of the agent (and consequently all the goals of Goals in the internal state of the agent) should be revised to take into account the agent's preferences and the perceived changes in the environment.

All the reasoning capabilities are formally specified in the model, the first 4 using abductive logic programming, and the last using logic programming with priorities. The formal specifications can be found in [9]. To give a flavour we give a simplified specification of the Planning capability.

Specification of the Planning capability:
KB, Goals, Plan, $(G_1, ..., G_n) \vdash_{plan} (PP_1, ..., PP_n)$ such that

- $P_{plan} \cup Goals \setminus G_i \cup Plan \cup PP_i \models_{LP} G_i$, for each i from 1 to n
- $P_{plan} \cup Goals \cup Plan \cup PP_1 \cup .... \cup PP_n \models_{LP} I_{plan}$

- There is a substitution σ for all the time variables in Goals, Plan, G_1, ..., G_n, PP_1,..., PP_n, that satisfies all temporal constraints in Goals, Plan, G_1, ..., G_n, PP_1,..., PP_n and allows all time variables of any actions in the PP_i to be instantiated by times in the future of Γ.

Here $\models_{plan}$ denotes the Planning capability and $\models_{LP}$ denotes any semantics for logic programming. The specification above states that the Planning capability takes as input

- the agent internal state
- a set G_1, ..., G_n of goals (to be planned for), which would be a subset of the goals in Goals
- a time Γ (the time the capability is called),

and produces as output a partial plan PP_i for each input goal G_i, such that

- each PP_i entails its associated goal G_i in the context of the state (without the G_i),
- all the partial plans together with the internal state entail all the integrity constraints in I_{plan},
- all the resulting temporal constraints, including any new ones generated (and any new instantiations of time parameters) are satisfiable together, and
- the temporal constraints of the new planned actions allow the actions to be performed in the future of Γ.

In a nutshell the Planning capability generates consistent, feasible partial plans for all the input goals. We gloss over exactly what a partial plan is. Examples have been given in Sections 1 and 3, and details are available in [9,14].

Notice that this specification is parametric on:

- $\models_{LP}$, i.e. some semantics for logic programs, and
- some semantics underlying constraint satisfaction.

In addition the formal specification of the Goal decision capability is parametric on some semantics $\models_{PR}$ for logic programs with priorities. The computational model of the KGP commits to concrete instances of the above: 3-valued completion semantics for $\models_{LP}$ and argumentation based semantics for a concrete framework, LPwNF [3] of $\models_{PR}$.

For the rest of the capabilities we give summary, informal specifications:

- The Temporal reasoning capability takes as input KB_{tr} and a timed fluent and determines if the fluent holds at the specified time.
- The Reactivity capability takes as input the internal state of the agent and a time of application of the capability, and returns as output all the "reactions" that are "fired" at that time from KB_{react}.
- The Identification of preconditions capability takes as input KB_{plan} and a set of timed action operators and returns the preconditions of those actions as determined by KB_{plan}.
- The Goal decision capability takes as input KB_{gd} and a time of application of the capability, and returns all the goals that are determined by KB_{gd} to have highest priority at that time.

5   The Transitions

Transitions use the capabilities and change the internal state of the agent. The model provides all the necessary specifications for the transitions. There are 8 transitions. They are:

1. Goal Introduction - GI: It replaces Goals in the state by the highest priority goals that the Goal decision capability generates.
2. Plan Introduction - PI: It uses the Planning capability and extends the state with the resulting partial plans for a selected set of goals.
3. Reactivity - RE: It extends the Goals and/or Plan components of the state with the reactions (goals and/or actions) that the Reactivity capability generates.
4. Action Execution - AE: It executes (a selected set of) actions and records their execution in KB0. It uses the Sensing capability for the execution of sensing actions.
5. Passive Observation Introduction - POI: It records in KB0 any (unsolicited) information observed in the environment or communication received from other agents. It uses the Sensing capability.
6. Active Observation Introduction - AOI: It senses the environment for a specific set of properties (fluents) and records the result in KB0. It uses the Sensing capability.
7. Sensing Introduction - SI: It adds new sensing actions to the Plan for sensing the environment to determine whether or not preconditions of some existing actions in Plan hold.
8. State Revision - SR: It revises the Goals and Plan components of the state by removing goals that are achieved or timed-out and their children, and actions that have been executed or timed-out. It uses the Temporal reasoning capability.

The transitions are specified in the following general form:

$$T: \quad \frac{S=<KB, Goals, Plan> , Input \quad \text{at a time } \tau}{S' =<KB',Goals',Plan'>}$$

denoting that the transition T takes a state S and an input at a time τ, and changes the state to S'. The Input may be missing from the specification of some of the transitions.

Transitions typically:

- call some capabilities and/or check for temporal constraint satisfaction, and
- have an input computed by *selection operators* (see Section 6).

The input is either a set of actions (to be executed in AE, for example), or a set of goals (to be planned for in PI), or a set of fluents (to be sensed in the environment in AOI, for example).

As an example we give the specification of the Plan Introduction (PI) transition below. Many details are glossed over, for lack of space.

$$PI: \quad \frac{S=<KB, Goals, Plan>, SGs \quad \tau}{S'=<KB,Goals',Plan'>}$$

where S' is determined as follows:

- The planning capability $\models_{plan}$ is utilised at time τ with input the set of goals SGs.
- $\models_{plan}$ will return partial plans for each goal G in SGs, the partial plans consisting of (sub)goals, actions and temporal constraints.
- The returned (sub)goals and actions are added to Goals and Plan, respectively, together with their temporal constraints.

6   Cycle Theories for Declarative Control

In the KGP model the agent control of the operations, i.e. the orchestration of the transitions, is via cycle theories. This is quite different compared with some other agent systems where a conventional control mechanism dictates a fixed sequence of operations. The KGP cycle theories determine the sequences of transitions *dynamically* and *declaratively*, providing flexible control that can be designed to capture specific agent behaviour profiles and to fit specific environments or applications.

The cycle theories are specified using logic programs with priorities. They are described in detail in [9], and in summary in [11]. Some behaviour profiles resulting from varying cycle theories are described in [15] and [1]. Here we give a summary with more emphasis on distinguishing what the model provides and what the user needs to add.

What the model provides:
A cycle theory is a (meta-)logic program with priorities T_{cycle} to reason about which transition should be chosen when. It consists of:

- a *basic* part T_{basic} to reason about which transition could be next (in some given state and at a given time), initially or after a transition that has just been executed,
- a *behaviour* part $T_{behaviour}$ to decide which transition (amongst the possibly many potential ones) will be next, and
- an auxiliary part, providing definitions of auxiliary predicates used in the other two parts.

T_{basic} consists of rules of the form:

```
r_{T1|T2} (S',X') : T2 (S',X') ← T1 (S,X,S'), EC(S', τ, X'),
                           time_now(τ)
```

where S, S' are states, T1, T2 are transition names (PI, GI, etc), X' is input to T2, and EC is a (possibly empty) conjunction of *enabling conditions* (defined in terms of the *core selection operators* described below).

The rule states that after transaction T1 has been performed with some input X and changing the state from S to S', then transition T2 is a possible follow-up provided at the current time the enabling conditions EC hold and produce an input X' for transition T2. The rule is given the name $r_{T1|T2}$ (S',X'). Notice the predicative representation of transitions in cycle theory rules. A transition represented as

$$T: \quad \frac{S=<KB, Goals, Plan>, Input \quad at\ a\ time\ \tau}{S'=<KB',Goals',Plan'>}$$

as seen in Section 5, is represented as an atom in the predicate T:

$T(S, Input, S', \tau)$

and sometimes, for brevity, with some parameters omitted.

$T_{behaviour}$ consists of rules of the form:

$$R^{T}_{N1|N2}: \quad r_{T|N1}(S,X1\ ) > r_{T|N2}(S,X2) \leftarrow BC(S,X1,X2,\tau),$$
$$time\_now(\tau)$$

where S is a state, N1, N2, T are transition names, X1 is input to N1, X2 is input to N2, BC is a (possibly empty) conjunction of *behaviour conditions* (defined in terms of the *heuristic selection operators* described below).

The rule states that after transition T, transition N1 is preferred to N2 when the behaviour conditions hold at the current time τ and produce inputs X1 and X2, respectively for N1 and N2. The behaviour rule is given the name $R^{T}_{N1|N2}$.

The auxiliary part of T_{cycle} consists of the definitions of any predicates occurring in the enabling and behaviour conditions, and rules of the form *incompatible(T(S,X), T'(S',X'))* stating that different transitions are incompatible with each other as are different calls to the same transition with different inputs (to be executed at the same time).

The enabling conditions of the rules in T_{basic} are defined in terms of the *core selection operators*. These selection operators compute the inputs to the transitions and help cycle theories to determine the next possible transition. There are 4 core selection operators:

- Action selection - $c_{AS}(S, \tau)$: selects a set of actions in the current state for execution.
- Goal selection - $c_{GS}(S, \tau)$: selects a set of goals in the current state to be planned for.
- Fluent selection - $c_{FS}(S, \tau)$: selects a set of fluents to be sensed in the environment.
- Precondition selection - $c_{PS}(S, \tau)$: selects a set of action preconditions to be sensed.

The definitions of these operators are given within the model. For example $c_{GS}(S, \tau)$ is the set of all goals in the state S at time τ which have not been achieved yet, are not timed out and are not the children of goals that have been achieved or are timed out. Analogous to the core selection operators there are 4 *heuristic selection operators* which are used to define the behaviour conditions in $T_{behaviour}$. The definitions of these are under the control of the user.

Given an agent's cycle theory T_{cycle}, the agent's behaviour is characterised as a (possibly infinite) sequence of transitions

$$T_1(S_0,X_1,S_1, \tau_1),....,T_i(S_{i-1},X_i,S_i, \tau_i), T_{i+1}(S_i,X_{i+1},S_{i+1}, \tau_{i+1}),....$$

such that

- S_0 is some initial state for the agent
- τ_i is given by some internal clock
- $T_{cycle}, T_i(S_{i-1},X_i, S_i, \tau_i), time\_now(\tau) \models_{pr} T_{i+1}(S_i,X_{i+1}, S_{i+1}, \tau_{i+1})$.

$\vDash_{pr}$ denotes some semantics for logic programs with priorities. The abstract KGP model is parametric with respect to this. The computational model chooses argumentation based semantics for a concrete framework of $\vDash_{pr}$ [3].

A complete specification of a cycle theory, called the *normal cycle theory*, can be found in [15]. We cannot reproduce it here for lack of space.
What the user has to provide:

The user can provide his own rules for all the 3 components of T_{cycle} conforming to the general syntax. The following are some examples.

Examples of T_{basic}:

```
r PI|AE(S',As): AE(S',As) ← PI(S,Gs,S'), As=c_AS(S', τ),

                                  As ≠ {}, time_now(τ)
```

This states that a Plan Introduction transition may be followed by an Action Execution transition, if there are actions to be executed (identified by the core selection operator for action selection c_{AS}).

```
r POI|RE(S',_): RE(S',_) ← POI(S,_,S')
```

This states that a Passive Observation Introduction transition may be followed by a Reactivity transition, unconditionally. Note that the Reactivity transition requires no input computed by any of the selection operators.

Examples of $T_{behaviour}$:

```
R^PI_AE|N: r_PI|AE(S,As) > r_PI|N(S,X) ← not unreliable_pre(As)
```

for all transitions $N \neq AE$.

```
R^PI_SI|AE: r PI|SI(S,Ps) > r PI|AE(S,As)) ← unreliable_pre(As)
```

These two rules state that after Plan Introduction, the transition Action Execution is preferred to any other, unless there are actions amongst the actions selected for execution whose preconditions are "unreliable" and need checking, in which case Sensing Introduction will be given preference. The predicate *unreliable_pre* has to be defined in the auxiliary part of T_{cycle}.

By varying the rules of the cycle theory the behaviour of the agent can be varied. Two different profiles of behaviour, called *focussed* and *careful*, obtained in this way are described in [15], where cycle theories are provided for each profile. With the focussed profile an agent concentrates on one goal at a time until it achieves it or it is convinced that it is unachievable. With the careful profile, after any transition the agent revises its state via the SR transition to ensure that unachievable or unnecessary goals and actions are revised away as soon as possible. A collection of other profiles, their properties and their associated cycle theories have been proposed in [1].

7   Conclusion

In this paper we have provided a tutorial on the KGP model of agency, concentrating on the abstract counterpart of the model. The tutorial has aimed to provide an overview of the model and give some user guidance. For each module of the abstract model we have summarised the domain-independent part which is provided by the model, and available through the implementation platform. In addition, for each module we have discussed the features of the domain-dependent part which the user has to provide in order to specify the particular requirements of the application.

This tutorial should help the user make a start on designing an agent in the KGP model. On its own, however, it is not sufficient for providing guidance up to and including the implementation stage. Further guidance on implementation is needed. This will become available when the platform becomes publicly accessible.

Acknowledgements

I am grateful to the anonymous reviewers for their helpful comments on an earlier draft of this paper. Work on the KGP model was funded by the IST programme of the EC, FET under the IST-2001-32530 SOCS project, within the GC proactive initiative.

References

1. M. Alberti, F. Athienitou, A. Bracciali, F. Chesani, U. Endriss, M. Gavanelli, A. Kakas, E. Lamma, W. Lu, P. Mancarella, P. Mello, F. Sadri, K. Stathis, F. Toni, P. Torroni: Verifiable Properties of Societies of Computees, Technical report, SOCS Consortium, Deliverable D13, U. Endriss, F. Sadri (eds.), will be available at http://lia.deis.unibo.it/research/socs/guests/publications/ (2005)
2. A. Bracciali, N. Demetriou, U. Endriss, A. Kakas, W. Lu, P. Mancarella, F. Sadri, K. Stathis, G. Terreni, F. Toni: The KGP Model of Agency for Global Computing: Computational Model and Prototype Implementation, Global Computing 2004 Workshop, Springer Verlag LNCS 3267 (2005) p. 342
3. Y. Dimopoulos, A.C. Kakas: Logic Programming Without Negation as Failure, in Logic Programming, Proceedings of the 1995 International Symposium, Portland, Oregon (1995) p. 369
4. U. Endriss, P. Mancarella, F. Sadri, G. Terreni, F. Toni: The CIFF Proof Procedure for Abductive Logic Programming With Constraints, JELIA'2004, International Conference on Logics in AI, Lisbon, Portugal, September 2004, Springer Verlag LNAI 3229 (2004) p. 31
5. U. Endriss, P. Mancarella, F. Sadri, G. Terreni, F. Toni: Abductive Logic Programming with CIFF: System Description, JELIA'2004, International Conference on Logics in AI, Lisbon, Portugal, September 2004, Springer Verlag LNAI 3229 (2004) p. 680
6. U. Endriss, P. Mancarella, F. Sadri, G. Terreni, F. Toni: Abductive Logic Programming with CIFF: Implementation and Applications, CILC04, Convegno Italiano di Logica Computazionale, 16-17 June 2004, Parma, Italy, Research Report Quaderno del Dipartimento di Matematica, Universita' di Parma, n. 390 (2004) p. 28
7. Gorgias: Argumentation and Abduction (http://www.cs.ucy.ac.cy/~nkd/gorgias)
8. A.C.Kakas, R.A. Kowalski, F. Toni: The Role of Abduction in Logic Programming, in Handbook of Logic in Artificial Intelligence and Logic Programming, D.M. Gabbay, C.J. Hogger, J.A. Robinson (eds.), volume 5, Oxford University Press (1998) p.235
9. A.C. Kakas, E. Lamma, P.Mancarella, P. Mello, K.Stathis, and F.Toni: Computational Model for Computees and Society of Computees, Technical report, SOCS Consortium, Deliverable D8, will be available at http://lia.deis.unibo.it/research/socs/guests/publications/ (2003)

10. A.C. Kakas, P.Mancarella, F. Sadri, K.Stathis, and F.Toni: A Logic-based Approach to Model Computees, Technical report, SOCS Consortium, Deliverable D4, will be available at http://lia.deis.unibo.it/research/socs/guests/publications/ (2003)

11. A. Kakas, P. Mancarella, F. Sadri, K. Stathis, F. Toni: The KGP Model of Agency, ECAI04, General European Conference on Artificial Intelligence, August 23-27, Valencia, Spain (2004) p. 33

12. A.C. Kakas, P.Mancarella, F.Sadri, K.Stathis, and F.Toni: Declarative Agent Control, 5th Workshop on Computational Logic in Multi-Agent Systems (CLIMA V), 29-30 September, J.Leite and P.Torroni (eds.) (2004) p. 212

13. R.A. Kowalski, M. Sergot: A Logic-based Calculus of Events, New Generation Computing, 4(1):67-95 (1986)

14. P.Mancarella, F.Sadri, G.Terreni, and F.Toni: Planning Partially for Situated Agents, 5th Workshop on Computational Logic in Multi-Agent Systems (CLIMA V), 29-30 September 2004, J.Leite and P.Torroni (eds.)

15. F. Sadri and F. Toni: Variety of behaviours Through Profiles in Logic-based Agents, in this volume

16. F. Sadri, K. Stathis, F. Toni: Normative KGP Agents: A Preliminary Report, Proc. NorMAS2005, 1st International Symposium on Normative Multi-Agent Systems, AISB convention (2005)

17. F. Sadri, K. Stathis, F. Toni: Normative KGP Agents, Computational and Mathematical Organization Theory (2006) (to appear)

18. Kostas Stathis, Antonis C. Kakas, Wenjin Lu, Neophytos Demetriou, Ulle Endriss, and Andrea Bracciali: PROSOCS: a Platform for Programming Software Agents in Computational Logic, in J. Müller and P. Petta (eds.), Proceedings of the Fourth International Symposium "From Agent Theory to Agent Implementation" (AT2AI-4 - EMCSR'2004 Session M), Vienna, Austria, 13-16 April (2004) p. 523

19. JXTA: http://www.jxta.org

Multi-threaded Communicating Agents in Qu-Prolog

Keith L. Clark[1], Peter J. Robinson[2], and Silvana Zappacosta Amboldi[1]

[1] Dept. of Computing, Imperial College, London
[2] School of ITEE, The University of Queensland, Brisbane

Abstract. In this tutorial paper we summarise the key features of the multi-threaded Qu-Prolog language for implementing multi-threaded communicating agent applications. Internal threads of an agent communicate using the shared dynamic database used as a generalisation of Linda tuple store. Threads in different agents, perhaps on different hosts, communicate using either a thread-to-thread store and forward communication system, or by a publish and subscribe mechanism in which messages are routed to their destinations based on content test subscriptions.

We illustrate the features using an auction house application. This is fully distributed with multiple auctioneers and bidders which participate in simultaneous auctions. The application makes essential use of the three forms of inter-thread communication of Qu-Prolog. The agent bidding behaviour is specified graphically as a finite state automaton and its implementation is essentially the execution of its state transition function. The paper assumes familiarity with Prolog and the basic concepts of multi-agent systems.

1   Introduction

Qu-Prolog is a multi-threaded Prolog designed specifically for developing distributed rational agent applications in which each agent can be multi-threaded. It started as a variant of Prolog for building interactive theorem provers and is the implementation language of the Ergo theorem prover [1]. We then added multi-threading and inter-thread communication via manipulation of the shared dynamic database and asynchronous messages [2] allowing the implementation of rational agent applications [3]. The final stage was to link Qu-Prolog with the Elvin [4] content-based message router to give us broadcast communication with message routing based on message pattern subscriptions. This also gave us a message interface to applications written in imperative programming languages such as C and Java since Elvin has APIs to many programming languages.

A key discriminator between object and agents is that agents have their own thread of control [5]. We go further, and believe that they are naturally multi-threaded. Each thread is used to encapsulate a key behavioural component of the agent. For example, we can have a thread for each other agent with whom the agent is interacting via messages. Each conversation thread then accesses and updates a shared belief store. On occasion it suspends waiting for a key update

F. Toni and P. Torroni (Eds.): CLIMA VI, LNAI 3900, pp. 186–205, 2006.

to be made by some other thread. Thus, an agent's internal threads coordinate using a Linda style belief store [6], which in Qu-Prolog is the database of dynamic clauses. There is a Qu-Prolog primitive, `thread_wait_on_goal`, which causes a thread to suspend until some goal dependent upon the dynamic database succeeds, usually after a clause is asserted or retracted. This generalises the Linda `rd` lookup operation but its implementation is very efficient as the dynamic database is internal to the agent.

Agent communication languages such a KQML [7] and Fipa ACL [8] assume agent to agent asynchronous communication. In Qu-Prolog this is supported by a thread to thread communication model. Each thread has a message buffer and a unique name similar to an email address. Messages sent to an internal thread are copied to the destination thread's buffer. Communication between threads in different Qu-Prolog processes uses McCabe's ICM [9] store and forward communication servers to route the message between processes, which can be on different hosts. Various message receive primitives enable a thread to periodically search and remove from its message buffer messages of interest. If need be it can suspend, with a timeout, until an acceptable message is received. Since we can have a thread for each conversation, a conversation thread can suspend waiting for a reply to its last outgoing message. It is automatically resumed when a reply is received.

Some agent applications require broadcast communication. That is, an agent wants to send a message to any other agent interested in the message content without knowing the agent's identity. An example is the contract net protocol [10]. For this style of communication, it is better to use a communications server that routes messages based on content rather that destination identification. Qu-Prolog's primitives for connecting to, subscribing, and sending notifications to an Elvin [4] server give us this facility. A thread registers content test subscriptions with the Elvin server. Any notification message sent to the server that satisfies one of these tests is then automatically routed to the thread and placed in its message buffer.

In this paper we illustrate the use of these three forms of inter-thread communication, and their utility in building agent applications. The application we use is an auction house with multiple simultaneous auctions comprising bidding agents and auctioneer agents. The application makes essential use of the three forms of inter-thead communication in Qu-Prolog. Bidding agents participate in multiple simultaneous auctions, each one conducted by its own auctioneer agent. A bidding agent starts with a wish list of items it wants to purchase with a maximum price it will pay for each item. It also has a limit to the total amount it can spend purchasing items in all the auctions. The bidding agents are multi-threaded with a thread for each auctioneer. Each bidder agent has its desires (the items it wants to buy), beliefs (about its purchases and unspent and committed funds) and intentions (its concurrently executing bidding threads). The application thus serves as an exemplar for the implementation of simple BDI agents concurrently executing intentions.

In the next section we sketch the structure of the auction application and the multi-threaded architecture of each bidding agent. In the section 3 we give an introduction to Qu-Prolog's thread spawning and inter-thread communication primitives illustrating their use with fragments of code from the application. In section 4 we specify the crucial bidding behaviour as a finite state automaton in which the state transitions are triggered by messages. In section 5 we show how the bidding agents and the auctioneers are implemented in Qu-Prolog. As we shall see, the bidding behaviour is essentially an execution of the finite state automaton transition function defined as a three argument relation. We summarise and mention some related agent implementation languages in section 6.

2   Auction Application

The overall architecture of the application and the architecture of each bidding agent is depicted in Figure 1. Each auction is conducted as an ascending English

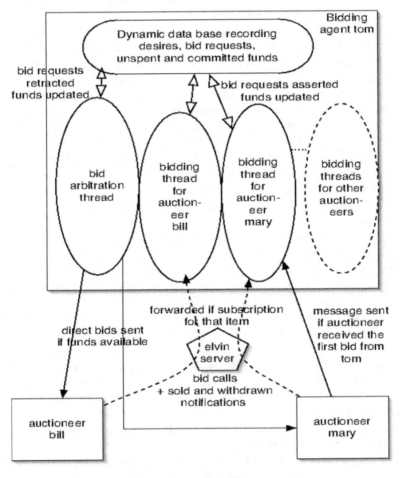

Fig. 1. Auction Architecture

auction. In each round the auctioneer calls for bids at a certain price. The sender of the first bid received at that price level becomes the potential purchaser. The auctioneer then raises the bid price and calls for bids at the new level. If no bids are received within a certain time limit the item is sold to the potential purchaser. The application is fully distributed, each bidding agent and each auctioneer runs as a separate Unix process, possibly on separate hosts.

An auctioneer agent broadcasts its bid calls, sold and withdrawn messages as notifications to an Elvin server. These are routed to the bidding thread for that auctioneer within each bidding agent because of subscriptions lodged by these threads with the Elvin server. Bids are sent directly to the auctioneer as ICM messages.

Before sending a bid each bidding thread must check that there are available funds. Funds are reduced each time a bidding thread wins the auction for an item. Funds are provisionally committed when a bid is made, and released if the bid does not result in a purchase at that bid level. In the later stages this means that a bidding agent may have to wait before bidding in one auction until committed funds are released from another, and it may even have to skip a bidding round. This is because the agent cannot overspend its initial allocation.

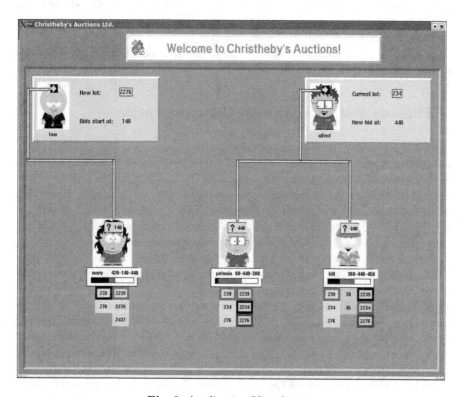

Fig. 2. Application Visualisation

The amount of the unspent and committed funds are held as dynamic clauses inside the agent. To allow the agent to make an overall judgement about which item it should continue bidding for when funds become tight, and more than one item of interest is currently being auctioned, the decision to commit funds for a particular bid call is made by a separate *bid arbitration* thread. When the auctioneer specific thread receives a bid call at a price below or at its maximum price for the item, it informs the agent's bid handling thread that it wants to make a bid by asserting a bid request fact.

The bid arbitration thread suspends until there is at least one bid request. Its role is to find and process pending requests for which there are sufficient avaliable funds as quickly as possible so as not to miss a bidding round. If there is such a request for which there is sufficient remaining budget taking into account provisionally committed funds, it removes the request, atomically increases the committed funds by the value of the bid, and immediately sends the bid to the appropriate auctioneer indicating that any response should be sent to the thread that posted the request. A response will be sent only if the bid was the first one to be received by the auctioneer at the current call price. If the arbitration thread cannot find a request for which there are sufficient available funds it re-suspends until either a new bid request is asserted (because this may be at a lower price that is within the available funds), or committed funds are released by one of the auctioneer linked threads. This behaviour is achieved using a `thread_wait_on_goal` call as illustrated in 3.1.

The entire application has been implemented with a Tcl/Tk GUI visualisation, which is illustrated in Figure 2.

3   Threads and Inter-thread Communication

Qu-Prolog has several predicates for creating and controlling threads. The predicate `thread_fork(Name, Goal)` creates a new thread and executes `Goal` within the thread. For the thread executing the fork the call is deemed to always succeed and the forking thread immediately continues with the next call. The forked thread is terminated when `Goal` terminates (either with success or failure). If `Name` (an atom) is supplied then this name can be used as part of the address of the thread when using ICM communication. If it is not supplied, the system generates a name for the thread and unifies it with `Name`.

The predicate `thread_exit(Name)` terminates the thread with the given name. If `Name` is not supplied then the current thread is terminated.

Sometimes, one thread may need to carry out a computation (such as making several changes to the database) before giving control to other threads. This can be achieved by using `thread_atomic_goal(Goal)`. When a thread enters such a call, no other thread will be given a time slice until `Goal` finishes executing (either in success or failure).

There are three mechanisms Qu-Prolog uses to communicate between threads. If the threads are within the same process then the threads can communicate using the dynamic database. Threads (in the same or different processes) can also communicate via messages using either ICM [9] or Elvin [4]. We now look at these in more detail.

3.1   Communication Using the Database

All threads within the same process share the dynamic database of the Qu-Prolog process and so when one thread asserts or retracts a clause, the effect is immediately visible to all the threads.

In some agent applications, the agent is implemented as several cooperating threads. One or more of these threads may be designed to wait for certain changes to the database before continuing with their execution. To achieve this behaviour we can use the single solution meta-call thread_wait_on_goal(Goal). If Goal fails, thread_wait_on_goal(Goal) suspends until the dynamic database is changed in some way. Goal is then retried and will be retried on each update of the dynamic database until it succeeds. Of course, the call may never succeed, in which case the thread executing the thread_wait_on_goal call suspends forever.

We can often specify exactly what dynamic database predicates Goal depends upon. In this case thread_wait_on_goal(Goal, PredList) can be used. This will only be retried if some change is made to at least one of the dynamic predicates in PredList. These are the *watch* predicates of the call.

The code for the arbitration thread within a bidding agent which is responsible for making bids on behalf of the bidding threads uses both thread_wait_on_goal/2 and thread_atomic_goal/1. The threads communicate by asserting and retracting bid_requests/3 facts and by changing the committed/1 and budget/1 facts.

```
handle_bid_requests :-
  repeat,
  thread_wait_on_goal(choose_bid, [bid_request/3,committed/1]),
  fail.

choose_bid :-
    thread_atomic_goal(
      bid_request(Auctioneer, Item, Price),
      budget(Budget),
      committed(Committed),
      Price =< Budget - Committed,
      retract(bid_request(Auctioneer, Item, Price)),
      retract(committed(Committed)),
      NewCommited is Committed + Price,
      assert(committed(NewCommitted)),
      send_bid(Auctioneer, Item, Price)
    ).
```

The committed/1 fact keeps track of the funds needed to cover sent bids that are not yet known to have succeeded or failed. The budget/1 fact records funds that have not been spent. This is decreased only when the bidder wins the auction for some item and is changed by the bidding threads.

The two dynamic relations `bid_request/3` or `committed/1` determine whether or not the call to `choose_bid` succeeds. If there are no outstanding `bid_requests`, or if the value of the committed funds is such that no such request can be covered from the remaining budget, the call to `choose_bid` suspends.

The call is resumed if either of these dynamic relations is updated (`budget/1` is never changed without `committed/1` being changed in the same atomic transaction). If the change was a new bid request, this may be for an amount that can be covered. If it was because the committed funds were reduced by a bidding thread when it learned its last bid did not result in a purchase at that price, funds may now be sufficient to cover a previous request.

The body of the `choose_bid` rule is executed as an atomic goal so that each time the call is entered or resumed no changes can be made to the dynamic database by the other bidder agent threads until it either succeeds or suspends; and, so that when it does succeed, the other threads will see a consistent update to the database. On success, a bid will have been sent, the `bid_request` that it has satisfied will have been retracted, and `committed` funds will have been increased by the amount of the bid. The `repeat/fail` iteration in the `handle_bid_requests` rule will now result in a new call of `choose_bid` inside the `thread_wait_on_goal`. It may immediately find another request it can satisfy. If not, it suspends until there is a change to one of the two dynamic relations it is watching for.

3.2   ICM Messages

The high-level peer-to-peer communication support of Qu-Prolog is based on the ICM. The ICM consists of one of more `icm` processes that act as message routers and an API that provides applications with ICM functionality. Using this, a process can register its name with an `icm` process and then send and receive messages via the `icm` processes.

ICM addresses have three main components: a thread name, a process name, and a machine address (the home of the process). An `icm` process uses the process name and home fields to determine the message destination. The process itself is responsible for managing the thread name field.

The Qu-Prolog implementation provides library support for the ICM API and manages an incoming message buffer for each thread within a Qu-Prolog process. The library provides two layers of support for ICM messages: a lower-level layer that provides the basic send and receive primitives, and a higher-level layer that further simplifies communication. In this paper we focus on the higher-level support.

In the higher-level layer the message send predicate is

```
Message ->> Address reply_to RTAddress
```

where `Message` is any Qu-Prolog term and `Address` is a Qu-Prolog term representing an ICM address. The `reply_to` part is optional and is used if the recipient of the message should forward a reply to some other thread.

The most general form for a Qu-Prolog address is

`ThreadName:ProcessName@HostName`

where the home part (`HostName`) can be dropped if the message is to another process on the same host. The process name (`ProcessName`) can also be dropped if the message is to another thread within the same process. The special address `self` can be used for a thread to send a message to itself. For agent applications, where each agent is a separate Qu-Prolog process, the process name is the agent name. Communication to local threads of a process does not use the ICM servers. The message is immediately placed at the end of the message buffer of the internal thread.

If a message is sent to a process that does not exist, one of the `icm` processes will store the message until the process is created. Similarly, if a message is sent to a thread that does not exist within a running process, the process will store the message until the thread is created.

In the `handle_bid_requests` clause given earlier, the `send_bid` action is defined by the clause:

```
send_bid(Auctioneer,Item,Price):-
    auctioneerAddress(Auctioneer,AuctioneerICMAdress),
    bid(Item,Price) ->> AuctioneerICMAdress reply_to Auctioneer,
    bid_sent(Item,Price) ->> Auctioneer.
```

`Auctioneer` is the name of the bidding thread that has made the bid request. The bidder has a relation, `auctioneerAddress` that stores the ICM address of the message interface threads of each auctioneer. It has facts such as:

```
auctioneerAddress(tom,thread0:tom@'zeus.doc.ic.ac.uk')
```

Here the name of the bidder thread `tom` is the name of the Qu-Prolog process that is the auctioneer agent.

The bid message is sent to the auctioneer agent, which will be on another host, with the `reply_to` set to be the bidding thread that made the request. This is so that the response the auctioneer will send, if this is the first bid received at that price, will go directly to that thread. In addition, a `bid_sent` message is put in the requesting thread's message buffer to alert it to the fact that a bid has been sent.

3.3   Elvin Messages

The high-level subscription/notification communication support of Qu-Prolog is based on Elvin. An Elvin notification is a list of field name, value pairs and is sent to an Elvin server that determines which processes are subscribed to this notification, and sends the notification to each of these processes. A process can subscribe to notifications they are interested in by using the Elvin subscription language. A subscription is a logical formula describing properties of notifications of interest - for example, notifications that contain a particular field or a particular value for a field.

Qu-Prolog threads can subscribe to Elvin notifications and any matching no-tifications are placed in that threads incoming message buffer. In order to distin-guish Elvin notifications from ICM messages in the threads incoming message buffer, the sender and reply-to addresses are both set to the atom `elvin`.

Unlike ICM, Elvin has no memory of past notifications. A thread only receives those notifications satisfying a subscription that are posted *after* it has registered the subscription with the server.

In the auction application the bidder thread corresponding to auctioneer `tom` will send subscriptions to Elvin such as:

```
elvin_add_subscription(auctioneer==tom && item==lot2239)
```

The Elvin router will then forward any notification that contains an `auctio-neer` field with value `tom` and an `item` field with value `lot2239` to this thread.

The auctioneer broadcasts to interested bidders by posting Elvin notifications with calls such as:

```
elvin_add_notification(
    [message_type=call,item=lot2239, price=204, auctioneer=tom])
```

The receiver of such a notification must make no assumption about the order of `field=value` pairs which may be changed by the Elvin server. So, a Pro-log recipient must extract pairs from the message list using the `member/2` list membership relation.

3.4   Processing the Message Buffer

There are several predicates that process the incoming message buffer for a thread. The simplest of these are:

```
Message <<- Address reply_to RTAddress
Message <<= Address reply_to RTAddress
```

where the reply-to fields are again optional.

A `<<-` call removes the first message in the message buffer and tries to unify the arguments with information contained in this message (including the ad-dresses). It suspends of there is no message, to be resumed when a message arrives. It fails if any of the unifications fail. A `<<=` call searches the message buffer looking for a message that unifies with the supplied patterns and removes the first such message. If no (unifying) message is found, the call suspends until a new message arrives. The second message receive never fails. Both are single solution calls.

Qu-Prolog also has a powerful `message_choice` operator that provides case analysis search of the message buffer with different response calls linked to differ-ent messages patterns. The program below is called by the auctioneer to handle bid messages in a bid round after it has broadcasted a bid call for an item `Item` at price `Price`.

```
handle_bids(Item, Price) :-
  message_choice (
    bid(Item, Price) <<- _ reply_to Bidder ->
      accept_bid(Item, Price, Bidder)
    ;
    bid(I,P) <<- _ :: (I\=Item;P\=Price)  ->
      handle_bids(Item, Price)
    ;
    timeout(7) ->
      bid_timeout_for(Item)
  ).
```

The argument of the `message_choice` operator has the same structure and similar semantics to the if-then-else construct in Prolog except that each test is a message pattern with an optional test following the `::` operator.

The first `->` rule matches any message of the form `bid(Item,Price)` which is a bid for `Item` at the current call price `Price`. The `reply_to` associated with the message, the address of the bidding thread within the bidder for this auctioneer, is assigned to the variable `Bidder`. It is used by `accept_bid` to record the bidder's identity and to send an acknowledgment message. The sender is ignored since this is the bidder's arbitration thread. The second `->` rule matches any `bid` message for a different item or a different price. This it so that such a message - usually a late bid for a previous round - can be discarded. The `handle_bids` program is then recalled to search for, and if need be wait for, the first valid bid for this round. The last rule specifies a timeout in seconds on how long the auctioneer will wait for a message that can be handled by the first two rules. If no such message has arrived within seven seconds then `bid_timeout/1` will be called.

Use of a timeout rule is optional, and if it is not supplied, `message_choice` will block until some message that can be handled by one of its rules arrives.

4 Bidding Behaviour

Figure 3 is a finite state automaton which characterises the bidding behaviour of a thread `A` within a bidding agent monitoring the announcements of auctioneer `AA`. The thread starts by posting Elvin subscriptions as given in section 3.3. These ensure that whenever `AA` broadcasts a message via Elvin about an item `I` the bidder wants to buy that message will appear in the thread's message buffer. Auctioneer announcements about items the bidder does not want to buy are not seen.

`A` then behaves in accordance with the finite state machine of Figure 3 starting at the `desire(I,MP)` node. `MP` is the maximum price it is prepared to pay for item `I`. It stays in that control state until it receives a message concerning any such item `I`. The state transitions are triggered by messages that `A` receives either via Elvin or directly. In the figure all messages are denoted as simple functor terms such as `call(I,P)` even though the actual message may be a list of attribute value pairs.

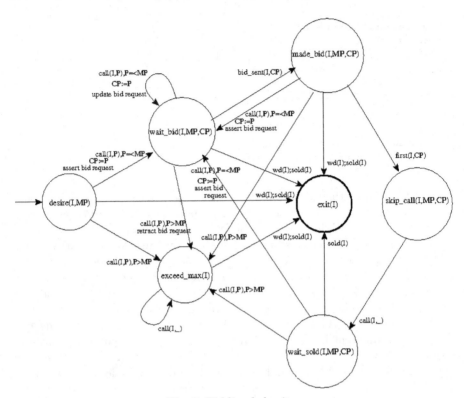

Fig. 3. Bidding behaviour

If the bidder agent has arrived at the auction after auctioneer **AA** has started, the first message it receives could be a **wd(I)** (withdrawn) or a **sold(I)** message for the item **I**. In this case the bidder enters the **exit(I)** state for the auction of **I** and then re-enters the finite state machine at the **desire** node to wait for a bid call for another item it wants to buy. It enters the **exit(I)** state whenever it receives either of these messages regarding item **I**. We assume that the auctioneer always starts the bidding at the reserve price for an item so that a withdrawn message is only sent when there are no bids received in the time the auctioneer allows for a bid response to a call.

More usually, the initial state is left when a **call(I,P)** message is the first message received asking for bids for item **I** at bid level **P**. If **P>MP** the behaviour moves into the **exceed_max(I)** state and subsequent bid calls for item **I** are ignored. The bidding behaviour moves into the **exceed_max(I)** state whenever a bid call is received for **I** at a price above the bidder's maximum price **MP**.

The other transition from the initial state is to the **wait_bid(I,MP,CP)** state. This happens if **call(I,P)** is received and **P=<MP**. **CP** just records the current bid price **P**. As part of the state transition the thread will also assert a **bid_request(A,I,CP)** fact. This is a request to the bid arbitration thread to send a **bid(I,CP)** message to the auctioneer **AA** on its behalf. The arbitration thread executes the program discussed in section 3.1.

In the wait_bid(I,MP,CP) state thread A may receive a bid_sent(I,CP) internal message from the arbitration thread. The arbitration thread places this message in A's message buffer immediately after sending the bid to auctioneer AA as an ICM message. In that case, the behaviour moves to the made_bid(I,MP,CP) state. Alternatively, it may first get a new message from its auctioneer concerning item I. This happens if the auctioneer AA has received a bid at the current bid price CP from another bidder, or no bids were received at this bid level within the auctioneer's time limit, *and* either event occurred before the arbitration thread decided to send a bid for item I and to inform A by inserting a bid_sent(I,CP) in its message buffer.

If the time limit was reached, auctioneer AA may broadcast a sold(I) message, indicating a sale to another bidder - the one that got in the first bid at the previous bid call price, or it broadcasts a wd(I) message (when no bids were received in time in response to its first call for bids for I).

If a new call(I,P) message is the first message to be received in the wait_bid (I,MP,CP) state, another bidder has got its bid in first. Thread A retracts its bid_request(A,I,CP), if it is still there. Then, if P=<MP, CP is updated to be the new P value, and a new bid request fact is asserted at the new CP level for consideration by the arbitration thread. If P>MP, the behaviour moves to the exceed_max(I) state.

The previous bid request fact may no longer be in the dynamic database because it has been retracted by the concurrently executing arbitration thread prior to sending A a bid_sent message and a (too late) bid to auctioneer AA. In this case the arbitration thread will also have added CP to the committed funds, so these will have to be reduced by this amount. As part of this roll back operation, the sent_bid(I,CP) message, that will have been placed in A's message buffer by the arbitration thread, might as well be removed from the buffer. If not, it will be repeatedly skipped over and ignored.

If a bid_sent(I,CP) message is the first message received in the state wait_bid (I,MP,CP), the behaviour moves into the made_bid(I,MP,CP) state to wait for a possible first(I,CP) message to be received from auctioneer AA letting it know that the bid(I,CP) message that was sent by the arbitration thread was the first bid received. If it gets this message, the behaviour moves into the skip_call(I) state as the bidder is now a potential purchaser of I and will win the auction if no one bids in response to the next bid call for I at the raised price. Receipt of the next call(I,_) message simply moves the behaviour from the skip_call(I) state to the wait_sold(I,MP,CP) state. In this state, a sold(I) message broadcast by the auctioneer indicates that no bids were received in response to the last bid call and hence that thread A has won the auction for item I. In the resulting transition to the exit(I) state, the committed and unspent funds are both decreased by amount CP, this double update being performed atomically.

The other message that might be received in the wait_sold(I,MP,CP) state is a new call(I,P) message. This will be broadcast by the auctioneer if it has received a bid in response to the raised price call. Bidding thread A has therefore not won the auction at price level CP. It now either moves into the exceed_max(I) or the wait_bid(I,MP,CP) state, with CP updated to the new call price P, depending upon whether or not P exceeds its maximum MP for item I. In either case, it decreases its committed funds by amount CP, releasing the allocation that was made for its last bid.

5   Auction Implementation in Qu-Prolog

5.1   The Bidding Agents

Each bidding agent program has facts for the predicates:

> auctioneer(A,AH): AH is the ICM handle for auctioneer A
> desire(A,I,MP):   Bidder wants item I from A at max. price MP

giving housekeeping details about the auctioneers and the purchasing desires of that bidder. It also has initial facts for dynamic predicates:

> budget(B) :   B is amount left to spend in all auctions
> committed(C) : C is amount currently committed in outstanding bids

The initial budget fact records the total amount each bidder has to spend when they arrive at the auction. The amount initially committed will be 0.

Each bidder agent starts by executing a call to the program:

```
bidder :-
    thread_fork(arbiter, handle_bid_requests),
    forall(auctioneer(Auctioner,_),
            thread_fork(Auctioner,
                          (post_subscriptions_for(Auctioneer),
                          monitor_auction) ).
```

The first thread_fork launches the bid arbitration thread executing the program given in section 3.1. The forall then launches a bidding thread for each auctioneer with the name of the auctioneer. This thread starts by posting subscriptions to the Elvin server as exemplified in 3.3 so that it will be sent just those Elvin messages for items it wants to buy from its auctioneer. It then executes the program monitor_auction.

```
monitor_auction :-
    bidding_behaviour_from(desire(I,MP)),
    monitor_auction.
```

The bidding_behaviour_from(desire(I,MP)) call is to a program that will follow the behaviour described by the finite state machine of section 4, starting at the state desire(I,MP). At this stage values of I and MP are unknown. They will be bound when the first message has been processed.

The call will terminate when the behaviour reaches the state `exit(I)`. The `monitor_auction` program then recurses to re-enter the bidding behaviour at the state `desire(I,MP)`[1].

The `bidding_behaviour_from` program is just a recursive program that walks over the finite state automaton of Figure 3 until the `exit` state is reached. We assume that the state transitions of the machine are defined by a `next_state/3` relation.

```
bidding_behaviour_from(exit(_)).
bidding_behaviour_from(State) :-
    essence_of_next_message(State, M),
    next_state(State, M, NxtState),!,
    bidding_behaviour_from(NxtState).
```

An example rule for `essence_of_next_message` is:

```
essence_of_next_message(desire(I,MP), Msg):-
    ElvinMsg <<= elvin,
    member(item=I, ElvinMsg),
    thread_symbol(A),       % get auctioneer name of this thread
    desire(A, I, MP),       % find bidder's max price for I
    ( elvin_call_message(ElvinMsg, P), Msg=call(I,P)
    ;
      elvin_sold_message(ElvinMsg), Msg=sold(I)
    ;
      elvin_withdrawn_message(ElvinMsg), Msg=wd(I)
    ).
```

where:

```
elvin_call_message(ElvinMsg, P) :-
    member(message_type=call, ElvinMsg),
    member(price=P,ElvinMsg).
elvin_sold_message(ElvinMsg) :-
    member(message_type=sold, ElvinMsg),
....
```

In the `desire` state only an Elvin message can be received. Its 'essence' is one of the terms used in the finite state machine of Figure 3. The term constructed for the Elvin message

```
[message_type=call, item=lot2239, price=204, auctioneer=tom]
```

is

```
call(lot2239,204).
```

---

[1] Our running auction implementation has the auctioneer broadcast an `auction_over` notification when it has no more items to auction. The above `monitor_auction` program suspends if the auctioneer just stops sending out calls for bids. It will terminate in failure, and hence cause the bidding thread to terminate, if an `auction_over` notification is broadcast.

Example `next_state` rules are:

```
next_state(desire(I,MP), call(I,P), wait_bid(I,MP,P)):-
    P=<MP,
    thread_symbol(A),
    assert(bid_request(A, I, P)).
next_state(desire(I,MP), call(I,P), exceed_max(I)):-
    P>MP.
next_state(desire(I,MP), M, exit(I)):- M=sold(I); M=wd(I).

next_state(wait_bid(I,MP,P), bid_sent(I,P), made_bid(I,MP,P)).
next_state(wait_bid(I,MP,P), call(I,NewP), wait_bid(I, MP, NewP)):-
    NewP=<MP,
    thread_symbol(A),
    thread_atomic_call(
      (remove_bid_request(A, I, P), assert(bid_request(A,I,NewP)).
next_state(wait_bid(I,MP,P), call(I,NewP), exceed_max(I)):-
    NewP > MP,
    thread_symbol(A),
    thread_atomic_call(remove_bid_request(A, I, P)).

remove_bid_request(A, I, P):-
    (retract(bid_request(A, I, P)) -> true
    ;        % retract failed, request already retracted by arb. thread
    retract(committed(F)),
    NewF is F-P,
    assert(committed(NewF)),
    bid_sent(I,P) <<= arbiter)).
```

A `remove_bid_request(A,I,P)` call removes P from the committed funds if the bid request message has already been deleted by the arbitration thread (the `retract` fails) and it also discards the `bid_sent` message which will be in its message buffer, as per the discussion in section 4.

As these example rules show, it is relatively easy to produce the `next_state` rules from the finite state machine and the discussion of section 4.

5.2   The Auctioneers

Each auctioneer program has facts for the predicate:

`item(I,RP)`: Item I has reserve price RP

detailing all the items that the auctioneer has to auction. The reserve price is the minimum price at which the item can be sold and is the price used to start the bidding. Each auctioneer program also has a fact for `my_name/1`, recording the auctioneer's name.

Compared to the bidding agents, the auctioneers execute a quite simple behavioural program. Each executes `auction`.

```
auction :-
    (retract(item(Item,RPrice)) -> send_bid_call(Item,RPrice) ; true).

send_bid_call(Item,Price) :-
    myname(Name),
    elvin_add_notification([message_type=call,item=Item,
                                auctioneer=Name,price=Price]),
    handle_bids(Item,Price).
```

where handle_bids is the program given in section 3.4.

As discussed there, this invokes accept_bid(Item,Price,Bidder) if the first bid received at the Price was from Bidder, and this was received within seven seconds of the call notification. This program asserts the fact:

potential_purchaser(Bidder,Item,Price)

after retracting any other such fact about Item. Bidder is now the potential purchaser of Item at Price. accept_bid also sends a first message directly to Bidder to inform them of this. It then increments Price by a fixed amount to give a new call price NewPrice and then executes send_bid_call(Item,NewPrice).

At some stage the timeout rule of handle_bids will be triggered when no bids are received in time. This invokes bid_timeout_for(Item). If a potential purchaser has been recorded for Item an Elvin notification is sent that the item has been sold and the potential_purchaser fact is replaced by a purchased fact; else a notification is sent that the item has been withdrawn. The latter only occurs if no bids are received in time following the first bid call. The auctioneer program then iterates with a new call to auction. It terminates when there are no more items to be auctioned.

6   Concluding Remarks

We trust we have demonstrated the expressiveness of Qu-Prolog for programming distributed agent applications in which the agents are subject to real time constraints, such as timely reaction to a bid call, and where agents may have to concurrently interact with several other agents taking into account limited shared resources, such as money to spend. Such agents can be programmed using multiple internal threads communicating via the shared dynamic database, or via messages, in order to co-ordinate access and use of the resources they must share.

In the case of our bidding agents a separate arbitration thread is in charge of allocating the shared money resource, and shared dynamic predicates and message passing are used to co-ordinate the threads. The program for the arbitration thread uses a simple strategy to allocate funds. It allocates to the first bid request it finds for which sufficient funds are available at that time. It is quite easy to change this to take into account preferences for items, and, say, the difference between the current call price and the maximum price the bidder is prepared to pay. It can then choose the pending request with maximum utility computed as a function of its preference rating and the price differential.

Qu-Prolog's interface to the ICM message servers enables us to seamlessly perform private agent to agent communication across the internet using symbolic names for threads similar to email addresses. Our application uses the ICM system to send private bid messages and acknowledgments for first bids. Using proxy servers, the ICM system [9] allows messages to be routed through fire walls and to be automatically downloaded to agents on mobile devices, such as laptops, when they connect to the network.

The interface to Elvin enables us to quickly build agent applications that need to use a message broadcast mechanism with messages routed to agents based on receiver subscriptions. It also gives us a mechanism for quickly building hybrid applications. One such might be an agent monitoring application in which sensor software written in Java or C posts notifications routed to the monitoring agents. The role and function of the monitoring agents can be changed without changing the sensor software simply by changing subscriptions.

Lodging appropriate subscriptions or sending notifications to the Elvin server gives an easy method for an agent to join an existing community of agents and components. Posting subscriptions is the joining mechanism for bidding agents at the auction. Posting notifications is the joining mechanism for the auctioneers.

To join the community an agent needs to know the message format being used. In open agent applications KQML or Fipa ACL based messages may be being used. The structure of Elvin notifications allows almost direct representation of such messages, which are also based on a list of attribute/value pairs. If the application uses KQML messages, the Elvin server takes over some of the role of a KQML facilitator [7].

The features of Qu-Prolog that support the writing of non-resolution inference systems are illustrated in [3] but they are more fully explained in the Qu-Prolog User Guide. The system and its documentation are down-loadable from:

`http://www.itee.uq.edu.au/~pjr/HomePages/QuPrologHome.html`

Qu-Prolog is used as the programming language used for a course on multi-agent systems at Imperial College and it was the language used by one of the winning submission [11] for the Agent Programming Competition of CLIMA VI. It is also being used in the ARC Center for Complex Systems at the University of Queensland for the simulation of insect behaviour, and for the proto-typing of free flight air traffic control in which aeroplane agents negotiate over flight levels and flight paths to avoid near misses and collisions. Currently the language does not have a finite domain constraints but it does have delayed calls linked to unbound variables and primitives to retrieve the delayed calls. We plan to add finite domain constraints using these features.

6.1   Some Related Languages

SICStus-MT [12] is a multi-threaded version of SICStus Prolog in which threads each have a single message buffer, called a port. As in Qu-Prolog, a thread can scan the buffer looking for a message unifying with a given message pattern, suspending if no such message is found. However, port communication is restricted to threads within the same Prolog process. SICStus Prolog does have a Linda package, but the Linda store is for external communication between different Prolog processes, or between a Prolog process and a process implemented in another programming language, not for internal thread coordination. For communication between processes in different languages we would use Elvin or the ICM API.

BinProlog[13] is a multi-threaded Prolog with a tight coupling to Java and communication between threads in Prolog or Java via Linda tuple stores. It also supports mobile agents via thread migration between different BinProlog processes.

QuP^{++} [14] is an object oriented extension of Qu-Prolog that allows a class structure with multiple inheritance to be used to construct multi-threaded agent applications. In QuP^{++} a class instance is an active object with at least one thread of control. This thread handles messages from other objects, can launch new internal threads, and can create new active objects.

Mozart-Oz[15] is a multi-paradigm distributed symbolic programming language with support for logic programming, functional programming and constraint handling. It is being used for distributed agent applications. Mozart-Oz is multi-threaded with the threads sharing a common store of values and constraints. The store is used for inter-thread communication. Constraints are posted to the store and the store can be queried as to whether some particular constraint is entailed by the current constraint store. A thread executing such a query will suspend until the store entails the constraint.

The CIAO system [16] uses the dynamic Prolog database for communicating between threads in the same process. Whereas Qu-Prolog uses `assert` and `retract` to update the database and `thread_wait_on_goal/2` to wait for changes to named dynamic predicates, the CIAO system requires the dynamic predicates that can lead to a thread suspension to be declared as `concurrent`. Changes to clauses for concurrent predicates are used for stream communication between threads. A normal call to a concurrent predicate will suspend if it cannot succeed, even on backtracking. Thus, a thread will suspend when a call to a concurrent predicate has 'seen' all the clauses for the predicate that have so far been asserted by the other threads. This allows the dynamic database to be used to communicate a stream of data between threads, as an incrementally asserted set of facts, with automatic suspension of consuming threads that run ahead of the producers. In Qu-Prolog we would achieve this by using ICM or Elvin message communication.

April [17] is a multi-threaded hybid functional/imperative programming language that also uses ICM servers to communicate messages between threads in different applications.

Erlang [18] is a functional multi-threaded language with a single message buffer for each thread. The `message_choice` operator of Qu-Prolog is modeled on the message receive primitive of Erlang.

Go! [19] is a multi-threaded multi-paradigm functional, logic and OO programming language in which threads can communicate using mailbox objects, or dynamic relation objects that act as Linda stores. Each mailbox, which is typically private to a thread, can have any number of linked dropbox objects that can be shared with other threads and used by them to post messages to the mailbox. A thread will suspend waiting for a particular message to be posted to a mailbox.

References

1. P. J. Robinson. Ergo Reference Manual. Technical report, ITEE, University of Queensland, http://www.itee.uq.edu.au/~pjr/HomePages/ErgoFiles/cover.html.
2. Keith L. Clark, Peter J. Robinson, and Richard Hagen. Multi-threading and message communication in Qu-Prolog. *Theory and Practice of Logic Programming*, 1(3):283–301, 2001.
3. P. J. Robinson, M. Hinchley, and K. L. Clark. Qu-Prolog: An Implementation Language with Advanced Reasoning Capabilities. In M. Hinchley et al, editor, *Formal Appraches to Agent Based systems, LNAI 2699*. Springer, 2003.
4. B. Segall et al. Content based routing with elvin4. In *Proceedings AUUG2K*. Canberra, Australia, ˆ Downloadable from http://elvin.dstc.com/doc/papers/auug2k/auug2k.pdf, 2000.
5. M. J. Wooldridge and P.Ciancarini. Agent Oriented Software Engineering: the State of the Art. In P.Ciancarini and M. J. Wooldridge, editors, *Agent Oriented Software Engineering*, volume 1957 of *LNCS*, pages 1–28. Springer-Verlag, 2001.
6. N. Carriero and D. Gelernter. Linda in context. *Communications of the ACM*, 32(4):444–458, 1989.
7. T. Finin, R. Fritzson, D. McKay, and R. McEntire. KQML as an agent communication language. In *Proceedings 3rd International Conference on Information and Knowledge Management*, 1994.
8. FIPA. Fipa communicative act library specification. Technical report, Foundation for Intelligent Physical Agents, www.fipa.org, 2002.
9. F.G. McCabe. *ICM Reference Manual*. Fujitsu laboratories Ltd. Downloadable from: http://sourceforge.net/projects/networkagent/, 1999.
10. Reid G. Smith. The contract net protocol: High-level communication and control in a distributed problem solver. In Alan H. Bond and Les Gasser, editors, *Readings in distributed aritficial intelligence*, pages 357–366. Morgan Kaufmann, 1988.
11. S. Coffey and D. Gaertner. Using pheromones, broadcasting and negotiation for agent gathering tasks. in this volume. 2006.
12. Jesper Eskilson and Mats Carlsson. SICStus MT—A Multithreaded Execution Environment for SICStus Prolog. In C. Palamidessi, H. Glaser, and K. Meinke, editors, *Programming Languages: Implementations, Logics, and Programs*, volume 1490 of *Lecture Notes in Computer Science*, pages 36–53. Springer-Verlag, 1998.
13. Paul Tarau. BinProlog 9.x Professional Edition: User Guide. Technical report, BinNet Corp., 2002. Available from http://www.binnetcorp.com/BinProlog.
14. K. L. Clark and P. J. Robinson. Agents as Multi-threaded Logical Objects. In T. Kakas and F. Sadri, editors, *Computational Logic: Logic Programming and Beyond*. LNAI 2699, Springer, 1998.
15. Peter Van Roy and Seif Haridi. Mozart: A programming system for agent applications. In *International Workshop on Distributed and Internet Programming with Logic and Constraint Languages*. http://www.mozart-oz.org/papers/abstracts/diplcl99.html, 1999. Part of International Conference on Logic Programming (ICLP 99).

16. D. Cabenza M. Hemenegildo and M. Carro. On the uses of attributed variables in parallel and concurrent logic programming systems. In L Sterling, editor, *Proceedings of ICLP95*, pages 631–645. MIT Press, 1995.

17. F.G. McCabe and K.L. Clark. April - Agent PRocess Interaction Language. In N. Jennings and M. Wooldridge, editors, *Intelligent Agents*, pages 324–340. Springer-Verlag, LNAI, 890, 1995.

18. J. Armstrong, R. Virding, and M. Williams. *Concurrent Programming in Erlang.* Prentice-Hall International, 1993.

19. K. L. Clark and F. G. McCabe. Go! – a Multi-paradigm programming language for implementing Multi-threaded agents. *Annals of Mathematics and Artificial Intelligence*, 41(2-4):171–206, 2004.

Variety of Behaviours Through Profiles in Logic-Based Agents

Fariba Sadri and Francesca Toni

Department of Computing, Imperial College, London
{fs, ft}@doc.ic.ac.uk

Abstract. In an earlier paper [6] we presented a declarative approach for agent control. In that work we described how control can be specified in terms of *cycle theories*, which define declaratively the possible alternative behaviours of agents, depending on their internal state and (their perception of) the external environment in which they are situated. This form of control has been adopted for logic-based *KGP agents* [8, 2]. In this paper we show how using this form of control specification we can specify different *profiles* of agents, how they would vary the *behaviour* of agents and what advantages they have with respect to factors in the application and in the environment, such as time-criticality.

1   Introduction

In an earlier paper [6] we described how to specify control of agents via cycle theories. The approach is based on representing and reasoning with preferences and allows flexible control of the operations of agents. This takes the control beyond a fixed one-size-fits-all approach and allows the operations of the agents to be chosen dynamically given the circumstances of the environment, the state of the agent and its preferences.

Cycle theories have been adopted as the means of control in the KGP agent model [8, 2] developed within the SOCS project[1]. KGP is a modular logic-based model developed to cater for the challenges of open global computing environments. It relies upon a collection of capabilities utilised within transitions controlled by cycle theories. All the components are defined within computational logic, some using abductive logic programming and others using logic programming with preferences. The capabilities are designed to provide functionalities such as planning, reactivity, temporal reasoning and goal decision, all of which have been envisaged useful, maybe even necessary, for coping and adapting in a dynamic open environment. The KGP model has been implemented within the PROSOCS platform [12].

The behaviour of KGP agents can be seen as the sequence of transitions or operations they perform, and this sequence is determined by the agents' cycle theories. Thus by varying the cycle theory one can vary the behaviour of the agent. We have explored a number of such variations resulting in different profiles of behaviour. In an earlier paper [6] we briefly mentioned three, the focussed, careful and impatient profiles. In this paper we detail the first two, and an additional one, that we refer to as full planner. We characterise them formally, show how to design cycle theories that achieve them and

---

[1] http://lia.deis.unibo.it/Research/Projects/SOCS/

F. Toni and P. Torroni (Eds.): CLIMA VI, LNAI 3900, pp. 206–225, 2006.

discuss their advantages depending on the features of the environment and application domains. Other profiles are described in [1].

The motivation for this work is threefold: 1) to explore the degree of heterogeneity that can be achieved by varying cycle theories; 2) to explore the advantages of different profiles of behaviour with respect to different parameters such as the dynamic nature of the environment and the time-critical nature of applications; 3) to explore how such analysis can provide guidelines for implementers who use the PROSOCS platform.

Environments and circumstances in which agents have to function can vary. Some environments can be fairly static and predictable, while others can be highly dynamic and unpredictable. Agents may or may not have strict deadlines for their activities, and agents' resources may be limited, thus constraining what they can do, or they may have few resource restrictions. What interests us in this paper is to explore what profiles of behaviour would be advantageous in what type of environment and under what circumstances. Moreover, we would like to explore how to define such profiles by varying the control strategies of agents defined via cycle theories.

The paper is organised as follows. In Section 2 we present two examples to motivate the careful, focussed and full planner profiles. In Sections 3 and 4 we describe the necessary background to our work. In Section 5 we describe the careful, focussed and full planner profiles in detail, show the characteristics of cycle theories that provably achieve these profiles, and discuss the advantages of the three behaviour profiles. In Section 6 we conclude.

2   Motivating Examples

In this section we motivate, in the context of concrete examples, the profiles we will study and formally define later, in Section 5.

2.1   Careful Profile

Intuitively an agent endowed with this profile frequently re-examines its commitments to ensure that he honours only those that are feasible and necessary and he is not encumbered by any infeasible or unnecessary commitments. The advantage of such a profile is evident in a dynamic, unpredictable environment.

Consider an agent c who has sent its registration form to a conference $conf05$ and thus believes that it has registered for the conference. But it now wishes not to be registered at the conference. It sets itself this goal, and plans for it by generating an action to cancel his registration at $conf05$. Suppose the agent knows that :

> *If it observes that the deadline for cancellation for a conference has reached and it expects to cancel its registration at the conference then it should contact its bank and tell them to stop its credit card payment to the conference.*

Suppose before it has a chance to execute the action of cancellation of its registration it receives a message from the conference secretary telling it that there was a problem with its initial attempt at registration (for example the registration form arrived corrupted) and so it is actually not registered.

An agent with the careful profile will immediately realise that there is no longer any need to cancel its registration and consequently will not contact its bank to tell them to stop the credit card payment. But, under the same circumstances, an agent with a different profile might execute the (unnecessary) acts of contacting the bank and canceling the payment.

2.2 Focused Profile

An agent may attempt to plan for multiple goals at once or may plan for one goal at a time. If the agent has limited resources it may be better off trying one goal at a time because typically it may not have enough resources for achieving multiple goals, and attempting to do so would only lead to time-wasting failures. This is the motivation behind our focussed profile. An agent endowed with the focussed profile focuses on one goal at a time.

Suppose an agent has two goals, one to have a particular book and the other to have a particular CD. Suppose the book costs £10 and the CD £15, and the agent has £20 available to spend. This agent cannot achieve both its goals, because due to its financial constraints it cannot form a consistent plan that would achieve both goals. If the agent has the focussed profile it will achieve one of them but if it has any other profile it may not achieve either goal.

2.3 Full Planner Profile

An agent may plan partially for its goals and interleave planning and action execution. This can have advantages in time-critical and dynamic environments. But it can also have some disadvantages. It can be wasteful, as the agent can execute actions of a partial plan without the certainty that it can develop the partial plan into a full one. Worse still execution of an action can end up blocking any alternative possible full plans. The third profile we describe allows the agent to prefer to plan fully before it starts executing the actions in its plan. This profile avoids the pitfalls of partial planning and is suitable for less dynamic and less time critical environments. In those environments it makes it more likely for the agent to achieve all its goals if its Planning capability can (possibly after multiple applications) generate a full consistent plan for all the goals.

As an example consider the following modification of the book and CD example, above. Suppose an agent wishes to read a book and listen to a CD. Suppose the CD is available in the library for free and in the shops for £15, and the book is available only in the shops for £20. Suppose the agent has £22. The agent might generate a partial plan for his goals consisting of the action of buying the CD. There is no way he can extend this plan to a complete plan. Also if it were to execute the action and buy the CD he has no way of satisfying his two goals as he can no longer exploit the alternative plan of borrowing the CD and buying the book.

3   The KGP Model of Agency

Here we briefly summarise the KGP model for agents. Formal details can be found in [8, 2]. This model relies upon

- an *internal (or mental) state*,
- a set of *reasoning capabilities*, in particular supporting planning, temporal reasoning, reactivity and goal decision,
- a *sensing capability*, allowing agents to observe their environment and actions by other agents,
- a set of *transition rules*, defining how the state of the agent changes, and defined in terms of the above capabilities,
- a set of *selection functions*, to provide appropriate inputs to the transitions,
- a *cycle theory*, for deciding which transitions should be applied when, and defined using the selection functions.

Internal State. This is a tuple $\langle KB, Goals, Plan, TCS \rangle$, where:

- KB is the knowledge base of the agent, and describes what the agent knows (or believes) of itself and of the environment. KB consists of various modules supporting the different reasoning capabilities of agents, and including KB_0, for holding the (dynamic) knowledge of the agent about the external environment in which it is situated.
- $Goals$ is the set of properties that the agent wants to achieve, each one with an associate time variable, possibly constrained by temporal constraints (belonging to TCS), defining when the goals are expected to hold.
- $Plan$ is a set of actions scheduled in order to satisfy goals. Each has an associated time variable, possibly constrained by temporal constraints in TCS, similarly to $Goals$, but defining when the action should be executed and imposing a partial order over actions in $Plan$. Each action is also equipped with the preconditions for its successful execution.
- TCS is a set of constraint atoms (referred to as *temporal constraints*) in some given underlying constraint language with respect to some structure equipped with a notion of *Constraint Satisfaction*. We assume that the constraint predicates include $<, \leq, >, \leq, =, \neq$. These constraints bind the time of goals in $Goals$ and actions in $Plan$. For example, they may specify a time window over which the time of an action can be instantiated, at execution time.

Goals and actions are uniquely identified by their associated time variable, which is implicitly existentially quantified within the overall state.

To aid revision and partial planning, $Goals$ and $Plan$ form a *tree*[2]. The tree is given implicitly by associating with each goal and action its parent. *Top-level* goals and actions are children of the root of the tree, represented by the (arbitrary) symbol $\perp$.

---

[2] In the detailed model we actually have two trees, the first containing *non-reactive* goals and actions, the second containing *reactive* goals and actions. All the top-level non-reactive goals are either assigned to the agent by its designer at birth, or they are determined by the Goal Decision capability, via the GI transition (see below). All the top-level reactive goals and actions are determined by the Reactivity capability, via the RE transition (see below). Here for simplicity we overlook the distinction amongst the two trees.

Reasoning Capabilities. These include:

- Planning, generating a plan, if one exists in the overall state, for any given set of input goals. These plans are *partial* or *total*. A partial plan consists of (temporally constrained) sub-goals and actions. A *total* plan consists solely of (temporally constrained) actions.
- Reactivity, reacting to perceived changes in the environment by modifying $Goals$, $Plan$, and TCS.
- Goal Decision, revising the top-most level goals by adapting the agent's state to changes in its own preferences and in the environment.
- Temporal Reasoning, reasoning about the evolving environment, and making predictions about properties holding in the environment, based on the partial information the agent acquires.

Transitions. The state of an agent evolves by applying transition rules, which employ capabilities and the Constraint Satisfaction. The transitions are:

- *Goal Introduction (GI)*, changing the top-level goals, and using Goal Decision.
- *Plan Introduction (PI)*, changing $Goals$ and $Plan$, and using Planning.
- *Reactivity (RE)*, changing $Goals$ and $Plan$, and using the Reactivity capability.
- *Sensing Introduction (SI)*, changing $Plan$ by introducing new sensing actions for checking the preconditions of actions already in $Plan$, and using Sensing.
- *Passive Observation Introduction (POI)*, changing KB_0 by introducing unsolicited information coming from the environment, and using Sensing.
- *Active Observation Introduction (AOI)*, changing KB_0 by introducing the outcome of (actively sought) sensing actions, and using Sensing.
- *Action Execution (AE)*, executing actions, and thus changing KB_0.
- *State Revision (SR)*, revising $Goals$ and $Plan$, and using Temporal Reasoning and Constraint Satisfaction.

The effect of transitions is dependent on the concrete time of their application. We briefly describe SR, as it will play an important role in section 5. Informally speaking, SR revises a state by removing (i) all timed-out goals and actions, (ii) all executed actions, (iii) all goals that have become obsolete because they are already believed to have been achieved, (iv) siblings (in the tree) of goals and actions deleted in (i), and (v) all descendants (in the tree) of goals deleted in (i)-(iv). A goal or action is *timed-out* if and only if the temporal constraints TCS of the state of the agent at the time of application of SR constrain the time of the goal or action to be less than or equal to the time of application of SR. A goal is *achieved* in a state if and only if it holds according to the Temporal Reasoning capability.

Selection Functions. Input to (some of the) transitions is given via selection functions, taking the current state S and time τ as input:

- *action selection function*, $c_{AS}(S, \tau)$, returning the set of actions in S to be executed by AE at time τ;
- *goal selection function*, $c_{GS}(S, \tau)$, returning the set of goals in S to be planned for by PI at time τ;

- *fluent selection function*, $c_{FS}(S, \tau)$, returning the set of properties in S to be sensed by AOI at time τ;
- *precondition selection function*, $c_{PS}(S, \tau)$, returning the set of preconditions of actions in S for which sensing actions are to be introduced by SI at time τ.

4 Cycle Theories

The behaviour of agents results from the application of transitions in sequences, repeatedly changing the state of the agent. These sequences are not fixed a priori, as in conventional agent architectures, but are determined dynamically by reasoning with declarative cycle theories, giving a form of flexible control. Cycle theories are given in the framework of Logic Programming with Priorities (LPP). For the purposes of this paper, we will assume that an *LPP-theory*, referred to as $\mathcal{T}$, consists of four parts:

(i) a low-level part P, consisting of a logic program; each rule in P is assigned a name, which is a term; e.g., one such rule, with name $n(X)$, could be
$$n(X) : p(X) \leftarrow q(X, Y), r(Y)$$

(ii) a high-level part H, specifying conditional, dynamic priorities amongst rules in P; e.g., one such priority rule, called $h(X)$, could be
$$h(X) : n(X) \succ m(X) \leftarrow c(X),$$
to be read: if (some instance of) the condition $c(X)$ holds, then the rule in P with name (the corresponding instance of) $n(X)$ should be given higher priority than the rule in P with name (the corresponding instance of) $m(X)$.

(iii) an auxiliary part A, defining predicates occurring in the conditions of rules in P and H and not in the conclusions of any rule in P;

(iv) a notion of incompatibility, here given as a set of rules defining the predicate *incompatible*, e.g.
$$incompatible(p(X), p'(X)),$$
to be read: any instance of the literal $p(X)$ is incompatible with the corresponding instance of the literal $p'(X)$. We refer to the set of all incompatibility rules as I.

Any concrete LPP framework is equipped with a notion of entailment, that we denote by $\models_{pr}$. Intuitively, $\mathcal{T} \models_{pr} \alpha$ iff α is the "conclusion" of a sub-theory of $P \cup A$ which is "preferred" with respect to $H \cup A$ in $\mathcal{T}$ over any other sub-theory of $P \cup A$ that derives a "conclusion" incompatible with α (with respect to I). Here, we are assuming that the underlying logic programming language is equipped with a notion of "entailment" that allows to draw "conclusions". In [10, 9, 7, 5, 3], $\models_{pr}$ is defined via argumentation.

Formalisation of Cycle Theories. Here and in the rest of the paper, we will use notation $T(S, X, S', \tau)$ to represent application of transition T at time τ in state S, given input X, resulting in state S', and notation $*T(S, X)$ to represent that transition T can be potentially chosen as the next transition in state S, with input X.

Formally, a cycle theory $\mathcal{T}_{cycle}$ consists of the following parts.

- An *initial* part $\mathcal{T}_{initial}$, that determines the possible transitions that the agent could perform when it starts to operate. Concretely, $\mathcal{T}_{initial}$ consists of rules of the form

$$*T(S_0, X) \leftarrow C(S_0, \tau, X), now(\tau)$$

which we refer to via the name $\mathcal{R}_{0|T}(S_0, X)$. These rules sanction that, if conditions C hold in the initial state S_0 at the initial time τ, then the initial transition could be T, applied to state S_0 and input X.

- A *basic* part $\mathcal{T}_{basic}$ that determines the possible transitions following given transitions, and consists of rules of the form

$$*T'(S', X') \leftarrow T(S, X, S', \tau), EC(S', \tau', X'), now(\tau')$$

which we refer to via the name $\mathcal{R}_{T|T'}(S', X')$. These rules sanction that, after transition T has been executed, starting at time τ in the state S and resulting in state S', and the conditions EC evaluated in S' at the current time τ' are satisfied, then transition T' could be the next transition to be applied in S', with input X'. EC are called *enabling conditions* as they determine when T' can be applied after T. They also determine input X' for T', via calls to selection functions.

- A *behaviour* part $\mathcal{T}_{behaviour}$ that contains rules describing dynamic priorities amongst rules in $\mathcal{T}_{basic}$ and $\mathcal{T}_{initial}$. Rules in $\mathcal{T}_{behaviour}$ are of the form

$$\mathcal{R}_{T|T'}(S, X') \succ \mathcal{R}_{T|T''}(S, X'') \leftarrow BC(S, X', X'', \tau), now(\tau)$$

with $T' \neq T''$, which we will refer to via the name $\mathcal{P}^T_{T' \succ T''}$. Recall that $\mathcal{R}_{T|T'}(\cdot)$ and $\mathcal{R}_{T|T''}(\cdot)$ are (names of) rules in $\mathcal{T}_{basic} \cup \mathcal{T}_{initial}$. Note that, with an abuse of notation, T could be 0 in the case that one such rule is used to specify a priority over the *first* transition to take place, in other words, when the priority is over rules in $\mathcal{T}_{initial}$. These rules in $\mathcal{T}_{behaviour}$ sanction that, at the current time τ, after transition T, if the conditions BC hold, then we prefer the next transition to be T' over T''. The conditions BC are called *behaviour conditions* and give the behavioural profile of the agent.

- An *auxiliary part* including definitions for any predicates occurring in the enabling and behaviour conditions.
- An *incompatibility part*, in effect expressing that only one (instance of a) transition can be chosen at any one time.

Hence, $\mathcal{T}_{cycle}$ is an LPP-theory where: (i) $P = \mathcal{T}_{initial} \cup \mathcal{T}_{basic}$, and (ii) $H = \mathcal{T}_{behaviour}$.

Operational Trace. The cycle theory $\mathcal{T}_{cycle}$ of an agent is responsible for its behaviour, in that it induces an *operational trace* of the agent, namely a (typically infinite) sequence of transitions

$$T_1(S_0, X_1, S_1, \tau_1), \ldots, T_i(S_{i-1}, X_i, S_i, \tau_i), T_{i+1}(S_i, X_{i+1}, S_{i+1}, \tau_{i+1}), \ldots$$

such that

- S_0 is the given initial state;
- for each $i \geq 1$, τ_i is given by the clock of the system ($\tau_i < \tau_{i+i}$);
- $(\mathcal{T}_{cycle} - \mathcal{T}_{basic}) \wedge now(\tau_1) \models_{pr} *T_1(S_0, X_1)$;
- for each $i \geq 1$
  $(\mathcal{T}_{cycle} - \mathcal{T}_{initial}) \wedge T_i(S_{i-1}, X_i, S_i, \tau_i) \wedge now(\tau_{i+1}) \models_{pr} *T_{i+1}(S_i, X_{i+1})$

namely each (non-final) transition in a sequence is followed by the most preferred transition, as specified by $\mathcal{T}_{cycle}$. If, at some stage, the most preferred transition determined by $\models_{pr}$ is not unique, we choose one arbitrarily.

Normal Cycle Theory. In defining profiles in section 5 we take the *normal cycle theory* as a starting point. This specifies a pattern of operation where the agent prefers to follow a sequence of transitions that allows it to achieve its goals in a way that matches an expected "normal" behaviour. Basically, the "normal" agent first introduces goals (if it has none to start with) via GI, then reacts to them, via RE, and then repeats the process of planning for them, via PI, executing (part of) the chosen plans, via AE, revising its state, via SR, until all goals are dealt with (successfully or revised away). At this point the agent returns to introducing new goals via GI and repeating the above process. Whenever in this process the agent is interrupted via a passive observation, via POI, it chooses to introduce new goals via GI, to take into account any changes in the environment. Whenever it has actions which are "unreliable", in the sense that their preconditions definitely need to be checked, the agent senses them (via SI) before executing the action. Whenever it has actions which are "unreliable", in the sense that their effects definitely need to be checked, the agent actively introduces actions that aim at sensing these effects, via AOI, after having executed the original actions. The full definition of the normal cycle theory is given in the appendix.

5   Behaviour Profiles

In this section we explore how cycle theories can be used to specify different profiles of behaviour. We concentrate on three profiles, the *careful*, the *focussed* and the *full planner*.

In the careful profile the behaviour of the agent is such that it would re-examine its commitments in terms of its goals and plans frequently to discard those that are no longer needed or have become infeasible. Intuitively, this profile would be suitable for a changing environment that intervenes in the agent's operations, and the frequent "self-examination" of the agent can help it avoid being occupied with unnecessary activity or activity which is bound to fail. It also ensures that the agent's operations are not hindered by superfluous items in the state and that reactive rules will not be triggered unnecessarily by goals/actions that are timed-out and not achieved/executed.

With the focussed profile the agent concentrates on one (top-level) goal at a time and only moves to other goals when that goal is achieved or is timed out. Intuitively this profile is useful when the agent has goals that have become mutually unachievable. By being focussed the agent increases its chances of achieving at least some of them.

With the full planner profile the agent plans fully for its goals before it starts to execute the actions in the plan. It thus ensures that when it executes an action it is guaranteed that there is a full plan backing that action.

Below we proceed to define each of the three profiles by giving a formal definition in terms of trace characteristics, followed by specification of cycle theories that will induce such traces. We then proceed to prove the advantages of the profile depending on particular characteristics of the application.

5.1   Careful Profile

Definition 1 (Careful profile: trace-based characterisation). *A careful agent is an agent that will never generate an operational trace with two consecutive transitions that are different from SR.*

In fact, this condition is stronger than strictly necessary: As long as there are no redundant or infeasible goals or actions no revision would be required. However, from a pragmatic point of view, Definition 1 nevertheless provides us with an appropriate characterisation of careful agents. This is so, because *checking* whether or not a state includes redundant or infeasible goals or actions to be revised is just as costly as performing a state revision in the first place.

Our next goal is to define a class of cycle theories that are guaranteed to induce an operational trace where every other transition is an SR. As we shall see this is not as straightforward a goal as it may seem. To illustrate the difficulties and to motivate our choices (which are eventually going to overcome these difficulties), we start by attempting to define a careful cycle theory as an extension of the normal cycle theory.

The Normal-Careful Cycle Theory. There are several ways of combining cycle theories (in this case the normal cycle theory with the core rules necessary for characterising the careful profile). One option would be to take the union of the two cycle theories (which are sets of basic and behaviour rules) and then, where necessary, to introduce additional behaviour rules that determine the agent's behaviour in case of conflict between the rules stemming from the different parts. Another way, which gives the profile designer less freedom but which results in much simpler cycle theories, would be to work at the level of basic rules as far as possible and to use suitable enabling conditions to control the agent's behaviour. This is the approach we are going to follow here.

To design a careful agent, we need to ensure that basic rules expressing that *SR* should follow any other transition T get priority over any conflicting rules. Instead of using behaviour rules to this effect, we are simply going to delete such conflicting rules in the first place. Hence, we end up with the following approach:

- **Step 1:** Take the normal cycle theory as a starting point.
- **Step 2:** Remove any basic rules (in $\mathcal{T}_{basic}$) that speak about two consecutive transitions both of which are different from *SR*.
- **Step 3:** Add the following basic rule (to $\mathcal{T}_{basic}$) for each T different from *SR:*

$$\mathcal{R}_{T|SR}(S', \{\}) : *SR(S', \{\}) \leftarrow T(S, X, S', \tau)$$

Note that there cannot be any enabling conditions in this kind of new rule: *SR* needs to be enabled under *any* circumstances. Note also that Step 3 might re-introduce rules which already belong to $\mathcal{T}_{basic}$. This causes no theoretical or practical problem. We thus end up with the following *normal-careful cycle theory:*

- $\mathcal{T}_{initial}$ is as for the normal cycle theory.
- $\mathcal{T}_{basic}$ consists of the above rules of the form $\mathcal{R}_{T|SR}$ and of the following rules:

$$\mathcal{R}_{SR|PI}(S', Gs) : *PI(S', Gs) \leftarrow SR(S, \{\}, S', \tau'),$$
$$Gs = c_{GS}(S', \tau), Gs \neq \{\}, now(\tau)$$
$$\mathcal{R}_{SR|GI}(S', \{\}) : *GI(S', \{\}) \leftarrow SR(S, \{\}, S', \tau'),$$
$$Gs = c_{GS}(S', \tau), Gs = \{\}, now(\tau)$$

$\mathcal{T}_{basic}$ does not contain any other rules, because all the remaining basic rules in the normal cycle theory speak about transitions that should follow transitions other than SR and these are fixed for the careful profile.

- $\mathcal{T}_{behaviour}$ is empty. Indeed, it turns out that also all of the rules in $\mathcal{T}_{behaviour}$ in the normal cycle theory are *redundant*, because they speak about what to do after a transition other than SR.

In summary, the normal-careful cycle theory will force an agent to alternate between SR and PI or GI (depending on whether there are currently goals to plan for or not). Such an agent would be careful, but not very useful. Below we improve the cycle theory to overcome this inadequacy.

The Core-Careful Cycle Theory. We improve the normal-careful cycle theory by adding that every transition except SR, itself, should be enabled after SR. Thus, $\mathcal{T}_{basic}$ in the *core-careful cycle theory* contains, in addition to the basic rules in the normal-careful cycle theory, the following rules:

$$
\begin{aligned}
\mathcal{R}_{SR|RE}(S', \{\}) : *RE(S', \{\}) &\leftarrow & SR(S, \{\}, S', \tau) \\
\mathcal{R}_{SR|AE}(S', As) : *AE(S', As) &\leftarrow & SR(S, \{\}, S', \tau'), \\
& & As = c_{AS}(S', \tau), As \neq \{\}, now(\tau) \\
\mathcal{R}_{SR|SI}(S', Ps) : *SI(S', Ps) &\leftarrow & SR(S, \{\}, S', \tau'), \\
& & Ps = c_{PS}(S', \tau), Ps \neq \{\}, now(\tau) \\
\mathcal{R}_{SR|AOI}(S', Fs) : *AOI(S', Fs) &\leftarrow & SR(S, \{\}, S', \tau'), \\
& & Fs = c_{FS}(S', \tau), Fs \neq \{\}, now(\tau) \\
\mathcal{R}_{SR|POI}(S', \{\}) : *POI(S', \{\}) &\leftarrow & SR(S, \{\}, S', \tau)
\end{aligned}
$$

The following proposition states the *correspondence* between the *core-careful cycle theory* and the (trace-based characterisation of the) careful profile given in Definition 1:

Proposition 1 (Careful profile). *The core-careful cycle theory induces the careful profile of behaviour: Any agent using this cycle theory will never generate an operational trace with two consecutive transitions that are different from SR.*

Proof. This follows immediately from the fact that the basic part of the cycle theory forces an SR after every other type of transition, and there is exactly one basic rule to determine the follow-up of any transition different from SR.

Other Careful Cycle Theories. The two careful cycle theories we have considered so far are just two examples; there is a range of cycle theories that conform to the careful behaviour profile. Our second example, the core-careful cycle theory is the most general cycle theory conforming to the careful profile.

For concrete applications, we may wish to combine the features of careful behaviour with other more specific features. We can construct a careful cycle theory of our choice by taking the core-careful cycle theory as a starting point and then imposing additional behaviour constraints using the following means:

- strengthening the enabling conditions in basic rules that determine the follow-up transition for an SR;

- deleting basic rules that determine the follow-up transition for an SR;
- adding any kind of behaviour rules;
- deleting rules that have become redundant due to other changes.

Note, however, that we *cannot* add any enabling conditions to the basic rules that state that *SR* has to follow any other transition. Otherwise, the resulting cycle theory cannot be guaranteed to conform to the careful profile of behaviour anymore. We also cannot delete such a rule, unless it has already become redundant due to other changes in the cycle theory. On the other hand, we do have complete freedom with respect to the behaviour rules we might wish to add, because the basic rules never admit any conflict as to what transition to choose after a transition different from *SR* in the first place.

Clearly, any such careful cycle theory will also induce the careful profile of behaviour in the sense of Proposition 1.

A Property of the Careful Profile. Informally, under certain circumstances:

- Careful agents will never generate a reaction via the reactivity transition to timed-out unachieved goals or timed-out unexecuted actions.
- Careful agents will never generate a reaction via the reactivity transition to actions that may not be timed out yet but which are unexecuted and are no longer necessary.

More formally:

Theorem 1. *The following will never contribute to the generation of a reaction (i.e. an action in* Plan *or goal in* Goals*) via the RE transition:*

1. *a timed-out unexecuted action,*
2. *a timed-out unachieved goal,*
3. *an unexecuted action whose execution is no longer needed, i.e.*
   (a) *with an ancestor which has already been achieved, or*
   (b) *with a sibling that has been timed-out, or*
   (c) *with an ancestor which has been timed-out,*

provided that no action and no goal is timed out between an SR transition and its immediate successor if that is an RE transition.

Proof. Let the assumption hold that no action and no goal is timed out between an SR transition and its immediate successor if that is an RE transition. Suppose a careful agent applies RE in a state $S = \langle KB, Goals, Plan, TCS \rangle$. Then by Definition 1, because SR must have been applied in the state immediately prior to S, no action or goal of the type specified in 1–3, above exists in state S. Therefore no such action or goal could possibly contribute to the generation of any reaction by RE.

5.2 Focussed Profile

In the *focussed* profile of behaviour an agent does not plan for more than one top-level goal at a time. More specifically, a focussed agent remains committed to a goal amongst its top-level goals until

- that goal has been successfully achieved, or
- that goal has become infeasible, or
- that goal is not preferred by the Goal Decision capability anymore, when invoked by the *GI* transition, or
- that goal has an empty plan in the state.[3]

The advantages of the focussed profile come into effect in highly time-critical domains as well as domains where an agent has several goals with mutually incompatible plans. In such situations, a focussed agent can be expected to achieve, at least, some goals, whereby an unfocussed agent may fail completely. This applies, in particular, to agents that have a preference for total planning. By concentrating planning on a single goal at a time, a focussed agent is likely to be faster and it will also avoid wasting computing resources over incompatible plans for other goals.

Formally, the focussed profile has the following characteristic: A focussed agent, under no circumstances, will generate an operational trace that includes a state with two distinct top-level goals with children, neither of which is either achieved or infeasible. Here, a goal G is called *feasible* iff neither itself nor any of its descendents is timed-out.

Note that this notion of infeasibility need not persist. A goal G may, at some point, be infeasible, because an action in its current plan is timed-out, but G may again become feasible later on, after the agent has revised its state and computed a new plan. Therefore, the only way to ensure that switching to a new top-level goal for planning is admissible (under the focussed profile) is to first check that infeasible goals will *stay* infeasible. This requires an SR. Hence, we can give the following alternative definition of the focussed profile, which is simpler than our earlier definition.

Definition 2 (Focussed profile: trace-based characterisation). *A focussed agent is an agent that, under no circumstances, will generate an operational trace that includes a state with two top-level goals with children.*

This definition is stronger (more restrictive) than our first definition, but as argued earlier, it is operationally equivalent to that definition, because an agent can only be sure that switching goals will not violate the focussed profile after having executed an SR (or after having performed an analogous check).

Possible Extensions. Note that, according to our definition, focussed agents do not deal with more than one top-level goal at a time, but may switch between top-level goals in some situations, as exemplified by the following example.

Example 1. Consider the following (portion of a) trace:

$$\ldots, SR(S, \{\}, S', \tau), PI(S', Gs, S'', \tau'), \ldots$$

with the top-level goals of S, S', S'' given by $\{G_1, G_2\}$. Assume that G_1 already has got a plan in S, i.e. the set of items in $Goals(S) \cup Plan(S)$ with ancestor G_1 is not empty. Assume also that G_2 has no plan in S, i.e. the set of items in $Goals(S) \cup Plan(S)$ with

---

[3] The need for this last item will become clear in Example 1.

ancestor G_2 is empty. Suppose that all items in the plan for G_1 in S are timed-out at τ, and thus S' is such that $Goals(S')$ is the set of all top-level goals in S' and $Plan(S') = \{\}$. Suppose also that neither G_1 nor G_2 are timed-out or achieved at τ', but PI is introducing a plan for G_2, so that the set of items in $Goals(S'') \cup Plan(S'')$ with ancestor G_2 is not empty. The agent with this trace is focussed according to definition 2. However, it does switch from dealing with goal G_1 to dealing with goal G_2, despite goal G_1 being still unachieved and feasible.

Definition 2 of focussed agent may be modified to prevent goal switching, by comparing successive agent states in traces and force that once an agent has been planning/executing for one top-most level goal in one state, it must stick to that goal in successive states, until the goal has been achieved or has become unachievable. This would amount to getting rid of the last item in the informal description of focussed agent at the beginning of Section 5.2 (and adding some other suitable conditions instead). This stronger definition of focussed agent would however force extending the notion of cycle theory and operational trace, either by looking at histories of transitions rather than individual transitions when deciding on the next transition, or by introducing additional information into cycle theories, such as variables holding the current top-level goal being dealt with. We therefore leave the stronger definition to future work.

Note also that our notion of focussed agent only refers to *top-level* goals, and not to sub-goals or actions. The notion of focussed agent could be extended so as to define agents that are focussed all the way, from top-level goals down.

Focussed Cycle Theories. To achieve the abstract specification, we need a cycle theory that ensures that before any PI an SR has been performed. This is to ensure that we can proceed with planning for a top-level goal even if some of its current children have become infeasible. However, rather than implementing this behaviour directly, we are going to ensure that PI is only enabled with respect to a set of goals that a focussed agent may plan for given its current state according to the Definition 2. (This, in effect, encourages an SR transition when a PI transition is not enabled.)

Definition 3 (Focussed cycle theories). *A cycle theory is called focussed iff the initial rule $\mathcal{R}_{0|PI}(S, Gs)$ (in $\mathcal{T}_{initial}$) and the basic rule (in $\mathcal{T}_{basic}$) $\mathcal{R}_{T|PI}(S, Gs)$ for any transition T include the enabling condition $focussed(Gs', S, Gs)$, where:*

- *given that Gs is the set of goals to which PI will be applied and $Gs' \supseteq Gs$ is the set of goals returned by the goal selection function, then*
- *the predicate $focussed(Gs', S, Gs)$ holds iff all the goals in Gs are descendants of the same top-level goal (possibly including that top-level goal itself) and no other top-level goal has got any children.*

The focussed variant of the normal cycle theory would have in $\mathcal{T}_{initial}$ the rule

$$\mathcal{R}_{0|PI}(S_0, Gs) : *PI(S_0, Gs) \leftarrow Gs' = c_{GS}(S_0, \tau),$$
$$focussed(Gs', S_0, Gs), Gs \neq \{\}, now(\tau)$$

instead of the original rule

$$\mathcal{R}_{0|PI}(S_0, Gs) : *PI(S_0, Gs) \leftarrow Gs = c_{GS}(S_0, \tau), Gs \neq \{\}, now(\tau)$$

Similarly, the focussed variant of the normal cycle theory would have in $\mathcal{T}_{basic}$ the rule

$$\mathcal{R}_{AE|PI}(S', Gs) : *PI(S', Gs) \leftarrow AE(S, As, S', \tau'), Gs' = c_{GS}(S', \tau),$$
$$focussed(Gs', S, Gs), Gs \neq \{\}, now(\tau)$$

instead of the original rule

$$\mathcal{R}_{AE|PI}(S', Gs) : *PI(S', Gs) \leftarrow AE(S, As, S', \tau'),$$
$$Gs = c_{GS}(S', \tau), Gs \neq \{\}, now(\tau)$$

The *correspondence* between the trace-based characterisation of the *focussed profile* and the class of focussed cycle theories may be stated as follows:

Proposition 2 (Focussed profile). *Any cycle theory that is focussed according to Definition 3 induces the focussed profile of behaviour according to Definition 2.*

Proof. The enabling condition $focussed(Gs', S, Gs)$ restricts the set of goals for which the agent may plan to precisely the set of goals that are available for planning according to the trace-based characterisation of the focussed profile. The claimed correspondence then follows immediately from the fact that PI is the only transition that can add non-top-level goals to a state.

A Property of the Focussed Profile. Let a focussed agent be one equipped with a focussed cycle theory, and a normal agent be one equipped with the normal cycle theory. Then if the two agents have a set of goals for which they have no compatible plans then the focussed agent may be able to achieve at least some of its goals while the normal agent may not be able to achieve any of the goals. The theorem below shows under what conditions the focussed agent is guaranteed to achieve more of its goals compared to the normal agent. Note that conditions 1-6 simply set the scene for the theorem whereas conditions 7-9 restrict features of the environment and the application.

Theorem 2. *Let f be a focussed agent and n be a normal agent. Let f and n be in a state $S = \langle KB, Goals, Plan, TCS \rangle$ at time τ such that all the conditions below hold:*

1. *Plan is empty.*
2. *Goals consists of top-level goals $G_1, \ldots, G_n$, $n > 1$[4].*
3. *The goal selection function, in state S, at all times τ', $\tau' \geq \tau$, selects the same set of k goals for some $1 < k \leq n$, until one or more such goals are achieved. Assume these goals are $\{G_1, \ldots, G_k\}$, without loss of generality.*
4. *The agents' PI transition produces a total plan for all its input goals.*
5. *At all times after τ, given input goals $\{G_1, \ldots, G_k\}$, the agents' PI transition returns no plan, because none exists in the overall state.*
6. *At all times after τ, given input goals $\{G_i\}$, $i = 1, \ldots k$, the agents' PI transition returns a (total) plan.*

---

[4] Conditions 1. and 2. can arise, for example, if f and n have just executed GI starting from the same initial state.

Then, f will achieve[5] at least one of the goals amongst $G_1, \ldots, G_n$, while n will achieve none of them, provided that:

7. *The agents' RE transition generates no goals or actions.*
8. *No POI, AOI transitions are performed, and no GI transition is performed after the establishment of top-level goals $G_1, \ldots, G_n$.*
9. *Goals and actions are non-time critical, i.e. no goal or action is ever timed out.*

Proof. (Sketch) Consider the case of the normal agent n: by conditions 3,5,7,8 the state of n remains the same (although time progresses). In this state, by conditions 3 and 5, n can never make any progress towards achieving any of its top-level goals.

Now consider the case of the focussed agent f: At some time τ_1, $\tau_1 \geq \tau$, f performs PI. By conditions 3 and 6 and the definition of the focussed profile a goal G_i, $i = 1, \ldots k$, is selected and PI succeeds in producing a complete plan for G_i, and updates its state by adding all the produced actions As to its $Plan$ and updating TCS appropriately. These new actions will then all be executed. They will not be timed-out by condition 9. So they may be removed from the state of the agent by SR only if their associated goal is achieved. Any new goals and actions that may be introduced by later applications of PI will not interfere with the execution of the actions in As. Therefore, finally, after all the actions are executed, it will be possible to prove by the Temporal Reasoning that goal G_i which was selected at time τ_1 is achieved.

Note that conditions 7–9 are sufficient but not necessary conditions. For example condition 8 can be replaced with one that requires only that any observation recorded as a result of a POI is "independent" of the goals $G_1, \ldots, G_n$, and allows GI transitions but imposes restrictions on their frequency. It is possible to construct examples where some, possibly many, of conditions 7–9 do not hold, but still the focussed agent performs better than the normal one in goal achievement terms.

5.3   Full Planner Profile

A full planner agent will not execute actions in its $Plan$ if there are still goals left in its $Goals$ that can be planned for. Formally:

Definition 4 (Full planner profile: trace-based characterisation). *A full planner agent is an agent that, under no circumstances, will generate a trace that includes a transition $T_i(S_{i-1}, X_i, S_i, \tau_i)$ where $T_i = AE$ and where $c_{GS}(S_{i-1}, \tau_{i-1}) \neq \{\}$.*

Full Planner Cycle Theories. To achieve the characterisation above we need cycle theories that disable Action Execution (AE) when the set of goals returned by the goal selection function is non-empty.

---

[5] Here achievement is intended in a *subjective* sense: the agent determines that a goal is achieved with respect to the information recorded in its knowledge base using its Temporal Reasoning capability. An alternative notion of achievement could be *objective*, requiring checking goal satisfaction in the environment.

Definition 5 (Full planner cycle theories). *A cycle theory is called full planner if*

– *all rules in $\mathcal{T}_{basic}$ enabling AE are of the form*

$$\mathcal{R}_{T|AE}(S', As) : *AE(S', As) \leftarrow T(S, X, S', \tau'), c_{GS}(S', \tau) = \{\}, now(\tau), Rest$$

with Rest a possibly empty conjunction of additional conditions;

– *all rules in $\mathcal{T}_{initial}$ enabling AE are of the form*

$$\mathcal{R}_{0|AE}(S', As) : *AE(S', As) \leftarrow c_{GS}(S_0, \tau) = \{\}, now(\tau), Rest$$

with Rest a possibly empty conjunction of additional conditions;

Proposition 3 (Full planner profile). *Any cycle theory that is full planner according to definition 5 induces the full planner profile of behaviour according to Definition 4.*

Proof. The *initial* and *basic* part of full planner cycle theories are defined in such a way that AE transitions are never enabled whenever the set of goals returned by the goal selection function is non-empty. This directly ensures that all traces generated by such cycle theories will induce the full planner profile.

A Property of the Full Planner Profile. In non-time critical and non-dynamic environments where the actions of the agents have the expected outcomes once the agent starts to execute actions it is guaranteed to achieve all its goals. The theorem below expresses this more precisely.

Theorem 3. *Suppose an agent has a set of goals Gs in a state S. If*

1. *goals and actions are non-time critical, i.e. no goal or action is ever timed out,*
2. *the agent executes at least one action in a state S', where S' is some state after S such that there has been no GI transition between S and S', and*
3. *there exists a state S'' which is either S' itself or is later than S' such that by the time the agent has reached S'' every action in S' has been either executed within an AE transition or revised away in an SR transition,*

then, if this agent is endowed with the full planner profile, all the goals in S are achieved in S''.

Proof. (Sketch) Once an action is executed in state S' it is guaranteed by the definition of the full planner profile that the agent has a full plan for all the goals in state S'. Any goals that are in S but not in S' must already have been achieved (and removed by SR), as no goals are timed out. Then condition 3 of the theorem ensures that all the goals in S' and thus in S are achieved.

An alternative stronger result that can be proven to hold is that, in an environment that is predictable in the sense that POI and AOI transitions always confirm what the agent expects, and a fairness property holds for the traces induced by cycle theories, then condition 3 in the earlier theorem is not necessary, and we are guaranteed the existence of such a state S''. We do not present this result formally for lack of space.

6 Conclusion

In this paper, building on our earlier work [6], we have further explored the use of cycle theories for declarative control of agents. We showed how in the case of KGP agents we can define concrete and useful agent profiles or personalities by varying the rules in cycle theories. We showed three such profiles in detail, careful, focussed and full planner, and exemplified and formally proved their advantages. The cycle theories for these three profiles are no more complicated than the normal cycle theory, and possibly, in the case of the careful profile, the cycle theory is simpler.

The careful profile is best suited to a dynamic unpredictable environment, but one in which the agent does not have strict deadlines. The focussed profile is best suited to resource-bounded agents. The full planner profile is best in non-time critical and non-dynamic environments, where the actions of the agents have the expected outcomes. The theoretical analysis of the profiles not only allows exploration of heterogeneity of agents, but it can also provide guidelines to designers of agents and implementers, for example those using the PROSOCS platform. There is scope for exploring a number of other profiles, some of which have been introduced in [1]. Exploring other profiles, parameterising their advantages and disadvantages according to factors in the environment and application domains and exploring how profiles can be usefully combined are subjects of current and future research. Currently we see no problem in combining the profiles proposed in this paper. Another avenue is to explore the relationships between profiles of behaviour and emotions.

Our work on profiles shares some of the objectives of the work on commitment strategies based on the BDI model [11]. Three commitment strategies have been defined, *blind*, *single minded*, and *open minded*. They are defined by expressing relationships between current and future intentions. A blindly committed agent, for example, maintains its intentions as long as it believes that it has achieved them, while a single minded agent maintains its intentions until it believes they are achievable. Our work on profiles and their consequences goes some way beyond these commitment strategies.

Our approach shares the aims of 3APL [4] to make it possible to program the agent cycle and make the selection mechanisms explicit. But it goes beyond 3APL by abandoning the concept of fixed cycles and replacing it with dynamic programmable cycle theories.

Acknowledgments

This work was partially funded by the IST programme of the EC, FET under the IST-2001-32530 SOCS project, within the GC proactive initiative. We are also grateful to A.C. Kakas and U. Endrich for early discussions regarding this work.

References

1. F. Athienitou, A. Bracciali, U. Endriss, A.C. Kakas, W. Lu, P. Mancarella, F. Sadri, K. Stathis, and F. Toni. Profile related properties. Technical report, SOCS deliverable, 2005.
2. A. Bracciali, N. Demetriou, U. Endriss, A.C. Kakas, W. Lu, P. Mancarella, F. Sadri, K. Stathis, G. Terreni, and F. Toni. The KGP model of agency for global computing: Computational model and prototype implementation. In *Global Computing 2004 Workshop*, page 342. Springer Verlag LNCS 3267, 2005.
3. Y. Dimopoulos and A. C. Kakas. Logic programming without negation as failure. In *Proc. ILPS*, pages 369–384, 1995.
4. K. V. Hindriks, F. S. de Boer, W. van der Hoek, and J. Ch. Meyer. Agent programming in 3APL. *Autonomous Agents and Multi-Agent Systems*, 2(4):357–401, 1999.
5. A. C. Kakas, P. Mancarella, and P. M. Dung. The acceptability semantics for logic programs. pages 504–519, 1994.
6. A. C. Kakas, P. Mancarella, F. Sadri, K. Stathis, and F. Toni. Declarative agent control. In *Proc. CLIMA V*, 2004.
7. A. C. Kakas and P. Moraitis. Argumentation based decision making for autonomous agents. pages 883–890, Melbourne, Victoria, July 14–18 2003.
8. A.C. Kakas, P. Mancarella, F. Sadri, K. Stathis, and F. Toni. The KGP model of agency. In *Proc. ECAI-2004*, 2004.
9. R.A. Kowalski and F. Toni. Abstract argumentation. *Artificial Intelligence and Law Journal, Special Issue on Logical Models of Argumentation*, 4:275–296, 1996.
10. H. Prakken and G. Sartor. A system for defeasible argumentation, with defeasible priorities. In *International Conference on Formal and Applied Practical Reasoning, Springer Lecture Notes in AI 1085*, pages 510–524. 1996.
11. A. S. Rao and M. P. Georgeff. Modeling rational agents within a BDI-architecture. In *Readings in Agents*, pages 317–328. 1997.
12. K. Stathis, A.C. Kakas, W. Lu, N. Demetriou, U. Endriss, and A. Bracciali. PROSOCS: A platform for programming software agents in computational logic. In *Proc. AT2AI*, 2004.

Normal Cycle Theory in Full

- $\mathcal{T}_{initial}$:

$\mathcal{R}_{0|GI}(S_0, \{\}) : *GI(S_0, \{\}) \leftarrow empty\_goals(S_0)$

$\mathcal{R}_{0|PI}(S_0, Gs) : *PI(S_0, Gs) \leftarrow Gs = c_{GS}(S_0, \tau), Gs \neq \{\}, now(\tau)$

$\mathcal{R}_{0|POI}(S_0, \{\}) : *POI(S_0, \{\}) \leftarrow poi\_pending(\tau), now(\tau)$

- $\mathcal{T}_{basic}$:

rules for deciding what might follow AE:

$\mathcal{R}_{AE|PI}(S', Gs) : *PI(S', Gs) \leftarrow AE(S, As, S', \tau'),$
$$Gs = c_{GS}(S', \tau), Gs \neq \{\}, now(\tau)$$

$\mathcal{R}_{AE|AE}(S', As') : *AE(S', As') \leftarrow AE(S, As, S', \tau'),$
$$As' = c_{AS}(S', \tau), As' \neq \{\}, now(\tau)$$

$\mathcal{R}_{AE|AOI}(S', Fs) : *AOI(S', Fs) \leftarrow AE(S, As, S', \tau'),$
$$Fs = c_{FS}(S', \tau), Fs \neq \{\}, now(\tau)$$

$\mathcal{R}_{AE|SR}(S', \{\}) : *SR(S', \{\}) \leftarrow AE(S, As, S', \tau')$

$\mathcal{R}_{AE|GI}(S', \{\}) : *GI(S', \{\}) \leftarrow AE(S, As, S', \tau')$

rules for deciding what might follow SR:

$\mathcal{R}_{SR|PI}(S', Gs) : *PI(S', Gs) \leftarrow SR(S, \{\}, S', \tau'),$
$$Gs = c_{GS}(S', \tau), Gs \neq \{\}, now(\tau)$$

$\mathcal{R}_{SR|GI}(S', \{\}) : *GI(S', \{\}) \leftarrow SR(S, \{\}, S'\tau'),$
$$Gs = c_{GS}(S', \tau), Gs = \{\}, now(\tau)$$

rules for deciding what might follow PI:

$\mathcal{R}_{PI|AE}(S', As) : *AE(S', As) \leftarrow PI(S, Gs, S', \tau'),$
$$As = c_{AS}(S', \tau), As \neq \{\}, now(\tau)$$

$\mathcal{R}_{PI|SI}(S', Ps) : *SI(S', Ps) \leftarrow PI(S, Gs, S', \tau'),$
$$Ps = c_{PS}(S', \tau), Ps \neq \{\}, now(\tau)$$

rules for deciding what might follow GI:

$\mathcal{R}_{GI|RE}(S', \{\}) : *RE(S', \{\}) \leftarrow GI(S, \{\}, S', \tau)$

$\mathcal{R}_{GI|PI}(S', Gs) : *PI(S', Gs) \leftarrow GI(S, \{\}, S', \tau'),$
$$Gs = c_{GS}(S', \tau), Gs \neq \{\}, now(\tau)$$

rules for deciding what might follow RE:

$\mathcal{R}_{RE|PI}(S', Gs) : *PI(S', Gs) \leftarrow RE(S, \{\}, S', \tau'),$
$$Gs = c_{GS}(S', \tau), Gs \neq \{\}, now(\tau)$$

$\mathcal{R}_{RE|SI}(S', Ps) : *SI(S', Ps) \leftarrow RE(S, \{\}, S', \tau'),$
$$Ps = c_{PS}(S', \tau), Ps \neq \{\}, now(\tau)$$

$\mathcal{R}_{RE|AE}(S', As) : *AE(S', As) \leftarrow RE(S, \{\}, S', \tau'),$
$$As = c_{AS}(S', \tau), As \neq \{\}, now(\tau)$$

$\mathcal{R}_{RE|SR}(S', \{\}) : *SR(S', \{\}) \leftarrow RE(S, \{\}, S', \tau')$

rules for deciding what might follow SI:

$\mathcal{R}_{SI|AE}(S', As) : *AE(S', As) \leftarrow SI(S, Ps, S', \tau'),$
$$As = c_{AS}(S', \tau), As \neq \{\}, now(\tau)$$

rules for deciding what might follow AOI:

$\mathcal{R}_{AOI|AE}(S', As) : *AE(S', As) \leftarrow AOI(S, Fs, S', \tau'),$
$$As = c_{AS}(S', \tau), As \neq \{\}, now(\tau)$$

$\mathcal{R}_{AOI|SR}(S', \{\}) : *SR(S', \{\}) \leftarrow AOI(S, Fs, S', \tau')$

$\mathcal{R}_{AOI|SI}(S', Ps) : *SI(S', Ps) \leftarrow AOI(S, Fs, S', \tau'),$
$$Ps = c_{PS}(S', \tau), Ps \neq \{\}, now(\tau)$$

rules for deciding when POI should take place:

$\mathcal{R}_{T|POI}(S', \{\}) : *POI(S', \{\}) \leftarrow T(S, X, S', \tau'), poi\_pending(\tau), now(\tau)$
for all transitions T;

rules for deciding what might follow POI:

$\mathcal{R}_{POI|GI}(S', \{\}) : *GI(S', \{\}) \leftarrow POI(S, \{\}, S', \tau)$

$\mathcal{R}_{POI|RE}(S', \{\}) : *RE(S', \{\}) \leftarrow POI(S, \{\}, S', \tau)$

$\mathcal{R}_{POI|SR}(S', \{\}) : *SR(S', \{\}) \leftarrow POI(S, \{\}, S', \tau)$

- $\mathcal{T}_{behaviour}$:

GI is given higher priority if there are no goals in *Goals* and actions in *Plan*:

$\mathcal{P}_{GI \succ T'}^T : \mathcal{R}_{T|GI}(S, \{\}) \succ \mathcal{R}_{T|T'}(S, X) \leftarrow empty\_goals(S), empty\_plan(S)$
for all T, T', with $T' \neq GI$ and T possibly 0;

GI is also given higher priority after a POI:

$\mathcal{P}_{GI \succ T}^{POI} : \mathcal{R}_{POI|GI}(S') \succ \mathcal{R}_{POI|T}(S, S')$ for all $T \neq GI$;

after GI, RE is given higher priority:

$\mathcal{P}_{RE \succ T}^{GI} : \mathcal{R}_{GI|RE}(S, \{\}) \succ \mathcal{R}_{GI|T}(S, X)$ for all $T \neq RE$;

after RE, PI is given higher priority:

$\mathcal{P}_{PI \succ T}^{RE} : \mathcal{R}_{RE|PI}(S, Gs) \succ \mathcal{R}_{RE|T}(S, X)$ for all $T \neq PI$;

after PI, AE is given higher priority, unless there are actions in the actions selected for execution whose preconditions are "unreliable" and need checking, in which case SI will be given higher priority:

$\mathcal{P}_{AE \succ T}^{PI} : \mathcal{R}_{PI|AE}(S, As) \succ \mathcal{R}_{PI|T}(S, X) \leftarrow not\, unreliable\_pre(As)$
for all $T \neq AE$;

$\mathcal{P}^{PI}_{SI \succ T} : \mathcal{R}_{PI|SI}(S, Ps) \succ \mathcal{R}_{PI|T}(S, As) \leftarrow unreliable\_pre(As)$
for all $T \neq SI$;

after SI, AE is given higher priority:
$\mathcal{P}^{SI}_{AE \succ T} : \mathcal{R}_{SI|AE}(S, As) \succ \mathcal{R}_{SI|T}(S, X)$ for all $T \neq AE$;

after AE, AE should be given higher priority until there are no more actions to execute in $Plan$, **in which case either AOI or SR should be given higher priority, depending on whether there are actions which are "unreliable", in the sense that their effects need checking, or not:**
$\mathcal{P}^{AE}_{AE \succ T} : \mathcal{R}_{AE|AE}(S, As) \succ \mathcal{R}_{AE|T}(S, X)$ for all $T \neq AE$;
$\mathcal{P}^{AE}_{AOI \succ T} : \mathcal{R}_{AE|AOI}(S, Fs) \succ \mathcal{R}_{AE|T}(S, X) \leftarrow empty\_executable\_plan(S),$
$\hphantom{\mathcal{P}^{AE}_{AOI \succ T} : \mathcal{R}_{AE|AOI}(S, Fs) \succ \mathcal{R}_{AE|T}(S, X) \leftarrow} unreliable\_post(S)$

for all $T \neq AOI$;
$\mathcal{P}^{AE}_{SR \succ T} : \mathcal{R}_{AE|SR}(S, \{\}) \succ \mathcal{R}_{AE|T}(S, X) \leftarrow empty\_executable\_plan(S),$
$\hphantom{\mathcal{P}^{AE}_{SR \succ T} : \mathcal{R}_{AE|SR}(S, \{\}) \succ \mathcal{R}_{AE|T}(S, X) \leftarrow} not \: unreliable\_post(S)$

for all $T \neq SR$;

after SR, PI should have higher priority:
$\mathcal{P}^{SR}_{PI \succ T} : \mathcal{R}_{SR|PI}(S, Gs) \succ \mathcal{R}_{SR|T}(S, \{\})$ for all $T \neq PI$;

after any transition, POI is preferred over all other transitions:
$\mathcal{P}^{T}_{PI \succ T'} : \mathcal{R}_{T||OI}(S) \succ \mathcal{R}_{T|T'}(S, X)$
for all T, T', with $T' \neq POI$ and T possibly 0;

in the initial state, PI is given higher priority:
$\mathcal{P}^{0}_{PI \succ T} : \mathcal{R}_{0|PI}(S, Gs) \succ \mathcal{R}_{0|T}(S, X)$ for all $T \neq PI$;

– The auxiliary part includes definitions for

$\qquad empty\_goals, unreliable\_pre, unreliable\_post,$
$\qquad empty\_executable\_plan, poi\_pending$ etc.

Note that $poi\_pending(\tau)$ holds when there is an input from the environment pending.

Contract-Related Agents

John Knottenbelt and Keith Clark

Dept of Computing, Imperial College London,
180 Queens Gate, London, SW7 2AZ, UK
{jak97, klc}@imperial.ac.uk

Abstract. We propose a simple event calculus representation of contracts and a reactive belief-desire-intention agent architecture to enable the monitoring and execution of contract terms and conditions. We use the event calculus to deduce current and past obligations, obligation fulfilment and violation. By associating meta-information with the contracts, the agent is able to select which of its contracts with other agents are relevant to solving its goals by outsourcing. The agent is able to handle an extendable set of contract types such as standing contracts, purchase contracts and service contracts without the need for a first-principles planner.

1 Introduction

Multi-agent systems is a growing research area and has already started to find application in industry in web services and the semantic web. There is also increased interest in agent coordination and choreography. Our approach sees contracts as a means of formally describing the relationships between agents in terms of obligations and permissions, as well as providing a coordination function.

By expressing the terms and conditions of a contract as a set of event-based rules – and so long as the participating agents agree on the history of events relevant to their contracts – an agent is able to obtain a completely unambiguous and indisputable view of the state of the contract at any given point in time.

We claim that the AgentSpeak(L) [13] architecture, with relatively few extensions, enables an agent to behave in a reactive manner (as is the case with service agents, where they react to obligations imposed on them) or a proactive manner where it makes use of agreed or newly proposed client contracts in order to impose obligations on other agents to do things for it. It may do this both to satisfy its own goals, or to discharged obligations it has arising from other contracts.

Starting off with a description of how contracts may be represented in the event calculus, we give an example of a short-term contract to conduct a purchase and a long-term standing contract to set-up short-term purchase contracts. In section 3 we discuss how the agents may communicate with each other and in section 4 we show how these communications can be used to effect the contract state (such as established facts, obligation fulfilment and violation). Section 5

F. Toni and P. Torroni (Eds.): CLIMA VI, LNAI 3900, pp. 226–242, 2006.

briefly presents the AgentSpeak(L) architecture and how we have used and extended it to incorporate reasoning about contracts. We give the plan libraries for the customer and vendor agents which are able to monitor a general class of purchase and standing contracts, of which the contracts presented in section 2 are instances. Finally we review related work and concluding remarks.

2 Contract Representation

The core of the contract representation language is the event calculus [12], where communications are events and the contract rules specify how the events initiate and terminate obligation fluents. We make an implicit assumption that an agent is *permitted* to perform any communication that, taking into account the history of the use of the contract up to this point, will initiate an obligation on another party to the contract. This assumption has been sufficient for the examples studied so far, however, we do intend to investigate explicit representation of permissions in future work. In this paper we are using the Prolog variable syntax convention where variables begin with an uppercase letter.

We are using the full event-calculus [14] without the `releases` predicate since the examples we have considered so far do not require the use of non-inertial fluents. We also dispense with the `initiallyP` and `initiallyN` predicates by providing a contract start event, and writing `initiates(start, F, T)` and `terminates` (`start, F, T`) respectively. Figure 1 summarises the axioms of the event calculus.

```
holdsAt(F,T) ↔ happens(E,T1) ∧ T1<T ∧
   initiates(E,F,T1) ∧ not clipped(T1,F,T).
notHoldsAt(F,T) ↔ happens(F, T1) ∧ T1<T ∧
   terminates(E, F, T1) ∧ not declipped(T1,F,T).
clipped(T0,F,T1) ↔ ∃T[T0≤T ∧ T<T1 ∧ terminates(E,F,T)].
declipped(T0,F,T1) ↔ ∃T[T0≤T ∧ T<T1 ∧ initiates(E,F,T)].
```

Fig. 1. Event Calculus Summary

The body of a contract is represented by a binary relation, `contractClause`, between the label of the contract and the clauses belonging to the contract. Variables can be shared between the contract label and the clauses – those appearing in the label are conceptually parameters to the contract. If we were representing the contracts directly in Prolog, there would be one `contractClause` definition for each rule of the contract. For example, Figure 2 shows the first rule of a short term contract about a purchase transaction.

The label of the contract is `customerVendorContract_purchase(...)`. The parameters to the left of the | are the principals of the contract, usually the offeror and the offeree in a normal two party contract. The rule reads that at the start of the contract, the vendor (V) is obliged to announce the invoice number (`invoice-no`) relating to the purchase within 100 time units. `start` is the event

```
contractClause(
   customerVendorContract_purchase(customer¹:C, vendor:V |
       vendorBank:VB, customerBank:CB, deliveryService:DS, item:I, price:P),
   initiates(start, oblig(V, achieve(value(invoice-no, _)), T+100), T).
```

Fig. 2. Contract Clause as Prolog

marking the start of the contract's lifetime. `oblig` is a 3-place fluent relation between the bearer, the goal to be performed and its deadline. `achieve` indicates a state of affairs is to be achieved. `value` is a binary fluent relating contract variables to their values.

For ease of presentation, we adopt a more compact syntax, where the label is written once at the beginning of the contract, and the rules are written inside the following brace delimited block. Macro definitions for frequently used terms are written in small caps and marked with ≡ and should be textually substituted by the reader as they occur.

```
customerVendorContract_purchase(
     customer:C, vendor:V |
     vendorBank:VB, customerBank:CB, deliveryService:DS, item:I, price:P) {
   PAID(R) ≡ paid(payer:C, payee:V, price:P, reference:R).
   DELIVERED(R) ≡ delivered(item:I, destination:C, invoice-no:R).
   INVOICEOBLIG(DL) ≡ oblig(V, achieve(value(invoice-no, _), DL).
   PAYOBLIG(R, DL) ≡ oblig(C, achieve(PAID(R)), DL).
   DELIVEROBLIG(R, DL) ≡ oblig(V, achieve(DELIVERED(R)), DL).

   initiates(start, INVOICEOBLIG(T+100), T).
   initiates(E, PAYOBLIG(R, T+100), T) ← initiates(E, value(invoice-no, R), T).
   initiates(E, DELIVEROBLIG(R, T+300), T) ← initiates(E, value(invoice-no, R), T).
   initiates(E, owns(owner:C, item:I), T) ←
       holdsAt(value(invoice-no, R), T) ∧ initiates(E, fulfilled(PAYOBLIG(R, _))).

   terminates(E, owns(owner:V, item:I), T) ←
       holdsAt(value(invoice-no, R), T) ∧ initiates(E, fulfilled(PAYOBLIG(R, _))).

   authoritative(V, value(invoice-no, _)),
   authoritative(VB, PAID(_)).
   authoritative(CB, PAID(_)).
   authoritative(DS, DELIVERED(_)).
}
```

Fig. 3. Simple Purchase Contract

2.1   Short-Term Contracts

Figure 3 shows the full text for a purchase contract, parameterised by the item being purchased, the price, the vendor, the customer, the vendor's and customer's bank, and a delivery service.

---

[1] To aid readability we employ the syntax `field:Value` to indicate a named field or parameter.

The first `initiates` rule, as described above, obliges the vendor to determine an invoice number and to signal this as an event notification for the contract. The vendor does this by sending an inform message to the customer (see sections 3 and 4.1). When the invoice number has been notified, the second and third `initiates` rules oblige the customer to concurrently pay within 100 time units and the vendor to deliver within 300 time units and to signal completion as contract related events.

The last `initiates` and the only `terminates` rule indicate that the customer will become the new owner of the item when the payment obligation has been fulfilled.

The `authoritative` clauses indicate which agents are authoritative for which fluents. The concept is related to controllable propositions [9] — the difference being that in our work the controlled proposition is limited in scope to a specific contract, rather than to the entire agent society. In the example, only the vendor has the authority to notify an invoice number. A notification by the customer would not be considered a contract event.

This mechanism is also useful to identify trusted-third parties: the banks are authoritative for the paid fluents (that is any payment from customer to vendor) and the delivery agent is authoritative for the proof of delivery fluent. An agent that is not authoritative for a fluent may attempt to communicate it, but the communication would have no effect in this contract.

2.2 Long-Term Contracts

It is useful to agree a contract about what contracts may be agreed in the future. In Figure 4 we give an example standing contract specifying prices for rolls of wire mesh, fixing screws and sheets of tin roofing. The vendor agent is constrained by the standing contract to accept any purchase proposals matching the agreed

```
customerVendorContract(customer:C, vendor:V |
    vendorBank:VB, customerBank:CB, deliveryService:DS) {

  initiates(E, oblig(V, do(X, replyTo(X, E)), T+100), T) ←
    proposeEvent(E, C, V, _).
  initiates(E, oblig(V, do(X, acceptEvent(X, E), T+100), T) ←
    proposeEvent(E, C, V,
        customerVendorContract_purchase(customer:C, vendor:V |
          vendorBank:VB, customerBank:CB,
          deliveryService:DS, item:I, price:P)) ∧
      agreedPrice(item:I, price:P).

  agreedPrice(item:wiremesh(width:10, height:10, gauge:10), price:10.00).
  agreedPrice(item:fixingscrews(gauge:5, amount:1000), price 6.99).
  agreedPrice(item:tinroofing(width:6, height:9), price 4.00).
}
```

Fig. 4. Standing Contract

criteria. The purchase proposal is a reference, by means of the contract label, to the simple purchase contract presented above.

The first `initiates` rule specifies that the vendor must reply to proposals (of any kind) from the customer within 100 time units. The important syntax here is the `do(...)` notation which indicates that the agent must bring about an event satisfying a particular constraint. In this case the event must satisfy the `replyTo` constraint, meaning that it must be a valid reply to the accept event (i.e. an accept or a reject). The following section defines the `replyTo`, `proposeEvent` and `acceptEvent` predicates, which are common to all agents. Similarly the second `initiates` rule specifies that the vendor must accept proposals meeting the `agreedPrice` criterion.

3   Communication

In our system, events are the act of sending messages. The messages are interpreted by the agents according to a shared ontology, the domain independent part of which is described here and in section 4. Only recorded events that are relevant to a contract may progress the contract state. Real world events, such as "the car leaving the drive way", may be put in the context of a contract by an inform event (or reported event, see below) to that effect.

We require that the events are observed by all contract principals because the state of the contract depends on the history of events relevant to it. In a two party contract, this requirement is trivially satisfied when one principal sends a message to another.

Although the exact format of a message and its transport details will vary from application to application and agent society to agent society, a well-formed message should include a time-stamp, a unique message identifier, a field identifying the message to which it is a reply (if any), message sender, message receiver, a message content, context and the interaction protocol or conversation identifiers. Messages relevant to a contract should include a context field corresponding to the contract label. This information can be inferred if the received message is in reply to an earlier message that was properly context-tagged. Figure 5 gives an example representation of an accept event for the long term contract between the customer and vendor (see Figure 4).

We list some predicates that can be used in the contract language and agent code either as tests on received messages, or as constraints on messages about to be sent (this commonly occurs when an agent is obliged to `do` a communication subject to some specified constraints). The predicates are implemented in terms of constraints on the message attributes above.

contractEvent(E, C) event E is in the context of contract C.

proposeEvent(PE, X, Y, P) PE is a propose event from X to Y for a proposal P. Proposals take the form of contract labels. Propose events must specify the propose protocol, which restricts the valid replies to accept or reject events.

acceptEvent(A, PE) A is an acceptance event in reply to a proposal event, PE. Accept events must specify the propose protocol. According to the protocol rules (see `replyTo` below), there can only be one reply to a proposal, so if there are any further accept or reject events they should be ignored. The receiving agent should check the validity of the proposal event.

rejectEvent(R, PE) R is a reject event in reply to a proposal event, PE. Like acceptEvents, rejectEvents should specify the propose protocol.

informEvent(IE, X, Y, F) IE is an inform event from X to Y that F is true. F is normally a fluent. Only agents that are authoritative about the fluent (see subsection 4.1) may establish it in the context of the contract.

replyTo(R, E) R is a reply to event E. If E specifies a protocol, `replyTo` constrains R to be a valid response in the protocol. R and E must share the same context and must agree on the protocol attribute. R's `in-reply-to` attribute must equal E's message identifier.

reportEvent(RE, E) indicates that RE is a report of an actual event E. This is most useful when E is an inform event from another contract that something has been achieved. Only events which actually occur may be reported – this constraint might be enforced by the requiring event senders to digitally sign their events.

requestEvent(E, A, F) E is a request event for agent A to bring about that F is true. A successful response is an inform event that F is now true.

```
accept(
  time:20050121144600, identifier:cv123, in-reply-to:cv122,
  sender:sales@wiremeshRus, receiver:jak97@imperial.ac.uk,
  content:propose(
    time:20050121130100,
    identifier:cv122,
    sender:jak97@imperial.ac.uk,receiver:sales@wiremeshRus,
    content:customerVendorContract(
      customer:jak97@imperial.ac.uk, vendor:sales@wiremeshRus,
      vendorBank:finance@bank1, customerBank:finance@bank2,
      deliveryService:deliver@pforce),
    protocol:propose),
  protocol:propose).
```

Fig. 5. Possible representation of an accept event

4   Contract Evaluation

An agent may have many contracts active at the same time. It is important to be able to consider the contracts independently of each other (for example to determine a contract's state), and also their combined effect (for example when outsourcing goals). For this reason we define a meta-interpreter predicate, `selon`[2], which evaluates queries relative to a specified contract. Subsection 4.3 describes how the individual contract effects are combined into the agent's belief store.

---

[2] From the French, *selon*, meaning "according to".

```
selon(C, happens(E, T)) ← happens(E, T) ∧ contractEvent(E, C).
selon(C, happens(start, T)) ← happens(E, T) ∧
  initiates(E, activeContract(C), T).
selon(C, R) ← contractClause(C, R ← S) ∧ selon(C, S).
selon(C, P ∧ Q) ← selon(C, P) ∧ selon(C, Q).
selon(C, not P) ← not selon(C, P).
selon(C, holdsAt(F, T)) ← selon(C, happens(E, T1)) ∧ T1<T ∧
  selon(C, initiates(E, F, T1)) ∧ selon(C, not clipped(T, F, T1)).
selon(C, clipped(T0, F, T1)) ← selon(C, happens(E, T)) ∧ T0≤T ∧ T<T1 ∧
  selon(C, terminates(E, F, T)).
```

Fig. 6. Contract meta-interpreter

Figure 6 shows the core of the meta-interpreter. The first parameter is the contract label, and the second is the formula to be evaluated. The agent can now query what obligations are current with respect to a contract by asking `selon(C, holdsAt(oblig(A, G, DL), Now))` where `Now` is a time point representing the current time and `C` is the label of an active contract.

The symbols `not`, `∧` and `←` are overloaded. Where they occur in a functional context (in the second argument to `selon`), they should be read as functional terms; where they occur in a logical context (as part of the definition of `selon`) they should be read as logical connectives. Further meta-interpreter rules are presented below defining the concepts of authoritative agents, reported events and obligation fulfilment and violation.

4.1   Authoritative Agents

In the simple purchase contract, the vendor was authoritative for the invoice number. We capture this authority with an extension to the meta-interpreter:

```
selon(C, initiates(E, F, T)) ←
  selon(C, authoritative(X, F)) ∧ informOrReportedEvent(E, X, F).

selon(C, terminates(E, G, T)) ← selon(C, incompatible(F, G)) ∧
  selon(C, authoritative(X, F)) ∧ informOrReportedEvent(E, X, F).

informOrReportedEvent(E, X, F) ← informEvent(E, X, _, F) ∨
  (reportEvent(E, I) ∧ informEvent(I, X, _, F)).
```

In the simple purchase contract, the delivery agent is authoritative for the delivery fluent. The delivery agent is not a principal of the contract, however, so in order for any delivery notification to have effect, it must be reported by one of the principals (in this case the customer or the vendor). Direct or indirect reporting of an inform event from the authoritative agent is deemed to be a valid contract event by virtue of the last rule.

We have borrowed the `incompatible` predicate, which states which fluents must be terminated in response to one being initiated, from the original event calculus [12].

4.2   Obligation Fulfilment and Violation

We adopt a similar semantics to Dignum et al. [8] with respect to deadlines. An obligation is fulfilled if the deadline has not yet expired. If the obligation was to achieve a state of affairs represented by a fluent fulfillment has to have been notified by an event that initiates the contract fluent. Where it was a more direct obligation to bring about an event characterized by a constraint, that the event has occurred is checked by showing that the constraint is now satisfied.

An obligation is violated if the deadline has elapsed and it has not been fulfilled. For simplicity's sake, we omit rules allowing a violation to be repaired (by meeting its sanction). We need three meta-interpreter rules to capture this: two for `achieve` and `do` fulfilment and one for violation.

```
selon(C, initiates(E,
    fulfilled(oblig(X, achieve(F), DL)), T)) ←
        selon(C, holdsAt(oblig(X, achieve(F), DL), T)) ∧
        T<DL ∧ selon(C, initiates(E, F, T)).
selon(C, initiates(E,
    fulfilled(oblig(X, do(E, Constraint), DL)), T)) ←
        selon(C, holdsAt(oblig(X, do(E, Constraint), DL), T))
        ∧ T<DL ∧ selon(C, Constraint).
selon(C, violated(oblig(X, G, DL), T)) ←
    selon(C, holdsAt(oblig(X, G, DL), T)) ∧ DL<T ∧
    not selon(C, holdsAt(fulfilled(oblig(B, G, DL)), T)).
```

4.3   Imported Fluents

Event calculus is used not only within the contract language definition, but also by the agent at the top-level to manage its beliefs. We need some rules to model that certain contracts have effects on the agent society outside of the contract itself. An example of this is the simple purchase contract which concludes with the transfer of ownership of the item from the vendor to the seller: reasoning solely with respect to the purchase contract will not allow the agent to realise that it does not own the item after selling it in the future. Since we need to track the ownership changes over the course of several contracts, we pool the ownership fluent into the agent's own belief store:

```
initiates(E, F, T) ← importedFluent(F) ∧
    holdsAt(activeContract(C), T) ∧ selon(C, initiates(E, F, T)).

terminates(E, F, T) ← importedFluent(F) ∧
    holdsAt(activeContract(C), T) ∧ selon(C, terminates(E, F, T)).

importedFluent(owns(_, _)).
importedFluent(activeContract(_)).
```

The `importedFluent` predicate selects which contract fluents should be imported into the agent's belief store. `activeContract` is a fluent predicate indicating which contracts are active. Marking it as an imported fluent allows contracts to spawn sub-contracts.

5   Agent Architecture

We now describe an agent architecture in the style of AgentSpeak(L) to enable agents to respond to events related to all their active contracts in a timely fashion. We give a brief introduction to a simplified version of AgentSpeak(L), and then propose a plan library for the customer agent that will allow it to make use of the standing and purchase contracts. AgentSpeak(L) is chosen as a basis because it has a well understood operational semantics and there are available implementations such as [18] and [5].

5.1   AgentSpeak(L)

An AgentSpeak(L) agent architecture can be viewed as multi-threaded event-triggered interruptible logic programming system [13].

There are two kinds of events, belief updates and new goal events. Belief updates are represented as `+b` or `-b` depending on whether the particular belief, `b`, is now true or false. Belief events model the changes in the environment as perceived by the agent. New goal events are represented as `+!g`, where `g` is the goal to achieve.

At the beginning of the agent cycle, the agent picks an event to handle from the set of unhandled events. The plan library is consulted to see if there are any plans that are triggered by the event. Each plan in the plan library has the syntax: `event:condition <- actions`.

For example, `+temperature(T) : T > 90 <- switch(heater, off).` is a plan from an environmental control agent. The plan is relevant to changes in temperature, and applicable when the temperature rises beyond 90 degrees. The action is to switch the heater off.

If the `event` in the head of the plan unifies with the selected event, the plan is said to be relevant. The `condition` is a formula in terms of the current beliefs of the agent and acts as a guard: the relevant plans whose condition formula evaluates to true are said to be applicable. Finally, one plan is selected from the applicable plans and an intention is created to monitor it.

The agent then picks an intention to execute, which involves executing the plan body (`actions`) one step at a time. A step may be either a physical action, an achieve goal (written `!goal`) or a test (written `?test`).

Goal achievement is handled by suspending the intention and adding a new goal event to the set of unhandled events. Future agent cycles will pick up the new goal event, and look in the plan library (as before) for an applicable plan to achieve it. The plan is then stacked on top of the intention that issued the achieve goal action, so that once the goal has been achieved, execution of that intention may continue.

Tests are queries to the agent belief store, and result in a set of variable assignments which are substituted into the remaining plan steps.

5.2   Extensions to AgentSpeak(L)

We extend the AgentSpeak(L) in the following ways:

- Plans may include belief update steps, of the form +b or -b. This effects the belief store of the agent in a similar way to Prolog's assert and retract.
- An agent may have an initial set of desires, which can be selected and posted as new goal events.
- In the example plan libraries below, we have also included some Prolog style horn clauses to ease readability. Since these definitions can be folded directly into the AgentSpeak(L) rules, they do not affect the operational semantics.
- "Fire and forget" goal execution, written !!goal. Instead of stacking the plan for the goal on top of the existing intention, create a separate intention for the achievement of the goal. This is useful when the agent requires simply to start off a process to achieve a goal, but not to wait for its achievement.
- The textually first applicable plan is selected if there is a choice and the agent commits to that plan.
- We implement the following physical actions:
  notify sends a message to all the principals of a given contract (see section 3), and logs it as a communication event.
  waitReply waits for a reply to a given notification message to be received, subject to a timeout.
  waitContractEvent waits for an event that is relevant to the specified contract. This is either an incoming communication event, or the lapsing of any of the current obligations' deadlines.
  fail abandons an executing plan and marks it as failed.

5.3   Meta-information About Contracts

Instead of writing a set of plans to address specific contracts, such as customer-VendorContract, we can write plans that address a general class of standing and purchase contracts. We do this by abstracting common behaviour into agent-specific meta-information about the contracts. We define a binary relation isa which is true iff a particular contract belongs to a more general class of contracts. The schematic rules below we say that customerVendorContract_purchase as an instance of purchaseContract and customerVendorContract as an instance of standingContract that can be used to create new customerVendorContract_purchase contracts, so long as the item and price information match up with the agreed prices in the standing contract.

```
customerVendorContract_purchase(X̄) isa purchaseContract(X̄).
customerVendorContract(Ȳ) isa standingContract(PC) :-
    PC isa purchaseContract(Ȳ, item:I, price:P)
    selon(customerVendorContract(Ȳ), agreedPrice(item:I, price:P)).
```

It is also useful to know when a contract is complete. This is dependent on the specific type of contract. For example, the standing contract above is open ended - it is never completed, whereas the purchase contract ends successfully with ownership of the item. complete is a binary predicate, first argument is the contract and the second argument is the time of evaluation.

```
complete(PC, T) :-
  PC isa purchaseContract(customer:C, _, item:I, _, _, _, _),
  selon(PC, holdsAt(owns(owner:C, item:I), T)).
```

5.4 Plan Library for Contract Execution

We now describe a plan library for executing arbitrary contracts. For each active contract, C, the agent must ensure that there is an intention to abide by it, by invoking a plan for the goal monitor(C).

In the case of the vendor, we assume an initial desire to abide by their standing contract, which will result in the goal to monitor it. However, as this standing contract does not impose any obligations on the customer agent, it is not necessary for that agent to actively monitor it. As we shall see, the customer may instead make use of the contract to achieve an ownership goal by creating an active purchase sub-contract that it will monitor.

```
+!monitor(C): now(Now) & complete(C, Now) <- true.
+!monitor(C): now(Now) & selon(C, holdsAt(oblig(Self, G, DL), Now)) &
              not(observed(C,oblig(Self, G, DL)))
<- +observed(C,oblig(Self, G, DL)) ; !G by DL in C ;
     !monitor(C).
+!monitor(C): now(Now) & selon(C, holdsAt(fulfilled(Oblig), Now)) &
              not(observed(C,fulfilled(Oblig))
<- +observed(C,fulfilled(Oblig)) ; !obligFulfilled(C, Oblig);
     !monitor(C).
+!monitor(C): now(Now) & selon(C, violated(Oblig, Now)) &
              not(C,observed(violated(Oblig)))
<- +observed(C,violated(Oblig)); !obligViolated(C, Oblig) ;
    !monitor(C).
+!monitor(C): true <- waitContractEvent(C) ; !monitor(C).
```

The conditions of the above plans query the state of the contract using the selon predicate. The now predicate gives the current time. When the contract is complete, as defined by the complete predicate in the contract meta-information, the first rule is applicable and the execution plan terminates.

The second rule states that if there is a new obligation on the agent, a goal of the form G by DL in C is posted. This goal event will be handled by other plans in the plan library (see customer and vendor agent's plan libraries below). When the plan to achieve the goal completes, the monitor(C) goal is reposted to carry on contract execution.

The third and forth rules monitor the contract for obligation fulfilment and violation. obligFulfilled and obligViolated goals are posted, which may be handled elsewhere in the agent's plan library to keep track of, for example, the reliability and reputation of the contract participants.

The last rule states that if the contract is not yet complete, the agent waits for a communication event or for the earliest outstanding obligation deadline to lapse before consulting the contract again. Although the condition of the last plan is always true, our plan selection function selects the textually first applicable plan.

5.5 Plan Library for Customer Agent

The role of the customer agent is to respond to desires to own an item. These desires are manifested by achievement goals, which gives rise to intentions to satisfy them. We show how the agent may make use of standing contracts (or other means of achieving ownership) in an example plan library.

```
+!owns(owner:Self, item:I) :
    now(Now) & not(holdsAt(owns(owner:Self, item:I), Now)) &
    holdsAt(activeContract(SC), Now) &
    SC isa standingContract(PC) &
    PC isa purchaseContract(customer:Self, vendor:V, item:I, price:P,
            vendorBank:VB, customerBank:SelfBank, deliveryService:DS) &
    reliable(V), reliable(DS) &
    fairPrice(item:I, price:P)
 <- ?proposeEvent(Proposal, Self, V, PC) ;
    notify(SC, Proposal) ;
    waitReply(Reply, Proposal, Now + 100) ;
    !enact(Reply, Proposal).

+!enact(timedOut, Proposal) : true <- +noResponseTo(Proposal).
+!enact(Reply, Proposal) : rejectEvent(Reply, Proposal) &
    proposeEvent(Proposal, Self, V, _) <- +rejected(Proposal).
+!enact(Reply, Proposal) : acceptEvent(Reply, Proposal) &
    proposeEvent(Proposal, Self, V, PC) <- !monitor(PC).
```

The plan above is applicable to the goal of achieving ownership of a particular item, if the agent does not already own it, and there is an agreed standing contract mandating an acceptable price for the item with a (believed) reliable vendor and delivery service. The plan body constructs a proposal event and sends it to the vendor in the context of the standing contract, waits for a reply and then acts on that reply. The vendor agent is obliged to respond with an accept event within 100 time units, and should they fulfill that obligation the resulting purchase contract will be monitored by the customer. If no response comes in time, or the proposal is rejected, a belief to that effect is stored effecting the customer's future reliability estimate of the vendor.

There is only one possible obligation on the customer arising from the purchase contract, and that is to pay for the item. We make the simplifying assumption that the customer has enough money in his account:

```
+!achieve(paid(payer:Self, payee:V, price:P, reference:R)) by DL in PC :
    now(Now) & holdsAt(activeContract(BC), Now) &
    BC isa bankContract(customer: C, bank:B)
<- ?requestEvent(Request, SelfBank, paid(payer:C, payee:V, price:P,
    reference:R)) ;
    notify(BC, Request) ; waitReply(Reply, Request, Now + 100);
    ?reportEvent(Report, Reply);
    notify(PC, Report).
```

After instructing the bank to transfer the money (in the context of the contract between the customer and their bank), the customer waits for an acknowledgement that this has been done and forwards it to the vendor in the context of the purchase contract. It is this reported event that causes the paid fluent to become established, and consequently for the customer to have fulfilled the payment obligation to the vendor (see section 4.1).

5.6   Plan Library for Vendor Agent

The following plan library enables the vendor to accept and reject proposals for purchase contracts. If the vendor is obliged to accept it, then by the generic contract execution plan library, a goal will be posted to of the form do(X, acceptEvent(X, E)) by DL in SC which is handled by the plan below.

```
+!do(X, acceptEvent(X, E)) by DL in SC: proposeEvent(E, C, Self, Proposal)
<- ?acceptEvent(X, E) ; notify(SC, X) ; !!monitor(Proposal).
```

The condition of this plan extracts the proposed contract from the content of the message, and the plan body constructs an accept event and sends it the customer in the context of the standing contract. A separate intention is then created to monitor the proposed contract. The plan for rejecting a proposal is similar, except no intention is created to monitor the proposed contract.

Now we consider that the standing contract also obliges the agent to reply to a proposal even if it is not obliged to accept it. We define two auxiliary predicates obligedToAccept which is true iff the vendor is obliged to accept the proposal, and shouldAccept which is true iff the it is in the vendor's interest to accept the proposal. shouldAccept includes checks like there is available stock, taking into account already committed stock, and that the proposed price of the item is at least twice the cost price.

```
obligedToAccept(SC, E, T) :-
    selon(SC, holdsAt(oblig(Self, do(X, acceptEvent(X, E)), DL), T)).

shouldAccept(Proposal, T) :-
    Proposal isa purchaseContract(customer:C, vendor:Self | price:P,
            vendorBank:SelfBank, customerBank:CB, deliveryService:DS),
    costPrice(item:I, price:CostPrice),
    warehouse(item:I, availability:Warehouse),
    committed(item:I, level:Committed),
    Warehouse - Committed > 0,
    P >= CostPrice * 2.
```

The following two plans make use of the predicates to decide whether to accept or reject the proposal. The plan bodies are simply goals to accept or reject which will be handled by the plans as the start of this subsection.

```
+!do(X, replyTo(X, E) by DL in SC: proposeEvent(E, C, Self, Proposal) &
    now(Now) & shouldAccept(Proposal, Now) &
```

```
    not(obligedToAccept(SC, E, Now))
<- +!do(X, acceptEvent(X, E)) by DL in SC.

+!do(X, replyTo(X, E) by DL in SC: proposeEvent(E, C, Self, Proposal) &
    now(Now) & not(shouldAccept(Proposal, Now)) &
    not(obligedToAccept(SC, E, Now))
<- +!do(X, rejectEvent(X, E)) by DL in SC.
```

There are two obligations that may result on the vendor during execution of the purchase contract. The first is an obligation to announce an invoice number, and the second is to arrange for delivery of the item.

```
+!achieve(value(invoice-no, _)) by DL in PC : true
<- -invoiceNo(Last) ;
    ?New is Last + 1; +invoiceNo(New) ;
    ?informEvent(E, Self, value(invoice-no, New)) ; notify(PC, E).    .
```

To achieve a fresh value for the invoice number, the vendor increments a belief atom, invoiceNo, and then creates an inform event asserting its value to send to the customer in the context of the purchase contract, PC.

```
+!achieve(delivered(item:I, destination:C, invoice-no:R)) by DL in PC :
    PC isa purchaseContract(customer:C, vendor:Self | price:P,
            vendorBank:SelfBank, customerBank:CB, deliveryService:DS) &
    now(Now) & holdsAt(activeContract(DC), Now),
    DC isa deliveryContract(customer:V, deliveryService:DS)
<- ?requestEvent(Request,DS,delivered(item:I,destination:C,invoice-no:R)) ;
    notify(DC, Request) ; waitReply(Reply, Request, Now + 100) ;
    ?reportEvent(Report, Reply) ; notify(PC, Report).
```

The vendor agent has no built-in capability to achieve delivery, so it must make use of a third party. The above plan checks that its has an active contract, DC, with the delivery service DS mentioned in the purchase contract (which we assume it will have).

The vendor must create a request event to achieve the delivery and sent it to DS in the context of DC. If successful, the delivery service will reply with an inform that the item has been delivered, which is then forwarded by the vendor to the customer in the context of the purchase contract, thus fulfilling the vendor's obligation to deliver the item.

6   Related Work

Our architecture shares the concepts of plan library, beliefs, intentions with AgentSpeak(L). The addition of contracts not only reifies the concept of obligations, but also extends the built-in behaviour of the agent by allowing it to outsource goals that it cannot achieve itself.

In Agent0 [15], agents are programmed by specifying a set of capabilities (commitment rules). Instead of building the commitment rules directly into the agent, our architecture allows these rules to be specified in the contract in the form of event calculus initiates and terminates rules.

Verharen's cooperative information agents [16, 17] are based on the language action perspective. The architecture specifies three main categories of activities: tasks (plans to achieve tasks organised with dependencies between the tasks), transactions (message sequences organised with temporal ordering constraints), and contracts, which are represented as deontic state machines of transaction transitions. Our system does not mandate such a conceptual break down, rather we envisage that higher level contract languages may be translatable into our simpler event calculus syntax.

Alberti et al propose a type of integrity constraint on the communicative acts uttered by agents in a society [1, 2]. These *social integrity constraints* take the form of implications which express when certain *expectations* (about future or past events) may arise. Positive expectations express events that should happen (or should have happened), and negative expectations express events that should never happen. Each event is associated with a time of occurrence which can be constrained by CLP constraints (for example to express a deadline relative to some other event that may not have happened already). Expectations differ from obligations in the sense that they do not necessarily require a creditor or debtor agent (for example, one could expect that the a society event, such as an auction opening should occur).

Like obligations, expectations can be fulfilled and violated, however, since there is no mandatory bearer of the expectation (as there is with an obligation), it is not always obvious how to assign blame to the violation of an expectation. Expectations are a more general concept than obligation, and should be viewed more as an expectation of the behaviour of an agent society than as the expectation of the behaviour of a particular agent (which is what an obligation is). It may be possible to relate certain classes of expectation, such as those where an action with a subject is expected in the future, to obligations. In this case a plan library of similar structure to the sort outlined in this paper ought to be applicable.

Artikis et al [3] describe a system for animating and specifying computational societies. The system takes a global perspective, and so in order to make inferences about the state of the society all the events relevant to it must be known. This is in contrast to our work, where conclusions are reached relative to each contract rather than the society as a whole.

Kollingbaum and Norman describe a system of supervised interaction [10] where agents are supervised by a third party called an authority. The authority registers contracts between the agents, witnesses the communications between the agents and enforces the norms specified in the contracts. Our system does not require this infrastructure, although it does admit a logging agent should the particular situation demand it. Furthermore the agents themselves are responsible for enforcing the contractual norms.

It is important that the contract is carefully constructed so that prohibitions do not completely prevent the fulfillment of obligations. It is feasible to statically check contracts for these kinds of potential conflicts [4]. The NoA architecture [11] solves conflicts by prioritising permissions over prohibitions — obligation consistency is determined by considering the action effects of plans to handle the obligation. If all plans include actions that are prohibited or interfere with other obligations, the obligation is found to be inconsistent and is not adopted.

Conflicts between obligations and desires may also emerge, and if so conflict resolution will be important. The BOID architecture [6] describes a method of resolving these conflicts. Beliefs, obligations, intentions and desires are represented as separate components with feedback loops between them. Each component builds extensions (closure under logical consequence) of their propositional theories, and conflicts between the components are resolved by prioritising the components one over the other.

7 Conclusion

Contracts are a powerful and high level approach to programming agent behaviour. Furthermore, specifying the contractual relationships between agents separately to the agents' capabilities is not only good software engineering, because concerns are separated, but also facilitates analysis and verification since the contracts are represented in a formal language, the event calculus. Event calculus is especially suitable for contract language representation because the semantics are unambiguous and, given a reliable log of events, the conclusions derived cannot be disputed.

The architecture mentioned here is currently being implemented in the Go! language [7], a language with logical, functional and object-oriented features. We are also investigating alternative plan types to the standard sequential plans of AgentSpeak(L) to offer more flexibility and facilitate plan recovery. We are implementing a full demonstration of this technology with vendor, customer, bank and delivery agents all mediated via contracts. We will report on the results of this work in a forthcoming paper.

Finally, our agent architecture provides a simple, powerful, extensible means to implement *passive* (by monitoring fulfilment and violation of obligations), *reactive* (by reacting to new obligations), *proactive* (by taking advantage of contracts to oblige other agents) and *opportunistic* (by accepting proposals that are in the agent's interest, but not necessarily obliged to accept) behaviours.

References

1. M. Alberti, D. Daolio, P. Torroni, M. Gavanelli, E. Lamma, and P. Mello. Specification and verification of agent interaction protocols in a logic-based system. In *SAC '04: Proceedings of the 2004 ACM symposium on Applied computing*, pages 72–78, New York, NY, USA, 2004. ACM Press.
2. M. Alberti, M. Gavanelli, E. Lamma, P. Mello, and P. Torroni. Specification and verification of agent interactions using social integrity constraints. In W. van der Hoek, A. Lomuscio, E. de Vink, and M. Wooldridge, editors, *Workshop on Logic and Communication in Multi-Agent Systems (LCMAS '03)*, volume 85 of *Electronic Notes in Theoretical Computer Science*, Eindhoven, Netherlands, June 2003. Elsevier.

3. A. Artikis, J. Pitt, and M. Sergot. Animated specifications of computational societies. In C. Castelfranchi and L. Johnson, editors, *Proceedings of Conference on Autonomous Agents and Multi-Agent Systems (AAMAS '02)*, pages 1053–1062. ACM Press, 2002.

4. A. K. Bandara, E. C. Lupu, and A. Russo. Using event calculus to formalise policy specification and analysis. In *Proceedings of the 4th IEEE International Workshop on Policies for Distributed Systems and Networks*, page 26. IEEE Computer Society, 2003.

5. R. H. Bordini and J. F. Hübner. Jason - A Java-based agentSpeak intepreter used with saci for multi-agent distribution over the net. http://jason.sourceforge.net, 2005.

6. J. M. Broersen, M. Dastani, J. Hulstijn, Z. Huang, and L. W. N. van der Torre. The BOID architecture: conflicts between beliefs, obligations, intentions and desires. In *Proceedings of the Fifth International Conference on Autonomous Agents*, pages 9–16. ACM Press, 2001.

7. K. L. Clark and F. G. McCabe. Go! – a Multi-paradigm programming language for implementing Multi-threaded agents. *Annals of Mathematics and Artificial Intelligence*, 41:171–206, August 2004. Issue 2-4.

8. F. P. M. Dignum, J. M. Broersen, V. Dignum, and J.-J. C. Meyer. Meeting the deadline: Why, when and how. In *Proceedings of the 3rd Conference on Formal Aspects of Agent-Based Systems (FAABS III)*, 5 2004.

9. V. Dignum, J.-J. C. Meyer, F. P. M. Dignum, and H. Weigand. Formal specification of interaction in agent societies. In *Formal Approaches to Agent-Based Systems*, number 2699 in LNAI. Springer, 2002.

10. M. J. Kollingbaum and T. J. Norman. Supervised interaction: creating a web of trust for contracting agents in electronic environments. In *Proceedings of the First International Joint Conference on Autonomous Agents and Multiagent Systems*, pages 272–279. ACM Press, 2002.

11. M. J. Kollingbaum and T. J. Norman. Norm consistency in practical reasoning agents. In *Proceedings of PROMAS Workshop on Programming Multiagent Systems (AAMAS '03)*, 2003.

12. R. A. Kowalski and M. J. Sergot. A logic-based calculus of events. *New Generation Computing*, 4(4):319–340, 1986.

13. A. S. Rao. AgentSpeak(L): BDI agents speak out in a logical computable language. In W. V. Velde and J. W. Perram, editors, *Agents Breaking Away (LNAI 1038)*, pages 42–55. Springer-Verlag, 1996.

14. M. Shanahan. The event calculus explained. In M. J. Wooldridge and M. Veloso, editors, *Artificial Intelligence Today*, volume 1600 of *LNAI*, pages 409–430. Springer Verlag, 1999.

15. Y. Shoham. Agent0: A simple agent language and its interpreter. In *Proceedings of AAAI-91*, pages 704–709, Anaheim, CA, 1991.

16. E. M. Verharen and F. P. M. Dignum. Cooperative Information Agents and communication. In P. Kandzia and M. Klusch, editors, *Cooperative Information Agents, First International Workshop*, number 1202 in LNAI, pages 195–209, 1997.

17. E. M. Verharen, F. P. M. Dignum, and S. Bos. Implementation of a cooperative agent architecture based on the language-action perspective. In M. Singh, editor, *Intelligent Agents IV*, volume 1365 of *LNAI*, pages 31–44. 1998.

18. M. Winikoff. An agentspeak meta-interpreter and its applications. In *Proceedings of the Third international Workshop on Programming Multi-Agent Systems*, 2005.

Specification and Verification of Agent Interaction Using Abductive Reasoning

Federico Chesani[1], Marco Gavanelli[2], Marco Alberti[2], Evelina Lamma[2], Paola Mello[1], and Paolo Torroni[1]

[1] DEIS - Dipartimento di Elettronica, Informatica e Sistemistica,
Facoltà di Ingegneria, Università di Bologna,
viale Risorgimento, 2, 40136 – Bologna, Italy
{fchesani, pmello, ptorroni}@deis.unibo.it
[2] DI - Dipartimento di Ingegneria,
Facoltà di Ingegneria, Università di Ferrara,
Via Saragat, 1, 44100 – Ferrara, Italy
{marco.gavanelli, marco.alberti, lme}@unife.it

Abstract. Amongst several fundamental aspects in multi-agent systems design, the definition of the agent interaction space is of the utmost importance. The specification of the agent interaction has several facets: syntax, semantics, and compliance verification.

In an open society, heterogenous agents can participate without showing any credentials. Accessing their internals or their knowledge bases is typically impossible, thus it is impossible to prove a priori that agents will indeed behave according to the society rules.

Within the SOCS (Societies Of ComputeeS) project, a language based on abductive semantics has been proposed as a mean to define interactions in open societies. The proposed language allows the designer to define open, extensible and not over-constrained protocols. Beside the definition language, a software tool has been developed with the purpose of verifying at execution time if the agents behave correctly with respect to the defined protocols.

This paper provides a tutorial overview of the theory and of the tools the SOCS project provided to design, define and test agent interaction protocols.

1 Introduction

Multi-Agent Systems (MAS) are recently emerging as a new programming paradigm. In the process of designing and developing a MAS, various facets of the system have to be studied and addressed: the architecture of the various agents, the interactions amongst the agents, the social organisation, the rules, the roles of the agents in the society.

According to Davidsson [27], there can be four types of societies:

Closed societies are predefined societies, in which no agent can enter. Only the designer of the society can create new agents in the society itself.

F. Toni and P. Torroni (Eds.): CLIMA VI, LNAI 3900, pp. 243–264, 2006.

Semi-closed are societies in which agents cannot enter, but they can nominate or spawn representatives in the society.

Semi-open are societies in which there exists one agent taking the role of gate-keeper, which receives the requests for entering the society. A potential member applies at the gate, can provide some credentials, and can possibly be admitted in the society by the gatekeeper.

Open are societies in which any agent can enter without restriction.

The classification by Davidsson is based on rules for entering the society, as this is the most pressing issue. Leaving the society could be done with a leaving protocol (in semi-open or semi-closed societies), or, in some cases, it can be considered as a way to punish misbehaving agents: when an agent does not comply to the rules, it is ejected from the society. Note that there are no given protocols to abandon an open society: agents may leave at any time without restrictions.

Clearly, open societies are the most flexible, but can also be very unstable. The set of members is not fixed, nor even computable in general, as new agents may join anytime, and current members could leave without any notification. Also openness à la Davidsson implies heterogeneity: any agent may join, so they are not required to share concepts such as beliefs, intentions, knowledge bases, or architectures. Some agents may exhibit powerful reasoning capabilities, while others may only be able to react to stimuli with predefined patterns. Foreign agents can join the society without restrictions and profit from interacting with the agents in the society. On the other hand, malicious agents could enter and disrupt the harmonious evolution of the society, threatening the usability of the whole MAS.

Thus, mastering open societies in order to drive them to a coherent, useful global behaviour is a challenge. The SOCS project accepted this challenge and provided theory, methods, and tools to raise from anarchy without overrestricting the agents' freedom. The goal is to point out unwanted behaviour without accessing the agent's mind. The aim is to orchestrate the agents' actions toward the user's goals without obliging agents to follow predefined rails.

A basic requirement for a meaningful society is that there exists a language of commonly understood utterances in the society. It is not necessary that all the agents understand the whole language: agents may understand subsets of the language, depending on the roles they want to play in the society, and on the type of interactions they want to start. The meaningful sequences of utterances make up the *interaction protocol*: agents are supposed to follow such protocols in order to get a coherent societal evolution. The MAS designer defines such protocols in a given language. Coherently with the concept of open society, protocols should be defined not to be over-restrictive, but should only guide the agents towards a desired behaviour. Note that agents cannot be forced to follow such protocols. While in non-open societies there are proposals that inspect the agent's mind and possibly update it to obtain a desired behaviour [32], in an open society any agent could join. The agent's implementation remains unrevealed to the society, so to change its mind and impose a desired behaviour is unimaginable. Agents, as well as humans, might not follow the protocol: this is a fact of life. It might happen due to malicious behaviour, because of erroneous design, because of ignorance of the society rules, or because of incapability to keep pace with tight deadlines. But, although unavoidable, protocol violation must not be accepted supinely, or the system will soon degenerate to chaos.

Of utmost importance is then to check that agents do not violate the protocols. Such a test cannot be executed in advance in an open society: even if we knew all the participants, we would still be unable to foresee the behaviour of members without knowing their implementation and their current (mental) state. Knowing the internals of the agents is against the concept of open society and, indeed, against that of multi-agent system research itself. The applicable check of compliance can be performed on-line: the society does not check beforehand the implementation of the agents, nor their internal mental states, but can only observe their external behaviour.

The SOCS project is aimed at developing Multi-Agent Systems for open societies and addresses two basic issues: it developed a model of a single agent [25], and a model for the society [10].

In this paper, we give taste of the society model, developed in the three-year SOCS project. In SOCS, the society model can be defined through a logic language, evolution of the IFF [34], called $\mathcal{S}$CIFF (Social Constrained IFF). The $\mathcal{S}$CIFF language can be used to define declaratively the interaction space, i.e., both the utterances of the agents and the protocols in the devised society, in a uniform way.

A corresponding proof-procedure can be used to verify that the agents behave according to the protocols, and detect possible violations. The $\mathcal{S}$CIFF proof-procedure is sound and complete with respect to its declarative semantics. Finally, practical issues have been taken into account, leading to an implementation and the development of a full-fledged software tool. The tool, called SOCS-SI, runs the implementation of the $\mathcal{S}$CIFF proof-procedure and it has been developed and interfaced with popular MAS systems. An intuitive Graphical User Interface (GUI) lets the user inspect both the history of happened events and the internal state of the proof-procedure.

This tutorial will not go deeply in the theoretical issues concerning the $\mathcal{S}$CIFF proof-procedure, but it will provide examples to clarify the concepts, together with pointers to previous publications, reports, and downloadable software to let the reader investigate the various facets of the SOCS society model and experiment with the provided tools.

The rest of the paper is organised as follows. After the introduction of the necessary background, we define the $\mathcal{S}$CIFF language, with motivating examples to smoothly learn how to define interaction space and protocols with $\mathcal{S}$CIFF. We then define the declarative semantics in Section 4, and the $\mathcal{S}$CIFF proof-procedure, with the SOCS-SI tool in Section 5. Discussion, related work and conclusions follow.

2   Background

We assume the reader has a basic familiarity with logics and logic programming; a good introduction is the book by Lloyd [46]. As it will be clear soon, the $\mathcal{SCIFF}$ proof-procedure is based on Abductive Logic Programming and on Constraint Logic Programming; we introduce the two concepts in an intuitive way, and provide pointers to the formal parts.

2.1   Abduction

Abduction is a powerful mechanism for hypothetical reasoning in the presence of incomplete knowledge, that is handled by labelling some pieces of information as "abducibles". Abducibles can be viewed as possible hypotheses which can be assumed, provided that they are consistent with the current knowledge base. The abduction process is typically applied when looking for an explanation about some observation. Starting from some observed facts, possible causes are hypothesised (they are abduced). Then it is possible to confirm the hypotheses by performing some additional observation: for example, the scientist postulates some theory, and then develops new experiments to confirm (or disconfirm) such theory. Another common application of abduction is *diagnosis*: the physician, by observing the symptoms, formulates some alternative hypothesis about the disease. The physician tries to find more facts by prescribing a patient another test, that will possibly support a smaller set of explanations. Some of the previously made hypotheses could be discarded because they are now incompatible with the new facts, or because some pairs of explanations cannot be assumed at the same time.

Formally, an *abductive logic program* (ALP) [40] is a triple $\langle P, Ab, IC \rangle$ where:

- P is a (normal) logic program, i.e., a set of clauses of the form $A_0 \leftarrow A_1, \ldots, A_m, not\ A_{m+1}, \ldots, not\ A_{m+n}$, where $m, n \geq 0$, each A_i $(i = 1, \ldots, m + n)$ is an atom, and all variables are implicitly universally quantified with scope the clause. A_0 is called the *head* and $A_1, \ldots, A_m, not\ A_{m+1}, \ldots, not\ A_{m+n}$ is called the *body* of any such clause;
- Ab is a set of *abducible predicates*, p, such that p is a predicate in the language of P which does not occur in the head of any clause of P;
- IC is a set of integrity constraints, that is, a set of formulae in the language of P.

Given an abductive logic program $\langle P, Ab, IC \rangle$ and a formula G, the goal of abduction is to find a (possibly minimal) set of ground atoms Δ (the *abductive explanation*), with $\Delta \subseteq Ab$, and which, together with P, entails G, and satisfies IC:

$$P \cup \Delta \models G \tag{1}$$

$$P \cup \Delta \models IC \tag{2}$$

The notion of entailment $\models$ depends on the semantics associated with the logic program P.

Several abductive proof procedures can be found in the literature (like the Kakas-Mancarella [41], limited to ground literals, SLDNFA [28], that can abduce literals with existentially quantified variables, ACLP [42] and $\mathcal{A}$-system [43], that integrate constraints, to cite some). The $\mathcal{S}$CIFF proof procedure, upon which the $SOCS$-SI application relies (see Section 5) is an extension of the if-and-only-if (IFF) abductive proof procedure [34]. The integrity constraints, in the IFF proof-procedure, are expressed as a set of implications of the form:

$$B_1 \wedge \ldots \wedge B_n \rightarrow A_1 \vee \ldots \vee A_m$$

where all variables are universally quantified, A_i and B_i are atoms (can be abducibles or defined predicates), but they cannot be the negation of an atom.

2.2   Constraint Logic Programming

Constraint Logic Programming [37, 38] (CLP) is a class of programming languages that extend logic programming by giving an interpretation to some of the symbols. In classical Logic Programming, the symbols are not interpreted, so the term 2+3 does not mean 5, but simply a structure whose functor is + and whose terms are 2 and 3. Unification performs a syntactical operation, and does not provide any interpretation, so the term 5 will not unify with the term 3+2, and the goal 5=3+2 simply fails.

In Constraint Logic Programming, a subset of the terms and atoms are given a standard interpretation: the symbol 5 stands for the number *five* and the symbol + represents the addition operation. Unification is extended, and treated as a *constraint*. For example, the goal $5 = A + 3$ succeeds in CLP, providing the answer $A = 2$. This behaviour is obtained by identifying syntactically the set of interpreted atoms, called *constraints*, and inserting them into a *constraint store* instead of applying resolution. The constraints in the store are then evaluated by a *constraint solver*, that detects possible failures and infers new constraints.

Each language of the CLP class is identified by a *domain*, representing the set of values that a variable subject to constraints can assume, the set of constraints, the set of interpreted symbols. For example, CLP(R) [39] is the instance of CLP that works on the reals; this means that a variable in CLP(R) can have a real value, and it can be subject to constraints on the reals. Current implementations typically employ the simplex algorithm as constraint solver.

CLP(FD) is the specialisation of CLP on the Finite Domains [30]. Variables are initially assigned a domain through the predicate $Variable :: Domain$. For instance $X :: [red, green, blue]$ states that X can take only the values *red*, *green* or *blue*. On numeric values, CLP(FD) languages typically interpret the symbols $<, \leq, =, \neq$, etc., plus the usual operations $+, -, *, /$. In CLP(FD), imposing constraints typically deletes inconsistent values from the domains of the variables; for example, if $A :: [0..10]$, $B :: [1..5]$, $A < B$ would remove the values that cannot satisfy the imposed constraint, in this case the values greater than 4 from the domain of A. When a domain becomes empty, there cannot be an assignment for the corresponding variable, so the system fails. Various languages and efficient solvers have been developed [30, 53]. Such languages have been successfully used for hard combinatorial problems, such as scheduling [24], planning [22], bioinformatics [47], and many others. These solvers typically deal only with problems that contain existentially quantified variables.

3   The $\mathcal{S}$CIFF Language

We will now give the syntax of the $\mathcal{S}$CIFF language, together with examples to clarify the various components. We first introduce the concept of happened event, that is the basic link between the society and the agents. Then, we introduce the concept of expectation, that is used to describe the correct evolution of the society. We define the Social Knowledge Base (Section 3.1) and the Social Integrity Constraints (Section 3.2), that are used to relate happened events and expected behaviour, and in particular can be used to define the interaction protocols that are valid in the society.

We will use, as a running example, an auction scenario; we can envisage the following utterances:

openauction(Item, Type) opens an auction for an *Item*, specifying the *Type* of auction, possibly with its own specific parameters;

bid(Item, Price) propose to buy the *Item* for the proposed *Price*;

answer(win/lose, Item, Price) communicate if a bid wins or loses the *Item* for the price *Price*;

deliver(Item) provide the *Item*;

pay(Item, Price) pay the *Price* for the *Item*;

The language for defining the society is based on computational logics, and is used to:

- Describe the events generated by agents in the society. Happened events are represented with the atom **H**(*Description, Time*), where *Description* is a term describing the type of event, its parameters, etc., and *Time* is an integer identifying the instant in which the event happened in the society. The collection **HAP** of all events happened in the society is called the *history*.
- Define the expected behaviour of agents.
- Relate the current history with the expected behaviour.

The expected behaviour is a conjunction of literals $[\neg]\mathbf{E}(Description, Time)$ and $[\neg]\mathbf{EN}(Description, Time)$.

- **E**(*Description, Time*) declares that an event matching with *Description* is expected to happen in the given *Time*. Note that *Time* could be a variable, possibly subject to CLP constraints, which may restrict the instants in which the event is expected to happen. This can be useful to express deadlines, time intervals, scheduling constraints, and any type of constraints existing in the adopted CLP language (possibly, user-defined). For instance:

$$\mathbf{E}(tell(luke, mark, answer(A, pen, 1), auction_1), T), T < 10$$

could mean that agent Luke is supposed to tell Mark an answer regarding its bid of 1€ for a pen, within time 10, in the context of $auction_1$. *Description* can be a term, possibly with variables, which can be possibly constrained. We often use the term $tell(Sender, Receiver, Content, DialogueId)$ to indicate communicative acts, however the formalism is open to any type of term. All the variables occurring in a literal **E** are existentially quantified: as soon as an action matching the expectation is performed, the expectation is fulfilled.

– **EN**(*Description*, *Time*) states that all matching events are violating the protocol: they are expected not to happen in order to fulfill the correct social evolution. Again, *Time* can be a (possibly constrained) variable and *Description* a term involving variables. Variables in **EN** are universally quantified (unless they also occur in **E** literals), expressing that all the matching events are forbidden in a compliant interaction. If a variable is shared between **E** and **EN**, it will be quantified existentially, as in

$$(\exists_{Auctioneer, Bidder, T_1} \forall_{T_2}) \; \mathbf{E}(tell(Auctioneer, Bidder, win, D), T_1),$$
$$\mathbf{EN}(tell(Auctioneer, Bidder, lose, D), T_2), T_2 > T_1$$

meaning that any auctioneer should tell any bidder that he wins the auction, and afterwards the same auctioneer should not tell the same bidder that he loses in the context of the same dialogue.

The current history and the set of current expectations are related through the rules of the society, that can be defined in the $\mathcal{S}CIFF$ language. Such language consists of a *Social Knowledge Base* and a set of *Social Integrity Constraints*, defined in the following sections.

3.1   The Social Knowledge Base

The Social Knowledge Base represents the pre-built, compile-time knowledge of the society. It is a set of rules that provide causal consequences of agents' behaviour. It provides properties that hold in the society when given conditions are met. For reasons that will be clear soon, the conditions are described by means of *expectations*, i.e., atoms describing the expected behaviour of the whole MAS.

We first give some motivating examples, then give the formal meaning and the scope rules. We can say that we have full occupation of the agents if none of them is idle, in any time:

$$full\_occupation : -\mathbf{EN}(idle(Agent), T). \tag{3}$$

meaning that

$$full\_occupation \leftarrow [\forall_{Agent, T} \; \mathbf{EN}(idle(Agent), T)].$$

We can say that an agent is busy if it is never idle:

$$busy(Agent) : -\mathbf{EN}(idle(Agent), T).$$

i.e.,

$$\forall_{Agent}\ busy(Agent) \leftarrow [\forall_T\ \textbf{EN}(idle(Agent), T)].$$

An agent in a society could be fairly served if it gets at least one resource within some given time limit:

$$
\begin{aligned}
&fairly(Agent) : -\textbf{E}(get(Agent, R), T), resource(R), T \leq 10.\\
&resource(printer).\\
&resource(window).\\
&\quad \cdots
\end{aligned}
\tag{4}
$$

where the first clause means:

$$\forall_{Agent}\ fairly(Agent) \leftarrow [\exists_{R,T}\textbf{E}(get(Agent, R), T), resource(R), T \leq 10],$$

or, equivalently,

$$\forall_{Agent,T,R}\ fairly(Agent) \leftarrow \textbf{E}(get(Agent, R), T), resource(R), T \leq 10.$$

Formally, the Social Knowledge base is a set of clauses (i.e., implications in the form $Head \leftarrow Body$) that can contain, in the body, expectations, literals or constraints. Variables are all quantified universally with the following scope rules. Variables that occur only in **EN** literals and constraints are quantified universally with the body as scope (this is coherent with the intuitive meaning of Eq. 3: in order to have full occupation, there should be no agent which is idle in any time). All other variables are quantified universally with the clause as scope (as in Eq. 4, in which one resource R is enough).

Note that the given clauses can also be interpreted in an abductive fashion to derive the expected behaviour given that we want a fair society. Stated otherwise, there could be a goal of the society (fairness, in this example), and expectations could be abduced describing the behaviour of the agents in a fair society. Then expectations could be communicated to the agents in order to guide them towards the desired behaviour. The generated expectations can then be matched on-line with the history to check if the current evolution of the society indeed provides the requested feature.

3.2 The Social Integrity Constraints

Social Integrity Constraints are a set of implications that relate the current history with the expected behaviour. They can involve the various elements in the SCIFF language, namely happened events, expectations, CLP constraints and predicates defined in the Social KB. Their syntax is given by the following grammar (where Literal and Term have the usual meaning as in Logic Programming [46] and Constraint is an atom in the language of constraints [37]):

$$\mathcal{IC}_S ::= [ic_S]^\star$$
$$ic_S ::= Body \rightarrow Head$$
$$Body ::= (EventLiteral \mid ExpLiteral) \ [\ \wedge \ BodyLiteral \ ]^\star$$
$$BodyLiteral ::= EventLiteral \mid ExpLiteral \mid Literal \mid Constraint$$
$$Head ::= HeadDisjunct \ [\ \vee HeadDisjunct \ ]^\star \mid false$$
$$HeadDisjunct ::= ExpLiteral \ [\ \wedge (ExpLiteral \mid Constraint)]^\star$$
$$EventLiteral ::= [\neg]\mathbf{H}(term, T)$$
$$ExpLiteral ::= [\neg]\mathbf{E}(term, T) \mid [\neg]\mathbf{EN}(term, T)$$

Social Integrity Constraints are the perfect tool to define both the semantics of the basic utterances and the interaction protocol in a uniform way.

Semantics of Communication Acts. When designing the interaction, we have to define:

- the set of communication acts commonly understood in the society
- the meaning of such communication acts.

Various works propose a semantics for communication acts. One of the most popular is the FIPA [33] proposal, based on the BDI (Beliefs, Desires, Intentions) model [48]. The semantics of the so-called *speech acts* is based on the Beliefs, Desires and Intentions of the agents. For instance, if agent A *informs* agent B about X, this means that A wants B to believe X. Intuitively, A is also implicitly stating that it believes X. Formally, speech acts are modeled in terms of *feasibility conditions* and *rational effects*, expressed through BDI logic formulas [58].

In open societies, as argued earlier, one cannot access mental states of the agents, so checking that an utterance is compliant with its semantics is impossible from the society viewpoint. We prefer a semantics based on observable events in the environment, and, in particular, which actions the agents perform. Hence, instead of mentalistic approaches, we prefer social approaches. One of the most successful is the semantics based on commitments [57, 29]; intuitively, by performing a communicative act, an agent implicitly commits to the truth of some statement, or to perform some further action. In the $\mathcal{S}$CIFF language, commitments are easily represented through expectations. In the auction example, with *openauction* an agent commits to renounce owning an *Item* in exchange for money. In the $\mathcal{S}$CIFF language, this means that when the auctioneer opens an auction, it knows that it will be *expected* to deliver the item, in case there is some bid which is declared as winning:

$$
\begin{aligned}
&\mathbf{H}(tell(A, \_, openauction(Item, \_), D), T_{open}) \ \wedge \\
&\mathbf{H}(tell(B, A, bid(Item, Price), D), T_{bid}) \ \wedge \\
&\mathbf{H}(tell(A, B, answer(win, Item, Price), D), T_{win}) \\
\rightarrow \ &\mathbf{E}(tell(A, B, deliver(Item), D), T_{deliv}) \ \wedge \\
&T_{deliv} < T_{win} + T_{deliver\_deadline}
\end{aligned}
\tag{5}
$$

We use the underscore for an unnamed variable (à la Prolog). Note that in an open society bidders may join the auction without invitation, so it is not important that the bidder was also addressee of the *openauction* message. The winning bidder might have obtained the information about the auction by another agent, from a blackboard, or advertisement.

Analogously, the bidder commits to pay in exchange for the item by declaring its *bid*:

$$\begin{aligned}
&\mathbf{H}(tell(B, A, bid(Item, Price), D), T_{bid}) \wedge \\
&\mathbf{H}(tell(A, B, answer(win, Item, Price), D), T_{win}) \wedge \\
&\mathbf{H}(tell(A, B, deliver(Item), D), T_{deliv}) \\
&\rightarrow \mathbf{E}(tell(B, A, pay(Item, Price), D), T_{pay}) \wedge \\
&T_{pay} < T_{deliv} + T_{pay\_deadline}
\end{aligned} \tag{6}$$

Note that these definitions are independent of the type of auction, which is defined by the protocol. The concept of expectation is not limited to represent the semantics of communicative acts, and, in particular, is not limited to express commitments, as we will see in the following.

Definition of the Protocol. Many works in the literature represent interaction protocols with Finite State Automata (FSA) [21]. The sequence of correct interaction moves can be interpreted as a phrase in the language recognised by the FSA. Clearly, FSA can recognise only regular languages, so there is a limit in the expressivity of the language for defining the protocol. On the other hand, the simple representation allows for powerful reasoning: proving properties of a protocol described as a FSA is probably easier than using a more sophisticated language. Model checking techniques, for example, have been used for this purpose by analysing protocols described as a FSA. Especially in the field of security protocol analysis, model checking-based techniques have been shown to be extremely successful [23].

Also, representing protocols as a graph means that every interaction which is not explicitly represented in the graph is considered *non compliant*. We believe that in open societies agents should be as free as possible: free to discuss in small groups with a language that is not recognised by the society, free to take shortcuts in long interaction runs (especially in presence of tight deadlines). A "whitelist" of allowed interaction moves is probably the best solution in the instance of security protocols; but in general it might be too restrictive.

The $\mathcal{S}$CIFF language gives the user more expressivity in the definition of the protocol: while in FSA an action can be only required or forbidden, in $\mathcal{S}$CIFF some actions are required ($\mathbf{E}$), some are forbidden ($\mathbf{EN}$) and all the others are *possible*. The *possible* state of an action provides the agent the freedom degrees to take shortcuts and to do actions not explicitly considered by the protocol designer. Uniformly to the semantics of communicative acts, the protocol can again be defined by means of Social Integrity Constraints.

Various protocols have a common core, which specialise into subtypes in different situations, with different properties. For example, the common concept of an auction can be implemented in a variety of ways, and in the real world various flavours of auctions are successfully employed (English, Dutch [54], first-price sealed bid, Vickrey, reverse, combinatorial [50, 35], just to name a few). On the other hand, all auction protocols share some core elements. From an engineering viewpoint, one could first try to define the common core, then refine the general protocol to obtain the desired specific features.

In the auction scenario, we can write rules that hold for all types of auctions, such as:

Before placing bids, there must have been an OpenAuction

$$\mathbf{H}(tell(B, A, bid(Item, Price), D), T_{bid})$$
$$\rightarrow \mathbf{E}(tell(A, \_, openauction(Item, \_), D), T_{open}) \tag{7}$$
$$\wedge \ T_{open} < T_{bid}$$

The auctioneer should reply to all bids

$$\mathbf{H}(tell(A, \_, openauction(Item, \_), D), T_{open}) \ \wedge$$
$$\mathbf{H}(tell(B, A, bid(Item, Price), D), T_{bid})$$
$$\rightarrow \mathbf{E}(tell(A, B, answer(Answer, Item, Price), D), T_{answer}) \ \wedge \tag{8}$$
$$Answer :: [win, lose]$$

The auctioneer should not give contradicting answers

$$\mathbf{H}(tell(A, B, answer(Answer_1, Item, Price), D), T_1)$$
$$\rightarrow \mathbf{EN}(tell(A, B, answer(Answer_2, Item, Price), D), T_2) \ \wedge \tag{9}$$
$$Answer_1 \neq Answer_2$$

Other rules specify the type of auction. One of the most used is the *English auction*. In an English auction, bids are increasing in value: a first bidder declares publicly its bid, then other bids can be placed, of increasing value. When no more bids are placed, the good is assigned to the last bid (which is also the highest). In order to decide that no other bids will occur, there exists a timeout τ: in human auctions, after each bid the auctioneer counts typically up to three and then declares the item sold.

The previous core of auction protocols can be easily specialised to the English auction instance by adding more Social Integrity Constraints, which refine the general auction protocol schema. In an English auction bids are in increasing order, so bidders should not place a bid which is lower than the previous ones:

$$\mathbf{H}(tell(A, \_, openauction(Item, english(\tau)), D), T_{open}) \wedge$$
$$\mathbf{H}(tell(Bidder_1, A, bid(Item, Price_1), D), T_1)$$
$$\rightarrow \mathbf{EN}(tell(Bidder_2, A, bid(Item, Price_2), D), T_2) \ \wedge \tag{10}$$
$$T_2 > T_1 \wedge Price_2 \leq Price_1$$

After a bid has been placed, the auctioneer waits for τ time units; either a better bid is placed within this time, or the auctioneer should declare the last bid as winning:

$$\mathbf{H}(tell(A, \_, openauction(Item, english(\tau)), D), T_{open}) \ \wedge$$
$$\mathbf{H}(tell(B_1, A, bid(Item, Price_1), D), T_1)$$
$$\rightarrow \mathbf{E}(tell(B_2, A, bid(Item, Price_2), D), T_2) \ \wedge$$
$$Price_2 > Price_1 \ \wedge \ T_2 < T_1 + \tau \tag{11}$$
$$\vee \ \mathbf{E}(tell(A, B_1, answer(win, Item, Price_1), D), T_{win}) \ \wedge$$
$$T_{win} = T_1 + \tau$$

It is well known that the English auction protocol might not terminate, so if there is a deadline, other auction protocols are used. The Dutch auction is used when the goods must be sold quickly. The Dutch auction follows a protocol which is nearly opposite to the English: the proposals are from the auctioneer, and they decrease in time. The auctioneer starts proposing a (very high) price. If one bidder accepts it, it wins the auction. If, within τ time units, no bidder replies, the auctioneer proposes a lower price.

In this case, we can exchange the order of the primitives *answer* and *bid*. The two utterances retain their meaning: $answer(win, Item, Price)$ still means that a bid for the *Item* and with the given *Price* wins, while $bid(Item, Price)$ means that the bidder would pay the *Price* for the *Item*. While retaining the original meaning, we can change the protocol: first the auctioneer declares a possible winning price, then the bidders place their bids.

Again, we refine the generic auction given by the semantics of the communication acts (5-6) together with the auction core (7-9) adding more Social Integrity Constraints specific for the Dutch auction.

In the Dutch auction, we must ensure that only one (valid) bid is placed; after the first bid is placed all other bids are illegal:

$$\begin{aligned}
&\mathbf{H}(tell(A, \_, openauction(Item, dutch(\tau)), D), T_{open}) \wedge \\
&\mathbf{H}(tell(A, \_, answer(win, Item, Price), D), T_a) \wedge \\
&\mathbf{H}(tell(B_1, A, bid(Item, Price), D), T_1) \\
&\rightarrow \mathbf{EN}(tell(\_, \_, bid(Item, \_), D), T_2) \wedge T_2 > T_1
\end{aligned} \quad (12)$$

Moreover, either a bid has been placed within τ time units, or the auctioneer should propose a new (lower) price:

$$\begin{aligned}
&\mathbf{H}(tell(A, \_, openauction(Item, dutch(\tau)), D), T_{open}) \wedge \\
&\mathbf{H}(tell(A, \_, answer(win, Item, Price_i), D), T_i) \\
&\rightarrow \mathbf{E}(tell(B, A, bid(Item, Price), D), T_{bid}) \wedge T_{bid} < T_i + \tau \\
&\vee \mathbf{E}(tell(A, \_, answer(win, Item, Price_{i+1}), D), T_{i+1}) \wedge \\
&\quad T_{i+1} = T_i + \tau \wedge Price_{i+1} < Price_i
\end{aligned} \quad (13)$$

Note that in this way the protocol is not overconstrained by a fixed sequence of communicative acts. Many freedom degrees are left to the agents, that may exploit them to converge faster to an agreement. For example, the auctioneer may start with a high price, bidders place their bids even if they do not match the price proposed by the auctioneer, and the auctioneer could choose one of them. Infinitely many hybrid auctions flavours could arise in an interaction. Of course, if this is not the intended meaning, and avoiding this double negotiation is necessary, the designer can refine the specification by adding more Social Integrity Constraints to avoid unwanted paths: *in the time interval between two answers, bidders can bid only the proposed price*, i.e., they cannot bid other prices:

$$\begin{aligned}
&\mathbf{H}(tell(A, \_, openauction(Item, dutch(\tau)), D), T_{open}) \wedge \\
&\mathbf{H}(tell(A, \_, answer(win, Item, Price_i), D), T_i) \\
&\rightarrow \mathbf{EN}(tell(B, A, bid(Item, Price), D), T_{bid}) \wedge \\
&\quad Price \neq Price_i \wedge T_i < T_{bid} < T_i + \tau
\end{aligned} \quad (14)$$

In this way, the bidders can place only bids whose prices match the prices proposed by the auctioneer.

4   Declarative Semantics

The SOCS social model is interpreted in terms of an *Abductive Logic Program (ALP)*. The idea is to exploit abduction for defining expected behaviour of the agents inhabiting the society, and an abductive proof-procedure to dynamically *generate* the expectations and perform the *compliance check*.

Classical abduction does not contemplate changes in the knowledge bases, while in a society the set of happened events dynamically grows. For this reason, we give abductive semantics to a society by associating an ALP to each possible history. We call *society instance* the grounding of a society on a given history:

Definition 1. *An instance $\mathcal{S}_{\mathbf{HAP}}$ of a society $\mathcal{S}$ is represented as an ALP, i.e., a triple $\langle P, Ab, \mathcal{IC}_S \rangle$ where:*

- *P is the Social Knowledge Base (SOKB) of $\mathcal{S}$ together with the history of happened events $\mathbf{HAP}$;*
- *Ab is the set of abducible predicates, namely $\mathbf{E}$, $\mathbf{EN}$, $\neg\mathbf{E}$, $\neg\mathbf{EN}$;*
- *$\mathcal{IC}_S$ are the social integrity constraints of $\mathcal{S}$.*

We give semantics to a society instance by defining those sets $\mathbf{EXP}$ (Δ in the abductive framework) of expectations which, together with the society's knowledge base and the happened events, imply an instance of the goal - if any - and *satisfy* the integrity constraints. Equations 1 and 2 can be rewritten as:

$$SOKB \cup \mathbf{HAP} \cup \mathbf{EXP} \models G \qquad (15)$$

$$SOKB \cup \mathbf{HAP} \cup \mathbf{EXP} \models \mathcal{IC}_S \qquad (16)$$

Moreover, we require the set $\mathbf{EXP}$ to be also

$\neg$-consistent: for any p, $\mathbf{EXP}$ cannot include $\{\mathbf{E}(p), \neg\mathbf{E}(p)\}$ or $\{\mathbf{EN}(p), \neg\mathbf{EN}(p)\}$ (which implements explicit negation), and

E-consistent: for any p, $\mathbf{EXP}$ cannot include $\{\mathbf{E}(p), \mathbf{EN}(p)\}$ (an event cannot be both expected to happen and expected not to happen);

At this point it is possible to define the concepts of fulfillment and violation of a set $\mathbf{EXP}$ of social expectations. Fulfillment requires all the $\mathbf{E}$ expectations to have a matching happened event, and all $\mathbf{EN}$ expectations not to have a matching $\mathbf{H}$ event in the history:

Definition 2. *Given a society instance $\mathcal{S}_{\mathbf{HAP}}$, a set of social expectations $\mathbf{EXP}$ that is $\neg-$consistent and $\mathbf{E}-$consistent, is fulfilled if and only if for all (ground) terms p:*

$$\mathbf{HAP} \cup \mathbf{EXP} \cup \{\mathbf{E}(p) \to \mathbf{H}(p)\} \cup \{\mathbf{EN}(p) \to \neg\mathbf{H}(p)\} \not\models false \qquad (17)$$

Symmetrically, we define violation as follows:

Definition 3. *Given a society instance $\mathcal{S}_{\mathbf{HAP}}$, a set of social expectations* **EXP** *is violated if and only if there exists a (ground) term p such that:*

$$\mathbf{HAP} \cup \mathbf{EXP} \cup \{\mathbf{E}(p) \to \mathbf{H}(p)\} \cup \{\mathbf{EN}(p) \to \neg\mathbf{H}(p)\} \models \textit{false} \qquad (18)$$

5   The *SOCS-SI* Tool for Compliance Checking

The *SOCS-SI* (SOCS-Society Infrastructure) application check the compliance of a given agent interaction with a given protocol definition. It uses the $\mathcal{S}$CIFF proof-procedure to perform the abductive reasoning, and it provides integration with multi-agent platforms. The $\mathcal{S}$CIFF is the logical "engine": by performing the abduction process, it generates the expectations (represented as abducibles) and verifies if they are fulfilled or violated.

While the *SOCS-SI* software heavily relies on the $\mathcal{S}$CIFF proof-procedure, this can be used instead as a stand-alone application. In fact, $\mathcal{S}$CIFF is a stand-alone abductive proof-procedure, that has been exploited for agent interaction compliance checking, but that can be used also to perform general abductive reasoning.

5.1   The $\mathcal{S}$CIFF Proof-Procedure

The operational semantics of the $\mathcal{S}$CIFF language is an abductive proof-procedure, i.e., it computes the set Δ introduced in Section 2.1. It is an extension of the IFF proof-procedure, but it also provides the following additional features:

- abduces atoms with variables universally quantified;
- deals with CLP constraints, also imposed as quantifier restrictions on universally quantified variables;
- is more dynamic, in fact new events may arrive, and the proof-procedure dynamically takes them into consideration in the knowledge base;
- has the new concepts, related to on-line verification, of *fulfillment* and *violation*.

As its ancestor IFF, the $\mathcal{S}$CIFF is a transition system that rewrites logic formulae into equivalent logic formulae. Each formula is a *Node* of the proof-tree, and it can be rewritten by one of the transitions into one or more nodes, logically in disjunction (so building an or-tree). The elements in a node are arranged as follows:

$$N \equiv \langle R, CS, PSIC, \mathbf{PEXP}, \mathbf{HAP}, \mathbf{FULF}, \mathbf{VIOL} \rangle \qquad (19)$$

where R is the resolvent, CS is the constraint store (as in CLP), PSIC is a set of implications (initially the set of all integrity constraints), **HAP** is the current history, **PEXP**, **FULF**, and **VIOL** are, respectively, the set of pending, fulfilled, and violated expectations. Reporting the transitions of the $\mathcal{S}$CIFF proof-proce-dure is beyond the scope of this paper, but the interested reader can refer to previous publications for more details [13].

$\mathcal{S}$CIFF has been implemented in SICStus Prolog [53], exploiting its CHR li-brary for defining the rewriting rules, and its CLP(FD) engine (suitably extended to deal with universally quantified variables) as underlying constraint solver.

5.2   The SOCS-SI Tool

SOCS-SI is a software tool that uses the $\mathcal{S}$CIFF proof procedure to check if an agent interaction is compliant with a given protocol definition. It is a full-fledged system, able to interface with multi-agent system like JADE [36] and PROSOCS [55], as well as the standard e-mail system (to verify interactions happening between human agents), and simple text files containing the log of the interaction. It provides a Graphic User Interface (GUI), that allows the user to observe the interaction in the form of the exchanged messages, to view the list of participants to the interaction, and to inspect the set of expectations generated by the proof-procedure: this set represents the expected behaviour at the society level.

Through *SOCS-SI*, it is possible to access a tree-view of the computation of the $\mathcal{S}$CIFF proof-procedure (Figure 1); interestingly, the shown tree bears both an operational and a logical interpretation. The operational interpretation is an intuitive graphical form of a log-file, showing the most significant computa-tional steps, useful for debugging purposes. The logical meaning is an or-tree (the branches of the tree are connected by logical disjunction) of the possible derivations timed by the incoming events. For each incoming event that enriches the knowledge base, the frontier of the explored proof-tree (which is a logical disjunction) is shown. The user can inspect each of the nodes, and see in the main window the state of the computation, i.e., the tuple given in Eq. 19.

SOCS-SI takes as input three types of information:

- The source of events, i.e. the multi agent system that is going to be observed.
- A file containing the Social Knowledge Base, as specified in Section 3.1.
- One or more files containing the specification of the protocol by means of Social Integrity Constraints (as discussed in Section 3.2).

SOCS-SI can be easily extended to support other multi-agent platforms, by simply adding interface modules, and selecting them as event sources. More details on *SOCS-SI*, on the output it generates and how to support new agent platforms can be found in [8].

SOCS-SI can be used at both design-time and run-time. The protocol designer can use *SOCS-SI* to support the development of a correct protocol: once this has been defined using the $\mathcal{S}$CIFF language, it is possible to check if the protocol does indeed allow only the desired interactions, and it excludes the wrong ones. Agent dialogues can be simulated by specifying on a log file the exchanged messages, and *SOCS-SI* can check the compliance of these interactions w.r.t. the protocol specification. Moreover, *SOCS-SI* provides a detailed view of the expectations

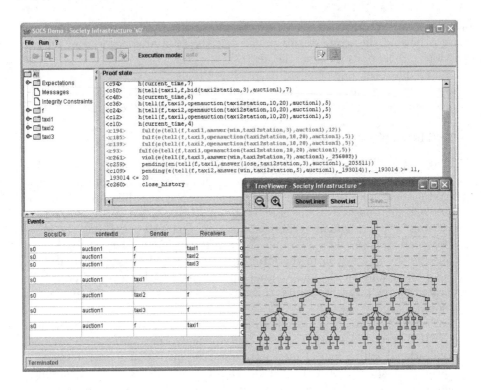

Fig. 1. The Logic or-Tree

generated at every step of the interaction and, in case of violations, indicates also the set of the possible causes.

Thanks to its integration with various agent platforms, *SOCS-SI* can be used at runtime to detect violations to the society protocols: in such cases proper measures can be taken against the culprit (e.g. excluding the culprit agent from the society).

6   Discussion

A number of papers describe in detail various aspects of the *SCIFF* proof-procedure; the details cannot be given here because of lack of space. In previous publications, the interested reader can find the definition of the general framework [15, 11, 10, 9], language and declarative semantics [14], the operational semantics [12, 13], and the implementation [8, 6]. The proofs of soundness, completeness and termination of the *SCIFF* proof-procedure can be downloaded from the *SCIFF* web page [51]. The concept of expectation, developed in the SOCS project, has been compared with that of obligation of deontic logic [17].

A plethora of different protocols has been tested with *SCIFF* and *SOCS-SI*, including various flavours of auctions (English, First Price Sealed Bid, Combinatorial Auctions [5]), resource sharing [16], e-commerce protocols (NetBill [15]), high level protocols (FIPA) and low-level ones (TCP/IP). The proof-procedure and the *SOCS-SI* application have been tested thoroughly; the systems have been subject to stress testing, varying the number of interacting agents and the exchanged messages [3].

SOCS-SI and $\mathcal{S}$CIFF can be downloaded from the web [1, 51].

7   Related Work

Opposite to mentalistic approaches [58], that give semantics to communication through the mental states of the agents, social approaches propose to focus on observable acts [57, 29]. The works on $\mathcal{S}$CIFF and SOCS-SI take the second view, and indeed belongs to such research stream. While other works [57] are based on temporal logics, we adopted a constraint solver, that is able to efficiently deal with scheduling constraints and to express a variety of real-life concepts, such as deadlines.

The idea of expected behaviour can be considered related to *deontic logic* [59]; however, our claim is that we do not need the full power of the standard deontic logic, but only constraints on events that are expected to happen or not to happen. We do not use deontic operators, but instead we map them into predicates (**E** for positive and **EN** for negative expectations).

Our work is very close for the objective and methodology to the notable work on computational societies presented and developed in the context of the ALFEBIITE project [18], and the work by Singh [60] where a social semantics is exemplified by using a commitment-based approach. With this work we share the same view of an open society as that of [20].

Artikis et al. [20] present a theoretical framework for providing executable specifications of particular kinds of multi-agent systems, called open computational societies, and present a formal framework for specifying, animating and ultimately reasoning about and verifying the properties of open computational societies: systems where the behaviour of the members and their interactions cannot be predicted in advance. Differently from [20], we do not explicitly represent the institutional power of the members and the concept of valid action. Permitted are all social events that do not determine a violation, i.e., all events that are not explicitly forbidden are allowed, and this implements a sort of "open world assumption" at a society level. Permission, when it needs to be explicitly expressed, is mapped into the negation of a negative expectation: $\neg$**EN**$(\ldots)$.

The semantics of our model can be directly mapped in an abductive framework, where expectations can be confirmed (fulfilled) or disconfirmed (violated) by the history of the happened social events.

Sadri et al. [49] propose a framework for agent negotiation based on dialogue. The dialogue of agents is defined in a two-part setting as an ordered sequence of communication primitives. The generation of dialogues results from an abductive reasoning process taking place inside each agent during the *think* phase of its life cycle (the cycle being inspired by [44]). Our work shares the view of integrity constraints that provide new abducible atoms, but in our case the abducibles are *expectations* of the society about the future behavior of the agents, while in [49] they are used as communication primitives.

Many abductive proof procedures have been proposed in the past; the reader can refer to the exhaustive survey by Kakas *et al.* [40]. The $\mathcal{S}$CIFF proof-procedure is mostly related to the IFF [34], which it extends in several directions, as explained in the paper.

Other proof procedures deal with constraints; in particular ACLP [42] and the $\mathcal{A}$-system [43] deeply focus on efficiency issues. Both use integrity constraints in the form of denials, instead of forward rules, and both only abduce existentially quantified atoms, which makes the $\mathcal{S}$CIFF in this sense more expressive.

The integration of the IFF with constraints has been explored, both theoretically [45], and in an implementation [31]. These works, however, do not deal with confirmation of hypotheses and universally quantified variables in abducibles.

Abdual [19] is a system for performing abduction from extended logic programs plus constraints adopting the well-founded semantics, but also capturing 2-valued generalized stable models. It handles only ground negated literals, and it relies on tabled evaluation.

8   Conclusions and Future Work

In this paper, we presented a tutorial overview of the methods and tools the SOCS project provided for defining the interaction space in an agent society. The reader interested in the theory can find the foundations of the $\mathcal{S}$CIFF language and proof-procedure in the given references. The practitioner interested in applying the tools can download the implementation of the proof-procedure and apply it to the check of compliance of interaction protocols, or to general abductive tasks. The *SOCS-SI* tool can be easily adapted to interact with popular multi agent systems, or with human communication tools, such as the e-mail exchange.

Current work follows multiple threads. A first thread is aimed at applying the developed tools to new applications, beside the check of compliance to protocols. Experiments are currently conducted in planning with the abductive event calculus [52], a classical application of abductive proof-procedures. Other applications involve checking protocols in other environments besides agents, like giving medical guidelines [4].

A second thread focuses on the evolution and optimisation of the proof-procedure. The aim is to reduce the branching factor of the $\mathcal{S}$CIFF proof-procedure by identifying a priori branches that will fail and whose exploration can be skipped. This goal could be obtained through powerful constraint propagation, or by encapsulating knowledge given by the experienced user on the application domain.

The third thread widens the properties the $\mathcal{S}$CIFF proof-procedure is able to prove. Besides on-line protocol conformance, the $\mathcal{S}$CIFF proof-procedure could also prove properties a-priori, by considering as input only the protocol (and not the history). The software engineering task of developing new protocols could be assisted by a tool that proves properties of the protocol. Such an approach has been widely used for detecting flawedness of security protocols [23]. Our aim is to extend the $\mathcal{S}$CIFF proof-procedure to also prove protocol properties, given as negated goals. The proof-procedure could find counterexamples if the proposed property is not entailed by the protocol definition, similarly to model checking in security protocols. The first experiments are very encouraging, as the $\mathcal{S}$CIFF proof-procedure was able to find attacks of flawed security protocols [7], although we believe that $\mathcal{S}$CIFF is better suited to prove properties of other protocols, such as e-commerce ones.

Finally, extensions of the framework could be considered, like communicating the expectations to the agents, or advertising to possible members the rules that should be followed in the society. Such rules would implicitly provide the accepted common language understood in the society.

References

1. SOCS-SI. `http://lia.deis.unibo.it/Research/socs_si/`.
2. C. Priami and P. Quaglia, editors, *Global Computing: IST/FET International Workshop*, volume 3267 of *LNAI*. Springer-Verlag, 2005.
3. M. Alberti and F. Chesani. The computational behaviour of the SCIFF abductive proof procedure and the SOCS-SI system. *Intelligenza Artificiale*, II(3):45–51, 2005.
4. M. Alberti, F. Chesani, A. Ciampolini, P. Mello, M. Montali, S. Storari, and P. Torroni. Protocol specification and verification by using computational logic. In *In Proceedings of Workshop dagli Oggetti agli Agenti (WOA'05)*, November 2005.
5. M. Alberti, F. Chesani, M. Gavanelli, A. Guerri, E. Lamma, P. Mello, and P. Torroni. Expressing interaction in combinatorial auction through social integrity constraints. *Intelligenza Artificiale*, II(1):22–29, 2005.
6. M. Alberti, F. Chesani, M. Gavanelli, and E. Lamma. The CHR-based implementation of a system for generation and confirmation of hypotheses. In A. Wolf, T. Frühwirth, and M. Meister, editors, *19th Workshop on (Constraint) Logic Programming*, pages 111–122, University of Ulm, Germany, 2005.
7. M. Alberti, F. Chesani, M. Gavanelli, E. Lamma, P. Mello, and P. Torroni. Security protocols verification in abductive logic programming: a case study. In O. Dikenelli, M.P. Gleizes, and A. Ricci, editors, *Proceedings of ESAW'05*, LNAI. Springer Verlag. to appear.
8. M. Alberti, F. Chesani, M. Gavanelli, E. Lamma, P. Mello, and P. Torroni. Compliance verification of agent interaction: a logic-based tool. In Trappl [56], pages 570–575. Extended version to appear in Applied Artificial Intelligence.
9. M. Alberti, F. Chesani, M. Gavanelli, E. Lamma, P. Mello, and P. Torroni. A logic based approach to interaction design in open multi-agent systems. In *Proceedings of WETICE-2004*, pages 387–392. IEEE Press, June 14–16 2004.
10. M. Alberti, F. Chesani, M. Gavanelli, E. Lamma, P. Mello, and P. Torroni. The SOCS computational logic approach for the specification and verification of agent societies. In Priami and Quaglia [2], pages 324–339.
11. M. Alberti, A. Ciampolini, M. Gavanelli, E. Lamma, P. Mello, and P. Torroni. A social ACL semantics by deontic constraints. In V. Mařík, J. Müller, and M. Pěchouček, editors, *CEEMAS 2003*, volume 2691 of *LNAI*, pages 204–213. Springer-Verlag, 2003.

12. M. Alberti, M. Gavanelli, E. Lamma, P. Mello, and P. Torroni. Abduction with hypotheses confirmation. In F. Giunchiglia, editor, *IJCAI-05*, pages 1545–1546.

13. M. Alberti, M. Gavanelli, E. Lamma, P. Mello, and P. Torroni. The *SCIFF* abductive proof-procedure. In S. Bandini and S. Manzoni, editors, *AI*IA 2005*, volume 3673 of *LNAI*, pages 135–147. Springer Verlag.

14. M. Alberti, M. Gavanelli, E. Lamma, P. Mello, and P. Torroni. An Abductive Interpretation for Open Societies. In A. Cappelli and F. Turini, editors, *AI*IA 2003*, volume 2829 of *LNAI*, pages 287–299. Springer-Verlag, 2003.

15. M. Alberti, M. Gavanelli, E. Lamma, P. Mello, and P. Torroni. Specification and verification of agent interactions using social integrity constraints. *Electronic Notes in Theoretical Computer Science*, 85(2), 2003.

16. M. Alberti, M. Gavanelli, E. Lamma, P. Mello, and P. Torroni. Modeling interactions using *Social Integrity Constraints*: A resource sharing case study. In J.A. Leite, A. Omicini, L. Sterling, and P. Torroni, editors, *Declarative Agent Languages and Technologies*, volume 2990 of *LNAI*, pages 243–262. Springer-Verlag, 2004.

17. M. Alberti, E. Lamma, M. Gavanelli, P. Mello, G. Sartor, and P. Torroni. Mapping deontic operators to abductive expectations. *Computational and Mathematical Organization Theory*. To appear.

18. ALFEBIITE: A Logical Framework for Ethical Behaviour between Infohabitants in the Information Trading Economy of the universal information ecosystem. IST-1999-10298, 1999. Home Page: http://www.iis.ee.ic.ac.uk/~alfebiite/.

19. J. Alferes, L. M. Pereira, and T. Swift. Abduction in well-founded semantics and generalized stable models via tabled dual programs. *Theory and Practice of Logic Programming*, 4:383–428, July 2004.

20. A. Artikis, J. Pitt, and M. Sergot. Animated specifications of computational societies. In Castelfranchi and Lewis Johnson [26], pages 1053–1061.

21. M. Barbuceanu and M.S. Fox. Cool: A language for describing coordination in multi-agent systems. In V. Lesser, editor, *Proceedings of the First Intl. Conference on Multi-Agent Systems*, pages 17–25. AAAI Press/The MIT Press, 1995.

22. R. Barruffi, M. Milano, and R. Montanari. Planning for security management. *IEEE Intelligent Systems*, 16(1):74–80, 2001.

23. D. Basin, S. Mödersheim, and L. Viganò. An on-the-fly model-checker for security protocol analysis. In E. Snekkenes and D. Gollmann, editors, *Computer Security - ESORICS 2003*, volume 2808 of *LNCS*, pages 253–270. Springer-Verlag, 2003.

24. F. Bosi and M. Milano. Enhancing CLP branch and bound techniques for scheduling problems. *Software Practice & Experience*, 31(1):17–42, 2001.

25. A. Bracciali, N. Demetriou, U. Endriss, A. Kakas, W. Lu, P. Mancarella, F. Sadri, K. Stathis, F. Toni, and G. Terreni. The KGP model of agency: Computational model and prototype implementation. In Priami and Quaglia [2], pages 340–367.

26. C. Castelfranchi and W. Lewis Johnson, editors. *Proceedings of the First International Joint Conference on Autonomous Agents and Multiagent Systems (AAMAS-2002)*, Bologna, Italy, 2002. ACM Press.

27. P. Davidsson. Categories of artificial societies. In A. Omicini, P. Petta, and R. Tolksdorf, editors, *Engineering Societies in the Agents World II*, volume 2203 of *LNAI*, pages 1–9. Springer-Verlag, 2001.

28. M. Denecker and D. De Schreye. SLDNFA: an abductive procedure for abductive logic programs. *Journal of Logic Programming*, 34(2):111–167, 1998.

29. V. Dignum, J. J. Meyer, and H. Weigand. Towards an organizational model for agent societies using contracts. In Castelfranchi and Lewis Johnson [26], pages 694–695.

30. M. Dincbas, P. van Hentenryck, H. Simonis, and A. Aggoun. The constraint logic programming language CHIP. In *Proceedings of the 2nd International Conference on 5th Generation Computer Systems*, pages 693–702, Tokyo, Japan, 1988.

31. U. Endriss, P. Mancarella, F. Sadri, G. Terreni, and F. Toni. The CIFF proof procedure for abductive logic programming with constraints. In J.J. Alferes and J.A. Leite, editors, *JELIA 2004*, volume 3229 of *LNAI*, pages 31–43. Springer-Verlag.

32. U. Endriss, N. Maudet, F. Sadri, and F. Toni. Protocol conformance for logic-based agents. In G. Gottlob and T. Walsh, editors, *IJCAI-03*. Morgan Kaufmann.

33. FIPA: Foundation for Intelligent Physical Agents. http://www.fipa.org/.

34. T. H. Fung and R. A. Kowalski. The IFF proof procedure for abductive logic programming. *Journal of Logic Programming*, 33(2):151–165, November 1997.

35. A. Guerri and M. Milano. Exploring CP-IP based techniques for the bid evaluation in combinatorial auctions. In F. Rossi, editor, *Principles and Practice of Constraint Programming - CP 2003*, volume 2833 of *LNCS*, pages 863–867. Springer-Verlag.

36. Java Agent DEvelopment framework. http://sharon.cselt.it/projects/jade/.

37. J. Jaffar and M.J. Maher. Constraint logic programming: a survey. *Journal of Logic Programming*, 19-20:503–582, 1994.

38. J. Jaffar, M.J. Maher, K. Marriott, and P.J. Stuckey. The semantics of constraint logic programs. *Journal of Logic Programming*, 37(1-3):1–46, 1998.

39. J. Jaffar, S. Michaylov, P.J. Stuckey, and R.H.C. Yap. The CLP(R) language and system. *ACM Transactions on Programming Languages and Systems*, 14(3):339–395, 1992.

40. A.C. Kakas, R.A. Kowalski, and F. Toni. The role of abduction in logic programming. In D.M. Gabbay, C.J. Hogger, and J.A. Robinson, editors, *Handbook of Logic in Artificial Intelligence and Logic Programming*, volume 5, pages 235–324. Oxford University Press, 1998.

41. A.C. Kakas and P. Mancarella. On the relation between Truth Maintenance and Abduction. In T. Fukumura, editor, *Proceedings of PRICAI-90*, pages 438–443. Ohmsha Ltd., 1990.

42. A.C. Kakas, A. Michael, and C. Mourlas. ACLP: Abductive Constraint Logic Programming. *Journal of Logic Programming*, 44(1-3):129–177, July 2000.

43. A.C. Kakas, B. van Nuffelen, and M. Denecker. $\mathcal{A}$-System: Problem solving through abduction. In B. Nebel, editor, *IJCAI-01*, pages 591–596, Seattle, Washington, USA, August 2001. Morgan Kaufmann.

44. R.A. Kowalski and F. Sadri. From logic programming towards multi-agent systems. *Annals of Mathematics and Artificial Intelligence*, 25(3/4):391–419, 1999.

45. R.A. Kowalski, F. Toni, and G. Wetzel. Executing suspended logic programs. *Fundamenta Informaticae*, 34:203–224, 1998.

46. J.W. Lloyd. *Foundations of Logic Programming*. Springer-Verlag, 2nd extended edition, 1987.

47. A. Dal Palù, A. Dovier, and E. Pontelli. Heuristics, optimizations, and parallelism for protein structure prediction in CLP(FD). In P. Barahona and A.P. Felty, editors, *Proc. of Principles and Practice of Declarative Programming*, pages 230–241. ACM, 2005.

48. A. Rao and M. Georgeff. An abstract architecture for rational agents. In C. Rich, W. Swartout, and B. Nebel, editors, *Proceedings of KR'92*, pages 439–449, 1992.

49. F. Sadri, F. Toni, and P. Torroni. An abductive logic programming architecture for negotiating agents. In S. Greco and N. Leone, editors, *Proceedings of JELIA'02*, volume 2424 of *LNCS*, pages 419–431. Springer-Verlag, September 2002.

50. T. Sandholm. Algorithm for optimal winner determination in combinatorial auction. *Artificial Intelligence*, 135(1-2):1–54, 2002.

51. The *SCIFF* abductive proof procedure.
    http://lia.deis.unibo.it/Research/sciff/.

52. M. Shanahan. The event calculus explained. In M. Wooldridge and M.M. Veloso, editors, *Artificial Intelligence Today: Recent Trends and Developments*, volume 1600 of *LNCS*, pages 409–430. Springer, 1999.

53. SICStus prolog user manual, release 3.11.0, 2003. http://www.sics.se/sicstus/.

54. C. Sierra and P. Noriega. Agent-mediated interaction. From auctions to negotiation and argumentation. In M. d'Inverno, M. Luck, M. Fisher, and C. Preist, editors, *Foundations and Applications of Multi-Agent Systems*, volume 2403 of *LNCS*, pages 27–48. Springer-Verlag, 2002.

55. K. Stathis, A.C. Kakas, W. Lu, N. Demetriou, U. Endriss, and A. Bracciali. PROSOCS: a platform for programming software agents in computational logic. In Trappl [56], pages 523–528. Extended version to appear in Applied Artificial Intelligence.

56. R. Trappl, editor. *Proceedings of the 17th European Meeting on Cybernetics and Systems Research, Symposium AT2AI-4*. Vienna, Austria, April 13-16 2004.

57. M. Venkatraman and M.P. Singh. Verifying compliance with commitment protocols. *Autonomous Agents and Multi-Agent Systems*, 2(3):217–236, 1999.

58. M. Wooldridge. *Introduction to Multi-Agent Systems*. John Wiley & Sons, Ltd., 2002.

59. G.H. Wright. Deontic logic. *Mind*, 60:1–15, 1951.

60. P. Yolum and M.P. Singh. Flexible protocol specification and execution: applying event calculus planning using commitments. In Castelfranchi and Lewis Johnson [26], pages 527–534.

Verification of Protocol Conformance and Agent Interoperability*

Matteo Baldoni, Cristina Baroglio, Alberto Martelli, and Viviana Patti

Dipartimento di Informatica, Università degli Studi di Torino,
C.so Svizzera, 185, I-10149 Torino, Italy
{baldoni, baroglio, mrt, patti}@di.unito.it

Abstract. In open multi-agent systems agent interaction is usually ruled by public protocols defining the rules the agents should respect in message exchanging. The respect of such rules guarantees interoperability. Given two agents that agree on using a certain protocol for their interaction, a crucial issue (known as "a priori conformance test") is verifying if their interaction policies, i.e. the programs that encode their communicative behavior, will actually produce interactions which are conformant to the agreed protocol. An issue that is not always made clear in the existing proposals for conformance tests is whether the test preserves agents' capability of interacting, besides certifying the legality of their possible conversations. This work proposes an approach to the verification of a priori conformance, of an agent's conversation policy to a protocol, which is based on the theory of formal languages. The conformance test is based on the acceptance of both the policy and the protocol by a special finite state automaton and it guarantees the interoperability of agents that are individually proved conformant. Many protocols used in multi-agent systems can be expressed as finite state automata, so this approach can be applied to a wide variety of cases with the proviso that both the protocol specification and the protocol implementation can be translated into finite state automata. In this sense the approach is general. Easy applicability to the case when a logic-based language is used to implement the policies is shown by means of a concrete example, in which the language DyLOG, based on computational logic, is used.

1 Introduction

Multi-agent systems (MASs) often comprise heterogeneous components, that differ in the way they represent knowledge about the world and about other agents, as well as in the mechanisms used for reasoning about it. Protocols rule the agents' interaction. Therefore, they can be used to check if a given agent can,

---

* This research has partially been funded by the European Commission and by the Swiss Federal Office for Education and Science within the 6th Framework Programme project REWERSE number 506779 (cf. http://rewerse.net), and it has also been supported by MIUR PRIN 2005 "Specification and verification of agent interaction protocols" national project.

F. Toni and P. Torroni (Eds.): CLIMA VI, LNAI 3900, pp. 265–283, 2006.

or cannot, take part in the system. In general, based on this abstraction, open systems can be realized, in which new agents can dynamically join the system. The insertion of a new agent in an execution context is determined according to some form of reasoning about its behaviour: it will be added provided that it satisfies the body of the rules within the system, intended as a society.

In a protocol-ruled system of this kind, it is, however, not necessary to check the interoperability (i.e. the capability of *actually* producing a conversation) of the newly entered agent with the other agents in the system if, as long as the rules are satisfied, the property is guaranteed. The problem which amounts to verifying if a given *implementation* (an agent interaction policy) respects a given *abstract protocol definition* is known as *conformance* testing. A conformance test can, then, be considered as a tool that, by verifying that agents respect a protocol, *should certify* their interoperability. In this perspective, we expect that two agents which conform to a protocol will *produce a conversation*, that is legal (i.e. correct w.r.t. the protocol), when interacting with one another.

The design and implementation of interaction protocols are crucial steps in the development of a MAS [24, 25]. Following [23], two tests must be executed in the process of interaction protocol engineering. One is the already mentioned conformance test, the other is the *validation* test, which verifies the consistency of an *abstract protocol definition* w.r.t. the *requirements*, derived from the analysis phase, that it should embody. In the literature validation has often been tackled by means of model checking techniques [10, 9, 29], and two kinds of conformance verifications have been studied: *a priori* conformance verification, and *run-time* conformance verification (or compliance) [14, 15, 21]. If we call a *conversation* a specific interaction between two agents, consisting only of communicative acts, the first kind of conformance is a property of the *implementation as a whole* –intuitively it checks if an agent will never produce conversations that violate the abstract interaction protocol specification– while the latter is a property of the *on-going conversation*, aimed at verifying if *that* conversation is legal.

In this work we focus on a priori conformance verification, defining a conformance test, based on the acceptance, of both the agent's policy and the public protocol, by a special finite state automaton. Many protocols used in multi-agent systems can be expressed as finite state automata, so this approach can be applied to a wide variety of cases with the proviso that both the protocol specification and the protocol implementation (policy) can be translated into finite state automata. In this sense the approach is general.

The application of our approach is particularly easy in case a logic-based declarative language is used to implement the policies. In logic languages indeed policies are usually expressed by Prolog-like rules, which can be easily converted in a formal language representation. In Section 4 we show this by means of a concrete example where the language DyLOG [7], based on computational logic, is used for implementing the agents' policies. On the side of the protocol specification languages, currently there is a great interest in using informal, graphical languages (e.g. UML-based) for specifying protocols and in the translation of such languages in formal languages [13, 16]. By this translation it is, in fact, possible to prove properties that the original representation does not allow. In this context, in [5] we have shown an easy algorithm for translating AUML sequence diagrams to finite state automata thus enabling the verification of conformance.

In [5] we already faced the problem of a priori conformance verification as a verification of properties of formal languages, but proposing a different approach with some limitations due to focussing on the legality issue. In fact, interpreting (as we did) the conformance test as the verification that all the conversations, allowed by an agent's policy, are also possible according to the protocol specification, does not entail interoperability. The next section is devoted to explain the expected relations among conformance and the crucial interoperability issue.

2   Conformant and Interoperable Agents

A *conversation policy* is a program that defines the communicative behavior of a specific agent, implemented in some programming language. A conversation *protocol* specifies the desired communicative behavior of a set of agents and it can be specified by means of many formal tools, such as (but not limited to) Petri nets, AUML sequence diagrams, automata.

More specifically, a conversation protocol specifies the sequences of speech acts that can possibly be exchanged by the involved agents, and that we consider as legal. In agent languages that account for communication, speech acts often have the form $m(ag_s, ag_r, l)$, where m is the performative, ag_s (sender) and ag_r (receiver) are two agents and l is the message content. It is not restrictive to assume that speech acts have this form and to assume that conversations are sequences of speech acts of this form. Notice that depending on the semantics of the speech acts, the conversation will take place in a framework based either on the *mentalistic* or on the *social state* approach [17, 28, 20]. However, the speech acts semantics does not play a role in our proposal, which concerns an orthogonal aspect of the interaction in Multi Agent Systems.

In the following analysis it is important to distinguish the incoming messages, w.r.t. a specific agent ag of the MAS, from the messages uttered by it. We respectively denote the former, where ag plays the role of the receiver, by $\mathsf{m}(\overleftarrow{ag})$, and the latter, where ag is the sender, by $\mathsf{m}(\overrightarrow{ag})$. We will also simply write $\overleftarrow{\mathsf{m}}$ (*incoming message*) and $\overrightarrow{\mathsf{m}}$ (*outgoing message*) when the agent that receives or utters the message is clear from the context. Notice that these are just shorthands, that underline the *role* of a given agent from the *individual perspective* of *that* agent. So, for instance, $m(ag_s, ag_r, l)$ is written as $\mathsf{m}(\overleftarrow{ag_r})$ from the point of view of ag_r, and $\mathsf{m}(\overrightarrow{ag_s})$ from the point of view of the sender but the three notions denote the same object.

A *conversation*, denoted by σ, is a sequence of speech acts that represents a dialogue of a set of agents.

Definition 1 (Conversation). *A conversation is a sequence σ of messages taken from a given set $\mathcal{SA}$ of speech acts.*

In this work we face the problem of conformance verification and interpret a priori conformance as a property that relates two *formal languages* [22], the language of the conversations allowed by the conversation policy of an agent, and the language of the conversations allowed by the specification of a communication protocol. Each of these languages represents a set of conversations. In the case of the protocol specification, it is intuitive that it will be the set of all the possible conversations allowed by the protocol among the partners. In the case of the single agent's policy, it will be the set of the possible conversations that the agent can carry on according to the policy. Of course, at execution time, depending on the interlocutor and on the circumstances, only one conversation at a time is actually expressed, however, for verifying conformance *a priori* we need to consider them all as a set.

Definition 2 (Policy language). *Given a policy p_{lang}^{ag}, where p is the policy name, lang is the language in which this is implemented, and ag is the agent that uses it, we denote by $L(p_{lang}^{ag})$ the set of conversations that ag can carry on according to p.*

Definition 3 (Protocol language). *Given a conversation protocol p_{spec}, where p is the protocol name, and spec is the language in which it is represented, we denote by $L(p_{spec})$ the set of conversations that a set of agents, that interact according to p, can carry on.*

The assumption that we make throughout this paper is that the two languages $L(p_{lang}^{ag})$ and $L(p_{spec})$ are *regular*. This choice restricts the kinds of protocols to which our proposal can be applied, because finite state automata cannot represent concurrent operations, however, it is still significant because a wide family of protocols (and policies) of practical use can be expressed in a way that can be mapped onto such automata. Moreover, the use of regular sets ensures *decidability*. Another assumption is that the conversation protocol encompasses only *two agents*. The extension to a greater number of agents will be tackled as future work. Notice that when the MAS is *heterogeneous*, the agents might be implemented in *different languages*.

We say that a conversation is legal w.r.t. a protocol specification if it respects the specifications given by the protocol. Since $L(p_{spec})$ is the set of all the legal conversations according to p, the definition is as follows.

Definition 4 (Legal conversation). *We say that a conversation σ is legal w.r.t. a protocol specification p_{spec} when $\sigma \in L(p_{spec})$.*

We are now in position to explain, with the help of a few simple examples, the intuition behind the terms "conformance" and "interoperability", that we will, then, formalize.

Definition 5 (Interoperability). Interoperability *is the capability of a set of agents of actually producing a conversation when interacting with one another.*

Often the introduction of a new agent in an execution context is determined according to some form of reasoning about its behaviour: it will be added provided that it satisfies a set of rules -the protocol- that characterize such execution context; as long as the new agent satisfies the rules, the interoperability with the other components of the system is guaranteed. Thus in protocol-based systems the interoperability of an agent with others can be proved by checking the communicative behavior of the agent against the rules of the system, i.e. against an *interaction protocol*. Such a proof is known as *conformance test*. Intuitively, this test must guarantee the following *definition of interoperability*. This work focuses on it.

Definition 6 (Interoperability w.r.t. an interaction protocol). Interoperability w.r.t. an interaction protocol P is the capability of a set of agents of producing a conversation that is legal w.r.t. P.

Let us begin with considering the following case: suppose that the communicative behavior of the agent ag is defined by a policy that accounts for two conversations $\{m_1(\overrightarrow{ag})m_2(\overleftarrow{ag}), m_1(\overrightarrow{ag})m_3(\overleftarrow{ag})\}$. This means that after uttering a message m_1, the agent expects one of the two messages m_2 or m_3. Let us also suppose that the protocol specification only allows the first conversation, i.e. that the only possible incoming message is m_2. Is the policy conformant? According to Definition 4 the answer should be no, because the policy allows an illegal conversation. Nevertheless, when the agent will interact with another agent that is conformant to the protocol, the message m_3 will never be received because the other agent will never utter it. So, in this case, we would like the a priori conformance test to accept the policy as *conformant* to the specification.

Talking about incoming messages, let us now consider the symmetric case, in which the *protocol specification* states that after the agent ag has uttered m_1, the other agent can alternatively answer m_2 or m_4 (agent ag's policy, instead, is the same as above). In this case, the expectation is that ag's policy is *not conformant* because, according to the protocol, there is a possible legal conversation (the one with answer m_4) that can be enacted by the *interlocutor* (which is not under the control of ag), which, however, ag cannot handle. So it does not comply to the specifications.

> **Expectation 1.** *As a first observation we expect the policy to be able to handle any incoming message, foreseen by the protocol, and we ignore those cases in which the policy foresees an incoming message that is not supposed to be received at that point of the conversation, according to the protocol specification.*

Let us, now, suppose that agent ag's policy can produce the following conversations $\{m_1(\overleftarrow{ag})m_2(\overrightarrow{ag}), m_1(\overleftarrow{ag})m_3(\overrightarrow{ag})\}$ and that the set of conversations allowed by the protocol specification is $\{m_1(\overleftarrow{ag})m_2(\overrightarrow{ag})\}$. Trivially, this policy is *not conformant* to the protocol because ag can send a message (m_3) that cannot be handled by any interlocutor that is conformant to the protocol.

> **Expectation 2.** *The second observation is that we expect a policy to never utter a message that, according to the specification, is not supposed to be uttered at that point of the conversation.*

Instead, in the symmetric case in which the policy contains only the conversation $\{m_1(\overline{ag})m_2(\overline{ag})\}$ while the protocol states that ag can answer to m_1 alternatively by uttering m_2 or m_3, *conformance holds*. The reason is that at any point of its conversations the agent will always utter legal messages. The restriction of the set of possible alternatives (w.r.t. the protocol) depends on the agent implementor's own criteria. However, the agent must foresee *at least one* of such alternatives otherwise the conversation will be interrupted. Trivially, the case in which the policy contains only the conversation $\{m_1(\overline{ag})\}$ is *not conformant*.

> **Expectation 3.** *The third observation is that we expect that a policy always allows an agent to utter one of the messages foreseen by the protocol at every point of the possible conversations. This means that it is not necessary that a policy envisions all the possible alternative utterances, but it is required to foresee at least one of them that allows the agent to proceed with its conversations.*

To summarize, at every point of a conversation, we expect that a conformant policy never utters speech acts that are not expected, according to the protocol, and we also expect it to be able to handle any message that can possibly be received, once again according to the protocol. However, the policy is not obliged to foresee (at every point of conversation) an outgoing message for every alternative included in the protocol but it must foresee at least one of them if this is necessary to proceed with the conversation. Incoming and outgoing messages are, therefore, *not handled in the same way*.

These expectations are motivated by the desire to define a minimal set of conditions which guarantee the construction of a conformance test that guarantees the *interoperability* of agents. Let us recall that one of the aims (often implicit) of conformance is, indeed, interoperability, although sometimes research on this topic restricts its focus to the legality issues. We claim –and we will show– that two agents that respect this minimal set of conditions (w.r.t. an agreed protocol) will *actually* be able to interact, respecting at the same time the protocol. The relevant point is that this certification is a property that can be checked on the single agents, rather than on the agent society. This is interesting in application domains (e.g. web services) with a highly dynamic nature, in which agents are searched for and composed at the moment in which specific needs arise.

3   Conformance Test

In order to decide if a policy is conformant to a protocol specification, it is not sufficient to perform an inclusion test; instead, as we have intuitively shown by means of the above examples, it is necessary to prove mutual properties of both $L(p_{lang}^{ag})$ and $L(p_{spec})$. The method that we propose for proving such properties consists in verifying that both languages are recognized by a special finite state automaton, whose construction we are now going to explain. Such an automaton is based on the automaton that accepts the *intersection* of the two languages. All the conversations that belong to the intersection are certainly legal. This, however, is not sufficient, because there are further conditions to consider, for instance there are conversations that we mean to allow but that do not belong to the intersection. In other words, the "intersection automaton" does not capture all the expectations reported in Section 2. We will extend this automaton in such a way that it will accept the conversations in which the agent expects messages that are not foreseen by the specification as well as those which include outgoing messages that are not envisioned by the policy. On the other hand, the automaton will not accept conversations that include incoming messages that are not expected by the policy nor will it accept conversations that include outgoing messages, that are not envisioned by the protocol (see Fig. 1).

3.1 The Automaton M_{conf}

If $L(p_{lang}^{ag})$ and $L(p_{spec})$ are regular, they are accepted by two *deterministic finite automata*, denoted by $M(p_{lang}^{ag})$ and $M(p_{spec})$ respectively, that we can assume as having the *same alphabet* (see [22]). An automaton is a five-tuple $(Q, \Sigma, \delta, q_0, F)$, where Q is a finite set of states, Σ is a finite input alphabet, $q_0 \in Q$ is the initial state, $F \subseteq Q$ is the set of final states, and δ is a transition function mapping $Q \times \Sigma$ to Q. In a finite automaton we can always classify states in two categories: *alive states*, that lie on a path from the initial state to a final state, and *dead states*, the other ones. Intuitively, alive states accept the language of the prefixes of the strings accepted by the automaton.

For reasons that will be made clear shortly, we request the two automata to show the following property: the edges that lead to the same state must *all* be labeled either by incoming messages or by outgoing messages w.r.t. *ag*.

Definition 7 (IO-automaton w.r.t. ag). *Given an automaton $M = (Q, \Sigma, \delta, q_0, F)$, let $E_q = \{m \mid \delta(p, m) = q\}$ for $p, q \in Q$. We say that M is an IO-automaton w.r.t. ag iff for every $q \in Q$, E_q alternatively consists only of incoming or only of outgoing messages w.r.t. an agent ag.*

Notice that an automaton that does not show this property can always be transformed so as to satisfy it, in linear time w.r.t. the number of states, by splitting those states that do not satisfy the property. We will denote a state q that is reached only by incoming messages by the notation $\overleftarrow{q}$ (we will call it an *I-state*), and a state q that is reached only by outgoing messages by $\overrightarrow{q}$ (an *O-state*).

Finally, let us denote by $M^\times(p_{lang}^{ag}, p_{spec})$ the deterministic finite automaton that accepts the language $L(p_{lang}^{ag}) \cap L(p_{spec})$. It is defined as follows. Let $M(p_{lang}^{ag})$ be the automaton $(Q^P, \Sigma, \delta^P, q_0^P, F^P)$ and $M(p_{spec})$ the automaton $(Q^S, \Sigma, \delta^S, q_0^S, F^S)$:

$$M^\times(p_{lang}^{ag}, p_{spec}) = (Q^P \times Q^S, \Sigma, \delta, [q_0^P, q_0^S], F^P \times F^S)$$

where for all q^P in Q^P, q^S in Q^S, and m in Σ, $\delta([q^P, q^S], m) = [\delta^P(q^P, m), \delta^S(q^S, m)]$. We will briefly denote this automaton by $M^\times$.

Notice that all the *conversations* that are accepted by $M^\times$ are surely *conformant* (Definition 4). For the so built automaton, it is easy to prove the following property.

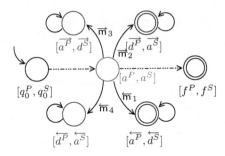

Fig. 1. A general schema of the M_{conf} automaton. From bottom-right, clockwise, cases (a), (b), (c), and (d).

Proposition 1. $M^{\times}(p_{lang}^{ag}, p_{spec})$ *is an IO-automaton w.r.t. ag if* $M(p_{lang}^{ag})$ *and* $M(p_{spec})$ *are two IO-automata w.r.t. ag.*

The definition of IO-automata is used in the following for the construction of the automaton M_{conf}.

Definition 8 (Automaton M_{conf}). *The finite state automaton* $M_{conf}(p_{lang}^{ag}, p_{spec})$ *is built by applying the following steps to* $M^{\times}(p_{lang}^{ag}, p_{spec})$ *until none is applicable:*

(a) *if* $\overleftarrow{q} = [\overleftarrow{a^P}, \overleftarrow{d^S}]$ *in Q is an I-state, such that* $\overleftarrow{a^P}$ *is an alive state and* $\overleftarrow{d^S}$ *is a dead state, we set* $\delta(\overleftarrow{q}, m) = \overleftarrow{q}$ *for every m in* Σ, *and we put* $\overleftarrow{q}$ *in F;*

(b) *if* $\overleftarrow{q} = [\overleftarrow{d^P}, \overleftarrow{a^S}]$ *in Q is an I-state, such that* $\overleftarrow{d^P}$ *is dead and* $\overleftarrow{a^S}$ *is alive, we set* $\delta(\overleftarrow{q}, m) = \overleftarrow{q}$ *for every m in* Σ, *without modifying F;*

(c) *if* $\overrightarrow{q} = [\overrightarrow{a^P}, \overrightarrow{d^S}]$ *in Q is an O-state, such that* $\overrightarrow{a^P}$ *is alive and* $\overrightarrow{d^S}$ *is dead, we set* $\delta(\overrightarrow{q}, m) = \overrightarrow{q}$ *for every m in* Σ *(without modifying F);*

(d) *if* $\overrightarrow{q} = [\overrightarrow{d^P}, \overrightarrow{a^S}]$ *in Q is an O-state, such that* $\overrightarrow{d^P}$ *is dead and* $\overrightarrow{a^S}$ *is alive, we set* $\delta(\overrightarrow{q}, m) = \overrightarrow{q}$ *for every m in* Σ, *and we put* $\overrightarrow{q}$ *in F.*

These four transformation rules can, intuitively, be explained as follows.

Rule (a) handles the case in which, at a certain point of the conversation, according to the policy it is possible to receive a message that, instead, cannot be received according to the specification (it is the case of message $\overleftarrow{m}_1$ in Fig. 1). Actually, if the agent will interact with another agent that respects the protocol, this message can never be received, so we can ignore the paths generated by the policy from the message at issue onwards. Since this case does not compromise conformance, we want our automaton to accept all these strings. For this reason we set the state as final.

Rule (b) handles the symmetric case (Fig. 1, message $\overleftarrow{m}_4$), in which at a certain point of the conversation it is possible, according to the specification, to receive a message, that is not accounted for by the implementation. In this case the state at issue is turned into a trap state (a state that is not final and that has no transition to a different state); by doing so, all the conversations that are foreseen by the specification from that point onwards will not be accepted by M_{conf}.

Rule (c) handles the cases in which a message can possibly be uttered by the agent, according to the policy, but it is not possible according to the specification (Fig. 1, message $\overrightarrow{m}_3$). In this case, the policy is not conformant, so we transform the current state in a trap state. By doing so, part of the conversations possibly generated by the policy will not be accepted by the automaton.

Rule (d) is the symmetric case of (c) (Fig. 1, message $\overrightarrow{m}_2$), it does not prevent conformance, in fact, an agent is free not to utter a message foreseen by the protocol. However, the conversations that can be generated from that point according to the specification are to be accepted as well. For this reason the state is turned into an accepting looping state.

Finally, to guarantee Expectation 3, we add the following requirement. The intuitive reason is that we would like an agent, which is supposed to utter a message at a certain point of its conversation, to actually do it, thus making the conversation, in which it is engaged, proceed.

Definition 9 (Complete automaton). *Let us denote by* $Messout(q)$ *the set:*

$$Messout(q) = \{m(\overrightarrow{ag}) \mid \delta(q, m(\overrightarrow{ag})) = p \wedge p \text{ is alive } \}$$

We say that the automaton M_{conf} *is* complete *iff for all states of form* $[q^P, q^S]$ *of* M_{conf}, *such that* $Messout(q^S) \neq \emptyset$, *the following holds:*

- $Messout(q^P) \neq \emptyset$;
- *if we substitute* $Messout(q^P)$ *to* $Messout(q^S)$ *in* M_{spec}, *the state* q^S *remains* alive.

One may wonder if the application of rules (b) and (c) could prevent the *reachability of states*, that have been set as accepting states by the other two rules. Notice that their application cannot prevent the reachability of *alive-alive* accepting states, i.e. those that accept the strings belonging to the intersection of the two languages, because all the four rules only work on dead states. If a state has been set as a trap state (either by rule (b) or (c)), whatever conversation is possibly generated after it by the policy is illegal w.r.t. the specification. So it is correct that the automaton is modified in such a way that the policy language is not accepted by it and that the final state cannot be reached any more.

3.2   Conformance and Interoperability

We can now discuss how to check that an agent conforms to a given protocol. The following is our definition of conformance test. It guarantees the expectations that we have explained by examples in Section 2.

Definition 10 (Policy conformance test). *A policy* p_{lang}^{ag} *is conformant to a protocol specification* p_{spec} *iff the automaton* $M_{conf}(p_{lang}^{ag}, p_{spec})$ *is complete and it accepts the union of the languages* $L(p_{lang}^{ag})$ *and* $L(p_{spec})$.

We are now in position to state that a policy that passes the above test can carry on *any* conformant conversation it is involved in.

Proposition 2. *Given a policy p_{lang}^{ag} that is conformant to a protocol specification p_{spec}, according to Definition 10, for every prefix σ' that is common to the two languages $L(p_{spec})$ and $L(p_{lang}^{ag})$, there is a conversation $\sigma = \sigma'\sigma''$ such that σ is in the intersection of $L(p_{lang}^{ag})$ and $L(p_{spec})$, when $L(p_{lang}^{ag}) \neq \emptyset$ and $L(p_{spec}) \neq \emptyset$.*

Proof. Since p_{lang}^{ag} is conformant, $L(p_{lang}^{ag})$ is accepted by M_{conf}. Then, by construction M_{conf} does not contain any state $[\overrightarrow{a^P}, \overrightarrow{d^S}]$, where a^P corresponds to an alive state in $M(p_{lang}^{ag})$ and d^S is a dead state in $M(p_{spec})$, due to illegal messages uttered by the agent. By construction it also does not contain any state $[\overrightarrow{d^P}, \overrightarrow{a^S}]$ due to incoming messages that are not accounted for by the policy. Obviously, no conversation σ accepted by states of the kind $[\overrightarrow{d^P}, \overrightarrow{a^S}]$ can belong to $L(p_{lang}^{ag})$ because the agent cannot utter the messages required to reach such states. Finally, no conversation produced by the agent will be accepted by states of the kind $[\overleftarrow{a^P}, \overleftarrow{d^S}]$ because by definition the protocol cannot utter illegal messages. Now, σ' is a common prefix, therefore it leads to a state of the automaton M_{conf} of the kind $[a^P, a^S]$ (i.e., both states are alive, see Figure 1). Due to *policy conformance*, all the incoming messages (w.r.t. the agent), that are labels of kind $m(\overleftarrow{ag})$ of outgoing edges, must be foreseen by the policy and in the case of outgoing messages (that is labels of kind $m(\overrightarrow{ag})$ of outgoing edges), the policy must foresee at least one of them in such a way that a^S is kept alive (*completeness* of M_{conf}). Therefore, either the above state $[a^P, a^S]$ is already a final state of M_{conf} and $\sigma'' = \varepsilon$ or from $[a^P, a^S]$ it is possible to perform one more common step, leading to a state of the same kind, i.e. composed of two alive states for the reasons exposed before. This an actual step ahead towards a final state due to conformance. In fact, for these properties there must be an edge outgoing from a^S, that leads to another alive state different from a^S, and the same edge must exist also in $M(p_{lang}^{ag})$; this edge will be one of the outgoing edges of a^P. We can choose to follow this edge also in the automaton M_{conf}. We can iteratively repeat this reasoning and, since the number of nodes is finite, we will eventually reach an accepting state, identifying a common conversation.   **q.e.d.**

Notice that the *intersection* of $L(p_{lang}^{ag})$ and $L(p_{spec})$ cannot be empty because of policy conformance, and also that Proposition 2 does not entail that the two languages coincide (i.e. the policy is not necessarily a full implementation of the protocol). As a consequence, given that the conversation policies of two agents ag_1 and ag_2, playing the different roles of an interaction protocol p_{spec}, are *conformant* to the specification according to Definition 10, and denoting by I the intersection

$$I = \bigcap_{ag_i}^{i=1,2} L(p_{lang_i}^{ag_i})$$

we can prove ag_1 and ag_2 *interoperability*, that is they will produce a legal conversation, when interacting with one another. The proof is similar to the previous one. Roughly, it is immediate to prove that every prefix, that is common to the two policies, also belongs to the protocol, then, by performing reasoning steps that are analogous to the previous proof, it is possible to prove that a common legal conversation must exist when both policies satisfy the conformance test given by Definition 10.

Theorem 1 (Interoperability w.r.t. an interaction protocol). *Given two policies $p_{lang_1}^{ag_1}$ and $p_{lang_2}^{ag_2}$ that are conformant to a protocol specification p_{spec}, according to Definition 10, for every prefix σ' that is common to the two languages $L(p_{lang_1}^{ag_1})$ and $L(p_{lang_2}^{ag_2})$, there is a conversation $\sigma = \sigma'\sigma''$ such that $\sigma \in I$.*

Proof. First of all, it is trivial that σ' is also a prefix of $L(p_{spec})$. By the previous property, we are sure that both ag_1 and ag_2 contain some legal conversations. We need to prove that at least of these is common. Let us consider the automaton that accepts the intersection of $M(p_{lang}^{ag_1})$ and $M(p_{lang}^{ag_2})$. Since σ' is a common prefix, there must be a path in such automaton, that leads to a state $[q^{ag_1}, q^{ag_2}]$. Due to *policy conformance*, all the incoming messages w.r.t. ag_1, foreseen by the protocol specification, must be foreseen also by the policy. On the other side, ag_2 must utter at least one of them, due to its conformance (its M_{conf} must be complete). Therefore, it is possible to continue the conversation at least one more common step. In the case of messages that are outgoing w.r.t. ag_1 the policy must foresee at least one of them in such a way that q^{ag_1} is kept alive (completeness of M_{conf}), while on the other side, ag_2 must be able to handle all the possible alternatives (conformance), therefore, also in this case it is possible to continue the conversation. In both cases all the performed steps are legal w.r.t. the protocol specification. Therefore, either the above state $[q^{ag_1}, q^{ag_2}]$ is a final state and $\sigma'' = \varepsilon$ or from $[q^{ag_1}, q^{ag_2}]$ it is possible to perform one more common step for the reasons exposed before. Proceeding in a way that is analogous to what done in the proof of Prop. 2, due to conformance and considering each agent as playing the role of the protocol specification w.r.t. to the other, this an actual step ahead towards a final state. Therefore, we will eventually reach an accepting state, that identifies a common conversation. **q.e.d.**

The *third expectation* is guarantedd by the completeness of M_{conf}. The role plaied by completeness is, therefore, to guarantee that two agents, playing the two roles of the same protocol, will be able to lead to an end their conversations. Without this property we could only say that whenever the two agents will be able to produce a conversation, this will be legal. We lose the certainty of the capability of producing a conversation.

Starting from regular languages, all the steps that we have described that lead to the construction of M_{conf} and allow the verification of policy conformance, are decidable. A naive procedure for performing the test can be obtained directly from Definitions 8 and 9 and from the well-known automata theory [22]. The following theorem holds.

Theorem 2. *Policy conformance is decidable when $L(p_{lang}^{ag})$ and $L(p_{spec})$ are regular languages.*

4 The DyLOG Language: A Case Study

In this section we show how the presented approach particularly fits logic languages, using as a case study the DyLOG language [7], previously developed in our group. The choice is due to the fact that this language explicitly supplies the tools for representing communication protocols and that we have already presented an algorithm for turning a DyLOG program in a regular grammar (therefore, into a finite state automaton) [5]. This is, however, just an example. The same approach could be applied to other logic languages. In the following we will briefly recall how interaction policies can be described in the language DyLOG. For examples and for a thorough description of the core of the language see [7, 4].

DyLOG [7] is a logic programming language for modeling rational agents, based upon a modal logic of actions and mental attitudes, in which modalities represent actions as well as beliefs that are in the agent's mental state. It accounts both for atomic and complex actions, or procedures, for specifying the agent behavior. DyLOG agents can be provided with a *communication kit* that specifies their communicative behavior [3, 4]. In DyLOG *conversation policies* are represented as procedures that compose speech acts (described in terms of their preconditions and effects on the beliefs in the agent's mental state). They specify the agent communicative behavior and are expressed as Prolog-like procedures:

$$p_0 \text{ is } p_1; p_2; \ldots; p_m$$

where p_0 is a procedure name, the p_i's in the body are procedure names, atomic actions, or test actions, and ';' is the sequencing operator.

Besides speech acts, protocols can also contain *get message actions*, used to read incoming communications. From the perspective of an agent, expecting a message corresponds to a query for an external input, thus it is natural to interpret this kind of actions as a special case of sensing actions. As such, their outcome, though belonging to a predefined set of alternatives, cannot be predicted before the execution. A get_message action is defined as:

get_message(ag_i, ag_j, l) is
    speech_act$_1(ag_j, ag_i, l)$ **or** ... **or** speech_act$_k(ag_j, ag_i, l)$

On the right hand side the finite set of alternative incoming messages that the agent ag_i expects from the agent ag_j in the context of a given conversation. The information that is actually received is obtained by looking at the effects that occurred on ag_i's mental state.

From the specifications of the interaction protocols and of the relevant speech acts contained in the domain description, it is possible to trigger a *planning* activity by executing *existential queries* of form Fs **after** $p_1; p_2; \ldots; p_m$, that intuitively amounts to determining if there is a possible execution of the enumerated actions after which the condition Fs holds. If the answer is positive, a

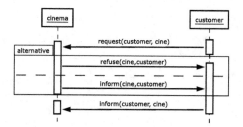

Fig. 2. AUML sequence diagram

conditional plan is returned. Queries of this kind can be given an answer by a
goal-directed proof procedure that is described in [3].

The example that we consider involves a reactive agent. The program of its
interlocutor is not given: we will suppose that it adheres to the public protocol
specification against which we will check our agent's conformance. The example
rephrases one taken from the literature, that has been used in other proposals
(e.g. [19]) and, thus, allows a better comprehension as well as comparison. We just
set the example in a realistic context. The agent is a web service [2] that answers
queries about the movies that are played. Its interlocutor is the requester of information (that we do not detail supposing that it respects the agreed protocol). This
protocol is described in Fig. 2 as an AUML sequence diagram [26]. The agent that
plays the role "cinema" waits for a request from another agent (if a certain movie
is played), then, it can alternatively send the requested information (yes or no) or
refuse to supply information; the protocol is ended by an acknowledgement message from the customer to the cinema. Hereafter, we consider the implementation
of the web service of a specific cinema, written as a DyLOG communication policy.
This program has a different aim: it allows answering to a sequence of information
requests from the same customer and it never refuses an answer.

(a) get_info_movie($cine, customer$) **is**
     get_request($cine, customer, available(Movie)$);
     send_answer($cine, customer, available(Movie)$);
     get_info_movie($cine, customer$)
(b) get_info_movie($cine, customer$) **is**
     get_ack($cine, customer$)

(c) send_answer($cine, customer, available(Movie)$) **is**
     $\mathcal{B}^{cinema} available(Movie)$?;
     inform($cine, customer, available(Movie)$)
(d) send_answer($cine, customer, available(Movie)$) **is**
     $\neg \mathcal{B}^{cinema} available(Movie)$?;
     inform($cine, customer, \neg available(Movie)$)

(e) get_request($cine, customer, available(Movie)$) **is**
     request($customer, cine, available(Movie)$)
(f) get_ack($cine, customer, ack$) **is**
     inform($customer, cine, ack$)

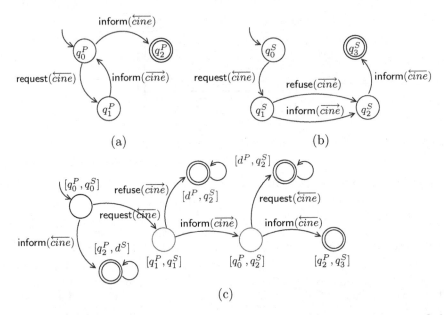

Fig. 3. (a) Policy of agent *cine*; (b) protocol specification; (c) M_{conf} automaton. Only the part relevant to the discussion is shown.

The question that we try to answer is whether this policy is *conformant* to the given protocol, and we will discuss whether another agent that plays as a customer and that is proved conformant to the protocol will actually be able to *interoperate* with this implementation of the cinema service. For what concerns the AUML sequence diagram, we have proved in [5] that diagrams containing only message, alternative, loop, exit, and reference to a subprotocol operators can be represented as a right-linear grammar, that generates a regular language. The automaton reported in Fig. 3(b) is obtained straightforwardly from this grammar. For what concerns the implementation, by applying the results reported in [5] it is possible to turn a DyLOG program in a context-free language. This grammar captures the structure of the possible conversations disregarding the semantics of the speech acts. When we have only right-recursion in the program, then, the obtained grammar is right-linear. So also in this case a regular language is obtained, hence the automaton in Fig. 3(a). Notice that all the three automata are represented from the perspective of agent *cine*, so all the short notation for the messages are to be interpreted as incoming or outgoing messages w.r.t. this agent.

The protocol allows only two conversations between *cine* and *customer* (the content of the message is not relevant in this example, so we skip it):

- request(*cus-tomer, cine*) inform(*cine, customer*) inform(*customer, cine*); and
- request(*customer, cine*) refuse(*cine, customer*) inform(*customer, cine*).

Let us denote this protocol by get_info_movie$_{AUML}$ (AUML is the specification language).

Let us now consider an agent (*cine*), that is supposed to play as cinema. This agent's policy is described by the above DyLOG program. The agent has a *reactive behavior*, that depends on the message that it receives, and its policy allows an infinite number of conversations of any length. Let us denote this policy by get_info_movie$_{DyLOG}^{cine}$. In general, it allows all the conversations that begin with a (possibly empty) series of exchanges of kind request($\overleftarrow{cine}$) followed by inform($\overrightarrow{cine}$), concluded by a message of kind inform($\overleftarrow{cine}$).

To verify its conformance to the protocol, and then state its interoperability with other agents that respect such protocol, we need to build the M_{conf} automaton for the policy of *cine* and the protocol specification. For brevity, we skip its construction steps and directly report M_{conf} in Fig. 3(c).

Let us now analyze M_{conf} for answering our queries. Trivially, the automaton is complete and it accepts both languages (of the policy, $L(\text{get\_info\_movie}_{DyLOG}^{cine})$, and of the specification, $L(\text{get\_info\_movie}_{AUML})$), therefore, get_info_movie$_{DyLOG}^{cine}$ is policy conformant to get_info_movie$_{AUML}$. Moreover, when the agent interacts with another agent *customer* whose policy is conformant to get_info_movie$_{AUML}$, the messages request($\overleftarrow{cine}$) and inform($\overleftarrow{cine}$) will not be received by *cine* in all the possible states it expects them. The reason is simple: for receiving them it is necessary that the interlocutor utters them, but by definition (it is conformant) it will not. The fact that refuse($\overrightarrow{cine}$) is never uttered by *cine* does not compromise conformance.

5   Conclusions and Related Work

In this work we propose an approach to the verification of the conformance of an agent's conversation policy to a public conversation protocol, which is based on the theory of *formal languages*. Differently than works like [1], where the compliance of the agents' communicative behavior to the protocol is verified at run-time, we tackled the verification of *a priori* conformance, a property of the *policy* as a whole and not of the on-going conversation only.

This problem has been studied by other researchers, the most relevant analysis probably being the one by Endriss et al. and reported in [15]. Here, the problem was faced in a logic framework; the authors introduce three degrees of conformance, namely *weak*, *exhaustive*, and *robust conformance*. An agent is weakly conformant to a protocol iff it never utters any dialogue move which is not a legal continuation (w.r.t. the protocol) of any state of the dialogue the agent might be in. It is *exhaustively conformant* to it iff it is weakly conformant to it and, for every received legal input, it will utter one of the expected dialogue moves. It is *robustly conformant* iff it is exhaustively conformant and for any illegal input move received it will utter a special dialogue move (such as not-understood) indicating this violation. Under the assumption that in their conversations the agents strictly alternate in uttering messages (ag_1 tells something to ag_2 which answers to ag_1 and so on), Endriss and colleagues show that by their approach it is possible to prove *weak conformance* in the case of logic-based agents and shallow protocols[1].

Our *Policy conformance* (Definition 10) guarantees that an agent, at any point of its conversations, can only utter messages which are legal w.r.t. the protocol, because of the M_{conf} construction step, given by rule (c). In this respect it entails *weak conformance* [15], however, our notion of conformance differs from it because it also guarantees that whatever incoming message the agent may receive, in any conversation context, its policy will be able to handle it.

A crucial difference concerns interoperability. In our framework, given two policies *each* of which is *conformant* to a protocol specification, their *interoperability* can be proved. Thus, we captured the expectation that conformance, a property of the single policy w.r.t. the public protocol, should in some way guarantee agents (legal) interoperability, while Endriss et al. do not discuss this issue and do not formally prove that interoperability is entailed by (all or some of) their three definitions of conformance. Moreover, we do not limit in any way the structure of the conversations (in particular, we do not require a strict alternation of the uttering agents).

This work is, actually, a deep revision of the work that the authors presented at [5], where the verification of a priori conformance was faced only in the specific case in which DyLOG [7] is used as the policy implementation language and AUML [26] is used as the protocol specification language. Basically, in that work the idea was to turn the problem into a problem of *formal language inclusion*. The two considered languages are the set of all the possible conversations foreseen by the protocol specification, let us denote it by $L(p_{AUML})$, and the set of all the possible conversations according to the policy of agent ag, let us denote it by $L(p_{dylog}^{ag})$. The conformance property could then be expressed as the following inclusion: $L(p_{dylog}^{ag}) \subseteq L(p_{AUML})$. The current proposal is more general than the one in [5], being independent from the implementation and specification languages. Moreover, as we have explained in the introduction, the interpretation of conformance as an inclusion test is too restrictive and not sufficient to express all the desiderata connected to this term, which are, instead, well-captured by our definitions of policy conformance.

The proposal that we have described in this paper is, actually, just a first step of a broader research. As a first step, we needed to identify the core of the problem, those key concepts and requirements which were necessary to capture and express the intuition behind a priori conformance, in the perspective of guaranteeing interoperability. Hence, the focus on interactions that involve two partners and do not account for concurrent operations. Under such restrictions, the choice of finite state automata fits very well and has the advantage of bearing along decidability.

Finite state automata, despite some notational inadequacy [20], are commonly used for representing protocols: for instance they have been used for representing both KQML protocols [8] and FIPA protocols [17]. In [5] we have presented an

---

[1] A protocol is shallow when the current state is sufficient to decide the next action to perform. This is not a restriction.

algorithm for translating AUML protocol specifications in finite state automata, focussing -on the side of sequence diagrams- on the operators used to specify FIPA protocols, which are: message, alternative, loop, exit, and reference to a sub-protocol. Some concrete example of application to the specification of complex protocols are the English Auction [27] and the Contract Net Protocol [18]. As a future work we mean to study an extension to policies (and protocols) that involve many partners as well as an extension to policies (and protocols) that use concurrent operators. For the latter problem in the literature there are well studied formalisms such as process algebras that can be used for representing protocols involving concurrency elements. It could be interesting to study how to import on the new basis the lessons learnt in the current research.

Concerning works that address the problem of verifying the conformance in systems of communicating agents by using model checking techniques (e.g. [19]), to the best of our knowledge, the issue of interoperability is not tackled or, at least, this does not clearly emerge. For instance, Giordano, Martelli and Schwind [19] based their approach on the use of a dynamic linear time logic. Protocols are specified, according to a social approach, by means of temporal constraints representing permissions and commitments. Following [21] the paper shows how to prove that an agent is compliant with a protocol, given the program executed by the agent, by assuming that all other agents participating in the conversation are compliant with the protocol, i.e. they respect their permissions and commitments. However, this approach does not guarantee interoperability.

Techniques for proving if the local agent's policy *conforms* to the abstract protocol specification can have an interesting and natural application in the web service field. In fact a need of distinguishing a global and a local view of the interaction is recently emerging in the area of Service Oriented Architectures. In this case there is a distinction between the *choreography* of a set of peers, i.e. a global specification of the way a group of peers interact, and the concept of *behavioral interface*, seen as the specification of the interaction from the point of view of an individual peer. The recent W3C proposal of the choreography language WS-CDL [30] is emblematic. In fact the idea behind it is to introduce specific *choreography languages* as languages for a high-level specification, captured from a global perspective, distinguishing this representation from the other two, that will be based upon ad hoc languages (like BPEL or ebXML).

Taking this perspective, choreographies and agent interaction protocols undoubtedly share a common purpose. In fact, they both aim at expressing *global interaction protocols*, i.e. rules that define the global behavior of a system of cooperating parties. The respect of these rules guarantees the interoperability of the parties (i.e. the capability of *actually* producing an interaction), and that the interactions will satisfy given requirements. One problem that becomes crucial is the development of formal methods for verifying if the behavior of a peer respects a choreography [11, 12]. On this line, in [6] we moved the first steps toward the application of the conformance test proposed in the present paper for verifying *at design time* (a priori) that the internal processes of a web service enable it to participate appropriately in the interaction.

Acknowledgement. The authors would like to thank the anonimous reviewers for their helpful suggestions and Francesca Toni for the discussion that we had in London.

References

1. M. Alberti, D. Daolio, P. Torroni, M. Gavanelli, E. Lamma, and P. Mello. Specification and verification of agent interaction protocols in a logic-based system. In *ACM SAC 2004*, pages 72–78. ACM, 2004.
2. G. Alonso, F. Casati, H. Kuno, and V. Machiraju. *Web Services*. Springer, 2004.
3. M. Baldoni, C. Baroglio, A. Martelli, and V. Patti. Reasoning about self and others: communicating agents in a modal action logic. In *ICTCS'2003*, volume 2841 of *LNCS*, pages 228–241. Springer, October 2003.
4. M. Baldoni, C. Baroglio, A. Martelli, and V. Patti. Reasoning about interaction protocols for customizing web service selection and composition. *Journal of Logic and Algebraic Programming, Special issue on Web Services and Formal Methods*, 2006. to appear.
5. M. Baldoni, C. Baroglio, A. Martelli, V. Patti, and C. Schifanella. Verifying protocol conformance for logic-based communicating agents. In *Proc. of 5th Int. Workshop on Computational Logic in Multi-Agent Systems, CLIMA V*, number 3487 in LNCS, pages 192–212. Springer, 2005.
6. M. Baldoni, C. Baroglio, A. Martelli, V. Patti, and C. Schifanella. Verifying the conformance of web services to global interaction protocols: a first step. In *Proc. of 2nd Int. Workshop on Web Services and Formal Methods, WS-FM 2005*, number 3670 in LNCS, pages 257–271, 2005.
7. M. Baldoni, L. Giordano, A. Martelli, and V. Patti. Programming Rational Agents in a Modal Action Logic. *Annals of Mathematics and Artificial Intelligence, Special issue on Logic-Based Agent Implementation*, 41(2-4):207–257, 2004.
8. M. Barbuceanu and M. Fox. Cool: A language for describing coordination in multiagent systems. In *Proceedings International Conference on Multi Agent Systems (ICMAS'95)*, pages 17–24. MIT Press, Massachusetts, USA, 1995.
9. J. Bentahar, B. Moulin, J. J. Ch. Meyer, and B. Chaib-Draa. A computational model for conversation policies for agent communication. In *Pre-Proc. of CLIMA V*, number 3487 in LNCS, pages 178–195. Springer, 2004.
10. R. Bordini, M. Fisher, C. Pardavila, and M. Wooldridge. Model Checking AgentSpeak. In *Proc. of 2nd International Joint Conference on Autonomous Agents and Multi-Agent Systems, AAMAS 2003*, 2003.
11. M. Bravetti, L. Kloul, and G. Zavattaro, editors. *Proc. of the 2nd International Workshop on Web Services and Formal Methods (WS-FM 2005)*, number 3670 in LNCS. Springer, 2005.
12. N. Busi, R. Gorrieri, C. Guidi, R. Lucchi, and G. Zavattaro. Choreography and Orchestration: a synergic approach for system design. In *Proc. the 3rd Int. Conf. on Service Oriented Computing*, 2005.
13. L. Cabac and D. Moldt. Formal semantics for auml agent interaction protocol diagrams. In *Proc. of AOSE 2004*, pages 47–61, 2004.
14. U. Endriss, N. Maudet, F. Sadri, and F. Toni. Protocol conformance for logic-based agents. In G. Gottlob and T. Walsh, editors, *Proc. of IJCAI-2003*, pages 679–684. Morgan Kaufmann Publishers, August 2003.

15. U. Endriss, N. Maudet, F. Sadri, and F. Toni. Logic-based agent communication protocols. In *Advances in agent communication languages*, volume 2922 of *LNAI*, pages 91–107. Springer-Verlag, 2004. invited contribution.
16. R. Eshuis and R. Wieringa. Tool support for verifying UML activity diagrams. *IEEE Trans. on Software Eng.*, 7(30), 2004.
17. FIPA. Fipa 97, specification part 2: Agent communication language. Technical report, FIPA (Foundation for Intelligent Physical Agents), November 1997.
18. L. Giordano, A. Martelli, and C. Schwind. Specifying and verifying interaction protocols in a temporal action logic. *Journal of Applied Logic (Special issue on Logic Based Agent Verification)*. Accepted for publication.
19. L. Giordano, A. Martelli, and C. Schwind. Verifying communicating agents by model checking in a temporal action logic. In *JELIA'04*, volume 3229 of *LNAI*, pages 57–69, Lisbon, Portugal, 2004. Springer.
20. F. Guerin. *Specifying Agent Communication Languages*. PhD thesis, Imperial College, London, April 2002.
21. F. Guerin and J. Pitt. Verification and Compliance Testing. In H.P. Huget, editor, *Communication in Multiagent Systems*, volume 2650 of *LNAI*, pages 98–112. Springer, 2003.
22. J. E. Hopcroft and J. D. Ullman. *Introduction to automata theory, languages, and computation*. Addison-Wesley Publishing Company, 1979.
23. M. P. Huget and J.L. Koning. Interaction Protocol Engineering. In H.P. Huget, editor, *Communication in Multiagent Systems*, volume 2650 of *LNAI*, pages 179–193. Springer, 2003.
24. A. Mamdani and J. Pitt. Communication protocols in multi-agent systems: A development method and reference architecture. In *Issues in Agent Communication*, volume 1916 of *LNCS*, pages 160–177. Springer, 2000.
25. N. Maudet and B. Chaib-draa. Commitment-based and dialogue-based protocols: new trends in agent communication languages. *Knowledge engineering review*, 17(2), 2002.
26. J. Odell, H. V. D. Parunak, and B. Bauer. Extending UML for agents. In *Proc. of the Agent-Oriented Information System Workshop at AAAI'00*. 2000.
27. J. Pitt, F. Guerin, and C. Stergiou. Protocols and intentional specifications of multi-party agent conversations for brokerage and auctions. In *Autonomous Agents 2000*, pages 269–276, Barcelona, 2000. ACM Prtess.
28. M. P. Singh. A social semantics for agent communication languages. In *Proc. of IJCAI-98 Workshop on Agent Communication Languages*, Berlin, 2000. Springer.
29. C. Walton. Model checking agent dialogues. In J. Leite, A. Omicini, P. Torroni, and P. Yolum, editors, *Declarative agent languages and technologies II, DALT 2004*, number 3476 in LNCS, pages 132–147. Springer, 2005.
30. WS-CDL. http://www.w3.org/tr/2004/wd-ws-cdl-10-20041217/. 2004.

Contextual Terminologies

Davide Grossi, Frank Dignum, and John-Jules Ch. Meyer

Utrecht University,
The Netherlands
{davide, dignum, jj}@cs.uu.nl

Abstract. The paper addresses the issue of contextual representations of ontologies, as it arises in the area of normative system specifications for modeling multiagent systems. To this aim, the paper proposes a formalization of a notion of contextual terminology, that is to say, a terminology holding only with respect to a specific context. The formalization is obtained by means of a formal semantics framework which enables the expressivity of common description logics to reason within contexts (intra-contextual reasoning), allowing at the same time the possibility to reason also about contexts and their interplay (inter-contextual reasoning). Using this framework, two complex scenarios are discussed in detail and formalized.

1 Introduction

The present research is motivated by problems concerning the specification of normative systems for modeling norm-governed multiagent systems. In [6, 22, 11] it has been variously stressed how the design of norm-governed multiagent systems has to cope with the inherent abstractness of norm formulations. This problem can be distilled in the question: how are norms specified by means of abstract terms ("persons driving vehicles may not access public parks") connected to norms specified via more concrete ones ("persons wheeling bicycles are allowed to access public parks")? In fact, normative systems of high complexity (for instance legal systems, or institutional ones) can be viewed not only as regulative systems, but also as systems specifying conceptualizations, or categorizations, of the domain of entities they are supposed to regulate (see for instance [2, 15]). In order to specify and represent such complex systems, it has been advocated in [7, 21], the notion of context plays a central role. Along these lines, in [13, 10], we proposed and applied a framework for representing this categorizing feature of normative systems via contextual taxonomic statements of the form "A counts as B in context C" taken from [19], where concept descriptions A and B displayed a very simple logical form (essentially boolean compositions of concepts). This work intends to pursue that research line further adding the necessary expressivity (essentially the possibility to deal with attributes or roles, i.e., binary relations besides concepts) to model more complex scenarios: from simple taxonomies to rich description logic terminologies.

The final aim consists in obtaining a framework in which to represent ontologies of different contexts and to reason about them both in isolation, i.e., within

F. Toni and P. Torroni (Eds.): CLIMA VI, LNAI 3900, pp. 284–302, 2006.

the contexts (intra-contextual reasoning), and in interaction, i.e. between contexts (inter-contextual reasoning). For instance, at the intra-contextual level a typical question would be of the form: given a set of subsumption relations holding in context C, is A a subconcept of B in context C? At an inter-contextual level instead, a typical question would be: given that context C is more concrete than context D, is A a subconcept of B in context C? With such a machinery it would then be possible to represent the ontological aspect of the regulating activity of institutions in a formal way, and the ontologies of different institutions could then be rigorously specified and reasoned about. To do this, we show that the approach proposed in [13] can be naturally applied to richer description logic languages thus providing the necessary expressive power we are interested in. In fact, the framework presented here consists in a contextualized version of the semantics of description logics. The proposal is tested in detail against two different examples.

The exposition is structured according to the following outline. In Section 2 two scenarios are introduced which exemplify in detail the issues addressed here, and some preliminary considerations are drawn. Section 3 is dedicated to the exposition of the framework, and Section 4 to the formalization of the two scenarios introduced in Section 2. Some concluding remarks follow.

2   Preliminaries

2.1   Scenarios

We now depict two scenarios in order to state, in clear terms, the kind of reasoning patterns we are aiming to capture formally. They exemplify quite typical forms of contextual conceptualizations occurring in the normative domain. The first scenario deals with a rule establishing sufficient conditions for a person to be liable of violating the regulation concerning access to public parks in three different municipalities. The second scenario deals with the refinement of a definition of "vehicle" from the abstract context of a general regulation to more concrete contexts of municipal regulations. From a logical point of view, they display description logic forms of reasoning at the level of the so-called taxonomical boxes (TBoxes)[1] (e.g., reasoning with value restriction and existential quantification, role subsumption) which were not yet available in our previous proposal [13].

Example 1 (**The public park scenario: "liability in parks"**). In the regulation governing access to public parks in region R it is stated that vehicles are not allowed within public parks and that: "persons using vehicles within public parks are liable for violating the regulation". In this regulation no mention is made of (possible) subconcepts of the concept vehicle, e.g., cars, bicycles, which may help in identifying an instance of vehicle, nor is it stated what it actually means to drive a vehicle: does the fact that I am wheeling my bicycle imply that I am driving it? In municipal regulations subordinated to this regional one, and

---

[1] Taxonomical boxes or *terminologies* are, in the description logic vocabulary, sets of inclusion relations between concepts.

therefore inheriting its global directives, specific subconcepts are instead handled. In municipality M1 and M2 the following rule holds: "persons driving bicycles within parks are liable of violating the regulation". In M3 instead, it holds that to drive a bicycle does not constitute any violation. On the other hand, in all M1, M2 and M3 it holds that cars are not allowed in public parks. Moreover, in M2 it holds that "persons wheeling bicycles into public parks are not liable for violating the regulation" despite liability arises in case bicycles happen to be driven. In M1 and M3 instead, to wheel a bicycle is considered a way of driving it.

Table 1. Liability in the public park scenario

	DRIVE VEHICLE	DRIVE CAR	DRIVE BICYCLE	WHEEL BICYCLE
R	liable	*not classifiable*	*not classifiable*	*not classifiable*
M1	liable	liable	liable	liable
M2	liable	liable	liable	not liable
M3	liable	liable	not liable	not liable

In this scenario the concept of `vehicle` gets various interpretations. Instances of `car` (w.r.t. the terminologies presupposed by M1, M2 and M3) are always instances of `vehicle`, while instances of `bicycle` are only in some contexts also instances of `vehicle`. What also gets various interpretations is the relation driving: somehow driving in M2 has a different meaning than in M1 and M3. Table 1 displays how liability comes down to be interpreted in three completely different ways by the contexts at issue, although in all contexts it holds that persons driving vehicles are to be considered liable. Note that context R cannot provide any qualification for actions such as driving or wheeling a bicycle simply because its language cannot express those notions.

Example 2 (**The public park scenario: "teenagers on skateboards"**). Consider again a regulation governing access to public parks in region R where it is stated that: "vehicles are not allowed within public parks". Also in this regulation no mention is made of (possible) subconcepts of the concept vehicle. Nevertheless, a (partial) definition, specifying necessary conditions for something to be a vehicle, is stated: "vehicles are conveyances which transport persons or objects". In municipal regulations subordinated to this regional one subconcepts are instead introduced. This is done inheriting the definition stated at the R level and refining it either incrementing the number of necessary conditions for something to be considered a vehicle or stating sufficient ones. In municipality M1 the definition of vehicle is refined in the following sense: "self-propelled conveyances which transport persons or objects are vehicles" and "vehicles are self-propelled". In M2, instead, the definition of vehicle is simply closed without any refinement: "conveyances which transport persons or objects are vehicles". Besides, in both M1 and M2, it holds that "skateboards are conveyances which are not self-propelled" and "teenagers are persons". These rules determine a different behavior of M1 and M2 with respect to concepts such as "skateboards transporting teenagers". With respect to this concept the following rule holds in M1: "skateboards transporting teenagers are not vehicles". In M2 instead, it holds that: "skateboards transporting teenagers are vehicles".

The second scenario displays some other aspects of contextual conceptualizations. The concept of vehicle gets again various interpretations and is first specified in its necessary conditions by context R and then completely defined in the two concrete contexts M1 and M2. The abstract regulation states that all vehicles are conveyances transporting persons or objects, leaving thus open the possibility for some of such conveyances not to be vehicles. This is the case of skateboards in M1 since M1 refines the abstract rule establishing more necessary conditions (being self-propelled) for conveyances to be classified as vehicles. Context M2 instead, simply closes the abstract rule through establishing that being a conveyance transporting persons or objects is sufficient for being a vehicle. Because of this, the two contexts M1 and M2 validate terminologies diverging on the conceptualization of the complex concept "skateboards transporting teenagers".

These two scenarios exemplify interesting nuances typical of complex context-dependent conceptualizations[2]. We will constantly refer back to them in the remainder of the work, and our central aim will be to develop a formal semantics framework able to represent analogous scenarios and to provide thus a rigorous understanding of the forms of reasoning therein involved.

2.2 Contextualizing Terminologies

We want to devise a language and a semantics for talking about contextual terminologies. More in detail, this turns out to devise a formal morphology and a formal semantics meeting the following requirements.

Firstly, it should support reasoning about the validity of TBoxes with respect to contexts giving a semantics to expressions of the type: "the concept bicycle is a subconcept of the concept vehicle in context M1". Besides this, the framework should be able to express the fact that concepts may be unclassifiable within specific contexts, that is, that specific subsumptions cannot be said to be valid or not valid: in the context R of the regional regulation, whether a person wheeling a bicycle within a public park is to be considered liable of violating the regulation corresponds to a non evaluable subsumption since the concept at issue is not part of the language of the context R (see Table 1). In some sense, it corresponds to a subsumption which is evaluated with respect to the wrong context. Therefore, we want the framework to be able to express whether a concept gets meaning within a context: "concept bicycle is meaningful with respect to context M1". Completely analogous expressions should be available in order to handle a contextualization of role (or attribute) hierarchies such as: "role wheel (wheeling) is a subrole of drive (driving) in context M2" and "role wheel is meaningful in context M2".

---

[2] It is instructive to notice that both scenarios represent instances of a typical form of contextual reasoning called "categorization" [4], or "perspective" [1], that is, the form of reasoning according to which a same set of entities is conceptualized in many different ways.

Secondly, it should provide a representation of context interplay. In particular, we will introduce: a *contextual disjunction* operator and a *contextual focus* operator[3]. The first one yields a union of contexts: the contexts "viruses" and "bacteria" can be unified on a language talking about microorganisms generating a more general context like "viral or bacterial microorganisms". The second one, which plays a central role in our framework, yields the context consisting of some information extracted from the context on which it is focused: the context categorizing "crocodiles", for instance, can be obtained via focusing the context which categorizes all reptiles on the language talking only about crocodiles and disregarding other reptiles. In other words, the operator prunes the information contained in the context "reptiles" focusing only on what is expressible in the language which talks about crocodiles and abstracting from the rest. Also *maximum* and *minimum* contexts will be introduced: these will represent the most general, and respectively the most specific, contexts on a language[4]. It is important to notice that all operations explicitly refer to a precise language on which the operation should take place. As we will see in the following section our formal language will be tuned to incorporate this feature.

Finally, it should represent specific relations between contexts. Examples 1 and 2 consider groups of contexts in which all contexts are specializations of an abstract one (R). This suggests the consideration of a generality relation between contexts[5] expressing that a context is at most as general as another one: the context of the abstract regulation R is somehow more general than the concrete ones M1 and M2[6].

These intuitions about the semantics of context operators will be clarified and made more rigorous in Section 3.2 where the semantics of the framework will be presented, and in Section 4 where the examples will be formalized deploying all these types of expressions.

3   A Formal Framework

Our proposal consists in mixing the semantics of description logic [3] with the idea of modeling contexts as sets of models [8], delivering a framework able to represent reasoning about sets of concept subsumptions, i.e., taxonomical boxes (TBoxes), in a contextual setting.

---

[3] In [13, 12] the *focus* operation is called *abstraction*. We decided to modify our terminology in order to avoid confusions with other approaches to notions of abstraction like for instance [9].

[4] In this paper, we limit the number of context operations to disjunction and focus. More operations are formalized in [13]. It is worth noticing, in passing, that similar operations and special contexts are discussed in [20].

[5] Literature on context theory often addresses this type of relation between contexts. See for instance [17, 4].

[6] As the discussion of the formalization of the examples will show (Section 4), there are some more subtleties to be considered since R is not only more general but is also specified on a simpler language.

3.1   Language

The language we are defining can be seen as a meta-language for TBoxes defined on $\mathcal{AL}$ description logic languages, which handle also concept union, full existential quantification (we want to deal with concepts such as "either car or bicycle" and "persons who drive cars") and role complement (we want to be able to talk about roles such as "not driving")[7].

The alphabet of the language $\mathcal{L}^{CT}$ (*language for contextual terminologies*) contains therefore the alphabets of a family of languages $\{\mathcal{L}_i\}_{0 \leq i \leq n}$. This family is built on the alphabet of a given "global" language $\mathcal{L}$ which contains all the terms occurring in the elements of the family. Moreover, we take $\{\mathcal{L}_i\}_{0 \leq i \leq n}$ to be such that, for each non-empty subset of terms of the language $\mathcal{L}$, there exist a $\mathcal{L}_i$ which is built on that set and belongs to the family. Each $\mathcal{L}_i$ contains two non-empty finite sets $\mathbf{A_i}$ of atomic concepts (A), i.e., monadic predicates, and $\mathbf{R_i}$ of atomic roles (R), i.e., dyadic predicates. These languages contain also concepts and roles constructors. As to concept constructors, each $\mathcal{L}_i$ contains the zeroary operators $\perp$ (bottom concept) and $\top$ (top concept), the unary operator $\neg$ (complement), and the binary operators $\sqcap$ and $\sqcup$. As to role constructors, each $\mathcal{L}_i$ contains the unary operator $\overline{R}$ (role complement). Finally, the value restriction operator $\forall R.A$ ("the set of elements such that all elements that are in a relation R with them are instances of A") applies to role-concept pairs.

Besides, the alphabet of $\mathcal{L}^{CT}$ contains a finite set of context identifiers $\mathbf{c}$, two families of zeroary operators $\{\perp_i\}_{0 \leq i \leq n}$ (minimum contexts) and $\{\top_i\}_{0 \leq i \leq n}$ (maximum contexts), one family of unary operators $\{\text{fcs}_i\}_{0 \leq i \leq n}$ (contextual focus operator), one family of binary operators $\{\curlyvee_i\}_{0 \leq i \leq n}$ (contexts disjunction operator), one context relation symbol $\preccurlyeq$ (context c_1 "is less general than" context c_2), two meaningfulness relation symbols ". $\downarrow^c$." (concept A is meaningful in context c) and ". $\downarrow^r$." (role R is meaningful in context c), and finally two contextual subsumption relation symbols ". $:$. $\sqsubseteq^c$." (within context c, concept A_1 is a subconcept of concept A_2) and ". $:$. $\sqsubseteq^r$." (within context c, role R_1 is a subrole of role R_2) for, respectively, concept and role subsumption[8]. Lastly, the alphabet of $\mathcal{L}^{CT}$ contains also the sentential connectives $\sim$ (negation) and $\wedge$ (conjunction)[9].

Thus, the set $\varXi$ of context constructs (ξ) is defined through the following BNF:

$$\xi ::= c \mid \perp_i \mid \top_i \mid \text{fcs}_i\, \xi \mid \xi_1\, \curlyvee_i\, \xi_2.$$

---

[7] This type of language is indeed an $\mathcal{ALC}$ conceptual language extended with role complement. See [3].

[8] We use superscripts here in order to distinguish between meaningfulness of concepts or roles, and subsumptions of concepts or roles. Nevertheless, in what follows, superscripts will be dropped when no confusion arises in order to lighten the notation.

[9] It might be worth remarking that language $\mathcal{L}^{CT}$ is, then, an expansion of each $\mathcal{L}_i$ language. Notice also that all operators on contexts are indexed with the language on which the operation they denote takes place.

Concept constructs and role constructs are defined in the standard way. The set P of roles descriptions (ρ) is defined through the following BNF:

$$\rho ::= R \mid \bar{\rho}.$$

The set Γ of concept descriptions (γ) is defined through the following BNF:

$$\gamma ::= A \mid \bot \mid \top \mid \neg\gamma \mid \gamma_1 \sqcap \gamma_2 \mid \forall\rho.\gamma.$$

Concept union and existential quantification are defined respectively as:

$$\gamma_1 \sqcup \gamma_2 =_{\text{def}} \neg(\neg\gamma_1 \sqcap \neg\gamma_2) \text{ and } \exists\rho.\gamma =_{\text{def}} \neg(\forall\rho.\neg\gamma).$$

Finally, the set $\mathcal{A}$ of assertions (α) is defined through the following BNF:

$$\alpha ::= \gamma \downarrow^c \xi \mid \rho \downarrow^r \xi \mid \xi : \gamma_1 \sqsubseteq^c \gamma_2 \mid \xi : \rho_1 \sqsubseteq^r \rho_2 \mid \xi_1 \preccurlyeq \xi_2 \mid {\sim}\alpha \mid \alpha_1 \wedge \alpha_2.$$

The set of atomic assertions of the language is then constituted by expressions enabling exactly the kind of expressivity required in Section 2.2: meaningfulness of concepts and roles in contexts, contextual subsumptions of concepts and roles, generality ordering between contexts.

3.2 Semantics

As exposed in the previous section, an $\mathcal{L}^{CT}$ consists of four classes of expressions: Ξ (context constructs), P and Γ (role and concept descriptions), $\mathcal{A}$ (assertions). Semantics of P and Γ will be the standard description logic semantics of roles and concepts, on which our framework is based. Semantics for Ξ will be given in terms of model theoretic operations on sets of description logic models, and at that stage the semantics of assertions $\mathcal{A}$ will be defined via an appropriate satisfaction relation. The structures obtained, which we call *contextual terminology models* or ct-models, provides a formal semantics for $\mathcal{L}^{CT}$ languages.

The firs step is then to provide the definition of a description logic model for a language $\mathcal{L}_i$ [3].

Definition 1. (Models for $\mathcal{L}_i$'s)
A model m for a language $\mathcal{L}_i$ is defined as follows:

$$m = \langle \Delta_m, \mathcal{I}_m \rangle$$

where:

- Δ_m *is the (non empty) domain of the model;*
- $\mathcal{I}_m$ *is a function* $\mathcal{I}_m : \mathbf{A_i} \cup \mathbf{R_i} \longrightarrow \mathcal{P}(\Delta_m) \cup \mathcal{P}(\Delta_m \times \Delta_m)$, *such that to every element of* $\mathbf{A_i}$ *and* $\mathbf{R_i}$ *an element of* $\mathcal{P}(\Delta_m)$ *and, respectively, of* $\mathcal{P}(\Delta_m \times \Delta_m)$ *is associated. This interpretation of atomic concepts and roles of* $\mathcal{L}_i$ *on* Δ_m *is then inductively extended:*

$$\mathcal{I}_m(\top) = \Delta_m$$
$$\mathcal{I}_m(\bot) = \emptyset$$
$$\mathcal{I}_m(\neg\gamma) = \Delta_m \setminus \mathcal{I}_m(\gamma)$$
$$\mathcal{I}_m(\gamma_1 \sqcap \gamma_2) = \mathcal{I}_m(\gamma_1) \cap \mathcal{I}_m(\gamma_2)$$
$$\mathcal{I}_m(\forall\rho.\gamma) = \{a \in \Delta_m \mid \forall b, <a,b> \in I_m(\rho) \Rightarrow b \in I_m(\gamma)\}$$
$$\mathcal{I}_m(\overline{\rho}) = \Delta_m \times \Delta_m \setminus \mathcal{I}_m(\rho).$$

A model m for a language $\mathcal{L}_i$ assigns a denotation to each atomic concept (for instance the set of elements of Δ_m that instantiate the concept `bike`) and to each atomic role (for instance the set of pairs of Δ_m which are in a relation such that the first element is said to "drive" the second element of the pair). Accordingly, meaning is given to each complex concept (for instance the set of elements of Δ_m that instantiate the concept `vehicle ⊔ bike`) and to each complex role (for instance the set of pairs listing elements related by role $\overline{\text{drive}}$).

3.3   Models for $\mathcal{L}^{CT}$

We can now define a notion of *contextual terminology* model (ct-model) for languages $\mathcal{L}^{CT}$.

Definition 2. (ct-models)
A ct-model $\mathbb{M}$ is a structure:

$$\mathbb{M} = \langle \{\mathbf{M_i}\}_{0 \leq i \leq n}, \mathbb{I} \rangle$$

where:

- *$\{\mathbf{M}_i\}_{0 \leq i \leq n}$ is the family of the sets of models $\mathbf{M}_i$ of each language $\mathcal{L}_i$. That is, $\forall m \in \mathbf{M}_i$, m is a model for $\mathcal{L}_i$.*
- *$\mathbb{I}$ is a function $\mathbb{I} : \mathbf{c} \longrightarrow \mathcal{P}(\mathbf{M}_0) \cup \ldots \cup \mathcal{P}(\mathbf{M}_n)$. In other words, this function associates to each atomic context identifier in $\mathbf{c}$ a subset of the set of all models in some language $\mathcal{L}_i$: $\mathbb{I}(c) = M$ with $M \subseteq \mathbf{M}_i$ for some i s.t. $0 \leq i \leq n$. Function $\mathbb{I}$ can be seen as labeling sets of models on some language i via atomic context identifiers. Notice that $\mathbb{I}$ fixes, for each atomic context identifier, the language on which the context denoted by the identifier is specified. We could say that it is $\mathbb{I}$ itself which fixes a specific index for each atomic context identifier c.*
- *$\forall m', m'' \in \bigcup_{0 \leq i \leq n} \mathbf{M}_i$, $\Delta_{m'} = \Delta_{m''}$. That is, the domain of all models m is unique. We assume this constraint simply because we are interested in modeling different conceptualizations of a same set of individuals.*

Contexts are therefore formalized as sets of models for the same language. This perspective allows for straightforward model theoretical definitions of operations on contexts.

3.4   Context Focus

We model focus as a specific operation on sets of models which provides the semantic counterpart for the *contextual focus* operator introduced in $\mathcal{L}^{CT}$. Intuitively, abstracting a context ξ to a language $\mathcal{L}_i$ yields a context consisting in that part of ξ which can be expressed in $\mathcal{L}_i$.

Let us first recall a notion of *domain restriction* ($\rceil$) of a function f w.r.t. a subset C of the domain of f. Intuitively, a domain restriction of a function f is nothing but the function $C \rceil f$ having C as domain and s.t. for each element of C, f and $C \rceil f$ return the same image: $C \rceil f = \{\langle x, f(x) \rangle \mid x \in C\}$.

Definition 3. (Context focus operation: $\rceil_i$)
Let M' be a set of models, then: $\rceil_i M' = \{m \mid m = \langle \Delta_{m'}, \mathbf{A}_i \cup \mathbf{R}_i \rceil \mathcal{I}_{m'} \rangle \ \& \ m' \in M'\}$.

The following can be proved.

Proposition 1. (Properties of context focus)
Operation $\rceil_i$ is: surjective, idempotent ($\rceil_i(\rceil_i M) = \rceil_i M$), normal ($\rceil_i \emptyset = \emptyset$), additive ($\rceil_i(M_1 \cup M_2) = \rceil_i M_1 \cup \rceil_i M_2$), monotonic ($M_1 \subseteq M_2 \Rightarrow \rceil_i M_1 \subseteq \rceil_i M_2$).

Proof. A proof is worked out in [12].

The operation of focus allows for shifting from richer to simpler languages and it is, as we would intuitively expect: surjective (every context, even the empty one, can be seen as the result of focusing a different richer context, in the most trivial case, a focus of itself), idempotent (focusing on a focus yields the same first focus), normal (focusing the empty context yields the empty context), additive (the focus of a context obtained via joining of two contexts can be obtained also joining the focuses of the two contexts), monotonic (if a context is less general then another one, the focus of the first is also less general than the focus of the second one). Notice also that operation $\rceil_i$ yields the empty set of models when it is applied to a context M' the language of which is not an expansion of $\mathcal{L}_i$. This is indeed very intuitive: the context obtained via focus of the context "dinosaurs" on the language of, say, "gourmet cuisine" should be empty.

A detailed comparison of our account of focus with approaches available in the literature on context theory is discussed in [12].

3.5   Operations on Contexts

We are now in a position to give a semantics to context constructs as introduced in Section 3.1. In Definition 2 atomic contexts are interpreted as sets of models on some language $\mathcal{L}_i$ for $0 \leq i \leq n$: $\mathbb{I}(c) = M \in \mathcal{P}(\mathbf{M}_0) \cup \ldots \cup \mathcal{P}(\mathbf{M}_n)$. The semantics of context constructs $\varXi$ can be defined via inductive extension of that definition.

Definition 4. (Semantics of context constructs)

Let ξ, ξ_1, ξ_2 be context constructs, then:

$$\mathbb{I}(\text{fcs}_i\ \xi) =]_i\mathbb{I}(\xi)$$
$$\mathbb{I}(\bot_i) = \emptyset$$
$$\mathbb{I}(\top_i) = \mathbf{M}_i$$
$$\mathbb{I}(\xi_1 \curlyvee_i \xi_2) =]_i(\mathbb{I}(\xi_1) \cup \mathbb{I}(\xi_2)).$$

The focus operator fcs_i is interpreted on the contextual focus operation introduced in Definition 3, i.e., as the restriction of the interpretation of its argument
to language $\mathcal{L}_i$. The $\bot_i$ context is interpreted as the empty context (the same on
each language); the $\top_i$ context is interpreted as the greatest, or most general,
context on $\mathcal{L}_i$; the binary $\curlyvee_i$-composition of contexts is interpreted as the lowest
upper bound of the restriction of the interpretations of the two contexts on $\mathcal{L}_i$.

In [17] the statement about the need for addressing "contexts as abstract
mathematical entities" was set forth. Here, moving from an analysis of contextual terminologies, we develop an account of context interplay based on model
theoretic operations. In some sense, we propose a view on contexts as "algebraic
entities". In fact, it is easy to prove, as we did in [12], that our contexts are
structured according to a Boolean Algebra with Operators [16]. This observation distills the type of conception of context we hold here: contexts are sets of
models on different concept description languages; on each language the set of
possible contexts is structured in a Boolean Algebra; adding operations of focus
on a finite number of sublanguages yields a Boolean Algebra with Operators.

3.6   Assertions

The semantics of assertions is defined as follows.

Definition 5. (Semantics of assertions: $\models$)

Let ξ, ξ_1, ξ_2 be a context constructs, $\gamma, \gamma_1, \gamma_2$ concept description, then:

$$M \models \gamma \downarrow \xi \quad \textit{iff} \quad \{D_c \mid \langle \gamma, D_c \rangle \in \mathcal{I}_m\ \&\ m \in \mathbb{I}(\xi)\} \neq \emptyset \tag{1}$$

$$M \models \rho \downarrow \xi \quad \textit{iff} \quad \{D_r \mid \langle \rho, D_r \rangle \in \mathcal{I}_m\ \&\ m \in \mathbb{I}(\xi)\} \neq \emptyset \tag{2}$$

$$M \models \xi : \gamma_1 \sqsubseteq \gamma_2 \quad \textit{iff} \quad M \models \gamma_1 \downarrow \xi, M \models \gamma_2 \downarrow \xi$$
$$\textit{and } \forall m \in \mathbb{I}(\xi)\ \mathcal{I}_m(\gamma_1) \subseteq \mathcal{I}_m(\gamma_2) \tag{3}$$

$$M \models \xi : \rho_1 \sqsubseteq \rho_2 \quad \textit{iff} \quad M \models \rho_1 \downarrow \xi, M \models \rho_2 \downarrow \xi$$
$$\textit{and } \forall m \in \mathbb{I}(\xi)\ \mathcal{I}_m(\rho_1) \subseteq \mathcal{I}_m(\rho_2) \tag{4}$$

$$M \models \xi_1 \prec \xi_2 \quad \textit{iff} \quad \mathbb{I}(\xi_1) \subseteq \mathbb{I}(\xi_2). \tag{5}$$

Clauses (1) and (2) specify when a concept, respectively a role, is meaningful
with respect to a context. This is the case when the set of denotations D_c and
D_r which the models constituting the context attribute to that concept (D_c
being a set of elements of the domain) or that role (D_r being a set of pairs of
elements of the domain), is not empty. If concept γ is not expressible in the

language of context ξ, then concept γ gets no denotation at all in context ξ. This happens simply because concept γ does not belong to the domain of functions $\mathcal{I}_m$, and therefore there exists no interpretation for that concept in the models constituting ξ. The same holds for a role ρ. Clauses (3) and (4) deal with satisfaction of contextual subsumptions. A contextual concept subsumption relation between γ_1 and γ_2 holds iff concepts γ_1 and γ_2 are defined in the models constituting context ξ, i.e., they receive a denotation in those models, and all the description logic models constituting that context interpret γ_1 as a subconcept of γ_2. Note that this is precisely the clause for the validity of a subsumption relation in standard description logics, but together with the fact that the concepts involved are actually meaningful in that context. Intuitively, we interpret contextual subsumption relations as inherently presupposing the meaningfulness of their terms[10]. A perfectly analogous observation holds also for the clause regarding contextual role subsumption relations.

With respect to clauses (3) and (4), it is important to notice their effect on the semantics of the negation of contextual subsumption statements: $\sim \xi : \gamma_1 \sqsubseteq \gamma_2$ and $\xi : \rho_1 \sqsubseteq \rho_2$. In fact, the statement $\sim \xi : \gamma_1 \sqsubseteq \gamma_2$ is true in model $\mathbb{M}$, iff either $\mathbb{M} \models \sim (\gamma_1 \downarrow \xi \wedge \gamma_2 \downarrow \xi)$ or it is simply not the case that $\forall m \in \mathbb{I}(\xi)\ \mathcal{I}_m(\gamma_1) \subseteq \mathcal{I}_m(\gamma_2)$. The same holds for contextual role subsumption. Out of technicalities, this means that to negate a contextual subsumption means to state *either* the undefinability of the concepts (roles) involved *or* that those concepts (roles) are not in such a relation with respect to that context. Therefore, the assertion to the effect that γ_1 and γ_2 are defined in ξ but γ_2 does not subsume γ_1 in ξ should be expressed as follows:

$$\gamma_1 \downarrow \xi \wedge \gamma_2 \downarrow \xi \wedge \sim \xi : \gamma_1 \sqsubseteq \gamma_2.$$

Notice that this very distinction is what marks the difference between the slots labeled with *"not classifiable"* and respectively *"not liable"* in Table 1. Further considerations on what and how can be expressed in $\mathcal{L}^{CT}$ about subsumption are provided in Section 3.7.

Finally, clause (5) gives a semantics to the $\preccurlyeq$ relation between context constructs interpreting it as a standard subset relation: $\xi_1 \preccurlyeq \xi_2$ means that context denoted by ξ_1 contains at most all the models that ξ_2 contains, that is to say, ξ_1 is *at most as general as* ξ_2. Clauses for boolean connectives are the obvious ones and notions of validity and logical consequence are classically defined.

3.7 Natural Expansions of $\mathcal{L}^{CT}$

The formal semantics machinery just exposed gives us space for the characterization of a number of notions which are not explicitly present in the syntax of $\mathcal{L}^{CT}$ as it is introduced in Section 3.1.

In [13] we have already shown how to characterize a form of vagueness within the framework, providing a formalization of the notions of *core* and *penumbra* of the meaning of a concept, that is, of what remains invariant and, respectively, of what varies in the meaning of concepts from context to context.

---

[10] For a more detailed discussion of these clauses we refer the reader to [13].

In this section we show how the language can be naturally expanded to include further notions concerning contextual subsumption for talking about TBoxes in contexts[11] which are used in the formal analysis of the examples exposed in Section 4.

What can be straightforwardly added is the concept contextual equivalence via the obvious definition:

$$\xi : \gamma_1 \equiv \gamma_2 \ =_{\text{def}} \ \xi : \gamma_1 \sqsubseteq \gamma_2 \ \wedge \ \xi : \gamma_2 \sqsubseteq \gamma_1.$$

This definition yields the following semantic characterization of contextual concept equivalence: for $\xi : \gamma_1 \equiv \gamma_2$ to be true, concepts γ_1 and γ_2 should be defined in ξ and $\forall m \in \mathbb{I}(\xi) \ \mathcal{I}_m(\gamma_1) = \mathcal{I}_m(\gamma_2)$.

An interesting direction for the expansion of the language consists in adding another class of expressions representing the negation of a subsumption relation: $\xi : \gamma_1 \not\sqsubseteq \gamma_2$ ("in context ξ, concept γ_1 is not subsumed by concept γ_2"). Our models can easily provide a semantics for this type of expressions:

$$\mathbb{M} \models \xi : \gamma_1 \not\sqsubseteq \gamma_2 \ \text{iff} \ \mathbb{M} \models \gamma_1 \downarrow \xi, \mathbb{M} \models \gamma_2 \downarrow \xi \ \text{and} \ \forall m \in \mathbb{I}(\xi) \ \mathcal{I}_m(\gamma_1) \not\subseteq \mathcal{I}_m(\gamma_2).$$

It is natural to confront this with the notion of negation already present in $\mathcal{L}^{CT}$, namely the one formalized by expressions of the form: $\sim \xi : \gamma_1 \sqsubseteq \gamma_2$. First of all, $\sim \xi : \gamma_1 \sqsubseteq \gamma_2$ statements are satisfied if the concepts γ_1 and γ_2 are not well-defined in ξ, while $\xi : \gamma_1 \not\sqsubseteq \gamma_2$ statements are not. Given that, instead, γ_1 and γ_2 are well-defined in ξ, the essential difference resides in the fact that the satisfaction condition for $\sim$ statements corresponds to $\exists m \in \mathbb{I}(\xi) \ \mathcal{I}_m(\gamma_1) \not\subseteq \mathcal{I}_m(\gamma_2)$, while for $\not\sqsubseteq$ statements it corresponds to the condition $\forall m \in \mathbb{I}(\xi) \ \mathcal{I}_m(\gamma_1) \not\subseteq \mathcal{I}_m(\gamma_2)$. It is therefore easy to prove that for all ct-models $\mathbb{M}$:

$$\mathbb{M} \models \xi : \gamma_1 \not\sqsubseteq \gamma_2 \Rightarrow \mathbb{M} \models \sim \xi : \gamma_1 \sqsubseteq \gamma_2.$$

At this point, readers acquainted with modal logic will have recognized that the difference between a $\sim$ and a $\not\sqsubseteq$ negation corresponds to the difference between placing a negation before or after a box operator[12].

On the basis of this notion of negation, a notion for strict contextual subsumption can also be added via simple definition:

$$\xi : \gamma_1 \sqsubset \gamma_2 \ =_{\text{def}} \ \xi : \gamma_1 \sqsubseteq \gamma_2 \ \wedge \ \xi : \gamma_2 \not\sqsubseteq \gamma_1.$$

Semantically, it is then easy to see that $\mathbb{M} \models \xi : \gamma_1 \sqsubset \gamma_2$ iff $\mathbb{M} \models \gamma_1 \downarrow \xi \wedge \gamma_2 \downarrow \xi$ and $\forall m \in \mathbb{I}(\xi) \ \mathcal{I}_m(\gamma_1) \subseteq \mathcal{I}_m(\gamma_2)$ but not vice versa.

This kind of expansions of $\mathcal{L}^{CT}$ bring the expressivity of the language much further the one of the $\mathcal{ALC}$ from which we started. In fact, they allow to deal not

---

[11] We confine ourselves to discuss expansions concerning concept subsumption. Perfectly analogous expansions can be discussed with respect to role subsumption.

[12] We actually investigated some relations between the framework presented here and the modal logic $\mathbf{KD45}_n^{i-j}$ in [14]. Notice though that, as it is introduced here, the $\not\sqsubseteq$ negation cannot be nested.

only with contextual subsumption statements ($\xi : \gamma_1 \sqsubseteq \gamma_2$), but also with their negated and strict versions ($\xi : \gamma_1 \not\sqsubseteq \gamma_2$ and $\xi : \gamma_1 \sqsubset \gamma_2$). This opens naturally the door to considerations about the complexity of the reasoning that can be carried out in the framework which constitute the focus of our present research on $\mathcal{L}^{CT}$ languages.

4 Contextual Terminologies at Work

4.1 Formalizing the First Scenario

We are now in the position to formalize Example 1.

Example 3 (**Sufficient conditions for "liability"**). To formalize the first scenario within our setting a language $\mathcal{L}$ is needed, which contains the following atomic concepts: person, liable, vehicle, car, bicycle; and the following atomic roles: drive and wheel. Four atomic contexts are at issue here: the context of the main regulation R, let us call it c_R; the contexts of the municipal regulations M1, M2 and M3, let us call them c_{M1}, c_{M2} and c_{M3} respectively. These contexts should be interpreted on two relevant languages (let us call them $\mathcal{L}_0$ and $\mathcal{L}_1$) s.t. $\mathbf{A}_0 = \{\text{person}, \text{liable}, \text{vehicle}\}$, $\mathbf{R}_0 = \{\text{drive}\}$ and $\mathbf{A}_1 = \{\text{person}, \text{liable}, \text{vehicle}, \text{car}, \text{bicycle}\}$, $\mathbf{R}_1 = \{\text{drive}, \text{wheel}\}$. That is to say, an abstract language concerning only persons, liability, vehicles and the action of driving, and a more detailed language concerning, besides liable persons, vehicles and driving, also cars, bicycles and the action of wheeling. The sets of all models for $\mathcal{L}_0$ and $\mathcal{L}_1$ are then respectively $\mathbf{M}_0$ and $\mathbf{M}_1$.

To model the desired situation, our ct-model should then at least satisfy the following $\mathcal{L}^{CT}$ formulas:

$$c_{M1} \curlyvee_0 c_{M2} \curlyvee_0 c_{M3} \preccurlyeq c_R \tag{6}$$

$$\sim (\text{car} \downarrow c_R) \wedge \sim (\text{bicycle} \downarrow c_R) \wedge \sim (\text{wheel} \downarrow c_R) \tag{7}$$

$$c_R : \text{person} \sqcap \exists \text{drive}.\text{vehicle} \sqsubseteq \text{person} \sqcap \text{liable} \tag{8}$$

$$c_{M1} \curlyvee_1 c_{M2} \curlyvee_1 c_{M3} : \text{car} \sqsubset \text{vehicle} \tag{9}$$

$$c_{M1} \curlyvee_1 c_{M2} : \text{bicycle} \sqsubset \text{vehicle} \tag{10}$$

$$c_{M3} : \text{bicycle} \sqsubseteq \neg\text{vehicle} \tag{11}$$

$$c_{M1} \curlyvee_1 c_{M3} : \text{wheel} \sqsubset \text{drive} \tag{12}$$

$$c_{M2} : \text{wheel} \sqsubseteq \overline{\text{drive}}. \tag{13}$$

Formula (6) plays a key role, stating that the three contexts c_{M1}, c_{M2}, c_{M3} are concrete variants of context c_R. It tells this by saying that the context obtained by joining the three concrete contexts on language $\mathcal{L}_0$ (the language of c_R) is at most as general as context c_R, that is: $]_0\mathbb{I}(c_{M1}) \cup]_0\mathbb{I}(c_{M2}) \cup]_0\mathbb{I}(c_{M3}) \subseteq \mathbb{I}(c_R)$ (see Section 3.2). As we will see in the following, this makes c_{M1}, c_{M2} and

c_{M3} inherit what holds in c_R. Formula (7) specifies what concepts and roles do not get interpretation in the abstract context c_R and make therefore the classification of specific complex concepts impossible (see Table 1). Formula (8) formalizes the abstract rule to the effect that persons driving vehicles (within public parks) are liable for a violation of the applicable regulation. Formulas (9)-(11) describe the different taxonomies holding in the three concrete contexts at issue, while formulas (12) and (13) describe the different role hierarchies holding in those contexts. The last formula can be seen as simply stating some background knowledge to the effect that to wheel a car is an empty concept.

To discuss in some more depth the proposed formalization, let us first list some interesting logical consequences of formulas (6)-(13). We will focus on subsumptions contextualized to monadic contexts, that is to say, we will show what the consequences of formulas (6)-(13) are at the level of the four contexts c_R, c_{M1}, c_{M2} and c_{M3} considered in isolation.

$$(7) \models \sim (\text{person} \sqcap \exists \text{drive.car} \downarrow c_R)$$
$$(7) \models \sim (\text{person} \sqcap \exists \text{drive.bicycle} \downarrow c_R)$$
$$(7) \models \sim (\text{person} \sqcap \exists \text{wheel.bicycle} \downarrow c_R).$$

$$(6,8) \models c_{M1} : \text{person} \sqcap \exists \text{drive.vehicle} \sqsubseteq \text{person} \sqcap \text{liable}$$
$$(9) \models c_{M1} : \text{person} \sqcap \exists \text{drive.car} \sqsubset \text{person} \sqcap \exists \text{drive.vehicle}$$
$$(10) \models c_{M1} : \text{person} \sqcap \exists \text{drive.bicycle} \sqsubset \text{person} \sqcap \exists \text{drive.vehicle}$$
$$(12) \models c_{M1} : \text{person} \sqcap \exists \text{wheel.bicycle} \sqsubset \text{person} \sqcap \exists \text{drive.bicycle}$$
$$(8,9) \models c_{M1} : \text{person} \sqcap \exists \text{drive.car} \sqsubset \text{person} \sqcap \text{liable}$$
$$(6,8,10) \models c_{M1} : \text{person} \sqcap \exists \text{drive.bicycle} \sqsubset \text{person} \sqcap \text{liable}$$
$$(6,8,10,12) \models c_{M1} : \text{person} \sqcap \exists \text{wheel.bicycle} \sqsubset \text{person} \sqcap \text{liable}$$
$$(9,10,12,13) \models (\text{car} \downarrow c_{M1}) \wedge (\text{bicycle} \downarrow c_{M1}) \wedge (\text{wheel} \downarrow c_{M1})$$

$$(6,8) \models c_{M2} : \text{person} \sqcap \exists \text{drive.vehicle} \sqsubseteq \text{person} \sqcap \text{liable}$$
$$(9) \models c_{M2} : \text{person} \sqcap \exists \text{drive.car} \sqsubset \text{person} \sqcap \exists \text{drive.vehicle}$$
$$(10) \models c_{M2} : \text{person} \sqcap \exists \text{drive.bicycle} \sqsubset \text{person} \sqcap \exists \text{drive.vehicle}$$
$$(13) \models c_{M2} : \text{person} \sqcap \exists \text{wheel.bicycle} \sqsubseteq \text{person} \sqcap \exists \overline{\text{drive.bicycle}}$$
$$(10,13) \models c_{M2} : \text{person} \sqcap \exists \text{wheel.bicycle} \sqsubseteq \text{person} \sqcap \exists \overline{\text{drive.vehicle}}$$
$$(8,9) \models c_{M1} : \text{person} \sqcap \exists \text{drive.car} \sqsubset \text{person} \sqcap \text{liable}$$
$$(6,8,10) \models c_{M2} : \text{person} \sqcap \exists \text{drive.bicycle} \sqsubset \text{person} \sqcap \text{liable}$$
$$(6,8,9,10,13) \models \sim c_{M2} : \text{person} \sqcap \exists \text{wheel.bicycle} \sqsubset \text{person} \sqcap \text{liable}$$
$$(9,10,12,13) \models (\text{car} \downarrow c_{M2}) \wedge (\text{bicycle} \downarrow c_{M2}) \wedge (\text{wheel} \downarrow c_{M2})$$

$$(6,8) \vDash c_{M3} : \text{person} \sqcap \exists\text{drive.vehicle} \sqsubseteq \text{person} \sqcap \text{liable}$$

$$(9) \vDash c_{M3} : \text{person} \sqcap \exists\text{drive.car} \sqsubseteq \text{person} \sqcap \exists\text{drive.vehicle}$$

$$(11) \vDash c_{M2} : \text{person} \sqcap \exists\text{drive.bicycle} \sqsubset \text{person} \sqcap \exists\text{drive.}\neg\text{vehicle}$$

$$(12) \vDash c_{M3} : \text{person} \sqcap \exists\text{wheel.bicycle} \sqsubset \text{person} \sqcap \exists\text{drive.bicycle}$$

$$(8,9) \vDash c_{M1} : \text{person} \sqcap \exists\text{drive.car} \sqsubset \text{person} \sqcap \text{liable}$$

$$(6,8,11) \vDash \sim c_{M3} : \text{person} \sqcap \exists\text{drive.bicycle} \sqsubset \text{person} \sqcap \text{liable}$$

$$(6,8,11,12) \vDash \sim c_{M3} : \text{person} \sqcap \exists\text{wheel.bicycle} \sqsubset \text{person} \sqcap \text{liable}$$

$$(9,10,12,13) \vDash (\text{car} \downarrow c_{M3}) \wedge (\text{bicycle} \downarrow c_{M3}) \wedge (\text{wheel} \downarrow c_{M3}).$$

These are indeed formulas that we would intuitively expect to hold in our scenario. The list displays four sets of formulas grouped on the basis of the context to which they pertain. Let us have a closer look to them. The first group of formulas pertains the abstract context c_R. Since the concepts of car and bicycle, and the role wheel cannot be expressed in the language $\mathcal{L}_0$ of c_R (7), the complex concepts which are central in the scenario (person driving a car, person driving a bicycle, person wheeling a bicycle) are not well-defined with respect to c_R. As to the consequences pertaining the three concrete contexts c_{M1}, c_{M2} and c_{M3}, we note that the first consequence of each group results from the generality relation expressed in (6), by means of which, the content of (8) is shown to hold also in the three concrete contexts: in simple words, contexts c_{M1}, c_{M2} and c_{M3} inherit the general rule stating the liability of persons driving vehicles (within public parks). Via this inherited rule, and via (9), it is shown that, in all contexts, who drives a car is also held liable (third formula from the bottom of each group). As to cars and driving cars then, all contexts agree. Where differences arise is in relation with how the concept of bicycle and the role of wheeling are handled.

In context c_{M1}, we have that it does not matter if somebody wheels or actually drives a bicycle, because in both cases this would count as driving a vehicle, and therefore of violating the regulation. In fact, in this context, a bicycle is a vehicle (10) and to wheel is a way of driving (11). Context c_{M2}, instead, expresses a different view. Since bicycles count as vehicles (10), to drive a bicycle is still a ground for liability. On the other hand, to wheel is actually classified as a way of refraining from driving (13), and therefore, there is no ground for considering persons wheeling bicycles to count as persons driving vehicles, and therefore to commit a violation. Context c_{M3} yields yet another terminology. Here bicycles are classified as objects which are not vehicles (11). Therefore, although to wheel is conceived as a way of driving (11), both to drive and to wheel a bicycle does not determine liability. With respect to this, it is instructive to notice that even though both in c_{M2} and c_{M3} to wheel a bicycle is not a sufficient reason for being held liable, this holds for two different reasons: in c_{M2} because of (13), and in c_{M3} because of (11). Finally, in each of the concrete contexts, the concepts car and bicycle, and the role wheel all get a meaning (last consequence of each group). This illustrates how our framework is able to cope with some quite subtle nuances that characterize contextual classifications.

4.2   A Model of the Scenario

In this section we expose a simple ct-model satisfying (6)-(13). Let us stipulate that the models m that constitute our interpretation of contexts identifiers consist of a domain $\Delta_m = \{a, b, c, d, e, f, g\}$. Being $\mathcal{L}_0$ and $\mathcal{L}_1$ the two languages at issue, the domain of the ct-models is $\mathbf{M}_0 \cup \mathbf{M}_1$. A ct-model would then be, for instance, a structure $\langle \mathbf{M}_0 \cup \mathbf{M}_1, \mathbb{I} \rangle$ where $\mathbb{I}$ is such that:

- $\mathbb{I}(c_{M1}) = \{m_1, m_2\} \subseteq \mathbf{M}_1$ s.t. $\mathcal{I}_{m_1}(\texttt{person}) = \{e, f, g\}$, $\mathcal{I}_{m_1}(\texttt{vehicle}) = \{a, b, c, d\}$, $\mathcal{I}_{m_1}(\texttt{bicycle}) = \{a, b\}$, $\mathcal{I}_{m_1}(\texttt{car}) = \{c, d\}$, $\mathcal{I}_{m_1}(\texttt{drive}) = \{< e, a >, < f, c >\}$, $\mathcal{I}_{m_1}(\texttt{wheel}) = \{< e, a >\}$, $\mathcal{I}_{m_1}(\texttt{liable}) = \{e, f\}$ and $\mathcal{I}_{m_2}$ agrees with $\mathcal{I}_{m_1}$ on the interpretation of $\texttt{person}, \texttt{bicycle}, \texttt{car}, \texttt{vehicle}$ and $\mathcal{I}_{m_2}(\texttt{drive}) = \{< f, c >, < g, d >\}$, $\mathcal{I}_{m_2}(\texttt{wheel}) = \{< g, d >\}$, $\mathcal{I}_{m_2}(\texttt{liable}) = \{f, g\}$.
- $\mathbb{I}(c_{M2}) = \{m_3, m_4\} \subseteq \mathbf{M}_1$ s.t. $\mathcal{I}_{m_3}$ and $\mathcal{I}_{m_4}$ agree with $\mathcal{I}_{m_1}$ on the interpretation of $\texttt{person}, \texttt{bicycle}, \texttt{car}, \texttt{vehicle}$ and $\mathcal{I}_{m_3}(\texttt{drive}) = \{< f, d >, < g, a >\}$, $\mathcal{I}_{m_3}(\texttt{wheel}) = \{< e, a >\}$, $\mathcal{I}_{m_3}(\texttt{liable}) = \{f, g\}$ and $\mathcal{I}_{m_4}(\texttt{drive}) = \{< e, c >\}$, $\mathcal{I}_{m_4}(\texttt{wheel}) = \{< f, a >\}$, $\mathcal{I}_{m_4}(\texttt{liable}) = \{e\}$.
- $\mathbb{I}(c_{M3}) = \{m_5\} \subseteq \mathbf{M}_1$ s.t. $\mathcal{I}_{m_5}$ agrees with $\mathcal{I}_{m_1}$ on the interpretation of $\texttt{person}, \texttt{bicycle}, \texttt{car}$ and $\mathcal{I}_{m_5}(\texttt{vehicle}) = \{c, d\}$, $\mathcal{I}_{m_5}(\texttt{drive}) = \{< e, a >, < f, c >, < g, d >\}$, $\mathcal{I}_{m_1}(\texttt{wheel}) = \{< e, a >\}$, $\mathcal{I}_{m_1}(\texttt{liable}) = \{f, g\}$.
- $\mathbb{I}(c_R) = \{m \mid m = \langle \Delta_m, \mathbf{A}_0 \cup \mathbf{R}_0 \rceil \mathcal{I}_i \rangle$ and $1 \leq i \leq 5\}$, that is, c_R is interpreted by the model as the union of all models constituting c_{M1}, c_{M2} and c_{M3} restricted to the language $\mathcal{L}_0$.

The model makes an interesting feature of our semantics explicit. In contexts c_{M1} and c_{M2} the set of liable persons do not coincide in the two models constituting the context; nevertheless only persons driving vehicles are indeed liable. This clearly shows that contexts can be viewed as clusters of possible situations all instantiating the same terminology[13].

4.3   Formalizing the Second Scenario

The formalization of the scenario introduced in Example 2 follows.

Example 4 (**Categorizing "teenagers on skates"**). The global language $\mathcal{L}$ needed contains the following atomic concepts: $\texttt{conv}, \texttt{person}, \texttt{obj}, \texttt{vehicle}, \texttt{teenager}, \texttt{skate}$; and the following atomic role: $\texttt{transp}$. Three are the atomic contexts at issue here: the context of the main regulation R, let us call it c_R; the contexts of the municipal regulations M1 and M2, let us call them c_{M1} and c_{M2} respectively. These contexts should be interpreted on two relevant languages (let us call them $\mathcal{L}_0$ and $\mathcal{L}_1$) s.t. $\mathbf{A}_0 = \{\texttt{conv}, \texttt{person}, \texttt{obj}, \texttt{vehicle}\}$, $\mathbf{R}_0 = \{\texttt{transp}\}$ and $\mathbf{A}_1 = \mathbf{A}_0 \cup \{\texttt{self\_prop}, \texttt{teenager}, \texttt{skate}\}$, $\mathbf{R}_1 = \mathbf{R}_0$. That is to say, an abstract language concerning only conveyances, persons, objects, vehicles and the attribute of transporting, and a more detailed language concerning, besides

---

[13] We developed this intuition also in a modal logic setting modeling contexts as sets of possible worlds. See [14].

this, also teenagers and skates. The sets of all models for $\mathcal{L}_0$ and $\mathcal{L}_1$ are then respectively $\mathbf{M}_0$ and $\mathbf{M}_1$. To model the desired situation, a ct-model should then at least satisfy the following $\mathcal{L}^{CT}$ formulas:

$$c_{M1} \curlyvee_0 c_{M2} \preccurlyeq c_R \tag{14}$$

$$\sim (\text{teenager} \downarrow c_R) \wedge \sim (\text{skate} \downarrow c_R) \tag{15}$$

$$c_R : \text{vehicle} \sqsubseteq \text{conv} \sqcap \forall \text{transp}.(\text{person} \sqcup \text{obj}) \tag{16}$$

$$c_{M1} : \text{vehicle} \sqsubseteq \text{self\_prop} \tag{17}$$

$$c_{M1} : \text{conv} \sqcap \exists \text{transp}.(\text{person} \sqcup \text{obj}) \sqcap \text{self\_prop} \sqsubseteq \text{vehicle} \tag{18}$$

$$c_{M2} : \text{conv} \sqcap \exists \text{transp}.(\text{person} \sqcup \text{obj}) \sqsubseteq \text{vehicle} \tag{19}$$

$$c_{M1} \curlyvee_1 c_{M2} : \text{teenager} \sqsubseteq \text{person} \tag{20}$$

$$c_{M1} \curlyvee_1 c_{M2} : \text{skate} \sqsubseteq \text{conv} \tag{21}$$

$$c_{M1} \curlyvee_1 c_{M2} : \text{skate} \sqsubseteq \neg\text{self\_prop} \tag{22}$$

We discuss the formalization of this scenario in fewer details than the previous one, stressing only the most important aspects. Formulas (14) and (15) are the analogous of formulas (6) and (7). Formula (16) represents the abstract constraints that context c_R imposes on the concept vehicle.

Formulas (17), (18) and (19) express the additional constraints on the concept vehicle holding in context c_{M1} and c_{M2} respectively: both contexts specify sufficient conditions and context c_{M1} adds also new necessary ones (17). Formulas (20) and (21) state the intuitive background knowledge common to the two concrete contexts. The point of the scenario consists in showing how teenagers on skateboards are conceptualized in the three contexts, that is to say: how are concept skate$\sqcap\exists$transp.teenager and concept vehicle related in each context? This can be easily shown via some relevant logical consequences of (14)-(22):

$$(14) \models \sim (\text{skate} \sqcap \exists \text{transp}.\text{teenager} \downarrow c_R)$$

$$(14, 16, 17, 18) \models c_{M1} : \text{conv} \sqcap \exists \text{transp}.(\text{person} \sqcup \text{obj})$$
$$\sqcap \text{self\_prop} \equiv \text{vehicle}$$

$$(14, 16, 17, 18, 20, 21, 22) \models c_{M1} : \text{skate} \sqcap \exists \text{transp}.\text{teenager} \not\sqsubseteq \text{vehicle}$$

$$(14, 16, 17, 18, 20, 21, 22) \models c_{M1} : \text{skate} \sqcap \exists \text{transp}.\text{teenager} \sqsubseteq \neg\text{vehicle}$$

$$(14, 16, 17, 18, 20, 21, 22) \models \sim c_{M1} : \text{skate} \sqcap \exists \text{transp}.\text{teenager} \sqsubseteq \text{vehicle}$$

$$(20, 21) \models \text{skate} \sqcap \exists \text{transp}.\text{teenager} \downarrow c_{M1}$$

$$(14, 16, 19) \models c_{M2} : \text{conv} \sqcap \exists \text{transp}.(\text{person} \sqcup \text{obj}) \equiv \text{vehicle}$$

$$(14, 16, 19, 20, 21) \models c_{M2} : \text{skate} \sqcap \exists \text{transp}.\text{teenager} \sqsubseteq \text{vehicle}$$

$$(20, 21) \models \text{skate} \sqcap \exists \text{transp}.\text{teenager} \downarrow c_{M2}.$$

Like in the previous example, the abstract context c_R cannot categorize the concept at issue. In the two concrete contexts c_{M1} and c_{M2} two different definitions of `vehicle` hold, and therefore two different conceptualizations of the concept `skate`$\sqcap\exists$`transp.teenager`: since skateboards are not, in c_{M1}, self-propelled, they are not only non classifiable as vehicles, but, more strongly, they are actually classifiable as objects which are not vehicles. In fact, the concept `vehicle` is defined via both necessary and sufficient conditions.

5   Conclusions and Future Work

We motivated and devised a formal framework for representing contextual ontologies via a contextualized version of description logic semantics. The key idea has been to show that the basic intuition of understanding contexts as sets of description logic models, which we presented in [13], works smoothly also with subsumption statements of more complex concept descriptions.

A next step will be to side contextual terminologies with appropriate contextual assertion boxes (ABoxes) in which to reason about contextual instantiations of concepts and roles. The main focus of on-going work consists though in investigating the meta-logical properties of the framework and especially complexity. To this aim, we are at the moment studying its relation with modal languages, exploiting the well established results about the correspondence between description and modal logics [18, 5] and some work we have already done in that direction [14].

Acknowledgments

We would like to thank the anonymous reviewers of CLIMA VI for their valuable comments and Prof. K. Clark for the useful comment during the presentation of the paper.

References

1. V. Akman and M. Surav. Steps toward formalizing context. *AI Magazine*, 17(3):55–72, 1996.
2. C. E. Alchourrón and E. Bulygin. *Normative Systems*. Springer Verlag, Wien, 1986.
3. F. Baader, D. Calvanese, D.L. McGuinness, D. Nardi, and P.F. Patel-Schneider. *The Description Logic Handbook*. Cambridge University Press, Cambridge, 2002.
4. M. Benerecetti, P. Bouquet, and C. Ghidini. Contextual reasoning distilled. *Journal of Experimental and Theoretical Artificial Intelligence (JETAI)*, 12(3):279–305, 2000.
5. G. De Giacomo and M. Lenzerini. TBox and ABox reasoning in expressive description logics. In L. Carlucci Aiello, J. Doyle, and S. Shapiro, editors, *KR'96: Principles of Knowledge Representation and Reasoning*, pages 316–327. Morgan Kaufmann, San Francisco, California, 1996.
6. F. Dignum. Agents, markets, institutions, and protocols. In *Agent Mediated Electronic Commerce, The European AgentLink Perspective.*, pages 98–114. Springer-Verlag, 2001.

7. F. Dignum. Abstract norms and electronic institutions. In *Proceedings of the International Workshop on Regulated Agent-Based Social Systems: Theories and Applications (RASTA '02)*, Bologna, pages 93–104, 2002.

8. C. Ghidini and F. Giunchiglia. Local models semantics, or contextual reasoning = locality + compatibility. *Artificial Intelligence*, 127(2):221–259, 2001.

9. C. Ghidini and F. Giunchiglia. A semantics for abstraction. In R. López de Mántaras and L. Saitta, editors, *Proceedings of ECAI'2004, including PAIS 2004*, pages 343–347, 2004.

10. D. Grossi, H. Aldewereld, J. Vázquez-Salceda, and F. Dignum. Ontological aspects of the implementation of norms in agent-based electronic institutions. In *Proceedings of NorMAS'05, Symposium on normative multi-agent systems.*, pages 104–116, Hatfield, England, April 2005. AISB.

11. D. Grossi and F. Dignum. From abstract to concrete norms in agent institutions. In M. G. et al. Hinchey, editor, *Formal Approaches to Agent-Based Systems: Third International Workshop, FAABS 2004*, Lecture Notes in Computer Science, pages 12–29. Springer-Verlag, April 2004.

12. D. Grossi, F. Dignum, and J-J. Ch. Meyer. Context in categorization. In *Proceedings of CRR'05, International Workshop on Context Representation and Reasoning*, volume 136 of *CEUR Workshop Proceedings*, Paris, July 2005.

13. D. Grossi, F. Dignum, and J-J. Ch. Meyer. Contextual taxonomies. In J. Leite and P. Toroni, editors, *Proceedings of CLIMA V Workshop, Lisbon, September*, LNAI 3487, pages 33–51. Springer, 2005.

14. D. Grossi, J-J. Ch. Meyer, and F. Dignum. Modal logic investigations in the semantics of counts-as. In *Proceedings of the Tenth International Conference on Artificial Intelligence and Law (ICAIL'05)*, pages 1–9. ACM, June 2005.

15. A. J. I. Jones and M. Sergot. On the characterization of law and computer systems. *Deontic Logic in Computer Science*, pages 275–307, 1993.

16. B. Jónsson and A. Tarski. Boolean algebras with operators: Part I. *American Journal of Mathematics*, 73:891–939, 1951.

17. J. McCarthy. Notes on formalizing contexts. In T. Kehler and S. Rosenschein, editors, *Proceedings of the Fifth National Conference on Artificial Intelligence*, pages 555–560, Los Altos, California, 1986. Morgan Kaufmann.

18. K. Schild. A correspondence theory for terminological logics: preliminary report. In *Proceedings of IJCAI-91, 12th International Joint Conference on Artificial Intelligence*, pages 466–471, Sidney, AU, 1991.

19. J. Searle. *The Construction of Social Reality*. Free Press, New York, 1995.

20. Y. Shoham. Varieties of context. pages 393–407. Academic Press Professional, Inc., 1991.

21. J. Vázquez-Salceda. *The role of Norms and Electronic Institutions in Multi-Agent Systems*. Birkhuser Verlag AG, 2004.

22. J. Vázquez-Salceda and F. Dignum. Modelling electronic organizations. In J. Muller V. Marik and M. Pechoucek, editors, *Proceedings CEEMAS'03. LNAI 2691*, pages 584–593, Berlin, 2003. Springer-Verlag.

Constitutive Norms in the Design of Normative Multiagent Systems

Guido Boella[1] and Leendert van der Torre[2]

[1] Dipartimento di Informatica, Università di Torino, Italy
guido@di.unito.it
[2] University of Luxembourg
leendert@vandertorre.com

Abstract. In this paper, we consider the design of normative multiagent systems composed of both constitutive and regulative norms. We analyze the properties of constitutive norms, in particular their lack of reflexivity, and the trade-off between constitutive and regulative norms in the design of normative systems. As methodology we use the metaphor of describing social entities as agents and of attributing them mental attitudes. In this agent metaphor, regulative norms expressing obligations and permissions are modelled as goals of social entities, and constitutive norms expressing "counts-as" relations are their beliefs.

1 Introduction

Legal systems are often modelled using regulative norms, like obligations, prohibitions, and permissions [1]. However, a large part of the legal code does not contain obligations, prohibitions and permissions, but definitions for classifying the commonsense world under legal categories, like contract, money, property, marriage. Regulative norms can refer to this legal classification of reality.

Consider the consequences for the design of legal systems. For example, in [2] we address the issue of designing obligations to achieve the objectives of the legal system. However, the problem has not been studied of how to design legal systems composed of both constitutive and regulative norms. For modelling constitutive norms, specialized formalisms for counts-as conditionals have been introduced [3, 4, 5], but it remains unclear how to relate them to regulative norms. In contrast, as Artosi *et al.* [3] argue, for constitutive norms to be norms it is necessary that "their conditional nature exhibits some basic properties enjoyed by the usual normative links". Thus constitutive and regulative norms should be more strictly related.

Obligations, prohibitions and permissions have a conditional nature. Their conditions could directly refer to entities and facts of the commonsense world, but they can rather refer to a legal and more abstract classification of the world, making them more independent from the commonsense view. E.g., they refer to money instead of paper sheets, to properties instead of houses and fields. This more natural and economical way to model the relation between commonsense reality and legal reality uses "counts-as" conditionals, and allows regulative norms to refer to the legal classification of reality. In this way, e.g., it is not necessary that each regulative norm refers to all the conditions

F. Toni and P. Torroni (Eds.): CLIMA VI, LNAI 3900, pp. 303–319, 2006.
© Springer-Verlag Berlin Heidelberg 2006

involved in the classification of paper as money or of houses and fields as properties. Moreover, it is not necessary that regulative norms manage the exceptions in the classification, e.g., that a fake bill is not money or that some field is not considered as a property. Finally, by referring to the legal classification of reality only, regulative norms are not sensitive anymore to changes in the classification: a new bill can be introduced without changing the regulative norms concerning money, or a new form of property or a new kind of marriage can be introduced without changing the relevant norms.

However, the trade-off and equivalences between systems made purely of regulative norms and those including also constitutive norms cannot be easily captured by specialized formalisms. They either consider only regulative norms, such as deontic logic, or only constitutive norms, such as logics of counts-as conditionals, or, finally, with formalisms using very different formalizations for modelling the two kinds of norms. This is a problem for the design of normative systems.

In [6], to model social reality, we have introduced constitutive norms in our normative multiagent systems. In this paper we use normative multiagent systems to model the design of legal systems. In particular, the research questions of this paper are: What properties have constitutive norms? In [6] we use rules satisfying the identity property, thus making the "counts-as" relation reflexive. This is a undesired property if constitutive norms provide a classification of reality in term of legal categories. In this paper we remedy this by modelling "counts-as" as input/output conditionals. This is an alternative solution with respect to the one proposed by Artosi *et al.* [3]. Secondly, how can regulative and constitutive norms be traded-off against each other in the design of legal systems? If we replace constitutive norms in a legal system with regulative ones, then we lose the abstraction provided by legal classification.

The main advantage of our approach in comparison with other accounts, is that we combine constitutive and regulative norms in a single conceptual model. As methodology we use our model of normative multiagent systems introduced in AI and agent theory to model social reality and agent organizations [7, 8]. The basic assumptions of our model are that beliefs, goals and desires of an agent are represented by conditional rules, and that, when an agent takes a decision, it recursively models [9] the other agents interfering with it in order to predict their reaction to its decision as in a game. Most importantly, the normative system itself can be conceptualized as an agent with whom it is possible to play games to understand what will be its reaction to the agent's decision: to consider its behavior as a violation and to sanction it. In the model presented in [6], regulative norms are represented by the goals of the normative system and constitutive norms as its beliefs. In this paper we discuss the properties of counts-as relations relating them to the properties of beliefs and how trade-off problem between constitutive and regulative norms can be handled by as the trade-off between beliefs and goals of the normative system. The cognitive motivations of the agent metaphor underlying our framework are discussed in [10].

The paper is organized as follows. In Section 2 we describe the agent metaphor. In Section 3 we introduce a logic which does not satisfy identity. In Section 4 we discuss the relation between constitutive and regulative norms. In Section 5 we introduce a formal model where we discuss the properties of constitutive norms and in Section 6 the trade-off with regulative ones. Comparison with related work and conclusion end the paper.

2   Attributing Mental Attitudes

We start with a well known definition: " *Normative systems* are sets of agents (human or artificial) whose interactions can fruitfully be regarded as norm-governed; the norms prescribe how the agents ideally should and should not behave [...]. Importantly, the norms allow for the possibility that actual behaviour may at times deviate from the ideal, i.e. that violations of obligations, or of agents rights, may occur" [1].

This definition of Carmo and Jones does not seem to require that the normative system is autonomous, or that its behavior is driven by beliefs and desires.

In [6] we use the agent metaphor which attributes mental attitudes to normative systems in order to explain normative reasoning in autonomous agents. The normative system is considered as an agent with whom the bearer of the norms plays a game. Henceforth, we can call it the normative agent.

Our motivation for using the agent metaphor is inspired by the interpretation of normative *multiagent* systems as dynamic social orders. According to Castelfranchi [11], a social order is a pattern of interactions among interfering agents "such that it allows the satisfaction of the interests of some agent". These interests can be a delegated goal, a value that is good for everybody or for most of the members; for example, the interest may be to avoid accidents. We say that agents attribute the mental attitude 'goal' to the normative system, because all or some of the agents have socially delegated goals to the normative system; these goals are the content of the obligations regulating it.

Moreover, social order requires *social control*, "an incessant local (micro) activity of its units" [11], aimed at restoring the regularities prescribed by norms. Thus, the agents attribute to the normative system, besides goals, also the ability to autonomously enforce the conformity of the agents to the norms, because a dynamic social order requires a continuous activity for ensuring that the normative system's goals are achieved. To achieve the normative goal the normative system forms the subgoals to consider as a violation the behavior not conform to it and to sanction violations. Norms, however, do not aim only at regulating behavior.

Searle argues that there are two types of norms: "Some rules regulate antecedently existing forms of behaviour. For example, the rules of polite table behaviour regulate eating, but eating exists independently of these rules. Some rules, on the other hand, do not merely regulate an antecedently existing activity called playing chess; they, as it were, create the possibility of or define that activity. The activity of playing chess is constituted by action in accordance with these rules. Chess has no existence apart from these rules. The institutions of marriage, money, and promising are like the institutions of baseball and chess in that they are systems of such constitutive rules or conventions" ([12], p. 131).

According to Searle, institutional facts like marriage, money and private property emerge from an independent ontology of "brute" natural facts through constitutive norms of the form "such and such an X counts as Y in context C" where X is any object satisfying certain conditions and Y is a label that qualifies X as being something of an entirely new sort. Examples of constitutive norms are "X counts as a presiding official in a wedding ceremony", "this bit of paper counts as a five euro bill" and "this piece of land counts as somebody's private property".

In our model, we define constitutive norms in terms of the normative system's belief rules and the institutional facts as the consequences of these beliefs rules.

The propositions describing the world are distinguished in two categories: first, what Searle calls "brute facts": natural facts and events produced by the actions of the agents. Second, "institutional facts": a legal classification of brute facts; they belong only to the beliefs of the normative system and have no direct counterpart in the world. Belief rules connect beliefs representing the state of the world to other beliefs which are their consequences. They have a conditional character and are represented in the same rule based formalism as goals and desires. In the case of the normative system the belief rules have as consequences not other beliefs about brute facts in the world (e.g., "if a glass drops, it breaks"), but new legal, institutional facts whose existence is related only to the normative system. These belief rules, moreover, can connect also institutional facts to other institutional facts.

This type of belief rules expresses the *counts-as* relations which are at the basis of constitutive norms. It is important that belief rules have a conditional character, since they must reflect the conditional nature of the counts-as relation as proposed by Searle: "such and such an X counts as Y in context C".

A fact p counts as an institutional fact q in context C for normative system $\mathbf{n}$ $counts\text{-}as_{\mathbf{n}}(p, q \mid C)$, iff agent $\mathbf{n}$ believes that $p \wedge C$ has q as a consequence.

The agent metaphor attributing mental attitudes to normative systems allows to understand how humans can conceive social reality by resorting to a better known domain. In [10], we discuss the cognitive basis of our model. In this way we are able to ground the ontology of social reality into a domain which can be modelled with the existing formal instruments. Most approaches, in contrast see social entities as black boxes, of which they describe the properties from an external point of view. In our model, instead, we explain the properties of normative systems as stemming from its conceptualization as an agent.

Mental attitudes of agents, however, have usually a private character: it is not possible to know which are the real goals and beliefs of an agent apart from inferring them from its behavior. In contrast, norms have a public character, otherwise it would not be possible to achieve a social order. When we map norms into beliefs and goals of the normative agent, we do not mean that they get a private character. The normative agent is only a socially constructed agent which exists only due to the collective acceptance by all the agents of the normative multiagent system.

Another advantage of considering normative systems as agents is that agents can play games with the normative system to understand whether they will be sanctioned.

The attribution of mental entities to normative systems is a methodology which can be grounded in different formal models, among which modal logic [13]. However, mental attitudes, as well as norms, are traditionally considered as conditional attitudes, thus we resort to a specialized logic which has been developed for this purpose: the Input/output logic.

We extend this approach advocated in [6] in two ways. First we give a logical analysis of counts-as, and we argue that it requires an identity free logic. Second we discuss the trade-off between the two kinds of norms.

3 Input/Output Logic

A disadvantage of the approach in [6] is that given the reflexivity of counts-as we have that "A counts as A", which is in contrast with our intuition and with other approaches (but see Section 7 for a discussion). In particular, since the counts-as relation classifies brute facts in legal categories, a brute fact A cannot be also a legal category: they are ontologically heterogeneous concepts, thus we keep them separate for the purpose of legal classification. We therefore want to use an identity free logic, for which we take a simplified version of the input/output logics introduced in [14, 15]. In this section we explain how it works. A rule set is a set of ordered pairs $P \rightarrow q$, where P is a set of propositional variables and q a propositional variable. For each such pair, the body P is thought of as an input, representing some condition or situation, and the head q is thought of as an output, representing what the rule tells us to be believed, desirable, obligatory or whatever in that situation. Makinson and van der Torre write (P, q) to distinguish input/output rules from conditionals defined in other logics, to emphasize the property that input/output logic does not necessarily obey the identity rule. In this paper we do not follow this convention.

In this paper, to keep the formal exposition simple, input and output are respectively a set of literals and a literal. In input/output logics, the input and output can be arbitrary propositional formulas, not just sets of literals and literal as we do here and additional rules for conjunction of outputs and for weakening outputs are added.

Definition 1 (Input/output logic). *Let X be a set of propositional variables, the set of literals built from X, written as $Lit(X)$, is $X \cup \{\neg x \mid x \in X\}$, and the set of rules built from X, written as $Rul(X) = 2^{Lit(X)} \times Lit(X)$, is the set of pairs of a set of literals built from X and a literal built from X, written as $\{l_1, \ldots, l_n\} \rightarrow l$. We also write $l_1 \wedge \ldots \wedge l_n \rightarrow l$ and when $n = 0$ we write $\top \rightarrow l$. For $x \in X$ we write $\sim x$ for $\neg x$ and $\sim(\neg x)$ for x. Moreover, let Q be a set of pointers to rules and $MD : Q \rightarrow Rul(X)$ is a total function from the pointers to the set of rules built from X.*

Let $S = MD(Q)$ be a set of rules $\{P_1 \rightarrow q_1, \ldots, P_n \rightarrow q_n\}$, and consider the following proof rules strengthening of the input (SI), disjunction of the input (OR), cumulative transitivity (CT) and Identity (Id) defined as follows:

$$\frac{p \rightarrow r}{p \wedge q \rightarrow r}SI \qquad \frac{p \wedge q \rightarrow r, p \wedge \neg q \rightarrow r}{p \rightarrow r}OR \qquad \frac{p \rightarrow q, p \wedge q \rightarrow r}{p \rightarrow r}CT \qquad \frac{}{p \rightarrow p}Id$$

The following output operators are defined as closure operators on the set S using the rules above.
out_1: SI (simple-minded output) out_3: SI+CT (simple-minded reusable output)
out_2: SI+OR (basic output) out_4: SI+OR+CT (basic reusable output)

Moreover, the following four throughput operators are defined as closure operators on the set S. out_i^+: out_i+Id (throughput) We write $out(Q)$ for any of these output operations and $out^+(Q)$ for any of these throughput operations. We also write $l \in out(Q, L)$ iff $L \rightarrow l \in out(Q)$, and $l \in out^+(Q, L)$ iff $L \rightarrow l \in out^+(Q)$.

A technical reason to distinguish pointers from rules is to facilitate the description of the priority ordering we introduce in the following definition.

Example 1. Given $MD(Q) = \{a \to x, x \to z\}$ the output of Q contains $x \wedge a \to z$ using the rule SI. Using also the CT rule, the output contains $a \to z$. $a \to a$ follows only if there is the Id rule.

The notorious contrary-to-duty paradoxes such as Chisholm's and Forrester's paradox have led to the use of constraints in input/output logics [15]. The strategy is to adapt a technique that is well known in the logic of belief change - cut back the set of norms to just below the threshold of making the current situation inconsistent.

In input/output logics under constraints, a set of mental attitudes and an input does not have a set of propositions as output, but a set of set of propositions. We can infer a set of propositions by for example taking the join (credulous) or meet (sceptical), or something more complicated. Besides, we can adopt an output constraint (the output has to be consistent) or an input/output constraint (the output has to be consistent with the input). In this paper we only consider the input/output constraints. The following definition is inspired by [16] where we extend constraints with priorities:

Definition 2 (Constraints). *Let $\geq: 2^Q \times 2^Q$ be a transitive and reflexive partial relation on the powerset of the pointers to rules containing at least the subset relation. Moreover, let out be an input/output logic. We define:*

- *$maxfamily(Q, P)$ is the set of $\subseteq$-maximal subsets Q' of Q such that $out(Q', P) \cup P$ is consistent.*
- *$preffamily(Q, P, \geq)$ is the set of $\geq$-maximal elements of $maxfamily(Q, P)$.*
- *$outfamily(Q, P, \geq)$ is the output under the elements of preffamily, i.e., $\{out(Q', P) \mid Q' \in preffamily(Q, P, \geq)\}$.*
- *$P \to x \in out_{\cup}(Q, \geq)$ iff $x \in \cup outfamily(Q, P, \geq)$*
  $P \to x \in out_{\cap}(Q, \geq)$ iff $x \in \cap outfamily(Q, P, \geq)$

In case of contrary to duty obligations, the input represents something which is inalterably true, and an agent has to ask himself which rules (output) this input gives rise to: even if the input should have not come true, an agent has to "make the best out of the sad circumstances" [17].

Example 2. Let $MD(\{a, b, c\}) = \{a = (\top \to m), b = (p \to n), c = (o \to \neg m)\}$, $\{b, c\} > \{a, b\} > \{a, c\}$, where by $A > B$ we mean as usual $A \geq B$ and $B \not\geq A$. $maxfamily(Q, \{o\}) = \{\{a, b\}, \{b, c\}\}$, $preffamily(Q, \{o\}, \geq) = \{\{b, c\}\}$, $outfamily(Q, \{o\}, \geq) = \{\{\neg m\}\}$

The *maxfamily* includes the sets of applicable compatible pointers to rules together with all non applicable ones: e.g., the output of $\{a, c\}$ in the context $\{o\}$ is not consistent. Finally $\{a\}$ is not in *maxfamily* since it is not maximal, we can add the non applicable rule b. Then *preffamily* is the preferred set $\{b, c\}$ according to the ordering on set of rules above. The set *outfamily* is composed by the consequences of applying the rules $\{b, c\}$ which are applicable in o (c): $\neg m$.

Due to space limitations we have to be brief on details with respect to input/output logics, see [14, 15] for the semantics of input/output logics, further details on its proof theory, its possible translation to modal logic, alternative constraints, and examples.

4   Constitutive Norms vs Regulative Norms

Why are constitutive norms needed in a normative system? In [6], we argue that, first, regulative norms are not categorical, but conditional: they specify all their applicability conditions. In case of complex and rapidly evolving systems new situations arise which should be considered in the conditions of the norms. Thus, new regulative norms must be introduced or existing ones revised each time the applicability conditions must be extended to include new cases. In order to avoid changing existing norms or adding new ones, it would be more economic that regulative norms could factor out particular cases and refer, instead, to more abstract concepts only. Hence, the normative system should include some mechanism to introduce new institutional categories of abstract entities for classifying possible states of affairs. Norms could refer to this institutional classification of reality rather than to the commonsense classification: changes to the conditions of the norms would be reduced to changes to the institutional classification of reality. Second, the dynamics of the social order which the normative system aims to achieve is due to the evolution of the normative system over time, which introduces new norms, abrogates outdated ones, and, as just noticed, changes its institutional classification of reality. So the normative system must specify how the normative system itself can be changed by introducing new regulative norms and new institutional categories, and specify by whom the changes can be done. This second aspect has been addressed in [7].

In this paper we discuss how constitutive norms, even if they can be replaced by regulative norms, allow to create a level of abstraction to which regulative norms can refer to, making to less sensitive to the changes in the legal system. The cons of introducing constitutive norms is that new rules are necessary, so that a trade-off must be found between the need of abstraction and the complexity of the normative system.

As a running example, consider a society where the fact that a field has been fenced by an agent counts as the fact that the field is property of that agent. In our model this relation is expressed as a belief attributed to the normative system. The fence is a physical "brute" fact, while the fact that it is a property of someone is only an institutional fact attributed to the beliefs of the normative system.

Assume now that the normative system has as goals that if a field is fenced, no one enters it and that if a fenced field is entered, this action is considered as a violation and the violation is sanctioned. These goals form an obligation not to trespass a fenced field. However, the same legal system could have been designed in a different way using the constitutive norm above: a fenced field counts as property. The constitutive norm introduces the legal category of property which an obligation not to trespass a property can refer to: it is obligatory not to trespass property. The two legal systems are equivalent in the sense that in the same situation, the same violations hold; on the other hand, they are different since the latter introduce a legal classification of reality; thus, the obligation has as condition the institutional fact that the field is a property: the field being a property is an institutional fact believed by the normative system, while entering the field is a brute fact.

Analogously, in the purely regulative legal system, a permission to enter a fenced field if it is close to a river could be added. This permission is an exception to the obligation not to trespass fenced fields. In the second legal system, the same purpose can be reached by adding a constitutive norm which states that a field close to the river, albeit fenced, is not a property. Note that this is different from saying that a field on the river is a property that can be trespassed, a fact which is expressed by a permission to enter a property close to the river.

The possibility that institutional facts appear as conditions in the goals of the normative system or as goals themselves explains the following puzzling assertion of Searle [18]: "constitutive rules constitute (and also regulate) an activity the existence of which is logically dependent on the rules" (p.34). How can constitutive rules *regulate* an activity, if this is the role played by regulative rules? E.g., Hindriks [19] argues that constitutive rules consist of also regulative ones.

In our model constitutive norms regulate a social activity since they create institutional facts that are conditions or objects of regulative norms. In our metaphorical mapping regulative norms are goals, and goals base their applicability in a certain situation on the beliefs of the agent: if the beliefs change, the goals which the agent pursues change too. Analogously, the institutional facts which are the consequences of constitutive rules determine what is obligatory, since the institutional facts determine which regulative rules are applicable. In the previous example, being a property indirectly regulates the behavior of agents, since entering a field is a violation only if it is a property; if a field is not a property, the goal of considering trespassing a violation does not apply.

Searle [18] interprets the creation institutional facts also in terms of what he calls "status functions": "the form of the assignment of the new status function can be represented by the formula 'X counts as Y in C'. This formula gives us a powerful tool for understanding the form of the creation of the institutional fact, because the form of the collective intentionality is to impose that status and its function, specified by the Y term, on some phenomenon named by the X term", (p.46).

Where "the ascription of function ascribes *the use to which we intentionally put these objects*", (p.20). Functions are usually defined in relation to goals. In our model, this teleological aspect of the notion of function depends on the fact that institutional facts make conditional goals relevant as they appear in the conditions of regulative norms or as goals themselves. The aim of fencing a field is to prevent trespassing: the obligation defines the function of property, since it is defined in terms of goals of the normative system. Hence, Searle's assertion that "the institutions [...] are systems of such constitutive rules" is partial: institutions are systems where constitutive (i.e., beliefs) and regulative (i.e., goals) rules interacts. In our model, they interplay in the same way as goals and beliefs do in agents.

From a knowledge representation point of view, constitutive norms behave as *data abstraction* in programming languages: types are gathered in new abstract data types; new procedures are defined on the abstract data types to manipulate them. So it is possible to change the implementation of the abstract data type without modifying the programs using those procedures. In our case, we have that regulative norms can be defined on abstract institutional facts: it is possible to change the constitutive norms defining the institutional facts without modifying the regulative norms which refer to those institutional facts. This analogy supports also our decision not to require identity as a property of counts-as. Data abstraction allows to hide the details concerning the implementation of the data type. Analogously, if the institutional facts are abstractions of the reality, they should hide the details consisting in the brute facts.

5   The Formal Model

The definition of the agents is inspired by the rule based BOID architecture [20], though in our theory, and in contrast to the BOID architecture, obligations are not taken as primitive concepts. Beliefs, desires and goals are represented by conditional rules rather then in a modal framework. We use in our model only goals rather than intentions since we consider only on decision step instead of having plans for the future moves.

We assume that the base language contains boolean variables and logical connectives. The variables are either *decision variables* of an agent, which represent the agent's actions and whose truth value is directly determined by it, or *parameters*, which describe both the state of the world and *institutional facts*, and whose truth value can only be determined indirectly. Our terminology is borrowed from Lang *et al.* [21].

Given the same set of mental attitudes, agents reason and act differently: when facing a conflict among their motivations and beliefs, different agents prefer to fulfill different goals and desires. We express these agent characteristics by a priority relation on the mental attitudes which encode, as detailed in [20], how the agent resolves its conflicts. The priority relation is defined on the powerset of the mental attitudes such that a wide range of characteristics can be described, including social agents that take the desires or goals of other agents into account. The priority relation contains at least the subset-relation which expresses a kind of independence among the motivations.

Definition 3 (Agent set). *An agent set is a tuple* $\langle A, X, B, D, G, AD, \geq \rangle$, *where:*

- *the agents A, propositional variables X, agent beliefs B, desires D and goals G are five finite disjoint sets.*
- *B, D, G are sets of pointers to rules. We write $M = D \cup G$ for the motivations defined as the union of the desires and goals.*
- *an agent description $AD : A \rightarrow 2^{X \cup B \cup M}$ is a total function that maps each agent to sets of variables (its decision variables), beliefs, desires and goals, but that does not necessarily assign each variable to at least one agent. For each agent $b \in A$, we write X_b for $X \cap AD(b)$, and B_b for $B \cap AD(b)$, D_b for $D \cap AD(b)$, etc. We write parameters $P = X \setminus \cup_{b \in A} X_b$.*
- *a priority relation $\geq : A \rightarrow 2^{M \cup B} \times 2^{M \cup B}$ is a function from agents to a transitive and reflexive partial relation on the powerset of the motivations containing at least the subset relation. We write $\geq_b$ for $\geq (b)$.*
  Since goals have priority over desires we have that given $S, S' \subseteq M$, for all $a \in A$, $S >_a S'$ if $S \setminus S' \subseteq G$ and $S' \setminus S \subseteq D$.

Example 3. $A = \{a\}$, $X_a = \{trespass\}$, $P = \{s, fenced\}$, $D_a = \{d_1, d_2\}$, $\geq_a = \{d_2\} \geq \{d_1\}$. There is a single agent, agent a, who can trespass a field. Moreover, it can be sanctioned and the field can be fenced. It has two desires, one to trespass (d_1), another one not to be sanctioned (d_2). The second desire is more important.

In a multiagent system, beliefs, desires and goals are abstract concepts which are described by rules built from literals.

Definition 4 (Multiagent system). *A multiagent system $\langle A, X, B, D, G, AD, MD, \geq \rangle$ is a tuple, where $\langle A, X, B, D, G, AD, \geq \rangle$ is an agent set, and the mental description*

$MD : (B \cup M) \rightarrow Rul(X)$ is a total function from the sets of beliefs, desires and goals to the set of rules built from X. For a set of mental attitudes $S \subseteq B \cup M$, we write $MD(S) = \{MD(q) \mid q \in S\}$.

Example 4 (Continued). $MD(d_1) = \top \rightarrow trespass$, $MD(d_2) = \top \rightarrow \neg s$.

In the description of the normative system, we do not introduce norms explicitly, but we represent several concepts which are illustrated in the following sections. Institutional facts (I) represent legal abstract categories which depend on the beliefs of the normative system and have no direct counterpart in the world. $F = X \setminus I$ are what Searle calls "brute facts": physical facts like the actions of the agents and their effects. $V_a(x)$ represents the decision of agent **n** that recognizes x as a violation by agent a. The goal distribution $GD(\mathbf{a}) \subseteq G_\mathbf{n}$ represents the goals of agent n the agent a is responsible for.

Definition 5 (Normative system). *A normative multiagent system, written as NMAS, is a tuple* $\langle A, X, B, D, G, AD, MD, \geq, \mathbf{n}, I, V, GD \rangle$ *where the tuple* $\langle A, X, B, D, G, AD, MD, \geq \rangle$ *is a multiagent system, and*

- *the normative system* $\mathbf{n} \in A$ *is an agent.*
- *the institutional facts* $I \subseteq P$ *are a subset of the parameters.*
- *the norm description* $V : Lit(X) \times A \rightarrow X_\mathbf{n} \cup P$ *is a function from the literals and the agents to the decision variables of the normative system and the parameters. We write* $V_a(x)$ *for* $V(x, a)$.
- *the goal distribution* $GD : A \rightarrow 2^{G_\mathbf{n}}$ *is a function from the agents to the powerset of the goals of the normative system, such that if* $L \rightarrow l \in MD(GD(\mathbf{a}))$, *then* $l \in Lit(X_\mathbf{a} \cup P)$.

Agent n is a normative system who has the goal that fenced fields are not trespassed.

Example 5 (Continued). There is agent n, representing the normative system.
   $X_\mathbf{n} = \{s, V_a(trespass)\}$, $P = \{fenced\}$, $D_\mathbf{n} = G_\mathbf{n} = \{g_1\}$, $MD(g_1) = \{fenced \rightarrow \neg trespass\}$, $GD(\mathbf{a}) = \{g_1\}$.
   Agent n can sanction agent a, because s is no longer a parameter but a decision variable. $V_a(trespass)$ represents the fact that the normative system considers a violation the action of a trespassing the field. It has the goal that fenced fields are not trespassed, and it has distributed this goal to agent a.

In the following, we use an input/output logic out to define whether a desire or goal implies another one and to define the application of a set of belief rules to a set of literals; in both cases we use the out_3 operation since it has the desired logical property of not satisfying identity.

Regulative norms are conditional obligations with an associated sanction and conditional permissions. The definition of obligation contains several clauses. The first and central clause of our definition defines obligations of agents as goals of the normative system, following the 'your wish is my command' metaphor. It says that the obligation is implied by the desires of the normative system **n**, implied by the goals of agent **n**, and it has been distributed by agent **n** to the agent. The latter two steps are represented by $out(GD(\mathbf{a}), \geq_\mathbf{n})$.

The second and third clause can be read as "the absence of p is considered as a violation". The association of obligations with violations is inspired by Anderson's reduction of deontic logic to alethic logic [22]. The third clause says that the agent desires that there are no violations, which is stronger than that it does not desire violations, as would be expressed by $\top \to V_{\mathbf{a}}(\sim x) \notin out(D_{\mathbf{n}}, \geq_{\mathbf{n}})$.

The fourth and fifth clause relate violations to sanctions. The fourth clause says that the normative system is motivated not to count behavior as a violation and apply sanctions as long as their is no violation, because otherwise the norm would have no effect. Finally, for the same reason the last clause says that the agent does not like the sanction. The second and fourth clauses can be considered as instrumental norms [23] contributing to the achievement of the main goal of the norm.

Definition 6 (Obligation). *Let $NMAS = \langle A, X, B, D, G, AD, MD, \geq, \mathbf{n}, I, V, GD \rangle$ be a normative multiagent system. Agent $\mathbf{a} \in A$ is obliged to see to it that $x \in Lit(X_{\mathbf{a}} \cup P)$ with sanction $s \in Lit(X_{\mathbf{n}} \cup P)$ in context $Y \subseteq Lit(X)$ in $NMAS$, written as $NMAS \models O_{\mathbf{an}}(x, s | Y)$, if and only if:*

1. *$Y \to x \in out(D_{\mathbf{n}}, \geq_{\mathbf{n}}) \cap out(GD(\mathbf{a}), \geq_{\mathbf{n}})$: if Y then agent $\mathbf{n}$ desires and has as a goal that x, and this goal has been distributed to agent $\mathbf{a}$.*
2. *$Y \cup \{\sim x\} \to V_{\mathbf{a}}(\sim x) \in out(D_{\mathbf{n}}, \geq_{\mathbf{n}}) \cap out(G_{\mathbf{n}}, \geq_{\mathbf{n}})$: if Y and $\sim x$, then agent $\mathbf{n}$ has the goal and the desire $V_{\mathbf{a}}(\sim x)$: to recognize it as a violation by agent $\mathbf{a}$.*
3. *$\top \to \neg V_{\mathbf{a}}(\sim x) \in out(D_{\mathbf{n}}, \geq_{\mathbf{n}})$: agent $\mathbf{n}$ desires that there are no violations.*
4. *$Y \cup \{V_{\mathbf{a}}(\sim x)\} \to s \in out(D_{\mathbf{n}}, \geq_{\mathbf{n}}) \cap out(G_{\mathbf{n}}, \geq_{\mathbf{n}})$: if Y and agent $\mathbf{n}$ decides $V_{\mathbf{a}}(\sim x)$, then agent $\mathbf{n}$ desires and has as a goal that it sanctions agent $\mathbf{a}$.*
5. *$Y \to \sim s \in out(D_{\mathbf{n}}, \geq_{\mathbf{n}})$: if Y, then agent $\mathbf{n}$ desires not to sanction. This desire of the normative system expresses that it only sanctions in case of violation.*
6. *$Y \to \sim s \in out(D_{\mathbf{a}}, \geq_{\mathbf{a}})$: if Y, then agent $\mathbf{a}$ desires $\sim s$, which expresses that it does not like to be sanctioned.*

The rules in the definition of obligation are only motivations, and not beliefs, because a normative system may not recognize that a violation counts as such, or that it does not sanction it: it is up to its decision. Both the recognition of the violation and the application of the sanction are the result of autonomous decisions of the normative system that is modelled as an agent.

The beliefs, desires and goals of the normative agent - defining the obligations - are not private mental states of an agent. Rather they are collectively attributed by the agents of the normative system to the normative agent: they have a public character, and, thus, which are the obligations of the normative system is a public information.

Since conditions of obligations are sets of decision variables and parameters, institutional facts can be among them. In this way it is possible that regulative norms refer to institutional abstractions of the reality rather than to physical facts only.

Example 6 (Continued). Let: $\{g_1, g_2, g_4\} = G_{\mathbf{n}}, G_{\mathbf{n}} \cup \{g_3, g_5\} = D_{\mathbf{n}}, \{g_1\} = GD(\mathbf{a})$

$MD(g_2) = \{fenced, trespass\} \to V_{\mathbf{a}}(trespass)$ $MD(g_3) = \top \to \neg V_{\mathbf{a}}(trespass)$
$MD(g_4) = \{fenced, V_{\mathbf{a}}(trespass)\} \to s$ $MD(g_5) = fenced \to \sim s$
$NMAS \models O_{\mathbf{an}}(\neg trespass, s \mid fenced)$, since:

1. $fenced \rightarrow \neg trespass \in out(D_n, \geq_n) \cap out(GD(a), \geq_n)$
2. $\{fenced, trespass\} \rightarrow V_a(trespass) \in out(D_n, \geq_n) \cap out(G_n, \geq_n)$
3. $\top \rightarrow \neg V_a(trespass) \in out(D_n, \geq_n)$
4. $\{fenced, V_a(trespass)\} \rightarrow s \in out(D_n, \geq_n) \cap out(G_n, \geq_n)$
5. $fenced \rightarrow \sim s \in out(D_n, \geq_n)$
6. $fenced \rightarrow \sim s \in out(D_a, \geq_a)$

Permissions are defined as exceptions to obligations [16], and can be overridden by obligations in turn. A permission to do x is an exception to an obligation not to do x if agent n has the goal that x is not considered as a violation under some condition. The permission overrides the prohibition if the goal that something does not count as a violation ($Y \wedge x \rightarrow \neg V_a(x)$) has higher priority in the ordering $\geq_n$ on goal and desire rules with respect to the goal of a corresponding prohibition that x is considered as a violation ($Y' \wedge x \rightarrow V_a(x)$):

Definition 7 (Permission). *Agent* $a \in A$ *is permitted by agent* n *to see to it that* $x \in Lit(X_a \cup P)$ *under condition* $Y \subseteq Lit(X)$*, written as* $NMAS \models P_{an}(x \mid Y)$*, iff* $Y \cup \{x\} \rightarrow \neg V_a(x) \in out(G_n, \geq_n)$*: if* Y *and* x *then agent* n *wants that* x *is not considered a violation by agent* a.

Example 7 (Continued). Let $P = \{fenced, river\}$, $\{g_6\} > \{g_2\}$,
$MD(g_6) = \{fenced, river, trespass\} \rightarrow \sim V_a(trespass)$
Then $\{fenced, river, trespass\} \rightarrow \sim V_a(trespass) \in out(D_n, \geq_n) \cap out(G_n, \geq_n)$
Hence, $NMAS \models P_{an}(trespass \mid fenced \wedge river)$

Constitutive norms introduce new abstract categories of existing facts and entities, called institutional facts. We formalize the counts-as conditional as a belief rule of the normative system n. Since the condition x of the belief rule is a variable it can be an action of an agent, a brute fact or an institutional fact. So, the counts-as relation can be iteratively applied.

Definition 8 (Counts-as relation). *Let* $\langle A, X, B, D, G, AD, MD, \geq, n, I, V, GD \rangle$ *be a normative multiagent system NMAS. A literal* $x \in Lit(X)$ *counts-as* $y \in Lit(I)$ *in context* $C \subseteq Lit(X)$*, NMAS* $\models$ *counts-as*$_n(x, y \mid C)$*, iff* $C \cup \{x\} \rightarrow y \in out(B_n, \geq_n)$*: if agent* n *believes* C *and* x *then it believes* y.

Example 8. $P \setminus I = \{fenced\}$, $I = \{property\}$, $X_a = \{trespass\}$, $B'_n = \{b'_1\}$,
$MD(b'_1) = fenced \rightarrow property$

Consequently, $NMAS \models$ counts-as$_n(fenced, property \mid \top)$. This formalizes that for the normative system a fenced field counts as the fact that the field is a property of that agent. The presence of the fence is a physical "brute" fact, while being a property is an institutional fact. In situation $S = \{fenced\}$, given B'_n we have that the consequences of the constitutive norms are $out(B'_n, S, \geq_n) = \{property\}$

As shown in the example, the logic of constitutive norms does not satisfy identity: *fenced* is not a consequence, since it represents a brute fact and not an institutional fact. Constitutive norms, in contrast, provide a legal classification of reality in terms of institutional facts only.

The institutional facts can appear in the conditions of regulative norms as the following example shows.

Example 9 (Continued). A regulative norm which forbids trespassing can refer to the abstract concept of property rather than to fenced fields: $O_{an}(\neg trespass, s \mid property)$.
Let: $\{g_1', g_2', g_4'\} = G_n'$, $G_n' \cup \{g_3', g_5'\} = D_n'$, $\{g_1'\} = GD(a)$
$MD(g_1') = property \rightarrow \neg trespass$ $MD(g_2') = \{property, trespass\} \rightarrow V_a(trespass)$
$MD(g_3') = \top \rightarrow \neg V_a(trespass)$ $MD(g_4') = \{property, V_a(trespass)\} \rightarrow s$
$MD(g_5') = property \rightarrow \sim s$
Then:

1. $property \rightarrow \neg trespass \in out(D_n, \geq_n) \cap out(GD(a), \geq_n)$
2. $\{property, trespass\} \rightarrow V_a(trespass) \in out(D_n, \geq_n) \cap out(G_n, \geq_n)$
3. $\top \rightarrow \neg V_a(trespass) \in out(D_n, \geq_n)$
4. $\{property, V_a(trespass)\} \rightarrow s \in out(D_n, \geq_n) \cap out(G_n, \geq_n)$
5. $property \rightarrow \sim s \in out(D_n, \geq_n)$
6. $property \rightarrow \sim s \in out(D_a, \geq_a)$

As the system evolves, new cases can be added to the notion of property by means of new constitutive norms, without changing the regulative norms about property. E.g., if a field is inherited, then it is property of the heir: $inherit \rightarrow property \in MD(B_n)$.

Since counts-as rules are beliefs and the logic is non-monotonic due to the priority ordering on the beliefs, counts-as can be used to express exceptions to the classification thus mirroring the relation between obligations and permissions as exceptions [2].

6 The Trade-Off Between Constitutive and Regulative Norms

In this section, we extend our scenario described in Example 8-9 to design a legal system equivalent to the one of Example 6-7.

Example 10 (Continued). $B_n' = \{b_2'\}$, $\{b_2'\} > \{b_1'\}$,
$MD(b_2') = fenced \wedge river \rightarrow \neg property$.
$out(B_n' = \{b_1', b_2'\}, \geq_n) = \{\{fenced \wedge river \rightarrow \neg property\}\}$ since
$maxfamily(B_n', S = \{fenced, river\}) = \{\{b_1'\}, \{b_2'\}\}$,
$preffamily(B_n', S = \{fenced, river\}, \geq_n) = \{\{b_2'\}\}$,
$outfamily(B_n', S = \{fenced, river\}, \geq_n) = \{\{\neg property\}\}$

Thus, $NMAS \models counts\text{-}as_n(fenced, \neg property \mid river)$ and this belief overrides the former one behind $counts\text{-}as_n(fenced, property \mid \top)$. This formalizes that the normative system does not consider as a property a fenced field if it is close to a river.

We show how a system containing constitutive and regulative norms like in Example 8-10 can be interchanged with an equivalent system of regulative norms only like the one of Example 6-7. By equivalence we mean that in the same state of the world the same violations hold. Since it is possible to replace constitutive norms with regulative norms only, a trade-off can be found between adding constitutive norms and achieving a sufficient level of abstraction.

Even if input/output logic is an inference system on rules we cannot directly prove the equivalence on the rules defining regulative and constitutive norms since they refer to different sets of rules: goal rules and belief rules. We provide the equivalence in an indirect way by considering the combined output of the rules.

Given the operation *out*, we define a combined output relation: $output(Q, Z, S, \geq_n) = out(Z, out(Q, S, \geq_n) \cup S, \geq_n)$ where $Q \subseteq B_n$, $Z \subseteq M_n$ and $S \subset Lit(X \setminus I)$. The institutional facts are the result of the reasoning of the normative system, so they cannot be present in the initial state composed of brute facts.

Note that we reintroduce the brute facts S as the input of the output operation on the motivations Z since the output operation on beliefs does not satisfy identity. We need S since the conditions of regulative norms can refer to brute facts as well as to the institutional facts which are the consequences of the constitutive norms. In this way we distinguish between the legal classification of reality and the information concerning commonsense, among which the brute facts which are the input to constitutive norms. Even if we attribute belief rules to the normative system these must be distinguished from the belief rules of agents: these belief rules concern the relation between brute facts and constitute their commonsense view of the work. The normative system as agent, in contrast, does not contain any knowledge of this kind. The relevant commonsense inferences are performed by the real agents playing roles in the normative system.

In our examples we have: $output(B_n, G_n, S, \geq_n) = output(B'_n, G'_n, S, \geq_n)$ for any $S \in Lit(X \setminus I)$.

Sketch of proof. We consider only the cases where the conditions of the goals and beliefs are satisfied. First, the normative system made of regulative norms only:

$output(B_n, G_n, S = \{fenced, trespass\}, \geq_n) = out(G_n, out(B_n, S, \geq_n) \cup S, \geq_n) = \{\neg trespass, V_a(trespass), s\}$
  from g_1, g_2, g_4, where $out(B_n, S, \geq_n) = \emptyset$ since $B_n = \emptyset$.

In contrast:

$output(B_n, G_n, S = \{fenced, river, trespass\}, \geq_n) = out(G_n, out(B_n, S, \geq_n) \cup S, \geq_n) = \{\neg trespass, \neg V_a(trespass), \sim s\}$
  (from g_1, g_5, g_6) where again $out(B_n, S, \geq_n) = \emptyset$.

In case of the legal system of Example 8 made of both constitutive and regulative norms:

$output(B'_n, G'_n, S = \{fenced, trespass\}, \geq_n) = out(G'_n, out(B'_n, S, \geq_n) \cup S, \geq_n) = \{\neg trespass, V_a(trespass), s\}$
  (from g'_1, g'_2, g'_4) where $out(B'_n, S, \geq_n) = \{property\}$ (from b'_1).

In contrast:

$output(B'_n, G'_n, S = \{fenced, river, trespass\}, \geq_n) = out(G'_n, out(B'_n, S, \geq_n) \cup S, \geq_n) = \{\neg trespass, \neg V_a(trespass), \sim s\}$
  (from g'_1, g'_3, g'_5) where $out(B'_n, S, \geq_n) = \{\neg property\}$ (from b'_2).

In summary, the trade-off between constitutive and regulative rules has to take into considerations, first, how many regulative rules share the same conditions. The design of the system of norms can be simplified by introducing abstractions representing the overlapping conditions. Second how frequently the normative system is updated. In case of dynamic situations, the preferred design of the system introduces constitutive rules introducing institutional facts which are abstractions which hide the details concerning the brute facts. In this way, new cases can be dealt with without changing the regulative part of the system, but only revising what counts as an institutional fact.

7 Related Work

While the formalization of regulative norms, like obligations, prohibitions and permissions, is often based in deontic logic on modal operators representing what is obligatory, forbidden or permitted, the formalization of constitutive norms is rather different. An attempt to make the notion of constitutive norm more precise is Jones and Sergot [5]'s formalization of the counts-as relation. For Jones and Sergot, the counts-as relation expresses the fact that a state of affairs or an action of an agent "is a sufficient condition to guarantee that the institution creates some (usually normative) state of affairs". As Jones and Sergot suggest, this relation can be considered as "constraints of (operative in) [an] institution", and they express these constraints as conditionals embedded in a modal operator. Jones and Sergot formalize this introducing a conditional connective $\Rightarrow_s$ to express the "counts-as" connection holding in the context of an institution s. They characterise the logic for $\Rightarrow_s$ as a classical conditional logic plus the axioms:

$$((A \Rightarrow_s B) \wedge (A \Rightarrow_s C)) \supset (A \Rightarrow_s (B \wedge C))$$
$$((A \Rightarrow_s B) \wedge (C \Rightarrow_s B)) \supset ((A \vee C) \Rightarrow_s B)$$
$$((A \Rightarrow_s B) \wedge (B \Rightarrow_s C)) \supset (A \Rightarrow_s C)$$

In addition, Jones and Sergot's analysis is integrated by introducing the normal KD modality D_s such that $D_s A$ means that A is "recognised by the institution s". Accordingly, it is adopted the schema: $(A \Rightarrow_s B) \supset D_s(A \supset B)$.

The limitation of this approach, according to Gelati *et al.* [24], is that the consequences of counts-as connections follow non-defeasibly (via the closure of the logic for modality D_s under logical implication), whereas defeasibility seems a key feature of such connections. The classical example is that in an auction if a person raises one hand, this may count as making a bid. However, this does not hold if he raises his hand and scratches his own head.

Finally, the adoption of the transitivity for their logic is criticized by Artosi *et al.* [3]. Artosi *et al.* [3]'s characterisation of the counts-as adopts a different perspective. Rather than introducing a logic for the counts-as connection, and then linking it with a D_s logic, they use one conditional operator $\Rightarrow$ to express any defeasible normative connections in any institutions. They use the same D_s operator as in [5] but they apply it to the components of normative links, to relativise them to a particular institution. Any institution can only state what normative situation holds for itself, given certain conditions, but according to a general type of conditionality. On the basis of $\Rightarrow$ they define a relativised $\Rightarrow_s$ operator: $(A \Rightarrow_s B) =_{def} (A \Rightarrow D_s B) \wedge (D_s A \Rightarrow D_s B)$

The connective $\Rightarrow$ is characterised by reflexivity and cumulative transitivity, whose combination does not prevent defeasibility. The system is completed by introducing a restricted version of the detachment of the consequent. To avoid losing non-monotonicity, Artosi *et al.* [3] do not accept the strengthening of antecedent property (SI in our input/output logic), thus making their logic weaker.

In contrast, in our model we accept the strengthening of antecedent (SI) rule and the cumulative transitivity (CT). We do not accept instead identity (Id). First of all, the adoption also of Id would make the system accepting also full transitivity. Non-monotonicity is achieved via the constraint mechanism which uses also a priority ordering on the mental attitudes. Secondly, we do not accept Id because we want to keep separate brute facts and institutional facts "whose nature - as also Artosi *et al.* [3] accept - is conceptually distinct from that of the empirical facts".

Our position is congruent also with Castelfranchi and Tummolini [25] who argue that counts-as rules regulate a cognitive activity, *viz.* the proper application of a concept:

> A constitutive rule describes, albeit very abstractly, a recognition process. [...] The application of a concept in fact can be represented in form of a rule that associates a specific set of stimuli ("something such and such") X with a linguistic label Y.

Since the stimuli and the linguistic label Y are ontologically heterogeneous, the "counts-as" relation cannot be reflexive.

Grossi and colleagues [26, 27] develop a notion of counts-as as a contextual classification in a modal logic setting, where for the classification aspect they use either description logic [26] or plain propositional logic [27]. They end up with a very strong logic for counts-as, satisfying rules not satisfied by Jones and Sergot's logic or the logic proposed in this paper, such as the identity rule (x counts-as x). They argue that the new rules are explained by their particular concept of counts-as as a contextual classification.

8   Conclusions

In this paper we discuss the design of legal systems composed of constitutive and regulative norms. We model legal systems as normative multiagent systems where the normative system is modelled as an agent using the agent metaphor: constitutive norms are defined by the beliefs of the normative system and the regulative norms by its goals. The characteristic of the counts-as relation is that it is not reflexive. The trade-off problem between constitutive and regulative norms can be handled by as the trade-off between beliefs and goals of the normative system. We show that constitutive norms, even if they can be replaced by regulative norms, allow to create a level of abstraction to which regulative norms can refer to, making it less sensitive to the changes in the legal system.

In [6] we extend this framework to model the problem of how the normative system itself specifies who can change the normative system. This specification is made by means of constitutive norms describe what facts count as the creation of new regulative and constitutive norms in the normative system. This work is at the basis of the definition of contracts we make in [7]. Future work is, for example, elaborating the notion of context to study which properties hold for it, and introducing hierarchies of normative systems composed of both constitutive norms and regulative norms, as we do for obligations and permissions in [16]. Moreover in [8] we discuss global policies about local policies in secure knowledge management. However, it has still to be studied global policies about constitutive rules.

References

1. Jones, A., Carmo, J.: Deontic logic and contrary-to-duties. In Gabbay, D., Guenthner, F., eds.: Handbook of Philosophical Logic. Kluwer (2001) 203–279
2. Boella, G., van der Torre, L.: Permissions and obligations in hierarchical normative systems. In: Procs. of ICAIL'03, New York (NJ), ACM Press (2003) 109–118

3. Artosi, A., Rotolo, A., Vida, S.: On the logical nature of count-as conditionals. In: Procs. of LEA 2004 Workshop. (2004)

4. Grossi, D., Dignum, F., Meyer, J.J.: Contextual taxonomies. In: LNCS n. 3487: Procs. of CLIMA'04 Workshop, Berlin, Springer Verlag (2004) 33–51

5. Jones, A., Sergot, M.: A formal characterisation of institutionalised power. Journal of IGPL **3** (1996) 427–443

6. Boella, G., van der Torre, L.: Regulative and constitutive norms in normative multiagent systems. In: Procs. of 10th International Conference on the Principles of Knowledge Representation and Reasoning KR'04, Menlo Park (CA), AAAI Press (2004) 255–265

7. Boella, G., van der Torre, L.: A game theoretic approach to contracts in multiagent systems. IEEE Transactions on Systems, Man and Cybernetics - Part C **36(1)** (2006)

8. Boella, G., van der Torre, L.: Security policies for sharing knowledge in virtual communities. IEEE Transactions on Systems, Man and Cybernetics - Part A (2006)

9. Gmytrasiewicz, P.J., Durfee, E.H.: Formalization of recursive modeling. In: Procs. of IC-MAS'95, Cambridge (MA), AAAI/MIT Press (1995) 125–132

10. Boella, G., van der Torre, L.: From the theory of mind to the construction of social reality. In: Procs. of CogSci'05, Mahwah (NJ), Lawrence Erlbaum (2005) 298–303

11. Castelfranchi, C.: Engineering social order. In: LNCS n.1972: Procs. of ESAW'00, Berlin, Springer Verlag (2000) 1–18

12. Searle, J.: Speech Acts: an Essay in the Philosophy of Language. Cambridge University Press, Cambridge (UK) (1969)

13. Boella, G., van der Torre, L.: Obligations as social constructs. In: LNAI n. 2829: AI*IA 2003 - Advances in Artificial Intelligence, Berlin, Springer Verlag (2003) 27–38

14. Makinson, D., van der Torre, L.: Input-output logics. Journal of Philosophical Logic **29** (2000) 383–408

15. Makinson, D., van der Torre, L.: Constraints for input-output logics. Journal of Philosophical Logic **30(2)** (2001) 155–185

16. Boella, G., van der Torre, L.: Rational norm creation: Attributing mental attitudes to normative systems, part 2. In: Procs. of ICAIL'03, New York (NJ), ACM Press (2003) 81–82

17. Hansson, B.: An analysis of some deontic logics. Noûs **3** (1969) 373–398

18. Searle, J.: The Construction of Social Reality. The Free Press, New York (1995)

19. Hindriks, F.: The constitutive rule revisited. In: Procs. of 3rd Conference on Collective Intentionality, Rotterdam (2002)

20. Broersen, J., Dastani, M., Hulstijn, J., van der Torre, L.: Goal generation in the BOID architecture. Cognitive Science Quarterly **2(3-4)** (2002) 428–447

21. Lang, J., van der Torre, L., Weydert, E.: Utilitarian desires. Autonomous Agents and Multi-agent Systems **5(3)** (2002) 329–363

22. Anderson, A.: The logic of norms. Logic et analyse **2** (1958)

23. Hart, H.: The Concept of Law. Clarendon Press, Oxford (1961)

24. Gelati, J., Governatori, G., Rotolo, N., Sartor, G.: Declarative power, representation, and mandate. A formal analysis. In: Procs. of JURIX 02, Amsterdam, IOS press (2002) 41–52

25. Castelfranchi, C., Tummolini, L.: The cognitive and behavioral mediation of institutions: Towards an account of institutional actions. In: Procs. of 4th Conference on Collective Intentionality. (2004)

26. Grossi, D., Dignum, F., Meyer, J.: Contextual terminologies. In this volume.

27. Grossi, D., Meyer, J., Dignum, F.: Modal logic investigations in the modal logic investigations in the semantics of counts semantics of counts-as as. In: Procs. of ICAIL'05, New York (NJ), ACM Press (2005) 1–9

Combining Answer Sets of Nonmonotonic Logic Programs

Chiaki Sakama[1] and Katsumi Inoue[2]

[1] Department of Computer and Communication Sciences,
Wakayama University, Sakaedani, Wakayama 640-8510, Japan
sakama@sys.wakayama-u.ac.jp
[2] National Institute of Informatics,
2-1-2 Hitotsubashi, Chiyoda-ku, Tokyo 101-8430, Japan
ki@nii.ac.jp

Abstract. This paper studies compositional semantics of nonmonotonic logic programs. We suppose the answer set semantics of extended disjunctive programs and consider the following problem. Given two programs P_1 and P_2, which have the sets of answer sets $\mathcal{AS}(P_1)$ and $\mathcal{AS}(P_2)$, respectively; find a program Q which has answer sets as minimal sets $S \cup T$ for S from $\mathcal{AS}(P_1)$ and T from $\mathcal{AS}(P_2)$. The program Q combines answer sets of P_1 and P_2, and provides a compositional semantics of two programs. Such program composition has application to coordinating knowledge bases in multi-agent environments. We provide methods for computing program composition and discuss their properties.

1 Introduction

Combining knowledge of different information sources is a central topic in multi-agent systems. In those environments, different agents generally have different knowledge and belief, then coordination among agents is necessary to form acceptable agreements. In computational logic, knowledge and belief of an agent are represented by a set of formulas. Combining multiple knowledge bases is then formulated as the problem of composing different theories. In multi-agent environments, individual agents are supposed to have incomplete information. Since theories including incomplete information are *nonmonotonic*, it is important and meaningful to develop a framework of composing nonmonotonic theories.

Suppose a multi-agent system in which each agent has a knowledge base written in a common logic programming language. When two programs do not contradict each other, they are combined into one by taking the union of programs. The resulting program is the collection of knowledge of two agents, and extends the original program of each agent with additional information from the other one. In nonmonotonic logic programs, however, simple merging does not always reflect the meaning of individual programs. To see the problem, consider the following scenario: there is a trouble in a system which consists of three components c_1, c_2, and c_3. After some diagnoses, an expert E_1 concludes that the

F. Toni and P. Torroni (Eds.): CLIMA VI, LNAI 3900, pp. 320–339, 2006.

trouble would be caused by either c_1 or c_2. On the other hand, another expert E_2 concludes that the trouble would be caused by either c_2 or c_3. E_1 (resp. E_2) has no knowledge on the component c_3 (resp. c_1). Two experts' diagnoses are then encoded as the following logic programs:

$$E_1 : \quad c_1 \,;\, c_2 \leftarrow,$$
$$E_2 : \quad c_2 \,;\, c_3 \leftarrow,$$

where ; represents disjunction. By merging two programs, the program $E_1 \cup E_2$ has two *answer sets* $\{c_2\}$ and $\{c_1, c_3\}$. The first one is the common minimal model between two experts, while the second one is produced as a result of merging programs. Two solutions thus have different grounds and would be acceptable to each expert. The story goes on: E_1 considers that the possible cause is either c_1 or c_2, but he knows that c_1 is older and more likely to disorder. Similarly, E_2 resolves the possible cause into either c_2 or c_3, but she empirically knows that c_2 is fragile and more likely to cause the trouble. Two experts then modify their diagnoses as

$$E_1' : \quad c_1 \leftarrow not\, c_2,$$
$$c_2 \leftarrow \neg\, c_1,$$
$$E_2' : \quad c_2 \leftarrow not\, c_3,$$
$$c_3 \leftarrow \neg\, c_2,$$

where *not* represents *negation as failure*. After the modification, E_1' is read as: c_1 is considered a cause if there is no evidence of c_2, and c_2 will not become a cause unless c_1 is explicitly proved to be false. E_2' is read in a similar way. Merging two programs, however, $E_1' \cup E_2'$ has the single answer set $\{c_2\}$, which reflects the result of diagnosis by E_2' but does not reflect E_1'. When two experts are equally reliable, the result might be unsatisfactory. In fact, E_2' puts weight on c_2 relative to c_3 and E_1' puts weight on c_1 relative to c_2. After integrating these diagnoses, there is no reason to conclude c_2 as the consensus of two experts. The problem is explained as follows: c_1 in E_1' and c_2 in E_2' are both *default* consequences derived from incomplete information in each program. However, simple merging has the effect of *preferring* c_2 to c_1 as the former is included in a relatively lower stratum than the latter. In logic programming consequences derived from a lower stratum are preferred in a single program, but the principle is not necessarily applied to the case of combining different programs. As observed in the above example, the local preference in E_1' or E_2' does not necessarily imply the global preference in $E_1' \cup E_2'$.

Thus, composition of nonmonotonic theories is not achieved by simply merging them. The problem is then how to build a compositional semantics of nonmonotonic theories. In this paper, we consider composition of *extended disjunctive programs* under the *answer set semantics* [16]. An answer set is a set of literals which corresponds to a belief set being built by a rational reasoner on the basis of a program [3]. A program may have multiple answer sets, and different agents have different collections of answer sets in general. We then capture composition of two programs as the problem of building a new program which combines answer sets of the original programs. Formally, the problems considered in this paper are described as follows:

Given: two programs P_1 and P_2;

Find: a program Q satisfying $\mathcal{AS}(Q) = min(\mathcal{AS}(P_1) \uplus \mathcal{AS}(P_2))$ where $\mathcal{AS}(P)$ represents the set of answer sets of a program P and $\mathcal{AS}(P_1) \uplus \mathcal{AS}(P_2) = \{S \cup T \mid S \in \mathcal{AS}(P_1) \text{ and } T \in \mathcal{AS}(P_2)\}$,

where $min(X) = \{Y \in X \mid \neg\exists Z \in X \text{ s.t. } Z \subset Y\}$. The program Q satisfying the above condition is called a *composition* of P_1 and P_2. The result of composition combines answer sets of two programs, which has the effect of amalgamating the original belief of each agent. We develop methods for constructing a program having the compositional semantics. Finally, we apply the theory to a logical formulation of multi-agent coordination.

The rest of this paper is organized as follows. Section 2 introduces basic notions used in this paper. Section 3 presents compositional semantics and its technical properties. Section 4 provides methods for building programs which reflect compositional semantics. Section 5 addresses permissible composition for multi-agent coordination. Section 6 discusses related issues and Section 7 summarizes the paper.

2   Preliminaries

In this paper, we suppose an agent that has a knowledge base written in logic programming.

A *program* considered in this paper is an *extended disjunctive program* (EDP) which is a set of *rules* of the form:

$$L_1 ; \cdots ; L_l \leftarrow L_{l+1}, \ldots, L_m, \, not \, L_{m+1}, \ldots, \, not \, L_n \quad (n \geq m \geq l \geq 0)$$

where each L_i is a positive/negative literal, i.e., A or $\neg A$ for an atom A, and *not* is *negation as failure* (NAF). *not* L is called an *NAF-literal*. The symbol ";" represents disjunction. The left-hand side of the rule is the *head*, and the right-hand side is the *body*. For each rule r of the above form, $head(r)$, $body^+(r)$ and $body^-(r)$ denote the sets of literals $\{L_1, \ldots, L_l\}$, $\{L_{l+1}, \ldots, L_m\}$, and $\{L_{m+1}, \ldots, L_n\}$, respectively. Also, $not\_body^-(r)$ denotes the set of NAF-literals $\{not \, L_{m+1}, \ldots, not \, L_n\}$. A disjunction of literals and a conjunction of (NAF-)literals in a rule are identified with its corresponding sets of literals. A rule r is often written as $head(r) \leftarrow body^+(r), not\_body^-(r)$ or $head(r) \leftarrow body(r)$ where $body(r) = body^+(r) \cup not\_body^-(r)$. A rule r is *disjunctive* if $head(r)$ contains more than one literal. A rule r is an *integrity constraint* if $head(r) = \emptyset$; and r is a *fact* if $body(r) = \emptyset$. A program is an *extended logic program* (ELP) if it contains no disjunctive rule. A program is *NAF-free* if no rule contains NAF-literals. A program with variables is semantically identified with its ground instantiation, and we handle propositional and ground programs only.

The semantics of EDPs is given by the *answer set semantics* [16]. Let Lit be the set of all ground literals in the language of a program. A set $S(\subseteq Lit)$ *satisfies* a ground rule r if $body^+(r) \subseteq S$ and $body^-(r) \cap S = \emptyset$ imply $head(r) \cap S \neq \emptyset$. In particular, S satisfies a ground integrity constraint r with $head(r) = \emptyset$ if either $body^+(r) \not\subseteq S$ or $body^-(r) \cap S \neq \emptyset$. S satisfies a ground program P if S satisfies every rule in P. Let P be a ground NAF-free EDP. Then, a set $S(\subseteq Lit)$ is an *answer set* of P if S is a minimal set such that (i) S satisfies every rule from P; and (ii) if S contains a pair of complementary literals L and $\neg L$, $S = Lit$. Next, let P be any ground EDP and $S \subseteq Lit$. For every rule r in P, the rule $head(r) \cap S \leftarrow body^+(r)$ is included in the *reduct* ^SP if $body^+(r) \subseteq S$ and $body^-(r) \cap S = \emptyset$. Then, S is an *answer set* of P if S is an answer set of ^SP.

Remark. The definition of a reduct presented above is different from the original one in [16]. In [16], the rule $head(r) \leftarrow body^+(r)$ is included in the reduct P^S (called Gelfond-Lifschitz reduction) if $body^-(r) \cap S = \emptyset$. A similar but different definition of reduct is in [15], where the rule $head(r) \leftarrow body^+(r)$ is included in the reduct if $body^+(r) \subseteq S$ and $body^-(r) \cap S = \emptyset$. Thus, disjunctive heads remain unchanged in the definition of [15].

Our reduction imposes additional conditions, but it produces the same answer sets as Gelfond-Lifschitz reduction does.

Proposition 2.1. *For any EDP P, S is an answer set of ^SP iff S is an answer set of P^S.*

Proof. If S is an answer set of P^S, it is a minimal set satisfying every rule in P^S. For any rule r in $^SP \setminus P^S$, it holds $body(r) = body^+(r) \subseteq S$ and $(head(r)' \leftarrow body(r)) \in P^S$ with $head(r) = head(r)' \cap S$. As S satisfies P^S, $body(r) \subseteq S$ implies $head(r)' \cap S \neq \emptyset$. So, S satisfies ^SP. Assume that there is a minimal set $T \subset S$ satisfying every rule in ^SP. Any rule r in $P^S \setminus ^SP$ satisfies either (a) $body(r) \not\subseteq S$ or (b) $body(r) \subseteq S$, $(head(r) \leftarrow body(r)) \in P^S$ and $(head(r) \cap S \leftarrow body(r)) \in ^SP$. In case of (a), $body(r) \not\subseteq S$ implies $body(r) \not\subseteq T$. Then, T satisfies r. In case of (b), as T satisfies ^SP, $body(r) \subseteq T$ implies $T \cap (head(r) \cap S) \neq \emptyset$, thereby $T \cap head(r) \neq \emptyset$. Thus, in each case T satisfies every rule in P^S. This contradicts the fact that S is a minimal set satisfying P^S. Then, S is also a minimal set satisfying every rule in ^SP. Hence, S is an answer set of ^SP.

Conversely, if S is an answer set of ^SP, S is a minimal set satisfying every rule in ^SP. For any rule r in $P^S \setminus ^SP$, it holds either (a) $body(r) \not\subseteq S$ or (b) $body(r) \subseteq S$, $(head(r) \leftarrow body(r)) \in P^S$ and $(head(r) \cap S \leftarrow body(r)) \in ^SP$. As S satisfies ^SP, $body(r) \subseteq S$ implies $head(r) \cap S \neq \emptyset$. Thus, in each case S satisfies every rule r in P^S. Assume that there is a minimal set $T \subset S$ satisfying every rule in P^S. For any rule r in $^SP \setminus P^S$, it holds $body(r) \subseteq S$ and $(head(r)' \leftarrow body(r)) \in P^S$ with $head(r) = head(r)' \cap S$. If $body(r) \not\subseteq T$, T satisfies r. Else if $body(r) \subseteq T$, $head(r)' \cap T \neq \emptyset$. As $head(r)' \cap T = head(r)' \cap S \cap T$, it holds that $head(r)' \cap S \cap T = head(r) \cap T \neq \emptyset$. Hence, T satisfies $head(r) \leftarrow body(r)$ in ^SP. This contradicts the fact that S is a minimal set satisfying ^SP. Then, S is an answer set of ^SP. □

Example 2.1. Let P be the program:

$$p; q \leftarrow,$$
$$q \leftarrow p,$$
$$r \leftarrow not\ p.$$

For $S = \{q, r\}$, P^S becomes

$$p; q \leftarrow,$$
$$q \leftarrow p,$$
$$r \leftarrow,$$

while $^S P$ becomes

$$q \leftarrow,$$
$$r \leftarrow.$$

Each reduct produces the same answer set S. Note that $\{p, q\}$ does not become an answer set of P.

The new reduct $^S P$ has the effect of (i) reducing any rule in P that is irrelevant to constructing S, and (ii) eliminating any disjunct in the head of a rule that is not a consequence in S. For technical reasons, we use the reduct $^S P$ for computing answer sets of P.[1]

A program has none, one, or multiple answer sets in general. The set of all answer sets of P is written as $\mathcal{AS}(P)$. Every element in $\mathcal{AS}(P)$ is *minimal*, that is, $S \subseteq T$ implies $T \subseteq S$ for any S and T in $\mathcal{AS}(P)$. A program having a single answer set is called *categorical* [3]. Categorical programs include important classes of programs such as *definite programs*, *stratified programs*, and *call-consistent programs*. Every NAF-free ELP has at most one answer set. An answer set is *consistent* if it is not Lit. A program P is *consistent* if it has a consistent answer set; otherwise, P is *inconsistent*. An inconsistent program has either no answer set or the single answer set Lit.

Proposition 2.2. *If a program P is consistent, $^S P$ contains no integrity constraint for any $S \in \mathcal{AS}(P)$.*

Proof. By the definition, for any integrity constraint $r \in P$, $\leftarrow body^+(r)$ is included in $^S P$ if $body^+(r) \subseteq S$ and $body^-(r) \cap S = \emptyset$. In this case, however, S does not satisfy r, so that it is not an answer set of P. Contradiction.   □

A literal L is a consequence of *credulous reasoning* in a program P (written as $L \in crd(P)$) if L is included in some answer set of P. A literal L is a consequence of *skeptical reasoning* in P (written as $L \in skp(P)$) if L is included in every answer set of P. Clearly, $skp(P) \subseteq crd(P)$ for any consistent program P.

---

[1] We will address the effect of this new reduct in Section 4.

Example 2.2. Let P be the program:

$$p; q \leftarrow,$$
$$r \leftarrow p,$$
$$r \leftarrow q,$$

where $\mathcal{AS}(P) = \{\{p, r\}, \{q, r\}\}$. Then, $crd(P) = \{p, q, r\}$ and $skp(P) = \{r\}$.

3   Combining Answer Sets

In this section, we introduce a compositional semantics of programs. Throughout the paper, different programs are assumed to have the same underlying language with a fixed interpretation.

Definition 3.1. Let S and T be two sets of literals. Then, define

$$S \uplus T = \begin{cases} S \cup T, & \text{if } S \cup T \text{ is consistent}; \\ Lit, & \text{otherwise.} \end{cases}$$

For two collections $\mathcal{S}$ and $\mathcal{T}$ of sets, define

$$\mathcal{S} \uplus \mathcal{T} = \{ S \uplus T \mid S \in \mathcal{S} \text{ and } T \in \mathcal{T} \}.$$

In particular, $\mathcal{S} \uplus \mathcal{T} = \emptyset$ if $\mathcal{S} = \emptyset$ or $\mathcal{T} = \emptyset$.

Definition 3.2. Let P_1 and P_2 be two programs. A program Q is called a *composition* of P_1 and P_2 if it satisfies the condition

$$\mathcal{AS}(Q) = min(\mathcal{AS}(P_1) \uplus \mathcal{AS}(P_2))$$

where $min(X) = \{ Y \in X \mid \neg \exists Z \in X \text{ s.t. } Z \subset Y \}$.

The set $\mathcal{AS}(Q)$ is called the *compositional semantics* of P_1 and P_2. By the definition, the compositional semantics is defined as the collection of minimal sets which are obtained by combining answer sets of the original programs. Note that the operation $min(\cdot)$ has the effect of making every element in $\mathcal{AS}(Q)$ incomparable under set inclusion.

Example 3.1. Let $\mathcal{AS}(P_1) = \{\{p\}, \{q\}\}$ and $\mathcal{AS}(P_2) = \{\{p\}, \{r\}\}$. Then, the compositional semantics becomes $\mathcal{AS}(Q) = \{ \{p\}, \{q, r\} \}$.

In what follows, when we refer a program Q to a composition of P_1 and P_2, it means a program Q satisfying the condition of Definition 3.2.

When categorical programs are composed, the resulting program is also categorical.

Proposition 3.1. *If P_1 and P_2 are two categorical programs, a composition Q of P_1 and P_2 is categorical.*

Proof. Let $AS(P_1) = \{S\}$ and $AS(P_2) = \{T\}$. Then, the compositional semantics becomes $AS(Q) = \{S \cup T\}$ if $S \cup T$ is consistent; otherwise, $AS(Q) = \{Lit\}$. In each case, Q has the single answer set, thereby categorical.   □

The following properties directly hold by the definition.

Proposition 3.2. *Let P_1 and P_2 be programs, and Q a composition of P_1 and P_2. Then,*

1. $AS(P_1) = \{Lit\}$ *and* $AS(P_2) \neq \emptyset$ *imply* $AS(Q) = \{Lit\}$.
2. $AS(P_1) = \emptyset$ *or* $AS(P_2) = \emptyset$ *implies* $AS(Q) = \emptyset$.

As shown in Proposition 3.2, if one of two programs is inconsistent, the result of composition is rather trivial. We thus consider compositions of consistent programs hereafter.

Proposition 3.3. *Let P_1 and P_2 be two consistent programs, and Q a composition of P_1 and P_2. Then, for any $S \in AS(Q)$, there is $T \in AS(P_i)$ for $i = 1, 2$ such that $T \subseteq S$.*

Proof. If Q is consistent, for any $S \in AS(Q)$ there exists $T \in AS(P_1)$ and $T' \in AS(P_2)$ such that $S = T \cup T'$ and $T \cup T'$ is consistent. Then, $T \subseteq S$ and $T' \subseteq S$ hold. Else if Q is inconsistent, $AS(Q) = \{Lit\}$. Then, $T \subset Lit$ and $T' \subset Lit$ for any $T \in AS(P_1)$ and any $T' \in AS(P_2)$.   □

Proposition 3.3 asserts that every answer set in the compositional semantics extends some answer sets of the original programs. On the other hand, the original programs may have an answer set which does not have its extension in their compositional semantics.

Example 3.2. Let $AS(P_1) = \{\{p, q\}\}$ and $AS(P_2) = \{\{p\}, \{q, r\}\}$. The compositional semantics of P_1 and P_2 becomes $AS(Q) = \{\{p, q\}\}$ which extends $\{p, q\}$ of P_1 and $\{p\}$ of P_2, but does not extend $\{q, r\}$ of P_2.

In the above example, $\{p, q\}$ absorbs $\{p\}$ and remains as a result of composition. Consequently, the set $\{p, q, r\}$, which combines $\{p, q\}$ of P_1 and $\{q, r\}$ of P_2, becomes non-minimal and is excluded from the result of composition.

Such cases are formally stated as follows.

Definition 3.3. *Let P_1 and P_2 be two consistent programs, and Q a composition of P_1 and P_2. When $AS(Q) = AS(P_1)$, P_1 absorbs P_2.*

In Example 3.2, P_1 absorbs P_2. If one program absorbs another program, the compositional semantics coincides with one of the original programs. The next proposition characterizes situations in which absorption happens.

Proposition 3.4. *Let P_1 and P_2 be two consistent programs, and Q a composition of P_1 and P_2. Then, P_1 absorbs P_2 iff for any $S \in AS(P_1)$, there is $T \in AS(P_2)$ such that $T \subseteq S$.*

Proof. For any $S \in \mathcal{AS}(P_1)$, suppose that there is $T \in \mathcal{AS}(P_2)$ such that $T \subseteq S$. As $S \cup T = S$, $\mathcal{AS}(P_1) \subseteq \mathcal{AS}(Q)$. Suppose any $T' \in \mathcal{AS}(P_2)$ such that $T' \not\subseteq S$ for any $S \in \mathcal{AS}(P_1)$. Then, $S \subset S \cup T'$. Since $S \in \mathcal{AS}(Q)$, $S \cup T' \notin \mathcal{AS}(Q)$. Thus, $\mathcal{AS}(Q) \backslash \mathcal{AS}(P_1) = \emptyset$. Hence, $\mathcal{AS}(Q) = \mathcal{AS}(P_1)$. Conversely, if $\mathcal{AS}(Q) = \mathcal{AS}(P_1)$, for any $S \in \mathcal{AS}(P_1)$ there is $T \in \mathcal{AS}(P_2)$ such that $S = S \cup T$. Then, $T \subseteq S$. □

Skeptical/credulous inference in compositional semantics has the following properties.

Proposition 3.5. *Let P_1 and P_2 be two consistent programs, and Q a composition of P_1 and P_2. When Q is consistent, the following relations hold.*

1. $crd(Q) \subseteq crd(P_1) \cup crd(P_2)$.
2. $skp(Q) = skp(P_1) \cup skp(P_2)$.

Proof. (1) Any literal included in a consistent answer set $S \in \mathcal{AS}(Q)$ is either included in an answer set $T \in \mathcal{AS}(P_1)$ or included in an answer set $T' \in \mathcal{AS}(P_2)$. (2) If any literal L is included in every answer set S in $\mathcal{AS}(P_1)$ or included in every answer set T in $\mathcal{AS}(P_2)$, it is included in every $S \cup T$ in $\mathcal{AS}(Q)$. Conversely, if any literal L is included in every consistent answer set U in $\mathcal{AS}(Q)$, L is included in every minimal set $S \cup T$ for some $S \in \mathcal{AS}(P_1)$ and $T \in \mathcal{AS}(P_2)$. Suppose $L \in S$ and there is $S' \in \mathcal{AS}(P_1)$ such that $L \notin S'$. If there is $T' \in \mathcal{AS}(P_2)$ such that $L \notin T'$, then $L \notin S' \cup T'$ so there is $V \in \mathcal{AS}(Q)$ such that $L \notin V \subseteq S' \cup T'$. Contradiction. Hence, $L \in T$ for every $T \in \mathcal{AS}(P_2)$. □

Thus, if the compositional semantics is consistent, it combines skeptical consequences of P_1 and P_2, and any information included in an answer set of Q has its origin in an answer set of P_1 or P_2. The above relations do not hold when Q is inconsistent.

Example 3.3. Let $\mathcal{AS}(P_1) = \{\{p, a\}, \{p, b\}\}$ and $\mathcal{AS}(P_2) = \{\{\neg p, a\}, \{\neg p, b\}\}$ where $crd(P_1) = \{p, a, b\}$, $skp(P_1) = \{p\}$, $crd(P_2) = \{\neg p, a, b\}$, and $skp(P_2) = \{\neg p\}$. The compositional semantics of P_1 and P_2 becomes $\mathcal{AS}(Q) = \{Lit\}$ where $crd(Q) = skp(Q) = Lit$.

As observed in the above example, the result of composition may become inconsistent even if the original programs are consistent. When $\mathcal{AS}(Q)$ has no consistent answer set, we consider that program composition fails. A necessary and sufficient condition to have a successful program composition is as follows.

Proposition 3.6. *Let P_1 and P_2 be consistent programs, and Q a composition of P_1 and P_2. Then, Q is consistent iff there are $S \in \mathcal{AS}(P_1)$ and $T \in \mathcal{AS}(P_2)$ such that $S \cup T$ is consistent.*

Proof. Q is consistent iff there is a consistent set $S \cup T$ in $\mathcal{AS}(P_1) \uplus \mathcal{AS}(P_2)$ for $S \in \mathcal{AS}(P_1)$ and $T \in \mathcal{AS}(P_2)$. Hence, the result follows. □

In program composition, the problem of interest is the case where one program does not absorb the other and the result of composition is consistent. In the next section, we present methods for computing program composition.

4   Composing Programs

In this section, every program is supposed to have a finite number of answer sets. We first introduce an additional notation used in this section.

Definition 4.1. Let $P_1, \ldots, P_k$ be programs. Then, define

$$P_1 ; \cdots ; P_k =$$
$$\{\, head(r_1); \cdots ; head(r_k) \leftarrow body(r_1), \ldots, body(r_k) \mid r_i \in P_i \ (1 \le i \le k) \,\}.$$

Thus, $P_1 ; \cdots ; P_k$ is an EDP which is obtained by disjunctively combining any rule from P_i $(1 \le i \le k)$ in every possible way. When all programs are NAF-free, the following properties hold.

Proposition 4.1. Let $P_1, \ldots, P_k$ be NAF-free programs. Then, $\mathcal{AS}(P_1 ; \cdots ; P_k) = min(\mathcal{AS}(P_1) \cup \cdots \cup \mathcal{AS}(P_k))$.

Proof. Let $S \in min(\mathcal{AS}(P_1) \cup \cdots \cup \mathcal{AS}(P_k))$. Then, $S \in \mathcal{AS}(P_i)$ for some $1 \le i \le k$. So, for any $r_i \in P_i$, either $head(r_i) \cap S \neq \emptyset$ or $body(r_i) \not\subseteq S$ holds. Correspondingly, for any $R = head(r_1); \cdots ; head(r_k) \leftarrow body(r_1), \ldots, body(r_k)$ in $P_1 ; \cdots ; P_k$, either $head(R) \cap S \neq \emptyset$ or $body(R) \not\subseteq S$ holds. Hence, S satisfies every rule in $P_1 ; \cdots ; P_k$. Next, suppose that there is a minimal set $T \subset S$ which satisfies every rule in $P_1 ; \cdots ; P_k$. Then, for any rule R of the above form, either $head(R) \cap T \neq \emptyset$ or $body(R) \not\subseteq T$ holds. On the other hand, by $T \not\in min(\mathcal{AS}(P_1) \cup \cdots \cup \mathcal{AS}(P_k))$, T satisfies no P_i. Then, for any P_i, there is a rule $r_i \in P_i$ such that $head(r_i) \cap T = \emptyset$ and $body(r_i) \subseteq T$. However, every such rule is combined into a rule $R = head(r_1); \cdots ; head(r_k) \leftarrow body(r_1), \ldots, body(r_k)$ in $P_1 ; \cdots ; P_k$, and it holds that $head(R) \cap T = \emptyset$ and $body(R) \subseteq T$. Contradiction. Hence, S is a minimal set satisfying every rule in $P_1 ; \cdots ; P_k$, and $S \in \mathcal{AS}(P_1 ; \cdots ; P_k)$.

Conversely, let $S \in \mathcal{AS}(P_1 ; \cdots ; P_k)$. If S satisfies no P_i $(1 \le i \le k)$, every P_i contains a rule r_i such that $head(r_i) \cap S = \emptyset$ and $body(r_i) \subseteq S$. Every such rule is combined into $R = head(r_1); \cdots ; head(r_k) \leftarrow body(r_1), \ldots, body(r_k)$ in $P_1 ; \cdots ; P_k$, and it holds that $head(R) \cap S = \emptyset$ and $body(R) \subseteq S$. So S does not satisfy $P_1 ; \cdots ; P_k$. Contradiction. Hence, S satisfies some P_i $(1 \le i \le k)$. Next, suppose that there is a minimal set $T \subset S$ satisfying P_i. Then, for any $r_i \in P_i$, it holds that either $head(r_i) \cap T \neq \emptyset$ or $body(r_i) \not\subseteq T$. In this case, T satisfies every $head(r_1); \cdots ; head(r_k) \leftarrow body(r_1), \ldots, body(r_k)$ in $P_1 ; \cdots ; P_k$. This contradicts the fact that S is a minimal set satisfying $P_1 ; \cdots ; P_k$. Hence, $S \in \mathcal{AS}(P_i)$. Suppose that $S \not\in min(\mathcal{AS}(P_1) \cup \cdots \cup \mathcal{AS}(P_k))$. Then, there is $S' \in \mathcal{AS}(P_j)$ $(1 \le j \le k)$ such that $S' \subset S$ and $S' \in min(\mathcal{AS}(P_1) \cup \cdots \cup \mathcal{AS}(P_k))$. In this case, $S' \in \mathcal{AS}(P_1 ; \cdots ; P_k)$ by the above proof. But this cannot happen, since $S \in \mathcal{AS}(P_1 ; \cdots ; P_k)$. Hence, $S \in min(\mathcal{AS}(P_1) \cup \cdots \cup \mathcal{AS}(P_k))$.   □

Corollary 4.2. Let $P_1, \ldots, P_k$ be NAF-free programs. Then, $P_1 ; \cdots ; P_k$ is consistent iff some P_i $(1 \le i \le k)$ is consistent.

Proof. The result follows from Proposition 4.1.   □

Definition 4.2. Let P_1 and P_2 be two programs such that $\mathcal{AS}(P_1) = \{\, S_1, \dots, S_m \,\}$ and $\mathcal{AS}(P_2) = \{\, T_1, \dots, T_n \,\}$. Then, define

$$P_1 \odot P_2 = R(S_1, T_1)\,; \; \cdots \,; \; R(S_m, T_n)$$

where $R(S, T) = {}^S P_1 \cup {}^T P_2$ and $R(S_1, T_1), \dots, R(S_m, T_n)$ is any enumeration of the $R(S_i, T_j)$'s for $S_i \in \mathcal{AS}(P_1)$ $(i = 1, \dots, m)$ and $T_j \in \mathcal{AS}(P_2)$ $(j = 1, \dots, n)$. In particular, $R(S, T) = \emptyset$ when $\mathcal{AS}(P_i) = \emptyset$ for $i = 1$ or $i = 2$.

$R(S, T)$ merges every NAF-free rule which contributes to the construction of an answer set S of P_1 and T of P_2. Those rules are then disjunctively combined for any $S_i \in \mathcal{AS}(P_1)$ and for any $T_j \in \mathcal{AS}(P_2)$ in every possible way. By the definition, $P_1 \odot P_2$ is computed in time $O(|P_1| \times |P_2| \times |\mathcal{AS}(P_1)| \times |\mathcal{AS}(P_2)|)$, where $|P|$ represents the number of rules in P and $|\mathcal{AS}(P)|$ represents the number of answer sets of P. In particular, if P_1 and P_2 respectively have the single answer set $\mathcal{AS}(P_1) = \{S\}$ and $\mathcal{AS}(P_2) = \{T\}$, it becomes $P_1 \odot P_2 = {}^S P_1 \cup {}^T P_2$.

The operator $\odot$ has the following properties.

Proposition 4.3. *The operation $\odot$ is commutative and associative.*

Proof. The commutative law $P_1 \odot P_2 = P_2 \odot P_1$ is straightforward. To see the associative law, both $(P_1 \odot P_2) \odot P_3$ and $P_1 \odot (P_2 \odot P_3)$ consist of rules of the form: $head(r_1)\,; \; \cdots \,; \; head(r_k) \leftarrow body(r_1), \dots, body(r_k)$ for $r_i \in R(S, T, U)$ $(1 \leq i \leq k)$ where $R(S, T, U) = {}^S P_1 \cup {}^T P_2 \cup {}^U P_3$ for any $S \in \mathcal{AS}(P_1)$, $T \in \mathcal{AS}(P_2)$, and $U \in \mathcal{AS}(P_3)$. Hence, $(P_1 \odot P_2) \odot P_3 = P_1 \odot (P_2 \odot P_3)$. □

Proposition 4.4. *Let P_1 and P_2 be programs. Then,*

1. $\mathcal{AS}(P_1) = \{Lit\}$ *and* $\mathcal{AS}(P_2) \neq \emptyset$ *imply* $\mathcal{AS}(P_1 \odot P_2) = \{Lit\}$.
2. $\mathcal{AS}(P_1) = \emptyset$ *or* $\mathcal{AS}(P_2) = \emptyset$ *implies* $\mathcal{AS}(P_1 \odot P_2) = \emptyset$.

Proof. (1) When $\mathcal{AS}(P_1) = \{Lit\}$, it becomes $P_1 \odot P_2 = R(Lit, T_1)\,; \cdots; R(Lit, T_n)$ for $\mathcal{AS}(P_2) = \{T_1, \dots, T_n\}$. Here, every $R(Lit, T_i)$ $(1 \leq i \leq k)$ has the answer set Lit, so that the result follows by Proposition 4.1. (2) When $\mathcal{AS}(P_1) = \emptyset$, $R(S, T) = \emptyset$ for any $T \in \mathcal{AS}(P_2)$ by Definition 4.2. Then, $\mathcal{AS}(P_1 \odot P_2) = \emptyset$ by Proposition 4.1. □

The program $P_1 \odot P_2$ generally contains useless or redundant literals/rules, and the following program transformations are useful to simplify the program: (i) Delete a rule r from a program if $head(r) \cap body^+(r) \neq \emptyset$ (*elimination of tautologies*: TAUT); (ii) Delete a rule r from a program if there is another rule r' in the program such that $head(r') \subseteq head(r)$ and $body(r') \subseteq body(r)$ (*elimination of non-minimal rules*: NONMIN); (iii) A disjunction $(L; L)$ appearing in $head(r)$ is merged into L, and a conjunction (L, L) appearing in $body(r)$ is merged into L (*merging duplicated literals*: DUPL). These program transformations all preserve the answer sets of an EDP [5].

Example 4.1. Consider two programs:

$$P_1 : p \leftarrow not\, q,$$
$$q \leftarrow not\, p,$$
$$s \leftarrow p,$$
$$P_2 : p \leftarrow not\, r,$$
$$r \leftarrow not\, p,$$

where $\mathcal{AS}(P_1) = \{\{p, s\}, \{q\}\}$ and $\mathcal{AS}(P_2) = \{\{p\}, \{r\}\}$. There are four $R(S, T)$'s such that

$$R(\{p, s\}, \{p\}) :\quad p \leftarrow,\quad s \leftarrow p,$$
$$R(\{p, s\}, \{r\}) :\quad p \leftarrow,\quad s \leftarrow p,\quad r \leftarrow,$$
$$R(\{q\}, \{p\}) :\quad q \leftarrow,\quad p \leftarrow,$$
$$R(\{q\}, \{r\}) :\quad q \leftarrow,\quad r \leftarrow.$$

Then, $P_1 \odot P_2$ contains the following seven rules (after applying DUPL):

$$p\,;\, q \leftarrow, \tag{1}$$
$$p\,;\, r \leftarrow, \tag{2}$$
$$p\,;\, q\,;\, r \leftarrow, \tag{3}$$
$$q\,;\, s \leftarrow p, \tag{4}$$
$$q\,;\, r\,;\, s \leftarrow p, \tag{5}$$
$$p\,;\, q\,;\, s \leftarrow p, \tag{6}$$
$$p\,;\, r\,;\, s \leftarrow p. \tag{7}$$

Further, rules (3), (5), (6), and (7) are eliminated by NONMIN. Consequently, the simplified program becomes

$$p\,;\, q \leftarrow,$$
$$p\,;\, r \leftarrow,$$
$$q\,;\, s \leftarrow p.$$

In the resulting program, the first rule $p\,;\, q \leftarrow$ corresponds to the rules $p \leftarrow not\, q$ and $q \leftarrow not\, p$ in P_1. The second rule $p\,;\, r \leftarrow$ corresponds to the rules $p \leftarrow not\, r$ and $r \leftarrow not\, p$ in P_2. On the other hand, one might wonder the effect of q in the head of the third rule $q\,;\, s \leftarrow p$. Without q, however, the set $\{p, q\}$, which is obtained by combining $\{q\} \in \mathcal{AS}(P_1)$ and $\{p\} \in \mathcal{AS}(P_2)$, does not become an answer set of the resulting program.

Now we show that the operator $\odot$ computes a composition of P_1 and P_2.

Lemma 4.5. *Let P_1 and P_2 be two consistent programs, and $S \in \mathcal{AS}(P_1)$ and $T \in \mathcal{AS}(P_2)$. Then, $S \uplus T$ is an answer set of $^S P_1 \cup {}^T P_2$.*

Proof. As P_1 and P_2 is consistent, neither $^S P_1$ nor $^T P_2$ contains integrity constraints (Proposition 2.2). When the NAF-free program $^S P_1 \cup {^T P_2}$ is inconsistent, it has the answer set *Lit*. Suppose that $S \cup T$ is consistent. Since S satisfies every rule in $^S P_1$ and T satisfies every rule in $^T P_2$, $S \cup T$ satisfies $^S P_1 \cup {^T P_2}$. Contradiction. So $S \cup T$ is inconsistent. Then, $S \uplus T = S \cup T = Lit$, and the result holds. Next, consider the case that $^S P_1 \cup {^T P_2}$ is consistent. Then, S is a minimal set satisfying $^S P_1$ and T is a minimal set satisfying $^T P_2$. As (i) $body(r) \subseteq S$ and $head(r) \subseteq S$ for any $r \in {^S P_1}$, and (ii) $body(r') \subseteq T$ and $head(r') \subseteq T$ for any $r' \in {^T P_2}$, it holds that $S \cup T$ satisfies $^S P_1 \cup {^T P_2}$. Suppose that there is $T' \subset T$ such that $S \cup T'$ satisfies $^S P_1 \cup {^T P_2}$. For any $L \in T \setminus T'$, if $L \notin S$, T' satisfies $^T P_2$. But this cannot happen, since T is a minimal set satisfying $^T P_2$. Then, $L \in S$, thereby $S \cup T = S \cup T'$. Thus, $S \cup T$ is a minimal set satisfying $^S P_1 \cup {^T P_2}$. As $^S P_1 \cup {^T P_2}$ is NAF-free and consistent, $S \uplus T = S \cup T$ becomes an answer set of it.   □

It is worth noting that the above lemma does not hold if we use Gelfond-Lifschitz reduction P^S instead of $^S P$. This is because $P_1^S \cup P_2^T$ may derive literals which are not in $S \cup T$. This is the reason why we use a new reduct in this paper.

Theorem 4.6. *Let P_1 and P_2 be two consistent programs. Then, $\mathcal{AS}(P_1 \odot P_2) = min(\mathcal{AS}(P_1) \uplus \mathcal{AS}(P_2))$.*

Proof. Let $U \in min(\mathcal{AS}(P_1) \uplus \mathcal{AS}(P_2))$. (i) If $U = Lit$, $S \cup T$ is inconsistent for any $S \in \mathcal{AS}(P_1)$ and for any $T \in \mathcal{AS}(P_2)$ (Proposition 3.6). Then, $R(S, T)$ has the answer set *Lit* for any $S \in \mathcal{AS}(P_1)$ and for any $T \in \mathcal{AS}(P_2)$ (Lemma 4.5), so $\mathcal{AS}(P_1 \odot P_2) = \{Lit\}$ by Proposition 4.1. (ii) Else if $U \neq Lit$, there is $S \in \mathcal{AS}(P_1)$ and $T \in \mathcal{AS}(P_2)$ such that $U = S \cup T$ is consistent (Proposition 3.6). By Lemma 4.5, U is an answer set of $R(S, T)$. Then, U satisfies $P_1 \odot P_2$. Suppose that there is a minimal set $V \subset U$ which satisfies $P_1 \odot P_2$. In this case, V is a minimal set satisfying some $R(S', T')$ in $P_1 \odot P_2$ (Proposition 4.1). It then holds that $V = S' \cup T'$ for some $S' \in \mathcal{AS}(P_1)$ and $T' \in \mathcal{AS}(P_2)$ (by Lemma 4.5). Since $V \in \mathcal{AS}(P_1) \uplus \mathcal{AS}(P_2)$ and $V \subset U$, $U \notin min(\mathcal{AS}(P_1) \uplus \mathcal{AS}(P_2))$. Contradiction. Thus, U is a minimal set satisfying $P_1 \odot P_2$, so $U \in \mathcal{AS}(P_1 \odot P_2)$.

Conversely, let $U \in \mathcal{AS}(P_1 \odot P_2)$. (i) If $U = Lit$, $R(S, T)$ is inconsistent for any $S \in \mathcal{AS}(P_1)$ and for any $T \in \mathcal{AS}(P_2)$ (by Corollary 4.2). Then, $S \cup T$ is inconsistent for any $S \in \mathcal{AS}(P_1)$ and for any $T \in \mathcal{AS}(P_2)$ (Lemma 4.5), thereby $min(\mathcal{AS}(P_1) \uplus \mathcal{AS}(P_2)) = \{Lit\}$. (ii) Else if $U \neq Lit$, U is a consistent minimal set satisfying some $R(S, T)$ in $P_1 \odot P_2$ (Proposition 4.1). It then holds $U = S \cup T$ for some $S \in \mathcal{AS}(P_1)$ and $T \in \mathcal{AS}(P_2)$ (by Lemma 4.5). Thus, $U \in \mathcal{AS}(P_1) \uplus \mathcal{AS}(P_2)$. Suppose that there is a minimal set $V \subset U$ such that $V = S' \cup T'$ for some $S' \in \mathcal{AS}(P_1)$ and $T' \in \mathcal{AS}(P_2)$. In this case, $V \in min(\mathcal{AS}(P_1) \uplus \mathcal{AS}(P_2))$, and V becomes an answer set of $P_1 \odot P_2$ by the proof presented above. This contradicts the assumption of $U \in \mathcal{AS}(P_1 \odot P_2)$. Hence, $U \in min(\mathcal{AS}(P_1) \uplus \mathcal{AS}(P_2))$.   □

Corollary 4.7. *Let P_1 and P_2 be two categorical programs such that $\mathcal{AS}(P_1) = \{S\}$ and $\mathcal{AS}(P_2) = \{T\}$. Then, $\mathcal{AS}(P_1 \odot P_2) = \{S \cup T\}$.*

Proof. When P_1 and P_2 are consistent, the result follows by Theorem 4.6. Suppose that either P_1 or P_2 is inconsistent. Let $AS(P_1) = \{Lit\}$. Then, $^{Lit}P_1$ is inconsistent. By $P_1 \odot P_2 = {}^{Lit}P_1 \cup {}^TP_2$, $P_1 \odot P_2$ is also inconsistent. Moreover, $^{Lit}P_1 \cup {}^TP_2$ contains no integrity constraint (Proposition 2.2), so that it has the inconsistent answer set Lit. Hence, the result holds. □

Example 4.2. In Example 4.1, $AS(P_1 \odot P_2) = \{\{p, q\}, \{p, s\}, \{q, r\}\}$, which coincides with the result of composition.

Two programs P_1 and P_2 are *merged* by taking their union $P_1 \cup P_2$. Program composition and merging bring syntactically and semantically different results in general, but there are some relations for special cases.

Proposition 4.8. *For two NAF-free programs P_1 and P_2, if $P_1 \cup P_2$ is consistent, $P_1 \odot P_2$ is consistent.*

Proof. If $P_1 \cup P_2$ is consistent, there is $^SP_1$ for $S \in AS(P_1)$ and $^TP_2$ for $T \in AS(P_2)$ such that $^SP_1 \cup {}^TP_2$ is consistent. Then, $P_1 \odot P_2$ is consistent by Corollary 4.2. □

The converse of Proposition 4.8 does not hold in general.

Example 4.3. Let $P_1 = \{p \leftarrow\}$ and $P_2 = \{\neg p \leftarrow p\}$. Then, $P_1 \odot P_2 = \{p \leftarrow\}$, but $P_1 \cup P_2$ has the answer set Lit.

In the general case, there is no relation for the "easiness" of inconsistency arising between composition and merging.

Example 4.4. Let $P_1 = \{p \leftarrow not \neg p\}$ and $P_2 = \{\neg p \leftarrow not p\}$. Then, $P_1 \cup P_2$ is consistent, but $P_1 \odot P_2 = \{p \leftarrow \ , \ \neg p \leftarrow\}$ is inconsistent. On the other hand, let $P_3 = \{p \leftarrow not q, \ q \leftarrow not r\}$ and $P_4 = \{r \leftarrow not p\}$. Then, $P_3 \cup P_4$ is inconsistent, but $P_3 \odot P_4 = \{q \, ; r \leftarrow\}$ is consistent.

For extended logic programs, the following syntactical and semantical relations hold.

Proposition 4.9. *For two NAF-free ELPs P_1 and P_2, $P_1 \odot P_2 \subseteq P_1 \cup P_2$.*

Proof. Any NAF-free ELP has at most one answer set. If $AS(P_1) \neq \emptyset$ and $AS(P_2) \neq \emptyset$, let $AS(P_1) = \{S\}$ and $AS(P_2) = \{T\}$. Then, $P_1 \setminus {}^SP_1 = \{r \mid r \in P_1$ and $body(r) \not\subseteq S\}$, and $^SP_1 \setminus P_1 = \emptyset$. This is also the case for P_2. Since $P_1 \odot P_2 = {}^SP_1 \cup {}^TP_2$, the result follows. Else if $AS(P_1) = \emptyset$ or $AS(P_2) = \emptyset$, $P_1 \odot P_2 \subseteq {}^SP_1 \cup {}^TP_2$. Then, the result also holds. □

Proposition 4.10. *Let P_1 and P_2 be two consistent NAF-free ELPs. If $AS(P_1 \cup P_2) \neq \emptyset$, then $U \subseteq V$ holds for the answer set U of $P_1 \odot P_2$ and the answer set V of $P_1 \cup P_2$.*

Proof. Let $AS(P_1) = \{S\}$ and $AS(P_2) = \{T\}$. Then, $AS(P_1 \odot P_2) = \{S \cup T\}$. If $P_1 \cup P_2$ is inconsistent, $AS(P_1 \cup P_2) = \{Lit\}$. So, $S \cup T \subseteq Lit$. Else if $P_1 \cup P_2$ has the consistent answer set V, $S \cup T$ is consistent by Proposition 4.8. Then, $S \cup T \subset V$ by Proposition 4.9. □

Example 4.5. Let $P_1 = \{p \leftarrow q\}$ and $P_2 = \{q \leftarrow\}$. Then, $P_1 \odot P_2 = \{q \leftarrow\}$ and $P_1 \cup P_2 = \{p \leftarrow q, \; q \leftarrow\}$. So $P_1 \odot P_2 \subseteq P_1 \cup P_2$ and $\{q\} \in \mathcal{AS}(P_1 \odot P_2)$ is a subset of $\{p, q\} \in \mathcal{AS}(P_1 \cup P_2)$.

5   Permissible Composition

In Section 3, we introduced the compositional semantics of two programs and Section 4 provided a method of composing programs. In this section, we argue permissible conditions for the compositional semantics in multi-agent coordination. First, we introduce a criterion for selecting answer sets in the compositional semantics.

Definition 5.1. Let P_1 and P_2 be two consistent programs, and Q a composition of P_1 and P_2. Then, any answer set $S \in \mathcal{AS}(Q)$ is *consenting* if it satisfies every rule in $P_1 \cup P_2$.

Example 5.1. Recall two programs P_1 and P_2 in Example 4.1:

$$P_1 : \; p \leftarrow not\, q,$$
$$q \leftarrow not\, p,$$
$$s \leftarrow p,$$
$$P_2 : \; p \leftarrow not\, r,$$
$$r \leftarrow not\, p,$$

where $\mathcal{AS}(P_1) = \{\{p, s\}, \{q\}\}$ and $\mathcal{AS}(P_2) = \{\{p\}, \{r\}\}$. The compositional semantics of P_1 and P_2 is $\mathcal{AS}(Q) = \{\{p, q\}, \{p, s\}, \{q, r\}\}$. Among them, $\{p, s\}$ and $\{q, r\}$ satisfy every rule in $P_1 \cup P_2$, so they are consenting. Note that $\{p, q\}$ is not consenting because it does not satisfy the third rule of P_1.

Consenting answer sets are good candidates for coordinative solutions, because they satisfy the original program of each agent. A consenting answer set is possibly inconsistent. Unfortunately, consenting answer sets do not always exist in the compositional semantics. For instance, in Example 5.1 if P_2 contains integrity constraints $\leftarrow s$ and $\leftarrow q$, no consenting answer set exists. Existence of no consenting answer set in general is not a serious flaw in the compositional semantics, however. In fact, different agents have different beliefs in a multi-agent environment, and it may happen that one agent must give up some original belief to reach an acceptable compromise. On the other hand, an agent may possess some *persistent* beliefs that cannot be abandoned. Those persistent beliefs are retained by each agent in coordination. Formally, persistent beliefs in a program P are distinguished as $PB \subseteq P$ where PB is the set of rules that should be satisfied by the compositional semantics. In this setting, a variant of the compositional semantics is defined as follows.

Definition 5.2. Let P_1 and P_2 be two programs, and PB_1 and PB_2 their persistent beliefs, respectively. A program Ω is called a *permissible composition* of P_1 and P_2 (sustaining PB_1 and PB_2) if it satisfies the condition

$$\mathcal{AS}(\Omega) = \{\, S \mid S \in min(\mathcal{AS}(P_1) \uplus \mathcal{AS}(P_2)) \text{ and } S \text{ satisfies } PB_1 \cup PB_2\}.$$

The set $\mathcal{AS}(\Omega)$ is called the *permissible compositional semantics* of P_1 and P_2. Any answer set in $\mathcal{AS}(\Omega)$ is called a *permissible answer set.* By the definition, permissible composition adds an extra condition to the compositional semantics of Definition 3.2. The permissible compositional semantics reduces to the compositional semantics when $PB_1 \cup PB_2 = \emptyset$. In particular, consenting answer sets are permissible answer sets with $PB_1 \cup PB_2 = P_1 \cup P_2$. Every permissible answer set satisfies persistent beliefs of each agent, and extends some answer sets of an agent by additional information of another agent.

Program composition that reflects the permissible compositional semantics is achieved by introducing every rule in $PB_1 \cup PB_2$ as a constraint to $P_1 \odot P_2$. Given a program P, let $IC(P) = \{\leftarrow body(r), not\_head(r) \mid r \in P\}$ where $not\_head(r)$ is the conjunction of NAF-literals $\{not\, L_1, \ldots, not\, L_l\}$ for $head(r) = \{L_1, \ldots, L_l\}$.

Theorem 5.1. *Let P_1 and P_2 be consistent programs, and Ω a permissible composition of P_1 and P_2. Then, $\mathcal{AS}(\Omega) = \mathcal{AS}((P_1 \odot P_2) \cup IC(PB_1) \cup IC(PB_2))$.*

Proof. By the definition of $\mathcal{AS}(\Omega)$ and the result of Theorem 4.6, $S \in \mathcal{AS}(\Omega)$
iff S is an answer set of $P_1 \odot P_2$ and satisfies $PB_1 \cup PB_2$
iff S is an answer set of $P_1 \odot P_2$ and satisfies $IC(PB_1) \cup IC(PB_2)$
iff $S \in \mathcal{AS}((P_1 \odot P_2) \cup IC(PB_1) \cup IC(PB_2))$.   □

Example 5.2. Consider two programs P_1 and P_2 in Example 5.1 where $PB_1 = \{s \leftarrow p\}$ and $PB_2 = \emptyset$. Then, $(P_1 \odot P_2) \cup IC(PB_1) \cup IC(PB_2)$ becomes

$$p\,;\, q \leftarrow,$$
$$p\,;\, r \leftarrow,$$
$$q\,;\, s \leftarrow p,$$
$$\leftarrow p,\, not\, s,$$

which has two permissible answer sets $\{p, s\}$ and $\{q, r\}$.

6   Discussion

A lot of studies exist for compositional semantics of logic programs (see [7, 12] for excellent surveys). A semantics is *compositional* if the meaning of a program can be obtained from the meaning of its components. The union of programs is the simplest composition between programs. However, semantics of logic programs is not compositional with respect to the union of programs even for definite logic programs. For instance, two definite logic programs $P_1 = \{p \leftarrow q\}$ and $P_2 = \{q \leftarrow\}$ have the least Herbrand models $\emptyset$ and $\{q\}$, respectively. But the least Herbrand model of the program union $P_1 \cup P_2$ is not obtained by the composition of $\emptyset$ and $\{q\}$. To solve the problem, a number of different compositional semantics have been proposed in the literature [7]. In composing nonmonotonic logic programs, difficulty of the problem is understood as: "*non-monotonic reasoning and compositionality are intuitively orthogonal issues that do not seem easy to be reconciled. Indeed the semantics for extended logic programs are typically non-compositional w.r.t. program union*" [7]. With this reason, studies for compositional semantics of nonmonotonic logic programs mainly concern with the issue of devising a compositional semantics that can accommodate (restricted) nonmonotonicity, or imposing syntactic conditions on programs to be compositional [6, 8, 9, 14, 23].

Compared with those previous studies, our approach is different in the following aspects. First, our primary interest is not simply merging two programs but building a new program that combines answer sets of the original programs. Second, our program composition is intended to coordinate meanings of different programs, rather than to synthesize a program by its component. One may wonder the practical value of such combination of answer sets aside from original programs. For instance, given two programs $P_1 = \{ \neg p \leftarrow not\, p \}$ and $P_2 = \{ p \leftarrow \}$, one would consider the meaning of a composed program as the answer set $\{p\}$ of $P_1 \cup P_2$. By contrast, our compositional semantics $P_1 \odot P_2$ becomes inconsistent, that is, combination of $\{\neg p\}$ and $\{p\}$ produces *Lit*. To justify our position, suppose the following situation: the agent P_1 does not believe the existence of an alien unless its existence is proved, while the agent P_2 believes the existence of aliens with no doubt. The situation is encoded by the above two programs. Then, what conclusion should be drawn after combining these conflicting beliefs of agents? If one simply merges beliefs by program union, the existence of alien is concluded by the answer set $\{p\}$. In our compositional semantics, two beliefs do not coexist thereby contradict. In multi-agent environments, different agents have different levels of beliefs. A cautious agent might have knowledge in a default form, while an optimistic agent might have knowledge in a definite form. In this circumstance, it appears careless to simply merge knowledge from different information sources. For another example, consider $P_3 = \{ p \leftarrow q \}$ and $P_4 = \{ p \leftarrow not\, q, \quad q \leftarrow \}$. Two agents have incompatible beliefs; P_3 believes that p holds if q holds, while P_4 believes that p holds if q does not hold. Now P_4 knows q, so that p is not believed. Merging two programs, however, p is derived from $P_3 \cup P_4$. This is rather an unexpected consequence for P_4. As argued in the introduction, simple merging of different programs does not always reflect the meaning of individual programs. We then took an approach of retaining belief of each agent and combine answer sets of different programs. As a result, the compositional semantics maintains information included in (at least one) answer set of the original programs. It precisely combines the results of skeptical consequences of original programs and does not introduce additional (unexpected) consequences (Proposition 3.5). Note that program composition should be distinguished from *revision* or *update*, in which one of two information sources is known more reliable. In the above example, it is reasonable to accept $P_1 \cup P_2$ as a result of revision/update of P_1 with P_2. Because in this case P_2 is considered new information which precedes P_1. In program composition P_1 and P_2 are supposed to have the same status, so there is no reason to rely P_2 over P_1. Several studies argue combining different theories having priorities [2, 11, 13, 19, 21]. Priorities are useful to resolve conflicts among agents, however, it generally introduces additional computational cost. Our compositional semantics does not handle programs with different priorities, but prioritized coordination is partly realized by permissible composition. If P_1 is more reliable than P_2, P_1 is put as persistent beliefs. Under the setting, every permissible answer set satisfies P_1.

Baral *et al.* [1] introduce algorithms for combining logic programs by enforcing satisfaction of integrity constraints. They request that every answer set of a resulting program to be a subset of an answer set of $P_1 \cup P_2$, which is different from our requirement. Moreover, their algorithm is not applicable to unstratified logic programs. The compositional semantics introduced in this paper does not enforce satisfaction of integrity constraints of original programs. One reason for this is that in nonmonotonic logic programs inconsistency may arise aside from integrity constraints. For instance, the integrity constraint $\leftarrow p$ has the same effect as the rule $q \leftarrow p, not\, q$ under the answer set semantics. Then, there seems no reason to handle integrity constraints exceptionally in a program. If desired, however, it is easy to have a variant of program composition satisfying constraints as $(P_1 \odot P_2) \cup IC_1 \cup IC_2$, where IC_i $(i = 1, 2)$ is the set of integrity constraints included in P_i. By the introduction of integrity constraints, every answer set which does not satisfy $IC_1 \cup IC_2$ is filtered out. This is also realized by a permissible version of the compositional semantics by putting $PB_1 = IC_1$ and $PB_2 = IC_2$. Combination of propositional theories has also been studied under the names of *merging* [18] or *arbitration* [20], but they do not handle nonmonotonic theories.

Buccafurri and Gottlob [10] introduce a framework of *compromise logic programs* which aims at reaching common conclusions and compromises among logic programming agents. Given a collection of programs $T = \{Q_1, \ldots, Q_n\}$, the joint fixpoints $JFP(T)$ is defined as $JFP(T) = FP(Q_1) \cap \cdots \cap FP(Q_n)$ where $FP(Q_i)$ is the set of all fixpoints of Q_i. Then, the *joint fixpoint semantics* of T is defined as the set of minimal elements in $JFP(T)$. The joint fixpoint semantics is different from our compositional semantics. For instance, when two programs $P_1 = \{p \leftarrow\}$ and $P_2 = \emptyset$ are given, by $FP(P_1) = \{\{p\}\}$ and $FP(P_2) = \{\emptyset\}$ their joint fixpoint semantics becomes $\emptyset$. Interestingly, however, if a tautology $p \leftarrow p$ is added to P_2, $FP(P_2)$ turns to $\{\emptyset, \{p\}\}$ and the joint fixpoint semantics becomes $\{\{p\}\}$. Thus, in their framework a rule $p \leftarrow p$ has a special meaning that "if p is required by another agent, let it be". With this reading, however, $P_1 = \{p \leftarrow\}$ and $P_3 = \{p \leftarrow p, \quad q \leftarrow\}$ have the joint fixpoint semantics $\{\emptyset\}$, that is, P_3 does not tolerate p when another irrelevant fact q exists in the program. By contrast, our compositional semantics becomes $\mathcal{AS}(P_1 \odot P_2) = \{\{p\}\}$ and $\mathcal{AS}(P_1 \odot P_3) = \{\{p, q\}\}$.

Sakama and Inoue [22] introduce a framework of coordination between logic programs. They study two problems as follows: given two programs P_1 and P_2, (i) find a program Q which has the set of answer sets such that $\mathcal{AS}(Q) = \mathcal{AS}(P_1) \cup \mathcal{AS}(P_2)$; and (ii) find a program R which has the set of answer sets such that $\mathcal{AS}(R) = \mathcal{AS}(P_1) \cap \mathcal{AS}(P_2)$. A program Q is called *generous coordination* and R is called *rigorous coordination* of two programs. They provide methods of building such programs. Compared with the program composition of this paper, generous/rigorous coordination does not change answer sets of the original programs. That is, generous one collects every answer set of each program, while rigorous one picks up answer sets that are common between two programs. By contrast, we combine answer sets of each program in every possible way. The resulting program and its compositional semantics are both different from generous/rigorous coordination. Aside from such differences, the present work is also applied to coordinate agents, so that it would be interesting to investigate relations among those different types of coordination.

The program composition introduced in Section 4 produces NAF-free EDPs. One may think this uneasy, because this is the case even for composing ELPs containing no disjunction. Disjunctive programs are generally harder to compute, so that it is desirable to have a non-disjunctive program as a result of composing non-disjunctive programs. Technically, the program $P_1 \odot P_2$ is transformed to a non-disjunctive program if $P_1 \odot P_2$ is *head-cycle-free*, that is, it contains no positive cycle through disjuncts appearing in the head of a disjunctive rule [4]. If $P_1 \odot P_2$ is head-cycle-free, the program is converted to an ELP by shifting disjuncts in the head of a rule to the body as NAF-literals in every possible way but leaving one in the head. For instance, the program $P_1 \odot P_2$ in Example 4.1 is converted to the ELP: $\{\, p \leftarrow not\, q, \;\; q \leftarrow not\, p, \;\; p \leftarrow not\, r, \;\; r \leftarrow not\, p, \;\; q \leftarrow p,\, not\, s, \;\; s \leftarrow p,\, not\, q \,\}$. The resulting program has the same answer sets as the original disjunctive program.

7   Conclusion

This paper has studied a compositional semantics of nonmonotonic logic programs. Given two programs, we first introduced combination of answer sets as the compositional semantics of those programs. Then, we developed a method of building a program which reflects the compositional semantics of the original programs. A permissible composition was also introduced for multi-agent coordination. The proposed framework provides a new compositional semantics of nonmonotonic logic programs, and serves as a declarative basis for coordination in multi-agent systems. From the viewpoint of answer set programming, program composition is considered as a program development under a specification that requests a program reflecting the meanings of two or more programs.

The approach taken in this paper requires computing every answer set of programs before composition. This may often be infeasible when a program possesses an exponential number of answer sets. The same problem arises in computing answer sets by existing answer set solvers, however. This paper considered compositional semantics as minimal sets that reflect the meaning of original programs. By contrast, a program may have *non-minimal* answer sets in the context of *general extended disjunctive programs* which possibly contain NAF in the heads of rules [17]. In this context, the compositional semantics would be defined as a collection of non-minimal answer sets. These extensions and variants of compositional semantics will be investigated in future study.

References

1. C. Baral, S. Kraus, and J. Minker. Combining multiple knowledge bases. *IEEE Transactions of Knowledge and Data Engineering*, 3(2):208–220, 1991.

2. C. Baral, S. Kraus, J. Minker, and V. S. Subrahmanian. Combining knowledge base consisting of first-order theories. *Computational Intelligence*, 8:45–71, 1992.

3. C. Baral and M. Gelfond. Logic programming and knowledge representation. *Journal of Logic Programming*, 19/20:73–148, 1994.

4. R. Ben-Eliyahu and R. Dechter. Propositional semantics for disjunctive logic programs. *Annals of Mathematics and Artificial Intelligence*, 12(1):53–87, 1994.

5. S. Brass and J. Dix. Characterizations of the disjunctive stable semantics by partial evaluation. *Journal of Logic Programming*, 32(3):207–228, 1997.

6. A. Brogi, S. Contiero, and F. Turini. Programming by combining general logic programs. *Journal of Logic and Computation*, 9(1):7–24, 1999.

7. A. Brogi. On the semantics of logic program composition. *Program Development in Computational Logic*, Lecture Notes in Computer Science, 3049, pp. 115–151, Springer, 2004.

8. A. Brogi, E. Lamma, P. Mancarella, and P. Mello. A unifying view for logic programming with nonmonotonic reasoning. *Theoretical Computer Science*, 184(1):1–59, 1997.

9. F. Bry. A compositional semantics for logic programs and deductive databases. *Proceedings of the Joint International Conference and Symposium on Logic Programming*, pp. 453–467, MIT Press, 1996.

10. F. Buccafurri and G. Gottlob. Multiagent compromises, joint fixpoints, and stable models. *Computational Logic: Logic Programming and Beyond*, Lecture Notes in Artificial Intelligence 2407, pp. 561–585, Springer, 2002.

11. F. Buccafurri, W. Faber, and N. Leone. Disjunctive programs with inheritance. *Proceedings of the 1999 International Conference on Logic Programming*, pp. 79–93, MIT Press, 1999.

12. M. Bugliesi, E. Lamma, and P. Mello. Modularity in logic programming. *Journal of Logic Programming*, 19/20:443–502, 1994.

13. M. De. Vos and D. Vermeir. Extending answer sets for logic programming agents. *Annals of Mathematics and Artificial Intelligence*, 42: 103–139, 2004.

14. S. Etalle and F. Teusink. A compositional semantics for normal open programs. *Proceedings of the Joint International Conference and Symposium on Logic Programming*, pp. 468–482, MIT Press, 1988.

15. W. Faber, N. Leone, and G. Pfeifer. Recursive aggregates in disjunctive logic programs: semantics and complexity. *Proceedings of the 9th European Conference on Logics in Artificial Intelligence*, Lecture Notes in Artificial Intelligence, 3229, pp. 200–212, Springer, 2004.

16. M. Gelfond and V. Lifschitz. Classical negation in logic programs and disjunctive databases. *New Generation Computing*, 9(3/4):365–385, 1991.

17. K. Inoue and C. Sakama. Negation as failure in the head. *Journal of Logic Programming*, 35(1):39–78, 1998.

18. S. Konieczny and R. Pino-Pérez. On the logic of merging. *Proceedings of the 6th International Conference on Principles of Knowledge Representation and Reasoning*, pp. 488–498, Morgan Kaufmann, 1998.

19. J. A. Leite. *Evolving Knowledge Bases, Specification and Semantics*. IOS Press, 2003.

20. P. Liberatore and M. Schaerf. Arbitration (or how to merge knowledge bases). *IEEE Transactions on Knowledge and Data Engineering*, 10(1):76–90, 1998.
21. S. Pradhan and J. Minker. Using priorities to combine knowledge bases. *Journal of Cooperative Information Systems*, 5(2&3):333–364. 1996.
22. C. Sakama and K. Inoue. Coordination between logical agents. *Proceedings of the 5th International Workshop on Computational Logic in Multi-Agent Systems*, Lecture Notes in Artificial Intelligence 3487, pp. 161–177, Springer, 2005.
23. S. Verbaeten, M. Denecker, and D. De. Schreye. Compositionality of normal open logic programs. *Proceedings of the 1997 International Symposium on Logic Programming*, pp. 371–385, MIT Press, 1997.

Speculative Constraint Processing with Iterative Revision for Disjunctive Answers

Martine Ceberio[1], Hiroshi Hosobe[2], and Ken Satoh[2]

[1] University of Texas at El Paso,
500 West University Avenue, El Paso, Texas 79968-0518, USA
mceberio@cs.utep.edu
[2] National Institute of Informatics,
2-1-2 Hitotsubashi, Chiyoda-ku, Tokyo 101-8430, Japan
{ksatoh, hosobe}@nii.ac.jp

Abstract. In multi-agents systems, incompleteness, due to either communication failure or response delay, is a major problem to handle. To face incompleteness, frameworks for speculative computation were proposed (see references [5, 6, 7]). The idea developed in such frameworks is to allow the asking agent, while waiting for the slave agents to reply, to reason using default beliefs until replies are sent.

In particular, K. Satoh and K. Yamamoto [7] proposed a framework that allows an agent not only to perform speculative computation, but also to accept iterative answer revision for yes/no questions. In this paper, we present an extension of the framework for more general types of questions using constraint logic programming (CLP).

1 Introduction

Multi-agent systems are very fashionable and convenient, because they make it possible, for instance, to take advantage of multi-processor machines, and also make it possible to design human-like efficient organizations of agents. The main limitation to such an approach is that, as also arises in human organizations, communication may be an issue: delayed or broken, it leads to incompleteness of the information in the reasoning structure.

This is a concrete concern when we consider distributed systems such as the Internet, in which communication is indeed not guaranteed, and even if we could guarantee it, communication may either take time, or agents themselves may delay their sending information.

For such non-ideal, but as we believe, practical situations, when problem-solving is at stake, frameworks for speculative computations were proposed: first for yes/no questions only [6], and then for general questions [5] using constraints.

K. Satoh et al. [6] and K. Satoh, P. Codognet, and H. Hosobe [5] only provided the possibility for the master agent to perform speculations and a returned answer from the slave agent is final and with no possibility of a change in answers. However, if we let every agent perform speculative computation, the asked agent may revise his answer since the previous answer sometimes depends on the asked

F. Toni and P. Torroni (Eds.): CLIMA VI, LNAI 3900, pp. 340–357, 2006.

agent's belief, which might turn out to be false. Therefore, a chain reaction of belief revision among agents might occur, which was firstly observed by K. Satoh and K. Yamamoto [7], and they provide a revisable speculative computation method for yes/no questions. The essential part of their work is a dynamic iterative belief revision mechanism that can handle a revision of an answer for query even during the execution.

Belief revision is indeed very important for both the sake of flexibility (information is processed before it is complete), and speed of computation (time is saved in case prior information is later entailed).

We combine the methods proposed by K. Satoh et al. [5, 7], and extend them, so that we can handle iterative answer revision for a query with constraints. We also complete these methods with the ability to incorporate disjunctive answers. So, the main contribution from this paper is the definition of the framework that enables to perform speculative computations on constraints, while handling belief revision, and that handles disjunctive answers as well. In particular, the main challenges with this framework are the following:

- First, processing speculative constraints, as shown by K. Satoh et al. [5], is manageable when belief revision is not considered. In our research, belief revision is made possible because it enables more speculative computation in multi-agent systems. This makes the problem much harder: the process management needs to be modified to enable changes in the computation at any time, while maintaining a reasonable balance between not being too space-consuming, and not loosing too much time (*i.e.*, we don't want to start from scratch all the time). The process management is presented in detail in this paper, as well as the results on the space complexity of our operational model.
- The second challenging point described in this paper is the way disjunction is now handled in the framework we propose. Indeed, considering the situation where each agent's behavior is specified as a CLP program, we need to handle alternative answers, since these answers may come from different derivations in CLP. By manipulating such alternative answers, we face another complication, in that we need to distinguish a revised answer of a previous answer, from an answer derived from an alternative derivation path. To solve this problem, we devise an answer entry that keeps track of the usage status of the answer in processes. This new feature impacts the way processes are managed, as described in Section 3, and therefore makes the problem more complicated.

For an iterative belief revision, many proposals have been described. As far as we know, existing frameworks separate reasoning and belief revision, except those by K. Satoh et al. [5, 6, 7] and that by F. Sadri and F. Toni [4]. Our framework in this paper is along the line of the works of K. Satoh et al. in a more general setting. F. Sadri and F. Toni proposed an abductive logic programming proof procedure, called LIFF, that enables the interleaving of belief revision and reasoning. The advantage of LIFF is that it allows the addition and deletion of rules, while our framework processes only the addition and deletion of constraints. However, our framework allows predicate cases, while LIFF handles only propositional cases. In addition, our framework does not require recomputation for constraint narrowing, whereas LIFF needs to recompute goals related to updated rules. Also, our framework performs computation along plausible paths by using default rules, while LIFF does not adopt such explicit control.

There are works on the formalization of an agent in terms of logic programming, such as that conducted by R. A. Kowalski and F. Sadri [3]. Although these works are important in their own right, our paper pursues another branch of investigation in the context of speculative computation.

The most closely related research would be constraint programming languages, such as Andorra Kernel Language (AKL) [2] and Oz [8], which perform a kind of speculative computation. AKL allows local speculative variable bindings in a guard of each clause until one of the guards succeeds, and Oz can control multiple computation spaces, each of which represents an alternative path of constraint processing. As far as we understand, however, speculative computation used in these languages is mainly meant for or-parallel computing, where all alternative paths of computation are executed in parallel, until one of the paths eventually succeeds. On the other hand, we regard a speculative computation as a default computation where the most plausible paths of computation are executed. Moreover, they do not consider any revision of the answers.

The structure of the paper is as follows. We firstly define the framework for speculative constraint processing and semantics of the framework. Then, we describe an operational model, show an example of an execution, and state correctness of our model. Finally, we discuss space complexity issues, before concluding.

2   Speculative Constraint Processing

In this section, we provide a framework of speculative constraint computation based on the CLP framework [1]. This framework is designed so that an agent not only performs speculative constraint processing but also accepts revised and alternative answers. We then define the semantics of this framework, in Sub-section 2.2.

2.1   Framework Definition

Definition 1. *Let Σ be a finite set of constants. We call an element in Σ a slave agent identifier. An atom is of the form either $p(t_1, ..., t_n)$ or $p(t_1, ..., t_n)@S$, where p is a predicate, $t_i (1 \leq i \leq n)$ is a term, and S is in Σ.*

We call an atom with an agent identifier an *"askable atom"*, and an atom without an identifier a *"non-askable atom"*.

Definition 2. *A framework for speculative constraint computation, in a master-slave system, is a triple $\langle \Sigma, \Delta, \mathcal{P} \rangle$, where:*

- *Σ is a finite set of constants;*
- *Δ is a set of rules of the following form, called* default rule w.r.t. Q@S:

$$Q@S \leftarrow C\|,$$

where Q@S is an askable atom, each of whose arguments is a variable, and C is a set of constraints, called default constraint for *Q@S;*

- $\mathcal{P}$ *is a constraint logic program, that is, a set of rules R of the form:*

$$H \leftarrow C \| B_1, B_2, ..., B_n,$$

where:

- *H is a non-askable atom; we refer to H as the* head *of R, denoted as head(R);*
- *C is a set of constraints, called the* constraint *of R, and denoted as const(R);*
- *each B_i of $B_1, ..., B_n$ is either an askable atom or a non-askable atom, and we refer to $B_1, ..., B_n$ as the* body *of R denoted as body(R).*

Note that a default is not necessarily specified for every askable atom. Moreover, we allow multiple defaults for the same askable atom.

Example 1. We consider the following example of a hotel room reservation. There is a master agent m: m asks travelers a and b. If both travel, m reserves a twin room. If only one of them travels, m reserves a single room. Agent m has default information about the status of a and b for days 1, 2 and 3, but the real status will be obtained directly from a and b, and the status is therefore likely to be changed.

This example can be represented as the following multi-agent system $\langle \Sigma, \Delta, \mathcal{P} \rangle$[1]:

- Σ is the set of slave agents. Here, there is one master agent, m, and two slave agents, a and b. Therefore, $\Sigma = \{a, b\}$.
- Δ is the set of default information (default rules), assumed by the master agent. In particular, let us suppose that m assumes that a is free on days 1 and 2, but busy on day 3, and that b is free on day 2, and busy on day 1. Then the corresponding set Δ is as follows:

$$\Delta = \{ \, d_1 : \; fr(D)@a \leftarrow D=1\|,$$
$$d_2 : \; fr(D)@a \leftarrow D=2\|, \;\; d_3 : \; bs(D)@a \leftarrow D=3\|,$$
$$d_4 : \; fr(D)@b \leftarrow D=2\|, \;\; d_5 : \; bs(D)@b \leftarrow D=1\|.\}$$

Let us remark that it is not necessary for default information to exist for all cases. In particular, m has no default information concerning the status of b on day 3.

- $\mathcal{P}$ is a constraint logic program, to be solved by agent m. In our case of the hotel room reservation with the two travelers, it is made of the following set of rules:

---

[1] A string beginning with an upper-case letter represents a variable and a string beginning with a lower-case letter represents a constant. We abbreviate "free" as fr, "busy" as bs, "travel" as $trvl$, "reserve" as rsv, "twin room" as tr, and "single room" as sr.

$$rsv(R, L, D) \leftarrow R=tr, L=[a, b] \| fr(D)@a, fr(D)@b.$$
$$rsv(R, L, D) \leftarrow R=sr, L=[a] \| fr(D)@a, bs(D)@b.$$
$$rsv(R, L, D) \leftarrow R=sr, L=[b] \| bs(D)@a, fr(D)@b.$$

In order to solve this constraint satisfaction problem, agent m will have to ask agents a and b about $fr(D)@a$, $bs(D)@a$, $fr(D)@b$, $bs(D)@b$.

2.2 Semantics of Speculative Constraint Processing

For the semantics of the above framework, we index the semantics of a constraint logic program by a *reply set*, which specifies a reply for an askable atom.

Definition 3. *A* reply set *is a set of rules in the form:*

$$Q@S \leftarrow C\|,$$

where $Q@S$ is an askable atom, each of whose arguments is a variable, and C is a constraint over these variables.

Let $\langle \Sigma, \Delta, \mathcal{P} \rangle$ *be a framework for speculative constraint computation, and $\mathcal{R}$ be a reply set. A belief state w.r.t. $\mathcal{R}$ and Δ is a reply set defined as:*

$$\mathcal{R} \cup \{ \text{``}Q@S \leftarrow C\|\text{''} \in \Delta \mid \neg\exists\, C' \text{ s.t. ``}Q@S \leftarrow C'\|\text{''} \in \mathcal{R}\}$$

and denoted as $BEL(\mathcal{R}, \Delta)$.

We introduce the above belief state since, if the answer is not returned, we use a default rule for an unreplied askable atom.

Definition 4. *A goal is of the form $\leftarrow C\|B_1, ..., B_n$, where C is a set of constraints and the B_i's are atoms. We call C the constraint of the goal and $B_1, ..., B_n$ the body of the goal.*

Definition 5. *A reduction of a goal $\leftarrow C\|B_1, ..., B_n$ w.r.t. a constraint logic program $\mathcal{P}$, a reply set $\mathcal{R}$, and an atom B_i, is a goal $\leftarrow C'\|B'$ such that:*

- *there is a rule R in $\mathcal{P} \cup \mathcal{R}$ s.t. $C \wedge (B_i = head(R)) \wedge const(R)$ is consistent[2];*
- *$C' = C \wedge (B_i = head(R)) \wedge const(R)$;*
- *$B' = \{B_1, ...B_{i-1}, B_{i+1}, ..., B_n\} \cup body(R)$.*

Definition 6. *A derivation of a goal $G =\leftarrow C\|Bs$ w.r.t. a framework for speculative constraint computation $\mathcal{F} = \langle \Sigma, \Delta, \mathcal{P} \rangle$ and a reply set $\mathcal{R}$ is a sequence of reductions "$\leftarrow C\|Bs$",..., "$\leftarrow C'\|\emptyset$"[3] w.r.t. $\mathcal{P}$ and $BEL(\mathcal{R}, \Delta)$, where in each reduction step, an atom in the body of the goal in each step is selected. C' is called an answer constraint w.r.t. G, $\mathcal{F}$, and $\mathcal{R}$. We call a set of all answer constraints w.r.t. G, $\mathcal{F}$, and $\mathcal{R}$ the semantics of G w.r.t. $\mathcal{F}$ and $\mathcal{R}$.*

---

[2] A notation $B_i = head(R)$ represents a conjunction of constraints equating the arguments of atoms B_i and $head(R)$.

[3] $\emptyset$ denotes an empty goal.

In the above definition, we only consider the most recent reply set, whereas a reply set might be varied during execution according to the slave agent's answer revision. We use the most recent reply set because it reflects the current situation of the slave agents. Let us remark that the order of reply messages is assumed to be preserved; that is, reply messages are always received by the master agent in the order that they are sent by the slave agent.

3   Operational Model for Speculative Computation with Iterative Answer Revision

3.1   Overview of the Operational Model

The execution of the speculative framework is based on two phases: a *process reduction phase* and a *fact arrival phase*. The process reduction phase is a normal execution of a program in a master agent, and the fact arrival phase is an interruption phase when an answer arrives from a slave agent.

For the operational model, we use the following two kinds of objects: a *process* and an *answer entry*.

Each *process* represents an alternative way of computation. Processes are created when a choice point of computation is encountered, such as case splitting, default handling, and answer arrival. A process becomes a finished process when the body of the associated goal with the process becomes empty. A process fails when some used default constraints are found to contradict the newly returned answer.

An *answer entry* is used to distinguish alternative answers and to detect which old answer corresponds to the newly revised answer. This detection is done by attaching an ID to each answer. If a new answer with an ID different from any existing answer comes, it is an alternative answer. Otherwise, the new answer is considered as a revised answer to the old answer with the same ID.

Figures 1–4 intuitively explain how processes are updated according to askable atoms. In the tree, each node represents a process, but we only show constraints associated with the process. The top node represents a constraint for the original process, and the other nodes represent added constraints for the reduced processes. Let us note that we specify *true* for non-top nodes without added constraints, since the addition of the *true* constraint does not influence the solutions of existing constraints. The leaves of the process tree represent the current processes. Therefore, the processes that are not in the leaves are deleted processes.

Figure 1 shows a situation of the processes represented as a tree when an askable atom, whose reply has not yet arrived, is executed in the process reduction phase. In this case, the current process, represented by the processed constraints C, is split into two different kinds of processes: the first one is a process using default information, C_d, and is called *default process*[4]; and the other one is the current process C itself, called *original process*, suspended at this point.

---

[4] In this figure, we assume that there is only one default for brevity.

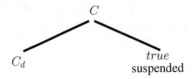

Fig. 1. When $Q@S$ is processed during the process reduction phase

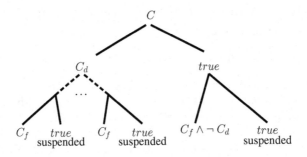

Fig. 2. When first answer C_f for $Q@S$ arrives

Note that, if there are multiple definitions of defaults, we will have more than one default process, but still only one suspended process. In addition, let us note that the reason for suspending the processes (which is, keeping them in memory), is that in case of a contradictory revision of the default, or the arrival of later alternative answers, it is essential to remember the original processes to be able to restore them.

When, after some reduction of the default processes (represented in Fig. 2 by dashed lines), the first answer comes from a slave agent, expressing constraint C_f for this askable literal, we update the default processes as well as the original suspended process as follows:

– Default processes are reduced to two different kinds of processes: the first kind is a process adding C_f to the problem to solve, and the other is the current process itself which is suspended at this point[5].
– The original process is reduced to two different kinds of processes as well: the first kind is a process adding $\neg C_d \wedge C_f$, and the other is the original process, suspended at this point.

Let us remark that although the tree of processes grows, only the leaves are kept in memory.

To intuitively explain the correctness of the above process update, we define the *frontier*, which represents the computation status of all alternative derivations. A *frontier* w.r.t. a goal $\leftarrow C\|Bs$, a framework for speculative constraint computation $\langle \Sigma, \Delta, \mathcal{P} \rangle$, and a reply set $\mathcal{R}$, is a set of goals defined as follows:

---

[5] Let us remark that this splitting process is similar to the splitting process above-described for the case of a first default used.

1. The set consisting of the initial goal, $\{\leftarrow C\|Bs\}$ is a frontier.
2. Let F be a frontier w.r.t. the above initial goal, the framework, and the reply set. If a goal G is in F, B is an atom in G, and $RGs = \{G'|\ G'$ is a reduction of G w.r.t. $\mathcal{P}$, $BEL(\mathcal{R}, \Delta)$, and $B\}$, then $F\backslash\{G\} \cup RGs$ is a frontier.

Then we have the following properties.

Lemma 1. *Let $\leftarrow C\|Bs$ be a goal, F be a frontier of this goal, and C' be a constraint. If we add C' to the constraints of every goal in F, then the disjunctions of all answer constraints of these modified goals is logically equivalent to the disjunction of all answer constraints of the goal $\leftarrow C \wedge C'\|Bs$.*

Lemma 2. *Let $\leftarrow C\|Bs$ be a goal, $\mathcal{R}$ be a reply set, and C' be a constraint. Then, the disjunction of answer constraints of $\leftarrow C \wedge C'\|Bs$ and $\leftarrow C \wedge \neg C'\|Bs$ is logically equivalent to the disjunction of all answer constraints of $\leftarrow C\|Bs$.*

Let $\leftarrow C\|Bs$ be a goal containing $Q@S$. Suppose that it is reduced into $\leftarrow C \wedge C_d\|Bs\backslash\{Q@S\}$ by a default rule "$Q@S \leftarrow C_d\|$". Let F be a frontier of $\leftarrow C \wedge C_d\|Bs\backslash\{Q@S\}$ when the first reply "$Q@S \leftarrow C_f\|$" is returned. Since our semantics considers the most recent replies, at this point, we should consider:

$$\leftarrow C \wedge C_f\|Bs\backslash\{Q@S\},$$

instead of:

$$\leftarrow C \wedge C_d\|Bs\backslash\{Q@S\}.$$

One possibility to implement this change is that we just discard F and invoke a new goal $\leftarrow C \wedge C_f\|Bs\backslash\{Q@S\}$. However, in this case, we throw every computation away before F is obtained. To retain the previous computation as much as possible, we propose the following execution.

1. We add C_f to the constraint of every goal in F. Let us remark that the disjunction of all answer constraints from this new frontier is logically equivalent to the disjunction of all answer constraints of $\leftarrow C \wedge C_d \wedge C_f\|Bs\backslash\{Q@S\}$, as Lemma 1 states. This computation keeps the previous computation, which is consistent with the new reply (C_f).
2. In addition to the above computation, we also start computing a new goal:

$$\leftarrow C \wedge \neg C_d \wedge C_f\|Bs\backslash\{Q@S\}$$

to guarantee completeness. This is because the disjunction of all answer constraints derived from $\leftarrow C \wedge C_d \wedge C_f\|Bs\backslash\{Q@S\}$ and $\leftarrow C \wedge \neg C_d \wedge C_f\|Bs\backslash\{Q@S\}$ is logically equivalent to the disjunction of all answer constraints derived from $\leftarrow C \wedge C_f\|Bs\backslash\{Q@S\}$, as Lemma 2 states.

When an alternative answer, with the constraint C_a, comes from a slave agent (Fig. 3), we need to follow the same procedure as when the first answer comes (Fig. 2), except that now the processes handling only default information are suspended. So, this is done by splitting the suspended default process(es), in order

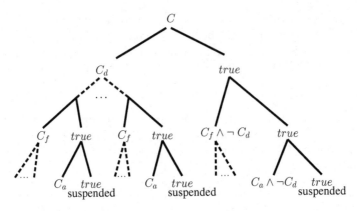

Fig. 3. When alternative answer C_a for $Q@S$ arrives

to obtain the answer constraints that are logically equivalent to the answer constraints of:

$$\leftarrow C \wedge C_d \wedge C_a \| Bs \backslash \{Q@S\},$$

as well as by splitting the suspended original process, in order to obtain the answer constraints that are logically equivalent to the answer constraints of $\leftarrow C \wedge \neg C_d \wedge C_a \| Bs \backslash \{Q@S\}$ (Fig. 3). By gathering these answer constraints, we can compute all answer constraints for the alternative reply.

On the other hand, when a revised answer with the constraint C_r arrives, all processes using the first (or current) answer are split, in order to obtain the answer constraints that are logically equivalent to the answer constraints of:

$$\leftarrow C \wedge C_f \wedge C_r \| Bs \backslash \{Q@S\},$$

and the suspended original process is split as well, in order to obtain the answer constraints that are logically equivalent to the answer constraints of $\leftarrow C \wedge \neg C_f \wedge C_r \| Bs \backslash \{Q@S\}$ (Fig. 4). By gathering these answer constraints, we can override the previous reply by the revised reply.

3.2 Preliminary Definitions

A process is either an *ordinary process* or a *finished process*. An *ordinary process* P is an expression of the form $\langle PID, C, GS, WA, AA \rangle$, where:

- PID: the ID for a process denoted as $pid(P)$;
- C: the current constraint in the goal denoted as $pconst(P)$;
- GS: the body in the goal denoted as $gs(P)$;
- WA: a set of pairs $\langle Q@S, WAID \rangle$, where $Q@S$ is an askable atom and $WAID$ is the ID of an answer entry whose answer is awaited by the process. We denote WA as $wa(P)$;
- AA: a set of pairs $\langle Q@S, AAID \rangle$, where $Q@S$ is an askable atom and $AAID$ is the ID of an answer entry whose answer is used in the process. We denote AA as $aa(P)$.

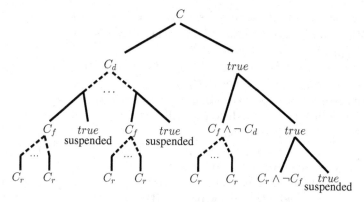

Fig. 4. When revised answer C_r for $Q@S$ arrives

A *finished process* FP is an expression of the form $\langle Query, FPID, C \rangle$, where:

- *Query*: an initial query for this process. It is used to send an answer to the asking agent;
- *FPID*: the ID for a process. This is also used when this answer is returned to the asking agent;
- *C*: the current constraint in the process.

For simplicity, an ordinary process is sometimes just called a process.

An *answer entry* A is an expression of the form $\langle Q@S, AID, C, UPIDs \rangle$, where:

- $Q@S$: the query given to the other agent denoted as $aq(A)$;
- AID: the ID for an answer entry denoted as $aid(A)$. We have the special IDs, "o" for the answer entry created when this query is firstly asked, and "d_1",... for default answers. We call an answer entry with the ID "o" an *original answer entry* for $Q@S$, an answer entry with an ID of "d_1",... a *default answer entry*, and other answer entries *ordinary answer entries*;
- C: the most recent answer constraint for $Q@S$ for answer entry A denoted as $aconst(A)$. The constraint of the original answer entry is defined as *true*;
- $UPIDs$: the set of IDs of processes using an answer in A denoted as $ups(A)$.

3.3 Process Reduction Phase

In the process reduction phase, we process the constraints in a regular CLP way. The only difference is that we may have to consider default information, or answers. In this subsection, we describe how we manage processes, following the above-given definitions.

We do the following until no more processes can be processed.

- When a query $Q_{init}@S_{self}$ is asked from another agent S', where S_{self} is the ID for this agent, we record Q_{init} as the initial query and S' as the asking agent. We then create a new process $\langle PID, true, Q_{init}, \emptyset, \emptyset \rangle$, where PID is a new process ID.

- If there is an ordinary process P such that $gs(P) = wa(P) = \emptyset$,
    1. We send an answer to the asking agent S' that is of the form:
       $\langle Q_{init}@S_{self}, pid(P), pconst(P)\rangle$.
    2. We change this process into a finished process of the form:
       $\langle Q_{init}@S_{self}, pid(P), pconst(P)\rangle$.
- Else if there is a process P such that $gs(P) \neq \emptyset$ and $wa(P) = \emptyset$, then we select
  an atom L in $gs(P)$ and reduce L as follows:
    - If L is a non-askable atom,
        1. For every rule R such that $pconst(P) \wedge (L = head(R)) \wedge const(R)$ is
           consistent, we do the following:
           (a) We create a new process $\langle newPID, newC, GS, \emptyset, AA\rangle$, where
               * $newPID$ is a new process ID;
               * $newC := pconst(P) \wedge (L = head(R)) \wedge const(R)$;
               * $GS := body(R) \cup gs(P)\backslash\{L\}$;
               * $AA := aa(P)$.
           (b) For every answer entry A s.t. $\langle aq(A), aid(A)\rangle$ in $aa(P)$,
               $ups(A) := ups(A) \cup \{newPID\}$.
        2. For every answer entry A s.t. $\langle aq(A), aid(A)\rangle$ in $aa(P)$,
           $ups(A) := ups(A)\backslash\{pid(P)\}$.
        3. We delete P.
    - If L is an askable atom $Q@S$,
        1. We do either of the following according to non-arrival/arrival of the
           answer.
           * If there is no ordinary answer entry of the form
             $\langle Q@S, AID, C, UPIDs\rangle$, then for each default "$Q@S \leftarrow C_d\|$"
             such that $pconst(P) \wedge C_d$ is consistent, we do the following:
             (a) We create a new process $\langle newPID, newC, GS, \emptyset, AA\rangle$, where
                 · $newPID$ is a new process ID;
                 · $newC := pconst(P) \wedge C_d$;
                 · $GS := gs(P)\backslash\{Q@S\}$;
                 · $AA := aa(P) \cup \{\langle Q@S, d\rangle\}$, where d is an ID for this default.
             (b) We associate the newly created process with a default d of $Q@S$
                 as follows:
                 · If there is a default answer entry
                   $A_d = \langle Q@S, d, C_d, UPIDs_d\rangle$, then
                   $ups(A_d) := UPIDs_d \cup \{newPID\}$.
                 · Else if there is no default answer of the form
                   $\langle Q@S, d, C_d, UPIDs_d\rangle$, we create an answer entry
                   $\langle Q@S, d, C_d, \{newPID\}\rangle$.
             (c) For every answer entry A s.t. $\langle aq(A), aid(A)\rangle$ in $aa(P)$,
                 $ups(A) := ups(A) \cup \{newPID\}$.
           * Else if there is an ordinary answer entry of the form
             $\langle Q@S, AID, C, UPIDs\rangle$, then for each ordinary answer entry
             $\langle Q@S, AID, C_a, UPIDs\rangle$ s.t. $pconst(P) \wedge C_a$ is consistent, we do
             the following:

(a) We create a new process $\langle newPID, newC, GS, \emptyset, AA \rangle$, where
- · $newPID$ is a new process ID;
- · $newC := pconst(P) \wedge C_a$;
- · $GS := GS \backslash \{Q@S\}$;
- · $AA := aa(P) \cup \{\langle Q@S, AID \rangle\}$.

(b) For every answer entry A s.t. $\langle aq(A), aid(A) \rangle$ in $aa(P)$,
$ups(A) := ups(A) \cup \{pid(P)\}$.

2. We associate P with $Q@S$ as follows:
- * If there is an original answer entry
  $A_o = \langle Q@S, o, true, UPIDs_o \rangle$, then
  $ups(A_o) := UPIDs_o \cup \{pid(P)\}$.
- * Else if there is no original answer entry of the form
  $\langle Q@S, o, true, UPIDs \rangle$, we create an answer entry
  $\langle Q@S, o, true, \{pid(P)\} \rangle$, and send a question Q to S.

3. $wa(P) := \{\langle Q@S, o \rangle\}$.

3.4   Fact Arrival Phase

Suppose that an answer is returned from an agent S for a question $Q@S$ of the form $\langle Q@S, AID, C \rangle$. Then, we do the following after one step of process reduction is finished.

- If there is no answer entry of the form $\langle Q@S, AID, C_f, UPIDs' \rangle^6$,
  1. We create an answer entry $\langle Q@S, AID, C, UPIDs \rangle$, where $UPIDs$ is initially set to $\emptyset$, but will be incremented as shown below.
  2. For every default answer entry for a default d of the form
     $\langle Q@S, d, C_d, UPIDs_d \rangle$ and for every process P_d such that $pid(P_d) \in UPIDs_d$, we do the following:
     - If P_d is a finished process of the form $\langle Q_{init}@S_{self}, PID, C_{Final} \rangle$ s.t. $C \wedge C_{Final} \neq C_{Final}$, we send an answer of the form $\langle Q_{init}@S_{self}, PID, C \wedge C_{Final} \rangle$ to the asking agent S'.
     - If P_d is an ordinary process, we do the following:
       (a) $wa(P_d) := wa(P_d) \cup \{\langle Q@S, d \rangle\}$.
       (b) $aa(P_d) := aa(P_d) \backslash \{\langle Q@S, d \rangle\}$.
       (c) If $C \wedge pconst(P_d)$ is consistent, we do the following:
           i. We create a new process $\langle newPID, newC, GS, WA, AA \rangle$, where
              * $newPID$ is a new process ID;
              * $newC := C \wedge pconst(P_d)$;
              * $GS := gs(P_d)$;
              * $WA := wa(P_d) \backslash \{\langle Q@S, d \rangle\}$;
              * $AA := aa(P_d) \cup \{\langle Q@S, AID \rangle\} \backslash \{\langle Q@S, d \rangle\}$.
           ii. $UPIDs := UPIDs \cup \{newPID\}$.
  3. Pick up the original answer entry of the form $\langle Q@S, o, true, UPIDs_o \rangle$.
  4. For every process P_o such that $pid(P_o) \in UPIDs_o$ and $C \wedge pconst(P_o) \wedge \bigwedge_{(Q@S \leftarrow C_d \parallel) \in \Delta} \neg C_d$ is consistent, do the following:

---

6 This means that the arriving answer is a first or alternative answer to the query $Q@S$.

(a) We create a new process $\langle newPID, newC, GS, WA, AA \rangle$, where
  - $newPID$ is a new process ID;
  - $newC := C \wedge pconst(P_o) \wedge \bigwedge_{(Q@S \leftarrow C_d\|) \in \Delta} \neg C_d$;
  - $GS := gs(P_o)$;
  - $WA := wa(P_o) \backslash \{\langle Q@S, o \rangle\}$;
  - $AA := aa(P_o) \cup \{\langle Q@S, AID \rangle\}$.
(b) $UPIDs := UPIDs \cup \{newPID\}$.
- Else if there is an answer entry of the form $\langle Q@S, AID, C_f, UPIDs' \rangle$[7],
  1. We change $\langle Q@S, AID, C_f, UPIDs' \rangle$ into $\langle Q@S, AID, C, UPIDs \rangle$, where $UPIDs := UPIDs'$ initially but will be incremented/decremented as shown below.
  2. For every process P such that $pid(P) \in UPIDs'$ do the following:
     - If P is a finished process of the form $\langle Q_{init}@S_{self}, PID, C_{Final} \rangle$ s.t. $C \wedge C_{Final} \neq C_{Final}$, we send an answer of the form $\langle Q_{init}@S_{self}, PID, C \wedge C_{Final} \rangle$ to the asking agent S'.
     - If P is an ordinary process, we do the following:
       * If $C \wedge pconst(P)$ is consistent, $pconst(P) := C \wedge pconst(P)$.
       * Otherwise, delete P and $UPIDs := UPIDs \backslash \{pid(P)\}$.
  3. Pick up the original answer entry of the form $\langle Q@S, o, true, UPIDs_o \rangle$.
  4. For every process P_o such that $pid(P_o) \in UPIDs_o$ and $C \wedge pconst(P_o) \wedge \neg C_f$ is consistent, we do the following:
     (a) We create a new process $\langle newPID, newC, GS, WA, AA \rangle$, where
       - $newPID$ is a new process ID;
       - $newC := C \wedge pconst(P_o) \wedge \neg C_f$;
       - $GS := gs(P_o)$;
       - $WA := wa(P_o) \backslash \{\langle Q@S, o \rangle\}$;
       - $AA := aa(P_o) \cup \{\langle Q@S, AID \rangle\}$.
     (b) $UPIDs := UPIDs \cup \{newPID\}$.

3.5 Execution Trace Example

We show a part of an execution trace for a question $rsv(R, L, D)$ in Example 1. In this trace, we consider a scenario that highlights process updates upon arrivals of an alternative answer and a revised answer. We firstly give the initial process $\langle p_0, true, \{rsv(R, L, D)\}, \emptyset, \emptyset \rangle$.

1. Select process p_0 and reduce it to p_1, p_2, p_3.
   Processes:
   $\langle p_1, \{R = tr, L = [a, b]\}, \{fr(D)@a, fr(D)@b\}, \emptyset, \emptyset \rangle$,
   $\langle p_2, \{R = sr, L = [a]\}, \{fr(D)@a, bs(D)@b\}, \emptyset, \emptyset \rangle$,
   $\langle p_3, \{R = sr, L = [b]\}, \{bs(D)@a, fr(D)@b\}, \emptyset, \emptyset \rangle$.

---

[7] This means that the arriving answer is a revised answer of one of the previous answers to the query $Q@S$.

2. Select p_1, and ask a question $fr(D)@a$, and create answer entries for $fr(D)@a$ and new processes p_4, p_5 for default answers.
   Answer entries:
   $\langle fr(D)@a, o, true, \{p_1\}\rangle$,
   $\langle fr(D)@a, d_1, \{D = 1\}, \{p_4\}\rangle$,
   $\langle fr(D)@a, d_2, \{D = 2\}, \{p_5\}\rangle$.
   Processes: p_2, p_3,
   $\langle p_4, \theta_{tr} \cup \{D = 1\}, \{fr(D)@b\}, \emptyset, \{\langle fr(D)@a, d_1\rangle\}\rangle^8$,
   $\langle p_5, \theta_{tr} \cup \{D = 2\}, \{fr(D)@b\}, \emptyset, \{\langle fr(D)@a, d_2\rangle\}\rangle$,
   $\langle p_1, \theta_{tr}, \{fr(D)@b\}, \{\langle fr(D)@a, o\rangle\}, \emptyset\rangle$.

3. Suppose that $\langle fr(d)@a, a_1, \{D=2\}\rangle$ is returned from agent a. We suspend p_4 and p_5 since they use a default answer and then create new processes p_6 from p_5 since the default answer used in p_5 is consistent with the returned answer. Note that we create no new process from p_1 since the returned answer contradicts one of the negations of default answers.
   Answer entries: $fra_o, fra_{d_1}, fra_{d_2}{}^9$,
   $\langle fr(D)@a, a_1, \{D = 2\}, \{p_6\}\rangle$.
   Processes: p_1, p_2, p_3,
   $\langle p_6, \theta_{tr2}, \{fr(D)@b\}, \emptyset, \{\langle fr(D)@a, a_1\rangle\}\rangle$,
   $\langle p_4, \theta_{tr1}, \{fr(D)@b\}, \{\langle fr(D)@a, d_1\rangle\}, \emptyset\rangle$,
   $\langle p_5, \theta_{tr2}, \{fr(D)@b\}, \{\langle fr(D)@a, d_2\rangle\}, \emptyset\rangle^{10}$.

4. Suppose that $\langle fr(D)@a, a_2, \{D = 3\}\rangle$ is returned from the agent a. Since this has a different answer ID from the previous answer in the last step, this answer is an alternative answer. Then, we create a new process from p_1 that is the original process for query $fr(D)@a$. Note that we create no new process from the processes created by default answers for $fr(D)@a$ since this answer contradicts the defaults.
   Answer entries: $fra_o, fra_{d_1}, fra_{d_2}, fra_{a_1}{}^{11}$,
   $\langle fr(D)@a, a_2, \{D = 3\}, \{p_7\}\rangle$.
   Processes: $p_1, p_2, p_3, p_4, p_5, p_6$,
   $\langle p_7, \theta_{tr} \cup \{D = 3, D \neq 1, D \neq 2\}, \{fr(D)@b\}, \emptyset, \{\langle fr(D)@a, a_2\rangle\}\rangle$.

5. Suppose that $\langle fr(D)@a, a_1, \{D = 1\}\rangle$ is returned from the agent a. The ID a_1 for the returned answer indicates that this answer is a revised answer for "$D = 2$". Therefore, we revise every process using a_1, which is recorded in the answer entry fra_{a_1}. This is p_6, but its associated constraint is contradictory to the returned answer, and therefore we kill this process. Then, we create a new process p_8 from p_1.

---

[8] $\theta_{tr} = \{R = tr, L = [a, b]\}$.

[9] $fra_o = \langle fr(D)@a, o, true, \{p_1\}\rangle$,
   $fra_{d_1} = \langle fr(D)@a, d_1, \{D = 1\}, \{p_4\}\rangle$,
   $fra_{d_2} = \langle fr(D)@a, d_2, \{D = 2\}, \{p_5\}\rangle$.

[10] $\theta_{tr2} = \theta_{tr} \cup \{D = 2\}$ and $\theta_{tr1} = \theta_{tr} \cup \{D = 1\}$.

[11] $fra_{a_1} = \langle fr(D)@a, a_1, \{D = 2\}, \{p_6\}\rangle$.

Answer entries: $fra_o, fra_{d_1}, fra_{d_2}, fra_{a_2}$ [12],
$\langle fr(D)@a, a_1, \{D = 1\}, \{p_8\}\rangle$.
Processes: $p_1, p_2, p_3, p_4, p_5, p_7$,
$\langle p_8, \theta_{tr} \cup \{D = 1, D \neq 2\}, \{fr(D)@b\}, \emptyset, \{\langle fr(D)@a, a_1\rangle\}\rangle$.

4   Correctness of the Operational Model

We guarantee that the above operational model gives a correct answer w.r.t. the most recent replies. Let us note that the order of reply messages is assumed to be preserved.

Theorem 1. *Let $\langle \Sigma, \Delta, \mathcal{P} \rangle$ be a framework for speculative constraint computation. Suppose that there is an ordinary process P such that $gs(P) = wa(P) = \emptyset$ for the initial query Q_{init}. Let*

$$\mathcal{R} = \{ \text{"}Q@S \leftarrow C\|\text{"} \mid there \ exists \ an \ answer \ entry \ \langle Q@S, AID, C, UPIDs \rangle$$
$$s.t. \ \langle Q@S, AID \rangle \in aa(P)\}.$$

Then, there exists an answer constraint C' w.r.t. Q_{init}, the framework, and $\mathcal{R}$ s.t. $\pi_V(pconst(P))$ entails $\pi_V(C')$, where V is the set of the variables that occur in Q_{init}, and π_V is the projection of constraints onto V.

Proof Sketch. See Appendix.   □

5   Space Complexity of Our Approach

Our approach, compared to traditional approaches (no belief revision), generates an additional cost in terms of space. In this section, we briefly show that the additional cost in space is linear. This cost is observed based on the size of the set PS of processes related to the revised or alternative answer to handle.

When a revised answer comes, say C_r, as shown in Fig. 4:

– If C_r entails the previous answer, say C_f, PS either remains the same size, or reduces (because some processes in PS may now have inconsistent constraints and therefore be killed);
– If C_r is inconsistent with C_f, then all the processes using C_f in PS are killed, the original suspended processes are duplicated and resumed with C_r, and therefore PS grows by at most, the number of original suspended processes;
– If C_r is consistent with C_f but does not entail it, PS grows by at most, the number of original suspended processes.

These three cases exhibit only linear (or less) behavior.

When an alternative answer comes, say C_a, as shown in Fig. 3, all the processes suspended by the first answer, as well as the original suspended processes, are duplicated and resumed with C_a. Therefore, PS grows by at most, the number of these suspended processes.

---

[12] $fra_{a_2} = \langle fr(D)@a, a_2, \{D = 3\}, \{p_7\}\rangle$.

As briefly covered here, the growth of the set of processes on the arrival of revised and alternative answers follows a linear behavior.

6   Conclusion

In this paper, we presented an operational model for speculative constraint processing with iterative revision for alternative answers. This paper is a generalization of two previous works; the work of revisable speculative computation for yes/no questions [7] and the work of non-revisable speculative computation for queries with constraints [5].

As for future work, we will prove the correctness and completeness for more general forms of multi-agent systems, where every agent can perform speculative computation. Our current framework is focused on master-slave multi-agent systems, and defines the operational model of the master agents. To handle a more general multi-agent system, we need to guarantee the appropriate computation of the overall system by additionally considering communication paths among agents. For another direction, we will also consider applications for this framework.

References

1. J. Jaffar, M. J. Maher, K. Marriott, and P. J. Stuckey. The semantics of constraint logic programs. *Journal of Logic Programming*, 37(1-3):1–46, 1998.
2. S. Janson and S. Haridi. Programming paradigms of the andorra kernel language. In *Proc. of ISLP'91*, pages 167–186, 1991.
3. R. A. Kowalski and F. Sadri. From logic programming towards multi-agent systems. *Annals of Mathematics and Artificial Intelligence*, 25:391–419, 1999.
4. F. Sadri and F. Toni. Interleaving belief revision and reasoning: Preliminary report. In *Proc. of Convegno Italiano di Logica Computazionale (CILC)*, 2005.
5. K. Satoh, P. Codognet, and H. Hosobe. Speculative constraint processing in multi-agent systems. In *Proc. of PRIMA2003*, volume 2891 of *LNCS*, pages 133–144, 2003.
6. K. Satoh, K. Inoue, K. Iwanuma, and C. Sakama. Speculative computation by abduction under incomplete communication environments. In *Proc. of ICMAS2000*, pages 263–270, 2000.
7. K. Satoh and K. Yamamoto. Speculative computation with multi-agent belief revision. In *Proc. of AAMAS2002*, pages 897–904, 2002.
8. C. Schulte. *Programming Constraint Services: High-Level Programming of Standard and New Constraint Services*, volume 2302 of *LNCS*. 2002.

Appendix

Proof Sketch of Theorem 1. To prove the property described in Theorem 1, we show that a more general property holds for any existing ordinary process at any "step" in the process reduction or fact arrival phase. By a "step", we mean the execution of operations in the process reduction or fact arrival phase from its beginning to its end, without returning to the beginning, and without transferring to the other phase. Then the property that we show is the following: at any n-th step, for any ordinary process P', there exists a sequence of reductions "$\leftarrow \|Q_{init}$", . . . ,

$$\text{"}\leftarrow C''\|\{Q@S \mid \langle Q@S, o\rangle \in wa(P')\} \cup gs(P')\text{"}$$

w.r.t. $\mathcal{P}$ and $BEL(\mathcal{R}_{P'}^{(n)}, \Delta)$, such that

$$\pi_V(pconst(P')) \text{ entails } \pi_V(C''),$$

where $\mathcal{R}_{P'}^{(n)}$ is the most recent reply set for P' at the n-th step, which is defined in the same way as $\mathcal{R}$ in Theorem 1.

Below we prove this property by induction on the progress of process reduction and fact arrival steps.

Induction base. When a query $Q_{init}@S_{self}$ is asked in the initial step, a process $P' = \langle PID, true, Q_{init}, \emptyset, \emptyset\rangle$ is created. This process corresponds to the initial goal "$\leftarrow \|Q_{init}$". The above property holds since $pconst(P') = true$ and $C'' = true$.

Induction step. Assume that, at the n-th step, the property holds.

Now consider the $(n+1)$-th step. It is straightforward to show that the property holds for the process reduction phase.

Here we consider the processing of a first or alternative answer in the fact arrival phase. Let the returned answer be $\langle Q@S, AID, C\rangle$. In this case, there is no answer entry in the form $\langle Q@S, AID, C_f, UPIDs'\rangle$.

Let $\langle Q@S, d, C_d, UPIDs_d\rangle$ be any default answer entry and P_d be any ordinary process such that $pid(P_d) \in UPIDs_d$. By the induction hypothesis, P_d satisfies the above property for some C'' and $\mathcal{R}_{P_d}^{(n)}$; that is, there is a sequence of reductions "$\leftarrow \|Q_{init}$", . . . , "$\leftarrow C_1\|\{Q@S\} \cup GS$", "$\leftarrow C_1 \wedge C_d\|GS$", . . . , "$\leftarrow C_1 \wedge C_d \wedge C_2\|\{Q'@S' \mid \langle Q'@S', o\rangle \in wa(P_d)\} \cup gs(P_d)$" w.r.t. $\mathcal{P}$ and $BEL(\mathcal{R}_{P_d}^{(n)}, \Delta)$, such that $\pi_V(pconst(P_d))$ entails $\pi_V(C_1 \wedge C_d \wedge C_2)$, where C_1 and C_2 are the constraints obtained before and after processing $Q@S$, respectively.

Assume that $C \wedge pconst(P_d)$ is consistent. Then a process $P' = \langle newPID, C \wedge pconst(P_d), gs(P_d), wa(P_d)\setminus\{\langle Q@S, d\rangle\}, aa(P_d)\cup\{\langle Q@S, AID\rangle\}\setminus\{\langle Q@S, d\rangle\}\rangle$ is created, and we have $\mathcal{R}_{P'}^{(n+1)} = \mathcal{R}_{P_d}^{(n)} \cup \{Q@S \leftarrow C\|\} \setminus \{Q@S \leftarrow C_d\|\}$. Then we can consider the sequence of reductions "$\leftarrow \|Q_{init}$", . . . , "$\leftarrow C_1\|\{Q@S\} \cup GS$", "$\leftarrow C_1 \wedge C\|GS$", . . . , "$\leftarrow C_1 \wedge C \wedge C_2\|\{Q'@S' \mid \langle Q'@S', o\rangle \in wa(P')\} \cup gs(P')$" w.r.t. $\mathcal{P}$ and $BEL(\mathcal{R}_{P'}^{(n+1)}, \Delta)$. Then, $\pi_V(pconst(P'))$ entails $\pi_V(C_1 \wedge C \wedge C_2)$ since $pconst(P') = C \wedge pconst(P_d)$ and $\pi_V(pconst(P_d))$ entails $\pi_V(C_1 \wedge C_d \wedge C_2)$. Thus, the above property holds for P'.

For the processing of a first answer, this step changes P_d by setting $wa(P_d) := wa(P_d) \cup \{\langle Q@S, d\rangle\}$ and $aa(P_d) := aa(P_d) \setminus \{\langle Q@S, d\rangle\}$, and hence we have $\mathcal{R}_{P_d}^{(n+1)} = \mathcal{R}_{P_d}^{(n)} \setminus \{Q@S \leftarrow C_d\|\}$. In the other case (that is, for processing an alternative answer), P_d is unchanged since $\langle Q@S, d\rangle \in wa(P_d)$ and $\langle Q@S, d\rangle \notin aa(P_d)$ hold for the original P_d, and therefore, we have $\mathcal{R}_{P_d}^{(n+1)} = \mathcal{R}_{P_d}^{(n)}$. In both cases, $BEL(\mathcal{R}_{P_d}^{(n+1)}, \Delta) = BEL(\mathcal{R}_{P_d}^{(n)}, \Delta)$ since "$Q@S \leftarrow C_d\|$" $\in \Delta$. Therefore, the above property is kept satisfied for P_d.

Next, let $\langle Q@S, o, true, UPIDs_o \rangle$ be the original answer entry and P_o be any ordinary process such that $pid(P_o) \in UPIDs_o$. By the induction hypothesis, P_o satisfies the above property for some C'' and $\mathcal{R}_{P_o}^{(n)}$; that is, there is a sequence of reductions "$\leftarrow \|Q_{init}$", ..., "$\leftarrow C''\|\{Q@S\} \cup gs(P_o)$" w.r.t. $\mathcal{P}$ and $BEL(\mathcal{R}_{P_o}^{(n)}, \Delta)$, such that $\pi_V(pconst(P_o))$ entails $\pi_V(C'')$. Since this step does not change P_o, the above property is kept satisfied for P_o.

Assume that $C \wedge pconst(P_o) \wedge \bigwedge_{(Q@S \leftarrow C_d\|) \in \Delta} \neg C_d$ is consistent. Then a process $P' = \langle newPID, C \wedge pconst(P_o) \wedge \bigwedge_{(Q@S \leftarrow C_d\|) \in \Delta} \neg C_d, gs(P_o), wa(P_o) \setminus \{\langle Q@S, o\rangle\}, aa(P_o) \cup \{\langle Q@S, AID\rangle\}\}\rangle$ is created, and we have $\mathcal{R}_{P'}^{(n+1)} = \mathcal{R}_{P_o}^{(n)} \cup \{Q@S \leftarrow C\|\}$. Then we can consider the sequence of reductions "$\leftarrow \|Q_{init}$", ..., "$\leftarrow C''\|\{Q@S\} \cup gs(P')$", "$\leftarrow C'' \wedge C\|gs(P')$" w.r.t. $\mathcal{P}$ and $BEL(\mathcal{R}_{P'}^{(n+1)}, \Delta)$. Then $\pi_V(pconst(P'))$ entails $\pi_V(C'' \wedge C)$ since $pconst(P') = C \wedge pconst(P_o) \wedge \bigwedge_{(Q@S \leftarrow C_d\|) \in \Delta} \neg C_d$ and $\pi_V(pconst(P_o))$ entails $\pi_V(C'')$. Therefore, the above property holds for P'.

The above property is kept satisfied for the other processes that are not handled in this case, since those processes and their most recent reply sets are unchanged.

Therefore, the above property holds for any processes after processing a first or alternative answer in the fact arrival phase.

Similarly, we can show that the above property holds for the processing of a revised answer in the fact arrival phase. Thus, the above property holds in all the cases.

Since the property described in Theorem 1 corresponds to the special case of the above property, where $gs(P') = wa(P') = \emptyset$, Theorem 1 holds. $\square$

Intention Recognition in the Situation Calculus and Probability Theory Frameworks

Robert Demolombe and Ana Mara Otermin Fernandez*

ONERA Toulouse,
France
Robert.Demolombe@cert.fr,
txantxita@hotmail.com

Abstract. A method to recognize agent's intentions is presented in a framework that combines the logic of Situation Calculus and Probability Theory. The method is restricted to contexts where the agent only performs procedures in a given library of procedures, and where the system that intends to recognize the agent's intentions has a complete knowledge of the actions performed by the agent.

An original aspect is that the procedures are defined for human agents and not for artificial agents. The consequence is that the procedures may offer the possibility to do any kind of actions between two given actions, and they also may forbid to perform some specific actions. Then, the problem is different and more complex than the standard problem of plan recognition.

To select the procedures that partially match the observations we consider the procedures that have the greatest estimated probability. This estimation is based on the application of Bayes' theorem and on specific heuristics. These heuristics depend on the history and not just on the last observation.

A PROLOG prototype of the presented method has been implemented.

1 Introduction

When two agents have to interact it is important for each agent to know the other agent's intentions because this knowledge allows to anticipate his future behavior. This information can be used either to help the other agent to do what he intends to do or to control whether what he does is compatible with his intention. Even if an agent can never be sure that he knows the other agent's intentions an uncertain information is much better than a complete ignorance when a decision has to be taken.

In this paper a method is proposed to recognize what are the agent's intentions in the particular context of a pilot that interacts with an aircraft. The first specificity of this context is that the pilot performs procedures that are very well defined in a handbook. The second specificity is that the procedures are defined in terms of commands that have to be performed (like to turn a switch

---

* Also student at: Universidad Politenica de Madrid.

F. Toni and P. Torroni (Eds.): CLIMA VI, LNAI 3900, pp. 358–372, 2006.

on) and it is reasonable to assume that the performance of these commands can be perceived thanks to sensors in the aircraft. Then, it is possible to design a system (for instance a part of the automatic pilot of the aircraft) that has the capacity to observe all the commands performed by the pilot.

Under this assumption the system can compare the sequence of observations with the procedure definitions in the handbook and it can determine the procedures that match with these observations. The procedures that have the "best" match are assigned to the agent's intentions.

To define a method to recognize the pilot's intentions we have to find solutions to three independent problems:

1. to select a language to represent the procedures in formal terms,
2. to define a formal characterization of the procedures that match with the observations,
3. to define a method to select the procedures that have the "best" match and are assigned to the agent's intention.

In a previous work Demolombe and Hamon [6, 10] have proposed solutions to problems 1 and 2 in the logical framework of the Situation Calculus. The Situation Calculus is a variant of classical first order logic, that is the reason why it is more convenient for computational logic than modal logics.

The contribution of this paper is to propose a solution to problem 3 in a framework that combines Situation Calculus and Probability Theory and which is based on Bayes' theorem. Probabilities have already been used in combination with Situation Calculus in [12] to deal with no deterministic actions, but that is a quite different problem.

There are many other works that have similar objectives in the field of plan recognition [13] and many of them make use of probabilities [4, 8, 1, 5] or use an utility function [15]. Baier in [3] also uses the framework of the Situation Calculus but without probabilities. Many of them have been designed in the particular context of natural language analysis [7, 2, 5] or game theory [1].

The original feature in our case is that the pilot's procedures may allow any other command in between a sequence of two prescribed commands and it may be specified that some commands are forbidden. Also it may happen that the pilot has the intention to perform several procedures in parallel. The consequence is that problems 2 and 3 are much more complex than the standard problem of plan recognition.

The paper is organized as follows. In sections 2 and 3 the solutions to problems 1 and 2 are recalled. In section 4 the method to solve problem 3 is presented. In that section we start with the analysis of a typical example, we define a general method to compute probabilities, we define heuristics to estimate the probabilities and finally we apply the method to the example to show that the results fit the intuitive requirements. Possible refinements or extensions of the method are presented in the conclusion.

Since the method can be applied to many other contexts we shall use the general term "agent" instead of "pilot", and "action" instead of "command".

2   A Brief Introduction to the Situation Calculus and to a GOLOG Extension

The logical framework of Situation Calculus [17] is used to represent the states of the world and the actions that are performed by the agent.

The Situation Calculus is a typed first order logic with equality (except some limited fragments that are of second order). In the language there are two kinds of predicates. The predicates whose truth value may change after performance of an action are called "fluents". They have exactly 1 argument of the type situation which is the last argument. The other predicates have no argument of the type situation.

For example, we may have the predicates:

$nationality(x)$: the nationality of the aircraft is x.

$gear.extended(s)$: in the situation s the landing gear is extended.

$altitude(x, s)$: in the situation s the aircraft altitude is x.

Here $altitude(x, s)$ and $gear.extended(s)$ are fluents, and $nationality(x)$ is not a fluent.

The terms of type situation may be constant or variable symbols of the type situation, or terms of the form $do(a, s)$ where do is a designated function symbol, a is a term of type action and s is a term of type situation.

For instance, if S_0 is a constant of type situation and $extend.gear$ and $retract.gear$ are constants of type action, the following terms are of type situation: S_0, $do(extend.gear, S_0)$, $do(extend.gear, s)$ and $do(retract.gear, do(extend.gear, S_0))$.

The term $do(retract.gear, do(extend.gear, S_0))$ denotes the situation where we are after performance of the actions $extend.gear$ and $retract.gear$.

As a matter of simplification we use the notation $do([a_1, \ldots, a_n], s)$ to denote $do(a_n, \ldots, do(a_1, s) \ldots)$.

The grammar of the formulas of the Situation Calculus is defined as usual for classical first order logics.

A successor relation[1] is defined on the set of situations. Intuitively $s \leq s'$ means that the situation s' is reached from the situation s after some sequence of action. In semiformal terms, $s \leq s'$ is the smallest relation that satisfies the following properties:

$$s \leq s' \stackrel{\text{def}}{=} (s < s') \vee (s = s')$$
$$\forall s \forall s' \forall a(s' = do(a, s) \rightarrow s < s')$$
$$\forall s \forall s' \forall s''((s < s') \wedge (s' < s'') \rightarrow (s < s''))$$

To define the truth value of the fluents in any situation a successor state axiom has to be given for each fluent. For example, for $gear.extended(s)$ we have:

$$\forall s \forall a(gear.extended(do(a, s)) \leftrightarrow a = extend.gear \vee gear.extended(s) \wedge \neg(a = retract.gear))$$

---

[1] In this paper the definition of the successor relation is the only part of the Situation Calculus that requires second order logic.

The intuitive meaning of this axiom is that the only action that can cause $gear.extended(do(a, s))$ to be true (resp. false) is the action $extend.gear$ (resp. $retract.gear$).

The GOLOG language [14] is a programming language for robots but it can be used for other kinds of agents. Its expressive power is the same as ALGOL and its semantics is defined in the logic of the Situation Calculus. Programs are terms that represent complex actions defined with several operators.

Here, for simplicity, we have only considered the operator of sequence (denoted by ";"), test (denoted by "ϕ?") and non deterministic choice (denoted by "|"). To represent what is called in the following "procedures" we have added the "negation" operator (denoted by "$-$") and the "any sequence of actions" term (denoted by "σ"). The motivation of this extension can be explained with the following example.

Let us, consider the procedure called "fire on board", which is described for a small private aircraft. The procedure says that in case of engine fire the pilot 1) turns off fuel feed, 2) sets full throttle, and 3) sets mixture off. These three primitive actions, or commands, are respectively denoted by $fuel.off$, $full.throttle$ and $mixture.off$, and the procedure is denoted by $fire.on.board$.

However, it is implicit in the procedure definition that between actions 1) and 2) or between 2) and 3) the pilot can do any other action. For example, he can call air traffic control. It is also implicit that after turning off fuel feed he must not turn on fuel feed. That is just common sense for a human being but it has to be made explicit to define a formal method that can be used by the system which observes the pilot.

Then, in the modified GOLOG language the "fire on board" procedure is represented by:

$$fire.on.board \stackrel{\text{def}}{=} fuel.off; (\sigma/fuel.on); full.throttle; (\sigma/fuel.on); mixture.off$$

where α_1/α_2 is an abbreviation for $\alpha_1 - (\sigma; \alpha_2; \sigma)$ which intuitively means that the sequence of actions which is a performance of α_1 must not contain a sequence of actions which is a performance of α_2.

In the case of programs for an artificial agent there is no need for the term σ nor for the operator "/" because **an artificial agent only does what is specified in the program**. That makes the basic difference between a program and what is called here a "procedure".

The formal definition of the modified GOLOG language is:

- atomic actions, test actions and σ are procedures,
- if α_1 and α_2 are procedures, then $(\alpha_1; \alpha_2)$, $(\alpha_1|\alpha_2)$ and $(\alpha_1 - \alpha_2)$ are procedures.

The formal definition of the procedures is defined by formulas of the Situation Calculus language. These formulas are denoted by the property $Do_p(\alpha, s, s')$ whose intuitive meaning is:

$Do_p(\alpha, s, s')$: s' is a situation that can be reached from the situation s after performance of the procedure α.

The formal semantics of $Do_p(\alpha, s, s')$ is:

$$Do_p(a, s, s') \overset{\text{def}}{=} s' = do(a, s) \text{ if } a \text{ is an atomic action.}$$
$$Do_p(\sigma, s, s') \overset{\text{def}}{=} s \leq s'$$
$$Do_p(\phi?, s, s') \overset{\text{def}}{=} \phi[s] \wedge s' = s$$
$$Do_p(\alpha_1; \alpha_2, s, s') \overset{\text{def}}{=} \exists s_1 (Do_p(\alpha_1, s, s_1) \wedge Do_p(\alpha_2, s_1, s'))$$
$$Do_p(\alpha_1 | \alpha_2, s, s') \overset{\text{def}}{=} Do_p(\alpha_1, s, s') \vee Do_p(\alpha_2, s, s')$$
$$Do_p(\alpha_1 - \alpha_2, s, s') \overset{\text{def}}{=} Do_p(\alpha_1, s, s') \wedge \neg Do_p(\alpha_2, s, s')$$

This modified GOLOG language gives a solution to the problem 1 that we have mentioned in the introduction.

3   Doing a Procedure

To characterize the fact that a sequence of performed actions "matches" a partial performance of a procedure, in the sense that this sequence **can be interpreted** as a partial performance of the procedure, we use the property $Doing(\alpha, s, s')$. However, this property does not guarantee that the agent is performing this procedure.

In informal terms the property $Doing(\alpha, s, s')$ holds if the three following conditions are satisfied:

1. The agent has begun executing a part α' of α between s and s'.
2. The agent has not completely executed α between s and s'.
3. The actions performed between s and s' do not prevent the continuation of the execution of α.

In a first step we define the property $Do_m(\alpha, s, s')$ whose intuitive meaning is that we have $Do_p(\alpha, s, s')$ and there is no shorter sequence of actions between s and s' such that we have Do_p for this sequence. We have:

$$Do_m(\alpha, s, s') \overset{\text{def}}{=} Do_p(\alpha, s, s') \wedge \neg\exists s_1 (Do_p(\alpha, s, s_1) \wedge s_1 \leq s')$$

Then, we define the property $Do_s(\alpha, s, s')$ whose intuitive meaning is that the sequence of actions between s and s' satisfies the above conditions 1, 2 and 3. We have:

$$Do_s(\alpha, s, s') \overset{\text{def}}{=} \exists \alpha' (start(\alpha', \alpha) \wedge$$
$$\exists s_1 (s_1 \leq s' \wedge Do_m(\alpha', s, s_1)) \wedge$$
$$\neg\exists s_2 (s_2 \leq s' \wedge Do_m(\alpha, s, s_2)) \wedge$$
$$\exists s_3 (s' < s_3 \wedge Do_m(\alpha, s, s_3)))$$

where $start(\alpha', \alpha)$ means that α can be reformulated into a procedure of the form: $(\alpha'; \alpha'')|\beta$ which has the same semantics as α, i.e. $\forall s \forall s' (Do_p(\alpha, s, s') \leftrightarrow Do_p((\alpha'; \alpha'')|\beta, s, s'))$.

The condition 1 is expressed by $\exists \alpha' (start(\alpha', \alpha) \wedge \exists s_1 (s_1 \leq s' \wedge Do_m(\alpha', s, s_1))$, the strict interpretation of condition 2 is expressed by $\neg\exists s_2 (s_2 \leq s' \wedge Do_m(\alpha, s, s_2))$, and the condition 3 is expressed by $\exists s_3 (s' < s_3 \wedge Do_m(\alpha, s, s_3))$.

Finally, the definition of $Doing(\alpha, s, s')$ is:

$$Doing(\alpha, s, s') \overset{\text{def}}{=} \exists s_1(s \leq s_1 \land Do_s(\alpha, s_1, s')) \land \neg\exists s_2(s \leq s_2 \land s_2 < s_1 \land Do_s(\alpha, s_2, s_1)))$$

The condition $\exists s_1(s \leq s_1 \land Do_s(\alpha, s_1, s'))$ expresses that there is an execution of α that has begun in s_1 and has not ended, and the condition $\neg\exists s_2(s \leq s_2 \land s_2 < s_1 \land Do_s(\alpha, s_2, s_1))$ expresses that there is no previous α execution which has started and not ended before s_1.

4 Intention Recognition

This section presents a method for choosing between several procedures, that satisfy the $Doing$ property, the one that can be assigned by the system to the agent's intention.

This assignment is never guaranteed to correspond to the true agent's intention, and due to this uncertainty it is sensible to make use of probabilities to make the choice.

Before going into the formal presentation of the method let us give a simple example to intuitively show what are the basic guidelines[2] and assumptions of the method.

4.1 A Simple Example

Let us consider the three following procedures[3].

$\alpha = a; \sigma; b; \sigma; c$
$\beta = d; \sigma; e$
$\gamma = a; \sigma; f$

Let us assume that we are in the situation s_5 where the following sequence of actions has been performed: $[f, a, d, b, c]$, that is in formal terms:

$$s_5 = do([f, a, d, b, c], s_0).$$

In the situation $s_1 = do(f, s_0)$ there is no procedure which is compatible with the performed action f. We have $\neg Doing(\alpha, s_0, s_1)$, $\neg Doing(\beta, s_0, s_1)$ and $\neg Doing(\gamma, s_0, s_1)$.

We have adopted the following assumption.

Assumption H1. If an agent has the intention to do a procedure α then he does the actions that are defined by the procedure α.

According to H1 in s_1 the system knows that the agent did not have the intention to do α in s_0, because if he had the intention to do α in s_0 he would

---

[2] These guidelines are expected properties and they should not be confused with the assumptions.

[3] In previous sections α, β and γ are procedure variables. Here specific constants are assigned to these variables.

have started to do α and he would have done the action a in s_1 instead of f. The same for β and γ.

Nevertheless in s_0 the system can accept that the probability that the agent has the intention to do α is not equal to 0. Then, we have accepted the additional assumption:

Assumption H2. If the agent in the situation s_i is not doing α, in the sense that $\neg Doing(\alpha, s_0, s_i)$, then in s_i the probability that he has the intention to do α is independent of s_i, and this probability is denoted by $\pi(\alpha)$.

Let us define the following notations.

$P(\phi)$: probability that ϕ holds.

$Int(\alpha, s_i)$: in the situation s_i the agent has the intention to do α^4.

In formal terms H2 can be expressed by:

$$\forall s \forall s' \forall \alpha (s \leq s' \wedge \neg Doing(\alpha, s, s') \rightarrow P(Int(\alpha, s')) = \pi(\alpha))$$

Since for any procedure α we have $\neg Doing(\alpha, s_0, s_0)$, from H2 we have: $P(Int(\alpha, s_0)) = P(Int(\alpha, s_1)) = \pi(\alpha)$, $P(Int(\beta, s_0)) = P(Int(\beta, s_1)) = \pi(\beta)$ and $P(Int(\gamma, s_0)) = P(Int(\gamma, s_1)) = \pi(\gamma)$.

In the situation $s_2 = do([f, a], s_0)$ we have $\neg Doing(\beta, s_0, s_2)$ and $P(Int(\beta, s_2)) = \pi(\beta)$, and now we have $Doing(\alpha, s_0, s_2)$ and $Doing(\gamma, s_0, s_2)$.

The fact that the action a has been performed is a good argument for the system to believe that the agent has the intention to do α and to believe that he has the intention to do γ. Then we should have $P(Int(\alpha, s_2)) > P(Int(\alpha, s_1))$ and $P(Int(\gamma, s_2)) > P(Int(\gamma, s_1))$.

It is sensible to assume that $P(Int(\alpha, s_i))$ and $P(Int(\gamma, s_i))$ increase in the same way from s_1 to s_2.

So, if $\pi(\alpha) = \pi(\beta) = \pi(\gamma)$, $Int(\alpha, s_2)$ and $Int(\gamma, s_2)$ have the same and the greatest probability and the system believes that the agent has the intention to do α and that he has the intention to do γ.

Let us use the following notation.

$BInt(\alpha, s_i)$: in the situation s_i the system believes that the agent has the intention to do α.

Using this notation we have: $BInt(\alpha, s_2)$, $\neg BInt(\beta, s_2)$ and $BInt(\gamma, s_2)$.

We have adopted the following general assumption.

Assumption H3. In a situation s_i such that $Doing(\alpha, s_0, s_i)$, if there is no procedure β such that $Doing(\beta, s_0, s_i)$ and $P(Int(\beta, s_i)) > P(Int(\alpha, s_i))$, then the system believes in s_i that the agent has the intention to do α (i.e. we have $BInt(\alpha, s_i)$).

H3 can be reformulated as:

$BInt(\alpha, s)$ iff $Doing(\alpha, s_0, s)$ and there is no procedure β such that $P(Int(\beta, s)) > P(Int(\alpha, s))$

In the situation $s_3 = do([f, a, d], s_0)$ we have $Doing(\alpha, s_0, s_3)$, $Doing(\beta, s_0, s_3)$ and $Doing(\gamma, s_0, s_3)$.

---

[4] To be more precise we should say that the agent has the intention to reach a situation where α has been done.

In s_3 we can assume that $P(Int(\beta, s_i))$ has increased from s_2 to s_3 in the same way as $P(Int(\alpha, s_i))$ and $P(Int(\gamma, s_i))$ have increased from s_1 to s_2.

For the procedures α and γ, in s_2 the agent has the choice between doing the next recommended action (that are respectively b and f) or doing any other action. We have assumed that if he does not do the recommended action, then the probability to do the corresponding procedure decreases, because the last observed action does not confirm that he has the intention to do this procedure.

Then, if $\pi(\alpha) = \pi(\beta) = \pi(\gamma)$ we have: $P(Int(\alpha, s_3)) < P(Int(\beta, s_3))$ and $P(Int(\gamma, s_3)) < P(Int(\beta, s_3))$, and therefore we have $BInt(\beta, s_3)$, $\neg BInt(\alpha, s_3)$ and $\neg BInt(\gamma, s_3))$.

In the situation $s_4 = do([f, a, d, b], s_0)$ we have $Doing(\alpha, s_0, s_4)$, $Doing(\beta, s_0, s_4)$ and $Doing(\gamma, s_0, s_4)$.

In that situation the action b is a recommended action for α but it is not a recommended action for γ. Then, if $\pi(\alpha) = \pi(\gamma)$ we should have $P(Int(\alpha, s_4)) > P(Int(\gamma, s_4))$.

If we compare the procedures α and β in s_4, there are two performed actions (a and b) that are recommended in α, and there is only one (a) which is recommended in β. The number of performed actions that are not recommended is the same for α and β (action d for α and action b for β). Therefore, if $\pi(\alpha) = \pi(\beta)$ we should have $P(Int(\alpha, s_4)) > P(Int(\beta, s_4))$. Then, we have $BInt(\alpha, s_4)$, $\neg BInt(\beta, s_4)$ and $\neg BInt(\gamma, s_4)$.

In the situation $s_5 = do([f, a, d, b, c], s_0)$ we have $\neg Doing(\alpha, s_0, s_5)$ (because α has been executed), $Doing(\beta, s_0, s_5)$ and $Doing(\gamma, s_0, s_5)$.

The number of recommended actions is 1 for β and γ in s_5, but the number of not recommended actions is 3 for γ and 2 for β. Then, if $\pi(\alpha) = \pi(\beta) = \pi(\gamma)$ we should have $P(Int(\beta, s_5)) > P(Int(\gamma, s_5))$ and $P(Int(\beta, s_5)) > P(Int(\alpha, s_5))$. Therefore we have $BInt(\beta, s_5)$, $\neg BInt(\alpha, s_5)$ and $\neg BInt(\gamma, s_5)$.

From this example we can derive some general guidelines that are expressed with the following terminology.

In a procedure definition we call an action a **prescribed** action if that action explicitly appears in the procedure and it is just preceded by an explicit action.

For example, if α has the form: $\ldots; a; b; \ldots$ then this occurrence of b is a prescribed action in α. Notice that in a given procedure some occurrences of b may be prescribed actions and others not, like in $\alpha = c; \sigma; b; a; b$.

In a procedure definition we call an action a **recommended** action if that action explicitly appears in the procedure and it is just preceded by a term of the form σ or σ/β.

For example, if α has the form: $\ldots; \sigma; a; \ldots$ or $\ldots; \sigma/(b|c); a; \ldots$ then this occurrence of a is a recommended action in α.

Let us call A the set of actions that can be done by the agent and can be observed by the system.

In a procedure definition we call an action a **tolerated** action if the procedure has the form: $\ldots; \sigma; a; \ldots$ and this action is in $A - \{a\}$.

For example, if $A = \{a, b, c, d, e\}$ and α has the form: $\ldots; \sigma; a; \ldots$, then the set of tolerated actions for this occurrence of σ is $\{b, c, d, e\}$.

In a procedure definition we call an action a **restricted tolerated** action if the procedure has the form: $\ldots; \sigma/(a_{i_1}|\ldots|a_{i_l}); a; \ldots$ and this action is in $A - \{a_{i_1}, \ldots, a_{i_l}, a\}$.

For example, if α has the form: $\ldots; \sigma/(b|d); a; \ldots$ the set of restricted tolerated actions for this occurrence of σ is $\{c, e\}$.

With these definitions we can formulate our basic guidelines in that way.

Guideline A. If in the situation s_i the last performed action is a prescribed action of α, then $P(Int(\alpha, s_i))$ should be much greater than $P(Int(\alpha, s_{i-1}))$.
Guideline B. If in the situation s_i the last performed action is a recommended action of α, then $P(Int(\alpha, s_i))$ should be greater than $P(Int(\alpha, s_{i-1}))$, but it should be less greater than in the case of a prescribed action.
Guideline C. If in the situation s_i the last performed action is a tolerated action of α, then $P(Int(\alpha, s_i))$ should be lower than $P(Int(\alpha, s_{i-1}))$.
Guideline D. If in the situation s_i the last performed action is a restricted tolerated action of α, then the fact that $P(Int(\alpha, s_i))$ is greater or lower than $P(Int(\alpha, s_{i-1}))$ depends on the cardinality of the set of restricted tolerated actions.

We also have adopted the following assumption about the evolution of the fact that the agent has the intention to do a procedure α.

Assumption H4. In a situation s_i such that we have $Doing(\alpha, s_0, s_i)$ it is assumed that the agent has in s_i the intention to do α iff he has the intention to do α in s_{i-1}.

The assumption H4 is expressed in formal terms as follows.

$(H4)\quad \forall s \forall s' \forall s'' \forall a \forall \alpha((Doing(\alpha, s, s'') \wedge s'' = do(a, s')) \rightarrow (Int(\alpha, s'') \leftrightarrow Int(\alpha, s')))$

H4 is logically equivalent to the conjunction of H'4 and H''4.

$(H'4)\quad \forall s \forall s' \forall s'' \forall a \forall \alpha(Doing(\alpha, s, s'') \wedge s'' = do(a, s') \wedge Int(\alpha, s') \rightarrow Int(\alpha, s''))$
$(H''4)\quad \forall s \forall s' \forall s'' \forall a \forall \alpha(Doing(\alpha, s, s'') \wedge s'' = do(a, s') \wedge Int(\alpha, s'') \rightarrow Int(\alpha, s'))$

The assumption H'4 means that the agent's intention is persistent as long as the procedure α is not completely performed. That corresponds to the notion of intention persistence proposed by Cohen and Levesque in [9] (see also [16]).

The assumption H''4 corresponds to a different idea. This idea is that if the action a performed by the agent is consistent with the fact that he is doing α and in the situation s'' the agent has the intention to do α, then he has performed the action a **because** in s' he had the intention to do α.

4.2   General Method to Compute the Probabilities

To present the general method we shall use the following notations.

$A = \{a_1, a_2, \ldots, a_N\}$: set of actions that can be performed by the agent and that can be observed by the system.

We adopt the following assumption.

Assumption H5. It is assumed that in the language definition the set of atomic action constant symbols is A.

The assumption H5 intuitively means that the actions performed by the agent that cannot be observed by the system are ignored by the system. This assumption is consistent with the fact that what the system believes about the agents' intentions is only founded on his observations.

o_i: ith observation action performed by the system.

$a_{j_i} = obs(o_i)$: a_{j_i} is the action performed by the agent that has been observed by the system by means of the observation action o_i.

O_i: short hand to denote the proposition $a_{j_i} = obs(o_i)$.

$O_{1,i} \stackrel{\text{def}}{=} O_1 \wedge O_2 \wedge \ldots \wedge O_i$

$O_{1,0} \stackrel{\text{def}}{=} true$

s_0: initial situation.

$s_i = do(a_{j_i}, s_{i-1})$

$P(Int(\alpha, s_i)|O_{1,i})$: probability that in the situation s_i the agent has the intention to do α if the sequence of observations is $O_{1,i}$.

From Bayes' theorem we have:

(1) $P(Int(\alpha, s_i)|O_{1,i}) = \frac{P(O_{1,i}|Int(\alpha,s_i)) \times P(Int(\alpha,s_i))}{P(O_{1,i})}$

From (1) we have:

(2) $P(Int(\alpha, s_i)|O_{1,i}) = \frac{P(O_i \wedge O_{1,i-1}|Int(\alpha,s_i)) \times P(Int(\alpha,s_i))}{P(O_i \wedge O_{1,i-1})}$

Then, we have:

(3) $P(Int(\alpha, s_i)|O_{1,i}) = \frac{P(O_i|O_{1,i-1} \wedge Int(\alpha,s_i))}{P(O_i|O_{1,i-1})} \times \frac{P(O_{1,i-1}|Int(\alpha,s_i)) \times P(Int(\alpha,s_i))}{P(O_{1,i-1})}$

If $\neg Doing(\alpha, s_0, s_i)$:

From H2 we have: $P(Int(\alpha, s_i)|O_{1,i}) = P(Int(\alpha, s_i))$. Then we have:

(4) $P(Int(\alpha, s_i)|O_{1,i}) = \pi(\alpha)$

If $Doing(\alpha, s_0, s_i)$:

From H4 we have: $Int(\alpha, s_i) \leftrightarrow Int(\alpha, s_{i-1})$.

Then, from (3) we have:

(5) $P(Int(\alpha, s_i)|O_{1,i}) = \frac{P(O_i|O_{1,i-1} \wedge Int(\alpha,s_{i-1}))}{P(O_i|O_{1,i-1})} \times \frac{P(O_{1,i-1}|Int(\alpha,s_{i-1})) \times P(Int(\alpha,s_{i-1}))}{P(O_{1,i-1})}$

Therefore we have:

(6) $P(Int(\alpha, s_i)|O_{1,i}) = \frac{P(O_i|O_{1,i-1} \wedge Int(\alpha,s_{i-1}))}{P(O_i|O_{1,i-1})} \times P(Int(\alpha, s_{i-1})|O_{1,i-1})$

If we adopt the notations:

$num_i(\alpha) \stackrel{\text{def}}{=} P(O_i|O_{1,i-1} \wedge Int(\alpha, s_{i-1}))$

$den_i(\alpha) \stackrel{\text{def}}{=} P(O_i|O_{1,i-1})$

$F_i(\alpha) \stackrel{\text{def}}{=} \frac{num_i(\alpha)}{den_i(\alpha)}$

We have:

(7) $P(Int(\alpha, s_i)|O_{1,i}) = F_i(\alpha) \times P(Int(\alpha, s_{i-1})|O_{1,i-1})$

The formula (7) allows to regress the computation of $P(Int(\alpha, s_i)|O_{1,i})$ until a situation s_j where we have $\neg Doing(\alpha, s_0, s_j)$[5].

4.3   Heuristics to Estimate the Probabilities

To define heuristics to estimate the value of $F_i(\alpha)$ we have restricted the set of procedures to procedures of the form:

---

[5] Notice that for any procedure α we have $\neg Doing(\alpha, s_0, s_0)$.

$$\alpha = A_1; \Sigma_1; \ldots; A_k; \Sigma_k; A_{k+1}; \ldots; A_s$$

where each A_k denotes an atomic action in A and Σ_k either is absent or denotes a term of the form $\sigma/(a_{i_1}|\ldots|a_{i_l})$ where each a_{i_j} is in A and l may be equal to 0. This form will be called in the following: "linear normal form".

Notice that this form is not a too strong restricted form because a procedure can be transformed by repeatedly applying the transformation rule that transforms $\alpha_1; (\alpha_2|\alpha_3); \alpha_4$ into $(\alpha_1; \alpha_2; \alpha_4)|(\alpha_1; \alpha_3; \alpha_4)$. At the end we get a procedure in the form $\alpha = \alpha_1|\alpha_2|\ldots|\alpha_p$. Then, the only difference between each α_i and a procedure in linear normal form is that the A_ks may denote either an atomic action or a test action, and the Σ_ks, when they are not absent, have in general the form σ/β where β may be any kind of procedure.

Now we are going to define the estimation of the term $F_i(\alpha)$ in the case where we have $Doing(\alpha, s_0, s_i)$.

The estimation of $F_i(\alpha)$ depends on the part α'_{i-1} of α which has already been performed in the situation s_{i-1}. This part is defined by the property $Done(\alpha'_{i-1}, \alpha, s_0, s_i)$ where the property $Done$ is defined as follows.

$Done(\alpha', \alpha, s, s') \stackrel{\text{def}}{=} Doing(\alpha, s, s') \land start(\alpha', \alpha) \land \exists s_1(s \le s_1 < s' \land Dos(\alpha, s_1, s') \land Do_p(\alpha', s_1, s'))$.

In this definition the condition $Dos(\alpha, s_1, s')$ guarantees that the part of α that is being performed in s has started his performance in s_1, and the condition $Do_p(\alpha', s_1, s')$ guarantees that there is no part of α that is longer than α' that has been performed between s_1 and s'. $Done(\alpha', \alpha, s, s')$ intuitively means that α' is the maximal part of α that has started between s and s' and that has ended in s'.

For instance, in the previous example in s_2 we have $Doing(\alpha, s_0, s_2)$ and for $\alpha'_2 = a$ we have $Dos(\alpha'_2, s_1, s_2)$ and $Do_p(\alpha'_2, s_1, s_2)$. In s_3 we have $\alpha'_3 = a; \sigma$ and in s_4 we have $\alpha'_4 = a; \sigma; b$.

To estimate $F_i(\alpha)$ we have accepted the following assumption.

Assumption H6. It is assumed that the ith observation 0_i is independent of the previous observations and each action in A has the same probability to be observed.

In formal terms H6 is expressed by: $den_i(\alpha) = P(O_i|O_{1,i-1}) = P(O_i) = \frac{1}{N}$.

We shall use the notation $O_i = A_k$ to express that the action a_{i_j} observed by the observation action o_i is the atomic action denoted by A_k, and we use the notation $O_i \in \Sigma_k$ to express that a_{i_j} is in the set $A - \{a_{i_1}, \ldots, a_{i_l}, a_{k+1}\}$, where a_{k+1} is the action denoted by A_{k+1}.

The terms $num_i(\alpha)$ and $F_i(\alpha)$ have to be estimated only in the case where we have $Doing(\alpha, s_0, s_i)$. We have to consider different cases.

Case 1. We have $\neg Doing(\alpha, s_0, s_{i-1})$.

In that case $\alpha'_{i-1} = A_1$ and, from the assumption H1, $Int(\alpha, s_{i-1})$ and $Doing(\alpha, s_0, s_i) \land \neg Doing(\alpha, s_0, s_{i-1})$ imply that in s_i the agent has performed the action A_1, and the observed action in O_i is A_1. Then, we necessarily have $O_i = A_1$.

Therefore we have $num_i(\alpha) = 1$ and $F_i(\alpha) = N$.

Case 2. We have $Doing(\alpha, s_0, s_{i-1})$.

– **Case 2.1.** α'_{i-1} has the form $\alpha'_{i-1} = \ldots; A_k$.
  • **Case 2.1.1.** α has the form
    $$\alpha = \ldots; A_k; A_{k+1}; \ldots.$$
    In that case Σ_k is absent in α. From the assumption H1, $Int(\alpha, s_{i-1})$ implies that the action performed in s_i is A_{k+1}. Then, we necessarily have $O_i = A_{k+1}$.
    Therefore we have $num_i(\alpha) = 1$ and $F_i(\alpha) = N$.
  • **Case 2.1.2.** α has the form
    $$\alpha = \ldots; A_k; \Sigma_k; A_{k+1}; \ldots.$$
    Case 2.1.2.1. $O_i = A_{k+1}$.
    The general form of Σ_k is $\sigma/(a_{i_1}|\ldots|a_{i_l})$.
    According to guideline B it is much more likely that the action performed by the agent in s_i is the recommended action A_{k+1} than any restricted tolerated action defined by Σ_k.
    Then we have $num_i(\alpha) = 1 - \epsilon$ where the value of ϵ is defined in function of the application domain and is supposed to be "small" with respect to 1.
    We have $F_i(\alpha) = N \times (1 - \epsilon)$.
    Case 2.1.2.2. $O_i \neq A_{k+1}$.
    Here we have adopted the following assumption.

    Assumption H7. It is assumed that when the agent has the intention to do α all the restricted tolerated actions have the same probability to be performed by the agent.
    According to H7 any action in $A - \{a_{i_1}, \ldots, a_{i_l}, a_{k+1}\}$ has the same probability to be done. Then, we have[6]: $num_i(\alpha) = \frac{\epsilon}{N-(l+1)}$.
    We have $F_i(\alpha) = \frac{N}{N-(l+1)} \times \epsilon$.

– **Case 2.2.** α'_{i-1} has the form $\alpha'_{i-1} = \ldots; \Sigma_k$.
    Case 2.2.1. $O_i = A_{k+1}$.
    We are in the same type of situation as in the case 2.1.2.1. Then we have $num_i(\alpha) = 1 - \epsilon$ and $F_i(\alpha) = N \times (1 - \epsilon)$.
    Case 2.2.2. $O_i \neq A_{k+1}$.
    We are in the same type of situation as in the case 2.1.2.2. Then we have $num_i(\alpha) = \frac{\epsilon}{N-(l+1)}$ and $F_i(\alpha) = \frac{N}{N-(l+1)} \times \epsilon$.

In the case where the action that has been performed by the agent in s_i is a prescribed action (cases 1. and 2.1.1.) we have $F_i(\alpha) = N$. This conforms the guideline A.

In the case where the performed action is a recommended action (cases 2.1.2.1. and 2.2.1.) we have $F_i(\alpha) = N \times (1 - \epsilon)$. To fulfill the guideline B, that is: $F_i(\alpha) > 1$, we have to assign to ϵ a value such that $\epsilon < \frac{N-1}{N}$.

---

[6] Notice that the case $N - (l + 1) = 0$ can be rejected because if $l = N - 1$ there is only one restricted tolerated action and the agent has no choice offered by Σ_k.

In the case where the performed action is a tolerated action (cases 2.1.2.2. and 2.2.2. and $l = 0$) we have $F_i(\alpha) = \frac{N}{N-1} \times \epsilon$. From the assumption $\epsilon < \frac{N-1}{N}$ we have $F_i(\alpha) < 1$ and this fulfills the guideline C.

In the case where the performed action is a restricted tolerated action (cases 2.1.2.2. and 2.2.2. and $l > 0$) we have $F_i(\alpha) = \frac{N}{N-(l+1)} \times \epsilon$.

Therefore we have $F_i(\alpha) < 1$ iff $\epsilon < \frac{N-(l+1)}{N}$ (therefore we also have $\epsilon < \frac{N-1}{N}$), and we have $F_i(\alpha) > 1$ iff $\epsilon > \frac{N-(l+1)}{N}$ (and this is consistent with $\epsilon < \frac{N-1}{N}$).

Therefore, according to guideline D we may have either $F_i(\alpha) < 1$ or $F_i(\alpha) > 1$ depending on the values of ϵ, l and N.

4.4   Coming Back to the Example

The method we have presented can be used to compute **iteratively** the values of $P(Int(\alpha, s_i)|O_{1,i})$, $P(Int(\beta, s_i)|O_{1,i})$ and $P(Int(\gamma, s_i)|O_{1,i})$.

If we use the notations $\Pi_i(\alpha) = P(Int(\alpha, s_i)|O_{1,i})$, $\Pi_i(\beta) = P(Int(\beta, s_i)|O_{1,i})$, $\Pi_i(\gamma) = P(Int(\gamma, s_i)|O_{1,i})$, and $R = N \times (1 - \epsilon)$, for recommended actions, and $T = \frac{N}{N-1} \times \epsilon$ for tolerated actions we get the following table

s_i	$\Pi_i(\alpha)$	$\Pi_i(\beta)$	$\Pi_i(\gamma)$
s_0	$\pi(\alpha)$	$\pi(\beta)$	$\pi(\gamma)$
s_1	$\pi(\alpha)$	$\pi(\beta)$	$\pi(\gamma)$
s_2	$N \times \pi(\alpha)$	$\pi(\beta)$	$N \times \pi(\gamma)$
s_3	$N \times T \times \pi(\alpha)$	$N \times \pi(\beta)$	$N \times T \times \pi(\gamma)$
s_4	$N \times R \times T \times \pi(\alpha)$	$N \times T \times \pi(\beta)$	$N \times T^2 \times \pi(\gamma)$
s_5	$\pi(\alpha)$	$N \times T^2 \times \pi(\beta)$	$N \times T^3 \times \pi(\gamma)$

We have $N > R > 1$ and $T < 1$.

If we have $\pi(\alpha) = \pi(\beta) = \pi(\gamma)$ we can determine what the system believes about the agents' intentions in these situations. As expected in 4.1 we get:

In s_0 we have $BInt(\alpha, s_0)$, $BInt(\beta, s_0)$ and $BInt(\gamma, s_0)$.
In s_1 we have $BInt(\alpha, s_1)$, $BInt(\beta, s_1)$ and $BInt(\gamma, s_1)$.
In s_2 we have $BInt(\alpha, s_2)$ and $BInt(\gamma, s_2)$.
In s_3 we have $BInt(\beta, s_3)$.
In s_4 we have $BInt(\alpha, s_4)$.
In s_5 we have $BInt(\beta, s_5)$.

5   Conclusion

We have presented a method to assign intentions to an agent which is based on the computation of the estimation of the probability that an agent has the intention to perform a procedure.

There are two parts in the computation method. The first part (section 4.2) is general and is based on the assumptions H1-H4. The second part (section 4.3) is based on heuristics and on the additional assumptions H5-H7 and requires to know the value of $\pi(\alpha)$ for each α. The values of N and l are determined by the application domain and the value of ϵ can be tuned by a designer.

A difference with other methods for plan recognition is that in the procedures we may have terms of the form σ/β. The property *Doing* allows the selection of the procedure that matches the observations $O_{1,i}$. To estimate the probability of the occurrence of the next observation O_i we consider the part α'_{i-1} of the procedure α that has already been performed. Therefore the estimated probabilities depend on the history and not just on the previous observation O_{i-1}. This is an important original aspect of the method.

The computation cost of the estimated probabilities and of the evaluation of the properties *Doing* and *Done* is linear with respect to the number of observations for a given procedure. That makes the computation very fast.

Finally, it is worth noting that a preliminary version of the method has been implemented in Prolog [11]. This implementation was of great help to check our intuition on simple examples.

Future works will be:

1) to remove the too strong assumption H6 about the independence of the observations O_i in order to have a better estimation of $\frac{P(O_i|O_{1,i-1}\wedge Int(\alpha,s_{i-1}))}{P(O_i|O_{1,i-1})}$,

2) to guarantee that after a long sequence of observations of tolerated actions $P(Int(\alpha, s_i)|O_{1,i})$ is never lower than $\pi(\alpha)$ and

3) to allow test actions ϕ? and temporal conditions in the procedure definitions.

Acknowledgment. We are very grateful to G. Eizenberg for his help in Probability Theory. If there are some errors they are the own responsibility of the authors.

References

1. D. W. Albrecht, I. Zukerman, and A. E. Nicholson. Bayesian models for keyhole plan recognition in an adventure game. In *User modeling and user-adapted interaction*, volume 8, pages 5–47. 1998.

2. D. E. Appelt and M. E. Pollack. Weighted abduction for plan ascription. In *User modeling and user-adapted interaction*, volume 2, pages 1–25. 1991.

3. J. A. Baier. On procedure recognition in the Situation Calculus. In *22nd International Conference of the Chilean Computer Science Society*. IEEE Computer Society, 2002.

4. M. Bauer. Integrating probabilistic reasoning into plan recognition. In *Proceedings of the 11th European Conference of Artificial Intelligence*. John Wiley and Sons, 1994.

5. N. Blaylock and J. Allen. Corpus-based, statistical goal recognition. In G. Gottlob and T. Walsh, editors, *Proceedings of the 18th Inernational Joint Conference on Artificial Intelligence*, pages 1303–1308, 2003.

6. C. Boutilier, R. Reiter, M. Soutchanski, and S. Thrun. Decision-theoretic high-level agent programming in the situation calculus. In *Proceedings of AAAI*. 2000.

7. S. Carberry. Incorporating default inferences into plan recognition. In *Proceedings of the 8th National Conference on Artificial Intelligence*, pages 471–478. 1990.

8. E. Charniak and R. P. Goldman. A Bayesian model of plan recognition. *Artificial Intelligence*, 64(1), 1993.
9. P. R. Cohen and H. J. Levesque. Persistence, Intention, and Commitment. In A. L. Lansky M. P. Georgeff, editor, *Reasoning about actions and plans*, pages 297–340, Timberline, USA, 1986.
10. R. Demolombe and E. Hamon. What does it mean that an agent is performing a typical procedure? A formal definition in the Situation Calculus. In C. Castelfranci and W. Lewis Johnson, editor, *First International Joint Conference on Autonomous Agents and Multiagent Systems*. ACM Press, 2002.
11. A. M. Otermin Fernndez. Reconocimiento de intenciones de un operador que interacta con un sistema. Technical Report, ONERA Toulouse, 2004.
12. A. Finzi and T. Lukasiewicz. Game theoretic GOLOG under partial observability. In F. Dignum, V. Dignum, S. Koenig, S. Kraus, and M. Wooldridge, editors, *Proceedings of the 4th International Conference on Autonomous Agents and Multi Agent Systems*. ACM Press, 2005.
13. H. A. Kautz. A formal theory of plan recognition and its implementation. In J. F. Allen, H. A. Kautz, R. N. Pelavin, and J. D. Tennemberg, editors, *Reasoning about plans*, pages 69–126. Morgan Kaufman Publishers, 1991.
14. H. Levesque, R. Reiter, Y. Lespérance, F. Lin, and R. Scherl. GOLOG: A Logic Programming Language for Dynamic Domains. *Journal of Logic Programming*, 31:59–84, 1997.
15. W. Mao and J. Gratch. A utility-based approach to intention recognition. In *Proceedings of the AAMAS 2004 Workshop on Agent Tracking: modeling other agents from observations*, 2004.
16. P. Pozos Parra, A. Nayak, and R. Demolombe. Theories of intentions in the framework of Situation Calculus. In *Proceedings of the AAMAS workshop on Declarative Agent Languages and technologies*, 2004.
17. R. Reiter. *Knowledge in Action: Logical Foundations for Specifying and Implementing Dynamical Systems*. MIT Press, 2001.

The First Contest on Multi-agent Systems Based on Computational Logic

Mehdi Dastani[1], Jürgen Dix[2], and Peter Novak[2]

[1] Utrecht University, P.O.Box 80.089,
3508 TB Utrecht, The Netherlands
mehdi@cs.uu.nl
[2] Clausthal University of Technology,
Julius-Albert-Str. 4,
38678 Clausthal-Zellerfeld, Germany
dix@tu-clausthal.de,
peter.novak@in.tu-clausthal.de

Abstract. This is a short report about the first contest of Multi-Agent Systems (MASs) that are based on computational logic. The CLIMA workshop series (which started in 1999) is a forum to discuss techniques, based on computational logic, for representing, programming, and reasoning about Multi-Agent Systems in a formal way. Now in its seventh year, it was felt that organising a competition for evaluating MASs based on computational logic was appropriate. The authors took on this task, which turned out to be quite difficult under the given time frame. We believe that this competition is a first (modest) step towards (1) collecting important benchmarks, (2) identifying advantages/shortcomings and, finally, (3) advertising the use of Computational Logic to the broader MAS audience, and foster integration of Computational Logic into existing agent-oriented software engineering frameworks.

1 Introduction

Multi-Agent Systems are beginning to play an important role in today's software development: The *International Journal of Agent-Oriented Software Engineering (IDOSE)* [1], the *International Workshop on Agent-Oriented Software Engineering (AOSE)* [2] and the *International Joint Conference on Autonomous Agents and Multi-Agent Systems* [3] are just examples for that trend.

The development of MASs requires efficient and effective solutions for different problems which can be classified into two classes: the problems related to (1) the development of individual agents and (2) the development of their interactions. Typical problems related to individual agents are how to specify, design and implement issues such as *autonomy, pro-active/reactive behaviour, perception and update of information, reasoning and deliberation,* and *planning.* Typical problems related to the interaction of individual agents are how to *specify, design and implement* issues such as *communication, coordination, cooperation* and *negotiation.*

F. Toni and P. Torroni (Eds.): CLIMA VI, LNAI 3900, pp. 373–384, 2006.
© Springer-Verlag Berlin Heidelberg 2006

This competition is a first attempt to stimulate research in the area of MASs by

1. identifying key problems, and
2. collecting suitable benchmarks

that can serve as milestones for testing new approaches and techniques from computational logic. While there already exist several competitions in various areas of artificial intelligence (theorem proving, planning, Robo-Cup, etc.) and, lately, also in specialised areas in agent systems (Trading Agent Competition (TAC) [4] and AgentCities competitions [5]), the emphasis of this contest is on the use of *computational logic* in MASs. We believe that approaches and techniques of computational logic are essential for the development of MASs for at least two reasons: (1) logical approaches have proven to be very useful for specifying and modelling MASs in a precise manner, and (2) the specification and models can be executed.

We expect to promote the development of MASs by first identifying difficult problems and then finding solutions by comparing different approaches from computational logic for solving them. While this idea seems very appealing, it is not an easy task to come up with a particular scenario that serves as a basis for a contest. Such a scenario should be *generic* enough to be applicable for a wide range of techniques of computational logic, but it should also be *precise* enough so that different approaches can be tested and compared against each other.

2   Scenario Description

This competition consisted of developing MASs to solve a *cooperative task in a dynamically changing environment*. The environment of the MAS is a grid-like world where agents can move from one slot to a neighbouring slot if there is no agent already in that slot. In this environment, food can appear in all but one of these slots. The special slot, in which no food can appear, is considered as a depot where the agents can bring and collect their food. An agent can observe if there is food in the slot it is currently visiting. Initially, food can be placed in some randomly selected slots. During the execution, additional food can appear dynamically in randomly selected slots except the depot slot. The agents may have/play different roles (such as explorer or collector), communicate and cooperate in order to find and collect food in an efficient and effective way.

We have encouraged submissions that specify and design a MAS in terms of high-level concepts such as goals, beliefs, plans, roles, communication, coordination, negotiation, and dialogue in order to generate an efficient and effective solution for the above mentioned application. Moreover, the MAS implementations should be based on computational logic techniques (e.g., logic programming, formal calculi, etc.) and they should reflect their design in a direct and intuitive way.

We are completely aware of the fact that this scenario can also be attacked by completely different methods and approaches (e.g., based on machine learning, neural nets, etc.). In fact, we believe almost all scenarios can be modelled in various languages and programming paradigms. One important aim of this contest is to find out where exactly computational logic helps in solving particular problems and where other approaches may be superior.

The challenge of this competition is thus to use computational logic techniques to provide implemented models for the abstract concepts that are used in the specification and design of MASs. These implemented models should be integrated to implement the above-mentioned application intuitively, directly, and effectively.

3   Submission Format

A submission consisted of two parts. The first part is a description of analysis, design and implementation of a MAS for the above application. Existing MASs methodologies such as Gaia [19], Prometheus [18] and Tropos [13] can be used (not demanded) to describe the analysis and design of the system. For the description of the implementation, it should be explained how the design is implemented. This can be done by explaining, for example, which computational logic techniques are used to implement certain aspects of the MAS (including issues related to individual agents).

The second part is an (executable) implementation of the application. We did not demand any particular way (data format, algorithm, mechanism) to implement the system as long as it is implemented as a MAS and as long as the environment is a 20x20 grid. Moreover, it should be possible to configure the initial state of the environment to place food in arbitrary slots. During the execution food should appear automatically every 20 seconds in a randomly selected slot. The MAS was run with 4 agents that were positioned initially at the corners of the grid. The implementation should be executable on a PC running either Microsoft Windows or Linux OS.

3.1   Received Submissions

We have received four submissions for this first edition of the CLIMA contest. From the received submissions, only one submission did use an existing multi-agent methodology to develop a running system. Moreover, some submissions did explain explicitly which techniques from computational logic were used to develop certain aspect of the MAS efficiently and effectively, while the use of computational logic techniques in other submissions seemed to be limited to the use of the language Prolog for the system implementation.

The submission from Carlos Cares [12] analyses the scenario and designs a MAS in a systematic manner using Tropos. The scenario is analysed in terms of multi-agent concepts and features such as actors, roles, beliefs, goals, plans, capabilities, commitments and resources. Based on these concepts, a system is designed in terms of instantiations of these concepts resulting in a set of agents. In this submission, the Tropos methodology was used to semi-automatically generate code which was then extended with a Prolog implementation phase.

This allowed the implementation of the Tropos-based architecture in terms of Prolog data structures such as lists, predicates, and rules.

The submission from Simon Coffey and Dorian Gaertner [14] does not use any existing MAS methodology to develop their system. They provide directly a system architecture consisting of BDI agents that sense the grid environment to update their beliefs, evaluate their intentions, communicate with other agents, and select and execute actions. The agents are able to negotiate over their intentions to improve the efficiency of food collection. They also introduce different roles that agents can play such as the scouting role: a role for finding food. Based on different agents roles, they discuss a second system that consists of two types of agents: the agents that can only play the scouting role and the agents that can find and collect foods. Although in the proposed system the agents are static and can play only one role, they discuss the possibility of agents that can play different roles and can change their roles dynamically. In this submission, the designed system is implemented using Qu-Prolog [6] that allows multi-threaded execution of agents.

The solution of Robert Logie, Jon G. Hall and Kevin G. Waugh [16] consisted of a purely reactive system of agents with no internal representation of the current state. Their system resembled Brook's subsumption architecture [11] and had the notion of a *role* (or policy) at its core. Agents use certain roles and can switch between them when the environment changes. They use the idea of pheromone trails in order to find interesting and successful paths (their agents do not have a memory). Although their system does not seem to use computational logic in an extensive way, it has been motivated from research on normative reasoning in deontic logic. An interesting idea is that for more complex systems, this might lead to agents that develop and create new roles (in addition to those originally specified).

The final submission, by Eder Mateus Nunes Goncalves and Guilherme Bittencourt [17], concentrated on the notion of coordination between agents in a MAS. Each agent maintains a knowledge base and updates it accordingly. The underlying notion is a high-level petri net. Agents start cooperating with the agent closest to the food (once it has been found). The cooperation ends when the food is delivered at the depot. Messages are FIPA compliant. One of the main results is the influence of the appearance of new food (and the time it takes to store food in the depot) to the impact of cooperation between the agents. If the time interval for new food to appear is small with respect to the time it takes to store it, than cooperation pays off.

4   Winning Criteria

The criteria used to evaluate submissions and to select the winners was as follows:

1. Original, innovative, and effective application of computational logic techniques in solving specific multi-agent issues identified in this application.
2. The performance of the executable implementation. The performance was measured based on the amount of food collected by the MAS in a certain

```
)(15, 12)(10, 8)(3, 6)(12, 19)(15, 17)(5, 8)(7, 8)(10, 13)(10, 10)] Status: storing
Agent 52 rescued: 23 --> [(13, 14)(14, 10)(10, 6)(9, 10)(6, 7)(7, 14)(14, 10)(15, 14)(5, 12)(12, 13)(10, 5)(8,
5)(16, 4)(7, 15)(10, 9)(6, 4)(12, 3)(13, 15)(16, 9)(6, 11)(12, 5)(14, 15)(17, 6)] Status: searching
Agent 53 rescued: 14 --> [(8, 12)(3, 10)(13, 12)(16, 13)(17, 6)(9, 13)(6, 5)(8, 17)(17, 3)(5, 5)(7, 4)(12, 9)(
10, 18)(18, 17)] Status: storing
Agent 54 rescued: 24 --> [(8, 7)(7, 6)(6, 11)(18, 5)(11, 17)(16, 5)(6, 11)(7, 9)(11, 17)(13, 14)(7, 13)(15, 13
)(12, 8)(12, 3)(3, 11)(8, 12)(12, 6)(6, 8)(4, 10)(14, 14)(10, 16)(7, 14)(9, 7)(17, 15)] Status: searching
==================================
Interaction: 925 -- Time: 19s
Food Positions: [(8, 18)(18, 11)(4, 15)(6, 7)(16, 17)(1, 2)(7, 6)(5, 17)(18, 7)(4, 2)(17, 3)(19, 11)(8, 16)(2,
3)(13, 19)(16, 15)(4, 11)(15, 9)(3, 17)(5, 5)(8, 14)(16, 12)(6, 16)(4, 16)(6, 4)(5, 2)(7, 19)(6, 15)(18, 8)(5
, 19)(18, 20)(14, 20)(20, 6)(3, 1)(13, 19)(7, 5)(10, 18)(5, 13)(9, 20)(19, 11)(17, 2)(3, 16)(12, 20)(2, 13)(17,
19)(19, 20)(1, 5)(15, 5)(18, 3)(18, 15)(18, 10)(3, 9)(6, 4)(20, 5)(8, 9)(18, 3)(18, 10)(16, 17)(4, 19
)(20, 1)(3, 3)(20, 9)(20, 7)(8, 19)(19, 9)(16, 18)(6, 18)(20, 18)(15, 19)(6, 16)(7, 4)(18, 10)(14, 20)(1, 7)(1,
12)(18, 3)(20, 1)(5, 17)(19, 11)(18, 15)(16, 18)(18, 15)(3, 12)(19, 16)(17, 1)(19, 14)(11, 20)(7, 17)(5, 2)(3
, 12)(17, 18)(5, 19)(2, 17)(1, 20)(14, 18)(1, 20)(3, 18)(1, 13)(17, 19)(7, 17)(20, 12)]
Number of slots with food: 102
Agent 51 Position: (10, 5)
Agent 52 Position: (11, 12)
Agent 53 Position: (10, 12)
Agent 54 Position: (6, 8)
Food Rescued: 82
Food in depot: 80
Agent 51 rescued: 21 --> [(14, 2)(17, 5)(13, 12)(14, 5)(6, 15)(9, 19)(7, 12)(8, 8)(9, 2)(14, 10)(13, 13)(11, 8
)(15, 12)(10, 8)(3, 6)(12, 19)(15, 17)(5, 8)(7, 8)(10, 13)(10, 10)] Status: storing
Agent 52 rescued: 23 --> [(13, 14)(14, 10)(10, 6)(9, 10)(6, 7)(7, 14)(14, 10)(15, 14)(5, 12)(12, 13)(10, 5)(8,
5)(16, 4)(7, 15)(10, 9)(6, 4)(12, 3)(13, 15)(16, 9)(6, 11)(12, 5)(14, 15)(17, 6)] Status: searching
Agent 53 rescued: 14 --> [(8, 12)(3, 10)(13, 12)(16, 13)(17, 6)(9, 13)(6, 5)(8, 17)(17, 3)(5, 5)(7, 4)(12, 9)(
10, 18)(18, 17)] Status: storing
Agent 54 rescued: 24 --> [(8, 7)(7, 6)(6, 11)(18, 5)(11, 17)(16, 5)(6, 11)(7, 9)(11, 17)(13, 14)(7, 13)(15, 13
)(12, 8)(12, 3)(3, 11)(8, 12)(12, 6)(6, 8)(4, 10)(14, 14)(10, 16)(7, 14)(9, 7)(17, 15)] Status: searching
===== Final Results ==================
Cycles: 926
Food Positions: [(5, 18)(19, 11)(4, 15)(6, 7)(16, 17)(1, 2)(7, 6)(5, 17)(18, 7)(4, 2)(17, 3)(19, 11)(8, 16)(2,
3)(19, 19)(16, 15)(4, 11)(15, 9)(3, 17)(5, 5)(8, 14)(19, 12)(6, 16)(4, 16)(6, 4)(5, 2)(7, 19)(6, 15)(18, 8)(5
, 19)(18, 20)(14, 20)(20, 6)(3, 1)(13, 19)(7, 5)(10, 18)(5, 13)(9, 20)(19, 11)(17, 2)(3, 16)(12, 20)(2, 13)(17,
19)(19, 20)(1, 5)(19, 19)(18, 3)(17, 15)(5, 5)(18, 14)(18, 10)(5, 3)(8, 9)(18, 3)(18, 10)(16, 17)(4, 19
)(20, 1)(3, 2)(20, 9)(20, 7)(9, 19)(9, 16)(18, 5)(18, 20)(2, 8)(18, 3)(18, 10)(16, 17)(4, 19
)(20, 1)(3, 3)(20, 9)(20, 7)(8, 19)(19, 9)(16, 18)(6, 18)(20, 18)(15, 19)(6, 16)(7, 4)(18, 10)(14, 20)(1, 7)(1,
12)(18, 3)(20, 1)(5, 17)(19, 11)(18, 15)(16, 18)(15, 19)(3, 12)(19, 16)(17, 1)(19, 14)(11, 20)(7, 17)(5, 2)(3
, 12)(17, 18)(5, 19)(2, 17)(1, 20)(14, 18)(1, 20)(3, 18)(1, 13)(17, 19)(7, 17)(20, 12)]
Number of slots with food: 102
Agent 51 Position: (10, 6)
Agent 52 Position: (11, 11)
Agent 53 Position: (10, 11)
Agent 54 Position: (6, 7)
Food Rescued: 82
Food in depot: 80
Agent 51 rescued: 21 --> [(14, 2)(17, 5)(13, 12)(14, 5)(6, 15)(9, 19)(7, 12)(8, 8)(9, 2)(14, 10)(13, 13)(11, 8
)(15, 12)(10, 8)(3, 6)(12, 19)(15, 17)(5, 8)(7, 8)(10, 13)(10, 10)] Status: storing
Agent 52 rescued: 23 --> [(13, 14)(14, 10)(10, 6)(9, 10)(6, 7)(7, 14)(14, 10)(15, 14)(5, 12)(12, 13)(10, 5)(8,
5)(16, 4)(7, 15)(10, 9)(6, 4)(12, 3)(13, 15)(16, 9)(6, 11)(12, 5)(14, 15)(17, 6)] Status: searching
Agent 53 rescued: 14 --> [(8, 12)(3, 10)(13, 12)(16, 13)(17, 6)(9, 13)(6, 5)(8, 17)(17, 3)(5, 5)(7, 4)(12, 9)(
10, 18)(18, 17)] Status: storing
Agent 54 rescued: 24 --> [(8, 7)(7, 6)(6, 11)(18, 5)(11, 17)(16, 5)(6, 11)(7, 9)(11, 17)(13, 14)(7, 13)(15, 13
)(12, 8)(12, 3)(3, 11)(8, 12)(12, 6)(6, 8)(4, 10)(14, 14)(10, 16)(7, 14)(9, 7)(17, 15)] Status: searching
==================================
```

Fig. 1. Screenshot from Concalves et al.

period of time. All programs ran on the same machine (Windows/Linux double boot machine).

3. The quality of the description of analysis, design and implementation of the MAS, the elegance of its design and implementation, and the ease of installation and execution of the program.

5   How to Determine the Winning System?

To determine a winner turned out to be a very difficult task. Three of the four systems were very close and we finally decided to select two of the three as winners. It should be noted that our decision was based on the packages we got, the problems we had to install them and our impression from the description of these packages and their underlying theory. We decided not to go into lengthy discussions with the authors as to the *why* and *how* of their systems.

While we did our best to achieve a fair evaluation, there are certainly no perfectly objective criteria we could have used: even the performance of the systems was not comparable. We believe that by using a server architecture for the second contest, we can at least measure the performance of the different approaches in a fair manner.

As an example, one of the criteria was the use of computational logic. Thus a system that seemed to be based on a simple reflex-architecture (as Logie et al. [16]) was not as highly ranked as others. But Logie-agents did use only a local view and no memory, so they might be much more efficient in unknown or changing environments.

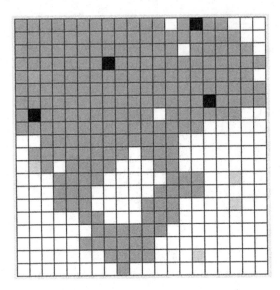

Fig. 2. Screenshot from Logie et al.

5.1   Technical Issues

In the call for submissions we did not impose any technical requirements on the implementation and installation procedure of the submitted softwares. Unfortunately, this turned out to be a serious bottleneck of the evaluation process. In fact, there were many technical problems varying from missing files for visualizing the simulation results (Cares et al.), using obsolete C++ compiler version (Concalves et al.), to using a number of not very well integrated external packages and libraries (Coffey et al.). The only submission without such technical problems was from Logie et. al. Fortunately, all the problems were finally solved in cooperation with the corresponding authors.

The authors used various supporting technologies for their implementations. While submissions of Logie et al. and Cares et al. were standalone MS Windows executables, submissions of Concalves et al. and Coffey et al. were source code packages for Linux OS. Although not required, most submitted softwares, except Concalves et al., did include a visualization component. Figures 2, 3 and 4 illustrate the screenshots of the visualization component of the submissions from Logie et al., Cares et al. and Coffey et al., respectively. While Logie et al. and Coffey et al. were visualizing the running system on-the-fly, the program from Cares et al. was generating a HTML file with embedded JavaScript code, which could be later viewed using standard HTML browser. The output generated by the submission from Concalves et. al. is illustrated in Figure 1.

5.2   Evaluation of Submitted Programs

Since participants of the contest used different approaches to implement the scenario, performance could not be considered as the most important criterion

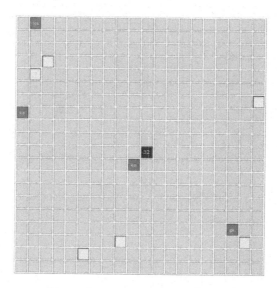

Fig. 3. Screenshot from Cares et al.

to compare them. Clearly, the systems in which each agent has a global view of the grid and is aware of its relative position with respect to the other agents (e.g. Cares et al.), has an advantage over the systems in which agents have only a local view and no memory (e.g. Logie et al.). Therefore, we rather evaluated the systems based on the originality of the idea and the strategy to collect food. The amount of collected food is then considered as a second-class criterion.

Table 1. Parameters of simulation used in the final evaluation

Overall duration of a simulation run	3 min.
Interval of random food generation	5 sec.
Amount of food seeded in one food generation	1 piece
Amount of food at starting configuration	0 pieces
Depot position	$\langle 10, 10 \rangle$
Number of agents	4
Starting positions of agents	grid corners

We executed simulations with the parameters presented in Table 1 on the same double-boot Windows XP/Linux computer with Intel Pentium 4 CPU with tact-frequency 2.80 GHz and 1GB of RAM. In some cases, it was not possible to comply with the simulation parameters set by the authors. For example, in the case of Logie et al., the depot position was not configurable. It was placed randomly at the beginning of the simulation. Also the simulation by Concalves et al. did not allow us to configure the details of the simulation and finished automatically after approximately 20 seconds with the exit status OK.

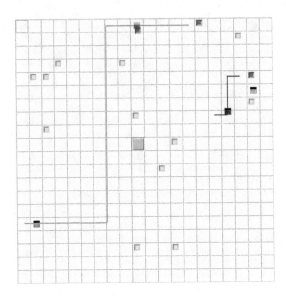

Fig. 4. Screenshot from Coffey et al.

5.3 Results and Winners

In the following, we describe the submitted multi-agent systems from a *black box* perspective. This means that we describe the behavior of the multi-agent simulations without considering their system descriptions. Note that the system descriptions are briefly summarized in subsection 3.1. Table 2 presents the results of evaluated simulation runs.

Table 2. Results of evaluated simulation runs

submission	collected food	food picked up	performed steps
Cares et al.	25	25	1066
Coffey et al.	15	47	not reported
Concalves et al.	165	165	1826
Logie et al.	4	6	3600

The best performance in terms of collected food was achieved by Concalves et al. However, this system exited unexpectedly before the allowed three minutes run time without any error message. Since it wasn't possible to configure the starting amount of the food in the grid and the interval of its generation, according to the simulation log, agents were able to collect 165 food items, although this is not in a correlation with the required interval of food generation (e.g. food item every 20 seconds as specified in the call for submissions). It was also not easy to verify the details of the simulation run because the program generated only a text stream to the standard output. Figure 1 shows the few lines of the simulation log. Because of these reasons and the fact that the use of computational logic techniques were quite limited, we decided not to consider this submission for the first rank.

The worst performer was the simulation submitted by Logie et al. In our opinion, the poor performance was due to the fact that the agents neither had an internal representation of the grid environment nor could communicate directly. Agents were randomly walking around in the grid and once they found a depot cell, they started to leave pheromone trail. This could help other agents to find the depot. At the beginning of the simulation, the paths of individual agents to the depot was not very direct, but after a while, a pheromone gradient could be observed in the grid. This was visualized as an orange gradient around the depot, where the saturation of yellow color in a particular cell was proportional to a strength of a pheromone marking in the cell. In this state of the simulation, agents were able to find their ways to the depot, after picking up a food item, more directly than at the beginning of the simulation. Unfortunately, this strategy was not performing very well in the short simulation runs, which was also a reason why this program did not qualify for higher ranking in the contest. Figure 2 shows a screenshot of the visualization component of the simulation by Logie et al. The four darkest cells are agents and the brightest cells (green) are available food. Since the depot position was not a configurable parameter of this simulation it was randomly placed to the position $\langle 2, 5 \rangle$ at the beginning of the simulation. Around the depot cell, the area marked by pheromone is visible.

The programs submitted by Cares et al. and Coffey et al. achieved approximately the same performance results using quite similar strategies. In the simulation by Cares et al., there were two types of agents: scout agent and ordinary agent. In this simulation, there was only one scout agent who did only explore the grid by columns to look for food. All the other agents in the simulation were ordinary agents. They were searching for food exploring rows one by one. When they found food, they delivered it directly to the depot cell. All agents knew the position of the depot cell. The agents in this simulation were informed about the position of the depot cell at the beginning of the simulation. The most interesting behaviour could be observed when a scout agent found food and later met an ordinary agent. The ordinary agent started immediately to walk directly toward the food, picked it up, and delivered it to the depot. Obviously the scout agent communicated the position of the found food to the ordinary agent. Figure 3 displays a screenshot of the visualization component of the simulation by Cares et al. Agents are depicted as red squares and the scout agent is marked as *ca* (position $\langle 1, 8 \rangle$). Dark blue cell is a depot displaying the number of already collected food items. Available food is depicted as yellow squares.

The approach by Coffey et al. did also use the idea of a scout agent. Here the scout agent as well as the agents that were not able to load any food (i.e. they were already carrying an item to the depot), marked the food they found and broadcasted its position to all other agents. The agents that did not load any food yet, started a negotiation and the winner of the bidding walked to pick up the food and deliver it to the depot. The interesting aspect of this submission is that when another food item was found, the negotiation was started all over again and agents possibly rearranged their claims on particular food items they were approaching. By this the agent team was able to optimize the overall cost of food delivery (i.e. overall number of steps to perform in order to deliver given set of food items to the depot) and thus improve its overall performance.

Contrary to the submission by Cares et al., agents from simulation by Coffey et al. were not informed about the position of the depot right from the beginning of the simulation. They spent a considerable amount of time until the depot was found by one of them. After that, agents were able to clear the grid of food quite quickly starting from the closest neighborhood of the depot to the borders of the grid. Figure 4 shows a screenshot of the visualization component of the simulation by Coffey et al. Lines show the connection between an agent and food it currently claims. Yellow boxes depict undiscovered food, dark purple boxes mean that the food item on a given position was discovered but not picked up yet. Finally agents carrying a food item are depicted as a double-box (e.g. the one in the first row of the grid). The scout agent (position $\langle 19, 6 \rangle$) recently found food in the cell above it. The blue agent (nearest one to the scout) won the bidding and gave up his intention to pick up the food item in the first row of the grid. This allowed the green agent to claim the abandoned food in the first row. The agent is now heading towards it.

Because of the elegance of the implemented approach, the use of MAS technology, the non-trivial amount of computational logic and, finally, their overall performance, both submissions by Cares et al. and Coffey et al. were chosen for the CLIMA Contest 2005 prize.

6   What Did We Learn for the Second Contest

As we already mentioned in Subsection 5.1, in the course of evaluation of submitted programs, we faced a number of difficulties. On the one hand we had to deal with various technical issues and, on the other hand, we recognized that since we had no common basis for evaluation, it was very hard (almost impossible) to compare the submitted programs exclusively on the basis of their performances. Difficulties with comparison are probably more serious, because a fair evaluation of submitted programs is only possible if conditions are equal for all participating simulations.

After carefully considering all the possibilities to solve the problems mentioned above, we decided to implement a supporting infrastructure for the next edition of the CLIMA Contest. This supporting infrastructure is a server system that runs the multi-agent system environment. Teams of agents can connect to this environment after which they can perform actions (including sense action). We allow multi-agent systems, which participate in the contest, to run on their own local platforms. The involved agents can then communicate with the server system, which runs the environment, via Internet using TCP/IP protocol.

Using this approach, participating multi-agent systems will be able to use their own specialized communication technology and infrastructure. Also implementing the simulation environment centrally will take off the burden of implementing the simulation from shoulders of contest participants and allow them to focus more on the strategy for the contest scenario. Moreover, the supporting infrastructure will allow us to evaluate participating MASs on a fair basis. It will also clearly divide a simulation scenario from the team of participating agents. We believe that such a supporting infrastructure also solve the technical issues related to installation and correct execution of submitted multi-agent systems.

In order to introduce an objective evaluation criterion, we decided to allow teams of agents to compete with each other in the simulation scenario. This allow participants to explore possibilities of more complex coordination strategies. We hope that all the mentioned factors will give rise to more flexibility on participants side and also to improve the fun-factor of the competition scenario.

7   Conclusion

Given the very tight schedule (from the announcement to the submission deadline) we were quite satisfied with the four submissions. We believe this contest will promote the use of techniques and approaches from computational logic to the development and implementation of MASs. Although the contributions for this contest may propose computational logic techniques and approaches that are specific for this particular scenario (application), they may be generalised and adopted to other MAS methodologies and programming languages. In particular, we believe that this contest will stimulate the use of computational logic techniques and approaches for research and design of programming languages that support the implementation of MASs in an effective and efficient manner.

There are several existing activities that aim at stimulating research and design of programming languages for MASs. Example of such activities are the *International Workshop on Programming Multi-Agent System* [7], the *AgentLink Technical Forum Groups on Programming Multi-Agent Systems* [8], and the various seminars and books dedicated to Multi-Agent Programming [9, 15, 10]. Our experience is that many of the existing programming languages for implementing MASs, such as IMPACT, 3APL, CLAIM, JACK, Jason, and Jadex [9], are based on techniques and approaches from computational logic. In these programming languages, computational logic techniques are used to model various mental attitudes of agents such as beliefs and goals, planning components, and reasoning components. The next CLIMA contest is a great opportunity to evaluate these approaches.

References

1. http://www.inderscience.com/browse/index.php.
2. http://www.agentgroup.unimore.it/aose05.
3. http://www.aamas-conference.org/.
4. http://www.sics.se/tac.
5. http://www.agentcities.org/EUNET/Competition.
6. http://www.itee.uq.edu.au/~pjr/HomePages/QuPrologHome.html.
7. http://www.cs.uu.nl/ProMAS.
8. http://www.cs.uu.nl/~mehdi/al3promas.html.

9. R. Bordini, M. Dastani, J. Dix, and A. E. Fallah-Seghrouchni. *Multi-Agent Progra-mming: Languages, Platforms, and Applications.* Number 15 in MASA. Springer, Berlin, 2005.

10. R. Bordini, M. Dastani, J. Dix, and A. E. Fallah-Seghrouchni. *Programming Multi-Agent Systems,* volume 3346. LNAI, Springer Verlag, 2005.

11. R. Brooks. How to build complete creatures rather than isolated cognitive simula-tors. In *Architectures for Intelligence,* pages 225–239. Lawrence Erlbaum Assosi-ates, Hillsdale, NJ, 1991.

12. C. Cares, X. Franch, and E. Mayol. Extending tropos for a prolog implementation: A case study using the food collecting agent problem. In this volume.

13. J. Castro, M. Kolp, and J. Mylopoulos. Towards requirements-driven information systems engineering: the TROPOS project. *Information Systems,* 27:365–389, 2002.

14. S. Coffey and D. Gaertner. Implementing pheromone-based, negotiating forager agents. In this volume.

15. M. Dastani, J. Dix, and A. E. Fallah-Seghrouchni. *Programming Multi-Agent Sys-tems,* volume 3067. LNAI, Springer Verlag, 2004.

16. R. Logie, J. G. Hall, and K. G. Waugh. Reactive food gathering. In this volume.

17. E. M. Nunes Gonçalves and G. Bittencourt. Strategies for multi-agent coordination in a grid world. In this volume.

18. L. Padgham and M. Winikoff. Prometheus: A methodology for developing in-telligent agents. In *Agent-Oriented Software Engineering III: Third International Workshop (AOSE'02).* Springer, LNAI 2585, 2003.

19. F. Zambonelli, N. R. Jennings, and M. Wooldridge. Developing multiagent sys-tems: The Gaia methodology. *ACM Transactions on Software Engineering and Methodology (TOSEM),* 12(3):317–370, 2003.

Implementing Pheromone-Based, Negotiating Forager Agents

Simon Coffey and Dorian Gaertner

Imperial College London, SW7 2AZ, United Kingdom

Abstract. We describe an implementation of distributed, multi-threaded BDI-style [RG95] agents cooperating efficiently in a foraging scenario. Using ant-style pheromone trails as the basis for a pseudo-random walk procedure, they explore the world uniformly and negotiate to allocate collection and delivery tasks. Global information is disseminated via a publish/subscribe mechanism. The system is implemented using the concurrent logic programming language Qu-Prolog.

1 Problem Description

The first CLIMA contest aimed to promote the development of multi-agent systems that employ approaches from computational logic to solve key problems in this field. These systems were to be specified in terms of high-level concepts such as goals, beliefs, plans, roles, communication, coordination, negotiation and dialogue. In order to specify the design of our system, we first have to define several assumptions we made about the scenario.

The contest requirements define the multi-agent environment to be a grid of 20 by 20 cells. Four agents start situated in the four corners of the grid and are able to walk into neighbouring cells unless these are occupied by another agent. They can also observe whether or not there is food in the cell they are currently visiting. Food can appear in all but one of these cells (the depot) and can be placed either in an initialisation phase or dynamically during execution at regular intervals. The agents can play various roles (such as explorer or collector) and their mission is to cooperate in order to find and collect the food and deliver it to the depot in an efficient and effective way.

We have made two additional assumptions. Firstly, we restrict the movement of agents to only the cells to the North, East, South and West of the cell they currently occupy (i.e. we exclude diagonal moves). Equipping them with extra sensory capabilities (such as looking two steps ahead or sensing the diagonally adjacent cells) would put more emphasis on the sensors rather than the reasoning ability of the agent. Secondly, we decided that each agent can only carry one item of food at a time.

The challenge of this competition is thus to use computational logic techniques to provide implemented models for abstract concepts that are often used in the specification and design of multi-agent systems.

F. Toni and P. Torroni (Eds.): CLIMA VI, LNAI 3900, pp. 385–395, 2006.

2   Design

A multi-agent system is typically characterised by the *distributed execution* of *autonomous, communicative agents* that are *situated* in an environment.

We decided to use multi-threaded, logic-based, autonomous pseudo-BDI agents that are situated in an environment without central control. This framework allows for a wide variety of agent techniques to be applied, as is seen later in the paper. The environment process seeds food into the world, maintains the pheromone trails (described in Sect. 2.8), sends percepts to the agents when requested and interfaces with the GUI.

2.1   Architecture

We designed our agents using an architecture loosely based on Rao and Georgeff's Beliefs-Desires-Intentions (BDI) model [RG95]. Each agent has *beliefs* about the state of the world including the location of food and the depot as well as beliefs about *claims* other agents have made. When an agent claims a certain piece of food, it informs the other agents about his *intention* to pick it up. Delivery of food and searching are two other examples of intentions. *Desires* in our implementation take the form of the two primary agent roles; scouts and gatherers (described in Sect. 2.7).

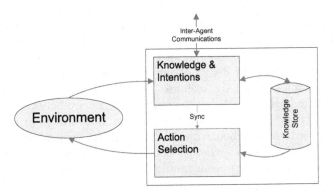

Fig. 1. Architecture design

Each agent consists of two primary threads and a dynamic database (Fig. 1). The knowledge thread receives percepts from the environment (*sensing*), updates the belief store depending on how it perceived the world, re-evaluates the intentions of the agent and communicates with other agents announcing certain events. The action selection thread then uses the current beliefs and intentions to decide which action to execute next. It informs the environment about its choice of action, which updates the world state and sends new percepts to the agent's knowledge thread.

2.2   Agent Language

We define actions, percepts, beliefs and intentions as sets of Prolog terms:

```
Action ::= [pickup, putout, move(Direction)]
```

where Direction is a variable representing north, south, east or west,

```
Percept ::= [depot_same_cell, food_same_cell, has_food, has_moved,
            north(N), south(S), east(E), west(W)]
```

where N, S, E, and W are variables that represent a cart, wall or pheromone level, and finally

```
Belief ::= [at(X,Y), depot_at(DX, DY), food_at(FX,FY), have_food,
           intends(Agent, Intention)]
```

```
Intention ::= [collect_food(X,Y), deliver_food]
```

where X and Y etc. represent coordinates. Note that there is no term to represent an exploring intention; rather, exploration is used as a default behaviour if no other intentions exist, and as such is never explicitly represented in the agent's intention state.

Intentions and beliefs are stored as Prolog terms in the agent's dynamic database, while percepts arrive as a list of terms belonging to the set of possible percepts. Percepts are immediately processed into beliefs, thus only **believes** and **intends** terms can appear in the body of clauses within the agent. To illustrate how these terms are used, see the scenario in Fig. 2.

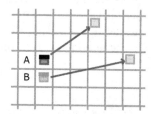

Fig. 2. Agent percept and state example

In the scenario above there are two agents, A and B, and it is agent A's turn to act next. Assuming it moved east last turn, it therefore receives the percept set:

```
[has_moved(east), north(pheromone(5)), south(cart),
 east(pheromone(4)), west(pheromone(2))]
```

where the entries for the unoccupied cells indicate the amount of pheromone in each cell. Assuming the agent has prior knowledge of agent B's intention, and knows the location of the food shown, its beliefs are then updated to:

```
believes('A', at(2,3)).
believes('A', food_at(5,5)).
believes('A', food_at(7,3)).
believes('A', intends('B', collect_food(7,3))).
```

Finally, the agent's intentions remain as follows:

```
intends('A', collect_food(5,5)).
```

This simple example elides details of communication; the agent's state may change in response to inter-agent messages as well as percepts, as discussed later.

2.3   Action Selection

Agents choose their actions using *teleo-reactive (TR) programs* [Nil94], consisting of a priority-ordered sequence of condition/action rules. A simplified version of the TR program used is shown in Fig. 3. This approach is particularly useful in scenarios like ours, in which durative behaviours (e.g. *explore*) are desired. It is important to note that at each percept/reaction cycle, the action chosen is only ever a single atomic one, belonging to the agent's set of allowed actions (defined in Sect. 2.2). For example, while walk_to(X,Y) appears to be a multi-step plan, it is in fact simply a set of rules which choose the agent's next atomic action; it must be repeatedly invoked in order to arrive at (X,Y). Thus, the right-hand side of the rules in Fig. 3 are all either atomic actions, or programs which return an atomic action.

Note that the action selection program does not manipulate beliefs, alter the intentions of the agent or handle negotiation in any sense; it operates solely on the current intentions and beliefs of the agent, returning only an action. All agent state manipulation is performed by the intentions thread (described in Section 2.4), which runs in parallel to the action thread, ensuring a consistent set of beliefs and intentions for the action selection program to use.

$$condition \rightarrow action$$

$$intends(deliver\_food) \wedge believes(agent\_at(depot)) \rightarrow putout$$
$$intends(deliver\_food) \wedge believes(depot\_at(X,Y)) \rightarrow walk\_to(X,Y)$$
$$intends(deliver\_food) \rightarrow explore$$
$$believes(at\_food) \rightarrow pickup$$
$$intends(collect\_food(X,Y)) \rightarrow walk\_to(X,Y)$$
$$\top \rightarrow explore$$

Fig. 3. Simplified action-selection TR program

2.4   Intention Selection and Knowledge Maintenance

The intention selection thread takes the form of a message-processing cycle, accepting inter-agent communication messages from the other agent threads, and percept messages from the environment. This is the only place in which modification of the agent's `believes(...)` and `intends(...)` dynamic predicates is permitted. While awaiting the next set of percepts, it listens for broadcast messages and negotiation requests from other agents, updating its beliefs and intentions accordingly. For example, if agent `red` receives a broadcast message informing him that agent `blue` is claiming food at location (5,9), it will add the term `believes(intends(blue, collect_food(5,9)))` to its dynamic knowledge base.

When a set of percepts is received, the agent first updates its beliefs about the world state using the new percepts. Since the set of percepts it can receive is relatively limited, this is achieved with an explicit set of handling routines for each type of percept. It then decides whether to send any negotiation requests, and finally re-evaluates its intentions accordingly. It does so using a series of declarative conditions, made possible by the backtracking operation of Prolog-style languages. For example, the delivery cost function for a particular item of food is simply written with two rules:

```
cost_of(food(X,Y),Cost) :-          % Depot location known
    believes(agent_at(AgX,AgY)),
    believes(depot_at(DepX,DepY)),
    manhattan(AgX,AgY,X,Y,C1),
    manhattan(X,Y,DepX,DepY,C2),
    Cost is C1 + C2.
cost_of(food(X,Y),Cost) :-          % Depot location not known
    believes(agent_at(AgX,AgY)),
    manhattan(AgX,AgY,X,Y,Cost).
```

where `manhattan(X1,Y1,X2,Y2,D)` gives the manhattan distance between two points. This cost function is then called to find the optimum choice of food at the start of each turn (assuming there is any known food). If this food is believed to be claimed by another agent, negotiations are initiated with that agent. If the negotiation is unsuccessful, the agent will claim the cheapest unclaimed food (or retain whichever food it had previously claimed). Every new claim is broadcast to the other agents, enabling them to contact the "claimant" of any food they wish to claim for themselves.

2.5   Communication

Communication between agents utilises two of the main communication paradigms: publish/subscribe, and point-to-point messaging. The former is used for global knowledge sharing, while the latter is used for efficient negotiation between specific agents, as well as agent/environment communication. Each agent places a *subscription* for messages about food/depot locations and agent commitments at a remote server. When one agent finds an item, or claims some known food, it will *publish* a notification about this event to the server which in turn will inform all other agents that have subscribed to this event. This allows for dynamic addition of new agents to the scenario without having to change the

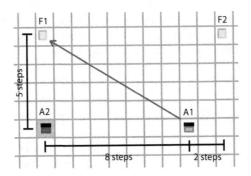

Fig. 4. Negotiation example

running system. Negotiation is achieved using asynchronous message-passing. This is more efficient than using the broadcast system, since negotiation is always bilateral in our implementation; there is no need for all agents to be party to the negotiation messages.

2.6 Negotiation

In order to most efficiently allocate the collection of known food to each agent, we allow our agents to negotiate over the targets of their intentions. The agents have a defined policy only with respect to individual negotiations, namely to minimise the combined cost of delivery for the two negotiating agents. This is achieved by examining each agent's next-best option, and optimising accordingly. The implicit global effect of this policy is to minimise the total delivery cost of all known deliveries. This is the result of a series of bilateral negotiations; no single agent takes responsibility for optimising the entire set of deliveries.

Figure 4 illustrates an example where negotiation can improve the efficiency of food collection. It shows a snapshot of the environment state, in which agent A_2 has just delivered some food, agent A_1 has claimed and intends to pick up food F_1 and some other agent that was already carrying food accidentally discovered and broadcasted the existence of food F_2. Without negotiation, A_2 would claim F_2 and collect and deliver it in 30 steps while A_1 drops off F_1 in 18 steps.

Note that A_1 would not volunteer to pick up F_2 since this would increase his personal delivery cost to 22 steps. We therefore allow A_2 to send a bid to A_1, requesting permission to collect F_1 instead. It sends its cost of collecting F_1, plus the delivery cost of its next-best option (in this case F_2). A_1 will then consider the request, ceding responsibility for F_1 if the total delivery cost after the swap is reduced. The re-allocation allows agent A_2 to pick up and deliver F_1 in 10 steps at the expense of a small increase in the other agent's delivery cost. The total number of steps to collect and deliver both items has been decreased from 48 to 32 and the longest individual delivery route has been reduced from 30 to 22.

In terms of welfare economics, the *utilitarian social welfare* of a system is defined as the sum of the utilities of all the individual agents, while the *egalitarian social welfare* is defined as the minimum utility of any of the agents in the system.

We take *utility* to be the negated cost of delivery, so that a shorter delivery yields a higher utility. The cost of delivery is the number of steps from the agent's location via the location of the food to the depot location.

The negotiation in our system leads to improvements to both utilitarian and egalitarian social welfare as the average number of steps per delivery, as well as the longest delivery route is reduced.

2.7   Agent Roles

After initial experimentation with all agents performing as described above (i.e. searching until they first find food, then immediately delivering it), it became obvious that except in the most food-rich environments, knowledge about food locations was almost non-existent. The agents thus simply randomly walk until they first find food, which they immediately pick up and deliver, giving no opportunity for task optimisation. We therefore implemented a second type of agent, a scout. Upon finding food, a scout will not pick it up, but will merely broadcast its location to the gatherer agents, and continue searching. This can be viewed as a second implicit desire, with the scout agent's desire being to gather information rather than food.

As implemented, the scout is statically determined; it may not switch to delivery mode. However, it is easy to envisage a scheme in which agents switch to scouting dynamically, thus completing the full BDI repertoire of mental attitudes. In a scenario in which all the agents are randomly searching, the first agent to happen upon food might switch to scout duty, combing the rest of the area while the other agents collect the food it has discovered. In this manner, unexplored areas (and hence concentrations of food) would be explored, rather than the first food simply being delivered and forgotten about.

2.8   Exploration

Initially the agents do not know where the depot is located or which cells of the grid contain food. They must therefore explore the world around them. If this world has a *rectangular* shape, then dividing the world into quadrants and assigning each agent to a quadrant would be the most efficient way to explore the world completely, but this ignores over-exploration of repeatedly visited areas (i.e. the area around the depot) and would not work in worlds with *irregular* shapes or *dynamically changing* shape. For this reason, a pseudo-random walk technique is used for exploration, utilising trail markers to ensure that agents prefer to explore cells that have not been as frequently visited.

A completely random walk based on Brownian motion would not be efficient enough since it tends to over-explore some areas at the expense of others. We chose to implement a more directed approach based on pheromones. Each agent drops a fixed amount of pheromone each time it enters a cell, similar to the methods used in ant colony optimisation ([DMC96], [GC05]). An agent can *smell* the concentration of pheromone in its neighbouring cells (those immediately to the east, west, north or south) and probabilistically decides to move in a direction which is under-explored. If there are one or more unexplored adjacent cells, it will always choose a move to one of these cells. This pseudo-random walking leads to the uniform exploration of the world. It also compensates for over-exploration of the area around the depot; the repeated trips of agents to this location mean it would be heavily over-explored if a quadrant-based strategy were used.

However, there is a disadvantage to simply counting all the visits to a cell since the start of the simulation. In an environment in which food is continuously appearing, the goal of a search algorithm must be to ensure each cell is visited as regularly as possible. In a system with permanent pheromones, a cell that has been visited only once, but very recently, appears more attractive to explore than a cell that was visited 10 times, 100 turns ago. In fact, the opposite is true, and the cell with "stale" pheromones should be explored preferentially. For this reason, a pheromone decay mechanism has been implemented and proved useful, whereby pheromone values decrease over time according to a variety of formulae. This ensures that cells which were over-explored in the past do not get unreasonably ignored in the future.

A further advantage of random walking is its use in avoidance of deadlocks. When two agents block each other's paths they will randomly move out of the way. While they may not successfully avoid each other instantly, due to the random choice of direction, the avoidance routine inevitably resolves the deadlock, since it is statistically impossible for both agents to choose the same move for ever. Each step that two blocking agents do in synchrony also adds extra pheromone to the cells they occupy and therefore increases the probability of opting to move in a different direction with their next move. In addition, this method is much simpler to implement than exhaustive characterisation of every possible deadlock, along with explicit strategies for resolving them.

Most importantly, using this flexible movement behaviour our implementation adapts very easily to unknown environments and even to worlds with dynamically changing shape. These scenarios are more relevant when thinking about real-world robotic exploration (e.g. on the battle-field or in disaster relief efforts), hence our focus on flexibility and adaptability.

3   Implementation

Our design required an implementation language that allows for the multi-threaded execution of agents. We chose *Qu-Prolog* [RW03, CRZ] because it allows for easy, declarative descriptions of the higher-level reasoning involved in intention selection and negotiation. Its flexible system of dynamic predicate manipulation also provides an unconstrained environment in which to construct and modify the simple agent language we have used, while simultaneously being descriptive enough to allow the lower level algorithms to be concisely expressed.

The publish/subscribe mechanism we described in Section 2.5 is realised using broadcasting via an *Elvin* [SAB+00] server. Direct negotiation between agents makes use of the Interagent Communication Model (ICM). Its communication server provides agent naming facilities and the means to encode, transport and queue symbolic messages.

Effectively, we are using three forms of communication—point-to-point communication for negotiations, broadcasting for events and knowledge sharing, and indirect communication via the environment using pheromones for exploration.

4   Analysis/Conclusion

The broadcast and negotiation techniques used here rely on a good supply of information about the environment. In scenarios where there is more known food than the agents can collect at once, these techniques have a potential to improve the utilisation of the agents, since the time spent conducting relatively unguided searches is limited. However, this knowledge of food locations needs first to be obtained, hence the introduction of a scout agent. The impact of the various techniques implemented is briefly assessed here.

For our quantitative analysis, we fixed the depot at location (10,10) and ran the simulation until 100 items of food had been collected and delivered. The agents were still required to discover the depot on each run. Ten runs of the simulation were conducted for each scenario. The average number of steps for one food delivery (μ_{steps}), the standard deviation of the number of steps (σ_{steps}) and the average number of successful negotiations per delivered food item (μ_{neg}) have been measured.

This shows that adding guidance to the randomly walking ants with the help of pheromones significantly improves their behaviour. However, adding negotiation does not seem to improve the results. We believe this is due to the low rate at which food is seeded into the environment. The negotiation usually improves a combined delivery of two ants by about 10%. However, the ants spent the majority of their time searching for food or the depot. Only about 10% of their time is spent collecting and delivering and so the improvement achieved by adding negotiation is only 10% of 10%, equivalent to 1% overall.

Table 2 shows the variation in scout performance at different seeding rates. In the high seeding-rate environment (with food seeded every 20 agent steps),

Table 1. Quantitative results when food is seeded every 60 simulated agent steps

Scenario	μ_{steps}	σ_{steps}	μ_{neg}
4 gatherers (no pheromone, no negotiation)	73.7	3.32	n/a
4 gatherers (pheromones, but no negotiation)	55.7	1.27	n/a
4 gatherers (pheromones and negotiation)	56.4	2.07	0.20
3 gatherers and 1 scout (pher. and neg.)	55.6	1.1	0.29

Table 2. Effect of permanent scout with varying seeding rates

Scenario	Seeding	μ_{steps}	σ_{steps}	μ_{neg}
4 gatherers	high	28.9	0.74	0.22
3 gatherers and 1 scout	high	31.6	1.28	0.18
4 gatherers	low	56.4	2.07	0.20
3 gatherers and 1 scout	low	55.6	1.1	0.29

having a dedicated scout agent proves significantly detrimental to the team performance. This is unsurprising, as with high rates of seeding, food is sufficiently abundant that the agents have no trouble finding food on their random walk. The team with a scout still performed better than would be expected of a team consisting solely of three gatherers, however, experiencing only a 9% performance drop despite effectively losing a quarter of the delivery capability.

In the low seeding-rate environment (with food seeded every 60 agent steps) however, the benefit of the scout agent completely compensated for the loss of delivery capacity, roughly equalling the delivery rate of four gatherers. In effect, the scout provides sufficient global knowledge to allow the agents to employ their high-level reasoning much more frequently, resulting in more efficient collection of the known food. As the delivery agents leave trails every time they visit the depot, the scout agent tends to explore the areas further from the depot, discovering concentrations of food that the delivery agents are unlikely to find.

As predicted, the usefulness of the scout agent depends on the rate of seeding. In an environment with a high rate of seeding, the food density is such that it becomes more efficient to simply have all agents collecting, since they are likely to find food soon after leaving the depot on their random search. Additionally, a scout agent in this situation tends to over-explore the edges, drawing the gatherer agents further from the depot than necessary. In a food-sparse (and thus information-poor) environment, however, the scout becomes more useful despite the loss of one agent's delivery capacity.

While these results do not show a scenario in which a scout agent provides a decisive advantage, they do indicate that there are situations in which a definite benefit exists. Accordingly, an initial attempt at an adaptive scouting strategy was implemented, wherein agents were allowed to change roles depending on the amount of knowledge they believed the team to have. In our first dynamic strategy, each agent is given a *scouting threshold* that controls whether it acts as a scout or a gatherer. This threshold depends on the amount of food the agents are collectively aware of. If the amount of known food drops below a particular agent's threshold, that agent will switch to scouting behaviour. By giving each agent a different threshold, a primitive dynamic scouting strategy is achieved. Results in several different scenarios are shown in Table 3.

It can be seen that allowing the agents to use an adaptive strategy all but eliminates the penalty for using scouts. In each scenario, the average cost of delivery is statistically identical, including the high seeding rate scenario which

Table 3. Effect of dynamic scouts with varying seeding rates

Scenario	Seeding	μ_{steps}	σ_{steps}	μ_{neg}
4 gatherers	high	28.7	0.72	0.07
Dynamic scouts	high	28.7	0.75	0.12
4 gatherers	medium	39.1	2.36	0.12
Dynamic scouts	medium	39.7	1.02	0.08
4 gatherers	low	54.4	0.94	0.03
Dynamic scouts	low	54.5	0.96	0.06

previously suffered from the use of scouts. While no definite improvement in performance has yet been shown when employing scouts, we believe this is primarily due to the simplicity of the contest's problem resulting in a lack of opportunities for negotiation. Since the benefit of negotiation in this world is small, the potential for scouts to improve the team's performance is consequently limited. In a world with a more complex set of tasks (e.g. one with different types of food, different delivery depots etc.), negotiation and hence scouting techniques are likely to prove much more valuable.

Acknowledgements

We would like to express our deepest gratitude to Silvana Zappacosta for allowing us to use and helping us to modify her visualisation written in Tcl/Tk, and to Peter Robinson for suggesting several improvements to our implementation. Furthermore, we are indebted to Keith Clark for encouraging us to participate in this contest and for many fruitful discussions.

References

[CRZ]   Keith L. Clark, Peter J. Robinson, and Silvana Zappacosta Amboldi. Multi-threaded communicating agents in Qu-Prolog. *In this volume.*

[DMC96]   Marco Dorigo, Vittorio Maniezzo, and Alberto Colorni. The Ant System: Optimization by a colony of cooperating agents. *IEEE Transactions on Systems, Man, and Cybernetics Part B: Cybernetics*, 26(1):29–41, 1996.

[GC05]   Dorian Gaertner and Keith Clark. On Optimal Parameters for Ant Colony Optimization Algorithms. In H. Arabnia and R. Joshua, editors, *Proceedings of the International Conference on Artificial Intelligence 2005*, volume 1, pages 83–89. CSREA, 2005.

[Nil94]   Nils J. Nilsson. Teleo-reactive programs for agent control. *Journal of Artificial Intelligence Research*, 1:139–158, 1994.

[RG95]   A. Rao and M. Georgeff. BDI agents: From theory to practice. *Proceedings of the 1st International Conference on Multi-Agents Systems*, pages 312–319, 1995.

[RW03]   Peter J. Robinson and Michael J. Walters. *Qu-Prolog 6.3 Reference Manual.* The University of Queensland, 2003.

[SAB⁺00] B. Segall, D. Arnold, J. Boot, M. Henderson, and T. Phelps. Content based routing with Elvin4. In *Proceedings of AUUG2K*, June 2000.

Extending Tropos for a Prolog Implementation: A Case Study Using the Food Collecting Agent Problem

Carlos Cares[1,2], Xavier Franch[1], and Enric Mayol [1]

[1] Dept. Llenguatges i Sistemes Informàtics, Universitat Politècnica de Catalunya,
Jordi Girona, 1-3 08034, Barcelona, Spain
Ph.: 43-93 413 7839
{ccares, franch, mayol}@lsi.upc.edu
[2] Dept. Ingeniería de Sistemas, Universidad de La Frontera,
Av. Francisco Salazar 01145, Casilla 54-D, Temuco, Chile
Ph.: 56-45 325000

Abstract. There is a recognized lack of Agent-Oriented Methodologies to translate a design into a computational logic implementation. In this paper we address this problem by extending Tropos, which is one of the most used methodologies to design agent systems. We show our proposal with the *Food Collecting Agent Problem* in which a team has to collect food in a grid-like world. Our solution includes autonomous behaviour, beliefs, multiple roles playing, communication and cooperation. The main contribution is the proposal to generate a Prolog implementation from a Tropos design by first extending the Tropos de-tailed design and second illustrating how to get a set of Prolog clauses for this design. In addition we show a performance evaluation of our Prolog implementation which confirms that our solution for the case study is effective and allows a simple configuration of the resulting program.

1 Introduction

Nowadays there is a recognized lack of Agent-Oriented Methodologies (AOM) at the implementation stage [1, 2]. Tropos [3, 4] is one of the most used AOM, however, it has an implementation stage oriented to an object-oriented implementation of the agent system, and therefore guidelines to derive declarative implementations from a Tropos design are not provided [5]. In this paper we address this situation and we propose a method to get a Prolog implementation starting from a Tropos design. To illustrate our method we use the Food Collecting Agent Problem (FCAP) as a case study, which is about a grid-like environment where agents can move just among neighbour slots and each slot can host at most one agent. In this world, food appears in a randomly way in any empty slot. There is a special slot, named the depot, where the agents may collect the food. In the next section we briefly show the stages of Tropos and our design for the FCAP, in section 3, an additional design step oriented to get a Prolog implementation is proposed and then we show how to convert this output into a computer program which is evaluated as a final point.

F. Toni and P. Torroni (Eds.): CLIMA VI, LNAI 3900, pp. 396–405, 2006.

2   Using Tropos for the FCAP

Tropos [3, 4] is an agent-oriented methodology for building software systems. It allows describing both the social (organizational) environment and the system itself. According to [5], Tropos covers from early requirements to implementation with a different focus on each stage: (1) Early Requirements focus on social context; (2) Late Requirements focus on system-to-be; (3) Architectural Design, focus on systems components; (4) Detailed Design and (5) Implementation, both focus on software agents.

Tropos uses the concepts of: *actor*, which can be organizational, human or software; *positions*, *roles* and *agents*, as specializations of actors; goals and social *dependencies* for representing the commitments or agreements of actors (*dependees*) to other actors (*dependers*). The type of the dependency is determined by on the intermediary element (*dependum*) between actors. It can be *goal* (hard or soft), *plan* or *resource*. Thus the basic structure of social representation is the *dependee-dependum-depender* relationship. In figures 1 and 2 we have illustrated the graphical representation of Tropos constructors according to their use. For further details about Tropos see [5].

In Tropos, at the Early Requirements stage, the analysis of the environment must be done. Since in the generic case the FCAP case study does not have a social context, we omit this stage here.

At the Late Requirements stage, the system-to-be is analyzed and the functional and non-functional requirements are specified. For FCAP we recognize two main actors, the *Food Provider* and the *Collector Team*. There are food dependencies representing a goal (*Food provided*) and two information resources (*Food depot* and *Food environment*). Moreover, the *Food Provider* delegates into the *Collector Team* the constraints about the agent's behaviour in the food environment. We build the models using our RiSD methodology [6]. Although there is an evolution of diagrams inside of this stage, we show the final output in figure 1.

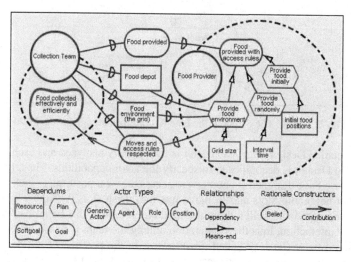

Fig. 1. Tropos: The output of the Late Requirements stage for the FCAP

Generally the FCAP problem does not consider the *Food Provider* as a system agent; however we do so because in the context of an Agent-Oriented Software Methodology, all actions should be executed by some system agent, although in specific cases, this agent does not become a software agent.

In the Architectural Design stage, the global architecture of the system is analyzed, new actors are incorporated and their main capabilities are identified. In our case we have added a *Team Member* position that represents all member of the team. Moreover we have decided to tackle the problem with the roles *Collector* (for gathering food and disposing it in the depot) and *Explorer* (for looking for food in the grid). Finally we have delegated in the *Rule Guard* role the goal to keep an adequate behaviour. When we specify that the position *Team Member* covers the *Rule Guard* role, it means that all the members of the team must play this role. In figure 2 we show the output of the Architectural Design. For simplicity of the drawing we have omitted the positive contributions from the *Team Member, Collector, Explorer* and *Rule Guard*'s goals to the main softgoal of the *Collection Team*.

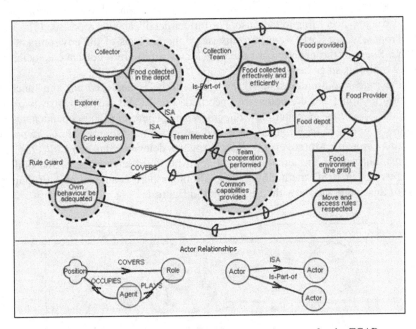

Fig. 2. Tropos: The output of the Late Requirements stage for the FCAP

At the Detailed Design stage, each actor is individually analyzed and each goal of the Architectural Design is decomposed to specify the actor capabilities. Thus, for the *Rule Guard* role, we have designed capabilities to access the own position, to pick up food, to know empty neighbour slots and to move just into these slots. For the *Team Member* role we have identified a belief about the food environment, this belief can be updated with agents' interaction, thus the cooperation among the team is based on sharing their beliefs. Moreover we have provided direct access to the position of the depot and we have designed the capability to advance towards a target point in the grid. For the *Collector* role we have the capabilities of disposing food in the depot, moving to the depot, moving for a guessed food position (based on its *belief*) and, in the case of not having food information, looking for it in unvisited slots. We have designed a main strategy, which specifies that collectors have different search spaces according to how many of them are in the grid and which is the size of the food environment.

Finally for the *Explorer* we have designed the simple capability of searching food through the grid (with the restriction again of moving just into adjacent slots), and the necessary data resources to support this capability have been identified. In figure 3 we show a partial view of the Detailed Design output, we illustrate this stage with the *Rule Guard* and *Team Member* roles, for simplicity of the drawing we have omitted the relationships and softgoal contributions among the actors and due to the simplicity of the *Explorer* behaviour we have omitted it too. In the next section we show our extension for the detailed design of the *Collector* role.

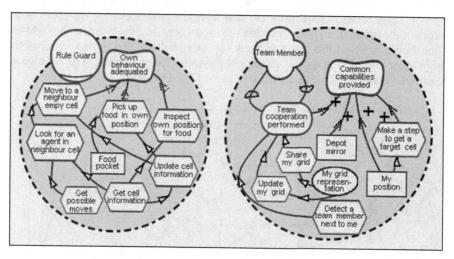

Fig. 3. Tropos: Detailed design for Rule Guard and Team Member roles

3   Extending Detailed Design

In this section we explain how to extend the Detailed Design stage to get a declarative implementation. First we propose to replace the Agent UML activity diagrams [7] used in Tropos by scenario sequences, which are based on Use Case Maps [8]; in [9] it is illustrated in an intuitive way how to put scenario sequences in these diagrams. We think that it is a simple way to specify sequences when they are needed. In a declarative implementation these sequences must have the convenient order to prove the logical goals, in addition this order could affect the system efficiency, and hence we consider an advantage to have a representation of these sequences at design time. In figure 4 we show a scenario sequence for the *Collector* role, represented by the black line crossing the *Collector* agent starting at the black circle and ending at the perpendicular line. Here the design indicates that the first goal to be proved is *Put food in the depot*, but this means to check that the agent is over the depot and has food in the buffer, otherwise the second goal, *Go to the depot*, should be proved, etc.

For *goal* and *plan* root elements we propose to specify when they must be executed, thus we propose four implementation attributes, namely *at begin, at end, at call* and *always. At call* means that the goal or plan is activated from another goal or plan. *At begin* and *at end* indicate that the selected goal or plan should be activated just one time, at start of run time or at the end. *Always* means that the goal or plan should be permanently executed.

Finally we propose to make the decisions about data representation. The design elements which require having a data representation are resource and belief. In Prolog we have two main choices: a data structure (generally a list) or the knowledge data base (KDB) included in Prolog. In our case, we have decided to represent the food environment with predicates and the rest of resource and belief elements with lists.

In figure 4 we show a partial view of the proposed extension, here we have some typical implementation decisions that we bring to design time, namely: (a) sequences of proofs using scenario sequences, (b) data representation decisions, the boxes at the bottom of the figure 4, and (c) execution time specifications, the boxes at the right top of the figure 4. From this point of view our extended detailed design enriches the design stage and their diagrams enhance the system documentation. The notation of the external attribute elements correspond to the GRL [10] proposal.

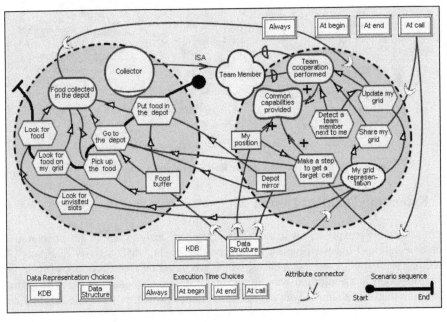

Fig. 4. Partial Extended Detailed Design for FCAP

4   The Prolog Implementation

To obtain an implementation from the extended detailed design we propose the following suggestions:

1. Generate the agents and their relationships with the predicates *agent, play, position, isa, cover,* etc., i.e. the actor types and actor relationships from Tropos. We have implemented some predicates to inherit resources and beliefs when *isa* is used and to replicate the data structures when the roles are assigned to agents. This predicates are generic and could be used in other agent applications. For FCAP we have generated a specific instantiation with five agents, a *food provider* agent (*fp*), an *explorer* agent (*ca*), and three *collectors* (*en, xa* and *ge*), we show this from lines 28 to 41 in figure 5.

2. Use the *define* predicate to implement *resource* and *belief* elements, identifying the name of the role as first argument, and a data structure which define the resources (e.g. lines 182 to 184 in figure 5).

3. Group root elements (*goal* and *plan*) under the identified activation times, each activation time is a predicate that needs the actor type (atom) and the agent name (variable); this is illustrated from lines 185 to 192 in figure 5.

4. Program the goals and plans using a set of predicates that act over the defined data structures and clauses. This step motivates the reuse of already programmed predicates but is not an automatic step because the specific clauses depend on the semantic of the each goal and plan. For example we show, in figure 5, the *amI* and *getResource* predicates that implement the *shareGrid* plan (lines 452 to 455).

5. Write the main program and call the predicates *runBegin, runEnd,* and *runAlways* (without parameters). These are simple predicates that execute the set of *begin, end* and *always* predicates of each agent. The implementation is generic and other agent applications could use the same predicates.

```
28 agent(fp).                           182 define(collector, [ [collector],
29 agent(ca).                           183                       [resources,
30 agent(xa).                           184                        [foodBuffer, 0]] ] ).
31 agent(en).                           185 begin(collector,_).
32 agent(ge).                           186 always(collector,MyName) :-
33 play(ge,collector).                  187             ( putFoodInDepot(MyName) |
34 play(xa,collector).                  188               goToDepot(MyName) |
35 play(en,collector).                  189               pickUpFood(MyName) |
36 play(ca,explorer).                   190               lookForFoodInMyGrid(MyName) |
37 play(fp,foodProvider).               191               lookForFood(MyName) ).
38 position(teamMember).                192 end(collector,_).
39 isa(collector,teamMember).           452 %------teamMember task--------------
40 isa(explorer,teamMember).            453 shareGrid(MyName,TheGrid) :-
41 cover(teamMember,ruleGuard).         454     amI(MyName,teamMember),
                                        455     getResource(MyName,mygrid,TheGrid).
```

Fig. 5. Implementation of the detailed design

We have implemented the system using WSI Prolog [11]. We have a set of parameters which are loaded from a text file; the parameters correspond to the *Food Provider* resources in fig. 1. Moreover we run the system in a batch mode, generating an HTML output where we can see what happened with the food collection in any web browser. Moreover, since some Prolog implementations allow a multithread execution we recommend to put each agent in a different thread getting data and execution time autonomy. In the following code segment we show the basic thread division imple-mented in SWI-Prolog (the symbol "..." means that we require a similar code line for each agent)

```
runThreads:-
    thread_create(ignore(run),IdAg_1,[alias(ag_1),detach(true)])
    , ...
    parameter(minutesRunning,TotalTime),
    T is TotalTime*60,
    sleep(T),
    thread_send_message(IdAg_1,stop),

    ...
    thread_join(IdAg_1,_),

    ...
```

To see the system output we add to the food provider agent a task that generates an HTML file with the different states of the grid. This output is showed in figure 6 with an 8x8 food environment and fifteen seconds of total time. The food depot is the dark slot with the number 0 at start and 8 at the end. The food is in the light slots and the agents are the slots with the strings ca, xa, en and ge.

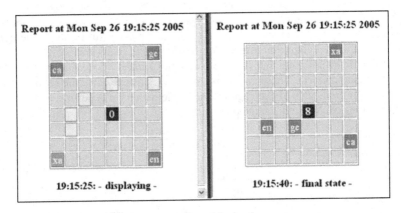

Fig. 6. Visualization of the html output

We have considered giving some performance results of our Prolog implementation. However a complete evaluation means to control many variables, for example the grid size, rate of food generation, amount of initial food in the grid, total time, and even some variations of the problem constraint, for example an unknown depot position, direct communications among agents (i.e., the agents do not need to be in neighbours slots to communicate their believes), etc. Also a general evaluation could consider other sophisticated variables and their implementation strategies but this work is out of the goal of this paper.

We just provide a simple evaluation scenario. We set the total time to one minute; the grid size to 15x15 without initial food in the grid; the rate of the random food generation to two seconds; and making the agents aware of the depot position. In this scenario we have made several executions interchanging the roles with different number of agents.

Thus we have different configurations to evaluate the system. Because we have a random system of food generation the performance is not always the same so it has been necessary to take a sample for each configuration over our random variable "amount of collected food". We have used a sample size 30. In figure 7 we show frequency graphics of the amount of collected food. We use the label *NeMc* for the configuration with *N* explorers and *M* collectors.

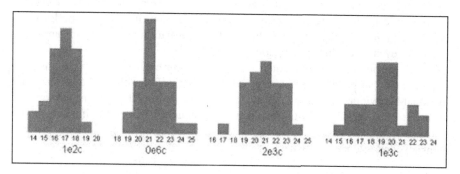

Fig. 7. Frequency graphics of collected food under 4 configurations

We have aimed to demonstrate that there is a statistical difference among configurations, i.e. we have a null hypothesis of means equality. In figure 7 it is possible to assume that our random variable has a normal probability distribution in spite of the fact that the standard deviation does not seem to be the same. In [12] it is reported that the Welch's test provides reasonable protection against type I errors (rejecting a true hypothesis) when the variances are heterogeneous. Thus we tried our set of null hypotheses using this statistical test. In figure 8 we illustrate the means of each configuration and also we show with a strong double arrow when the null hypothesis has been rejected with an error probability less than 1% ($\alpha=0.01$) and with a segmented line when there was not possible to reject the equality assumption with the same probability.

Based on these results, we can see that there is a better performance when we increase the total amount of agents, but also it seems that a limit exists. Another observation is that there is not a real difference when the roles are changed. We think that

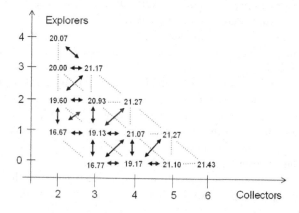

Fig. 8. Significance of the roles and number of agents over the amount of collected food

this similar performance means that the roles are not significantly different, since maybe the collectors look for food when they do not have food information and, in a small grid it is relatively fast to go to the depot. On the other hand, the vertical differences seem very interesting because, although the explorer spends CPU time and it does not collect food, there are 4 cases in which the system improves its performance when an explorer is added, which indicates that information interchange is an important factor, even when this information is not updated.

Finally, in spite of these outcomes, we think that our evaluation is modest and it is not possible to get general laws, mainly because we think that the global strategy and individual behaviours are more relevant variables to improve the system performance, but at the same time, this initial evaluation is enough to show our implementation performance and flexibility to move the quantity of agents, general food provider parameters and role interchange.

5 Conclusions

In this paper we have proposed a specific way to get a Prolog implementation from a Tropos design on two steps, first extending Tropos, specifically at the detailed design with new elements: sequences, execution times and data representation; and second, proposing translation suggestions to get the Prolog implementation from this Tropos-extended detailed design. Although we have used the FCAP, the approach is a generic developing proposal based on the atomicity and clarity of the elements in the extended detailed design. However a set of different projects should be carried out to get stronger evidence about its utility and wide range of applications.

On the other hand the program architecture is always the same, and there are a common set of predicates already programmed and other ones that we can get from the detailed design, thus a relevant part of the code could be generated automatically and the rest could be sufficiently documented for programming aid. This means that detailed de-sign and implementation are very close and, hence, the detailed design conforms a good documentation of the implementation stage.

We think that our proposal is very simple, repeatable in many problems and, hence, easy and convenient to establish in software developing teams which are developing agent-oriented systems.

About FCAP we have designed a solution using multiple roles playing (*Team member*, *Rule guard* plus *Collector* or *Explorer*). The agents cooperate in the solutions sharing information about their belief of the world. Besides, the similar behaviour is grouped in the *Team member* role, being an efficient solution to implement common features. Moreover we have tested the system with different roles configurations showing the performance and flexibility of the implementation as the result of a case study of our methodological proposal. On the other hand we think that a complete agent strategy description and evaluation is necessary to find an optimal agent solution to FCAP.

Acknowledgement

This work has been done in the framework of the research project UPIC, ref. TIN2004-07461-C02-01, supported by the Spanish Ministerio de Ciencia y Tecnología. Carlos Cares wants to acknowledgment to MECE-SUP FRO0105 Project of the chilean government and the University of La Frontera, who supports his stand at Universitat Politècnica de Catalunya.

References

1. Dastani M., Hulstijn J., Dignum F., Meyer J.: Issues in Multiagent Systems Development. Third International Conference AAMAS04, Columbia, USA, July (2004), 920-927
2. Hoa, K., Winikoff, M.: Comparing Agent-Oriented Methodologies. In the proceedings of the Fifth International Bi-Conference Workshop on Agent-Oriented Information Systems, AAMAS'03. Melbourne, Australia, July (2003)
3. Castro, J.,Kolp M., Mylopoulos, J.: A Requirements-Driven Development Methodology. In Advanced Information Systems Engineering: 13th International Conference, CAiSE'01. In-terlaken, Switzerland. (2001), 108-123
4. Perini A.,Bresciani P.,Giunchiglia P., Giorgini P., Mylopoulos J.: A knowledge Level Soft-ware Engineering Methodology for Agent Oriented Programming. In Proceedings of the Fifth International Conference on Autonomous Agents, Montreal, Canada, May (2001).
5. Sannicoló, F., Perini, A., Giunchiglia, F.: The Tropos modelling language - A User Guide. Technical report DIT-02-0061, University of Trento, February (2002)
6. Gemma Grau, Xavier Franch, Enric Mayol, Claudia Ayala, Carlos Cares, Mariela Haya, Fredy Navarrete, Pere Botella, Carme Quer. "RiSD: A Methodology for Building i* Strategic Dependency Models". In Proceedings of The 17th Int. Conf. on Software Engineering and Knowledge Engineering (SEKE'05). 14-16 July. Taipei, Taiwan, (2005) 259-266.
7. Odell, J., Parunak H.v.D., Bauer, B.: Extending UML for Agents. In Proceedings of the Agent-Oriented Information System Workshop at the 17th National Conference on Artificial Intelligence. Austin, USA. (2002) 3-17
8. Amyot, D., Mussbacher, G.: URN: Towards a New Standard for the Visual Description of Requirements. Proc. of the 3rd Int. Workshop on Telecommunications and beyond: The Broader Applicability of SDL and MSC., Aberystwyth, UK, June 24-26, (2002) 21-37
9. Liu L., Yu E.: Designing Web-Based Systems in Social Context: A Goal and Scenario Based Approach. Lecture Notes in Computer Science **2348**, Jan (2002) 37-51
10. GRL web site. http://www.cs.toronto.edu/km/GRL/.
11. Wielemaker, J.:SWI-Prolog 5-1: Reference Manual. SWI, University of Amsterdam, Roetersstraat 15, 1018 WB Amsterdam, The Netherlands, (1997)-(2003)
12. Kirk, R.E.: Experimental Design. Brooks/Cole Publishing Company, 2nd Edition (1982)

Reactive Food Gathering

Robert Logie[1], Jon G. Hall[2], and Kevin G. Waugh[2]

[1] Osaka Gakuin University, Faculty of Computer Science,
2-36-1 Minami Kishibe, Suita Shi Osaka 564-8511, Japan
rob@utc.osaka-gu.ac.jp
[2] The Open University, Department of Computing,
Faculty of Mathematics and Computing, Walton Hall,
Milton Keynes MK7 6BJ, England

Abstract. This short paper describes a simple agent system aimed at addressing the food gathering problem set for the 2005 CLIMA contest. Our system is implemented as a collection of reactive agents which dynamically switch between a number of behaviours depending on interaction with their environment. Our agents maintain no internal representation of their environment and operate purely in response to their immediate surroundings. The agents collectively map the environment co-operating indirectly via environmental markers and they use these markers to assist them in locating the depot when they discover food. The required behaviour emerges from the interaction between agents and the marked environment. Despite the simplicity of the agents and their behaviours formal description is difficult. We concentrate more on identifying interesting problems in characterising system exhibiting emergent behaviour and outline possible logic approaches to dealing with them.

The application (and one or two other systems addressing the same problem in a different manner) can be downloaded from:
http://219.1.164.219/~robert/pwBlog/wp-content/CLIMAbuild.zip

1 Introduction

As multi-agent systems become more complex designers are increasingly having to deal with difficulties introduced by heterogeneous systems. Agents may not behave as they are 'supposed' to for many reasons[1], they may have been programmed by different organisations, they may have competing interests or be operating with a different set of agent level experiences. Given these differences the task of designing and maintaining multi-agent systems may be made less difficult if there was a method of specifying agent behaviour in respect of desired system behaviour. Recent research in normative systems and, particularly, normative reactive systems may provide this means of describing and constraining agent behaviour in a manner which allows us to address this difficulty. Our system has been built as a tool for investigating such approaches, we have constrained the world in a number of ways in an attempt at simplifying our initial investigations. Our agents are purely reactive, they maintain no internal model of their environment and operate entirely on the basis of local

F. Toni and P. Torroni (Eds.): CLIMA VI, LNAI 3900, pp. 406–413, 2006.

information. This makes learning about the environment difficult and our agents achieve this by making learning a partially external group activity, agents mark the environment with a simple indication of their internal state. This removes the difficulties associated with different sets of agent level experiences problem mentioned above.

For many problems in a tightly bounded environment – problems such as industrial process control or safety systems – reactive agents may be ideal and a fuller understanding of their potential behaviour will be beneficial in allowing their use in increasingly complex scenarios. The CLIMA contest scenario provides such an environment and is, we feel, ideal for the application of reactive agents. Jennings *et al.* [2] note that a major selling point of purely reactive agent systems is that overall behaviour emerges from interactions between component behaviours and the agent's environment. This inherent simplicity makes reactive agents attractive but it also masks a number of difficulties. The most notable are those of designing agents in such a way that they can take account of non-local information and in such a way as to be able to improve their agent level performance over time. Jennings *et al.* further note that agents using a large number of behaviours can quickly become too complex to understand.

Reactive agents generally operate by having predetermined behaviours or sequences of actions intended to deal with the various circumstances that the agent may encounter. As circumstances change an agent may switch behaviours. Our agent design involves identifying problems within the environment and designing behaviours to address them. Switching between behaviours brings a number of constraints. If an agent's behaviour involves maintaining a record of data and the agent switches to another behaviour, that does not maintain this data, then this data may become outdated. In a dynamic environment such internal world data may be dangerously out of date when the agent returns to using it and maintaining the data my be expensive for a resource bounded agent concentrating on other tasks. We avoid such problems by letting agents use only very local data and data about their internal state or history.

2   The Problem — A General Approach

We approached the problem by identifying sub-problems which we could associate with agent roles. The roles assigned were those of locating food and, when food has been found, transporting it to the depot. Both of these roles involve searching the environment, the former for food which may be at random locations and the latter for the depot which remains at a fixed location. Clearly it is in the system's benefit to have all agents aware of the depot so when one agent finds it some means of indicating its presence to others will be a valuable asset. Our intention is to make the agents purely reactive and one of the consequences of this is that communications options are rather restricted. In addition we limit each agent to being able to carry only one food unit.

We have assumed that the depot location is unknown initially but that it remains at a fixed position throughout a run, when an agent discovers the depot it discovers its permanent location. This leads to a minor difficulty, our agents operate using only very local data and do not know their absolute position in the world[1] which means that they cannot remember an exact depot location. We address this by letting agents leave local markers in the environment. Agents use a random walk to search for the depot. When an agent finds the depot it initialises a 'dropper' which allows it to leave a trail of pheromone like weightings on the cells that it visits between leaving the depot cell and finding a piece of food. Despite the extreme simplicity of this system it allows agents acting only with local data to co-operate in mapping their environment in a way that facilitates the task of carrying food to the depot.

The depot location problem within the food transport role is addressed by three agent behaviours; *depot-searching, depot-marking* and *depot-seeking*. These behaviours, respectively, involve a random walk looking for the depot cell, a random marker laying walk searching for food and a directed pheromone gradient following walk whilst carrying food back to the depot.

The second search problem – that of finding food – cannot be approached in the same way since food is deposited randomly by the system. This random placement precludes structured search behaviour by the agents. Food may well appear in a location already searched. The specification indicates that food can only be seen on a cell that an agent is visiting so this rules out giving food a smell that agents can detect. We address this problem with a simple random walk and there is one *food-searcher* behaviour assigned to the food locating role. This behaviour may be concurrent with the depot-searcher and depot-marker behaviours.

Searcher behaviours involve random walks and seeker behaviours involve trail following. We assume that cells will not have multiple food units, when an agent picks up food then thet cell has been cleared. There is, thus, no need to lay trails to food and consequently there is no food-seeker behaviour, food searching is always a random process and its performance will not improve over time. Seeker behaviours involve using environmental markers left by agents to track previously located objects with persistent locations. It is expected that the performance of seeker type behaviours will improve over time as the environment is more accurately mapped during the random walks of food-searchers.

The food searcher and depot searcher behaviours can operate concurrently. Considering the agent's behaviour in this manner provides a convenient method for analysing behaviour transitions, these are shown in figure 1.

Bonabeau *et al.* [3, page 26] describe a broadly similar process where ants influence or *recruit* other ants so as to guide them towards persistent food sources, such recruitment based solely on pheromones is known as *mass recruitment*. The depot-marking behaviour is an instance of this mass recruitment as depot-searchers (agents that have yet to find the depot) make use of the pheromone trails from agents that have already located the depot. We have also briefly

---

[1] Co-ordinate values are only used as a means of keeping agents in bounds and displaying user friendly data. Beyond ensuring that the agent doesn't try to move out of bounds they are not used in any of the agent's operating decisions.

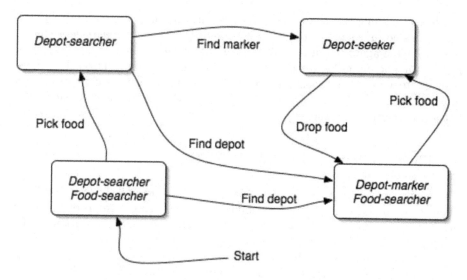

Fig. 1. Agent behaviour transitions

experimented with other environmental marking methods but felt that these were uncomfortably close to requiring global knowledge or data, something which we are trying to avoid.

3 The Agents

Our agents have two modules, a simple reactive core and a move manager. The reactive core senses details of the agent's immediate environment and takes actions depending on these percepts. The agent's roles and component behaviours have been briefly described in section 2. The agent's 'cycle' involves sensing its environment, selecting a behaviour, executing that behaviour then making either a directed or random move. Behaviour selection is very dynamic and an agent may switch behaviours on each cycle through its core module. In this environment all behaviours either execute concurrently (such as food-searcher and depot-searcher), or one is suppressed by historic actions (such as having located and picked up food the food-searcher behaviour is suppressed in favour of the depot-searcher behaviour).

Our agent's pheromone tracking behaviour is very simple, finding the depot triggers the agent's depot-marking behaviour causing the agent to prime its trail marker and reinforce any environmental markers in locations it passes through. It will reinforce other agent's markers but does not reinforce its own so as to prevent creating strong local maxima if the agent repeatedly moves between a small number of cells. Finding food will trigger the depot-seeker behaviour causing the agent to stop marking and try to return to the depot by following marker gradients. The other environment marking methods, mentioned in section 2 that we briefly experimented with were of comparable complexity.

The move manager is coupled to the agent core and simply makes sure that the agent does not move out of the world's boundaries, This coupling is loose in the sense that the agent doesn't monitor what the move manager does and merely requests a pheromone gradient directed move or a random move. The move manager may introduce a small element of non-determinism by not executing a directed however this in inconsequential as agents operate in cycles, each cycle is a sense, select, act sequence.

4   The Problem — Logical Aspects

The agents have a small set of behaviours defined *a-priori* and the logical aspects of our work are early steps in an attempt at characterising systems of emergent behaviour in a sequence of logics beginning with a deontic description of the system. We have an idea of what agents *ought* to; they *ought* to take food to the depot and they *ought* to do this in as efficient a manner as possible. We also have an idea of what they ought not to do - wander aimlessly and unproductively.

Adopting an *ought to do / ought not to do* partitioning may allows us consider deontic logic as an initial means of characterising the system. This approach, however, brings difficulties, Horty[4, page 36] notes that standard deontic logic partitions the system's possible future worlds into sets that are either ideal or non ideal. Agents either take food to the depot or they do not, there is no means of characterising notions of good and bad ways of doing this and, consequently, no notion of improving performance.

Although deontic logic provides a useful framework for partitioning agent behaviours it does not really help us to group these behaviours and, more importantly, behaviour transitions into appropriate sets. If we consider the deontic approach as being an absolutely prescriptive starting point we need some means of describing the system such that prescriptive constraints can be flexibly evaluated. Logical norms may provide this bridge: van der Torre and Tan[5] note that norms are prescriptive whilst *normative propositions* are descriptive. This is useful as propositions are a step closer to something that can be used to specify agent behaviour. They further note that prescriptive obligations can be interpreted dynamically whereas descriptive obligations are interpreted statically. This may be a key to describing systems of emergent behaviour, an agent's set of actions may be static and these can be used to describe possible interactions with its environment. The set of actions which an agent may use in different sets of circumstances will be dynamic and change as an agent learns or its environment changes. An additional attraction is that norms are typically a social phenomena [6] which makes them intrinsically a multi agent concept.

Does a normative view provide a means of partitioning behaviours less brutally than standard deontic logic? Boella and van der Torre [7] indicate that an important feature of norms is that they allow for behaviour that deviates from ideal. A normative system that specifies deontically ideal behaviour will tolerate less than ideal behaviour and will, thus, provide guidelines for agents to use as they improve their performance. Our agents are extremely simple, they have fixed transitions between behaviours (see figure 1) and their 'pure' reactivity means that there are no internal systems to allow considered choice. This operation appears to be constrained rather than norm governed. The agents are constrained to drop food on the depot but their route from a food pickup to the depot is free. Agents are always capable of taking food back to the depot – in this bounded environment a random walk would eventually locate the depot – but they are not constrained to taking the best route. As agents mark their routes after visiting the depot they are setting up external triggers for their behaviour transitions and we think that this can be considered as generating norms that govern their behaviour.

When every cell has been marked the agents are confined to a subset of their available behaviours, the depot-searcher is no longer required and transitions are only between depot-seeker and depot-marker/food-searcher behaviours. We feel that this can be described as an emergent norm which influences agents by guiding them away from the depot-searcher behaviour. If this characterisation holds then the system may be thought of as a meta-agent – a collective normative authority. Our simple agents delegate the task of improving their performance to an emergent norm and they contribute to its emergence. This system may be a very simple and may be a degenerate example of what Boella and van der Torre describe in [8].

Lomuscio and Sergot[9] note that most of the highly respected theories for modelling aspects of agent systems are based on earlier work in philosophical logic. This is understandable given the complexity of the capabilities required by agents in a complex environment. Halpern[10], however, notes that pragmatic concerns – such as those frequently encountered in system building – are not really addressed by the philosophical literature. Deontic and normative approaches, for example, are useful for specifying and reasoning about systems but they do not really provide a methodology for building systems. Additionally, our agents have no real concept of their environment but this does not prevent them from carrying out their task or – more interestingly – improving their performance over time. A different semantic view may help us step towards a way of characterising emergent behaviours. The commonly used Kripke semantics are based on possible alternatives for future worlds. A world based view may be useful when considering a system in its entirety but may not be helpful at the agent level, especially in this case where the agents, as we have noted, have no concept of their environment. One possible approach is to view this as an *interpreted system* (see [11] which allows us to consider the system by specifying the states in terms of states the agents and their environment. The level of specification is open which allows us to characterise things as precisely or as loosely as required.

Indeed a fairly loose specification is sufficient for us to see, intuitively, where problems may arise. If, for example, the world state contains one or more looped paths that do not lead to the depot and the full set of agents is in the trail following state then there is a danger that the system will livelock. Clearly this aggregate world state is not desirable.

5   Observations

Our system performance evaluation had two criteria, the directness of the route taken by agents carrying food back to the depot and whether or not food accumulated in the environment. Test runs were carried out by seeding the environment with a few food units then starting the agents. Initial agent performance is rather poor, agents rely on random searches for both the depot and food. Agents that have found food wander at random and do not appear to be doing anything useful whilst food continues to appear. When one agent finds the depot and begins marking the environment other agents gradually move from random depot-searching to pheromone gradient following depot-seeking. At first this means following, in reverse, another agent's random walk so as to reach the depot. Over a period of time the gradient mapping becomes smoother and spreads more widely, this allows agents to begin taking more direct routes to the depot with a concomitant performance improvement.

Agents will occasionally become trapped by a 'livelock'. This livelocking manifests itself when an agent appears to walk repeatedly over the same looped path. This only occurs when a food carrying agent is following a pheromone gradient and encounters local maxima. Because the agent follows gradients without backtracking these local maxima may trap the agent. Livelock may be broken by another agent passing through a cell adjacent to the loop and altering pheromone levels sufficiently to weaken the local maxima thereby allowing the trapped agent to escape. The system has only four agents and if there is a high food density then there is a risk that all four will become livelocked especially where local maxima form within a few grid squares of the depot, a location to which depot-seeker agents are already drawn.

Intuitively if there is a non food carrying agents then there is a chance of a livelock being broken. Designing a system where agents can detect that they are livelocked whilst maintaining a local data only approach is an interesting problem.

6   Future Work

Our system was developed solely for the CLIMA contest but it contains elements of an ongoing research project into emergent behaviour. This combination has pointed to a number of interesting areas for further investigation. Even with a very small number of component behaviours the observation by Jennings et. al. [2] in section 1 holds and interactions within the system cause fairly complex overall behaviour to emerge. Identifying potential emergent behaviour is difficult and a normative approach may provide a means of better understanding the potential interactions in reactive systems. A fully normative approach may, however, be inadequate for reasons that have been outlined above. An interpreted approach allows us to look more closely at agent level details leaning more towards design and implementation. Lomuscio and Sergot's work[9] has shown that it is possible to consider an interpreted system deontically. This system is now being investigated by 'looking up' from the agent level and an interpreted description and 'looking down' from a deontic systems level description so as to identify and attempt to close the gap where these approaches meet.

Despite their simplicity our agents do, what we consider, a good job at carrying food to the depot and improving their performance over time. We have concentrated on the depot and not paid much attention to food location simply leaving this to an unstructured, random search. Dealing with the occasional appearance of livelock whilst maintaining a local data only approach presents an interesting problem. Adopting a normative approach we could prohibit livelock. This ought implies that agents can avoid livelock which is not easy when relying on purely local data. One possible approach is to have 'defender agents' [12] which look for possible livelocks and release trapped agents. The difficulty of doing this using only local data is obvious. Our agents are very simple but considering them as a normative system gives a rich view of their interactions and raises a number of questions about how best to improve their performance. If an agent finds food and is unable to pick it up then marking that food location – in a similar manner to the depot – may intuitively seem to be a good step but this may lead to a greater possibility of all agents becoming livelocked.

References

1. Lomuscio, A., Sergot, M.: Deontic interpreted systems. Studia Logica **75** (2003) 63–92
2. Jennings, N., Sycara, K., Wooldridge, M.: A roadmap of agent research and development. Autonomous Agents and Multi-Agent Systems **1** (1998) 7–38
3. Bonabeau, E., Dorigo, M., Theraulaz, G.: Swarm Intelligence - from nature to artificial systems. Santa Fe institute studies in the sciences of complexity. OUP (1999)
4. Horty, J.: Agency and deontic logic. OUP (2001)
5. van der Torre, L.W.N., Tan, Y.: An update semantics for deontic reasoning. In Prakken, H., McNamara, P., eds.: Norms, Logics and Information Systems. New Studies in Deontic Logic and Computer Science. IOS Press, Amsterdam (1998)
6. Conte, R., Castelfranchi, C.: Cognitive and social action. UCL press (1995)
7. Boella, G., van der Torre, L.W.N.: Fulfilling or violating obligations in normative multiagent systems. In: IAT, IEEE Computer Society (2004) 483–486
8. Boella, G., van der Torre, L.W.N.: Attributing mental attitudes to normative systems. In: AAMAS, ACM (2003) 942–943
9. Lomuscio, A., Sergot, M.: Investigations in grounded semantics for multiagent systems specfications via deontic logic. Technical report, Imperial College, London (2000)
10. Halpern, J.Y.: Reasoning about knowledge: a survey. In: Handbook of Logic in Artificial Intelligence and Logic Programming. Oxford University Press (1995) 1–34
11. Fagin, R., Halpern, J.Y., Moses, Y., Vardi, M.Y.: Reasoning About Knowledge. MIT Press (1995)
12. Boella, G., van der Torre, L.W.N.: Norm governed multiagent systems: The delegation of control to autonomous agents. In: IAT, IEEE Computer Society (2003) 329–335

Strategies for Multi-agent Coordination in a Grid World Using Petri Nets

Eder Mateus Nunes Gonçalves and Guilherme Bittencourt

UFSC - Federal University of Santa Catarina,
DAS - Automation and Systems Department,
88040-900 Florianópolis, SC, Brazil
{eder, gb}@das.ufsc.br

Abstract. In this work, we describe strategies for multi-agent coordination, where adequate coordination means a system performance increase. In the main strategy, when an agent cannot perform an action, for whatever reason, it chooses the agent more capable in the environment to execute this action. All the specification of the multi-agent system, from the social strategy to the actions in the environment, is made using a particular Petri Net model. The results show the strategy efficacy especially when the environment increases the necessity for a reaction.

1 Introduction

The advantages obtained with a multi-agent approach can be easily lost if an adequate coordination process between agents can not be established. To explore the real possibilities of a multi-agent strategy, the agents in the society must be able to cooperate in a coordinated way. In the Artificial Intelligence literature, several research problems were proposed in which these coordination strategies can be implemented and tested, e.g., robot soccer, rescue and surveillance activities, etc. One common artificial environment consists of a world in a grid format, that agents should explore to find resources, normally associated with "food units". The idea of all these problems is to measure how the performance of the agents, in this case the quantity of food items that is collected, increases with coordination, i.e., what is the impact of team work.

In this context, we have developed a software[1] that simulates a grid world, with twenty lines and twenty columns, where food units can appear at a randomly chosen cell of the world at regular time intervals. Four agents should coordinate their actions in order to collect the maximimal quantity of food units in a given period of time. Any agent, that finds a food unit, should depose it into a given storage cell. To evaluate the coordination strategies we can modify the environment conditions to determine the better moment to use the strategy.

The software was implemented in C++, using object orientation. The agents are implemented by a knowledge-based system, whose rules are explicitly codified

---

[1] The software can be downloaded from:
http://www.das.ufsc.br/~eder/clima.src.tar.gz.

F. Toni and P. Torroni (Eds.): CLIMA VI, LNAI 3900, pp. 414–419, 2006.

into the software main program using a restricted *predicate logic* as knowledge representation formalism. The knowledge bases of these agents are specified using a particular model of Petri Nets. This methodology permits to develop all the system with a unique tool, from the social strategy to the actions in the environment. As a base case, the performance without any cooperation strategy is considered. In this case, the agents search for food alone, without taking into account the other agents. As a first cooperation strategy we propose some actions to be taken when an agent already loaded finds food in its way to the depot.

The paper is organized in the following way. In the next section, it is described the Grid World and its constraints. In section 3 the strategies used to solve the problem of the Grid World, in a multi-agent approach specified by Petri Nets, are presented. In section 4 the results of the simulations in the Grid World are presented. Finally, section 5 presents the conclusions and future perspectives.

2   The Environment: A Grid World

The environment consists of a grid, a matrix with twenty lines and twenty columns. The intersection between a line and a column is called a *case*. At each moment, each agent is located in exactly one case. One case is chosen to be the depot case, where all collected food units should be stored. The simulation occurs in cycles, i.e., the temporal unit is a cycle. In a cycle, an agent can perform one, and only one, action, that can be either a movement to an adjacent case, or the emission of a message. Initially, the agents are located in the grid corners and the case depot is located in the center of the grid, in position (10,10).

According to the environment rules, one food unit appears automatically every n cycles, where n is a simulation parameter. The experiments showed that the strategy efficacy varies with this parameter value.

Others constraints were considered to create a problem more adequate to the multi-agent approach. All simulations were performed using a time interval of twenty seconds. The agents can carry only one food unit at a time. Once an agent collected a food unit, it can only leave it in the depot. There is no direct communication, all communication traffic is carried out by a communication manager. When an agent needs to send a message, this message is transmitted to a mailbox, and the communication manager delivers it to the message receiver. An agent can receive several messages, but it can participate in only one cooperation process at each time, i.e., during one cooperation process, the agent can not engage into a new cooperation process.

The software was implemented in the C++ programming language [1], using an object-oriented approach. A total of seven classes were implemented. The classes are:

- **Position:** indicates a position in the grid;
- **Food:** contains the list of positions in the grid where the food is located;
- **Message:** contains constructors for messages with different performatives;
- **Mailbox:** used by the environment to manage the agent's messages;

- **Clock:** implements the environment clock;
- **Interface:** verifies and validates the agent's actions in the environment, besides providing the input information for the agents;
- **Agent:** provides the agent internal variables and the actions in the environment, including movements and message exchanges.

The main program implements the four agents and their interactions with the environment, besides providing the interface with the exterior. This interface is in command-line form. In every cycle, the system updates the environment state, i.e, the simulation time, the cases with food units, the agent's positions, the number of foods collected, the number of food units already stored in the depot and the number of food units collected individually by each agent and the positions where they were collected.

For simplicity, the program was implemented in a totally sequential way. A more realistic approach would consider five different processes, one for each agent and one for the environment, however the sequential approach response was satisfactory with respect to the constraints described in this section.

3   The Cooperation Strategy

Each agent encapsulates a knowledge-based system. Nevertheless, the multi-agent system is a homogeneous one, in which all the agents have the same knowledge about the domain. In each cycle, the agent is allowed to perform only one action, that can be either a movement to a new case, or a message emission to another agent, through the environment mailbox.

As a first strategy we consider that there is no cooperation between the agents. Each agent searches for food independently. Once the agents have the same knowledge about the environment, they have the same specification.

This specification is carried out using a methodology described in [2], where a High-Level Petri Net is used to specify the agent's knowledge in a multi-agent system. The Petri Net that specifies the agent knowledge can be seen in the figure 1.

The token represents the knowledge base (k). When this token enables a transition, an *Ask* is made to the k, that must return an answer. This answer is represented by a directive *Tell*, where the inference engine returns the results to k. Besides that, an action in the environment is also inferred.

The knowledge base is built in the following way. Each transition in the net represents a rule. The *Ask* field in the transition corresponds to the rule premise, and the *Tell* field corresponds to the rule conclusion. Besides that, if there is an *Action* directive, it represents an action executed in the environment. After the Petri Net is simulated to detect structural problems, it is automatically translated in to a knowledge base.

According to the specification presented in the figure 1, if an agent finds a food unit while it goes to the depot, it must follow its way, and the second food found is not collected.

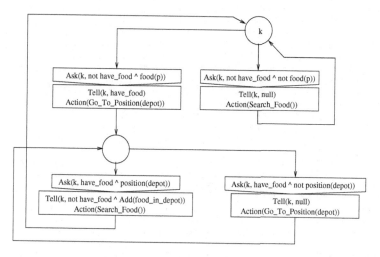

Fig. 1. The knowledge base of each agent represented by a Petri net in the blind strategy

In the second strategy, when this situation happens, a cooperation process is started, represented by the inclusion of the transition $t5$ in figure 2.

Considering the methodology [2], the multi-agent specification starts with the definition of a social strategy. This strategy is also represented by a Petri Net, just like the individual specification. However, in a multi-agent specification, the social strategy corresponds to the social knowledge that must be instantiated to each agent, in order to compose the individual knowledge bases. The difference between the individual knowledge of each agent is determined by the role of the agent in the environment.

In this sense, the specification presented in figure 2 corresponds to the social strategy adopted in the Grid World. Now, when an agent finds a food unit on its way to the depot, it sends a message to the other agents with the food position. The agents answer this message telling the distance between them and the food position. The closest agent is considered the winner and starts a cooperation. When the food is stored in the depot, the cooperation is finished.

Following the FIPA-ACL [3], a message is constituted by a performative field, a sender field, a receiver field and a content field. The content field contains the agent position or the distance between the agent and the food. The sender and receiver fields contain, respectively, the identification of the agent that has sent the message and the identification of the agent that receives it. When the receiver field contains "all", all the agents receive the message.

The performative field describes the type of communication act intended with the message. A *request* is used when a cooperation is requested. A request should be answered with a *propose* or with a *refuse*. In the first case, the sender agent makes a proposal telling its distance from the food unit. In the second case, the agent is not ready to cooperate, because it is either carrying a food unit or involved in another cooperation process. The requesting agent receives the

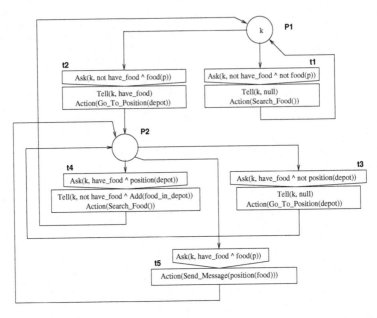

Fig. 2. The knowledge base of each agent represented by a Petri net in a multi-agent strategy

proposals and chooses the best one. In a last step, it sends a message with an *accept* performative to the winner and one with a *reject* performative to all the others. It is important to consider that only one message is delivered per cycle.

Once the agents have the same roles in the environment and also a simple reactive behavior, the social specification corresponds exactly to the individual specification. Hence, all the agents possesses the same knowledge base.

4   Results

The simulations were ran on a computer with Intel Celeron 2 Ghz processor, 256MB of RAM memory, running Mandrake Linux 10.0, using the gcc-2.96. The results are summarized in table 1.

The performance of the system is measured by the number of cycles that the system needs to store a food unit. Considering a period of n =80 cycles for the appearance of a new food items, the four agents, without any cooperation strategy need 80.7 cycles to collect and store a food unit in the depot. If we

Table 1. Results of the simulations for different n

n	Blind Strategy	Multi-agent Strategy
80	80.7	80.6
40	41.1	41.1
10	15.2	14.8
5	10.9	10.1

consider the cooperation strategy the mean is the same: 80.6. The same results are obtained if we diminish the period down to 10 cycles. With a period of 40 cycles, the multi-agent system needs 41.1 cycles to collect and store one food unit, with or without the cooperation strategy.

With a period of 10 cycles between each new food unit, the strategy starts to make some difference. Without cooperation, the agents need 15.2 cycles to find and store a food unit. Using cooperation, this is reduced to 14.8 cycles, still a small difference. When the period is set to 5 cycles, a greater difference appears: 10.9 cycles without cooperation and 10.1 cycles with cooperation. In fact, the smaller the cycle period, the greater is the number of times a conflict occurs. We have a conflict when an agent carrying a food to the depot finds another food unit in its way.

5   Conclusion

There are many ways of cooperating to solve the given grid problem. However this work focuses on one approach and analyzes its impact. This strategy consists in starting a cooperation strategy when an agent finds a food in its way to the depot. In this case, the agent is still carrying a resource and is not able to take another one. In this case it sends a message to the other agents to discover which is the closest agent. Once this agent is determined, it should go to food case and collect it.

In fact, this is a special case inside the environment dynamics. It almost never happens. However, if the period between the introduction of two successive food items is diminished, the probability that this situation happens is increased, and the cooperation turns into an alternative to improve the system performance. This is the main conclusion of the results presented. The smaller the period between food appearances, the greater is the effect of the cooperation strategy.

It is important to note that this is not the only way to cooperate in this setting. Others ways include designating a fix collector that must collect the foods found by the others agents. In other cases, when an agent finds a food item, it can ask the others what they are doing. If there is an agent that is storing the food, it is informed with the position of the new food, and then goes to it. In others words, the collector role, in this case, is dynamic.

The approach presented here can model situations in real problems, like collecting robots and intelligent routing in networks.

References

1. Stroustrup, B.: The C++ Programming Language. Addison Wesley Longman (1999) ISBN 0-201-88954-4.
2. Gonalves, E.M.N., Bittencourt, G.: A planning-based knowledge acquisition methodology. In: Congress of Logic Applied to Technology (LAPTEC), IOS Press (2005)
3. Foundation for Intelligent Physical Agents http://www.fipa.org: FIPA ACL Message Structure Specification. (2002)

Multi-agent Systems in Computational Logic: Challenges and Outcomes of the SOCS Project

Francesca Toni

Department of Computing, Imperial College London,
180 Queen's Gate, SW7 2BZ London, UK
ft@doc.ic.ac.uk

Abstract. The SOCS project (A computational logic model for the description, analysis and verification of global and open SOcieties of heterogeneous ComputeeS), funded by the European Commission under the Fifth Framework, Future and Emerging Technologies programme, has been one of the main sponsors of CLIMA VI. This short article outlines the project's main challenges and its main outcomes.

1   Introduction

The SOCS project [35] was concerned with the development of a computational logic model for the description, analysis and verification of global and open SOcieties of heterogeneous ComputeeS, where computees are agents realised in computational logic. SOCS was funded by the European Commission under the Fifth Framework, Future and Emerging Technologies programme, within the Global Computing (GC) proactive initiative. GC research provides the foundations for the development of large-scale general purpose computer systems that have dependably predictable behaviour, for the needs of a distributed world [27]. SOCS addressed the challenges of the GC initiative with a consortium composed of six European partners, based in Italy, the UK, and Cyprus.[1] Its original aims were:

- To provide a computational logic model for the description, analysis and verification of global and open societies of heterogeneous computees, intended as abstractions of the entities that populate open and global computing environments;
- To provide prototype implementations of computees and their societies;
- To run experiments based on various scenaria to ground and test the model.

SOCS interpreted the GC challenges under an agent-oriented perspective, with a Logic Programming (LP)-based approach. In particular, the project adopted variants of Abductive Logic Programming, Constraint Logic Programming and

---

[1] These were, respectively, the universities of Pisa, Bologna and Ferrara (Italy), Imperial College London and City University London (UK), and Cyprus University. The project was coordinated by Imperial College London. The project started in January 2002 and finished in June 2005.

F. Toni and P. Torroni (Eds.): CLIMA VI, LNAI 3900, pp. 420–426, 2006.

Logic Programming with Priorities, appropriately integrated to deal with agents and GC scenaria.

In this short article, we give an overview of the project, its main challenges and outcomes.

2   The KGP Model of Agency

The KGP model of agency [28, 29] gives concrete guidelines for the formal specification of the knowledge of computees (via a modular computational logic-based knowledge base, partitioned in modules devoted to the different reasoning tasks of planning, reactivity, goal decision, temporal reasoning and identification of preconditions of actions) and of the behaviour of computees (via a computational logic-based cycle theory providing the flexible, declarative control for the operation of computees [30]). The model can be seen at two different levels: on one hand, it is rather concrete, as it exactly specifies what the internal configuration of the computee is; on the other hand, its control component can be varied to obtain heterogeneous behaviour, and is abstract, in that it can be used also for other agent models, independently of their structure/configuration/design.

We have tested the KGP model satisfactorily on a number of applications (including e-commerce and ambient intelligence scenaria [37]). More insights about how to specify and execute computees can be found in this book in the tutorial paper [33].

3   The SOCS Model of Agent Societies

The SOCS society model [32, 9] gives concrete guidelines for the formal specification of the interaction among computees that form a society, and for the definition of a computational logic-based architecture for computee interactions. A layered architecture is proposed where the society defines the allowed interaction protocols, which in turn are defined by means of *Social Integrity Constraints* (ICs). The society's knowledge is defined as an abductive logic program [15], where ICs are used in order to express constraints on the communication patterns of computees, and expected communicative acts ("*expectations*") are expressed as abducible predicates.

Expectations, whose intuition recalls the usual deontic operators of permission, obligation, and prohibition [14], are used to provide a semantics to both agent communication languages and to interaction protocols [12]. The resulting model is based on a declarative (logic) representation and therefore it is easy to understand, and close to an operational model and suitably usable in order to achieve an implementation of societies of computees based on their formal specifications [8]. Finally, thanks to the link between formal specification and implementation, the model provides a good ground for the automatic verification and formal proof of properties [16].

We have tested the society model satisfactorily on a number of applications (including resource exchange [17], e-commerce protocols [13], combinatorial auctions [6]). A repository of protocols specified using ICs is being maintained and is publicly available through the project's home page.[2] More insights about how to specify and execute societies of computees can be found in this book in the tutorial paper [20].

4   Computational Models

Both the KGP model and the society model are equipped with correct computational counterparts ([19] and [18], respectively). These computational models are heavily based upon proof procedures for (various extensions of) logic programming. In particular, the operational model for KGP agents relies upon CIFF [22], a proof procedure for abductive logic programming with constraints, and Gorgias [21], for logic programming with priorities, and the operational model for societies of agents relies upon SCIFF [1], a proof procedure for abductive logic programming with events and expectations. These procedures have been obtained by adapting and suitably extending two existing proof procedures for logic programming, namely Fung and Kowalski's IFF procedure for abductive logic programming [25], for CIFF and SCIFF, and Kakas and Toni's argumentation-based procedure for negation as failure in logic programming [31], for Gorgias. The overall operational models are sound and (in some cases) complete with respect to the abstract KGP model and model for societies of agents, respectively, and form a solid bridge between the models and their implementations within the PROSOCS and SOCS-SI platforms (see section 6 below).

5   Properties

A great deal of the project activities has been devoted to formalising and studying properties of agents and agent systems. The SOCS approach to properties is formal, and it aims at exploiting the potential of the declarative LP paradigm for giving a precise specification of properties and for allowing their formal verification. Moreover, the double declarative and operational reading of LP supports both an abstract description of systems and their (expected) properties, and mechanisms to implement them. Descriptions and mechanisms are closely related to each other so that properties enjoyed by the models are easily reflected in the implementations.

We have compiled a catalogue of concrete properties, demonstrating:

1. The effectiveness of our logic programming approach to modeling computees and their societies. This facilitates the formalisation of formal properties and prediction of behaviour without resorting to empirical methods.
2. The consequences of some of the design choices. For example, we have identified coherence properties for computees showing some of the benefits that result directly as a consequence of the choice of goal and action selection

---

[2] http://edu59.deis.unibo.it:8079/SOCSProtocolsRepository/jsp/index.jsp

functions in the computee model. Another example concerns the design of the social infrastructure that provably allows verification of protocol properties automatically [11].

3. The versatility of the computee and society models. For example, we have investigated how we can specify different profiles of behaviour in computees and how such profiles could alter the behaviour of computees [34].

We have identified three broad areas for investigating properties of (societies of) computees [26, 3]:

- Properties of individual computees (agents), including agent profiles [34];
- Properties of the society infrastructure;
- Properties related to protocol conformance [23].

These properties help showing the effectiveness of the computational logic approach in modeling computees and societies, in the sense of facilitating formalisation of properties and prediction of behaviour without the need to resort to empirical methods. They also help exploring the consequences of our design choices.

6   Implementation and Experimentation

We have developed a prototype implementation [5] and platform for computees and societies (PROSOCS [36] and SOCS-SI [10, 2]), which implement the models and have been used for extensive experimentation in the later phases of the project. The experimentation [4] has also been conducted to confirm or disprove properties of the models. The SOCS prototype has also been used to provide a practical basis for the design of combinatorial auctions, which require aggregate behaviour of computational entities and tools.

The PROSOCS platform provides the reasoning and communication capabilities a computee needs in order to operate in a GC environment. The agent developer, as a result, is only required to specify the set of logic theories that describe the background knowledge necessary for the agent to operate within a specific application domain. PROSOCS uses SICStus Prolog for inference-based components (CIFF and Gorgias).

Analogously, SOCS-SI supports the declarative formalisation and the automated verification of the social aspects of a SOCS application. SOCS-SI is general in its scope, and has been interfaced to other implemented agent platforms, such as Jade and tuProlog, and to other non-agent related communication platforms. SOCS-SI uses SICStus Prolog, and in particular its CHR library [24], for the reasoning and verification part [7].

Both PROSOCS and SOCS-SI use JXTA for inter-agent communication and agent discovery, and Java to implement the supporting applications, integrate Prolog and build the GUIs. SOCS-SI and PROSOCS communicate through JXTA.

7   SOCS Dissemination Meeting at CLIMA VI

The SOCS dissemination event presented several key aspects of the project's approach, and discussed some open issues. The speakers Antonis Kakas,[3] Andrea Bracciali,[4] and Marco Alberti[5] presented the operational models for agents and multi-agent systems and the formal properties of agents and agent systems developed within SOCS. Paolo Torroni[6] discussed possible guidelines for evaluating intelligent systems of reasoning agents, building on the SOCS experience.

Acknowledgments

This work was funded by the IST programme of the EC, FET under the IST-2001-32530 SOCS project, within the GC proactive initiative. The author is grateful to all participants of the SOCS consortium for inputs to this article and for their hard work throughout the project. The author is also grateful to Paolo Torroni for some helpful suggestion for an earlier version of this article.

References

1. The $\mathcal{S}CIFF$ abductive proof procedure home page.
   http://lia.deis.unibo.it/research/sciff/, 2005.
2. The SOCS-$\mathcal{S}$I (socs social infrastructure) home page.
   http://lia.deis.unibo.it/research/socs_si/, 2006.
3. M. Alberti, F. Athienitou, A. Bracciali, F. Chesani, U. Endriss, M. Gavanelli, A. Kakas, E. Lamma, W. Lu, P. Mancarella, P. Mello, F. Sadri, K. Stathis, F. Toni, and P. Torroni. Verifiable properties of societies of computees. Technical report, SOCS Consortium, 2005. Deliverable D13. Available from the SOCS project web site: http://lia.deis.unibo.it/research/socs/guests/publications/.
4. M. Alberti, A. Bracciali, F. Chesani, A. Ciampolini, U. Endriss, M. Gavanelli, A. Guerri, A. Kakas, E. Lamma, W. Lu, P. Mancarella, P. Mello, M. Milano, F. Riguzzi, F. Sadri, K. Stathis, G. Terreni, F. Toni, P. Torroni, and A. Yip. Experiments with animated societies of computees. Technical report, SOCS Consortium, 2005. Deliverable D14. Available from the SOCS project web site: http://lia.deis.unibo.it/research/socs/guests/publications/.
5. M. Alberti, A. Bracciali, F. Chesani, U. Endriss, M. Gavanelli, W. Lu, K. Stathis, and P. Torroni. SOCS prototype. Technical report, SOCS Consortium, 2003. Deliverable D9. Available from the SOCS project web site: http://lia.deis.unibo.it/research/socs/guests/publications/.
6. M. Alberti, F. Chesani, M. Gavanelli, A. Guerri, E. Lamma, P. Mello, and P. Torroni. Expressing interaction in combinatorial auction through social integrity constraints. Intelligenza Artificiale, II(1):22–29, 2005.

---

[3] University of Cyprus, http://www2.cs.ucy.ac.cy/~antonis/
[4] University of Pisa, Italy, http://www.di.unipi.it/~braccia/
[5] University of Ferrara, Italy http://www.ing.unife.it/docenti/malberti.html
[6] University of Bologna, Italy, http://lia.deis.unibo.it/~pt/

7. M. Alberti, F. Chesani, M. Gavanelli, and E. Lamma. The CHR-based Implementation of a System for Generation and Confirmation of Hypotheses. In A. Wolf, T. Frühwirth, and M. Meister, editors, *19th Workshop on (Constraint) Logic Programming W(C)LP 2005*, number 2005-01 in Ulmer Informatik-Berichte, pages 111–122, 2005.

8. M. Alberti, F. Chesani, M. Gavanelli, E. Lamma, P. Mello, and P. Torroni. A logic based approach to interaction design in open multi-agent systems. In *Proceedings of the 13th IEEE international Workshops on Enabling Technologies: Infrastructures for Collaborative Enterprises (WETICE-2004)*, pages 387–392, Modena, Italy, June 14–16 2004. IEEE Press.

9. M. Alberti, F. Chesani, M. Gavanelli, E. Lamma, P. Mello, and P. Torroni. The SOCS computational logic approach for the specification and verification of agent societies. 3267:324–339, 2005.

10. M. Alberti, F. Chesani, M. Gavanelli, E. Lamma, P. Mello, and P. Torroni. Compliance verification of agent interaction: a logic-based tool. *Applied Artificial Intelligence*, 20(4-5), 2006.

11. M. Alberti, F. Chesani, M. Gavanelli, E. Lamma, P. Mello, and P. Torroni. Security protocols verification in Abductive Logic Programming: a case study. In O. Dikenelli, M.-P. Gleizes, and A. Ricci, editors, *Proceedings of ESAW'05, Kuşadası, Aydın, Turkey, October 26-28, 2005*, Lecture Notes in Artificial Intelligence. Springer-Verlag, 2006.

12. M. Alberti, A. Ciampolini, M. Gavanelli, E. Lamma, P. Mello, and P. Torroni. A social ACL semantics by deontic constraints. *Lecture Notes in Artificial Intelligence*, 2691:204–213, 2003.

13. M. Alberti, D. Daolio, M. Gavanelli, E. Lamma, P. Mello, and P. Torroni. Specification and verification of agent interaction protocols in a logic-based system. In H. M. Haddad, A. Omicini, and R. L. Wainwright, editors, *Proceedings of the 19th Annual ACM Symposium on Applied Computing (SAC 2004)*, pages 72–78, Nicosia, Cyprus, Mar. 14–17 2004. ACM Press.

14. M. Alberti, M. Gavanelli, E. Lamma, P. Mello, G. Sartor, and P. Torroni. Mapping deontic operators to abductive expectations. *Computational and Mathematical Organization Theory*, 2006.

15. M. Alberti, M. Gavanelli, E. Lamma, P. Mello, and P. Torroni. An Abductive Interpretation for Open Societies. *Lecture Notes in Artificial Intelligence*, 2829:287–299, 2003.

16. M. Alberti, M. Gavanelli, E. Lamma, P. Mello, and P. Torroni. Specification and verification of agent interactions using Social Integrity Constraints. *Electronic Notes in Theoretical Computer Science*, 85(2), 2003.

17. M. Alberti, M. Gavanelli, E. Lamma, P. Mello, and P. Torroni. Modeling interactions using *Social Integrity Constraints*: A resource sharing case study. *Lecture Notes in Artificial Intelligence*, 2990:243–262, 2004.

18. M. Alberti, M. Gavanelli, E. Lamma, P. Mello, and P. Torroni. The SCIFF abductive proof-procedure. *Lecture Notes in Artificial Intelligence*, 3673:135–147, 2005.

19. A. Bracciali, N. Demetriou, U. Endriss, A. Kakas, W. Lu, P. Mancarella, F. Sadri, K. Stathis, F. Toni, and G. Terreni. The KGP model of agency: Computational model and prototype implementation. *Lecture Notes in Artificial Intelligence*, 3267:340–367, 2005.

20. F. Chesani, M. Gavanelli, M. Alberti, E. Lamma, P. Mello, and P. Torroni. Specification and verification of agent interaction using abductive reasoning. In this volume.

21. N. Demetriou and A. C. Kakas. Argumentation with abduction. In *Proceedings of the fourth Panhellenic Symposium on Logic*, 2003.

22. U. Endriss, P. Mancarella, F. Sadri, G. Terreni, and F. Toni. The CIFF proof procedure for abductive logic programming with constraints. *Lecture Notes in Artificial Intelligence*, 3229:680–684, 2004.

23. U. Endriss, N. Maudet, F. Sadri, and F. Toni. Protocol conformance for logic-based agents. In G. Gottlob and T. Walsh, editors, *Proceedings of the Eighteenth International Joint Conference on Artificial Intelligence, Acapulco, Mexico (IJCAI-03)*. Morgan Kaufmann Publishers, Aug. 2003.

24. T. Frühwirth. Theory and practice of constraint handling rules. *Journal of Logic Programming*, 37(1-3):95–138, Oct. 1998.

25. T. H. Fung and R. A. Kowalski. The IFF proof procedure for abductive logic programming. *Journal of Logic Programming*, 33(2):151–165, Nov. 1997.

26. M. Gavanelli, E. Lamma, P. Torroni, P. Mello, K. Stathis, P. Moraïtis, A. C. Kakas, N. Demetriou, G. Terreni, P. Mancarella, A. Bracciali, F. Toni, F. Sadri, and U. Endriss. Computational model for computees and societies of computees. Technical report, SOCS Consortium, 2003. Deliverable D8. Available from the SOCS project web site: `http://lia.deis.unibo.it/research/socs/guests/publications/`.

27. Global Computing, Future and Emerging Technologies. Co-operation of autonomous and mobile entities in dynamic environments. Home Page: `http://www.cordis.lu/ist/fetgc.htm`, 2000.

28. A. Kakas, P. Mancarella, F. Sadri, K. Stathis, and F. Toni. A logic-based approach to model computees. Technical report, SOCS Consortium, 2003. Deliverable D4. Available from the SOCS project web site: `http://lia.deis.unibo.it/research/socs/guests/publications/`.

29. A. Kakas, P. Mancarella, F. Sadri, K. Stathis, and F. Toni. The KGP model of agency. In R. Lopez de Mantaras and L. Saitta, editors, *Proceedings of the Sixteenth European Conference on Artificial Intelligence, Valencia, Spain (ECAI 2004)*. IOS Press, Aug. 2004.

30. A. C. Kakas, P. Mancarella, F. Sadri, K. Stathis, and F. Toni. Declarative agent control. *Lecture Notes in Artificial Intelligence*, 3487:96–110, 2005.

31. A. C. Kakas and F. Toni. Computing negation as failure via argumentation. *Journal of Logic and Computation*, 9:515–562, 1999.

32. P. Mello, P. Torroni, M. Gavanelli, M. Alberti, A. Ciampolini, M. Milano, A. Roli, E. Lamma, F. Riguzzi, and N. Maudet. A logic-based approach to model interaction amongst computees. Technical report, SOCS Consortium, 2003. Deliverable D5. Available from the SOCS project web site: `http://lia.deis.unibo.it/research/socs/guests/publications/`.

33. F. Sadri. Using the KGP model of agency to design applications. In this volume.

34. F. Sadri and F. Toni. Variety of behaviours through profiles in logic-based agents. In this volume.

35. SOcieties of ComputeeS (SOCS). A computational logic model for the description, analysis and verification of global and open SOcieties of heterogeneous ComputeeS. IST-2001-32530. `http://lia.deis.unibo.it/research/socs/`, 2002-2005.

36. K. Stathis, A. Kakas, W. Lu, N. Demetriou, U. Endriss, and A. Bracciali. PROSOCS: A platform for programming software agents in computational logic. *Applied Artificial Intelligence*, 20(4-5), 2006.

37. K. Stathis and F. Toni. Ambient Intelligence using KGP Agents. *Lecture Notes in Artificial Intelligence*, 3295:351–362, 2004.

Author Index

Lecture Notes in Artificial Intelligence (LNAI)